Challenging the conventional wisdom conveyed by Western environmental historians about China, this book examines the relationships between economic and environmental changes in the southern Chinese provinces of Guangdong and Guangxi (a region historically known as Lingnan, "South of the Mountains") in imperial China, focusing on the period from 1400 to 1850, but also providing substantial background from 2 CE on. Robert Marks discusses the impact of population growth on land-use patterns, the agroecology of the region, and deforestation; the commercialization of agriculture and its implications for ecological change; the impact of climatic change on agriculture; and the ways in which the human population responded to environmental challenges. This book is a significant contribution to both Chinese and environmental history. It is groundbreaking in its methods and in its findings.

STUDIES IN ENVIRONMENT AND HISTORY

Tigers, Rice, Silk, and Silt

STUDIES IN ENVIRONMENT AND HISTORY

Editors

Donald Worster *University of Kansas*
Alfred W. Crosby *University of Texas at Austin*

Other books in the series

Donald Worster, *Nature's Economy: A History of Ecological Ideas*
Kenneth F. Kiple, *The Caribbean Slave: A Biological History*
Alfred W. Crosby, *Ecological Imperialism: The Biological Expansion of Europe, 900–1900*
Arthur F. McEvoy, *The Fisherman's Problem: Ecology and Law in the California Fisheries, 1850–1980*
Robert Harms, *Games Against Nature: An Eco-Cultural History of the Nunu of Equatorial Africa*
Warren Dean, *Brazil and the Struggle for Rubber: A Study in Environmental History*
Samuel P. Hays, *Beauty, Health, and Permanence: Environmental Politics in the United States, 1955–1985*
Donald Worster, *The Ends of the Earth: Perspectives on Modern Environmental History*
Michael Williams, *Americans and Their Forests: A Historical Geography*
Timothy Silver, *A New Face on the Countryside: Indians, Colonists, and Slaves in the South Atlantic Forests, 1500–1800*
Theodore Steinberg, *Nature Incorporated: Industrialization and the Waters of New England*
J. R. McNeill, *The Mountains of the Mediterranean World: An Environmental History*
Elinor G. K. Melville *A Plague of Sheep: Environmental Consequences of the Conquest of Mexico*
Richard H. Grove, *Green Imperialism: Colonial Expansion, Tropical Island Edens and the Origins of Environmentalism, 1600–1860*
Mark Elvin and Tsui'jung Liu, *Sediments of Time: Environment and Society in Chinese History*

TIGERS, RICE, SILK, AND SILT

ENVIRONMENT AND ECONOMY IN LATE IMPERIAL SOUTH CHINA

Robert B. Marks

Whittier College

CAMBRIDGE UNIVERSITY PRESS
Cambridge, New York, Melbourne, Madrid, Cape Town, Singapore, São Paulo

Cambridge University Press
The Edinburgh Building, Cambridge CB2 2RU, UK

Published in the United States of America by Cambridge University Press, New York

www.cambridge.org
Information on this title: www.cambridge.org/9780521591775

First published 1998
This digitally printed first paperback version 2006

A catalogue record for this publication is available from the British Library

Library of Congress Cataloguing in Publication data
Marks, Robert B., 1949–

Tigers, rice, silk, and silt: environment and economy in late imperial south China/Robert B. Marks.

p. cm. – (Studies in environment and history)
Includes bibliographical references and index.
ISBN 0-521-59177-5 (hb)

1. Economic development – Environmental aspects – China – History. 2. Nature – Effect of human beings on – China – History. 3. Human beings – Effect of environment on – China – History. 4. Kwangtung Province (China) – Economic conditions. 5. Kwangsi Chuang Autonomous Region (China) – Economic conditions. 6. China – History – Ming dynasty, 1368–1644. 7. China – History – Ch'ing dynasty, 1644–1912. I. Title. II. Series.
HC427.6.M37 1997 96-53322
333.73′0951′2 – dc21 CIP

ISBN-13 978-0-521-59177-5 hardback
ISBN-10 0-521-59177-5 hardback

ISBN-13 978-0-521-02776-2 paperback
ISBN-10 0-521-02776-4 paperback

CONTENTS

MAPS, FIGURES, AND TABLES

Maps

Figures

Tables

DYNASTIES, QING DYNASTY EMPERORS' REIGN DATES, WEIGHTS AND MEASURES

The dynasties of imperial China, 221 BCE 1911 CE

Qin	221–207 BCE
Han	202 BCE–220 CE
Sui	589–618
Tang	618–907
Song	960–1279
Yuan	1279–1368
Ming	1368–1644
Qing	1644–1911

Qing dynasty emperors' reign dates

Shunzhi	1644–1661
Kangxi	1662–1722
Yongzheng	1723–1735
Qianlong	1736–1795
Jiaqing	1796–1820
Tongzhi	1821–1850
Xianfeng	1851–1861
Tongzhi	1862–1874
Guangxu	1875–1907
Xuantong	1908–1911

Weights and measures

Area	*Volume*
100 *mu* = 1 *qing*	1 *shi* = 1 *picul* ≈ 1 bushel
6 *mu* ≈ 1 acre	1 *shi* = 10 *dou*
100 *qing* ≈ 16 acres	1 *dou* = 10 *sheng*

Length
1 *zhang* ≈ 10 feet

Weight
1 *jin* ≈ 1.33 pounds
16 *liang* = 1 *jin*
1 *dan* = 100 *jin*
1 *shi* ≈ 170 pounds

Currency
1 silver *liang* = 10 *qian*
1 *qian* = 10 *fen*
1 silver *liang* = 1 *tael*
1,000 copper *wen* ≈ 1 silver *liang*

ACKNOWLEDGMENTS

The intellectual, emotional, and institutional debts that I have accumulated while writing this book are enormous. For the probity of their questioning, I want to thank James Lee, John Siedensticker, and two anonymous readers. Through their questions and comments, Mark Elvin and Pierre-Etienne Will convinced me that I was on the right track. Richard Archer, Patrick Caffrey, Alfred Crosby, Christopher Hill, J. Donald Hughes, Joyce P. Kaufman, John R. McNeill, Rhoads Murphey, J. Richard Penn, and Kenneth Pomeranz did me the honor of reading and commenting upon the entire manuscript, for which I am exceedingly grateful; they helped in ways too numerous to mention.

Others critiqued parts of the manuscript in various stages of preparation, and I thank each of them: Robert Antony, William Atwell, Thomas Buoye, Cao Shuji, Chen Chunsheng, Helen Dunstan, Joseph Esherick, Robert Gardella, Philip Huang, James Lee, Lillian Li, Katherine Lynch, John D. Post, Mary Rankin, Thomas Rawski, G. William Skinner, Kathy Walker, Yeh-chien Wang, and R. Bin Wong. Participants at various conferences where I presented preliminary findings – the Fourth International Conference on Qing Social and Economic History at Shenzhen in 1987, the February 1993 Southern California China Colloquium, and the 1993 Conference on the History of the Environment in China – also provided helpful comments, and I thank them all.

Special thanks go to Gordon Jacoby and Rosanne D'Arrigo for sharing with me their reconstruction of northern hemisphere temperature trends and then reading a draft chapter that incorporated their findings. Qiu Yuanyou, head librarian at Beijing Teacher's College (now Capital Normal University), introduced me to the archives at the Number One Historical Archives in Beijing; fellow researchers at the Number One – Jack Wills, Tom Buoye, Lillian Li, Robert Antony, and David Kelly – shared ideas and experiences. Helen Dunstan graciously allowed me to use and quote from a wonderful manuscript she is working on, and Tom Buoye shared with me harvest data he collected in Beijing. Yeh-chien Wang made available his rice price data, which I used to corroborate the data I collected; and Betty Wiens graciously gave me a copy of her late husband's (Herold J. Wiens's) book. Whittier College students Keith Black and Susan Ingersoll entered data, and the former helped with preliminary statistical analyses.

Building the digitized maps and geocoding the data that undergirds much of this book would have been impossible without the help of numerous people. Robert Hartwell selflessly shared with me both what he had learned about geographic information systems (GIS), as well as his coding system for China's counties. Larry Crissman has been extraordinarily helpful, offering not only advice and base maps, but also the good offices of the Australian Centre for Asian Spatial Information and Analysis Network (ASIAN) at Griffith University in translating my ARC/INFO files to MapInfo (neither a small nor, for me, insignificant feat). Qin Tang of CITAS (China in Time and Space) at the University of Washington provided technical assistance, as did Noel Paul and Nadja Leibers at ASIAN. Eric Patrick helped me to learn and use ARC/INFO at Whittier College's W. M. Keck Image Processing Laboratory.

Professor Chen Chunsheng, chair of the History Department at Zhongshan University in Guangzhou, has been of enormous help and support for this work. Indeed, he has had a greater influence on my understanding and conceptualization of this work than any other person. His interests and mine overlap, and collaborating with him over the past decade has been delightful. I have learned much about rice prices, granaries, Guangzhou, the Pearl River delta, Zhujigang, and the nature of international collaboration and friendship from him. I would like to thank Professor Ye Xian'en for first introducing us in 1985 when I passed through Guangzhou, and then bringing us together at the Fourth International Conference on Qing Social and Economic History in 1987, where we shared our interest in, and enthusiasm and respect for, each other's work. A grant from the Committee on Scholarly Communication with the People's Republic of China (CSCPRC) enabled Chen Chunsheng to spend six months in the United States in early 1993, and Professor Philip C. C. Huang arranged for Chen to affiliate with the Center for Chinese Studies at UCLA; we thank both for their support. Chen hosted me at Zhongshan University in early 1994 for two weeks of field work in Lingnan, and I thank him and his wife, Liu Hong, for their hospitality. Chen also introduced me to Liu Zhiwei, his colleague in the History Department, who is exceptionally knowledgeable about the history of the Pearl River delta; I thank Liu for sharing both his ideas, especially about the Pearl River delta and the migrations from northern Guangdong into the delta, and his written work with me.

Without libraries and archives, and their staffs, none of this book would have been possible. I would like to thank the Number One Historical Archives in Beijing, especially Ju Deyuan and his staff, including Liu Wei and Wang Daorui; the National Palace Museum in Taibei; the Library of Congress, especially Chu Mi Wiens, Robert Dunn, and David Hsü in the Asian Division, and Pam Vanee and the staff of the Geography and Map Division; Ann Topjon of the Bonnie Bell Wardman Library at Whittier College; Ramon Myers and the staff at the Hoover Institution Library at Stanford University; the University of Wisconsin Library; the Gest Library at Princeton University; and the Yale University Library.

At Cambridge University Press, Frank Smith made the process of getting the manuscript to print a delight, Camilla T. K. Palmer saw it through production, and Robert Racine helped sharpen my prose and argument and saved me from making several errors.

Generous financial support gave me the time to do the research and to write. A Graves Award (administered for the American Council of Learned Societies by Pomona College) in 1985 supported two months of research at the Number One Historical Archives in Beijing, followed two years later by another month's research there. A Stanford University grant allowed me to use the Hoover Institution Library. A 1990 NEH Travel-to-Collections grant supported work at the National Palace Museum in Taibei, and a 1991–92 NEH Fellowship for College and University Teachers (FB-28715-91) supported the writing of this book. Support from the Chiang Ching-kuo Foundation enabled me to travel to Hong Kong to attend the Conference on the History of the Environment in China in 1993. The indulgence of two Whittier College presidents granted me the time to pursue my scholarly interests by releasing me from my more bureaucratic duties, and a sabbatical leave of absence from Whittier College provided another semester of time. Whittier College also granted me funds to purchase computer hardware and software. Grant McNaughton made his mountain home near to the John Muir Wilderness available to me, and completing the final revisions of this book there was pleasurable indeed.

Finally, permission to use material previously published is gratefully acknowledged: from E. J. Brill for material from my and Chen Chunsheng's article, "Price Inflation and Its Social, Economic, and Climatic Context in Guangdong Province, 1707–1800," *T'oung pao* 81, no. 1 (1995); and from the Society of Qing Studies for material from "Rice Prices, Food Supply, and Market Structure in Eighteenth-Century South China," *Late Imperial China* 12, no. 2 (Dec. 1991).

To all of these friends, colleagues, students, institutions, libraries, colleges, universities, and granting agencies, I say, "Thank you." Whatever errors or questionable interpretations that remain are mine alone.

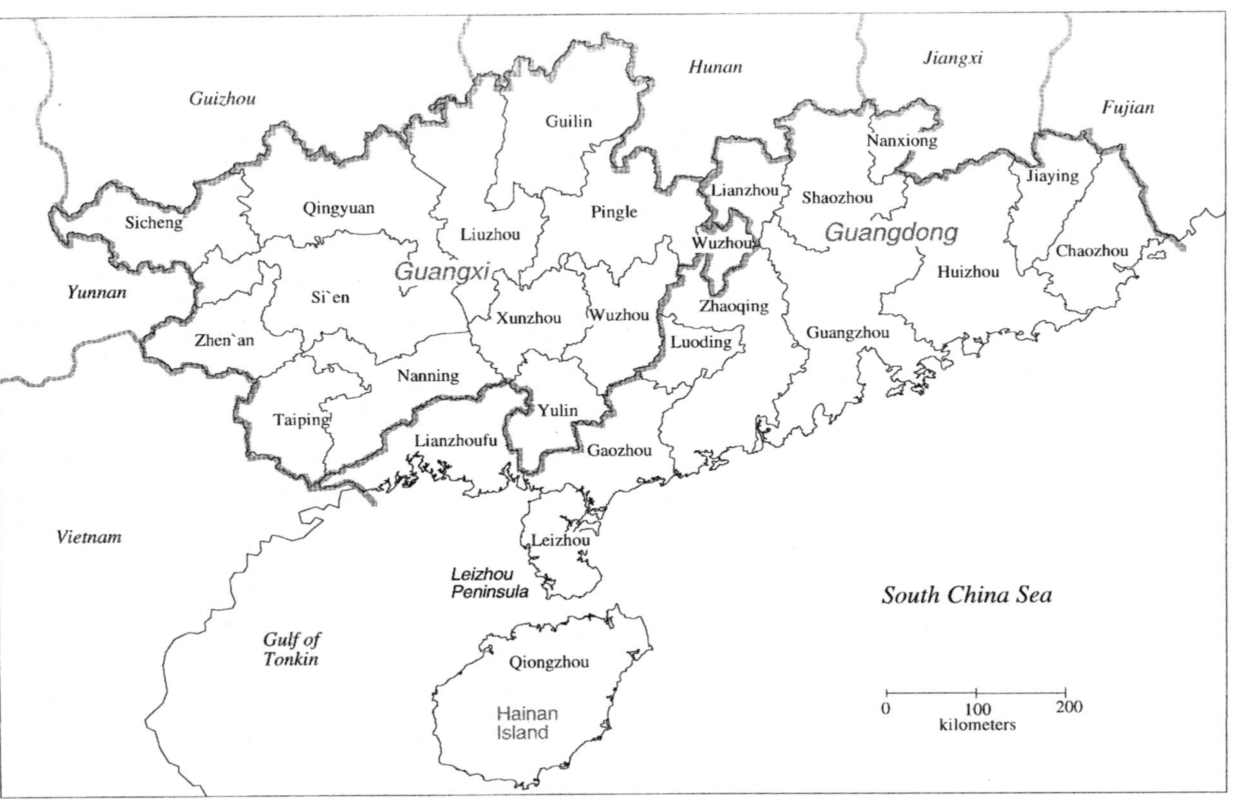

Lingnan prefectures, ca. 1820

Map key *Lingnan counties, ca. 1820*

County	Key	County	Key	County	Key	County	Key	County	Key	County	Key
Anding	64	Fengshun	51	Huitong	181	Luorong	44	Shangsi	160	Xingning	34
Anping	141	Fengyang	165	Jiangzhou	137	Luoyang	145	Shangxiadong	153	Xingye	198
Baishan	84	Fengyi	83	Jiaying	25	Maoming	158	Shicheng	168	Xinhui	128
Beiliu	200	Fogang	63	Jie'an	123	Maping	188	Shixing	18	Xining	107
Binzhou	193	Fuchuan	27	Jielun	115	Mingjiang	162	Shunde	117	Xinning	147
Bobai	202	Gan'en	185	Jieyang	68	Nadi	31	Si'en	15	Xinning	152
Boluo	82	Gaoming	118	Kaijian	76	Nama	99	Sihui	88	Xinxing	133
Bose	73	Gaoyao	100	Kaiping	138	Nan'ao Is.	79	Siling	170	Xinyi	140
Cangwu	69	Gongcheng	22	Laibin	191	Nandan	14	Suixi	172	Xiuren	61
Cenxi	114	Guangning	75	Lechang	9	Nanhai	104	Taiping	146	Xuanhua	124
Changhua	183	Guanyang	6	Lehui	182	Nanxiong	8	Teng	77	Xuwen	174
Changle	54	Gui	195	Lianping	40	Ningming	161	Tianbao	101	Yaizhou	187
Changning	55	Guide	120	Lianshan	37	Panyu	96	Tianhe	35	Yangchun	139
Chaoyang	80	Guiping	194	Lianzhou	24	Pingle	39	Tianzhou	67	Yangchun	116
Chenghai	72	Guishan	92	Lin'gao	178	Pingnan	78	Wanzhou	184	Yangjiang	159
Chengmai	177	Guishun	102	Lingchuan	7	Pingyuan	20	Wancheng	129	Yangli	136
Chongshan	151	Guling	93	Lingshan	201	Puning	81	Wenchang	175	Yangshan	30
Chongzuo	142	Guohua	110	Lingshui	186	Qianjiang	190	Wengyuan	38	Yangshuo	32
Conghua	71	Haifeng	97	Lingui	17	Qinzhou	156	Wuchuan	171	Yingde	50
Danzhou	179	Haikang	173	Lingyun	36	Qingyuan	59	Wulu	105	Yining	12
Dapu	26	Haiyang	57	Lipu	48	Qiongshan	176	Wuxuan	85	Yishan	45
Deqing	98	He	41	Liucheng	46	Quanzhou	2	Xialei	131	Yong'an	62
Dianbai	167	Hechi	43	Long'an	111	Quanming	134	Xiangzhou	66	Yongfu	28
Ding'an	180	Hengzhou	197	Longchuan	29	Qujiang	19	Xiangshan	130	Yongkang	135
Dingluo	103	Heping	33	Longmen	70	Raoping	47	Xiangwu	113	Yongning	16
Dong'an	112	Hepu	169	Longsheng	3	Renhua	10	Xiaozhen'an	106	Yongshun	58
Dongguan	108	Heshan	125	Longying	132	Rong	11	Xiashixi	166	Yong'an	74
Donglan	49	Heyuan	53	Longzhou	155	Rong	196	Xilin	52	Yulin	199
Dujie	121	Hua	90	Luchuan	149	Ruyuan	23	Xilong	42	Zengcheng	87
Dukang	127	Huazhou	163	Lufeng	86	Sanshui	94	Xin'an	122	Zhaoping	60
Duyang	65	Huaiji	56	Luobai	164	Shanglin	192	Xincheng	189	Zhenping	21
Enping	143	Huaiyuan	5	Luocheng	13	Shanglin	109	Xing'an	4	Zhenyuan	119
Fengchuan	89	Huilai	95	Luoding	126	Shanglong	144	Xinglong	91	Zhongzhou	157

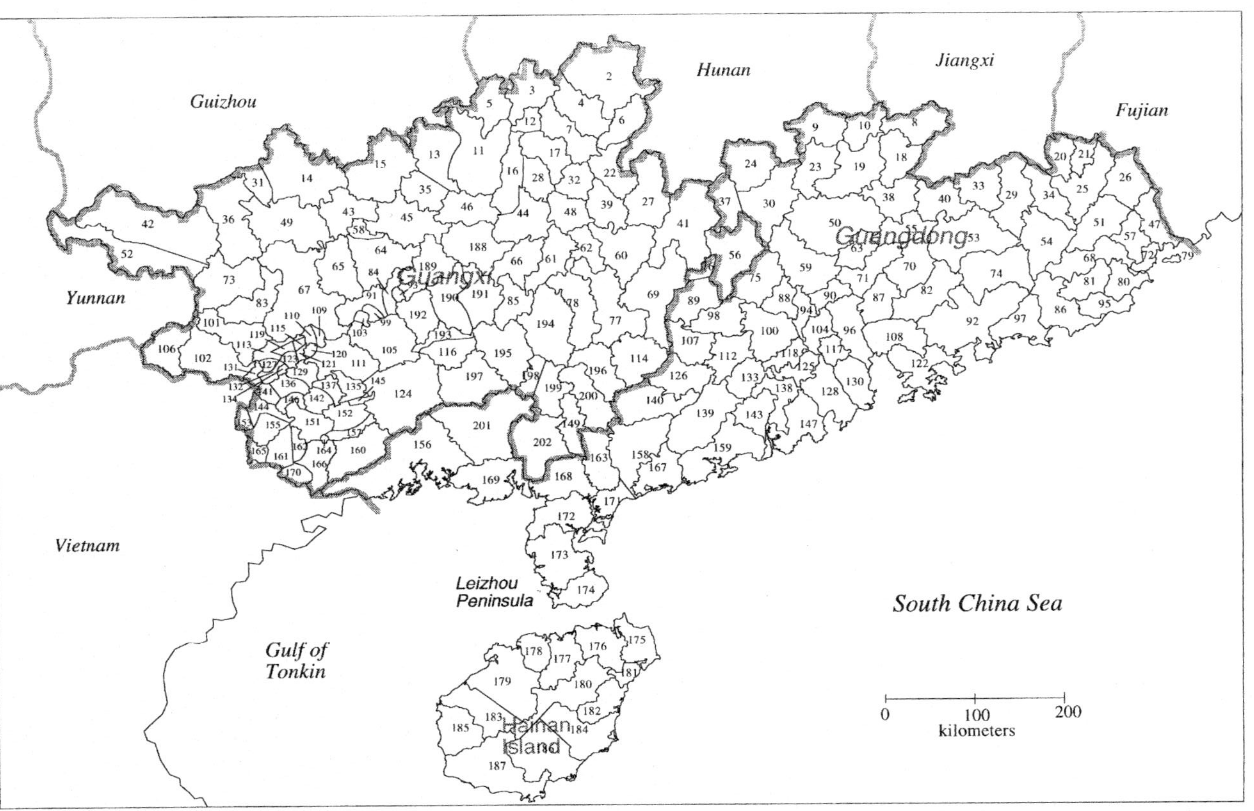

Lingnan counties, ca. 1820

Tigers, Rice, Silk, and Silt

INTRODUCTION

While prominent environmental historians in the West have referred to China's mode of agriculture as a model of sustainable development, that is a dubious claim. Rather, as this history of south China will show, by the turn of the nineteenth century, biodiversity in Lingnan had declined significantly, and the region was "leaking" huge amounts of energy that could only be replenished with massive rice imports to feed the booming human population. Simply put, agriculture in late imperial south China was unsustainable without increasingly greater inputs, and the drive to keep the system in balance led to a substantial remaking of both the environment and the economy of south China over the centuries covered in this book.

By way of defining (and defending) my choice of the two large and inclusive concepts of "environment" and "economy" both in the title and for the focus of this book, let me begin by explaining how the book came to be. I wish I could say I had the plan worked out when I began the research for it some 10 years ago, but that is not the case. In fact, what I have ultimately written is the result of an intellectual journey that began with the problem of food supply: How did the Chinese economy supply food, usually in sufficient quantity, to sustain a growing population during the late imperial period, and what were the economic and social consequences of producing too little or too much food?

The problem of food supply struck me as a good one for exploring the relationships among population growth, commercialization of agriculture, and rural class relations, each of which has been identified by one historian or another as constituting the driving force of long-term historical change. Indeed, the National Endowment for the Humanities was sufficiently convinced by this initial problematic to support me with two grants, for which I am exceedingly grateful. While I am still interested in these broader issues of social and economic history – and most have been incorporated in this book – along the way other topics and problems thrust themselves into my consciousness, resulting in a reconceptualization of my analytic framework.

In particular, while reconstructing eighteenth-century rice prices from the grain lists preserved in large quantities in the archives in Beijing and Taibei, I began taking notes from the equally voluminous "rain and grain" (*yu liang*) memorials in which provincial officials reported weather conditions and estimated harvest yields. My first effort to make sense of Chinese officials' harvest yield estimates and their connection to rice prices led a sympathetic reader of a draft chapter to ask just one simple question: What role did climatic factors have in determining the size of the harvest? All I could offer by way of an answer was to confess my ignorance.

But that simple question sent me into the vast literature on climatic change, where I discovered that Chinese climatologists had produced some of the earliest and most comprehensive studies of the history of climate. With findings from this scientific literature in hand, I returned to my analyses of harvest yields and rice prices, thinking in the process that I might just broaden the focus of my book to include a more general consideration of the impact of climate and climatic change on the economy of late imperial south China. And there I left the conceptualization of the book – until some months later once again I was asked a few simple questions.

While trying to gain perspective on the amount of land under cultivation in Guangdong and Guangxi provinces during the Ming (1368–1644) and Qing (1644–1911) dynasties, I was reading the annual chronicles in the various provincial and prefectural gazetteers. As those familiar with China's local gazetteers know, these chronicles include brief notations of major events in any given year, from floods and droughts to bandit "uprisings" and epidemics. With chronicles covering centuries, the gazetteers are a rich source of climatological data; indeed, they constitute an important source for the story I will tell here. But at the time I was rereading the Ming-era chronicles for Guangxi province, not for the climatological data (which I had already gathered), but for clues about the extent of land clearance: noting the vast number of accounts of aboriginal uprisings in the fifteenth century, it struck me that aboriginal resistance to Chinese occupation of the land was a very rough indicator of when and where Chinese had "reclaimed" the land for their style of cultivation.

As I pondered these fifteenth-century events and their relevance to land reclamation, I was drawn back to another kind of notation in the annual chronicles that I had found interesting but had overlooked as not relevant to my concerns: reports of tiger attacks on villages. The entries on tiger attacks and aboriginal uprisings had a striking similarity in the eyes of the Chinese chroniclers: both represented intrusions into and disruptions of the Chinese occupation of the land, and from the point of view of the Chinese authors of the gazetteers, aborigines and tigers were all part of the same threat to their culture of settled agriculture. If the reports of aboriginal uprisings roughly charted Chinese penetration of the Guangxi frontier, I reasoned, might not the reports of tiger attacks be a more sensitive indicator?

Being quite ignorant of tiger behavior, I did some initial reading but soon decided I needed to talk with tiger experts. Fortunately, one of the world's greatest authorities on tigers was almost literally in my own backyard. Living in Washington, DC, while writing most of this book, I called Dr. John Siedensticker at the National Zoo, and after explaining my project and questions about tigers, he invited me to visit him near the tiger house at the zoo.

That visit precipitated another reconceptualization of my project. After talking with Dr. Siedensticker about China and my project, he asked me three simple questions that led me once again into new areas of research: Tigers inhabit forests, he said, so what were the forests like? As anyone who has traveled in south China knows, there are no forests there any more. What were the forests like 400 years ago, I repeated? I felt the same pain of ignorance as when I had been asked about climate, and Dr. Siedensticker wasn't even finished yet. Next he said that tigers prey on large game like deer or wild boar, and asked me which large game inhabited the forests and swamps of south China. Again I admitted my ignorance. The last question he asked had less to do with tigers than with humans: in the other parts of the world where he has studied tigers, an environmental danger to the North American and European scientists is malaria, and so he wondered about the prevalence of malaria there. Once again, I could not answer, although I later came to understand that his questions were the ones any good ecologist would ask about the relationships among living things in an ecosystem.

These questions about the relationship of climate and climatic change to historic harvest yields, tigers and forests, and malaria sent me into the literature on environmental history, and there I discovered rich monographic studies and thoughtful reflections on both the history of the environment and the methods and scope of environmental history. My intellectual journey was not yet complete, but by the time I read these works I was quite prepared to understand that the primary goal of environmental history, in the words of one practitioner, is to anchor human institutions – states, economies, societies – in "the natural ecosystems which provide the context for those institutions."[1] And that is just what I intend to do with this book.

As anyone who has read or studied Chinese history knows, nature is rarely part of the story.[2] Until I was asked these questions about climate, forests, tigers, and malaria and began reading in the secondary literature, I was not fully

[1] William Cronon, "Changes in the Land: Indians," *Colonists, and the Ecology of New England* (New York: Hill & Wang, 1983), vii.

[2] A significant exception is the work of Edward H. Schafer, whose works on south China during the Tang and Song dynasties (roughly the eighth through the twelfth centuries) attempted to convey something of the sensibilities of Chinese intellectuals about the exotic world they encountered in south China. See especially *The Vermilion Bird: T'ang Images of the South* (Berkeley and Los Angeles: University of California Press, 1967), and *Shore of Pearls* (Berkeley and Los Angeles: University of California Press, 1970).

aware how little nature has figured into Chinese history. Where has nature been? Where does the natural environment fit into the story? Why has it been left out? Having grown up in a small town in northern Wisconsin, I had loved the "woods," as we called the northern forest that surrounded the town and provided it with the raw materials for its basic industry, paper making. But as I moved away from that small town, first to the university and then to my first academic position in the urban sprawl of southern California, I became ever more removed from contact with the processes of nature. Perhaps our urban existence accounts in part for the disappearance of the natural environment from the histories we have written. But re-reading my Chinese sources – the local gazetteers, travelogues, and officials' memorials – with these new questions about the environment in mind opened up a whole new vista on late imperial Chinese history. When queried, these sources speak and provide some answers to John Siedensticker's questions.

And that, in brief, is how I came to write a history of the environment and economy of south China. To the questions about food supply, harvest yields, and agricultural production with which I started, I have added questions about climatic change and the environmental history of China. These questions are interesting enough in themselves, but the significant questions have to do with the relationships between humans and their environment: In what ways did the environment condition the ways in which people settled south China and provided for their subsistence? And what has been the impact of people upon the environment of south China?

Until recently, these large questions have not been the province of historians, but of anthropologists, geographers, and ecologists.[3] But this book is a history, and as a historian I would like to locate questions about China's environment in the context of my discipline by viewing three "triptychs": (1) Fernand Braudel's division of historical time into three layers; (2) Donald Worster's identification of the three levels upon which environmental history can proceed; and (3) a discussion of three different but related pairs of concepts – "ecology and technology," "nature and culture," and "environment and economy."

Fernand Braudel In his preface to *The Mediterranean and the Mediterranean World in the Age of Philip II*, Braudel divided his book into three parts, each representing separate layers "of overlapping histories, developing simultaneously." "The first . . . is . . . a history whose passage is almost imperceptible, that of man in his relationship to the environment, a history in which all change is slow, a history of constant repetition, ever-recurring cycles." The second layer, which Braudel called "social history," concerned the history of human groups

[3] See especially B. L. Turner II et al., eds. *The Earth as Transformed by Human Action: Global and Regional Changes in the Biosphere of the Past 300 Years* (Cambridge University Press, 1990).

and groupings: "economic systems, states, societies, civilizations and . . . warfare." Braudel considered the last layer to be the traditional history of individuals, "that is, the history of events: surface disturbances, crests of foam that the tides of history carry on their strong backs."[4]

Braudel of course has had an enormous impact upon historians, and he stands as perhaps the preeminent historian of the twentieth century. Many have learned from him and incorporated insights from his work, especially by locating their historical studies in terms of the "*longue durée*," the long-term view of social history. But despite Braudel's appropriation of the environment as belonging within the purview of the historian, few followed his lead in this direction. Without claiming that this book compares in any way with Braudel's *Mediterranean*, I think it can be usefully located in terms of Braudel's first two "layers" of history. To be sure, at some points in the book I will delve into the connections between social history and the "history of events," especially when considering the mid-seventeenth-century general crisis, but that realm is not the focus of this book. Here we look at the relationship between the environment and the economy.

Donald Worster. Braudel did not conceive of *The Mediterranean* as a history of the environment or as environmental history, in part because he had a larger agenda and in part, perhaps, because the field of environmental history had not yet taken form when he wrote. But by the time *The Mediterranean* was translated and published in English in 1972, some historians had begun to write what they considered to be "environmental history." Among these was the American historian Donald Worster, whose *Dust Bowl: The Southern Plains in the 1930s*,[5] was a pioneering and highly regarded work. In reflecting upon and trying to define the new field of environmental history that he helped create with his book, Worster recently argued that the new history proceeds along three lines of inquiry. "The first involves the discovery of the structure and distribution of natural environments of the past." This task is a prerequisite for writing environmental history, both because of the paucity of source materials and because doing so is not easy. "To make such a reconstruction," Worster advises, "the environmental historian must turn for help to a wide array of the natural sciences and must rely on their methodologies, sources, and evidence."[6] As I have already related, I have found all of that to

4 Fernand Braudel, *The Mediterranean and the Mediterranean World in the Age of Philip II*, Siân Reynolds trans. (New York: Harper and Row, 1972), 20–21. As much of the literature on global change now shows, the pace of environmental change both now and in the past has not been so slow as to be as "imperceptible" as Braudel thought.

5 Donald Worster, *Dust Bowl: The Southern Plains in the 1930s* (New York: Oxford University Press, 1979).

6 Donald Worster, *The Wealth of Nature: Environmental History and the Ecological Imagination* (New York: Oxford University Press, 1993), 48.

be true, and to be good advice as well. As environmental historians, we must rely on the work of scientists, and we must synthesize large amounts of scientific work for our purposes. Thus, to write this book I have relied on the work of climatologists, geologists, physical geographers, botanists, soil scientists, and zoologists, to mention just a few, to learn about climatic changes, forests, elephants and tigers, malaria, and the growth rates of rice plants. I can only hope that I have fairly and accurately synthesized the scientific research and conveyed it in a way that is understandable to those interested in Chinese history.

The second panel in Worster's triptych "focuses on productive technology as it interacts with the environment." The historian's tasks here, according to Worster, are to understand "how technology has restructured human ecological relations" and to analyze "the various ways people have tried to make nature over into a system that produces resources for their consumption. In that process of transforming the earth, people have also restructured themselves and their social relations."[7] In this book I am concerned mostly with agricultural technologies, including the use of fire to clear the forests and the construction of the vast and impressive water control and irrigation works necessary for wet-rice cultivation. An important part of that story is not only the human effort to produce enough food to support a large and growing population, but the ways in which that effort transformed the physical environment of south China.

From physical geography and the working of technology upon it, Worster turns in the third panel of his triptych to a consideration of the "more intangible, purely mental type of encounter in which perceptions, ethics, laws, and myths have become part of an individual's or group's dialogue with nature."[8] I wish I could have spent more time considering Chinese and non-Chinese conceptions of the environment within which they found themselves – from their explanations of diseases like malaria to attitudes toward forests and beliefs about the morality of land clearance – for they do raise important questions. Did their belief that the best use of land was for agriculture provide the Chinese with the moral justification for expropriating the lands of non-Chinese forest dwellers? Or did they not even feel the need for justification? Did beliefs about the causes of drought devalue tigers and remove compulsions about killing them off? I do not know the answers to questions like these. The most I am able to do is pose them and speculate about possible answers. I hope that readers will not feel shortchanged; perhaps others will take up a study of Chinese "mental encounters" with their environment, for such a study surely is needed.

The third triptych that I use to locate the subject matter of this book is a discussion of three related but different pairings – "ecology and technology,"

pairings

[7] Worster, *The Wealth of Nature*, 49. [8] Ibid.

"nature and culture," and "environment and economy" – each of which I considered as possible subtitles; I chose only the last as most apt, and I would like to explain why. First, the pairings themselves indicate that I am interested in exploring relationships, not just one or the other element. It is entirely possible, for example, to write a history of technology without considering the impact of technology upon ecosystems or to write the history of an economy without consideration of the environment, as any casual perusal of the books under the Library of Congress classification "HC" or "HD" will reveal. These three pairings thus represent a problematic conveyed by the tiny word "and": What was the relationship between the development of the economy *and* the environment? Was there a causal relationship that ran one way or the other, or a more complex and less certain relationship? The "and" in the subtitle therefore is highly problematic and not easily analyzed, regardless of which concepts are linked through it.

Environment and Economy. I have chosen to use the term "environment" rather than "ecology" or "nature" not just because it includes climate and climatic change, but also because the field has defined itself as "environmental history." To be sure, if "ecology" is the study of the relationship between living things and their environment, then it includes human beings. But "environmental history" has come to connote specifically the relationship of people to their environment, and so "environment" conveys a more precise meaning here than "ecology." By "economy" I do not mean to include all forms of production, distribution, and consumption, although that of course is its general definition, but rather in the context of late imperial China I want to emphasize the agricultural economy. I do so on the grounds not only that the economy was overwhelmingly based on agriculture and thus that the cycles of agriculture for the most part determined larger economic cycles, but also that agriculture is the economic activity most closely connected to the environment. Indeed, a whole field of study (and a journal) is devoted to "agricultural ecology." "Agriculture" or even "agricultural economy," though, would be too narrow, for in the scope of this book I include markets and grain prices, both of which are more properly included in the concept of economy; on the other hand, "agricultural economy" is often conceived in terms of the ways in which farming households make cropping and marketing decisions. Hence, for the title of the book at least, "economy" seems more appropriate and "economical" than other choices.

Time and Place. I would like now to return to a more personal narrative to explain my choices of time and place for the book. China, with an eighteenth-century population about the same as all of Europe west of the Urals, is too large and complex to analyze as a single unit. Merely because it remained a unified empire with a single name rather than fragmenting into countless political units that would become independent states, as happened in Europe, is not a good reason to attempt to write the history of "China" as if it were an undifferentiated whole. Like Europe, China is best analyzed in smaller units. The question is not whether to conceive of China in smaller units, but how best to do so. The strongest case so far has been developed by G. William Skinner, who analyzed China in terms of eight physiographic "macroregions" and then provided considerable empirical evidence that demographic and economic cycles of development occurred within those regions. As I will argue in various places in the book, Skinner's macroregional analysis is compelling and provides a starting point for analyzing China's economic and environmental history.

The region discussed here is called "Lingnan," which can be translated as South of Mountains. I will discuss the meaning and location of Lingnan more in Chapter 1, so for now it will suffice to identify it as the region roughly within a 200-mile radius of Hong Kong. I chose historic Lingnan for two basic reasons. Despite the compelling rationale for analyzing Chinese economic history in terms of macroregions, the Chinese state reported demographic and economic data according to political units – provinces, prefectures, and counties. Fortunately, Lingnan as a physiographic region is nearly coterminous with two provinces – Guangdong and Guangxi – so that collecting data has been significantly simplified. The two terms – "Lingnan," as defined physiographically, and "Liangguang," or the "Two Guang" provinces – are not exactly the same, so I will at times note and discuss the differences, but even these designations provide opportunities to test some of the hypotheses generated by a macroregional analysis.

I also chose Lingnan because I already knew something about the region and its history[9] and because few other scholars are focusing their attention on its history. Because this region of China is currently undergoing the most rapid and transforming economic development, an environmental history of Lingnan thus can provide an important context for understanding contemporary developments in the People's Republic of China.

Originally I had conceived of the book as focusing on just the eighteenth century, the period for which archival sources are most rich. But as I worked on the problems of the economy I realized I had to extend my analysis both earlier and later into the middle of the nineteenth century, with the bulk of the study on the period beginning about 1400 and ending in 1850. As Braudel pointed out, the history of the environment can best be told on the scale of centuries, while that of the economy requires long periods to chart the changes too. On these grounds alone, four and a half centuries would seem defensible. But they are not just any 450 years: they begin with the first reasonably

[9] Robert B. Marks, *Rural Revolution in South China: Peasants and the Making of History in Haifeng County, 1570–1930* (Madison: University of Wisconsin Press, 1984).

good, disaggregated population data and end with the mid-nineteenth-century Opium War, the Taiping Rebellion, and important changes in global temperatures.

Most of the book thus concerns the period of Chinese history most scholars now call "late imperial China." But a 1994 trip to Lingnan convinced me that it was necessary to extend the period of study even earlier. I visited three elements of the Lingnan landscape that had emerged in my mind as significant in defining the region: the Meiling Pass in northern Guangdong, "chiseled" through the mountains in 716 CE; the Ling Qu Canal in northern Guangxi, linking the Xiang River flowing north into the Yangzi River drainage system to the Li River flowing south into Lingnan's drainage system and constructed during the Qin dynasty (ca. 215 BCE); and the alluvial fields (*shatan*, or "sand flats") of the Pearl River delta, one of the most agriculturally rich and productive areas of China. The first two chapters thus cover aspects of the environmental history of Lingnan from the Qin (221–207 BCE) through the Yuan dynasty (1279–1368 CE), including the story of how the Pearl River delta came to be "made."

Problems and Perspectives

The central problematic of this book can be summarized as follows: What was the nature and extent of environmental change in south China? Did the activities of people contribute to environmental change? How can those changes be documented? Did climatic changes affect the environment and the economy? If so, how? And finally, did the environment and the changes (both naturally caused and anthropogenic) in the environment affect people, their choices, and, hence, their history? The picture of the relationship between people and the environment that emerges from this book is dialectical, not unidirectional. Just as people changed their environment, so too did the environment condition and shape the society and economy of south China. I explore this broad theme in terms of four major topics that are interwoven throughout the book: climatic change, population dynamics, commercialization of the economy, and the role of the state.

Climate. The sharpest way to phrase the question is: To what extent has climate change affected the course of history? In the context of current concerns about global warming and its possible dangers, this question is of more than passing interest. Answers so far have ranged from "slight, perhaps negligible,"[10] to "an important (and neglected) historical force."[11] The issue

[10] Emmanuel Le Roy Ladurie, *Times of Feast, Times of Famine: A History of Climate since the Year 1,000*, Barbara Bray trans. (Garden City: Doubleday, 1971) 119.

[11] The position attributed by Jan deVries to John Post and Christian Pfister, in "Measuring the Impact of Climate on History: The Search for Appropriate Methodologies," in R. I. Rothberg

has been highly controversial, stimulating debate over both data and methodologies.[12]

While these issues inform the work on climate that I present in this book, I do not suppose for one moment that my work will resolve the question. But I think it does contribute to the debate in at least two ways. First, nearly all of the work exploring the connection between climate and history has focused upon Europe. And while Europe and Europeans turned out to have been historically significant for the world, it seems to me imprudent to generalize from the history of that highly unusual peninsula of Asia. Bringing the Chinese historical record to bear should thus serve to broaden the base from which generalizations are made. Second, the evidence from south China leads me to take a middling position in the controversy. I certainly will not present a "climatic determinist" argument, but I do think that climatic fluctuation and change have affected human societies, especially those like late imperial China that were based upon agriculture. The problem is not merely to determine the specific linkages of climatic change to the ways a society or economy functioned, but also to document the ways in which humans responded to a changing climate, building and sustaining institutions that buffered people from unwanted consequences of climatic fluctuations, especially upon food supplies. Thus, rather than seeing humans as unresponsive, passive objects in the face of climatic changes (or vice versa), I think it makes more sense to think about the ways that climate and human society interacted. This does not mean that climatic fluctuations or changes were insignificant, but neither does it suppose that climate changes alone account for the course of historical change in south China (or elsewhere for that matter).

Population. Demographers are beginning to demonstrate similarly complex interrelationships between population dynamics and economic conditions;[13] one has even begun to probe the ways in which grain prices affected vital rates.[14] The point of this recent work is that population dynamics are

and T. K. Rabb, eds., *Climate and History: Studies in Interdisciplinary History* (Princeton: Princeton University Press, 1981), 23.

12 See the essays in Rothberg and Rabb, eds., *Climate and History*, and in T. M. L. Wigley, et al., eds., *Climate and History: Studies in Past Climates and Their Impact on Man* (Cambridge University Press, 1981). The debate, of course, is much older, going back at least to Ellsworth Huntington's *Climate and Civilization* (New Haven: Yale University Press, 3rd revised edition, 1924).

13 See especially three articles by Patrick Galloway: "Annual Variations in Deaths by Age, Deaths by Cause, Prices, and Weather in London, 1670–1830," *Population Studies* 39 (1985): 487–505; "Long-Term Fluctuations in Climate and Population in the Preindustrial Era," *Population and Development Review* 12, no. 1 (Mar. 1986): 1–24; and "Basic Patterns in Annual Variations in Fertility, Nuptiality, Mortality, and Prices in Pre-industrial Europe," *Population Studies* 42 (1988): 275–303.

14 James Lee, Cameron Campbell, and Guofu Tan, "Infanticide and Family Planning in Late Imperial China: The Price and Population History of Rural Liaoning, 1774–1873," in Thomas

related to broader conditions and are not exogenous forces acting upon the economy or environment; there are feedback loops that affect not merely mortality, but fertility and nuptiality as well. As readers will soon discover, I think that the size and distribution of the human population is a significant element in understanding the processes of environmental change in south China, and many chapters begin with a consideration of the size and growth of the population. But I am not a demographer, and I lack the data to explore the interrelationships in Lingnan between economic conditions and fertility, for example. Because I do not explore these questions and thereby limit my inquiry about population to its size and distribution, I may leave the impression that I think that population is exogenous to the processes of economic and environmental change that I am documenting. I do not believe that to be so, but I will have to leave it to others to probe the ways in which the economy and environment affected demographic vital rates.

Commercialization (without Capitalism). Coupled with the size and distribution of the population of south China, I see the commercialization of the economy as critically important in understanding the processes of environmental change. And Lingnan certainly became commercialized, not only with exports of silk to Southeast Asia and Europe and of sugar to central China, but also with rice trading in local markets throughout the region, flowing from the West River valley in Guangxi into Guangzhou and the Pearl River delta. Historians of China generally agree that the economy of late imperial China had become quite commercialized from about 1500 to 1850, and there is much agreement over the sources of that commercialization; they disagree, however, over what that commercialization signifies. And mostly, it seems to signify something about capitalism.

Capitalism – to use that term surely opens the biggest of historical cans of worms. Let me assure readers at the outset that I am familiar with the complexity of, disagreement over, and historiography about the concept, and hence understand that a brief attempt to define the term is fraught with danger and difficulty. But I must do so, however cursorily, to explain what I mean by "commercialization without capitalism." Most important, I do not equate commerce, specialization, markets, and profit seeking with capitalism.[15] Following Braudel, who, like Marx, Wallerstein, and a host of others, sees capitalism historically as a complex with particular modes (Braudel calls them "rules") of movement, change, and motion, it seems to me that commerce and commercialization are necessary, but not sufficient, for capitalism to exist. If we think,

G. Rawski and Lillian M. Li, eds., *Chinese History in Economic Perspective* (Berkeley and Los Angeles: University of California Press, 1992), 145–76.

15 This definition, of course, is the one usually thought of by those working within the framework developed by the followers of Adam Smith.

as Braudel does, of economic activity in world-economies[16] as occurring in three, ultimately connected and interconnected layers (i.e., in a hierarchy) – material life, commerce and markets, and large-scale finance and production – then late imperial China and early modern Europe (both world-economies) shared many commonalities in the first two realms, including extremely healthy, competitive markets supplied by small-scale, oftentimes household production units; Hill Gates calls this the "petty capitalist mode of production."[17] Where Europe and China differ fundamentally is in the third realm: the Chinese imperial state controlled large-scale finance, production, and much foreign trade through what Gates terms the "tributary mode of production,"[18] while the war-driven European state system allowed, enabled, and required[19] those activities to be controlled by private persons, thus producing capitalism. To me, the fact that China remained an empire makes all the difference: an extraordinarily competitive and efficient market system could develop (i.e., the process of commercialization), while simultaneously the imperial state, rather than capitalists, controlled the "commanding heights of the economy" (to borrow Lenin's phrase). Hence, "commercialization without capitalism" seems to me to an apt characterization of China's late imperial economy.

The reason this distinction is important is because prominent Western environmental historians have attributed environmental changes to the workings of the "capitalist mode of production."[20] The story that I will tell here certainly documents massive environmental changes in Lingnan, changes in land use and land cover such as the deforestation that led to the loss of species or the human creation of the Pearl River delta. But in south China, these changes were neither driven by, nor attributable to, the capitalist mode of production. Rather, we must look to the specifics of how the economy and environment in south China actually interrelated to be able to understand the nature of historical and environmental change there. Thus, the environmental history of Lingnan serves once again as a caution about generalizing only from the

[16] As understood in the Braudelian–Wallersteinian sense. See Fernand Braudel, *The Perspective of the World*, vol. 3 of *Civilization and Capitalism, 15th-18th Century*, Siân Reynolds, trans. (New York: Harper and Row, 1984), 21–70; Immanuel Wallerstein, *The Modern World System*, vol. 1, *Capitalist Agriculture and the Origins of the European World-Economy in the Sixteenth Century* (New York: Academic, 1977). Braudel and Wallerstein disagree regarding the origins of the European world economy, Wallerstein locating it with the failure of the Hapsburg quest for empire in the mid-sixteenth century, and Braudel in thirteenth-century Italy.

[17] Hill Gates, *China's Motor: A Thousand Years of Petty Capitalism* (Ithaca: Cornell University Press, 1996), 13–41.

[18] Ibid.

[19] See Charles Tilly, *Coercion, Capital and European States, AD 990–1990* (Cambridge, MA: Basil Blackwell, 1990).

[20] For one such argument, see Worster, *The Wealth of Nature*, 45–63.

experiences of Europe or North America and should prompt some revision of the larger story being told about how and why humans have changed the environment.

The State. To be sure, the rise of capitalism and the processes of making states are central themes in modern world history. But if those themes become significant in Chinese history after the middle of the nineteenth century, as Kenneth Pomeranz has so elegantly shown,[21] in the period before 1850 the rhythms of empire and the concerns of traditional Confucian statecraft animated the Chinese state. Nonetheless, by the beginning of the eighteenth century, new problems – in particular the growing population and the commercialization of the economy, to name the most important in south China – began to challenge Confucian statecraft practices. State officials from the emperors down to county magistrates had to respond to new situations, devising policies and approaches to new problems – especially those dealing with land reclamation – that affected the processes of environmental change.

The late imperial state thus took an active role in constructing both the economy and the environment. But "the state," while it may have been monomorphic, was neither monolithic nor monochromatic. Indeed, differences between the Yongzheng and Qianlong emperors (reigned 1723–35 and 1736–95, respectively) regarding land reclamation policies had significantly different impacts upon the environment. Nonetheless, I have been impressed with the reach of the late imperial state, which set up a data-gathering enterprise to help not merely in monitoring the economic pulse of the empire, but also in managing the economy. In China, the state mattered. But once again, in contrast to the major themes of European history, the expanding scope of the Chinese state had more to do with the patterns of empire formation and dissolution than with the making of the modern world.

Themes. While this book therefore addresses themes that may sound familiar to those more accustomed to European or American history, readers must remember that these themes played themselves out in China, where the empire and Confucian statecraft rather than capitalism and state making provided the critical context. Indeed, world-system theory is helpful in reminding us not only that all parts of the physical world were not parts of the capitalist world economy, but that in the centuries considered here, from 1400 to 1850, there was another world system centered on China.

The big theme of this book thus is the way in which climatic change, population, commercialization, and state action interacted to cause environmen-

big theme

[21] Kenneth Pomeranz, *The Making of a Hinterland: State, Society, and Economy in Inland North China, 1853–1937* (Berkeley and Los Angeles: University of California Press, 1993).

tal and economic change in south China, leading to an agroeconomic system that because it was not sustainable, resulted in severe environmental degradation and loss of biodiversity. No one of these factors alone is the single cause of this outcome, for what is interesting and historically significant are the interactions among all of these forces and the ways in which humans then responded to change, thereby affecting the environment (including climatic conditions), population dynamics, the economy, and state policies. These interrelationships will not be explored in each chapter, but will build up layer by layer throughout the book.

Organization of the Book. In Chapter 1, I describe the natural environment of Lingnan, focusing on the defining physical characteristics of the region, in particular the mountains and river systems, and I reconstruct the forests and wildlife populations of Lingnan, before bringing the human population into the story in Chapter 2. In this chapter I take a broad overview of the size and distribution of the population from 2 to 1400 CE, and consider the environmental circumstances that patterned the Han Chinese settlement of Lingnan, including the creation of the Pearl River delta. Chapter 3 focuses upon the population and economic history of Lingnan during the Ming dynasty (1368–1644 CE), examining the linkages between the growth of the economy and changes in land use and cropping patterns, as well as the increasing commercialization of the economy.

In Chapter 4, I locate the transition from the Ming to the Qing (1644–1911) dynasty and the attendant wars of conquest in the context of a general crisis of the mid-seventeenth century, as well as explore both the environmental causes and consequences of the great loss of population during those decades. Chapter 5 examines the resurgence of economic growth that began in the late seventeenth century, which I argue was caused by the rapid expansion of overseas trade, changing cropping patterns caused by trade in silk and sugar, and the emergence of a marketing system that linked all of Lingnan into a single economic unit. In Chapter 6, I reconstruct the patterns of climatic change affecting Lingnan and explore the linkages between climatic fluctuations and harvest yields, focusing upon the eighteenth century. Chapters 7 and 8 then take up two ways in which the people of Lingnan responded to the variations in harvest yields caused by the climatic fluctuations: the state granary system and the private market for rice. Chapter 8 also documents the commercialization of rice and the generally rising price of rice during the eighteenth century.

Faced with both rising grain prices and a growing population, state officials felt pressure to resolve what seemed to them an impending crisis by designing and implementing various land reclamation schemes, the topic of Chapter 9. In Chapter 10, I examine the ecological consequences of land clearance, including deforestation, the increased incidence of flood and drought, and the extinction of species. In the Conclusion I summarize the processes of environmental change described in the previous chapters and then return to a consideration of the broader issues raised in the Introduction.

Finally, a note about conventions. First, I use pinyin romanization throughout, with one exception: as I write, Hong Kong remains under British control, and thus will not become Xiang Gang until July 1, 1997. Second, with regard to place names, I have tried to use their late imperial (i.e., Ming and Qing dynasty) forms, with a preference whenever possible to use the ca. 1820 forms. This convention may open me to the charge of anachronism, but I think it will reduce confusion for the nonexperts among the readers, and it does simplify (the often extremely complex) task of mapping and geographic information system (GIS) analysis. Also, although there were various names (*xian*, *ting*, etc.) for the lowest-level political unit in the late imperial state, I translate all as "county." Finally, instead of BC and AD for dating, I use "BCE" ("before the common era") and "CE" ("common era").

1

"FIRS AND PINES A HUNDRED SPANS ROUND":

THE NATURAL ENVIRONMENT OF LINGNAN

To begin this study with a chapter subtitled "the natural environment" followed by one on "human settlement" presents something of a false dichotomy between nature on the one hand and people on the other, for as ecologists have insisted, human beings are a part of a broader ecosystem. Moreover, people are "in" the environment in another sense as well: as the observers. To describe the natural environment of south China requires looking through two lenses, one of which has been crafted in our times, the other of which is provided by Chinese sources. Our times focus the description in a particular way. Historians have only lately begun to locate their work within the context of "environmental history," and with good reason, for it was in the 1960s and 1970s that scientists' warning bells about the dangers of environmental degradation began to be heard. Historians cannot be blamed too much for creating the field of environmental history only in the context of these contemporary concerns about pollution of the land and air, depletion of energy sources, deforestation of the tropics, and global warming. Given this context, the kinds of questions environmental historians have been asking about the past have been conditioned by these contemporary concerns. I too have been concerned about global warming, the destruction of forests and wetlands, and the fate of the large cats, and these concerns have found their way into this book, certainly opening up some avenues of investigation, but just as surely closing down others.

Just as the issues of our times filter the ways in which we perceive the environment, so too did the concerns and views of the people who left written records select out what they saw and reported in their documents, whether these observers lived in the tenth or the eighteenth century. For better or worse, these observers were mostly Chinese, with all of the literary and organizational skills they possessed, but also with beliefs, biases, and prejudices about other peoples and about nature. Thus, even if we want to know more about forests and the way of life of non-Chinese inhabitants, for instance, we have to do so through the eyes of people who placed the highest value on settled agriculture. Sometimes we might learn what we want to know, but at other times the Chinese observers may have been blinded by their value system and so failed to report about phenomena we might think were interesting or relevant.

The limitations of traditional historical sources can be augmented, at least with respect to significant aspects of the environment, by more recent observations and by scientific studies. To see the mountains and the delta, to sense the amount and timing of the rains, to see the rice grow, or to hear the snarl of the tiger outside a village wall, we need not rely solely upon sources from the period under consideration, but may without too many caveats draw upon sources from other times and places.

The purpose of this section on the environment thus neither is intended to be, nor could it be, a description of all of the interlocking ecosystems that historically comprised the south China environment. The task would be too gargantuan, even if I wanted to do it. I am a historian, not an ecologist, and the approach taken here is open to the charge of being anthropocentric, for I am indeed interested here in the environment insofar as it related to the human activity of securing a livelihood from the soil. With that caveat in mind, let us turn our attention to the south of China.

Physical Landscape

Braudel entitled the first section of his book on the Mediterranean in the Age of Philip II, "Mountains Come First."[1] That holds for us too, not just because it makes geologic or historical sense, but also because it causes us to change the perspective from which we view south China. For if we first examine a standard map of China and locate the space now occupied by the two provinces of Guangdong and Guangxi, we see that the region of our concern is coastal, straddling the Tropic of Cancer. Indeed, most Americans and Europeans looking at a map of China will read it first from the east or southeast looking toward the west or northwest, as if on a plane flying westward to China. This reading of the map conforms both to the direction most Americans read and tell their own history – from the east looking west[2] – and to the way in which Europeans first encountered China. From this perspective, the first elements we see are the coasts and the coastal cities, and only later, after some exploration of this fringe, do our eyes move inland to the great river systems and mountain ranges of China.

But if instead of the usual east-to-west reading of China, we adopt a Chinese reading of their own geography, then we will begin to see it from the north looking toward the south. Chinese civilization originated north of the

[1] Fernand Braudel, *The Mediterranean and the Mediterranean World in the Age of Philip II*, Siân Reynolds, trans. (New York: Harper and Row, 1972), vol. 1: 25–52.

[2] Dee Brown made this point elegantly in *Bury My Heart at Wounded Knee* (New York: Holt, Rinehart, & Winston, 1970), xvi.

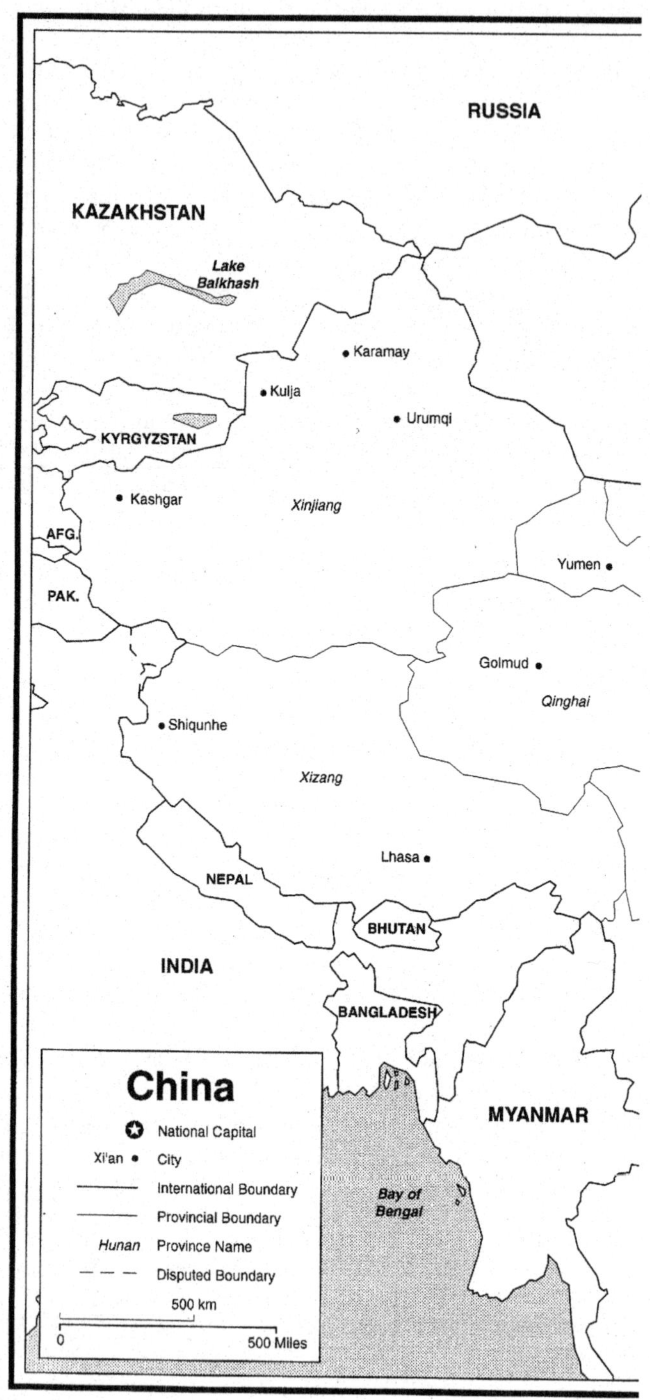

Map 1.1a. South China, ca. 1990

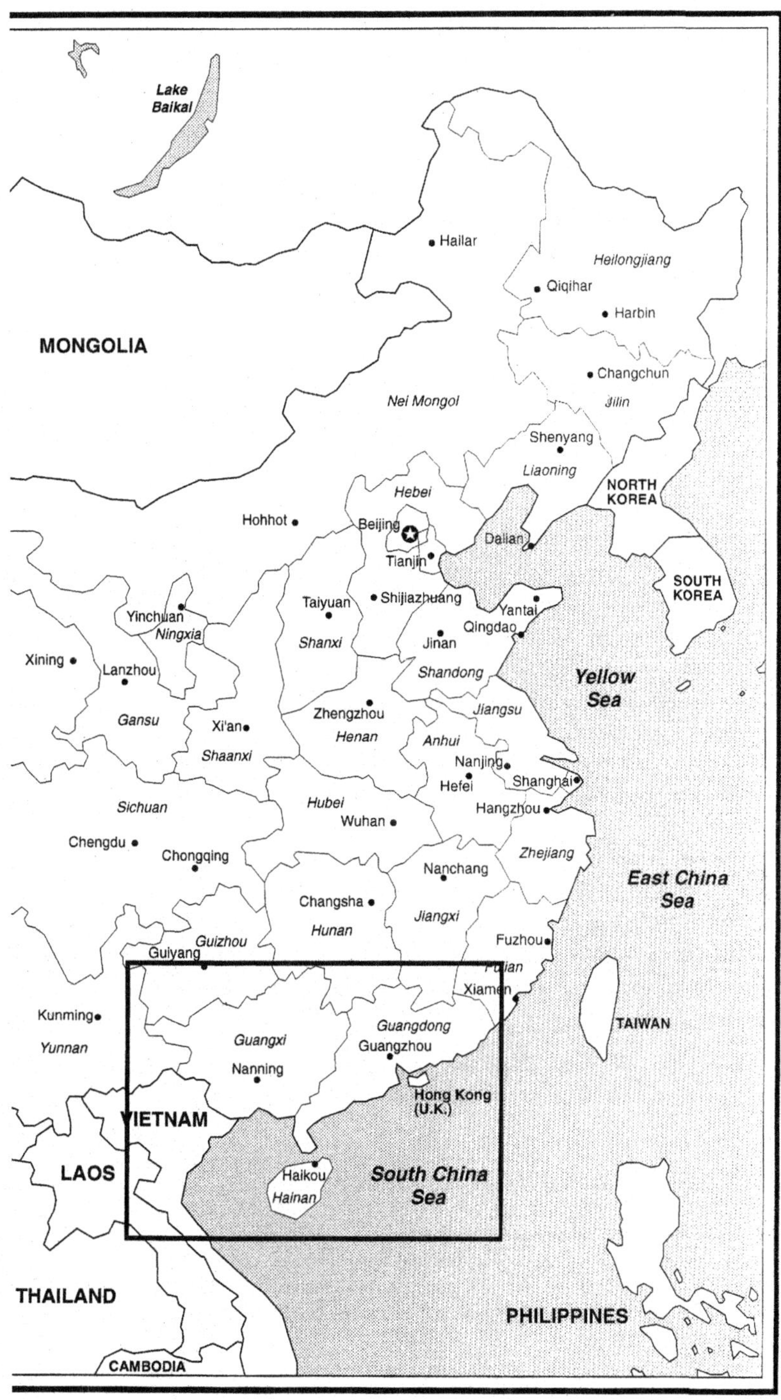
Lake Baikal
MONGOLIA
Hailar
Heilongjiang
Qiqihar
Harbin
Changchun
Jilin
Nei Mongol
Shenyang
Liaoning
NORTH KOREA
SOUTH KOREA
Hebei
Hohhot
Beijing
Dalian
Tianjin
Taiyuan
Shijiazhuang
Yantai
Qingdao
Yinchuan
Ningxia
Shanxi
Jinan
Shandong
Xining
Lanzhou
Yellow Sea
Gansu
Zhengzhou
Henan
Jiangsu
Xi'an
Shaanxi
Anhui
Nanjing
Hefei
Shanghai
Sichuan
Hubei
Wuhan
Hangzhou
Chengdu
Chongqing
Zhejiang
Nanchang
East China Sea
Changsha
Jiangxi
Hunan
Guizhou
Guiyang
Fuzhou
Fujian
Xiamen
Kunming
Yunnan
Guangdong
Guangxi
Guangzhou
TAIWAN
Nanning
Hong Kong (U.K.)
VIETNAM
LAOS
Haikou
Hainan
South China Sea
THAILAND
PHILIPPINES
CAMBODIA

Qinling Mountains, gradually spreading south into the Yangzi River valley around Suzhou and Hangzhou in the region more generally known as Jiangnan, or "south of the river." By Tang times (618–907 CE), when a material and cultural civilization centered in Jiangnan arose and flourished, the southern extent of its world was marked by a low mountain range the Chinese at the time called the Nanling, the "southern ranges," or "southern mountains." To the south of the Nanling Range was the region known as Lingnan, the area "south of the mountains," which was more backward and less culturally refined than Jiangnan. While not uninhabited and having been governed as part of the Chinese empire since the First Emperor, Qin Shi Huang Di, first conquered it around 230 BCE, still, in Song times, the authorities considered Lingnan sufficiently far from the cultured center of Chinese civilization to be an appropriate place to banish political enemies.

Among the most famous – if not the first[3] – of political exiles to Lingnan was the renowned Song poet Su Dongbo. Sent in 1094 to serve as a county magistrate in Lingnan as punishment for some politically incorrect commentaries on the emperor, Su headed south from the capital in Kaifeng, pausing first around Nanjing and then continuing up the Yangzi River to Poyang Lake in Jiangxi. From Poyang Lake, Su headed south, up the Gan River toward the Nanling Mountains. From the base of the Nanling Range at the headwaters of the Gan River in Nan'an prefecture could be seen a saddle between the higher peaks of the Nanling, marking the Meiling Pass through the Dayu Mountains. According to his biographer, Lin Yutang, Su stopped to rest when he reached the pass: "It was a sentimental place where many travelers scribbled poems on the rocks. Standing there on the peak of the mountain, so close to the sky and the clouds, Su [Dongbo] felt that he was living in a dream world" (see Map. 1.1a).[4]

Centuries later, in 1793, Sir George Staunton and the rest of the MacCartney Mission to Beijing were among the first Westerners to follow the route south from Beijing, like Su Dongbo passing through Nanjing and up the Gan River to the Meiling Pass.[5] In his book about the MacCartney Mission, Staunton described the view from the Meiling Pass looking south into Lingnan:

> The mountain is clothed [on the Jiangxi side] with plantations of trees to its utmost height, from whence an extensive and rich prospect opens at once to

[3] For a description of the political exiles in Tang Lingnan, see Schafer, *The Vermilion Bird*, ch. 3.

[4] Lin Yutang, *The Gay Genius: The Life and Times of Su Tungpo* (New York: John Day, 1947), 346.

[5] The MacCartney Mission was not the first group of Westerners to travel up the Gan River to the Meiling Pass. In 1549, several Portuguese were taken prisoner in Fujian and transported overland to Guilin, probably traveling over the Meiling Pass. See the chronicle of Galeote Pereira in Charles R. Boxer, *South China in the Sixteenth Century* (London: Hakluyt Society, 1953), esp. 30–32.

> the eye. A gentle and uniform descent of several miles on every side, almost entirely clothed with lively verdure, and crowned with towns, villages, and farm-houses, is, as it were . . . "laid at the feet of the spectator," whilst distant plains of unbounded extent, with mountains rising out of the horizon, terminate the view. Towards the southerly point of the compass appeared, however, a tract of waste and barren ground. The hills scattered over the plain appeared, comparatively to the vast eminence from whence they were viewed, like so many hay-ricks;[6] as is, indeed, the distant appearance of many other Chinese hills. The town of [Nan'an], which the travelers had lately left, from their present situation, seemed merely to be a heap of tiles, while the river that passed by it was like a shining line. The mountain, so superior to the surrounding objects, must be of much higher elevation above the surface of the sea. It cannot be less than one thousand feet higher than the source of the [Gan River] . . . up which the party had navigated.[7]

From the Meiling Pass, both Su Dongbo and George Staunton looked south into Lingnan and commented upon the natural environment – the peak of the mountain, the verdant hills, the rivers – as well as the human elements in the environment: the villages, the farmhouses, and the path leading up to the pass. Their views of the south raise questions for us not only about the environment they saw – what were the forests like? What kind of animals lived in the forests? What was the climate like? – but also about the relationship between the people living there and the environment, for as perceived by these two observers, the environment was not purely "natural," if by that we mean the absence of human influence, but included people in the landscape. Indeed, the very place from which they recorded their first views of China "south of the mountains" was in fact a human creation: the Meiling Pass.

The Meiling Pass had been "chiseled" (*zao*) by human labor during the Tang dynasty (in 716 CE) under the leadership of the engineer and state minister, Zhang Jiuling. A native of Shaozhou in northern Lingnan, a place some 90 miles southwest of the pass, Zhang ascended the ranks of the Tang bureaucracy and ultimately found himself positioned to be able to "improve" the pass, the main link between the Yangzi River valley and Lingnan. As might be imagined, the path over the Meiling Pass originally had been a single, rugged mountain trail winding over steep precipices. As Zhang Jiuling described it, Meiling was

> Formerly, an abandoned road in the east of the pass,
> Forbidding in the extreme, a hardship for men.
> An unswerving course; you clambered aloft

[6] In Chinese, this section of the Nanling Range is called the Dayu Ling, or "Big Grain-Stack Mountains," a name conveying a similar image.

[7] Sir George L. Staunton, *An Authentic Account of an Embassy from the King of Great Britain to the Emperor of China* (Philadelphia, 1799), vol. 2: 213–14.

On the outskirts of several miles of heavy forest,
With flying bridges, clinging to the brink
Halfway up a thousand fathoms of layered cliffs.[8]

As trade between Lingnan and areas to the north picked up after the Tang reestablished political unity and stability in the seventh century, the amount of silk and porcelain flowing into Lingnan increased, as did exports of furs, pelts, incense, and medicinal herbs. With more trade, the need to improve the route over the Meiling Pass arose, and in 716 CE state minister Zhang Jiuling began to cut a less steep, broader gradient over the Meiling Pass, lowering the solid rock by some 20 yards to create a pass about 3 yards wide (Figure 1.1). Not only did Zhang chisel the pass through solid rock, he paved the road on either side with small stones. The pass effectively linked the Gan River in Jiangxi with the North River in Lingnan. According to Ye Xian'en, the Tang opening of the Meiling Pass reoriented shipping routes in Lingnan: the North River became increasingly busy, while the former route through Guangxi fell into disuse.[9] Singing the praises of his own work, Zhang Jiuling boasted after he cut the pass:

The several nations from beyond the sea
Use it daily for commercial intercourse;
Opulence of teeth, hides, feathers, and furs;
Profits in fish, salt, clams, and cockles.[10]

Thus, to Chinese and even the first Western travelers overland from the Yangzi valley into south China, the Nanling Mountains do come first, if I may paraphrase Braudel. For at least a millennia, all of China "south of the mountains" was called Lingnan, an area stretching from westernmost Guangxi province into Fujian province on the east, and culminating in the sea or in tributary countries "beyond the south sea." But the Nanling Mountains defined Lingnan not just in the Chinese sense we have been discussing so far, but also in terms of its physical geography.

Mountains and highlands

Three distinct ranges define the northern, western, and southwestern boundaries of Lingnan: the Nanling Mountains in the north, the Yunnan–Guizhou Plateau to the west, and the low coastal Yunkai Range in the south and southwest.

[8] Translated and quoted in Schafer, *The Vermilion Bird*, 22.

[9] Ye Xian'en, Tan Dihua, and Luo Yixing, *Guangdong hang yun shi* (Beijing: Renmin jiaotong chuban she, 1989), 51–53.

[10] Translated and quoted in Schafer, *The Vermilion Bird*, 22.

Figure 1.1. The Meiling Pass, 1994.

The Nanling Mountains, a sinuous belt of several ranges the Chinese sometimes called the "Five Ranges" (Wu Ling) because of the names of five sections of the range, divides the Yangzi valley from Lingnan in a generally east–west alignment between latitudes 25° and 26° N. Today, weathered and rounded or gullied, the Nanling Range averages about 3,000 feet above sea level, with some of the peaks rising to 6,000 feet. These mountains are, however, fairly old and in terms of internal structure and genesis can be compared with the Appalachians in eastern North America.[11] Thus, as mountains they are not large or rugged, and they have served less as a barrier and more as an obstacle to commerce between central and south China.

In the grand scope of geological time, the area that is now south China was still covered with ocean some 200 million years ago when north China already had become continental land. When the uplift of south China began in the early to middle Jurassic, hundreds of millions of years of sediment had been deposited and formed into sandstone or limestone, and then tectonic pressures folded and refolded the sedimentary rocks into low mountains in a generally east-to-west configuration. The geological processes that created the Nanling Range were complex (and still not fully understood), resulting in three separate regions in the range. The western Nanling, separating the Guizhou Plateau from the Guangxi Basin, follows a mainly east–west orientation. In the central section, roughly from the border of eastern Guangxi westward to the Guangdong–Jiangxi border, the range zigzags southward and then northward again before resuming in its eastern section an irregular east–west alignment to the junction with the southeastern uplands.

Delineating the eastern edge of the Nanling Range, the southeastern uplands comprise a separate geologic formation and follow a southwest–northeast direction covering southern Jiangxi, the whole of Fujian, and eastern Guangdong province. Topographically distinct from the rest of Lingnan, the rivers of the southeastern upland have a distinctive pattern, flowing southeasterly in trellis-tributary patterns to the sea. Included in this region are Chaozhou and Jiaying prefecture in eastern Guangdong province. The border between the two regions is defined by the watershed between the Han River, which flows directly into the sea like the other river systems in the southeast coastal region, and the East River, which has its outlet in the Pearl River delta. To the Chinese, Lingnan thus included the area occupied by easternmost Guangdong province and all of Fujian province. Geologically and physiographically, though, that part of south China is distinct from the rest of Lingnan. To give the term "Lingnan" more geographic rigor than that used by Chinese observers, we will restrict it here to mean the Nanling Range and the three other physiographic subregions south of the mountains that for the most part lie within Guangdong and Guangxi provinces. Thus excluded from Lingnan proper are the Qing-era Guangdong prefectures of Chaozhou and Jiaying.[12]

[11] K. J. Hsü, "Origin of Sedimentary Basins of China," in X. Zhu, ed., *Chinese Sedimentary Basins* (Amsterdam: Elsevier, 1989), caption to Fig. 17.2 on p. 211.

[12] This definition of Lingnan follows that developed by G. William Skinner in two articles, "Regional Urbanization in Nineteenth-Century China," and "Cities and the Hierarchy of Local Systems," both in G. William Skinner, ed., *The City in Late Imperial China* (Stanford: Stanford University Press, 1977), 282.

The Yunnan–Guizhou plateau rises in the western part of Guangxi province, and to the south a low coastal range of mountains arc from present-day Vietnam through the border with Guangdong, enclosing the Guangxi Basin. Most of the surface of the basin is a tableland with an average elevation of about 1,000 feet, although in the western part of the basin a sharp step up in elevation toward the Yun–Gui plateau is marked by the Yao Hills, which run north-northeast on a line just to the west of the cities of Nanning and Liuzhou. The Guangxi Basin is essentially the drainage basin for the West River, with the tributaries all ultimately converging at the city of Wuzhou into a single trunk. The West River basin constitutes a well-defined subphysiographic region, connected to Guangdong province through the single point in Wuzhou where the West River flows out of Guangxi and into Guangdong (see Map 1.1b).

The southern border of Lingnan is a long coastal zone of varying width running southwest from the Pearl River delta to the Vietnam border, separated from the rest of Lingnan by a range of low folded sandstone rocks metamorphosed by granitic or igneous intrusions. The coastal belt, largely the Leizhou Peninsula, contains considerable lowlands drained by short rivers flowing into the South China Sea or the Gulf of Tonkin. Some 15 miles offshore lies Hainan Island, an essentially mountainous continuation of the same geological structure as the southeastern coastal region, with peaks in the central range reaching 5,500 feet. Narrow alluvial lowlands, mostly in the north facing the Leizhou Peninsula, ring the island.

As a physiographic unit, then, Lingnan is composed of subregions that more or less fit together. I say "more or less" because the region is not simply a basin surrounded by mountains, as one might conceive of Sichuan province or a single river valley. Rather, two features constrain the physical unity of Lingnan. First, the low coastal range that forms the southern rim of the Guangxi basin forms a watershed, forcing the West River drainage system to remain within Guangxi and dividing southwestern Guangdong from the rest of Lingnan. Without this low range, the West River drainage system might well have flowed directly into the Gulf of Tonkin. While denied a coastal outlet by the low hills, the West River constituted the most important linkage of Guangxi to Guangdong. Physiographically, this single connection between the Guangxi Basin and the Pearl River delta may be seen as a weak link, formed only because of the flow of water into the West River drainage system. One might think of the West River basin as being precariously stuck to western Guangdong with a single pin near the city of Wuzhou. Without sufficient amounts of water, the Guangxi Basin may well not have been connected to the rest of Lingnan at all. And the reason there is plenty of water to fill the rivers – usually, that is – is because of the climate of south China.

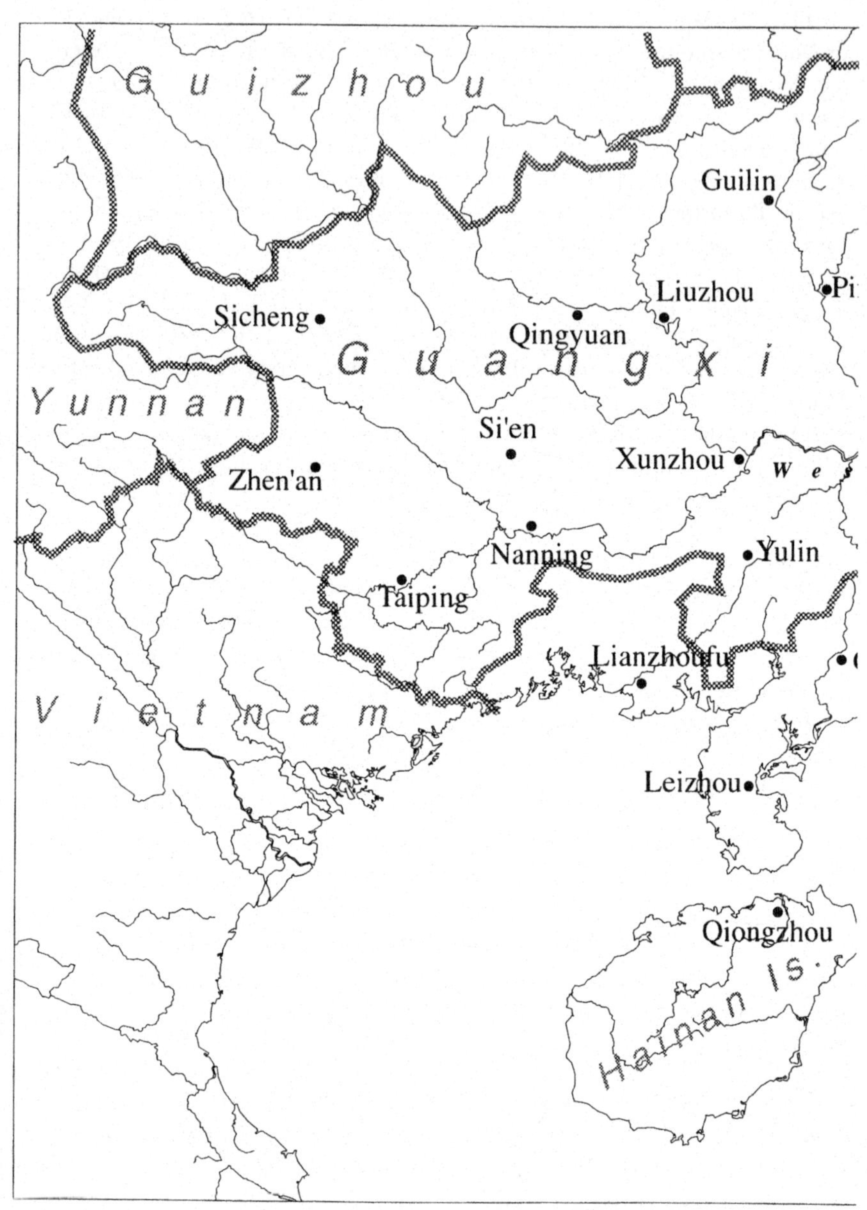

Map 1.1b. South China, ca. 1820

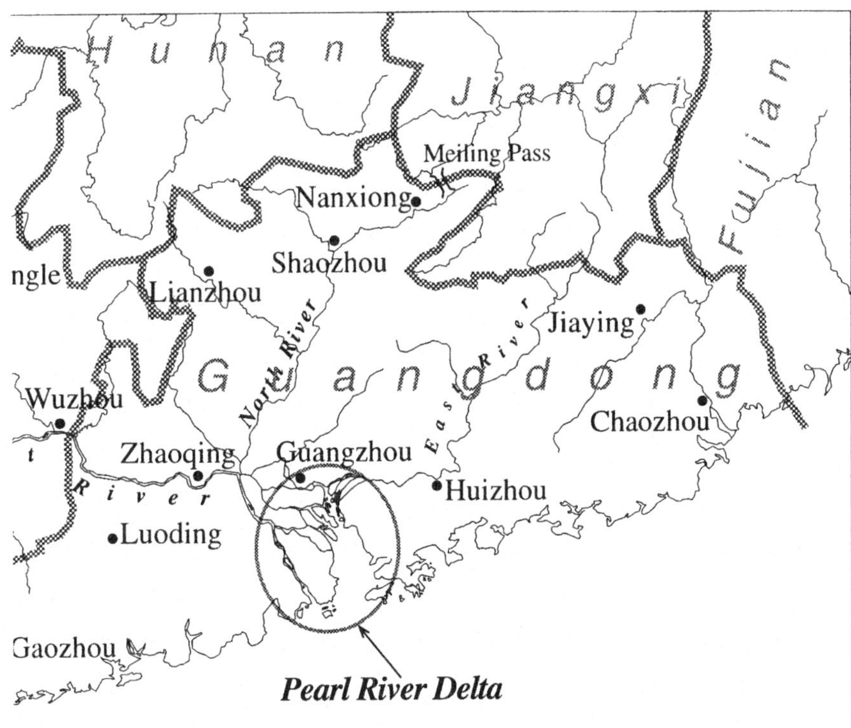

South China Sea

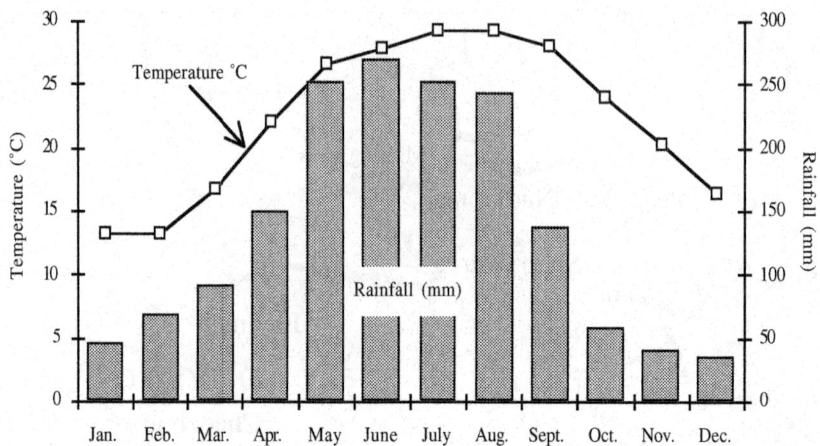

Figure 1.2. Mean monthly temperature and rainfall at Guangzhou. Source: International Rice Research Institute, *Rice Research and Production in China* (Los Banos, Philippines: IRRI, 1979), 25.

Climate

The present climate of Lingnan is classified broadly as subtropical to tropical; Guangdong and Guangxi provinces straddle the Tropic of Cancer, while the more southerly positioned Leizhou Peninsula and Hainan Island have a tropical climate.[13] Current monthly mean temperatures throughout the region range from about 10 to 30°C, and plentiful rainfall (about 1,600 mm annually) falls mostly during the agricultural growing season. Although the region is not frost free, the growing season ranges from 250 to 320 days (10°C is the minimum temperature for growing rice).[14] Figure 1.2 summarizes present climatological data (temperature and rainfall) for the city of Guangzhou.

While the Nanling Mountains separate Lingnan from central China, too much emphasis should not be placed on the mountains as a climatic dividing line, for the dominant feature of climate throughout China, and not just Lingnan, is the summer and winter monsoons. As we have seen, the Nanling Range actually is not very high, allowing for a significant exchange of air

[13] For a classification of China's climatic zones, see Zhang Jiacheng and Lin Zhiguang, *Climate of China*, Ding Tan, trans. (New York: Wiley, 1992), 285.

[14] In northern Guangdong province, because of higher altitudes and exposure to cold currents in the winter, there are only about 225 frost-free days, and the growing season is hence shorter. See International Rice Research Institute, *Rice Research and Production in China* (Los Banos, Philippines: IRRI, 1979), 25.

masses from north to south over the mountains and vice versa. Not high enough to be a climatic barrier, the low-lying Nanling Range enables monsoon winds to flow north into central China instead of being blocked or directed elsewhere. Each winter, a continental air mass located in Siberia sends cold, dry winds from the north, while in the early summer through autumn winds from the south and southeast bring moisture-laden air from the Pacific Ocean over the Asian landmass, defining China's monsoonal climate.[15]

The summer monsoon has a definite annual cycle and brings 80 percent of China's rain, nearly all of it in the summer months. In the winter months, a cold polar front with dominant winds blowing from the inland northwest blocks the moisture-laden southeasterly winds from reaching China. China's rainy season begins in the spring as the polar front recedes northward with warmer temperatures. In late spring, the clockwise circulation of air around the high pressure system brings rains to south China, and in early summer the high directs rain toward central China and the Yangzi Valley. By July and August, the northernmost retreat of the subtropical high brings rain to north China. With cooling northern hemisphere temperatures in the fall, the advancing polar front pushes the Pacific subtropical high southward, and in September and October typhoon rains hit south and southwest China. As the polar front advances further in the winter months, nearly all of China is rain free (except for drizzle in the Yangzi Valley).[16]

When the North Pacific subtropical high moves in this regular annual cycle, "normal" and predictable rainfall patterns appear. For Lingnan, the monsoon brings a considerable amount of rain, ranging from over 80 inches in Hong Kong on the coast to 51 inches in Wuzhou and 67 inches in Guangzhou. By any standards, that is a lot of precipitation. Not only is there a lot of rain, it is concentrated in just five or six months of the year, from April through October. Since neither evaporation nor soil permeability or retention could contain the vast quantities of water that falls upon Lingnan, it runs off the surface and fills the natural lines of drainage. As Fenzel succinctly and aptly concluded, "consequently, extended river systems had to develop themselves in order to ensure the removal of the water."[17]

[15] A monsoon is defined as "alternating winds between winter and summer, the direction of which varies more than 120°." Manfred Domrös and Peng Gongping, *The Climate of China* (Berlin: Springer, 1988), 41.

[16] This paragraph is based on Zhang Jiacheng and Thomas B. Crowley, "Historical Climate Records in China and the Reconstruction of Past Climates," *Journal of Climate* 2 (Aug. 1989): 835. See also Zhu Kezhen and Zhang Baogun, *Zhongguo zhi yuliang* (Beijing: Ziyuan weiyuan hui, 1936), 1–12.

[17] G. Fenzel, "On the Natural Conditions Affecting the Introduction of Forestry as a Branch of Rural Economy in the Province of Kwangtung, Especially in North Kwangtung," *Lingnan Science Journal* 7 (June 1929): 72.

Table 1.1. *The Pearl River drainage basin, compared with the Yangzi and Yellow Rivers*

River	Drainage area (sq. km)	Flow (cu. m/sec.)	Suspended (kg/cu. m)	Silt carried (kg/sec.)	Silt carried (ton/sq. km/yr.)
Yangzi River	1,705,383	28,500	0.575	16,388	1,686
Yellow River	687,869	1,350	37.700	50,895	293
West River	329,705	6,294	0.321	2,020	201
North River	38,363	1,280	0.126	161	n.a.
East River	25,325	697	0.136	95	n.a.
Pearl River system	393,393	8,271	<0.321	2,276	>201

Source: Chen, *Zhongguo ziran dili*, vol. 4, *Dibiao shui*: 71–75, 108–11.

Rivers and Soils

Lingnan's "extended river systems" consist primarily of three rivers – the East, the North, and the West – which converge in the Pearl River delta and then empty into the South China Sea. As can be readily seen from Map 1.1b, the drainage basin of the West River is the largest and most important, followed by those of the North and the East Rivers. The catchment basins and the structure of these major river systems conform to the topography of Lingnan, with most of the river systems contributing to the flow of water into the Pearl River. Shorter, smaller rivers in southwest Lingnan flow directly into either the South China Sea or the Gulf of Tonkin. While the West River system constitutes the largest drainage in Lingnan, in comparison with other drainage systems in the rest of China, it ranks third behind the Yellow River and Yangzi River systems.

Besides the length of its rivers and area of its drainage basins, the Lingnan system exhibits three other characteristics that differentiate it from the Yellow and Yangzi Rivers. First, the amount of water flowing into Lingnan's river systems fluctuates wildly with the monsoon, rising rapidly in the rainy season and falling equally dramatically in the dry season.[18] A sense of how dramatic the swings are can be seen in the West River water level at Wuzhou. As will be recalled, by the time the West River reaches Wuzhou, the water from all its tributaries in Guangxi has entered the stream; from Wuzhou, the West River spills into Guangdong province. At flood stage, up to 2 million cubic feet per second flow past Wuzhou, with the water level an average of 60 feet above the dry-season level. In extremely wet years, the West River could rise even higher;

[18] For the comparative data, see Chen Binyi, editor in chief, *Zhongguo ziran dili*, vol. 4, *Dibiao shui* (Beijing: Kexue chuban she, 1981), 73–77.

in 1915, for instance, the water rose to 82.3 feet above the dry-season level, and when the West River spilled into Guangdong province that year, massive flooding occurred.[19]

Second, the Lingnan rivers carry (and have carried) the least amount of silt of any major river system in China (see Table 1.1). Although the Pearl River drainage system (which includes the West, North, and East Rivers) is the third largest in China, it carries but 12 percent of the amount of silt in the Yangzi River, though this is partly because of the greater flow of the Yangzi system.[20] Before the forest cover of Lingnan was removed (a story I take up in later chapters), anecdotal evidence from the Tang era indicates that the rivers ran clear.[21] But even in the nineteenth and twentieth centuries, after the forests had been removed, the hills were not barren, but covered with a tough grass that held much of the soil in place. Comparatively, then, the Pearl River drainage system washed less soil to the ocean than the Yellow and Yangzi Rivers, but it carried enough silt that it settled out and began forming a delta.

Indeed, during the summer monsoon, enough soil was washed into the rivers, especially the West, to lend them a muddy appearance. "So," in the words of a twentieth-century observer,

> during the summer months, the swelled rivers carry along with their brown, turbid waters enormous quantities of sedimentary materials and, in the lower courses, where the rivers transverse the delta at a much slower speed, and split up into a network of channels, these materials are deposited quickly. In this deposition, however, though it leads to a steady growth of the land at the cost of the rivers and the back waters of the bays, which gradually lead over to the open sea, a strict boundary between the firm land and the water is lacking nearly everywhere, and extremely high waters inundate even areas which have long since been regarded as finally dry and secure from floods.[22]

The amount of silt carried by these rivers thus was significantly less than that carried by the Yellow River, but the Pearl River system nonetheless did carry enough silt to be deposited at the mouths of the rivers to form a delta. Moreover, the amount of silt varied from one historical epoch to another as people settled and cleared the land. Indeed, the pace by which the Pearl River delta formed, as I will discuss in more detail in the next chapter, hastened concurrent with the clearance of land in the upper reaches of the North and West Rivers, which increased the amount of silt flowing downstream.

19 G. W. Olivercrona, "The Flood Problem of Kwangtung," *Lingnan Science Journal* 3, no. 1 (1925): 1–2.

20 Chen, *Zhongguo ziran dili*, vol. 4, 111.

21 Zeng Zhaoxian, "Cong lishi dimaoxue kan Guangzhou cheng fazhan wenti," *Lishi dili* 4 (1986): 29.

22 Fenzel, "On the Natural Conditions Affecting the Introduction of Forestry," 74.

A third difference with the Yellow and Yangzi Rivers is that because of the amount and concentration of the rain in just a few months, the river beds often lie in valleys with sides cut too steep for cultivation, a characteristic particularly evident throughout much of the West River drainage system in Guangxi,[23] in the upper reaches of the North River, and in the East River east of Huizhou. Had the climate provided a more even or less intensive rainfall, the rivers of Lingnan might have eroded the old hills and mountains at a more leisurely pace, creating wider, more level valleys. But the particular combination of Lingnan's topography with the climatic patterns conspired on the one hand to leave little valley land in Lingnan fit for cultivation, but on the other to create the alluvial soils that have been captured to create the Pearl River delta.

The Pearl River Delta. Carrying considerably less silt than China's other major rivers, the West, North, and East Rivers nonetheless converged to create a common delta in central Guangdong. These three rivers at one time had independent outlets, but subsidence of the coastal region after the Jurassic lifting created a common bay into which they all emptied. The subsidence left the tops of many of the original hills above sea level, now at most a thousand feet, but the alluvium brought down by the rivers slowly filled in the bay, creating the delta. With its "curious combination," as the British Naval Intelligence termed it, of alluvium, hills, islands, and bay, the Pearl River delta is not a true or pure delta, but a rather unique structure.[24] Indeed, in terms of geologic time, the Pearl River delta is a very recent creation. Just 3,000 years ago, the delta was perhaps half its current size and even 1,000 years ago had not increased much beyond that; in the past millennium, though, the Pearl River delta has doubled in size, largely as a result of human action. How that happened is an interesting story that will be told in the next chapter; suffice it to say here that the Pearl River drainage system carried so little silt that the delta originally formed very slowly, with the pace quickening only when the lower reaches of the West, North, and East Rivers were altered to meet human needs, and pioneers began to settle in the delta.

Navigation. Lingnan's rivers not only carried sediment to be deposited in the alluvial plains; they also carried boats. Navigation on the extensive river system provided the basic means of communication, travel, and trade through the otherwise impassable folded hills of the Lingnan interior. Each of the

[23] Zhao Songqiao, *Geography of China: Environment, Resources, Population, and Development* (New York: Wiley, 1994), 157.

[24] Great Britain Naval Intelligence Division, *China Proper*, vol. 1, *Physical Geography, History, and Peoples*, Geographical Handbook Series (London, 1941), 119–22. Because it is a filled-in bay rather than a true delta, this source calls the Pearl River delta an "embayment."

major rivers was navigable, if by that we mean that small dugouts or rafts could float downstream until the river widened and deepened to accommodate boats of deeper draft. The MacCartney Mission, for instance, took small boats from Nanxiong downriver to Shaozhou, where they boarded larger boats to complete the journey to Guangzhou, passing through some stretches of narrows where the North River coursed over rapids. Rapids and shallower water could be found on the East River above Huizhou and on many of the tributaries to the West River in Guangxi.

It was of course easier going downstream than up. Sailing junks could maneuver in the Pearl River estuary and up the West River most of the way to Wuzhou, but after that poles and pullers were needed. The same was true for the North River. Likewise, to take the Gui River upstream from Wuzhou to Guilin was not impossible, but it was "inconvenient," if I may borrow a phrase from current Chinese bureaucratic usage. In 1729, for instance, when the Manchu governor-general of Yunnan and Guizhou provinces, E-er-tai, toured Guangxi soon after it was added to his bailiwick and wanted to travel from Yunnan to Guilin, his route took him from the Yunnan–Guangxi border downstream through Bose to Nanning, where he crossed overland through Liuzhou to Guilin. "Large boats (*da chuan*) can travel from Bose through Nanning to Wuzhou and [upriver] through Pingle to Guizhou," he said. "But the route is rather roundabout."[25]

The monsoons also regulated the shipping calendar. Clearly, when the rivers were at flood stage in the spring and summer with 2 million cubic feet per second flowing through Wuzhou, travel either up- or downstream was difficult and dangerous. But the dry season also posed its challenges, as water levels in the channels dropped, sometimes to levels too low for boats. And when those boats carried rice down the rivers to markets, low water levels affected rice prices: "Grain prices are rising," an official reported in early 1763. "Investigation shows that with clear days in the winter, the rivers are dry or shallow, and outside trade is minimal. Also, it is difficult to transport and sell rice . . . In the spring when rains raise the rivers, [prices] for rice in the cities and villages alike will fall uniformly."[26]

Linkages to the Yangzi River System. The Lingnan river system was such an important part of the transportation system of the entire Chinese empire that from very early times links were established between it and the Yangzi River valley. The earliest was the construction of the Ling Qu Canal connecting the upper reaches of the southward-flowing Li River above Guilin with

[25] Memorial dated YZ8.1.13 in *Gongzhongdang Yongzheng chao zouzhe*, Gugong bowuyuan, comp. (Taibei: Guoli gugong bowuyuan, 1977–88), vol. 15: 463–67. Hereafter cited as YZCZZ.

[26] Memorial dated QL28.12.18 IN *Gongzhongdang Qianlong chao zouzhe*, Gugong bowuyuan, comp. (Taibei: Guoli gugong bowuyuan, 1982–86), vol. 20: 99–100. Hereafter cited as QLCZZ.

the Xiang River, which flowed north through Hunan province and into the Yangzi River. Built initially around 230 BCE by Shi Lu, an engineer in Qin Shi Huang Di's army, the Ling Qu was (and remains) a masterpiece of ingenuity. Even an extended description of the Ling Qu Canal cannot do justice to the way in which the Xiang and Li Rivers were connected, so suffice it to say that Joseph Needham translated the character in its name (Ling) as "magic," rather than the less grandiose but still apt "ingenious." Used first to transport Qin troops and warships into Lingnan, the Ling Qu was later used to transport goods to and from Lingnan from north China via the Yangzi River.[27]

Natural processes could do only so much with the raw material of Lingnan in providing a river system adaptable to human use. The natural river systems endowed Lingnan with a transport network upon which to move goods from one part of the region to another, facilitating agricultural specialization and the shipment of bulk items like grain down the West River to the city of Guangzhou, with accessible sources of water for irrigation and with a mechanism for creating rich soils, all of which could be considered advantageous to human settlement of the region. Over the millennia the vast amount of water flowing into the West River basin found an outlet through a fault in hills near the city of Wuzhou, thereby not only draining the basin, but establishing a water link between the two major parts of Lingnan. But for the people inhabiting Lingnan, these natural processes proved insufficient in linking Lingnan to the rest of China, and so people created two additional links: the Ling Qu Canal and the Meiling Pass.

The Lingnan river system thus was not ideal. Besides not connecting Lingnan with the Yangzi River valley to the north, the rivers cut mostly deep ravines into the hills, leaving little level space for alluvial valleys to spread out, thereby limiting the amount of land that could be given over to agriculture and challenging those who would attempt to inhabit the flood plains. The gush of water through the system brought by the summer monsoon virtually ensured flooding wherever the rivers could overflow their banks, thereby depositing their alluvium, a potentially fertile and rich soil.

Soils. Soil is composed of a mixture of varying proportions of decomposed rock, decaying organic matter, and living organisms, which then interact to form various chemical compounds.[28] But despite the fact that, in Lingnan, rocks of various kinds – mostly granites, sandstone, limestone –

[27] Joseph Needham, *Science and Civilization in China*, vol. 4, part 3, *Physics and Physical Technology: Civil Engineering and Nautics* (Cambridge University Press, 1971), 299–306.

[28] This section is woefully brief and does not do justice to the complexity of soils. As Edward O. Wilson recently observed: "The very soils of the world are created by organisms. Plant roots shatter rocks to form much of the grit and pebbles of the basic substrate. But soils are much

contribute different bases for the soils, the rainfall and humidity exercise the greatest influence on the kind of soil that predominates. Because of the large amount of rainfall, soluble materials in the upper layers of the soil leached into lower levels, leaving slightly acidic soils that are red or brown in color. When exposed to the air, these soils either develop a hard crust upon which little vegetation can grow, or contain a hardpan called "laterite" just below the surface that can be exposed by erosion; this may have been what Staunton saw from the Meiling Pass when looking south he described "a tract of waste and barren ground." The original vegetation probably had been burned off, exposing the earth to the rains and eroding the topsoil down to the hardpan.

The soil covering the hardpan was generally yellow or red podzolized earth, a soil type found throughout south China, including Lingnan. None are particularly fertile and, with the hardpan, are at best difficult to work. Tropical soils generally are poor, and those in Lingnan were no different. The reason for the infertility is that most of the organic matter in tropical ecosystems is tied up in the trees that constitute the tropical forest, and the nutrients from decaying matter are quickly leached from the soil by the heavy rainfall.

Forests and Wildlife

In the 1930s, according to estimates made at the time by Chinese and Western botanists, cultivated land took up about 10–15 percent of the land surface of Lingnan, while most of the rest of Lingnan – being hills or mountains – was savanna, and only a very small proportion, maybe as little as 1 percent but perhaps as much as 5 percent of the land, was forested. However much forest did exist in the 1930s, the scientists agree that most was a secondary growth of pine forests – the scrubby-looking Mason's pine (*Pinus massoniana*, see Figure 1.3) – sometimes intermixed with some broadleafs.[29] To those in the 1930s looking at the vast expanse of treeless hills, the question was whether the

more than fragmented rock. They are complex ecosystems with vast arrays of plants, tiny animals, fungi, and microorganisms assembled in delicate balance, circulating nutrients in the form of solutions and tiny particles. A healthy soil literally breathes and moves. Its microscopic equilibrium sustains natural ecosystems and croplands alike." Edward O. Wilson, *The Diversity of Life* (Cambridge, MA: Harvard University Press, 1992), 308. Similarly, Donald Worster has written, "Few . . . would deny that a topsoil is an organization of life, fundamentally akin to a mountain forest, a coral reef, or a school of minnows." Donald Worster, "A Sense of the Soil," in Worster, *The Wealth of Nature*, 82. For an extended argument about the centrality of soil conservation in the rise and fall of civilizations, see Edward Hyams, *Soil and Civilization* (New York: Harper Colophon, 1976). The brief summary provided here of the soils of Lingnan is based upon: Great Britain Naval Intelligence, *China Proper*, vol. 1: ch. 7, and to a lesser degree upon Fenzel, "On the Natural Conditions Affecting the Introduction of Forestry," 50–63.

29 Ling Daxie, "Wo guo senlin ziyuan de bianqian," *Zhongguo nongshi* 2 (1983): 34–35.

Figure 1.3. *Pinus massoniana.*

savanna was the natural vegetation of Lingnan or whether instead the region ever had been covered by forest. As a result of investigations in the 1930s and after 1949, botanists and foresters have concluded that the grasslands represent a "climax" vegetation established after earlier existing forests had been burned off.[30]

Given the virtual absence by the twentieth century of any natural forest, reconstructing what kind of forests originally (i.e., some 1,000–3,000 years ago, before human populations dramatically altered the environment) might have covered Lingnan was not easy, requiring botanists to examine climatic conditions, compare conditions in Lingnan with regions elsewhere in the world, investigate the few, inaccessible mountain areas where forest still stood, consult

[30] Chen, *Zhongguo ziran dili*, vol. 10: 21–23; Guangdong sheng zhiwu yanjiuso, ed., *Guangdong zhipei* (Beijing: Kexue chuban she, 1976), 16–17; Zhang Yongda, et al., *Leizhou bandao de zhipei* (Shanghai: Xinhua shu ju, 1957), 83–84. Changes in the extent of forest cover have been studied by Ling, "Wo guo senlin ziyuan de bainqian." Unfortunately, Ling does not describe his methods for estimating the extent of forest cover at various points in time. Given the sticky issues of definition, not to mention sources, this oversight is regrettable. For a discussion of the changing definitions of "forest" in China, see S. D. Richardson, *Forests and Forestry in China* (Washington, DC: Island Press, 1990), 89–93.

historical records, and conduct field experiments. While much uncertainty remains, to date the most extensive considerations of the issue have been conducted by Wang Chi-wu[31] and by Chinese scientists whose synthesized findings were published in 1982.[32] According to these studies, the original forests of Lingnan included three main types: (1) an evergreen broadleafed forest composed mainly of evergreen oaks (and associated trees like the laurel), which grew on the inland hills of northern Guangdong and throughout much of Guangxi; (2) a tropical rain forest, growing in the lower elevations (below 300 feet) in the southern parts of Guangdong and Guangxi, and on Hainan Island, composed of many species of straight-trunked trees forming a high canopy above the forest floor; and (3) a littoral forest on the coast, including brackish-water mangrove swamps.

Despite the nearly total deforestation of Lingnan by the 1930s, remnants of forests remained protected by Buddhist temples, and one in particular – on Dinghu Mountain some 45 miles northwest of Guangzhou – has provided Chinese botanists with a laboratory from which to reconstruct some of the botanical "combinations" of trees, shrubs, and grasses that may have comprised some of the original forests of Lingnan. The area has been designated a Biosphere Reserve under the UNESCO program "Man and the Biosphere," and scientists at a research station have been investigating, among other topics, the structure of the forest community. Although people have slightly modified the forest (some fruit trees have been planted, and some trees removed for lumber or fuel), ecologists consider this forest to be close to what originally covered much of Lingnan.[33] If so, two points are worth emphasizing.

First, the evergreen broadleafed forest is comprised of many different kinds of plants – in the language of ecologists, it is "species rich."[34] According to Wang Chi-wu, "The composition of the rain forest is characterized not only by the exceedingly rich flora but by the great diversity of plant species in a unit area, features which are not surpassed in any other type of plant community. The forest contains a wide range of life-forms to fit every possible niche . . . It is, in fact, a community of communities."[35] Second, this forest is the kind that would have covered only the inland hills of Lingnan. While those hills indeed comprise much of the land area of Lingnan, the lowlands – both

[31] Wang Chi-wu, *The Forests of China* (Cambridge, MA: Harvard University Press, 1961). See also the summary of Wang's work in Richardson, *Forests and Forestry in China*, ch. 2.

[32] Chen, *Zhongguo ziran dili*, vol. 10.

[33] For a brief description of the reserve, see E. F. Bruenig et al., *Ecological-Socioeconomic System Analysis and Simulation: A Guide for Application of System Analysis to the Conservation, Utilization and Development of Tropical and Subtropical Land Resources in China* (Bonn: Deutsches Nationalkomitee für das UNESCO Programm Der Mensch und die Biosphäre, 1986).

[34] Fenzel, "On the Natural Conditions Affecting the Introduction of Forestry," 37–97.

[35] Wang, *The Forests of China*, 159.

along the coast and in the river valleys – comprised two other ecosystems. The coastal lowlands, belonging to a more tropical climate, probably had forests similar to those on Hainan Island, remnants of which remain. Like the evergreen broadleafed forest, the tropical forest is species-rich, composed of at least four levels of growth, climaxing in a canopy 40–60 m above the floor of the forest.

The forest most difficult to reconstruct – and hence about which the greatest uncertainty lies – would have stood in the river valleys. Unlike the inland hills, where Buddhist temples protected remnants of the hill forest, or the coastal lowlands, where tropical forests on Hainan serve as an indicator of the natural vegetation, the river valleys have been subjected to so much human alteration over the millennia, from changing the river courses to clearing the land for agriculture, that few clues remain regarding the kind of forest that once stood there. The evidence that does exist, thin though it is, indicates that the river valleys – especially the lower reaches of the West, North, and East Rivers and the upper reaches of the Pearl River delta – were covered with a forest filled with a massive tree that the Chinese call the "water pine" (*shui song*, lat. *Glyptostrobus pensilis*: see Figure 1.4). The *Nan fang cao mu zhuang*, a fourth-century text, mentions the water pine as "coming from Nanhai [i.e., Lingnan]," and archeological excavations of a third-century boat-building site indicate the extensive use of water pine in boat construction. The water pine is a freshwater tree, apparently once at home in the freshwater swamps of the lower reaches of the three major rivers, but not extending its reach into the brackish water pushed into the Pearl River delta by the tides; there, mangrove swamps typified the forest community.[36]

Certainly, this sketch of the kinds of forests that may have covered Lingnan does not do justice to the diversity of forests or to the fine gradations between them. Nonetheless, I must continue to paint with a broad brush to convey an image of Lingnan's forests. To do so, I use a 1976 map of the vegetation cover of Guangdong province[37] and then make some inferences about Lingnan's original forest cover from that map (see Map 1.2). I have simplified the original to show but three types of vegetation – forest, grassland, and agriculture – covering the land ca. 1970. We can assume that the areas currently forested – nearly all in mountainous regions – probably were like the evergreen broadleaf forest on Dinghu mountain. Moreover, it seems reasonable to conclude that the grasslands now covering the inland hills had also previously been evergreen broadleaf forest (the reasons will be discussed in more detail later),

[36] Chen, *Zhongguo ziran dili*, vol. 10: 22. The Chinese biologists reached their conclusions using textual sources; as far as I know, no palynological studies have been conducted.

[37] For reasons that are somewhat baffling, Chinese botanists have divided their natural world into the arbitrary provincial boundaries of the modern nation-state, leaving us with the map of vegetation covering Guangdong province, not with maps that make more ecological sense.

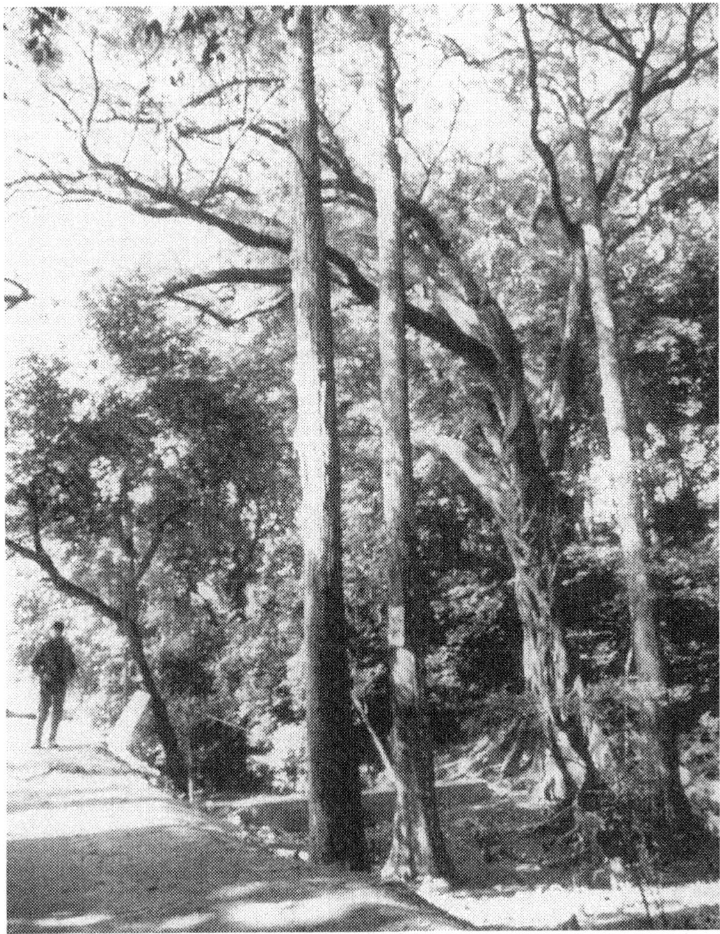

Figure 1.4. Water pine (*shui song*).

and that the coastal grasslands had been tropical forest. Finally, the land currently given over to agriculture occupies the river valleys, once the location of the lowland evergreen broadleaf and water pine forests. With a little imagination, this 1976 vegetation map can be transformed into the tropical and subtropical forests covering Lingnan when Chinese from the north first peered over the Meiling Pass into Lingnan, with the areas labeled "grasses and scrub" being the evergreen broadleaf forests and the "cultivated" areas in the river valleys the domain of water pine forests.

The ways in which Chinese first saw and recorded these forests differs substantially from the ways in which modern ecologists reconstruct forest

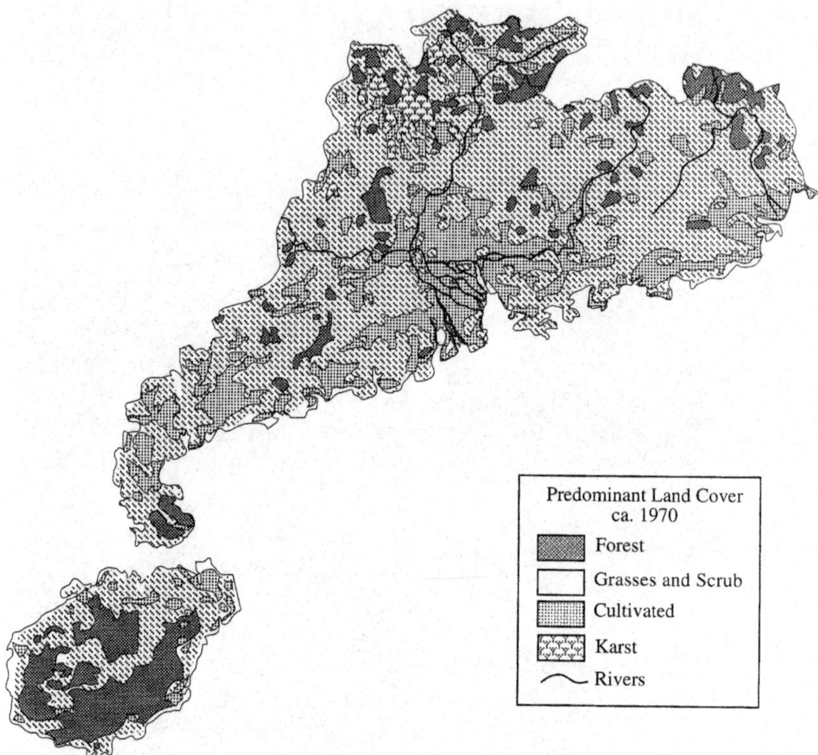

Map 1.2. Guangdong land cover, ca. 1970. Source: Guangdong sheng zhiwu yanjiuso, ed., *Guangdong zhipei* (Beijing: Kexue chuban she, 1976), folded map insert

communities. On the one hand, the lush tropical forests of Lingnan simply were radically different from anything that Chinese from the north had seen or experienced. Edward Schafer elegantly addresses how the south China environment clashed with northern sensibilities in his books about the south, so suffice it here to quote the eighth-century view of Yuan Jie, who wrote of Lingnan:

> At times you hear sounds as of some kind of cicada or fly, but as you listen to them, they are no longer there. Here and there you see great valleys and long rivers, level fields and deep abysses; firs and pines a hundred spans round; dense stands of this or that kind of juniper; blue sedge by white sand;

> grottoes and caves in vermilion banks; cold springs, flying and flowing; strange bamboos and variegated flowers.[38]

On the other hand, though, the forests of Lingnan yielded a rich trove of trees and plants that were of economic or medical importance[39] and much of the detail about Lingnan's flora is described from this perspective, especially in the "local products" (*tu chan* or *wu chan*) sections of local gazetteers (*fangzhi*). In the earliest extant gazetteer for Lingnan, the *Nanhai zhi*, printed during the Yuan dynasty in 1304, the compiler comments in the preface to the "local products" section (*wu chan*) that "in each of the four corners of the earth, the climate is different; thus so too are the local products. Southerners do not know the camel, and northerners do not know the elephant, the pear tree, or the cuckoo."[40]

Two Ming-era Guangdong province gazetteers (published in 1558 and 1602) list over 60 different kinds of trees. For several, the 1558 edition also glossed their uses and their relative abundance. Pine (*song*) was most plentiful; camphor (*zhang*) grew so tall (50–60 feet) that half the lumber for a house could be cut from one tree; cedar (*bo*) could be used to carve Buddhas; cypress (*shan*) was used for lumber to build houses, boats, and furniture; *gao* was very suitable for furniture; and the cutting tung tree (*la tong*) yielded good lumber. Writing in 1178, Zhou Qufei identified the remarkable *wu lan* wood found in Qinzhou, that was

> used for making the rudders of great ships . . . Rudders that are produced elsewhere do not exceed 30 feet in length and are adequate to control a ship of 10 thousand piculs capacity . . . Only rudders produced in Qinzhou are close-grained, sturdy, and almost 50 feet in length . . . Ten to twenty percent of purchasers come to the spot because the length of the materials makes it difficult to transport by sea.[41]

To be useful, not all trees required being cut, for many trees provided oils and varnishes (the lacquer tree and the tung-oil tree, for instance), or their leaves or bark could be distilled for spirits (the *zhi fo* tree), or they yielded seeds or leaves used in medicine (from the *dang* tree) or pesticides (from the *yuan* tree). Still others provided raw material for weaving into cloth (the *mu mian*, or kapok, tree and the *guang lang* palm). Ironically, the banyan (*yong*) was included as a "local product" precisely because its economic uselessness did lend it a usefulness of sorts: "The wood is twisted and turned, and cannot be used to make

[38] Translated and quoted in Schafer, *The Vermilion Bird*, 167.

[39] On the economic uses of tropical trees, see Wang, *The Forests of China*, 164.

[40] *Nanhai zhi*, 1304 ed., juan 7: 1a, reprinted in *Song Yuan fangzhi congkan* (Beijing: Zhonghua shuju, 1990), vol. 8.

[41] Quoted in Shiba Yoshinobu, *Commerce and Society in Sung China*, Mark Elvin, trans. (Ann Arbor: University of Michigan Press, 1970), 8.

utensils, nor as lumber. It does not burn, and so cannot be used as fuel. It has absolutely no use, so it is not harmed. It can shade over 10 *mu*, though, so people rest under it."[42]

Forest as Habitat. Whether the Lingnan forests were virgin or secondary growth, what precise combination of trees comprised the three major forest types and where the lines between them were probably will never be known, in large part because very little physical evidence remains. Nonetheless, from more traditional historical sources we do know that the forests provided habitat for at least two large animal species (not including humans) at the top of the food chain: elephants and tigers. Elephants once roamed through much of Lingnan, probably in the open space under the canopy of the rain forest.[43] According to Liu Xun, a Tang official writing in the early tenth century, "There are many elephants in Chaozhou and Xunzhou [Qing-era Huizhou] prefectures [in eastern and northeast Guangdong]."[44] Two centuries later, Zhou Qufei, writing about Guangxi, described the process by which the inhabitants living near the mountain range separating Lingnan from Vietnam lured elephants into a trap to capture them for their tusks and trunks.[45] And in 1171, "several hundred wild elephants [in Chaozhou] ate the rice plants."[46] The Nanning prefecture gazetteer mentions within the entry for the year 1383 that "an elephant [or elephants, the text is unclear] emerged from the Shiwan Mountains in Shangsi; 20,000 troops were called out to capture it [them]."[47] Also in Guangxi, an early-fifteenth-century Nanning gazetteer mentions inhabitants of southern and western Guangxi killing elephants for their tusks and trunks.[48]

Various species of large deer foraged in Lingnan's very numerous river valleys, seeking cover in the forests and swamps. Deer were so plentiful even into the seventeenth century that more deerskin products were produced in Guangdong province and exported elsewhere than in any other part of the empire.[49] The descriptions of the deer in the various local gazetteers do not

[42] *Guangdong tongzhi*, 1561 ed., juan 23: 15a–20a.

[43] For an overview of the evidence, see Zeng, "Cong lishi dimaoxue kan Guangzhou cheng fazhan wenti," 28–29.

[44] Liu Xun (897–946 CE), *Ling biao lu yi*, reprinted in *Qin ding si ku quan shu* (Taibei: Shangwu yinshu guan, 1975), vol. 138: shang juan, 10a.

[45] Zhou Qufei, *Ling wai dai ta*, 1178 ed., reprinted in *Qin ding si ku quan shu* (Taibei: Shangwu yinshu guan, 1975), vols. 138–39, juan 9: 1a–b.

[46] Cited in *Guangdong sheng ziran zaihai shi liao* (Guangzhou: Guangong sheng wenshi yanjiu guan, 1961), 153.

[47] *Nanning fuzhi*, 1742 ed., juan 39, entry for HW16 (1383 CE).

[48] *Nanning zhi*, ca. 1407, *Yongle da dian* edition, vol. 4: 2080ff.

[49] Song Yingxing, *Tiangong kaiwu*, trans. by E-tu Zen Sun and Shiou-Chuan Sun as *T'ien-kung k'ai-wu: Chinese Technology in the Seventeenth Century* (University Park: Pennsylvania State University Press, 1966), 67–69.

go much beyond simply saying "deer" (*li*), so it is not easy to determine which species roamed about in Lingnan, but some describe a "white deer" (*bai li*) and a "mountain horse" (*shan ma*), an animal that looked like a deer but was as big as a horse.[50]

While the elephants had no natural predators, the deer were not so fortunate, for at the top of the food chain in the Lingnan biome was the tiger.[51] Being very adaptable animals, tigers lived throughout much of Lingnan (except on Hainan Island)[52] and everywhere preyed on large animals, deer being their favorite. In the twelfth century, Zhou Qufei mentioned that "there are tigers in much of Guangdong,"[53] and Ming-era gazetteers for Guangdong and Guangxi provinces, as we will see, are replete with references to tigers.

"*Star Species.*" Just as the tropical forest in Lingnan was species rich in flora, so too was it rich in fauna; further down the food chain from tigers and elephants, smaller predators such as leopards and foxes preyed on yet smaller mammals, and so on, each species comprising communities within communities of living organisms. But rather than describe all of the various ecosystems and communities of plants and animals, I will stop my description of the wildlife with the elephants and tigers. These are the "star species" of Lingnan.[54]

The reason for focusing on the star species is that their existence can act as a barometer of human intrusion into and destruction of the natural environment. Both the elephant and the tiger required vast expanses of habitat to sustain themselves. Elephants consumed huge amounts of foliage each day,

50 The "mountain horse" may have belonged to a species known as Schomberg's deer, a very large deer with horselike features, now extinct.

51 The south China tiger, *Panthera tigris amoyensis*, is one of eight subspecies. Three species are already extinct, and the south China tiger is endangered. Some are kept in zoos, but perhaps only 20–30 survive in the north Guangdong–Guangxi–Hunan border region. See the articles by Xiang Peilon, Tan Bangjie, and Jia Xianggang, "South China Tiger Recovery Program"; Lu Houji, "Habitat Availability and Prospects for Tigers in China"; and Tan Bangjie, "Status and Problems of Captive Tigers in China," all in Ronald L. Tilson and Ulysses S. Seal, eds., *Tigers of the World: The Biology, Biopolitics, Management and Conservation of an Endangered Species* (Park Ridge, NJ: Noyes, 1987), 323–28, 71–74, 134–48, respectively.

52 *Qiongtai zhi*, 1521 ed., reprinted in *Tian yi ge Ming dai fangzhi xuan kan*, vols. 60–62 (Shanghai: Gu ji shudian, 1982), juan 7: 12b.

53 Zhou, *Ling wai dai ta*, juan 9: 3b.

54 "Star species" is a term used by Edward O. Wilson to relate preservation of endangered species more broadly to protection of ecosystems: "The cutting of primeval forest and other disasters, fueled by the demands of growing human populations, are the overriding threat to biological diversity everywhere . . . when the *entire* habitat is destroyed, almost all of the species are destroyed. Not just eagles and pandas disappear but also the smallest, still uncensused invertebrates, algae, and fungi, the invisible players that make up the foundation of the ecosystem . . . The relationship is reciprocal: when star species like rhinoceros and eagles are protected, they serve as umbrellas for all the life around them." Wilson, *The Diversity of Life*, 259.

and herds of elephants grazed through miles of territory daily. To accommodate elephants, a forest needs lots of trees with plenty of leaves, implying the obverse relationship that where there are elephants, there are forests. The same was true of tigers. While female tigers were territorial, male tigers roamed widely in search of prey. The amount of territory required to support each tiger varied with the density of large prey – the more deer, for instance, the more tigers – and recent studies estimate that it requires from 20 to 100 square kilometers under good conditions to support a single tiger.[55] As the habitat required to support the tiger and the elephant declined, in the past just as today, so too did the animal populations. Edward O. Wilson cites biological studies showing a "rigorous connection" in the decline of rain forest habitat to that of species, so that when the rain forest is reduced to 10 percent of its original size, the number of species will have been reduced by 50 percent.[56] Traditional historical sources familiar to most historians of China can be used to chart the location of tigers and elephants, at least insofar as the Chinese observers who left the records were aware, and thereby provide additional evidence concerning the timing and extent of changes in the Lingnan environment.

The tiger, especially, will play an important role in the story, in large part because it has managed to avoid extinction and therefore appears periodically in the written historical record. Wherever and wherever tigers appear, we can be certain that sufficient forest provided those tigers with the habitat necessary to sustain the species. On the other hand, when tigers begin to disappear from the historical record, we can begin to suspect that their habitat too has disappeared. Unlike the tiger, the elephant – the other star species of the south China biome – will not play much of a part in this book, not because I am less interested in elephants, but because, unfortunately, they disappeared from Lingnan before the late imperial period (i.e., 1400–1850) that is the focus of the book.

The Disappearance of the Elephant: Human or Natural Causes? Although elephants once roamed through much of Lingnan, as the evidence cited earlier indicates, by the end of the fourteenth century it is not clear whether elephants still existed anywhere in Guangdong province, for the only references I have found locate them in Guangxi. In the early Ming, the Nanning gazetteer mentions inhabitants of southern and western Guangxi killing elephants for their tusks and trunks.[57] Indeed, the last notation I have found for elephants in

55 John Seidensticker, "Large Carnivores and the Consequences of Habitat Insularization: Ecology and Conservation of Tigers in Indonesia and Bangladesh," in S. D. Miller and D. D. Everett, eds., *Cats of the World: Biology, Conservation, and Management* (Washington, DC: National Wildlife Federation, 1986), 20–21.

56 See Wilson, *The Diversity of Life*, 275–78.

57 *Nanning zhi*, ca. 1407, *Yongle dadian* edition, vol. 4: 2080ff.

Lingnan is the 1383 mention of troops being called out to deal with rogue elephants in southern Guangxi province. Perhaps other evidence might be found, but it seems to me most likely that, by the fifteenth century, elephants had become extinct in Lingnan.

There may be some question as to what caused the elimination of elephants from Lingnan, for the clues that we have – the timing and direction of their disappearance – can be read in at least three different ways, all consistent with the available evidence. The elephants disappeared around 1400, and they did so in a north-to-south direction, with earlier references placing them further north in Lingnan and later references placing them only in the south. Hunting, elimination of habitat (either by human action or climatic change), or climatic changes (or any combination of the three) may have been responsible; let me consider each in turn.

Hunting certainly killed off a substantial number of elephants. Ivory was prized, and both elephants and elephant tusks were listed as "local products" from Lingnan in the Tang, Song, and Yuan dynasties; indeed, roasted elephant trunk was considered a delicacy. Moreover, there is clear evidence that elephants had been hunted by what can only be called professionals who had learned how to entrap and kill the elephants. Zhou Qufei, writing in the twelfth century, for instance, describes hunters in southern Guangxi province enticing elephants into a dead-end, stone enclosure, where they were trapped and killed.[58] While hunters no doubt killed a large number of elephants, if hunting were the primary cause of their disappearance, would they not have disappeared in all directions simultaneously, leading to references of elephants in the lowlands throughout Lingnan, not just in the south?

What about the elimination of habitat as a cause of the elephants' disappearance? As we will see in more detail later, people certainly changed the Lingnan environment in important ways, especially in the eighteenth and nineteenth centuries. However, the herds of elephants cited in eastern Guangdong roamed the forests during the twelfth century, concurrent with the population peak of the Song dynasty, while the human population decline of the late thirteenth century left large tracts of forest undisturbed. In fact, by 1400 the human population of Lingnan probably had not recovered to the level it had reached during the Song dynasty three centuries earlier. In other words, there is no direct relationship between the increase in the human population (and hence of changes in the environment) of Lingnan and the disappearance of the elephant.

Climate change is another possible cause of the disappearance of the elephant. By 1400, when the last reliable evidence places elephants in Lingnan, the climate had begun turning cooler. While it is possible that either elephants

[58] Zhou, *Ling wai dai ta*, juan 9: 1a–b.

or their food supply were sensitive to temperature changes, both being affected by this cooling trend, the climate had already gone through periods of cooling (see Zhu Kezhen's reconstruction of temperatures in Figure 1.6, cited later) coinciding with elephant sightings in Lingnan. On the other hand, recent work regarding rainfall patterns (to be discussed in more detail next), indicating a major change after 1230 toward a drier climate, does coincide (more or less) with the disappearance of the elephants. Might a slightly drier climate or longer, more intense periods of drought remove a major source of food for elephants? With the evidence available, the question remains.

Although climatic change, hunting, and elimination of habitat are possible explanations for why elephants disappeared from Lingnan, in the final analysis the question is not easy to answer, and separating out natural from human causes of ecological change, at least in this instance, is problematic. My reason for discussing the disappearance of the elephant, though, was not to offer an answer to the puzzle, but to illustrate the complexities of determining the causes of ecological change. Were the changes "natural" or induced by human activity? While anthropogenic causes of environmental change will take up most of the rest of the book, here I want to introduce the question of nonanthropogenic sources of ecological change.

Ecological Change

Before Chinese settlement of Lingnan in the Qin and Han dynasties – and probably for centuries afterwards, too – Lingnan was a tropical wilderness, teeming with all kinds of exotic life. By the twentieth century – and centuries earlier, too, as we will see – most of the forest and much of the wildlife were gone. In their place emerged a different landscape, nearly all of which had been touched, if not worked and reworked countless times, by human hands. The questions that we must ask thus do not concern whether there was massive environmental change in Lingnan, for that much is quite certain, but rather when and why the changes occurred, the role people had in effecting those changes, and the consequences – both for the environment and for the society and economy – that those changes wrought.

Although we shall be looking primarily at the location of people in their environment and the role of human agency in forcing environmental change, we must be aware at the outset that changes in the environment have natural causes too. Mostly, the pace of natural change is slow, and imperceptibly slow to people. The erosion and weathering of the mountains, the meandering of the courses of rivers, and the deposition of silt in the delta all must be measured in geologic time. But other kinds of natural change happen faster. Fires sparked by lightning could remove vast expanses of forest, which then might take centuries to recover. Floods and earthquakes (and sometimes climate changes too) occurred suddenly, precipitating changes in environments. Disease – then as now – might decimate animal or plant species, forever altering the ecosystems in which they were embedded.

The whole Lingnan region – not just the mountains, forests, and large animals described here, but including all living things – constituted a series of interlocking and nested ecosystems. As defined by Eugene Odum in his classic text on the subject, an ecosystem is "any unit that includes all of the organisms (i.e., the 'community') in a given area interacting with the physical environment so that a flow of energy leads to clearly defined trophic structure, biotic diversity, and material cycles (i.e., exchange of materials between the living and non living parts) with the system."[59] In Odum's view, ecosystems developed in successive stages toward a "climax stage" of homeostasis into a "mature ecosystem."[60] The Lingnan ecosystem, if we can imagine it before too many people lived there when forests covered the land surface, might have constituted such a "mature ecosystem."

A major implication of Odum's ecological view of the world is that because it tends toward order, stability, and maturity, the primary cause of its disruption was the hand of human beings. In recent years, though, this view of the "balance of nature" has been challenged by biologists working in wildlife population and chaos theories. According to these studies, there is no evidence of "mature ecosystems," but plenty of evidence of change leading nowhere in particular, and of unpredictable fluctuations in wildlife populations. Random disturbances of all kinds, these scientists argue, intrude into nature, rendering the idea of an ecological stability and maturity predating human interference moot.[61] Among the most powerful of these nonhuman agents of disorder, in the eyes of these biologists, has been climatic change. As will become clear in the rest of this book, I think that human action was the primary cause of environmental change in Lingnan and that what happened there cannot be dismissed as nothing more than random disturbances to the environment. Nonetheless, climatic change is important to consider, for changes in the climate not only affected the natural environment, but also were critical for the success or failure of agriculture. My reason for examining climate change thus is not to lend credence to the chaotic view of ecological change, but because, as will become clear in later chapters, people too had to deal with climatic challenges.

59 Eugene P. Odum, *The Fundamentals of Ecology*, quoted in Worster, *The Wealth of Nature*, 159.

60 The discussion in these two paragraphs is based upon Donald Worster, "The Ecology of Order and Disorder," in Worster, *The Wealth of Nature*, ch. 13.

61 Worster makes the valuable point that these newer conceptions of nature serve the ideological purposes of those who wish to disassociate themselves from reform-minded environmentalism and its nagging, inconvenient criticisms of the human impact on nature. Ibid., 166–67.

Climatic Change

Until quite recently, historians (and scientists too) considered climate to have been more or less constant, especially in historic times: climate in Roman and Han times seemed to have been similar to our climate, most assumed, so the question of changes in climate was not really considered. However, the debate during the past 20 years concerning the likelihood, causes, and significance of global warming has prompted climatologists to reconstruct past climates and to assess the impact of climatic change on human societies. The results of these efforts include chronologies of climatic change, annual mean temperature reconstructions going back to the mid-seventeenth century, and model and empirical studies of the response of agriculture to climatic change.[62]

When charting climatic change, climatologists focus on two main elements – temperature and rainfall – with most of the scholarly energy devoted to temperature change. Not only is climate and climate change crucial for understanding the environment, but the physical responses of plants and animals to changes in temperature and rainfall – such as changes in tree-ring growth, the incidence of pollen, and even the droppings of beetles – constitute the proxy evidence used to reconstruct past climates.[63]

Cold and Warm Periods. As a result of this recent research, we now know that the climate of the world has not been constant and that even since the end of the last ice age 12,000 years ago, there have been some periods warmer and some substantially cooler than the present.[64] Temperatures 5,000–8,000 years ago may have been 3–5°C warmer than present, but annual mean temperature variations in historical times have been 1–1.5° on either side of present annual mean temperatures.

[62] For an accessible synthesis of the results of these studies, see H. H. Lamb, *Climate, History and the Modern World* (London: Methuen, 1982). For the most recent temperature reconstruction, see Gordon C. Jacoby and Rosanne D'Arrigo, "Reconstructed Northern Hemisphere Annual Temperature since 1671 Based on High-Latitude Tree-Ring Data from North America," *Climatic Change* 14 (1989); 39–59. See also Hugh W. Ellsaesser et al., "Global Climatic Trends as Revealed in the Recorded Data," *Reviews of Geophysics* 24, no. 4 (Nov. 1986), 745–92. For an example of studies of the impact of climatic change on agriculture, see Sally Kane, John Reilly, and James Tobey, "An Empirical Study of the Economic Effects of Climatic Change on World Agriculture," *Climatic Change* 21 (1992), 17–35; and Diana Liverman, "Forecasting the Impact of Climate on Food Systems: Model Testing and Model Linkage," *Climatic Change* 11 (1987): 267–85.

[63] For a summary of the kinds of proxy evidence, see Lamb, *Climate, History and the Modern World*, 67–100.

[64] For discussions of the causes of temperature changes, see John A. Eddy, "Climate and the Changing Sun," *Climatic Change* 1 (1977), 173–90; and H. H. Lamb, "Volcanic Dust in the Atmosphere: With a Chronology and an Assessment of its Meteorological Significance," *Philosophical Transactions of the Royal Society of London*, Series A, 266 (1970), 425–533.

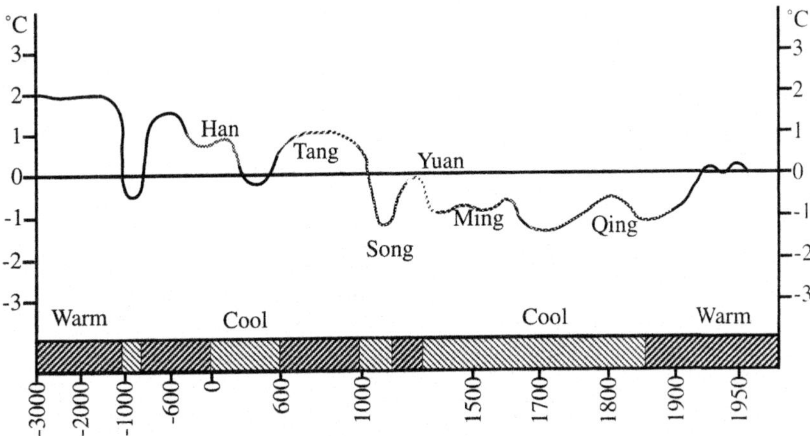

Figure 1.5. Temperature changes in China, 3000 BCE–1950 CE. Source: Manfred Domrös and Peng Gongping, *The Climate of China* (Berlin: Springer, 1988), 137.

Not only are the broad outlines of global climatic change known, but Chinese climatologists have produced pioneering studies of the history of climate in China, the foremost being Zhu Kezhen's 1972 reconstruction of China's temperature fluctuations for the past 5,000 years (see Figure 1.5). Based upon archeological evidence for the earliest millennia, documentary sources recounting phenological data and the freezing of Yangzi Valley rivers and lakes, and twentieth-century instrumental readings, Zhu's reconstruction has continued to be cited by climatologists not just for his methods but also for his findings.[65]

As can be seen in Figure 1.5, temperature change in China during the past 5,000 years can be characterized by four periods (the scale indicates temperature departures in °C from the 1950–80 mean), but the general trend following the warm period of 3000–800 BCE was toward cooler temperatures until about 1700 CE. Severe cold dropped annual mean temperatures significantly in three periods: 1000–800 BCE, 400–600 CE, and 1000–1200 CE. Following a brief warming period in 1200–1300, temperatures in China trended downward to 1700, beginning a sustained rise again only in the middle of the nineteenth century.

[65] Zhu Kezhen, "Zhongguo jin wuqian nian lai qihou bianqian de chubu yanjiu," *Kaogu xuebao*, no. 1 (1972), reprinted in Zhu Kezhen, *Zhu Kezhen wen ji* (Beijing: Kexue chuban she, 1979). For a discussion in English of Zhu's findings, see Domrös and Peng, *The Climate of China*, 130–38.

Rainfall Patterns. Unlike temperature change, which tends to exhibit hemispheric (if not global) regularity, rainfall patterns are particular to places. Although climatologists have suggested a relationship between 20-year Asian and North American precipitation cycles,[66] to understand rainfall patterns in China, specific attention must be paid to the North Pacific subtropical high, which governs the summer monsoon in Asia (discussed earlier). The monsoon, though, could be somewhat unpredictable and not "normal." As every historian of China knows, floods and droughts of varying intensities occur, disrupting agriculture, causing widespread damage, and initiating subsistence crises. Where historians tend to see the occurrence of floods and droughts as accidental events impinging on the course of history, climatologists have found scientific explanations and regularity to the patterns of floods and droughts in China.[67]

The key to the "anomalous" patterns of flood and drought is variation from the "normal" annual migration of the North Pacific subtropical high.[68] Briefly put, when the subtropical high is pushed further to the north or east than its usual position, floods tend to occur north of the Yangzi Valley; when the subtropical high advances westward toward the south China coast, central and south China suffer from a greater frequency of floods. And when the high-pressure system intensifies, rainfall increases in and to the south of the Yangzi Valley.[69] Colder winter temperatures and a strong polar front tend to cut off the normal circulation of the subtropical high, resulting in drought conditions that can spread over all of China depending on the strength of the blocking pattern.[70]

Chinese climatologists have assembled two massive databases, related to the incidences of floods and droughts, that form the basis of intriguing analyses of rainfall patterns in China over the past 2000 years. The first, an impressive scholarly feat headed by China's Bureau of Meteorology, quantified and mapped nearly 300,000 meteorological citations contained in China's local

66 J. M. Lough, H. C. Fritts, and Wu Xiangding, "Relationships between the Climates of China and North America of the Past Four Centuries: A Comparison of Proxy Records," in Ye Duzheng et al., eds., *The Climate of China: Proceedings of the Beijing International Symposium on Climate* (Berlin: Springer), 89–105.

67 S. Hameed et al., "An Analysis of Periodicities in the 1470 to 1974 Beijing Precipitation Record," *Geophysical Research Letters* 10, no. 6 (June 1983), 436–39. The periodicities of recurrent climatic patterns are statistically determined by means of "power spectrum analysis." For a discussion of this analytic method, see M. B. Priestly, *Spectral Analysis and Time Series* (London: Academic, 1981). For an example of its application, see R. P. Kane, "Spectral Characteristics of the Series of Annual Rainfall in England and Wales," *Climatic Change* 4 (1988), 77–92.

68 Huang Jia-you and Wang Shao-wu, "Investigations on Variations of the Subtropical High in the Western Pacific during Historic Times," *Climatic Change* 7 (1985), 427–40.

69 See Zhang and Crowley, "Historical Climate Records," 835, and Lough et al., "Relationships between the Climates of China and North America," 104.

70 Zhang and Crowley, "Historical Climate Records," 843.

gazetteers for the 510-year period from 1470 to 1980.[71] Since the publication of this work in 1981, researchers have analyzed the data for periodicities and regularities in the patterns of floods and droughts[72] and have classified the characteristic modes of the summer monsoon into six types.[73] (These data are important for reconstructing the historical climate of Lingnan in Ming and Qing times and will be useful later in this book.)

The second database, compiled over the past decade by a research team led by Professor Zhang Peiyuan at China's Institute of Geography, is even larger and more comprehensive than the first, adding over 500,000 citations to those already compiled by the Bureau of Meteorology. This second database has not yet been published, but the group has begun to disseminate some of its findings. Constructing and analyzing a rainfall index for the past 2,000 years, Zhang's group has reached three major conclusions: first, that the long-term trend has been toward increasing aridity in China; second, that three distinct periods with defining characteristics can be identified; and third, that the climatic changes between those periods were abrupt and can be rather precisely dated. In the first period, from the beginning of the database in 137 BCE to the 280s CE, the climate was stable and relatively wet. The second period, from 280 to 1230, was more arid, but since the duration of periods of wet or dry fluctuated rapidly and randomly, the researchers classify the climate in this period as unstable. In the third period, from 1230 to the present, the drying trend continued, but in a more stable pattern, with longer and more regular periodicities of lighter flooding but more severe drought.[74]

The question, of course, is what impact these climatic changes had on the environment and on human society. And that question raises many others. How did colder temperatures affect agriculture? How can we know? And how did people respond to climatic changes? Did those responses begin to shield the human society of south China from adverse climatic impacts? It will take

[71] *Zhongguo jin wubai nian han lao fenbutu ji*, Zhongyang qixiang ju, comp. (Beijing: Kexue chuban she, 1981).

[72] See especially Gong Gaofa, Zhang Jinrong, and Zhang Peiyuan, "Ying yong shiliao feng qian jizai yanjiu Beijing diqu jiang shui liang dui dong xiaomai shoucheng de yingxiang," *Qixiang xuebao* 41, no. 4 (Nov. 1983): 444–51; Hameed et al., "An Analysis of Periodicities in the 1470 to 1974 Beijing Precipitation Record," 436–39; and Huang and Wang, "Investigations on Variations of the Subtropical High in the Western Pacific during Historic Times," 427–40.

[73] Wang Shao-wu and Zhao Zong-ci, "Droughts and Floods in China, 1470–1979," in T. M. L. Wigley et al., eds., *Climate and History: Studies in Past Climates and Their Impact on Man* (Cambridge University Press, 1981), 271–88. The six types are: (1a) flood in most of China; (1b) drought in most of China; (2) drought in the Yangzi Valley, flood in other parts; (3) flood in the Yangzi Valley, drought in other parts; (4) flood in south China, drought in north China; (5) drought in south China, flood in north China.

[74] Zhang Peiyuan et al., "Climate Change and Its Impact on Capital Shift during the Last 2000 Years in China," paper presented at the Conference on the History of the Environment in China, Hong Kong, December 13–18, 1993.

most of the rest of the book to examine these questions, so suffice it to say here that the climate of south China did change over the centuries considered here and that people did respond to the likelihood of those changes by creating some very effective and interesting institutions.

Conclusion

Before proceeding to consider the place of people in the processes of environmental change in south China, it might be helpful to summarize the salient features of Lingnan's natural environment as reconstructed here. Separated from the Yangzi River valley by the Nanling Mountains but connected by two major man-made structures, Lingnan was drained by an extensive, well-developed river system that cut through folded hills. The lowlands were periodically and regularly flooded in monsoon rains, while the uplands drained well. Unlike other parts of China, where lowlands are consolidated and ringed by hills and uplands, in Lingnan both lowlands and upland areas followed the rivers and were intermixed throughout the region, providing two different environments for human settlement. Tropical forests filled the river valleys and the coastal plain, while evergreen broadleafed forests covered the higher elevations, providing habitat to support star species like elephants and tigers and the whole ecosystems that undergird those marvelous animals. Humans too have been part of the Lingnan environment for millennia, and as we have seen, reconstructing the "natural" environment of Lingnan has, at the very least, implied the presence of people as observers. Now it is time to make that presence explicit, turning in the next chapter to a consideration of both the size and distribution of the human population of Lingnan.

2

"ALL DEEPLY FORESTED AND WILD PLACES ARE NOT MALARIOUS":

HUMAN SETTLEMENT AND ECOLOGICAL CHANGE IN LINGNAN, 2–1400 CE

Late imperial Lingnan was dominated by Han Chinese, and it was the Chinese who mostly remade the natural environment into one that supported the settled agricultural practices and cultures commonly understood as Chinese: irrigated paddy fields from which two or more crops of rice could be harvested from the same plot of land with little or no fallow period. But if the Han Chinese predominated, they were not the only ethnic group to inhabit Lingnan: Yao, Miao, Li, and Zhuang are all peoples (now called "national minorities") who also lived in Lingnan. By the late imperial period, the Han Chinese had come to occupy the richest farmland in the river valleys and the Pearl River delta, while the non-Chinese held lands in the hills of northern and eastern Guangdong and in the western half of Guangxi. But while this ethnic mix and distribution of people in Lingnan is the one we have become most accustomed to thinking about, it was the result of a long and interesting historical process.

Tracing that process is the purpose of this chapter. What we will see is that for centuries before the late-thirteenth-century Mongol conquest, the pattern of settlement was reversed from the late imperial pattern, with Chinese inhabiting the northern hill regions around Guilin in Guangxi and in Nanxiong and Shaozhou in Guangdong. Even through the migrations of the Tang (618–907) and Song (960–1279) periods, the movement of Han Chinese down into the river valleys was inhibited both by swamps and by the fear (and reality) of tropical diseases, especially malaria. The efforts that removed these obstacles to Han Chinese settlement also created the most fertile farmland in Lingnan (the Pearl River delta), a process that was greatly accelerated when the Mongol invasion of the south in the 1270s made swamps and malaria less risky to the Han Chinese than staying in the path of the invading army. The establishment of settled Chinese agriculture in the river valleys of Lingnan and in the Pearl River delta by 1400 is thus the story of Han Chinese encounters with other ethnic groups defending their lands, with swamps and malaria, and with Mongol invaders.

The Original Inhabitants

Lingnan was first inhabited not by Chinese but by other ethnic groups. To be sure, Chinese had settled in Lingnan as early as the creation of the first Chinese empire by the Qin (ca. 221 BCE), albeit in small numbers, but even then they were invading territory inhabited for millennia by various non-Chinese ethnic groups. In the lowlands of the river valleys and along the coast were various Tai peoples, the largest group now called the Zhuang, with a smaller group called the Li in the littoral belt on the Leizhou Peninsula and the coastal strip on Hainan Island.[1] Over the centuries extensive interaction between Han Chinese conquerors and settlers and the Zhuang and the Li – including intermarriage, trade, and the spread of the Chinese language, if not the actual adoption of Chinese cultural practices – rendered some of the aboriginal peoples less alien than others, giving rise by the Song to the distinction between the "cooked" (*shu*) and the "raw" (*sheng*) Li or Zhuang, the former refering to those who had accepted Chinese overlordship, the latter to those still beyond the influence of Chinese culture.[2]

Whereas the Zhuang and the Li were aboriginal in the sense of being the original human inhabitants of Lingnan, at least as far as is now known, other non-Chinese groups migrated into Lingnan in later periods and were seen by the Chinese as "barbarians" (*man*), and later historians sometimes mistook that Chinese characterization as meaning "aborigines." The most important of the non-Chinese immigrants into Lingnan were the Yao. Dating their arrival in Lingnan is controversial, some placing it in the Han and others in the Yuan or even the Ming. The latest Chinese assessment is that the Yao first migrated in small numbers during the Han dynasty, but came from the north in larger numbers in the tenth century during the wars that gave birth to the Song dynasty.[3] Whenever they first arrived, by the Ming the Yao had successfully colonized the uplands of northern Lingnan. In his mid-seventeenth-century work on strategic geography, Gu Yanwu lists by name each of the mountains that the Yao had occupied: 106 in Qingyuan county, or 41 in Xinyi county, for instance.[4]

Whenever the Yao arrived in Lingnan, their preferred habitat was the hills and mountains, where they organized themselves into villages, or at best into

[1] For a history of the Li on Hainan Island, see Anne Csete, *A Frontier Minority in the Chinese World: The Li People of Hainan Island from the Han through the High Qing*, Ph.D. dissertation, State University of New York at Buffalo, 1995.

[2] Taiwan is another case where these categories applied; see John Robert Shepherd, *Statecraft and Political Economy on the Taiwan Frontier, 1600–1800* (Stanford: Stanford University Press, 1993), 7–8.

[3] Mo Naiqun, ed., *Guangxi nonye jingji shi gao* (Nanning: Guangxi minzu chuban she, 1985), 24.

[4] Gu Yanwu, *Tianxia junguo li bing shu*, part 3 (*xia*) of the Guangdong section (Shanghai: Shangye yinshu guan, 1936), 11a–17b.

groups of villages that might be called "tribes," that practiced slash-and-burn, shifting agriculture. In contrast, the lowland Tai peoples grew wet rice,[5] cast bronze, wove silk, and by about 300 BCE had organized themselves into a state called Yue. With a state system and knowledge of sericulture and metallurgy, the Tai were the only people whom the Chinese did not consider barbarians. But that did not prevent the Qin from conquering them, which they did over a period of years (234–222 BCE). The Tai ruling elite fled south to organize another state in Thailand, leaving behind the Zhuang agriculturists in the lowlands.

How many indigenous people inhabited Lingnan before it was brought under control of the Chinese empire and, thus, before Chinese began settling there is not known. If the average density was as low as one person per square kilometer, then there may have been about half a million people in Lingnan around 200 BCE. In the Han dynasty (206–200 CE), a 2 CE count of households (adjusted for the boundaries of Lingnan) placed the total at 72,000 households, or 350,000–400,000 people, depending on assumptions about household size.[6] Citing earlier studies, Harold Wiens thought that the Han totals included both the few Chinese who had settled in Lingnan and the indigenous people, although the total omitted a significant number of non-Chinese.[7] A guess at a half million thus is not unreasonable.

Predating (or concurrent with, in the case of the Yao) Chinese settlement of Lingnan, then, the half million or so non-Chinese peoples had developed two different agricultural regimes, one for the lowlands and one for the uplands.[8] In the lowlands, the Zhuang planted wet rice, maybe in paddies and maybe in the same plot year after year, while in the uplands the Yao slashed and burned their way through the hills, probably waiting 20–25 years before burning them once more (swidden will be discussed more later), and on the coastal littoral and Hainan Island, Li peoples pursued a more desultory approach to growing food.

[5] Indeed, among the earliest pieces of archeological evidence indicating that rice was cultivated comes from coastal Haifeng county. See *Archeological Discovery in Eastern Kwangtung: The Major Writings of Fr. Rafael Maglioni (1891–1953)* (Hong Kong: Hong Kong Archeological Society, 1975), 23–24.

[6] The population figures are given as "households" (*hu*) rather than "people" (*ren*) or "mouth" (*kou*) because the count of households is generally considered to have been more accurate than *ren* or *kou*. The purpose here, in any event, is to gain a perspective on the movements in population, a purpose served just as well by enumerating households as people. For those interested in population estimates, it is not unreasonable to assume each household to have been comprised of 5–6 people. For a discussion, see Robert M. Hartwell, "Demographic, Political, and Social Transformations of China, 750–1550," *Harvard Journal of Asiatic Studies* 42, no. 2 (Dec. 1982): 369.

[7] Harold J. Wiens, *Han Chinese Expansion in South China* (Shoe String Press, 1967), 180–81.

[8] This classification was first suggested by George Moseley, *The Consolidation of the South China Frontier* (Berkeley and Los Angeles: University of California Press, 1973), 12.

Chinese Migration into and Settlement of Lingnan

Chinese migration into Lingnan came in three principal waves, the first a small one following the Qin subjugation of the Yue kingdom around 225 BCE, when a hundred thousand or so troops occupied Lingnan and then intermarried with local Tai women. The second wave came in the early fourth century, when nomadic tribesmen invaded north China and sacked the Chinese imperial capital at Luoyang, bringing on the "Yongjia Panic," when inhabitants of north China fled south. The third wave began similarly in the twelfth century, when central Asians – this time the Jin armies (predecessors of the Mongols) – in 1126 CE took the Song capital in Kaifeng, forcing the Song to relocate their capital south of the Yangzi River in Hangzhou; this third wave continued in the 1270s, when the Mongols began their push to conquer all of China.[9] As many historians have noted, when northern nomadic invaders pressed south of the Great Wall, they set off a chain reaction wave of Chinese migration south.[10] Many of those fleeing the war and disorder in the north found their way through the Nanling passes and into Lingnan.

Taking a *tour d'horizon* of Lingnan's population over the fourteen centuries from 2 to 1391 CE, we can see the impact both of the waves of in-migration and of war (see Figure 2.1). From the Han (2 CE) to the Tang (742 CE), the population had fluctuated higher and lower than the Han figure of 72,000 households, probably reaching a nadir late in the third century, from which the population increased by the Tang (in the eighth century) to 319,000 households, largely as a result of in-migration from the north. The population growth over the three centuries from the Tang to the Song (742 to 1080) most likely was not the result of much in-migration, but of the natural increase in the base population. My estimate for the population in 1200 may well be low, given the massive influx of refugees after the 1126 Song loss of their capital in Kaifeng. Whatever the population may have been at the peak of the Southern Song around 1200 – and it certainly was higher than it had been in 1080 – it declined substantially after the Mongols subdued south

9 For a brief discussion, see Li Zhuanshi, Li Minghua, and Han Qiangfu, eds., *Lingnan wenhua* (Shaoguan: Guangdong renmin chuban she, 1993), 171–205. Li et al. also claim that a fourth wave of immigrants arrived in the late Ming, but cite no evidence to support the claim; I have not found any either, and so do not include it here.

10 The Russian historian L. N. Gumilev has suggested that the movements of central Asian nomads across the steppe were caused mainly by changing patterns of rainfall in central Asia: "It is easy to understand what an enormous part such changes in steppe climate played in the history of the nomads of Eurasia. Livestock cannot live without grass, grass cannot grow without water, or nomads exist without livestock. Consequently, all these form a single system in which the key link is water." L. N. Gumilev, *Searches for the Imaginary Kingdom of Prester John*, R. E. F. Smith, trans. (Cambridge University Press, 1987), 23.

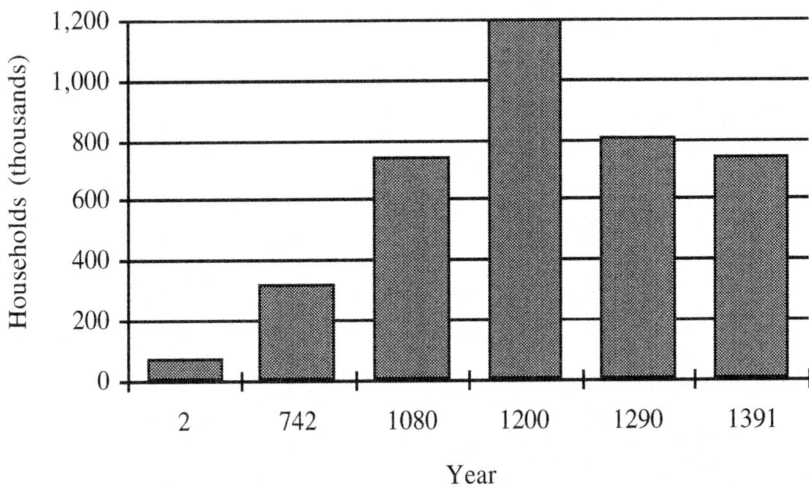

Figure 2.1. Population (recorded) of Lingnan, 2–1391 CE. Sources: For 2 CE, *Han Shu*, Dili zhi, juan 8 xia; for 742 CE, *Xin Tang Shu*, juan 33; for 1080 CE *Yuanfeng Jiu Yu Zhi*, juan 9; for 1290 CE, *Yuan Shi*, juan 62–63; for 1391, Liang Fangzhong, *Zhongguo lidai hukou tiandi tianfu tongji* (Shanghai: Renmin Chuban She, 1980): 277–78.

China in 1278 and again a century later during the establishment of the Ming dynasty.

By 1400, then, the population of Lingnan had gone through a great cycle, increasing more or less steadily from the Tang to the Southern Song, and then declining for another two centuries until the beginning of the Ming. Relative to the population peak in the Southern Song, Lingnan in 1400 had become relatively depopulated and, as we will see in the next chapter, had reached a low point from which the population increased slowly but steadily for another 250 years.

The human population was not spread evenly over the landscape, and an analysis of the differing population densities can tell us something both about when and where Chinese settled Lingnan and about the long-term processes of environmental and economic change. As Robert Hartwell has argued in his important study of general demographic trends in China from 750 to 1550, "The separate territories of a physio[graphic] region experienced quite different patterns of population growth and decline in each period."[11] Adapting Hartwell's methodology, I have correlated the population figures for Tang, Song, and Yuan administrative units with the equivalent Qing-era prefectural-

[11] Hartwell, "Demographic, Political, and Social Transformation of China, 750–1550," 373.

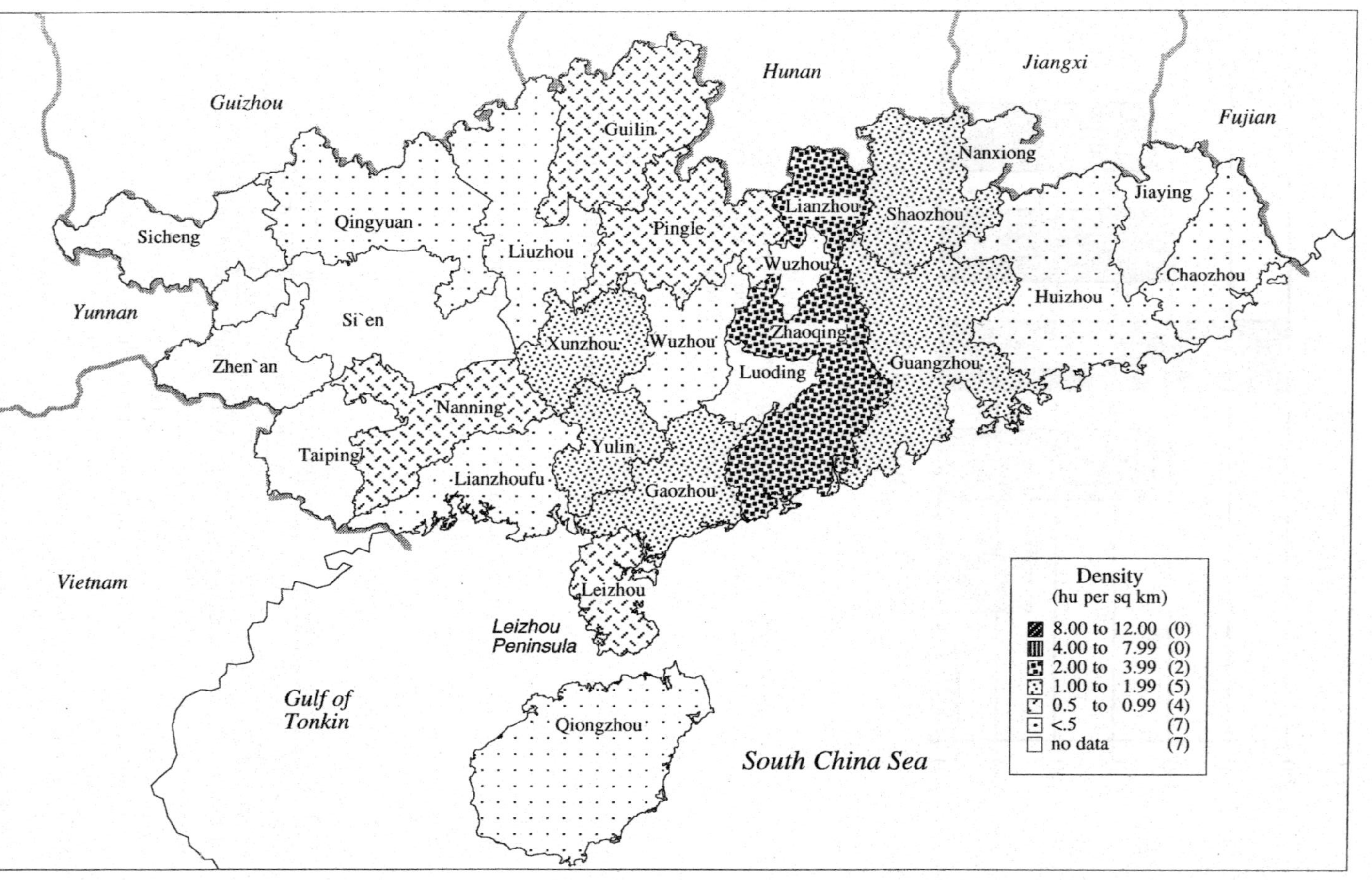

Map 2.1a. Population density, ca. 742

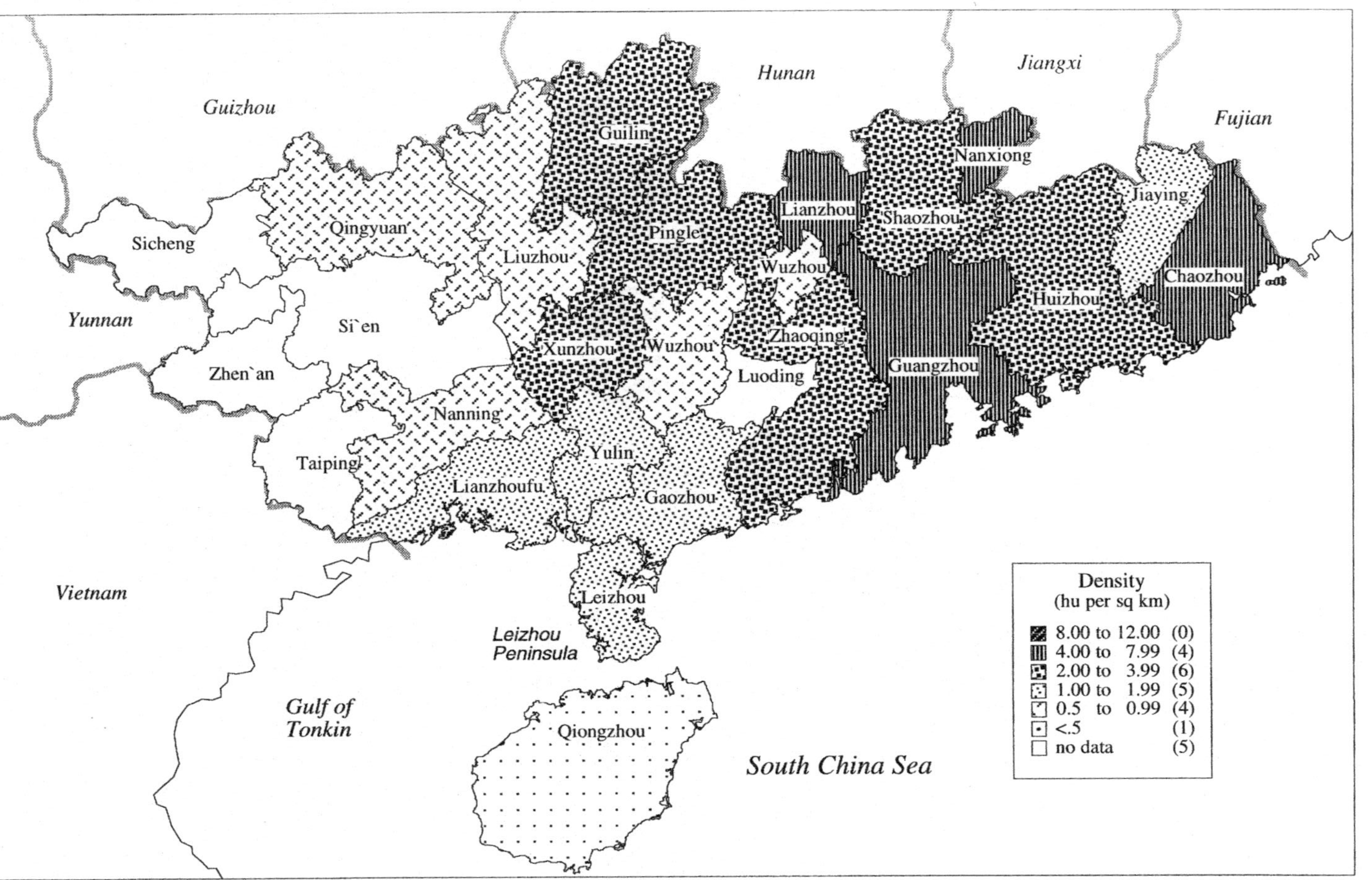

Map 2.1b. Population density, ca. 1080

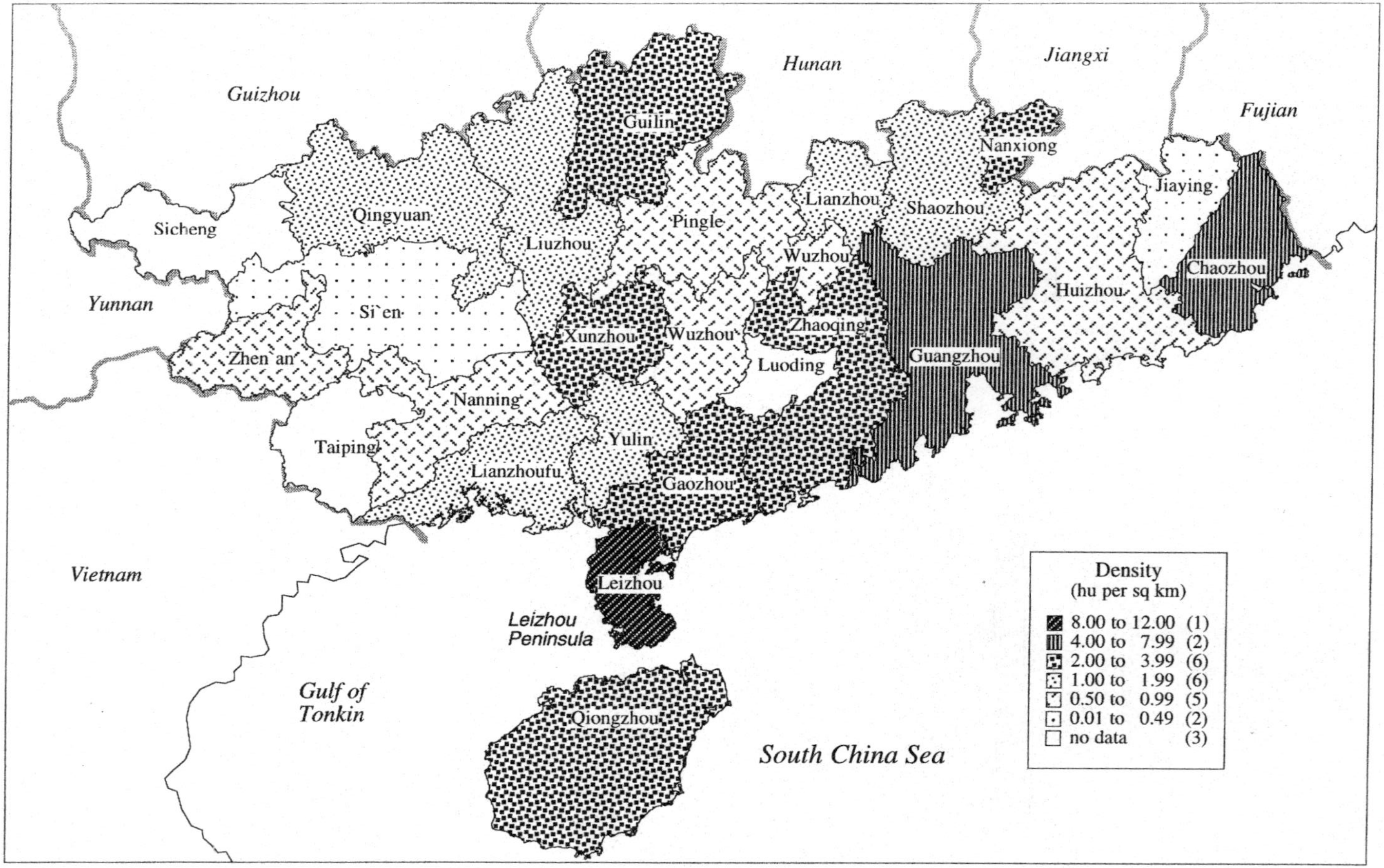

Map 2.1c. Population density, ca. 1290

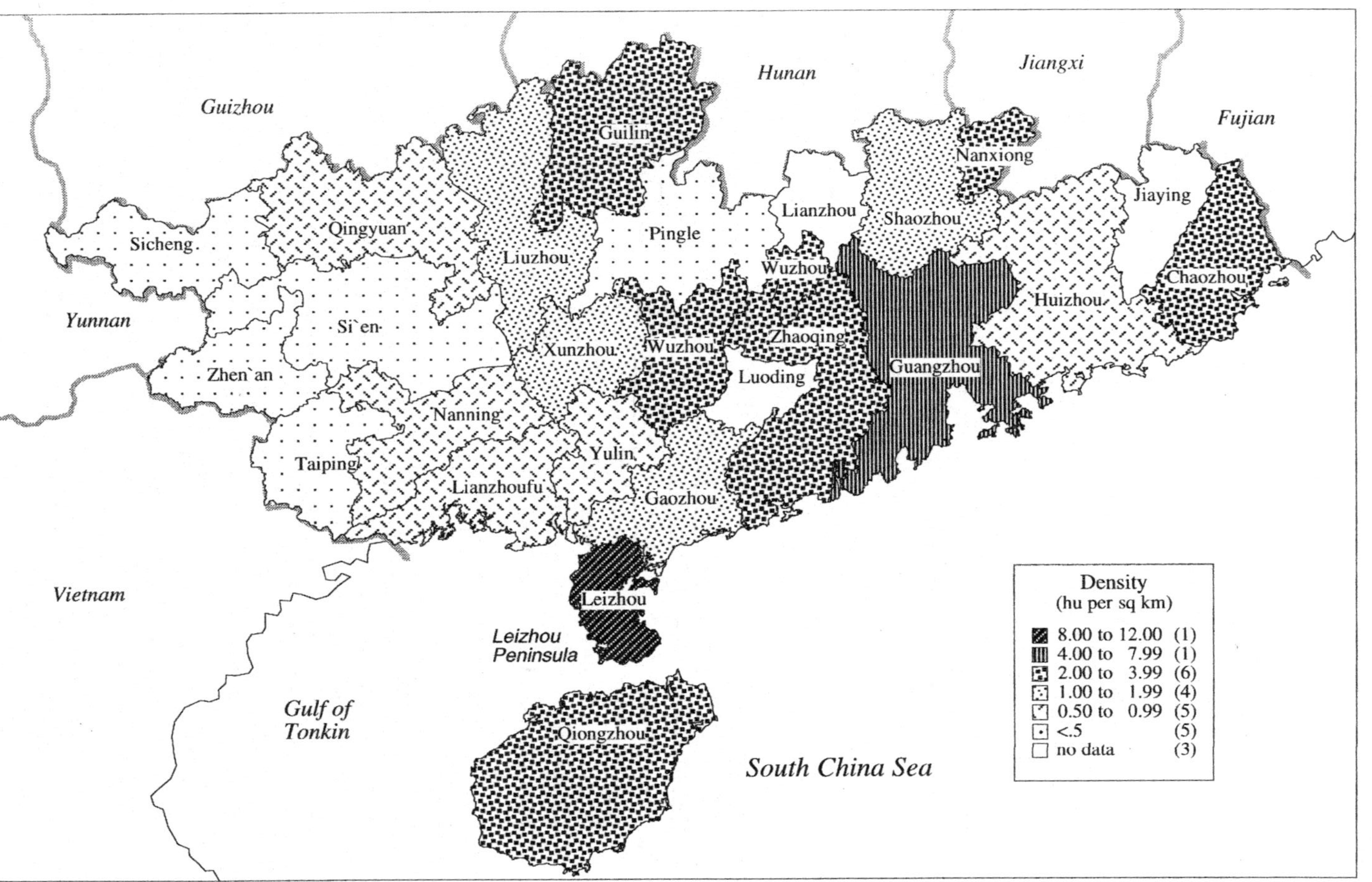
Guizhou
Hunan
Jiangxi
Fujian
Guilin
Nanxiong
Jiaying
Qingyuan
Sicheng
Liuzhou
Pingle
Lianzhou
Shaozhou
Wuzhou
Chaozhou
Huizhou
Yunnan
Si`en
Xunzhou
Wuzhou
Zhaoqing
Zhen`an
Luoding
Guangzhou
Nanning
Yulin
Taiping
Lianzhoufu
Gaozhou
Vietnam
Leizhou
Leizhou
Peninsula
Density
(hu per sq km)
8.00 to 12.00 (1)
4.00 to 7.99 (1)
2.00 to 3.99 (6)
1.00 to 1.99 (4)
0.50 to 0.99 (5)
<.5 (5)
no data (3)
Gulf of
Tonkin
Qiongzhou
South China Sea

Map 2.1d. Population density, ca. 1391

level units and computed population densities to ensure comparability across both time and space.[12] While not exact fits and with but one significant distortion,[13] I believe my reassignments to be generally accurate.

2 CE. The Han administrative units were much larger than even the Qing prefectures, so it is not possible to reconfigure the population figures to be comparative with later ones. What the Han tabulation does show, though, is that most of the population of Lingnan was in northeastern Guangxi around Guilin and in northern Guangdong around Shaozhou. The least-populated area was the region called Nanhai, or the whole area of Qing-era (1644–1911) Guangzhou, Huizhou, Nanxiong, Lianzhou, and Chaozhou prefectures. Even the coastal littoral had a larger population than the area that would become Guangzhou and the Pearl River delta. The Red River delta, in what is now northern Vietnam, also had 10 times more people than Nanhai. There is a reason, I think, for this distribution of the population, but I will discuss it only after describing Lingnan's population patterns in the other time periods.

742 CE. As G. William Skinner has theorized, the density of the population can be seen as a rough indicator of the relative level of resources in various areas when compared with each other: the more dense the population, the wealthier and hence more "developed" one area is likely to be than another. Population densities can also give us a sense of where population is tending to concentrate (or dissipate) from one period to the next and, hence, of differential rates of development. When the Tang population densities of Lingnan are sorted and arrayed in a simple graph, a certain hierarchy and

12 The idea for keeping land boundaries constant was developed first by Robert Hartwell in "Demographic, Political, and Social Transformation of China, 750–1550." Hartwell used the Song-era administrative map. But because this book points toward the Ming and Qing dynasties, I have chosen to use instead the Qing-era prefecture-level political units.

13 The one significant distortion is for the Qing-era prefecture of Nanning. In nearly all other cases, the Tang, Song, and Yuan administrative units were smaller than the Qing units, enabling me to correlate them with the Qing prefectures. To be sure, this procedure is not exact: the Tang administrative unit for eastern Guangdong, Xun, is not exactly the same as Huizhou, with some Xun areas actually belonging in Chaozhou or Jiaying. By and large, though, the procedure works – except for Nanning. In this case, the Tang and Song administrative units for western Guangxi were larger than the Qing prefectures. Where the Qing created five prefectures (Sicheng, Si'en, Taiping, Zhen'an, and Nanning), the Tang had just one (Yong). Moreover, where Qing-era Nanning was in the lowlands along the Yu River (a major tributary of the West River), the other prefectures were all in the western Guangxi upland border region. Until the creation of these additional prefectures in the Ming, then, "Nanning" may best be understood more generally as the upland border region of western Guangxi (Sicheng, Si'en, Taiping, and Zhen'an prefectures).

clustering are apparent.[14] The densities range from a high of 2.9 households per square kilometer in Lianzhou (northern Guangdong) to a low of 0.05 in northwest Guangxi. Using the clusters of densities as a guide, a marked regional pattern emerges (see Maps 2.1a–d).

As had been the case in the Han dynasty, the hill region of northern Guangdong had both the largest and most dense population. Northern and eastern Guangxi, while gaining some population from the relatively high population levels in the Han, was no longer as important. Having developed in the meantime were western and central Guangdong (Zhaoqing and Guangzhou), and the parts of the West River valley and its tributaries (Xunzhou and Yulin). Very sparsely populated areas included the southwestern littoral (Leizhou and Lianzhoufu), eastern Guangdong (Huizhou and Chaozhou), and Hainan Island. One of the more interesting features of this regional structure is that the population density in northern Guangdong continued to outweigh that of Guangzhou. To be sure, the population of Guangzhou had increased substantially since the Han population tabulation, but it still did not equal that of Zhaoqing, let alone the northern hill region. Furthermore, if Schafer is right that the city of Guangzhou attained a population approaching 200,000 in the Tang,[15] then it is conceivable that most of the Guangzhou population (tabulated at 42,200 households) was concentrated in the city, with few farming families indeed.

1080 CE. By 1080, the regional structure had changed significantly, with Guangzhou emerging as the most populous and most densely populated region of Lingnan.[16] While still increasing, the population density of northern Guangdong fell substantially below that of Guangzhou, while that of western and eastern Guangdong (Zhaoqing and Huizhou, respectively) rose to that of northern Guangdong. The prefectures along the West River and its major tributaries (i.e., Guilin, Pingle, Xunzhou, and Yulin) more or less equalized, while the southwestern littoral (Gaozhou, Leizhou, and Lianzhoufu), Hainan Island, and western Guangxi all remained less densely populated.

Besides Guangzhou, the fastest growing regions were Huizhou and Chaozhou prefectures in eastern Guangdong. The reason, of course, as will be discussed more later, especially in the next chapter, is that water control and irrigation sped the development of agriculture in all three prefectures. For now,

14 "Let the data themselves . . . speak" was Skinner's advice in his "Presidential Address: The Structure of Chinese History," *Journal of Asian Studies* 45, no. 2 (Feb. 1985): 288. Although Skinner was speaking specifically about economic data, his comment applies to population (and other) data as well.

15 Schafer, *The Vermilion Bird*, 28.

16 For an excellent discussion of Song-era Lingnan, see Han Maoli, "Song dai Lingnan diqu nongye dili chutan," *Lishi dili* (1993.11): 30–34.

Table 2.1. *Population densities by prefecture, 742–1391 (households/sq. km)*

742		1080		1290		1391	
Lianzhou	3.87	Guangzhou	5.05	Leizhou	11.28	Leizhou	11.48
Nanxiong	n.a.						
Shaozhou	1.77	Chaozhou	4.80	Guangzhou	5.68	Guangzhou	6.69
Zhaoqing	2.23	Nanxiong	4.57	Chaozhou	4.09	Chaozhou	2.74
Guangzhou	1.41	Shaozhou	3.29				
		Lianzhou	4.44	Nanxiong	2.42	Nanxiong	2.00
Gaozhou	1.85			Shaozhou	1.12	Shaozhou	1.08
Xunzhou	1.71	Huizhou	3.42	Lianzhou	1.26	Lianzhou	n.a.
Yulin	1.65	Zhaoqing	3.00				
				Huizhou	0.68	Huizhou	0.73
Guilin	0.77	Pingle	2.68	Zhaoqing	3.04	Zhaoqing	3.44
Pingle	0.57	Xunzhou	2.39				
Wuzhou	0.37	Guilin	2.05	Pingle	0.75	Pingle	0.26
		Yulin	1.85	Xunzhou	3.07	Xunzhou	1.00
Leizhou	0.54			Guilin	3.43	Guilin	2.50
Lianzhoufu	0.37	Leizhou	1.74	Yulin	1.15	Yulin	0.61
		Jiaying	1.17				
Huizhou	0.30	Gaozhou	1.39	Gaozhou	2.27	Gaozhou	1.45
Chaozhou	0.28	Lianzhoufu	1.08	Lianzhoufu	1.17	Lianzhoufu	0.71
Jiaying	n.a.						
		Wuzhou	0.74	Wuzhou	0.55	Wuzhou	2.52
Liuzhou	0.23						
Nanning	0.98	Liuzhou	0.61	Liuzhou	1.73	Liuzhou	1.53
Qiongzhou	0.25	Qingyuan	0.60	Qingyuan	1.01	Qingyuan	0.66
		Qiongzhou	0.31	Qiongzhou	2.72	Qiongzhou	2.02
Qingyuan	0.05	Nanning	0.90	Nanning	0.81	Nanning	0.65
				Jiaying	0.23	Jiaying	n.a.

Source: Same as Figure 2.1.

it is important to note that, by 1080, Huizhou had reached the same level of population density as Zhaoqing, in the second tier behind Guangzhou, and Chaozhou rocketed ahead, from 0.31 to 5.19 households per square kilometer. When all prefectures are sorted by density (see Table 2.1), Chaozhou falls just after Guangzhou.

In Table 2.1, I have sorted and grouped prefectures by population density and geographic proximity to show what might be called the "core–periphery" structure of Lingnan in different historical periods. Although the most densely populated core area of Lingnan differed in these periods, with 1080 being the only time when Guangzhou clearly was the most densely populated region, the periphery was almost always westernmost Guangxi. Furthermore, the northern regions around Nanxiong in Guangdong and Guilin in Guangxi continuously became relatively less densely populated, showing a movement of the population from the hilly, northern sections of Lingnan into the river valleys in the southern and central parts of Lingnan.

1290 CE. The Mongol invasions of China in the thirteenth century rearranged the regional structure of Lingnan. Previously populated regions – especially northern Guangdong (Shaozhou, Nanxiong, and Lianzhou), Huizhou, Pingle, and Yulin – all were decimated. Refugees from Pingle and Yulin probably headed northwest into Liuzhou, which recorded a modest increase in population from 1080 to 1290. But the greatest population surge came in the southwestern littoral (Leizhou) and Hainan Island (Qiongzhou prefecture), whose total population surpassed that of Guangzhou in 1290. Some of the increase in Leizhou and Qiongzhou no doubt came from those displaced from Huizhou, but the vast majority no doubt were northerners who fled nomadic invaders into the southwest and to Hainan in two great waves after 1126 and 1278. When most of these newcomers arrived is not clear – maybe in the twelfth century or maybe only after 1278 – but whenever they came, they swelled the population living on the Leizhou Peninsula and Hainan Island. Since these areas had been relatively sparsely populated, and since the space was already occupied by the non-Chinese Li people, the influx of Chinese refugee settlers pushed the Li off the mainland and into the interior of Hainan Island, where they remained from Ming times on.

1391 CE. By the time of the early Ming population count that has given us the 1391 figures, Lingnan continued to bear the scars of the Mongol invasion. The Leizhou Peninsula was still the most densely populated area, while northern Guangdong, Huizhou, Pingle, and Yulin all remained relatively depopulated when compared with the extent of settlement reached in the Song. Guangzhou, on the other hand, continued to grow, increasing its population density over that of the rest of Lingnan. If Leizhou is removed from the picture, what the Mongol invasion appears to have done to the regional population structure was to elevate the importance of Guangzhou and flatten the differences among the rest of the prefectures in Lingnan (see Table 2.1). Even Chaozhou, which in 1080 was beginning to look out of place in Lingnan, again took on the same levels as the rest.

Summary. This broad overview reveals significant changes over time in the population distribution of Lingnan, at least as it can be indicated by population densities. Several changes are noteworthy. In retrospect, only the 1080 CE population distribution resembles that of Lingnan in the nineteenth or the twentieth century, with Guangzhou as the "core" and population densities decreasing in a more or less orderly fashion from Guangzhou to the periphery of the Lingnan physiographic region. All of the other snapshots reveal rather different patterns. First, the early population center was in the north (especially Nanxiong), just south of the Nanling Mountains, primarily in northern Guangdong but also around Guilin, and not, as might have been expected, in Guangzhou prefecture. That area emerged as a population center only during the Song, for most of the population during the Tang was in the city of Guangzhou, and that was sacked and burned by the rebel Huang Chao in the fall of 879. By the Song dynasty, though, Guangzhou prefecture clearly was the population center of Lingnan, a position it held despite being temporarily eclipsed by the Leizhou Peninsula as a result of the thirteenth-century wave of refugees settling there. In the meantime, the Mongol invasion dealt a blow to northern Guangdong as a population center from which it would never recover, while other prefectures that had been effectively depopulated by the Mongol invasion did regain population after peace was restored in the Ming dynasty. The modern array of population in Lingnan with which we are most familiar – the centrality of Guangzhou with population thinning toward the periphery – thus was not the result of a linear continuation from early settlement patterns of Lingnan. Indeed, if earlier trends had continued, northern Guangdong – or perhaps even the Leizhou Peninsula or Hainan Island – might have emerged as the densely populated core. The question thus arises: How did Guangzhou emerge as the population core of Lingnan? The answer to that question links changes in the distribution of population in Lingnan to significant environmental change in what came to be the Pearl River delta.

The Making of the Pearl River Delta

For the first millennium after Chinese settlers moved into Lingnan, what we now call the Pearl River delta and know as one of the most agriculturally rich and productive regions of China, second only to the Yangzi River delta, was not yet a delta, but in fact still open sea, albeit a fairly shallow bay. Residents of Guangzhou, then called Nanhai, or "the south sea," looked out onto a bay dotted with islands, probably appearing much the way the South China Sea looks today from Repulse Bay on the back side of Hong Kong Island (see Figure 2.2).

To be sure, silt carried downstream in the West, North, and East Rivers had been settling out in the bay, slowly creating the upper reaches of the delta. But because the silt content of these rivers was exceptionally low, the natural processes by which the delta was being created worked extremely slowly. Then, beginning in the eleventh century (during the Song dynasty), the delta began to grow more rapidly and in the fourteenth century (during the Yuan dynasty) accelerated even faster. The series of four maps of the Pearl River delta (Map 2.2), chosen to correspond with the dates for which we have population data,

Figure 2.2. The South China Sea.

shows the build-up of the delta. During the seven centuries from the Han to the Tang, the delta barely changed, with the bay remaining filled with water. By the Song dynasty, however, enough of the delta had emerged south of Guangzhou to block the view of the ocean, and by the Yuan dynasty alluvial sand bars appeared off the coast of Dongguan, where the East River emptied into the bay. Certainly, though, the largest increases in the size of the Pearl River delta occurred from the Yuan dynasty on. Where virtually no change had occurred in the nine centuries after the founding of the Han, in the 300 years from 1290 to 1582, what had been the island of Xiangshan became connected to the mainland.[17] Both the change in the shape of the delta over time and the rate of the change itself are interesting and significant: What accounts for both?

[17] Zhou Yuanhe, "Zhujiang sanjiaozhou de chenglu guocheng," *Lishi dili* 5 (1987): 58–69.

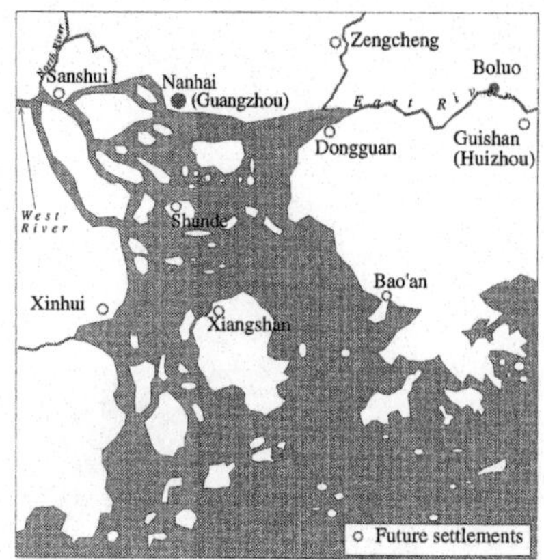

2 CE

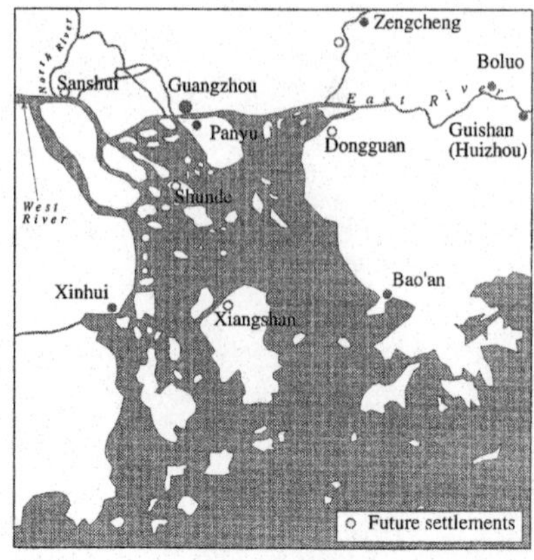

742 CE

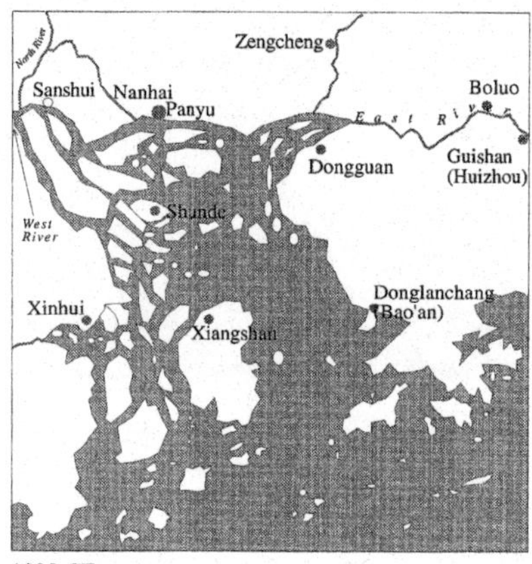

1290 CE

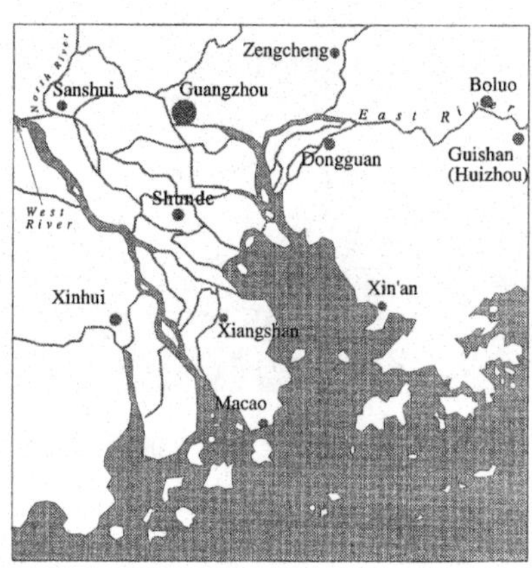

1820 CE

Map 2.2. The Pearl River Delta, ca. 2, 742, 1290, and 1820. Source: Tan Qixiang, editor in chief, *Zhongguo lishi ditu ji* (Historical maps of China) (Shanghai: Ditu chuban she, 1975–82)

In the title to this section, I referred to the "making" of the Pearl River delta. I chose the word "making" specifically to refer to the action of human beings, for more than anything else, people made the Pearl River delta. Involved in this story are, in chronological order: the early settlement patterns and agricultural technology of the Chinese in-migrants in northern Guangdong; the building of water control projects in the lower reaches of the West, North, and East Rivers from the Song on; the Mongol invasion of south China in the 1270s and the consequent displacement of the Chinese population from northern Guangdong to islands in the Pearl River estuary; and the creation of new lands off the islands in the estuary by the refugees.

Slash-and-Burn Agriculture. Slash-and-burn, the earliest and most rudimentary form of agriculture, was practiced in Lingnan until the techniques of wet-rice agriculture spread to Lingnan in the eleventh century. When Chinese migrated into Lingnan, first in Han times and later in greater numbers in the fourth century, they settled in the upland areas around Nanxiong and Guilin, rather than near the swamps in the river valleys further south (the reasons for this will be discussed later). Burning off tracts of land, settlers broadcast millet, barley, and wheat (and maybe rice) seeds onto the ash and then harvested a crop for two or three years until the fertility of the soil was depleted. Abandoning the burned-off ground, the settlers then moved on, and a new tract was burned, the process starting over again. The fires must have been impressive, as this eighth-century poem describing the process in Lianzhou in northern Guangdong graphically illustrates:

> Wherever it may be, they like to burn off the fields,
> Round and round, creeping over the mountain's belly.
> When they bore the tortoise and get the "rain" trigram,
> Up the mountain they go and set fire to the prostrate trees.
> Startled muntjacs run, and then stare back;
> Flocks of pheasants make *i-auk* sounds.
> The red blaze forms sunset clouds far off,
> Light coals fly into the city walls.
> The wind draws it up to the high peaks,
> It licks and laps across the blue forest.
> The blue forest, seen afar, dissolves in a flurry,
> The red light sinks – then rises again.
> A radiant tarn brings forth an old *kau*-dragon;
> Exploding bamboos frighten the forest ghosts.
> In the color of night we see no mountain,
> Just an orphan glow by the Starry Han [Milky Way]:
> It is like a star, then like the moon,
> Each after the other, until at daybreak the wind dies away.
> Then first comes a light which beats on the stones,
> Then follows a heat which glows up to heaven.
> They drop their seeds among the warm ashes;
> These, born by the "essential heat" [yang],
> Burst into buds and shoots.
> Verdant and vivid, after a single rain,
> Spikes of trumpet vine come out like a cloud.
> The snake men chant with folded hands;
> Neither plowing nor hoeing involve their hearts.

From the first they have found the temper of this land,
Whose every inch holds an excess of "essential cold" [yin].[18]

Chinese settlers in the north at first adopted the slash-and-burn techniques of the non-Chinese hill peoples, the Yao and Miao, both of whom practiced various forms of slash-and-burn, shifting cultivation, along with hunting and gathering. Setting fire to forested hillsides during the dry winter months, groups of families then broadcast or drilled dry rice seed into the ash and harvested crops for a few years. They then moved on to another patch, leaving the depleted ground to return to forest, relocating their encampment as well. Remnants of this system were observed in the early twentieth century, with the Yao planting seedlings and leaving the reforested area alone for 20 years after burning it off and planting it for 2 years.[19] The reason for such a long "fallow," as scientists later learned, is that hillsides burned off too regularly turned into grassland with dense root systems very difficult to break up and plant, unlike the soft, easily poked soils under a forest. Even for agriculture, forest was better than grassland, and the Yao seem to have discovered that.

How much of the original forest the settlers burned off is not at all clear, nor is it clear whether the forest was given sufficient time to recover its composition of broadleafed evergreens before being burned off again, or whether the scrubby mason's pine (*Pinus massoniana*) took the place of the broadleafs. What does seem to be quite certain, though, is that the slash-and-burn agriculture practiced in the upper reaches of the drainage system opened the hills to greater erosion and hence to a higher silt content flowing downstream in the West, North, and East Rivers.[20]

Until the eleventh century, much of this silt did not reach the Pearl River delta, but rather was deposited in the flood plains in the lower reaches of the West, North, and East Rivers. Much like the end of a garden hose under high pressure, the lower courses of these rivers flopped around from one outlet to another when monsoonal rains sent water gushing through the system, filling the flood plains with silt-laden water. When the flood waters receded, the silt was left behind. Clearly, the flood plains of the lower reaches of these rivers, especially the area near the confluence of the West and North Rivers, thereby contained fertile soils with great agricultural potential. But they had two related problems: flooding and malaria. Before the upper reaches of the future Pearl River delta could become the densely populated, agriculturally rich center of the Lingnan regional economy, the Chinese would have to either change the swampy environment of the flood plains of the West, North, and East Rivers or else adapt to that environment, for the south China lowlands were not hospitable to northern Chinese people.

[18] Liu Yuxin, translated and quoted in Schafer, *The Vermilion Bird*, 54–55.
[19] Fenzel, "On the Natural Conditions Affecting the Introduction of Forestry," 45.
[20] This conclusion is reached by Chinese hydrologists in Chen, *Zhongguo ziran dili*, vol. 4: 243.

Malaria. To Chinese from the north, all of Lingnan looked diseased. In the words of Liu Xun (whom we have already cited regarding tigers and elephants): "The mountains and rivers of Lingbiao [i.e., Lingnan] are twisted and jungly; the vapors concentrate and are not easily dispersed or diffused. Therefore there is much mist and fog to cause pestilence."[21] As is now known, of course, malaria is caused by a parasite transmitted to humans from a particular kind of mosquito, the genus *Anopheles*. Because of the linkages among parasite, mosquito, and human host, malaria requires a specific set of environmental conditions to exist and cannot spread beyond those limits. Malaria thus is not a communicable disease like plague, smallpox, or cholera that can spread broadly and fast through human populations regardless of where they reside, but is limited to certain environments.

Tropical forests such as those originally covering Lingnan are especially good breeding grounds for parasites of all kinds. But the particular parasites that cause malaria in humans – several species of the single-celled protozoa belonging to the genus *Plasmodium* – were not there just waiting for human hosts to invade, but rather arrived with their human hosts when they migrated into south China. To be sure, malaria is found in monkeys, apes, rats, birds, and reptiles, many of which inhabited Lingnan's tropical forests, but these forms are not infectious to humans. Human malaria is a very old disease, not merely evolving with humans, but even influencing the process of natural selection.[22] The disease probably originated in tropical Africa and only later spread elsewhere with the Neolithic revolution. According to Bruce-Chwatt, the preeminent historian of the disease, in Neolithic times the infection established itself in Mesopotamia, India, the Nile River valley (from which it invaded the Mediterranean), and south China.[23] Whether it was brought into Lingnan by the original settlers in the area or was spread among an indigenous population by later arrivals is not known. But however and whenever malaria became established among the human population of south China, it was there among the indigenous Tai population long before the first Chinese migrants arrived.

Anopheles mosquitoes carry three species of plasmodium harmful to humans, and each causes a different kind of malaria. Two cause intermittent fevers and are not particularly virulent, even in nonimmune populations, but

[21] Liu Xun, *Lingbiao lu yi*, shang: 1.

[22] William H. McNeill, *Plagues and Peoples* (New York: Doubleday, 1976), 47–48.

[23] From these five foci the disease spread throughout the tropics and into temperate climates. L. J. Bruce-Chwatt, "History of Malaria from Prehistory to Eradication," in Walther H. Wernsdorfer and Sir Ian McGregor, eds., *Malaria: Principles and Practice of Malariology* (Edinburgh: Churchill Livingstone, 1988), vol. 1, 3. By the end of the nineteenth century, malaria covered two-thirds of the world, becoming (and remaining) what many consider to be "the most important disease in the world." Brian Maegraith, *Adams and Maegraith: Clinical Tropical Diseases* (Oxford: Blackwell Scientific, 1989), 201.

one – the malignant tertian, or pernicious, malaria, caused by *P. falciparum* – "is the most dangerous form of malaria."[24] Depending on the parasite, the clinical manifestations of malaria (including fever with or without paroxysm, sweating, and chills, vomiting and diarrhea, anemia, and hardening of the spleen) occur as the brood of the parasite undergo schizogony together.[25] That all three forms of malaria were found in Lingnan is clear from the classification of fevers given by Zhou Qufei in the late twelfth century. In the "lighter kind (*qingzhe*), the fevers come and go." In the "serious kind (*zhongzhe*), there is only fever and no chill." And in the "really serious kind (*geng zhongzhe*), fever continues without letting up."[26] Zhou may have been in error about ranking the severity based solely on the periodicity of fever, but clearly he identifies three kinds of fever, all consistent with scientific understandings of malaria. Which of the three was predominant in Lingnan can only be guesswork, but given what is known about the general epidemiology of the parasites and the fact that the malaria in Lingnan was often fatal to newcomers in the region, *P. falciparum* probably was the most prevalent.

With rainfall coming in the spring and summer when temperatures were in the range considered optimal for mosquitoes to breed, with pools of water forming in depressions in the earth's surface but especially in the swamps left by the annual flooding of the river systems, and with relatively high humidity, both the parasite and the anopheles mosquito could flourish in Lingnan.[27] Since the parasite lived in both the mosquito and in humans, the environmental conditions which brought both into contact provided the environment for malaria. Human beings, as host to the parasite, thus are a prerequisite to the existence of malaria: no humans, no malaria.[28]

24 Maegraith, *Clinical Tropical Diseases*, 201.

25 Ibid., 210–20.

26 Zhou Qufei, *Ling wai dai ta*, juan 4, 3b–4a.

27 For a discussion of the general conditions favorable for anopheles, see L. Molineaux, "The Epidemiology of Human Malaria as an Explanation of Its Distribution, Including Some Implications for Its Control," in Wernsdorfer and McGregor, eds., *Malaria*, vol. 2, 915.

28 Although it seems a simple proposition that mosquitoes breed in warm, wet surroundings and thus that malaria should exist nearly everywhere where those conditions prevail and people live, nature is not that simple. Indeed, the issue is so complex that scientists still cannot pinpoint the precise conditions that breed the anopheles mosquito. Indeed, even the particular species of anopheles responsible for malaria has been shown to be six "sibling" subspecies, only two of which carry plasmodium and infect humans. The plasmodium-carrying siblings are nearly indistinguishable from other *Anopheles maculipennis* except for laying their eggs separately upon the surface of water rather than in "rafts." Certainly differences in mosquito habitat – however minute – have favored one kind of reproductive strategy over the other. Variables such as whether the water is standing or moving, the amount of sunlight or shade, the presence of gases or minerals dissolved in the water, and the salinity of the water all affect whether or not the anopheles mosquito will breed. Other factors include competition for habitat by other species of mosquitoes, such as the nonthreatening genus *Culex*, and predation by insects and fish. Those

That malaria was prevalent throughout much of Lingnan is certain, as Liu Xun's comment makes clear. Some areas were known as being particularly virulent, such as around Qingyuan up the North River from Guangzhou. Other places mentioned malaria in the "climate" section of their gazetteers, such as Chaozhou in eastern Guangdong, where malaria was prevalent in the hills.[29] But it was also apparent to Chinese observers that malaria was not found in all areas of Lingnan. In the Song dynasty toward the end of the twelfth century, for instance, Zhou Qufei could write: "Not all deep[ly forested] and wild (*shen guang*) places in Ling[nan] are necessarily malarious. For example, Qiongzhou on Hainan Island and, on the north side of the sea [i.e., on the mainland across from Hainan], Lianzhoufu, Leizhou, and Huazhou are described as *shen guang*, but there is little malaria." But other *shen guang* places – Nanning, Yulin, Qinzhou, and Guiping (all in Guangxi) – all had it.[30] Although malaria had spread to Hainan Island by the nineteenth century, even in the fifteenth it was still described as a place free of malaria. The littoral belt of southwestern Guangdong (or at least part of it) – described by Gu Yanwu as an area with "very little malaria"[31] – was still free from malaria in the late nineteenth century.[32] The area around Guilin seems to have been free of malaria: according to Fan Chengda, writing in the twelfth century, "Everywhere south [of Guilin] is the home of malaria."[33] Northern Guangdong province, in particular Nanxiong, Lianzhou, and Shaozhou prefectures, also was free of malaria. Local ecological factors, such as elevation,[34] played the critical role in accounting for the presence of malaria in one area or its absence in another, even if we cannot now be sure exactly what those ecological differences were.

caveats aside, though, it seems that the anopheles tends to favor stagnant water: small pools of water formed after rains, or the swamps left after floods. See Marston Bates, "Ecology of Anopheline Mosquitos," in Mark Boyd, ed., *Malariology* (Philadelphia: Saunders, 1949), 302–30; Richard Fiennes, *Man, Nature and Disease* (London: Weidenfeld and Nicolson, 1964), 77; L. Molineaux, "The Epidemiology of Human Malaria as an Explanation of Its Distribution, Including Some Implications for Its Control," in Wernsdorfer and McGregor, eds., *Malaria*, vol. 2: 916.

29 *Chaozhou fuzhi*, 1762 ed., juan 2: 1b, 4b.

30 Zhou Qufei, *Ling wai dai ta*, juan 4: 2b–3a.

31 Gu Yanwu, *Tianxia junguo li bing shu*, juan 98: 28a.

32 "The earliest Customs Records for Pakhoi [Beihai] (1889) state that there was no malaria there and that there was not likely to be any outbreak since the Pakhoi peninsula consisted of dry sandy ground." Ernest Carrol Faust, "An Inquiry into the Prevalence of Malaria in China," *China Medical Journal* 40, no. 10 (Oct. 1926): 938–56. Four years later, though, there was.

33 Fan Chengda, *Gui hai yu heng zhi*, 28a, translated and quoted in Schafer, *The Vermilion Bird*, 132.

34 J. R. McNeill has found that, in the Mediterranean, malaria did not extend above 500 meters elevation. See J. R. McNeill, *The Mountains of the Mediterranean World: An Environmental History* (Cambridge University Press, 1992), 350. More research needs to be conducted to determine the elevations in Lingnan above which malaria ceased.

The Chinese immigrants to Lingnan understood neither the causes of malaria, nor the environmental link to the mosquito, but they did have enough knowledge of where the disease was and where it wasn't to guide decisions about where to settle – and where to remain. Most came to Lingnan via either the Meiling Pass or the Ling Qu Canal and then settled in northern Guangdong and Guangxi provinces. This was in part because those were the first regions "south of the mountains" they encountered and in part because those regions were free of malaria. Once settled, they tended to remain there, and the primary reason given was the fear of malaria in other parts of Lingnan. According to the genealogies of several lineages that trace their roots to Nanxiong, during Song times the fear of malaria kept them from migrating elsewhere in Lingnan, even in the face of mounting population pressure in northern Guangdong.[35]

In the southern part of Lingnan, significant Han population densities were found not in the Guangzhou region, but along the largely malaria-free southwestern littoral, including the Leizhou Peninsula and the areas to its east and west. As noted earlier in this chapter, Guangzhou prefecture was not initially the most densely populated part of Lingnan, despite the fact that by the Ming dynasty it (in particular the Pearl River delta) was to become the core of the Lingnan macroregion. Certainly one possible explanation for the reticence of Chinese immigrants to settle the Pearl River delta was malaria. In terms of its original physical environment, the flood plains in the lower reaches of the West, North, and East Rivers seem to have been nearly ideal for the anopheles mosquito. In other parts of the world where the mouths of rivers created deltas and swamps, malaria thrived, such as in the south of France and in much of Italy.[36]

Settlement patterns also provide indirect evidence that malaria existed in the flood plains in the lower reaches of the West and North Rivers.[37] Malaria

[35] Chen Lesu, "Zhujigang shi shi," [Guangdong] *Xueshu yanjiu* (1982), no. 6.

[36] Bruce-Chwatt, "History of Malaria from Prehistory to Eradication," 12–13. In a malaria epidemic in 1865 in Mauritius, according to Scott: "The sequence was similar to that which is seen to occur in other tropical regions at the present day. Low-lying, badly drained areas near the coast became converted into swamps by the heavy rains. This condition would vary in extent and duration with the nature of the soil, the amount of slope, the drainage and the rainfall, but would usually persist for several weeks and the swamps became the home of innumerable insects. Among the first to breed would be the mosquitoes." A medical doctor and scientist, Scott concluded that "the general principle may be summed up by saying that . . . the disease prevails on low-lying land, becomes less as we ascend . . . Hence an outbreak will decline as a damp or marshy soil dries up, as it will also when the ground is completely covered [with water], to reappear as the surface clears and puddles and ponds form." H. Harold Scott. *A History of Tropical Medicine* (Baltimore: Willliams and Wilkins, 1939), vol. 1: 131–32.

[37] Anopheles mosquitoes were collected in the Pearl River delta in the early twentieth century, but that is not proof that they had been there long before. See Faust, "Mosquitoes in China and Their Potential Relationship to Human Disease," 133–37.

cannot exist without human hosts to provide a "reservoir of malaria infection,"[38] so areas uninhabited by humans thus could not have been malarial. As noted earlier, an indigenous population of Tai peoples lived in the river valleys and along the coast,[39] providing the infectious reservoir of humans that allowed malaria to become endemic: uninfected anopheles mosquitoes picked up the parasite from an infected human and passed it along to a person uninfected or not recently infected. Interestingly, though, communities in which malaria is endemic also develop a certain immunity to the disease.[40]

The indigenous Tai population of Lingnan, especially those who lived in the lower reaches of the river valleys, thus would have acquired a certain level of immunity to malaria before Han Chinese even appeared on the scene. But for those without acquired immunity – such as Chinese migrants from north China – the disease would have been deadly. Besides malaria, other tropical diseases also no doubt ravaged newcomers from the north, posting warning signs for later migrants. Indeed, the Yao also settled in the hills and avoided the flood plains, perhaps as much because of their fear of tropical diseases as because of their preference for the hills. If malaria was one reason that Chinese (and Yao) initially avoided the area around the Pearl River estuary, then to settle there Chinese had to either acquire immunity to malaria like the indigenous Tai peoples or change the ecological conditions so they were no longer so conducive to breeding anopheles mosquitoes. The best piece of direct evidence for the gradual acquisition of immunity comes from a Ming-era author Wang Linting, who claimed that "in the Tang and Song, malaria in Lingnan was wherever [Chinese] in-migrants lived. But by the end of the Song, when the worthies and ministers fled [in the face of the Mongol invasion], [the earlier migrants] had become more like the locals [in not contracting malaria]."[41]

38 Maegraith, *Clinical Tropical Diseases*, 201.

39 "The largest series of open-air [dwelling] sites with early pottery is in the Hsi-chiao-shan area at the delta of the Pearl River south of Canton." Kwang-chih Chang, *The Archeology of Ancient China*, 4th edition (New Haven: Yale University Press, 1986), 106.

40 "In the indigenous population of a malarious area the active disease is usually rare in very young infants, possibly because of a combination of the high proportion of haemoglobin F in the infant, the passive transfer of immune bodies from the mother and of the inhibitory effect of the breast or other milk diet itself on the multiplication of the malaria parasite. Malaria as a disease becomes more common and severe in the latter half of the first year of life and in the first few years of childhood, when attacks are very severe and not infrequently fatal. As the surviving children grow older, however, the attacks get milder and, provided there is continued reinfection by the same form of parasite, the overt disease eventually becomes very much modified and ameliorated in the older child and adult." Maegraith, *Clinical Tropical Diseases*, 204–205.

41 Quoted in Su Guangchang, "Song dai de Guangxi shehui jingji," *Guangxi shifan xueyuan xuebao* (1981): 75–84.

Malaria by itself might have proved sufficient to keep Chinese out of the Pearl River delta, but the fact was that the lower reaches of the West, North, and East Rivers were sufficiently swampy and difficult to farm whether or not they were malaria infested. It is not that the river valleys were unpopulated, for the non-Chinese Tai people had inhabited those regions for millennia. Also, of course, there was the Chinese city of Guangzhou, which, being set upon a hill overlooking the Pearl River estuary,[42] was probably free of malaria, as may have been the area north of the city walls. But Chinese settlement of the nearby malarial valleys required levees to control flooding and to drain swamps, opening the flood plains to Chinese-style settled agriculture. Human beings were about to alter the environment to make it more hospitable to them, as well as inhospitable to the anopheles mosquito;[43] ecological change cut both ways.

Flood Control. Lingnan experienced two kinds of water control problems: too much water, resulting in flooding, and too little or irregular supplies of water during the growing season; the summer monsoon rainfall pattern and the Lingnan drainage system accentuated both. When the monsoons brought the rain to Lingnan, most fell in the four summer months, swelling the ofttimes nearly dry river beds. From the west, all of the rain gathered into the catchment basin that emptied into the West River, and then spilled from Wuzhou down into Guangdong province. From the north, all of the rain gathered into the North River. The West and the North River joined at Sanshui (three rivers) some 10 miles west of the city of Guangzhou, forming the beginning of the Pearl River delta. From the east, rain drained into the East River basin, pouring into the Pearl River estuary to the east of Guangzhou.

The normal rainfall patterns thus poured huge amounts of water into the system in a very short period of time. Naturally, the floodplain from Zhaoqing (on the West River) down to Sanshui flooded every year, depositing ever greater amounts of silt eroded from the burned-off hills further upriver. As early as 809 (the Tang dynasty), levees constructed downstream from Zhaoqing prevented the West River from following the southern of two branches to the confluence with the North River, restricting the flow to the northern branch.[44] The levee not only opened a floodplain to agriculture, but also sent all of the silt-

[42] Zeng, "Cong lishi dimaoxue kan Guangzhou cheng fazhan wenti," 28–41.

[43] Other scholars have proposed this idea as well. Tuan Yi-fu, citing earlier studies, wrote: "New irrigation methods evolved with the spread of rice. The practice of periodic draining destroyed malarial mosquitoes. This meant that large areas which were unhealthy before, say, the year 1000, could now be settled and absorb large population." Tuan Yi-fu, *China* (London: Longman Group, 1970), 129.

[44] Chen, *Zhongguo ziran dili*, vol. 10: 183.

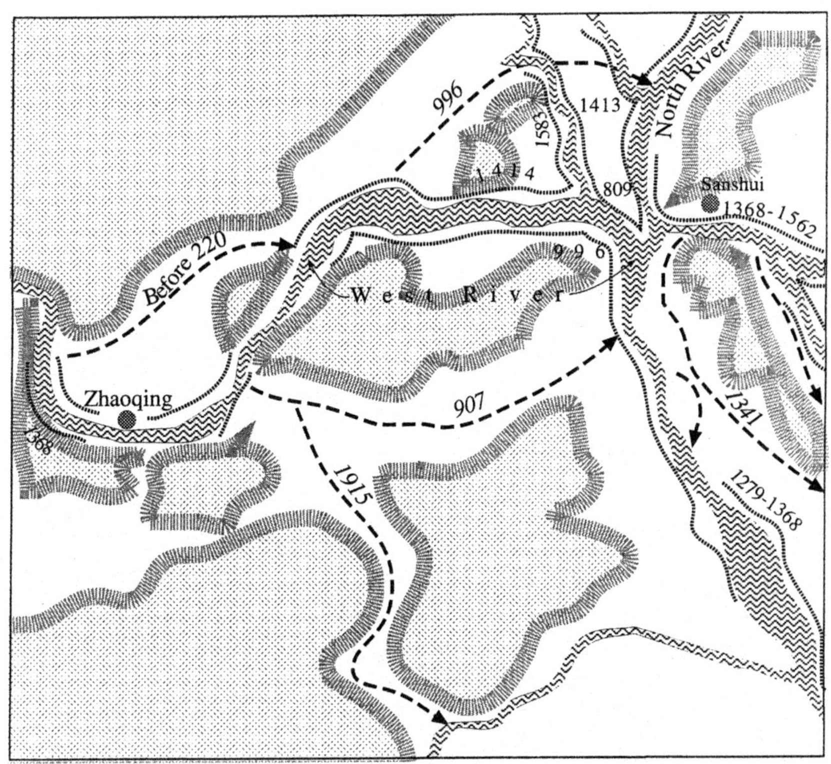

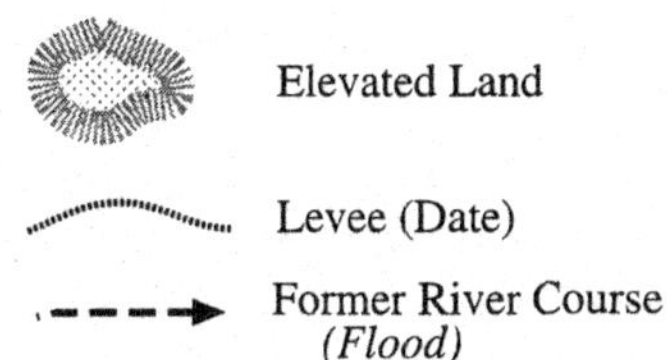

Map 2.3. Levees on the West River, Tang–Ming dynasties

laden floodwaters further downstream, thereby increasing the pressure and flooding around Sanshui (see Map 2.3). Controlling the flooding at the confluence of the West and North Rivers thus was among the first large-scale water control projects in Lingnan to be tackled.

Around 1100, work commenced on the Sang Yuan Wei (or Mulberry Garden enclosure). When it was completed, it was about 28 miles in length and protected some 6,500 *qing* (about 100,000 acres) of land from flooding,[45] inaugurating a new era of agricultural development in that part of Lingnan. About the same time that the Sang Yuan Wei was being built, seawalls along the coast in Leizhou prefecture and in western Dongguan county also were under construction. In Leizhou, nearly 25,000 *zhang* (about 48 miles) of seawall was constructed during the Shaoxing era (1131–62 CE), creating some 10,000 *qing* (about 160,000 acres) of arable land by protecting it from periodic inundation by tides and typhoons, and no doubt eliminating the mangrove forests there as well.[46] In Dongguan, the 12,806-*zhang* (about 24-mile) Xian Chao (Salt-Tide) dike was built in 1089, making 21,028 *qing* (about 300,000 acres) of land arable.[47]

According to statistics compiled by Ye Xian'en and Tan Dihua, in Song times 28 earthenwork dikes or embankments were built in the upper reaches of the Pearl River delta, totaling 66,024 *zhang* (about 125 miles) in length and protecting 24,322 *qing* (nearly 400,000 acres) of land; during the Yuan dynasty an additional 34 embankments were built, adding 50,526 *zhang* (about 96 miles) to the length and 2,320 *qing* in area.[48] In other words, the embankments extended for about 200 miles (or about 100 miles of river, if dikes were on both banks), and protected about 20 percent of the cultivated land in Yuan-era Guangdong. Additionally, in Chaozhou prefecture in eastern Guangdong, 22 sections of river dikes restrained the floodwaters of the Han River in Haiyang and Jieyang county, protecting another 88,000 *qing* of land.[49]

These flood control levees had the effect of pinning each river diked into a single course, so that rather than meandering and spilling into numerous courses during the monsoon season, rivers ran straight for the bay. The floodplains, of course, then were opened for agricultural production. But these waterworks begun in the Song had other environmental consequences as well. Draining the swampy backwaters that had remained after the floodwaters receded altered the ecological conditions that had favored the malaria-carrying anopheles mosquito, rendering the areas less deadly to Chinese originally from the north.

Equally important, though, the flood control works channeled the silt away from the former floodplains and directed it further downstream to the beginning of the Pearl River estuary. As a consequence of both the slash-and-burn agriculture in the hills and the water control works, the amount of silt pouring into the Pearl River thus increased significantly from the eleventh century on.

45 Wang Ping, "Qing ji Zhujiang sanjiaozhou de nongtian shuili," in *Jindai Zhongguo quyu shi yanjiu taolunhui wenji* (Taibei: Academica Sinica Institute of Modern History, 1986), 569–71.

46 *Guangdong tongzhi*, 1822 ed., juan 26.

47 Wang Ping, "Qing ji Zhujiang sanjiaozhou de nongtian shuili," 581–82.

48 Ye Xian'en and Tan Dihua, "Ming Qing Zhujiang sanjiaozhou nongye shangyehua yu xushi de fazhan," *Guangdong shehui kexue*, 2 (1984): 73.

49 *Guangdong tongzhi*, 1822 ed., juan 26.

The changes to the Pearl River delta that the increased amount of silt precipitated are evident in the maps of the delta. What is not evident, however, is that while more silt entered the upper reaches of the estuary, it just might have continued to flow further into the bay had it not been "captured," as explained later, by pioneers who fled to the rocky islands in the bay in the aftermath of the Mongol invasion of the 1270s.

Present at the Creation: The Delta Lineages from Zhujigang

Many of the large, powerful families that came to dominate the economic, social, and political life of the Pearl River delta by the Ming and Qing dynasties traced their origins to the Nanxiong area in northern Guangdong, in particular to the small but important village of Zhujigang, which sat astride the road to the Meiling Pass.[50] All traffic flowing between Lingnan and the Yangzi River over the Meiling Pass – and that was a considerable amount of foot traffic, carrying products made from the natural wonders of Lingnan north and bringing the porcelains from Jingdezhen south – had to pass through Zhujigang. Perhaps the village had acquired its name – "Pearl Alley" – either from pearl merchants who may have operated there or from the small, rounded stones inlaid into the ground to form the road. Qu Dajun claims the village was named after an especially filial Tang-era man from Nanxiong who was so fat he had "a belly like a pearl."[51] However the village obtained the "pearl" part of its name, it literally straddled the road, with travelers forced to walk between the rows of houses and shops lining the "alley." Zhujigang served as a resting place for merchants and other travelers before beginning or ending the one-day journey over the pass and, we would assume, exercised some control over who passed through and how easily they did so. Nanxiong had been the first area in Lingnan settled by Han Chinese, and the population swelled after the Jin invasion of north China in the 1120s sent refugees fleeing south; many of those who took up residence in Zhujigang, according to later chroniclers, were among the most wealthy and powerful families from north China. Resources and wealth thus concentrated in Zhujigang – until the 1270s and the Mongol invasion, at least.

Perhaps because the wealthy families of Zhujigang had settled there in the first place out of fear of northern invaders, when Kubilai Khan's armies began moving south in the 1270s, many residents decided to flee in 1273–74, a couple of years before the Mongol armies pushed south to the Nanling Mountains.[52] When the Mongol armies crossed over the Meiling Pass in 1276, those resi-

50 For a brief discussion, see Li Zhuanshi et al., eds., *Lingnan wenhua*, 183–92.

51 Qu Dajun, *Guangdong xin yu*, juan 2: 65 (Hong Kong: Zhonghua shuju, 1974 ed.), 59.

52 *Xinhui xiang tuzhi* (Hong Kong: Gangzhou xuehui, 1970 reprint of late Qing edition), 84–85.

dents of Zhujigang who could flee did so; those who failed to flee probably died in the battles that devastated much of Nanxiong and Shaozhou. According to the traditions recorded in several genealogies, 97 families (*jia*) with 33 different surnames (*xing*) fled south into the area that would become the Pearl River delta.[53]

Fearing the Mongols more than malaria or adversity, and perhaps hoping to find additional maritime escape routes, these families settled on the small islands that dotted the Pearl River estuary; many of the large lineages in Xinhui county, for instance, trace their origins to Zhujigang.[54] Even today, the relics of that settlement pattern can be seen in the towns situated on what once were islands, but now are hills in an ocean of alluvial soil. Most expressive of this is the town of Shawan, which hugs the southern slope of the island/hill where the town of Panyu also was built; to its west was a mouth of the North River.[55] Shawan means "bay of sand," which in 1276 no doubt it was.

How much cultivable land was available to the settlers of places like Shawan in the fourteenth century is not known. No doubt some alluvium had been deposited by natural processes, perhaps speeded up a bit by the slash-and-burn agriculture practiced in the hill regions around places like their former home in Zhujigang. As the water from the West and North Rivers flowed into the bay and around the islands, the current slowed on the "leeward" side, allowing the silt to settle out. But the new residents in the bay were not content to let natural processes create their agricultural land.

Shatan. In what became the Pearl River delta, settlers created new fields from the sandbars that formed wherever the current slowed sufficiently for the transported sediment to settle, but mostly on the downstream side of islands, or on the outward side of river bends. Called *shatan*, or "sand flats," these fields truly were new, having literally arisen from the water. Unlike polders or enclosed fields that had been reclaimed from swamps or coastal flats, the *shatan* "grew" in the Pearl River, adding land where none had previously existed.

[53] Chen Lesu, "Zhujigang shi shi," 144–49.

[54] *Xinhui xiang tuzhi*, 85–87.

[55] Liu Zhiwei, "Zongzu yu shatian kaifa – Panyu Shawan He zu de ge'an yanjiu," *Zhongguo nongshi* 4 (1992): 34–41. Professor Liu argues that the shatian of the He lineage of Shawan can reliably be traced back only to the late sixteenth century at the latest, not the early fourteenth century as implied in the oral traditions of the lineage's origins. Certainly most of the shatian was added from the mid-Ming on, becoming epecially pronounced in the eighteenth century. But that does not obviate the point that it began to be created after the Mongol invasion disrupted the previous settlement patterns with most of Lingnan's population occupying in the northern hills. Professor Liu's work has recently been translated and published in English as "Lineages on the Sands: The Case of Shawan," in David Faure and Helen F. Siu, eds., *Down to Earth: The Territorial Bond in South China* (Stanford: Stanford University Press, 1995), 21–43.

The particular topographical and hydrological conditions of the Pearl River estuary and the modifications to both caused by diking contributed to the creation of *shatan*. Before the Sang Yuan Wei and other dikes had been built at the entrances of the delta, the floodwaters of the West and North Rivers spilled over the river banks, depositing the sediment in the swamps bordering the river channels. Some of the silt was carried further down into what was then a bay, creating the delta. But when the dikes were built to prevent flooding, the river course was fixed and the sediment did not settle until further downstream. In Ming and Qing times, this occurred mostly in southern Panyu, northern Xiangshan, Shunde, eastern Xinhui and western Dongguan counties, and it is in these counties where *shatan* emerged.

Certainly, some of the *shatan* emerged by natural processes, but the majority were constructed. The method of creating *shatan* was relatively simple, but did require years until the land was usable. When a sandbar arose by natural means close to the water level, rocks were thrown around its perimeter not merely to fix the existing sand in place, but also to capture more sediment. After a more substantial enclosure was built, the sediment was "transformed" by planting legumes (which fix nitrogen in the soil). After three to five years, the *shatan* would be ready for rice.[56] According to the seventeenth-century writer Qu Dajun, a three-year fallow period followed three years of growing rice.[57]

Once one *shatan* was created, more silt would build up on its downstream side. This silt would be captured by the process just described to create more *shatan*, and so on, until a whole series of *shatan* extended the cultivated land area to several tens of thousand *mu*. These connected *shatan* were called "mother and child" (*mu zi*) *shatan*, rendering metaphorical the relationship between the original *shatan* and the one to which it had given birth. Continuing the Chinese metaphor, one could say that over time whole families or even lineages of *shatan* constituted the Pearl River delta. But more to the point, the delta had been built by people working with natural processes, but in the unusual conditions created by the Mongol invasion of south China.

Curiously, the abandonment of northern Guangdong farms in the face of the Mongol armies may have hastened the creation of *shatan* in the years or decades following. J. R. McNeill has shown that the soil of farms abandoned in the Mediterranean hill country in the aftermath of the fall of the Roman empire eroded rapidly, contributing both to the degradation of the mountains and to the deposition of silt in the lowlands at the mouths of rivers.[58] A similar process may have occurred in Lingnan following the Mongol invasion, with

[56] The method is described in Peng Yuxin, *Qing dai tudi kaiken shi* (Beijing: Nongye chuban she, 1990), 164.

[57] Qu, *Guangdong xin yu*, juan 2: 57.

[58] McNeill, *The Mountains of the Mediterranean*, 85, 191, 312, 319–22.

increased erosion from abandoned northern Guangdong farms sending silt down the North River to the Pearl River delta. But an important difference with the Mediterranean experience should be noted. In the lowlands of the Mediterranean, the silt was not captured and turned into new land, but rather formed swamps and marshes, creating the conditions for malaria and rendering the lowlands uninhabitable until swamp drainage projects in the eighteenth and nineteenth centuries eliminated the disease. In the Pearl River delta, by contrast, the new settlers captured the silt and turned it into *shatan*, perhaps preventing the creation of conditions favoring malaria in the first place.

Before leaving our discussion of the Pearl River delta, one further aspect of its creation deserves note. Because of the large amount of labor required to create *shatan*,[59] most projects were undertaken by wealthy families. All of the evidence comes from the Ming and Qing dynasties, but that should not obviate the point. Professor Liu Zhiwei details the case of the He lineage in Panyu county,[60] while Professors Ye Xian'en and Tan Dihua cite additional evidence about another He family, this one in Dongguan, which built or accumulated some 28,000 *mu* of *shatan* during the Kangxi, Yongzheng, and Qianlong reigns in the Qing dynasty.[61] But not all *shatan* were created by wealthy lineages; Helen Siu discovered a stele in Xinhui county making reference to military colonies established in the mid-Ming for the purpose of settlement and land reclamation in that part of the delta.[62]

Conclusion

The Pearl River delta thus was not created by purely natural processes and had not been simply waiting for Chinese to migrate from the north and reclaim it for agriculture. Rather, the creation of the delta was the result of a complex causal chain. Chinese immigrants into Lingnan preferred to settle in the hills of northern Guangdong, fearful of the diseases in the river valleys further to the south. Their land clearing eventually increased the silt content of the rivers flowing south, but most of that alluvium never reached the bay, being deposited instead by floods in the lower reaches of the North, East, and West River valleys. Only the construction of flood-control dikes and levees there in the Song directed the silt-laden waters into the upper reaches of the Pearl River

59 C. K. Yang documents the 1936 creation of new fields by the members of one lineage of Nanjing village south of Guangzhou. See C. K. Yang, *Chinese Communist Society: The Family and the Village (A Chinese Village in Early Communist Transition)* (Cambridge: MIT Press, 1959), 26.

60 Liu Zhiwei, "Zongzu yu shatian kaifa," 34–41.

61 Ye Xian'en and Tan Dihua, "Lun Zhujiang sanjiaozou de zu tian," in *Ming Qing Guangdong shehui jingji xingtai yanjiu* (Guangzhou: Guangdong renmin chuban she, 1985), 34–35; Peng Yuxin, *Qing dai tudi kaiken shi*, 168.

62 Helen Siu, *Agents and Victims in South China: Accomplices in Rural Revolution* (New Haven: Yale University Press, 1989), 25.

estuary. Even then, that silt might have continued to flow further out into the bay had it not been captured by refugees from the north who had fled from the Mongols to the islands in the bay. The creation of the Pearl River delta and its later emergence as the densely populated, agriculturally rich core of Lingnan was thus a historically contingent, rather than naturally determined, outcome. One can only speculate as to whether or not the same pattern would have been followed had it not been for the "historical accident" of the Mongol invasion. Whatever the outcome may have been, by the time the Mongols were driven from China and the Chinese peasant army leader Zhu Yuanzhang succeeded in establishing the Ming dynasty in 1368, the development of the Pearl River delta had begun.

3

"AGRICULTURE IS THE FOUNDATION":

ECONOMIC RECOVERY AND DEVELOPMENT OF LINGNAN DURING THE MING DYNASTY, 1368–1644

If the first two chapters skimmed the surface of more than a thousand years of Chinese history, in the remainder of the book the pace will slow down to allow a more detailed examination of the environmental and economic history of Lingnan during the four and a half centuries from 1400 to 1850, a period usually glossed by historians as "late imperial China." In this chapter we will see that in the Ming dynasty (1368–1644), Han Chinese aggressively occupied lands in Guangxi and in the southwestern littoral previously held by non-Chinese, bringing those lands under not only Chinese suzerainty but Chinese plows as well. Moreover, commercial development especially was becoming one of the primary engines of ecological change: agricultural exports represented energy drains that had to be replaced by imports of energy from outside the ecosystem – in particular, food for the human population. The commercialization that began to fuel economic growth from the middle of the sixteenth century on, though, was cut short by the disasters attending the mid-seventeenth-century Manchu wars of conquest, thereby also attenuating the anthropogenic processes of ecological change until more peaceful conditions returned in the late 1600s. Nonetheless, the Ming pattern of economic development began pointing toward greater deforestation, large-scale extinction of other species, significant reduction of biodiversity, and the creation of a single Lingnan agroecosystem. While the shattering of the biological old regime was to be a legacy of the seventeenth and eighteenth centuries, the factors that created that dynamic were all present in embryo by the end of the Ming.

Population and Land, 1400 1600

To provide a context for the developments during the Ming dynasty, I want to begin by summarizing the relation of the people of Lingnan to their environment in terms of population and cultivated land figures. As we saw in the pre-

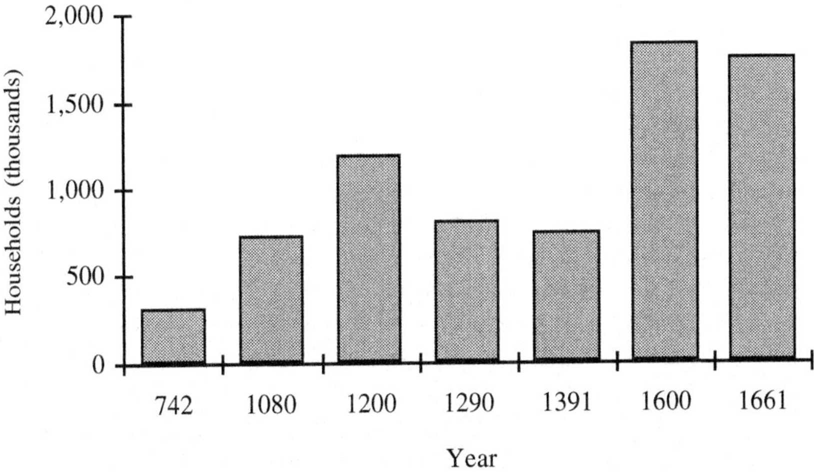

Figure 3.1. Lingnan population, 742–1661.

ceding chapter (see Figure 2.1), the population of Lingnan peaked first during the Southern Song dynasty and then declined until the beginning of the Ming dynasty. Most of China at the beginning of the Ming dynasty was relatively depopulated from the levels reached prior to the Mongol conquest; in Lingnan, vast regions had been laid waste, while others had been swelled with refugees from the north. With a lasting peace established during the Ming, the population not only grew slowly and steadily (at least until the disruptions of the Ming–Qing transition in the middle of the seventeenth century), but also sometime – probably in the late sixteenth century – surpassed the levels that had been attained in the Song dynasty (see Figure 3.1).

But whether the Ming level of cultivated land ever surpassed Song levels is questionable. Cultivated land figures for Song-era Lingnan do not exist, but assuming that the amount of land under cultivation varied more or less directly with the population size (given virtually the same agricultural technology), then certainly the amount of land cultivated at the beginning of the Ming was considerably less than had been cultivated in the Song. By the end of the Ming, the population was one-third greater than the Song level, an increase that could have been sustained quite easily by increased crop yields achieved during the Ming, especially in the Pearl River delta. It is likely, therefore, that in the Ming the amount of land cleared for agriculture in Lingnan never exceeded that of the Song (excluding the new *shatan* created in the Pearl River delta). That being the case, then it is reasonable to think that in Lingnan, the amount of forest cleared for agriculture also did not exceed the limits reached in the Song. Moreover, with the population decline and consequent abandonment of farms in northern Lingnan (in Nanxiong and Guilin prefectures) after the

Mongol invasion, forests had more than a century to reestablish themselves before population increased again.

In a significant departure from earlier periods, the growth of population during the Ming came not from waves of in-migration by people from the north, but rather by the slow increase in the size of the existing population. The reason for this difference was another legacy of Mongol rule: with so much abandoned land for the taking throughout much of north China, along the southeast coast, and in the middle and upper reaches of the Yangzi River valley from Jiangxi to Sichuan, northern Chinese did not venture "south of the mountains" in search of good agricultural land.[1] Thus, whatever population growth occurred in Lingnan during the Ming came largely from the natural rate of increase of those who had inhabited the region at the beginning of the dynasty.

Soon after proclaiming the establishment of the new Ming dynasty in 1368, Zhu Yuanzhang declared that "agriculture is the foundation of the nation"[2] and implemented policies to secure that foundation. From the point of view of the Chinese state, it was not merely agriculture that was to be the foundation of the nation, but a particular kind of settled agriculture characterized by peasant family management of the land. As other Chinese dynasties had come to understand, small peasant-farmers provided a stable tax base and a source of army recruits and conscripts, all essential to the stability and longevity of the dynasty. From the perspective of the Chinese agriculturalists, the conversion of land for agricultural purposes was variously called *kaidi*, *kaiken*, or *kaihuang*, all of which had slightly different meanings depending on whether or not the land had been farmed before – opening new land, opening wasteland, or reclamation of fallow fields – but all of which were considered "good." In biological terms, these processes of land conversion captured energy flows within an ecosystem in order to sustain human life, changing natural ecosystems into agricultural ecosystems.

The remainder of this chapter explores the relationships among population size and distribution, agricultural systems, land use patterns, improvements to agriculture, and the growth and change of the agricultural economy during the Ming dynasty, as a means of assessing the relationship between the people of Lingnan and their environment. Since so many issues regarding the environment and economy are directly or indirectly related to the size and distribution of the population, I will begin with a consideration of

[1] Robert M. Hartwell, "Societal Organization and Demographic Change: Catastrophe, Agrarian Technology, and Interregional Population Trends in Traditional China," a revised version of a paper presented under the same title at the 2eme Congrès international de demographie historique, Paris, June 4–5, 1987. I thank Professor Hartwell for sharing this unpublished paper with me.

[2] Huang Tisong et al., *Guangxi lishi dili* (Guilin: Guangxi minzu chuban she, 1984), 125.

Lingnan's population around 1400. From there I will discuss the cultivated land area and land use patterns, including the development of water control and irrigation works, and conclude by examining the commercialization of agriculture that began in the mid-sixteenth-century but that was cut short by the mid-seventeenth-century general crisis (the subject of the next chapter).

Population and Its Growth, 1400 1640

Based upon official population figures compiled by the new Ming state, we can estimate that about 4 million people lived in Lingnan around 1400, about a half million more if the residents of Chaozhou prefecture in eastern Guangdong province are included. From this base – which was about the same as a century earlier, although distributed differently – the population began to grow, slowly at first but with a faster pace by the middle of the sixteenth century, reaching perhaps 12 million by 1640.[3] The distribution of the population changed too, only slowly approaching the form it would have in the Qing dynasty (1644–1911).

Spatial Distribution of the Population, ca. 1400 to 1600. To chart the density and distribution of the population of Lingnan during the Ming dynasty, it would be ideal to have reliable population and cultivated land data from various times disaggregated down to the smallest reporting unit, the county. Unfortunately, those data do not exist in a form sufficiently detailed to include

[3] The 1640 figure is an estimate only, based on the official 1391 figures and on assumptions about likely rates of increase. For the entire Ming period, Ho Ping-ti has suggested that the population of the southern provinces grew at a rate faster than the 0.34% for northern provinces. See Ho Ping-ti, *Studies on the Population of China, 1368–1953* (Cambridge, MA: Harvard University Press, 1959), 263–64. For Guangdong and Guangxi, we know in addition that the economy began to improve substantially after about 1550 (to be discussed later), leading me to suspect that the population grew slightly faster as well. And unlike north China, there is nothing in the historical record to suggest that the rate of growth slowed around 1600; indeed, there is no reason to think that the population of Guangdong and Guangxi provinces did not keep increasing right up to 1644. Guangxi probably had a lower rate of population increase for two reasons: there is evidence of substantial social unrest and warfare in Guangxi during the first half of the fifteenth century, and throughout the entire period mortality was higher because of malaria. For the period from 1391 to 1542, then, I assume that the population of Guangdong and Guangxi provinces increased at 0.4% and 0.3% annual rates, respectively, increasing afterwards to 0.5% and 0.4% from 1542 to 1640. During the Qing dynasty, the population of Guangxi was about 40 percent that of Guangdong; the differential rates of increase during the Ming bring the populations of the two provinces into that ratio. Kang Chao adopts a 0.6% rate of increase for the period from 1391 to 1590. Despite Chao's claims otherwise, that rate seems to me to be too high. See *Man and Land in Chinese History: An Economic Analysis* (Stanford: Stanford University Press, 1986), 37.

all counties in Guangdong and Guangxi provinces.[4] To paint a picture of the population density at the county level thus requires using proxy data; fortunately two reasonably good sets are available: the enumeration of the number of *li* for each county in the early Ming, and county-level cultivated land figures dating from 1581. Before using these figures, I should explain what they represent, starting with the *li*.

Even before the formal establishment of the Ming dynasty in 1368, its founder, Zhu Yuanzhang, began to count the population and to survey the cultivated land in areas under his control.[5] After the final defeat of his rivals in 1368, Zhu extended these initiatives throughout China. Local officials created forms called *hu tie*, or "household placards," upon which each household was to record the total number of people and the property owned.[6] The *hu tie* placards became the basis for combining the population into taxpaying units known as the *li-jia* (a *jia* was a group of 10 *hu*, and a *li* 11 *jia*). Every 10 years the population was to be refigured and new *hu tie* produced, providing the basis once again for a national population count and the decennial rotation of *li-jia* leadership responsibilities. The household (*hu*), population (*kou*), and *li* figures were all reported, providing the mechanism for taxation. An incomplete count was first done in 1381, and an empire-wide tally was completed in 1391 and reported in 1393; the *li* figures from the 1393 reports are used here. By regulation, 110 households were to form one *li*, but in actual practice the numbers ranged between 140 and 160 *hu* per *li* throughout China.[7] For Lingnan, the data from six early Ming prefectural gazetteers which listed population figures by county can be combined with the county-level *li* figures reported in the *Da Ming huidian* to determine how many households (*hu*) comprised each *li* in Lingnan.[8]

Just as the founder of the Ming dynasty was determined to have an adequate count of the entire population for taxation purposes, so too did he want an accurate survey of the cultivated land acreage. The cultivated land figures

4 The 1602 edition of the Guangdong provincial gazetteer does report both population and land figures for 1391 and 1581, for the most part down to the county level. But for both the population and land figures, sometimes only the prefectural totals and not the disaggregated county totals are given. Even with its faults, the raw data available for Guangdong province is better than that for Guangxi, which does not even exist.

5 See Ho, *Studies on the Population of China*, ch. 1.

6 Ho analyzes one surviving example of a *hu tie* in *Studies on the Population of China*, 5–7. Another example is provided in Wang Yumin, "Ming chu quan guo renkou kao zhi yi," *Lishi yanjiu* 3 (1990): 55–64.

7 See Otto van der Sprenkel, "Population Statistics of Ming China," *Bulletin of the School of Oriental and African Studies* 15, no. 2 (1953): 289–326.

8 The number of households (*hu*) per *li* varied throughout Lingnan. The variation, however, was not random: the greater the number of *li* per county, the greater the number of *hu* per *li*. The relationship, in fact, is nearly linear: the trend line explains most of the variation in the data ($R^2 = 0.933$) at the 95% confidence level.

produced during Zhu Yuanzhang's reign and reported along with the 1391 population tally, though, were not the result of a national survey of the land.[9] Although it is clear that Zhu Yuanzhang dispatched students of the Imperial Academy to Zhejiang and Anhui provinces to survey land and assign tax quotas, there is little evidence that land was actually surveyed in other parts of the realm. Rather, according to Ho Ping-ti (He Bingdi), local officials relied upon the self-reported figures provided by landowners to compile land records into registers known as "fish-scale registers" (*yu-li tu ce*).[10]

The decennial population updates based upon the *li-jia* system quickly fell into disuse after 1391, rendering official population data for the rest of the Ming too unreliable to use. But toward the end of the sixteenth century, the Ming state did survey and report cultivated land areas. For Guangdong province, the results of the 1581 tally were recorded in the 1602 edition of the provincial gazetteer, but, like the 1391 population figures, are not complete down to the county level. Fortunately, the 1581 cultivated land figures were the basis upon which the Qing state calculated its tax basis in the early eighteenth century, and these figures (known as the *yuan-e*, or "original tax targets," for the land tax) not only have been preserved, but in addition have the virtue of having been adjusted for Qing-era county boundaries. With the 1391 *li* and the Qing-era *yuan-e*, then, I have been able to construct a complete data set for all counties in Guangdong and Guangxi provinces. From these data the percentage of cultivated land area for each county can be calculated and, assuming that percentage to have varied directly with the population density, compared with the ca. 1400 *li* density figures. In short, it seems defensible to compare the 1400 population densities of *li* with the percentage of cultivated land ca. 1600 to analyze changing patterns in population densities.

Around 1400 (see Map 3.1), the population of Lingnan was arrayed into three or four "cores," each with its own periphery. Clearly, Guangzhou and the Pearl River delta counties constituted one core region. But parallel to it were the counties of Chaozhou prefecture to the east. To be sure, Chaozhou is physiographically separated from the rest of Lingnan, as I have already shown in Chapter 1, and these data too show that it was not integrated into a

9 Although Ho Ping-ti pointed this out in 1959, the belief in China that the cultivated land figures were the result of an actual survey went unchallenged since 1961, when Wei Qingyuan published an influential article. In 1985, though, Ho published a two-part article in China's influential journal *Zhongguo shehui kexue* in which he not only convincingly demolishes the idea of a national land survey, but also shows how the belief that one was conducted was passed from the compilers of the *Ming shi* to Wei Qingyuan. See Ho Ping-ti (He Bingti), "Nan Song zhi jin duti shuzi de kaoshi he pingjia," *Zhongguo shehui kexue* 2 (1985): 133–65 and 3 (1985): 125–60.

10 Ibid., 2: 152–54. Although He's conclusion is a deduction from circumstantial evidence, the argument is convincing. The registers are so named because when showing the plots of land on a sheet of paper, the resulting map took on the appearance of being laid out like fish scales.

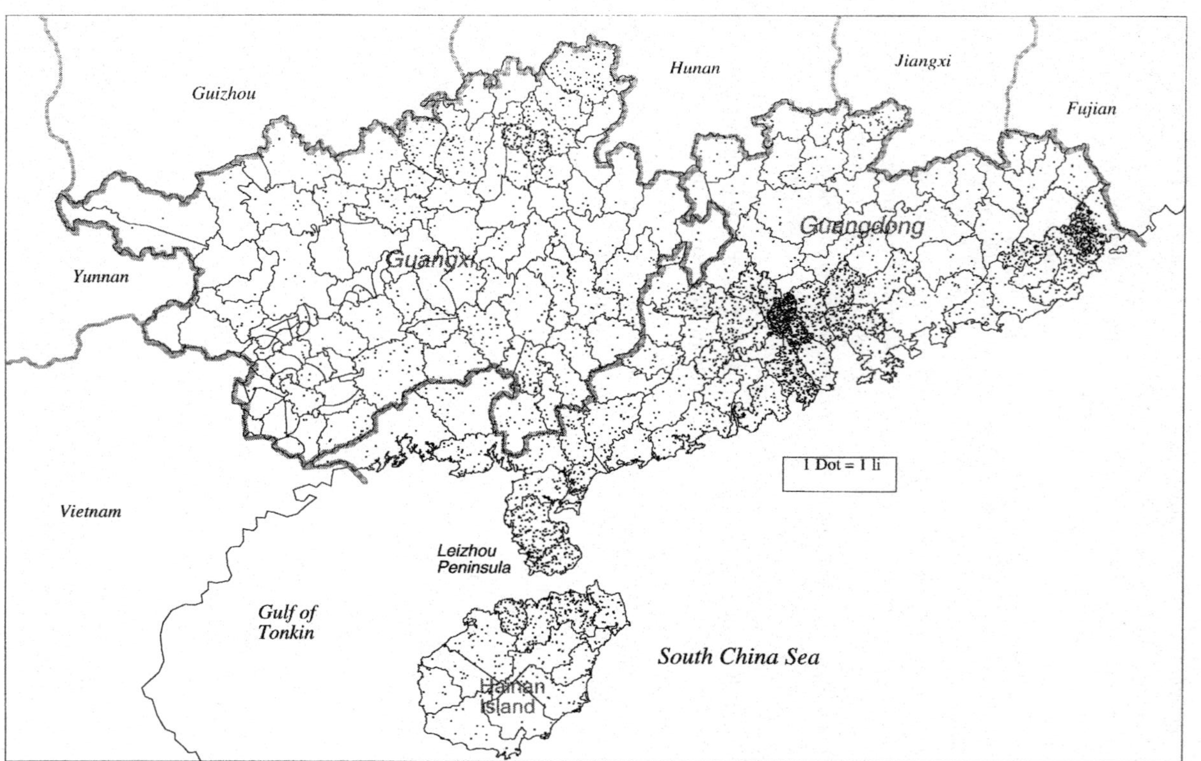

Map 3.1. Population density, ca. 1391

structure centered upon Guangzhou. Northern Guangxi, the region centered upon Guilin, also constituted a separate subregion; given the historical settlement patterns of Lingnan, this should not be surprising. Perhaps more surprising is the appearance of the Leizhou Peninsula and Hainan Island with relatively high population densities. We have already had occasion to comment upon the large populations of Leizhou and Qiongzhou prefectures; the county-level *li* densities confirm the relative, and perhaps surprising, weight of the southwestern littoral in the early Ming regional population structure of Lingnan. Thus, rather than exhibiting a clear hierarchical structure with a single core surrounded by varying degrees of periphery, Lingnan in 1400 had at least three core regions, four if Chaozhou is included.

Mapping the percentage of land cultivated (Map 3.2) provides not just a view of population density, but also a sense of Lingnan's agricultural landscape around 1600. Not surprisingly, the most intensely cultivated area was the Pearl River delta: three-quarters of the land in Nanhai and Shunde counties was being cultivated, two-fifths in Sanshui and Panyu, a third in Dongguan and Xinhui, and a quarter in Zengcheng and Sihui. In Guangxi, the most intensively cultivated counties were in Guilin prefecture (11–17 percent), while in the West River valley less than 10 percent of the land was being cultivated, and that no doubt was literally along the river. In western and southwestern Guangxi, so little land was being cultivated that rounding brought the figures to zero percent.[11]

Comparing the 1391 county-level *li* densities with the 1581 percentage of land cultivated highlights three significant changes over time. First, in Guangxi previously sparsely populated counties in the West River valley and in Yulin, all areas that had been relatively depopulated around 1400, gained significant population by 1600. Second, relatively depopulated areas in Guangdong – the northern prefectures of Shaozhou, Nanxiong, and Lianzhou, as well as Huizhou prefecture – all surged up in population. Third, the counties on the Leizhou Peninsula and Hainan Island all dropped precipitously into peripheral status. These changes in population distribution reflect significant historical developments in Lingnan and need to be examined in more detail.

Land Clearance in Guangxi: Han and Non-Han. "Taking agriculture as the base" (*nong wei guo ben*), Zhu Yuanzhang and his successors encouraged land reclamation in Guangxi by Han Chinese and the diffusion by local officials of

[11] These percentages were calculated by converting *mu* into hectares and then dividing by the total land area of each county. The percentages for the Pearl River delta counties actually were higher by some unknown amount because for total land area I used figures calculated for boundaries in 1820, by which time the total land area had increased because of the creation of *shatan*.

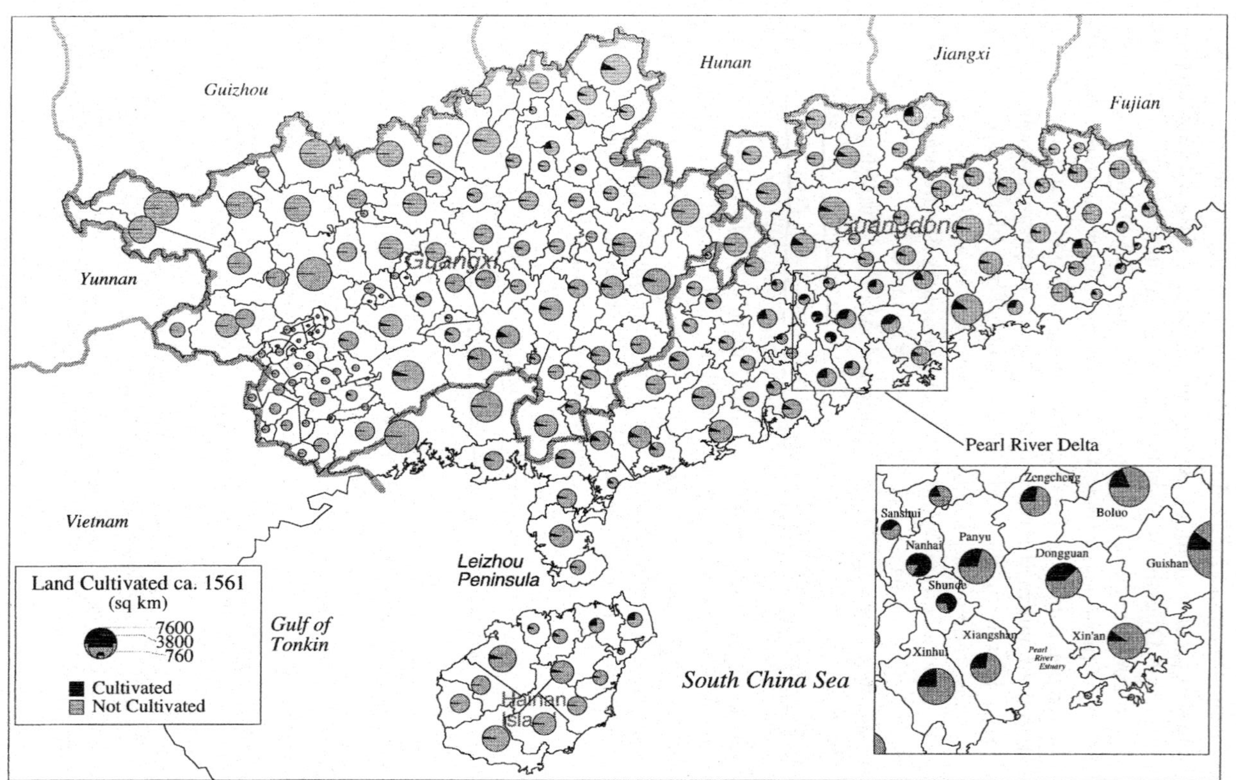

Map 3.2. Cultivated land, ca. 1561

techniques for improving agriculture. In Rong county, for example, the magistrate disseminated sericulture techniques, and in Yangchun officials taught farmers how to plant hemp (for spinning flax) and millet (*su*).[12] With a three-year exemption from taxes and corvée labor obligations for new land brought into production, clearing land and filling in swamps and lakes proceeded apace as the population grew. A lake to the west of Guilin was finally completely filled in by the sixteenth century, while in other areas Han settlers pushed in "to fill up the land."[13]

Not surprisingly, the expansion in Guangxi of Han settlements by land clearance and swamp drainage came at the expense of the aboriginal and non-Han peoples. The 1391 population figures for Guangdong and Guangxi provinces certainly omitted an unknown number of these non-Han inhabitants from the official tabulation. The aboriginal people of Guangxi and northern Guangdong, cited in Chinese sources as early as 100 BCE under various names, by Song times had come to be known generally as "Zhuang."[14] Others – Yao and Miao, along with Hui (Moslems) – had migrated into Guangxi and Guangdong provinces at different times. All told, 10 different tribal peoples – some aboriginal but others more recent immigrants – inhabited Guangxi.[15]

As a proportion of the total population of Guangxi province, early Qing sources guessed that half were Zhuang, 30 percent Yao, and 20 percent Han. Ming sources indicate that 80–90 percent of the population of Guilin prefecture was Yao, and 70–80 percent of Liuzhou too was Yao. By the 1940s, Han Chinese constituted about 60 percent of the population and the Zhuang, 37 percent.[16] As a rule of thumb, the population then of the western half of Guangxi was predominantly non-Han Chinese tribal peoples, while the eastern half was predominantly Han. In Guangdong, by the early Ming there were fewer non-Han Chinese, except in the northern region around Lianzhou, as well as on Hainan Island, where about 20 percent of the population was comprised of the Li people.

The new Ming state distinguished between those tribal peoples who had accepted Chinese suzerainty and those who remained independent and refused to submit. The tribal and aboriginal peoples living in the eastern half of Guangxi province thus probably were included in the 1391 Ming population

[12] Both examples cited in Huang Tisong et al., *Guangxi lishi dili*, 126.

[13] Ibid., 127.

[14] The written character for Zhuang meant a certain kind of dog, and when the character meant "dog" it was read *tong*. But when referring to the tribal people of Guangxi, the character was read "Zhuang." To remove the derogatory denotation, in 1965 Premier Zhou Enlai changed the written form of Zhuang to the character meaning "strong" or "able bodied." See Mo Naiqun, *Guangxi nongye jingji shi gao* (Nanning: Guangxi minzu chuban she, 1985), 30, n. 26.

[15] Ibid., 23.

[16] Sources cited in ibid., 26–27.

Table 3.1. *Early Ming population returns for Hainan Island* (households)

		1413	
County	1377	Chinese	Li
Qiongshan	14,932	16,228	2,169
Chengmai	8,367	8,519	3,169
Ding'an	4,270	4,363	954
Wenchang	6,276	6,770	308
Huitong	1,145	1,116	0
Lehui	1,783	1,716	433
Lin'gao	7,985	8,638	2,707
Danzhou	13,876	13,843	4,377
Changhua	1,944	1,484	960
Wanzhou	5,539	5,645	157
Lingshui	1,165	1,178	73
Yaizhou	4,349	4,374	4,020
Gan'en	1,589	1,589	1,995
Reported total	68,522	71,212	17,394
Calculated total	73,220	75,463	21,322

Source: Qiongtai zhi (Zhengde 16; 1521 ed.), juan 10–11.

count, since these regions were under Chinese administration. In the western half of the province, though, the early Ming administrative system recognized some 49 "*ji mi*," or "loosely controlled," administrative districts (*zhou*), which were governed by hereditary tribal chiefs who nominally reported to the nearest Chinese military post and were liable for paying taxes.[17] Whether these ever were included in the population registers of Guangxi province is open to question. With the Li on Hainan Island, though, we can be quite sure that most were included in the population registers.

The population returns for Qiongzhou prefecture (Hainan Island) for 1377 and 1413 (Table 3.1) clearly show that the Li were included in the 1413 count. Whereas the 1377 figures are only for households without any further notation, the 1413 data are broken down into Chinese "Han" and aboriginal "Li" categories. For the Han majority, the number of households reported increased from 68,522 in 1377 to 71,212 in 1413, when in addition 17,394 Li households were reported, for a grand total of 88,606 households. From these data it is clear that the Li – some 20 percent of the 1413 total – had been excluded from the 1377 (and probably the 1391) totals. Whether these figures included all Li is doubtful. As we saw in the preceding chapter, the Li were divided into the

[17] Huang et al., *Guangxi lishi dili*, 119.

unassimilated "raw" and the "cooked"; even in the eighteenth century, the Qing state knew little about the "raw" Li living in the interior mountains of Hainan Island.[18]

How much land Chinese settlers took from the non-Han as they pressed into Guangxi simply is not known. But it was not coincidental that the Yao, Zhuang, and Li resisted Chinese advances as best they could, resorting to armed resistance when necessary – and if the record of military encounters is any gauge, the Yao and Zhuang resistance was stiff. In northeastern Guangxi, near Guilin, Zhuang "uprisings" are recorded for a 70-year period from 1450 to 1520, while around Xunzhou on the West River the high point of military encounters between Han Chinese and the Yao occurred in the 1460s. So large and threatening did the Yao resistance become that in 1465 the Ming state mobilized 200,000 troops (160,000 from outside the area) to suppress the "rebellion," in the process occupying over 300 places formerly held by the Yao.[19]

The Han Chinese appropriation of aboriginal land engendered a certain enmity that was palpable; according to du Halde, the non-Han "have Reason to be dissatisfied with the Chinese, who have taken from their best Land, and who continue to seize on whatever they find is for their Conveniency."[20] Records of Chinese military action against the tribal peoples fill the gazetteers of Guangxi province, while an early Ming gazetteer for Hainan Island has two entire sections devoted to the Li.[21] Like the Zhuang and the Yao in Guangxi, on Hainan the Li (to once again quote du Halde) "have been obliged to abandon their Plains and champaign Country to the Chinese, and to retire in the Mountains in the Centre of the Island . . . These Islanders never appear, unless it be sometimes when they make Irruptions into the Villages which are nearest to the Chinese."[22] Or as the Li leader of a 1767 uprising stated in his confession: "Much of the land of us Li people is occupied by Ke [i.e., Chinese] (who come in from the outside) . . . The Li people of every village have all nursed grievances for a long time already. I often think about gathering Li people to kill and force out these outsider Ke [Chinese] people. (Then) the profits from the mountain lands will return to the Li people."[23]

Thus, how much land the Chinese took in the fifteenth century is not at all clear. But it seems certain that the record of the encounter of Han Chinese

[18] See Anne Csete, "Qing Management of a Multi-Ethnic Society: The Case of Han–Li Conflict on Hainan in 1767," paper presented at the Asian Studies annual meeting, Washington, DC, April 7, 1995.

[19] Huang, *Guangxi lishi dili*, 123–24.

[20] Jean Baptiste du Halde, *The General History of China* (London, 1741), vol. 1: 70–71.

[21] *Qiongtai (Qiongzhou) zhi*. The 1982 Shanghai reprint, intentionally or not, has "omitted" those two sections.

[22] Du Halde, *The General History of China*, vol. 1: 247.

[23] Quoted in Csete, "Qing Management of a Multi-Ethnic Society."

with the non-Han – from the Han Chinese point of view, of course – is a rough index to Han Chinese occupation and use of the land, turning "wasteland" into agriculturally productive land. As for the Zhuang and the Yao who had resisted the Chinese advance and lost, they retreated further to the west and higher into the hills, where they subjected the forest to their agricultural routine, probably some form of shifting slash-and-burn agriculture.[24]

The story of the Chinese and non-Han encounter in the Ming and the Qing surely is one of the important chapters in China's environmental history. Clearly the Li and the Yao had different conceptions of property rights, land tenure systems, and hence land use practices than the dominant Chinese, and when Chinese conceptions displaced those of the Li or the Yao, changes in land use followed. For the Li, these conceptions concerned the best ways to use mountainous areas, while for the Yao they concerned both lowland and upland land use practices. Here I have been able only to scratch the surface of this encounter and its significance for south China's environment.[25]

The Northern Guangdong Hill Region. By the Southern Song (ca. 1200), about 150,000 households inhabited Guangdong's northern hill region (comprised of Nanxiong, Shaozhou, and Lianzhou); after the Mongol invasion, two-thirds of their members had either died or fled. The population size drifted even lower during the Yuan dynasty (1279–1368), so that less than 40,000 households were counted in the 1391 Ming tabulation. During that century of depopulation, we can imagine the abandoned farmland being covered first with pioneering species of plants, then giving way to a secondary forest in which pines and firs dominated; perhaps even enough time had elapsed for the broadleafed evergreens to begin to reestablish themselves. As evidence we may cite the experience of the Dinghu Mountain Biosphere Reserve near Zhaoqing, where "random single to grouped patterns of broadleaf species [established themselves in] the degraded land under the shelter of the pine and protection from fire after establishment of the biosphere reserve."[26]

[24] David Faure, who has been studying the Ming Yao wars in Guangxi, has written that "I have yet to find the reasons for the retreat of the Yao from the late Ming to the early Qing. Into the early seventeenth century, Guangdong was still threatened by Yao 'uprisings.' However, the Yao gradually retreated towards the upland areas in Guangxi and northern Guangdong. I suspect the close connection between land registration and the development of rice cultivation had much to do with the sinicization of the Yao and this apparent retreat, but this will have to be substantiated." David Faure, abstract for "The Yao Wars and the Rise of Orthodoxy from the Mid-Ming to the Early Qing," *Association for Asian Studies, Inc. Abstracts of the 1995 Annual Meeting*, p. 107.

[25] For an example of the important work that can be done, see Shepherd, *Statecraft and Political Economy on the Taiwan Frontier, 1600–1800*. Shepherd's work does not focus on the environment, but he nicely analyzes the differences between Han and aborigines regarding property rights and land use patterns and how those changed during the Qing dynasty.

[26] Bruenig et al., *Ecological-Socioeconomic System Analysis and Simulation*, 12.

From the low level around 1400, the population in the northern hill region recovered over the next two centuries. Using the early Ming *li* and the 1581 cultivated acreage figures to demonstrate the increase, the two counties in Nanxiong moved in rank from 25th and 104th (out of 135 counties for which there are data) in terms of *li* to 10th and 53rd in terms of cultivated acreage. Certainly we are on shaky ground trying to reconstruct the size of the population around 1600, but since the cultivated acreage increased at a rate faster than many other parts of Lingnan, it is not unreasonable to think that no fewer than 100,000 families then lived and farmed in these three prefectures. Since that figure is less than the total achieved in the Southern Song, we can conclude that while the forest cover certainly was removed during the Ming by the increasing population, there probably was more forest there around 1600 than there had been in 1200.

The Southwestern Littoral. Where regrowth of forest may have accompanied the population decline and then recovery in the northern hill region, in the southwest the expansion of the population after the Mongol invasion caused such permanent environmental damage – turning much of the Leizhou Peninsula into an eroded desert – that even with the peaceful conditions established during the Ming dynasty, the population declined and never recovered. The economic decline – one is almost tempted to say "development of underdevelopment" – of the Leizhou Peninsula and Hainan Island during the course of the Ming dynasty was the result not of geographical determinism, but of a combination of other factors. When the population of this region surged at the end of the thirteenth century in the face of the Mongol onslaught, there was both virgin land, especially on the Leizhou Peninsula, and a healthy foreign trade to sustain the population growth.

Hainan Island sat astride the shipping routes linking the South China Sea to the Indian Ocean and benefited from the trade centered on Guangzhou. As the author of an early Ming Guangzhou gazetteer makes clear, Guangzhou had been an important trading post for Arab and other merchants from Tang times on. Indeed, during the Tang dynasty there was such a large resident Muslim population in Guangzhou that they built a mosque, for centuries the tallest and most easily recognizable landmark to people sailing up the Pearl River estuary to the city. Scores of "large foreign ships" anchored off Guangzhou, and the city even was called "Little Tang."[27] The trade routes remained open during the Song and Yuan dynasties, benefiting not only Guangzhou but other coastal areas as well. Maps of the Hainan Island city of Qiongshan (which functioned as the prefectural city), situated on the coast facing the mainland, show at least two harbors, a large, fortified city, and numerous surrounding villages. Chinese naval and land forces also were sta-

[27] *Guangzhou zhi*, in *Yongle dadian* (ca. 1407; 1980 Tokyo reprint), vol. 3: 1639.

tioned on the island. The local gazetteer lists several kinds of products, including spices, silver, copper, and linen, that were exported – whether to Guangzhou or directly to foreign traders stopping at the port is not known.[28] With a population of nearly 400,000 by 1400, the island was not self-sufficient in grain and had to import it from the mainland: the closest source was the Leizhou Peninsula.[29]

The demand for food, not just from Hainan Island but also from the large population that had settled on the Leizhou Peninsula, produced a surge in land reclamation – wholesale clearing of the tropical rain and mangrove swamp forests. Presumably the clearance was accomplished by burning off the forest. Just how much land was cleared in the fourteenth century may never be known, but I think we do have clues from the condition of the peninsula in the twentieth century and from an 1820 report by shipwrecked British sailors.

According to surveys in the early twentieth century, about half of the Leizhou Peninsula then was covered with grassland – mostly the tough *Eromochloa ciliaris*, which the Chinese call *wusong cao*. Botanists have concluded that the Leizhou Peninsula once had been a tropical monsoon rain forest, which was burned off, replaced then by camphor trees, and finally by grassland,[30] if not being completely denuded, as in nearby Dianbai county, described in the mid-twentieth century as a "barren, eroded . . . area under constant threat of flood."[31] As is now well known, the soil on the floor of a rain forest is not fertile, and once the forest cover is removed, the soil gets depleted quickly, providing sufficient nutrients only for grasses.

When did those transformations of the Leizhou environment occur? Certainly it had happened well before the nineteenth century. According to the detailed reports of the shipwrecked English Captain Ross, who blew ashore with his crew on the eastern shore of Hainan Island and then hiked overland (except for the boat passage from Qiongzhou to the Leizhou Peninsula) to Guangzhou in late 1819 and early 1820, "The whole of the country thus far [i.e., the Leizhou Peninsula], may be considered as one undivided plain of not less than a hundred miles in length, two-thirds of which appears to be used for pasturage, and the other appropriated to cultivating rice and sugar cane."[32] Captain Ross mistakenly assumed that the grasslands he saw were pasture for cattle, but the fact remains that in his estimation at least, two-thirds of the peninsula in 1819 was grassland, and even that may have been an improvement over conditions earlier. Commenting on land reclamation plans in the

[28] *Qiongtai zhi*, in *Yongle dadian*, vol. 4. [29] Schafer, *Shore of Pearls*, 81.

[30] Zhang Yongda et al., *Leizhou bandao de zhipei*, 83–84.

[31] Bruenig et al., *Ecological-Soioeconomic System Analysis and Simulation*, 44.

[32] J. Ross, "Journal of a Trip Overland from Hainan to Canton in 1819," *Chinese Repository* 18, no. 5 (May 1849): 225–53.

1740s, the Qianlong emperor noted that much of the land on the peninsula was "barren and very difficult to reclaim."[33] If the population history of the peninsula is a guide – with low population densities until the Mongol invasion, then population totals and densities as high as anywhere else in Lingnan around 1400, and the population declining afterwards – then I would suspect that the environmental damage had been done with the massive influx of people during the fourteenth and fifteenth centuries.

With the Ming closure of the coast to trade and exploration in the first quarter of the fifteenth century and with the depletion of the agricultural potential of the Leizhou Peninsula, the fate of the southwestern littoral and Hainan Island was sealed, becoming the peripheral backwater it was known as from the Qing dynasty into the twentieth century.[34] Was this predetermined? Probably not. Had the foreign trade continued, the Leizhou Peninsula might have generated sufficient wealth to pour additional resources into agriculture, ensuring the continued productivity of the land through irrigation and greater inputs of fertilizer. As it turned out, the land died, and with it the relative weight of its population in Lingnan.

Summary. During the course of the Ming dynasty, the population of Lingnan nearly tripled and spread out from a few densely settled regions to more evenly inhabit the land. In Guangdong, population moved into Huizhou and Chaozhou prefectures, which came to have larger proportions of the total population than around 1400, the population in the northern hill region recovered, while the population of Guangzhou and Zhaoqing prefectures too increased in density. Only on the Leizhou Peninsula and on Hainan Island did the pace of population growth slow so much that it became less developed relative to the rest of the region. In Guangxi, after the fifteenth-century wars to remove or subdue the non-Han peoples, the Chinese population spread from Guilin and Liuzhou prefectures into the West River valley and other parts of the province previously inhabited by non-Han ethnic groups.

Comparing the bare statistics on population and cultivated land areas from 1400 and 1600 thus tells an important story. But we must remember that the story that they tell for the most part is that of the Han Chinese. For from their point of view, the story is one of progressively penetrating the Lingnan frontier and bringing increasingly greater amounts of land under cultivation; from the point of view of the non-Han peoples it was a story of being forced from their lands; and from the point of view of tigers and other wildlife (if I may

[33] *Da Qing shi chao sheng xun*, Gaozong huangdi, juan 71: 1b (Taibei: Wenhai chuban she, 1965), vol. 3: 1060.

[34] The conventional (i.e., wrong) wisdom, perhaps best conveyed by the 1988 *Encylopedia of Asian History*, reasons that "because of its unhealthy tropical climate, . . . Hainan remained for most of its history relatively sparsely populated and underdeveloped."

be permitted to anthropomorphize), it was a story of the destruction of their habitat.

If environmental change followed in the wake of the changes in population densities during the course of the Ming dynasty – land clearance in the river valleys of Guangxi, reforestation and then reclearance in northern and eastern Lingnan, and desertification in the southwestern littoral – there was a more gradual, continued creation and economic development of the Pearl River delta. Indeed, as we will see, the Pearl River delta became so productive that it could support an extraordinarily dense population.

Land Use and Cropping Patterns

When thinking about agricultural systems, it seems almost natural to think first about the amount of cultivated land. But as Boserup has shown, that starting point often assumes that any increases in agricultural output come only by bringing less productive, marginal land into production. Rather, Boserup suggests:

> The relevant classification for analysis of agricultural systems is not between new land and land which is sown and cropped each year, but the frequency at which a given piece of land is sown and cropped. Both in the past and today, we have a continuum of agricultural systems, ranging from the extreme case of land which is never used for crops, to the other extreme of land which is sown as soon as the previous crop is harvested.[35]

In Lingnan ca. 1400, this whole continuum of land use could be found, from hunting and gathering to double cropping. For analytic purposes, land use patterns in Lingnan can be classified into four broad categories, depending upon the intensity of use: (1) hunting, fishing, and gathering; (2) logging; (3) mining; and (4) agriculture. The evidence to be examined indicates that by 1600 a pattern of intensive agricultural cultivation in the Pearl and Han River deltas and in the West River valley around Nanning and Xunzhou, with dryland and less intensive, long-fallow slash-and-burn farming in the hill regions to the north and northeast of Guangzhou, and in similar regions in Guangxi, with less intensive, nonagricultural uses such as gathering, logging, and mining in the sparsely populated hill and mountain regions. Indeed, Boserup also points out the "positive correlation between intensity of [the] food system and population density": "Systems such as hunting, pastoralism, and long-fallow agriculture can support only a sparse population. Unless they rely on imported food, densely populated areas must employ systems of intensive agriculture,

[35] Ester Boserup, "Agricultural Growth and Population Change," in Ester Boserup, *Economic and Demographic Relationships in Development*, T. Paul Schultz, ed. and intro. (Baltimore: Johns Hopkins University Press, 1990), 12.

such as annual cropping or multicropping."[36] The continuum of land use patterns from least-intensive to most-intensive forms thus parallels population density as well, from sparsely to more densely populated.

Hunting, Fishing, and Gathering. For the earliest, non-Han Chinese inhabitants of Lingnan, hunting, fishing, and gathering no doubt were the primary means of obtaining a subsistence, but those activities continued in the Ming and Qing periods. Large game provided opportunities for skillful hunters. At least two kinds of deer grazed in the river valleys, wild pigs foraged in the hills, and mountain sheep occupied higher land. Deerskin was produced and exported in large quantities from Guangdong, and bear and sable pelts also had value, as did tiger skins for decorating military officers' uniforms and monkey fur reserved for the emperor's caps.[37] In the mountains bordering current-day Vietnam, villagers rounded up wild horses and traded them at frontier outposts.[38] The streams and rivers draining the Lingnan region teemed with many varieties of fish, as did the ocean. The seabeds off the eastern coast of the Leizhou Peninsula also yielded oysters and pearls, as did the coastal waters off Lianzhoufu.[39] From the forests, hills, and mountains, people gathered fungus and herbs (for both medicinal purposes and food) and picked wild flowers too.

Logging. Hunting, fishing, and gathering for the most part left the environment unchanged, as did the serendipitous gathering of felled tree limbs for fuel. More extensive logging of trees for fuel, for burning charcoal, and for constructing buildings and ships, though, did destroy woodlands as the population grew during the Ming and Qing. The history of China's timber industry, its impact on the environment, and its more problematic relationship to energy supplies and economic development has not been written, so we really know very little about what actually happened in China as a whole, let alone in Lingnan.[40] Adshead has suggested that for the empire as a whole, the three major sources of timber were Fujian, Hunan, and Sichuan provinces, each of which devoted a section of its gazetteers to *mu zheng*, or "timber administration," and was required to supply timber of varying kinds and amounts to the Ming and Qing states for their imperial building programs. In her study of

[36] Ester Boserup, *Population and Technological Change: A Study of Long-Term Trends* (Chicago: University of Chicago Press, 1981), 15. See also her classic work, *The Conditions of Agricultural Growth: The Economics of Agrarian Change under Population Pressure* (New York: Aldine, 1965).

[37] Song, *Tiangong kaiwu*, 67–69.

[38] *Nanning zhi*, in *Yongle dadian*, vol. 4: 2080ff.

[39] Song, *Tiangong kaiwu*, 296–98.

[40] The latest volume of Joseph Needham's *Science and Civilization in China*, vol. 6, *Biology and Biological Technology*, part 3, *Agro-industries and Forestry*, by Christian Daniels and Nicholas K. Menzies (Cambridge University Press, 1996), begins to meet this need, but arrived too late for its find-

long-distance trade in the Ming and Qing, Fan I-chun has shown that "the timber trade may have constituted more than one fifth of the trade volume carried through the customs houses of the Yang[zi] system in the high [Qing]."[41]

The *mu zheng* referred solely to state acquisition of lumber, not private logging and trading. Neither the Guangdong nor Guangxi provincial gazetteers include sections on *mu zheng*, so it is unlikely that Lingnan was expected to provide timber for imperial uses. But that does not mean timber was not cut and logs sold privately. The "local products" sections of the gazetteers all list "wood products," *mu chan*, or logs and poles cut from various kinds of trees and floated in large rafts down the North and West Rivers to Guangzhou. By Ming times, the most frequently mentioned were pine and fir, although more exotic tropical hardwoods had been cut and exported from Hainan Island as early as the tenth century, when magnates that Schafer calls "lumber millionaires" monopolized the trade.[42]

Mining. Mining of various ores was of sufficient importance to warrant mention in fifteenth-century gazetteers. Gold, silver, and lead came from mines in the mountains west of Nanning, while a large iron mining and smelting operation was centered around Lianzhou northwest of Guangzhou. The largest iron mines were located in northern Guangdong province in Lianzhou and in Qingyuan county. Additional iron and silver mines could be found in northeastern Haifeng county. Although one of the counties in Lianzhou (Yangshan) was described as "the poorest place under heaven . . . no one lives outside of the town,"[43] several thousand miners dug enough iron ore from Bin Mountain to keep 15 furnaces pouring out 700,000 *jin* (about 465 tons) of pig iron (*sheng tie*) each year during the early Ming.[44] No doubt this iron was shipped down the North River and made into iron implements and pots at the Foshan ironworks, which in turn were exported to all parts of China.

In northern Guangxi, tin was washed from a mountainside in Nandan and panned from the nearby river. According to Song Yingxing's early-seventeenth-century account:

ings to be incorporated in this work. See also S. A. M. Adshead, "An Energy Crisis in Early Modern China," *Ch'ing shih wen-t'i*, 3 no. 2 (Dec. 1974): 21–28.

41 Fan I-chun, *Long-Distance Trade and Market Integration in the Ming–Ch'ing Period, 1400–1850* (Stanford University, Ph.D. dissertation, 1992), 212–13.

42 Schafer, *Shore of Pearls*, 80–81.

43 *Guangzhou zhi*, in *Yongle dadian*, vol. 3: 1644.

44 The 700,000 *jin* figure is specifically for the year 1372 (Hongwu 5). *Guangzhou zhi*, in *Yongle dadian*, vol. 3: 1807. Without coal, one wonders how much of the surrounding forest was cut down to fuel the furnaces.

> Mountain tin produced at Nan-tan [Nandan] is found in the shady side of the mountain there. As there is no water for concentration of the ore, some hundred lengths of bamboo are connected to form an aqueduct. Water is conducted here from the sunny side of the mountain and the gangue materials of the ore are washed away. The concentrated ore is then smelted in a furnace.
>
> For smelting tin, a blast furnace is fed with several hundred catties each of tin and of charcoal in alternate layers. When the right temperature is reached and the ore does not melt immediately, a small amount of lead added to the mixture will induce it to flow freely.[45]

How much tin was mined or how many mountains were washed into the rivers to get it is unclear, but there was substantial demand: Song Yingxing estimated that Guangxi produced about 80 percent of the tin used in the Chinese empire in the early seventeenth century. How much of an environmental impact did the tin mining and smelting operation have? Were hillsides first denuded of trees to make the charcoal and then washed away to obtain the ores? If so, these operations may have left permanent scars in the mountains around Nandan and, together with the iron mining and smelting in Lianzhou, would comprise an important story that has yet to be told.

Agriculture

While hunting, logging, and mining represented more extensive uses of land in Lingnan, agriculture certainly was the most intensive use of the land. Three basic agricultural regimes were practiced – slash-and-burn, dry land, and irrigated rice paddy – and although the proportion of the land under cultivation devoted to each varied with time and place, all could be found in Lingnan during the early Ming dynasty.

Slash-and-Burn. In the previous chapter, I discussed slash-and-burn agriculture in relation to the increased erosion and silting in northern Guangdong that had contributed to the creation of the Pearl River delta, and quoted a Tang poem describing the impressive fires set to clear the land. In the early 1400s, inhabitants of northern Guangzhou prefecture – in Qingyuan county and in Lianzhou – still practiced slash-and-burn.[46] In the same period in Wulu county in Nanning prefecture, "slash-and-burn agriculture is practiced because the land is infertile."[47] But in Xiangshan county, although land there too was described as infertile and "the people the poorest," slash-and-burn was not mentioned. Slash-and-burn was used in the hill regions in Qingyuan, Heyuan, and Xining, and, one can imagine, in similar locations in Guangxi province

[45] Song, *Tiangong kaiwu*, 251. [46] *Guangzhou zhi*, in *Yongle dadian*, vol. 3: 1642–44.
[47] *Nanning zhi*, in *Yongle dadian*, vol. 4: 2064–65.

too. In Gaoyao where "the hills are high and the waters deep," most inhabitants fished rather than farmed for scanty yields.[48] In the southwestern littoral, farmers "do not fertilize or hoe, but broadcast seed upon the land; relying on the forces of nature, they still harvest 1–2 *shi* per *mu* . . . After a few years the soil is depleted and [they] move to another place. Thus productive fields are few and fallow (*huang*) fields abound. This is the reason there is so much land and so few people."[49] Similar comments about swidden and low yields can be found in contemporaneous records from Shaozhou, Qinzhou, Zhaoqing, Lianzhou, and parts of Huizhou prefectures.[50]

Certainly not all land thus was brought into production by slash-and-burn, but it was a common enough practice to be cited in a ditty by local poet Li De: "In May we harvest rice from the burned-off fields; at 6 a.m. the watchman reports the rooster's crow."[51] In mid-sixteenth-century Huizhou prefecture, slash-and-burn agriculture was regularly practiced in Boluo, Heyuan, and Changle counties, where there were "sparsely populated, deep forests."[52] Even in the early twentieth century, aerial photographs of the far western reaches of Guangxi province indicate that the residents practiced slash-and-burn, completely denuding the hills.[53]

Dry-Land Farming. Dry-land farming differed from slash-and-burn to the extent that the same plot of land was tilled year after year. Whether dry-land farming developed from slash-and-burn or represented a separate development is not clear, but successful dry-land farming did require higher population densities, reducing the land required to sustain life and increasing the amount of labor available to be lavished on the fields in hoeing, weeding, and fertilizing. Zhou Qufei, whose twelfth-century observations on malaria and elephants I cited in Chapters 1 and 2, describes dry-land farming in the westernmost region of Guangdong province:

> The farmers of [Qinzhou] are careless. When they work the soil with an ox they merely break up the clods; and when the time comes for sowing they go to the fields and broadcast the grain. They do not transplant seedlings. There is no more wasteful use of seed than this. After they have planted it, they neither hoe nor irrigate it, but place their reliance on the forces of nature.[54]

48 *Zhaoqing fuzhi*, quoted in Wu Jianxin, "Ming Qing Guangdong liangshi shengchan shuiping shitan," *Zhongguo nongshi* 4 (1990): 32.

49 *Lianzhou fuzhi*, quoted in Wu Jianxin, "Ming Qing Guangdong liangshi shengchan shuiping shitan," 32.

50 Sources cited in Wu Jianxin, "Ming Qing Guangdong liangshi shengchan shuiping shitan," 32.

51 *Guangzhou zhi*, in *Yongle dadian*, vol. 3: 1791.

52 *Huizhou fuzhi*, 1556 ed., juan 5: 48a–49b.

53 Wiens, *Han Chinese Expansion in South China*, photo p. 13.

54 Translated and quoted in Mark Elvin, *The Pattern of the Chinese Past* (Stanford: Stanford University Press, 1973), 114.

In the eighteenth century, dry-land farming (probably with a bit more technique and care than that evident from Zhou Qufei's text) continued to be the primary mode throughout the hills of Guangdong and in most of Guangxi. In 1724, for example, a regional military commander of Guangxi province noted that "the harvest yield in Guangxi is dependent upon rainfall [not irrigation]."[55] (Dry-land farming received an additional impetus with the sixteenth-century importation of New World crops, but that part of the story will be told later.)

Not all farming technique was rudimentary, and much required considerable labor inputs. In the Pearl River delta, peasant-farmers "exerted themselves in spreading fertilizer" and "worked the fields." Comments in Ming genealogies provide insight into the care with which the land was prepared: "Plow twice, early and without let-up . . . level the ground everywhere . . . work the land, and fertilize heavily. That's the way to being a superior farmer."[56] But no matter how important working the soil may have been, the most important improvement to agriculture came not with more labor or fertilizer inputs, but with irrigation.

Water Control and Irrigation. To make the transition to wet-rice cultivation from the dry-land farming techniques just described and not "waste" seed – by transplanting rice seedlings from preparation beds into rice paddies – required extensive water control and irrigation projects. From the time Chinese and other settlers moved into Lingnan until the tenth or eleventh centuries, slash-and-burn and dry-land farming had been the dominant forms of agriculture. But during the Song, the more sophisticated techniques of wet-rice cultivation that had developed in Jiangnan gradually spread to Lingnan. Indeed, official exhortations to bring the wet-rice techniques of Jiangnan to Lingnan began in earnest in 991,[57] and as late as 1100, Su Dongbo (the famous poet who was then in exile in Huizhou) was trying to introduce the use of the "floating horse" to facilitate transplanting rice seedlings into the flooded paddy.[58]

With the levees discussed in the preceding chapter controlling the river channels, irrigation works could be constructed. In low-lying areas of the Pearl River delta – such as in Nanhai, southern or "lower" Panyu, Xinhui, and Sanshui county, where *shatan*, or "sand flats," had been created – the preferred technique was building *wei tian*, or "enclosed fields". Clearly, the *shatan* could be easily irrigated. The *wei tian* embankments were constructed of earth, or reinforced with lumber and stones, with sluice gates for keeping unwanted

55 Memorial dated YZ2.6.14 in YZCZZ, vol. 2: 750.

56 "Huo shi zongbentang zongpu," quoted in Wu Jianxin, "Ming Qing Guangdong liangshi shengchan shuiping shitan," 32.

57 *Guangdong tongzhi*, 1561 ed., juan 26.

58 Lin Yutang, *The Gay Genius*, 357.

floodwaters out and letting freshwater in. Not all of Lingnan was alluvial delta, of course, and other water control techniques had to be used. The most commonly used method was to obstruct a river or stream with a stone and wooden structure called a *pi*, backing the water up so it could be let into fields either by a sluice gate or hoisted above the *pi* by waterwheels.

Commenting on the reasons for the difference between *wei tian* and *pi*, the author of a brief entry in the Guangdong gazetteer wrote: "There was much low-lying land in Nanhai, so dikes [*ji wei*] were constructed [to keep the water out]. In [northern] Panyu, there was much high, dry land, so waterwheels [*shui che* or *zhuan lun*] are used to lift the water into the fields. They are commonly called *che pi*, and they are everywhere."[59] The counties north of Guangzhou used the *che pi* combination: in Longmen, "residents along the stream construct *pi* to irrigate their fields . . . and those along the White Sand River construct *pi* and use waterwheels to irrigate the fields."[60]

Other methods varied by place, but could include dams (*ba*), pools (*shi*), ditches (*gou*), and wells (*jing*), all of which (and more) are mentioned in the section on "water control" in the 1558 edition of the Guangdong provincial gazetteer. Generally speaking, the more sophisticated and capital-intensive methods could be found in the Pearl and Han River delta regions, with more simple and presumably less effective means in the less densely populated hill regions. In Changning and Yong'an counties in northern Huizhou prefecture, for instance, the residents "build ditches (*qu*) to conduct the water [from the streams to the fields], but do not construct weirs [*pi*] or reservoirs [*tang*]."[61]

Having begun in the Song dynasty, the building of water control and irrigation works in Lingnan thus continued in the Ming. While it is difficult to quantify how many new works were constructed in the Ming over the base established in the Song, a listing of waterworks in the 1558 edition of the Guangdong gazetteer provides a picture of the number and distribution of irrigation works then in existence. By the mid-sixteenth century water control or irrigation works existed in every prefecture (if not county) in Guangdong province (see Table 3.2). The density of these projects of course varied, with more in the heavily populated prefectures than in the more remote hill country. But even in northernmost Nanxiong prefecture, there were 13 *pi* and 8 *tang*, and on Hainan Island 35 *pi*.

The data summarized in Table 3.2 can convey only a very rough approximation of the extent of waterworks in Guangdong (see also Map 3.3a and b). The large number of waterworks in Shaozhou, a prefecture in northern

[59] *Guangdong tongzhi*, 1822 ed., juan 115: 11b. In the *shui che* waterwheel, the wheel was vertically aligned with an axle parallel to the ground; the *zhuan lun* had the wheel horizontal with an axle perpendicular to the ground.

[60] Ibid., 1822 ed., juan 115: 12a–b. [61] Ibid., 1731 ed., juan 15.

Table 3.2. *Waterworks in Guangdong, ca. 1561*

Prefecture	Counties	W/Water	Number	Per 1,000 sq. km
Guangzhou	14	9	133	10.94
Nanxiong	2	2	11	4.70
Shaozhou	6	6	262	18.98
Huizhou	13	4	22	1.49
Chaozhou	11	4	92	13.21
Zhaoqing	13	8	85	8.46
Gaozhou	6	5	88	7.28
Leizhou	3	3	48	6.37
Qiongzhou	13	12	69	2.35
Lianzhoufu	3	3	7	0.52
Lianzhou	3	3	22	2.57

Note: W/water means "counties with waterworks."

Guangdong, for instance, does not mean that it had more irrigated land than Guangzhou prefecture, but that there were many small works there. Even in Nanhai county in the Pearl River delta, waterworks varied in size from a 3,000-*zhang* (about six-mile) section of the Sang Yuan Wei levee irrigating 13,000 *mu* (slightly more than 2,000 acres), to the Fu You Zhang dike at 50 *zhang* in length watering 200 *mu* (about 30 acres).[62]

The large flood control projects, such as the Sang Yuan Wei levee protecting the western approaches to Guangzhou, the levees along the East River, the seawalls in Leizhou, or the Han River levees in Chaozhou (all discussed in the preceding chapter), had been organized and perhaps even financed by the state. A few of the smaller embankments also clearly were listed as belonging to the state (*guan you*), but most of the smaller irrigation projects were private affairs. For some, the initiative for and ownership of the project can be found in their names, such as the Luo Jia (Luo family) dike or the Chen Cun (Chen village) reservoir. For the others, though, the ownership and control is not explicit. Presumably, the larger a project became, the more the cooperation of various social groups – families (*hu*), villages (*xiang*), or districts (*du*) – was required to construct and manage it. One project in Chaozhou prefecture, for instance, the San Ji (three waterworks) Stream, was so called because it required the cooperation of three counties to manage.[63]

The investment of time, energy, and capital to create the waterworks of course varied with size and complexity. Even individuals or families of great

[62] Wang Ping, "Qing li Zhujiang sanjiaozhou de nongtian shuili," in *Jindai Zhongguo quyu shi yan taolunhui wen ji* (Taibei: Academica Sinica Institute of Modern History, 1986), 571–72, 581–82.

[63] Ibid., 1822 ed. Whether this waterworks was this large in the Ming is not clear from the source.

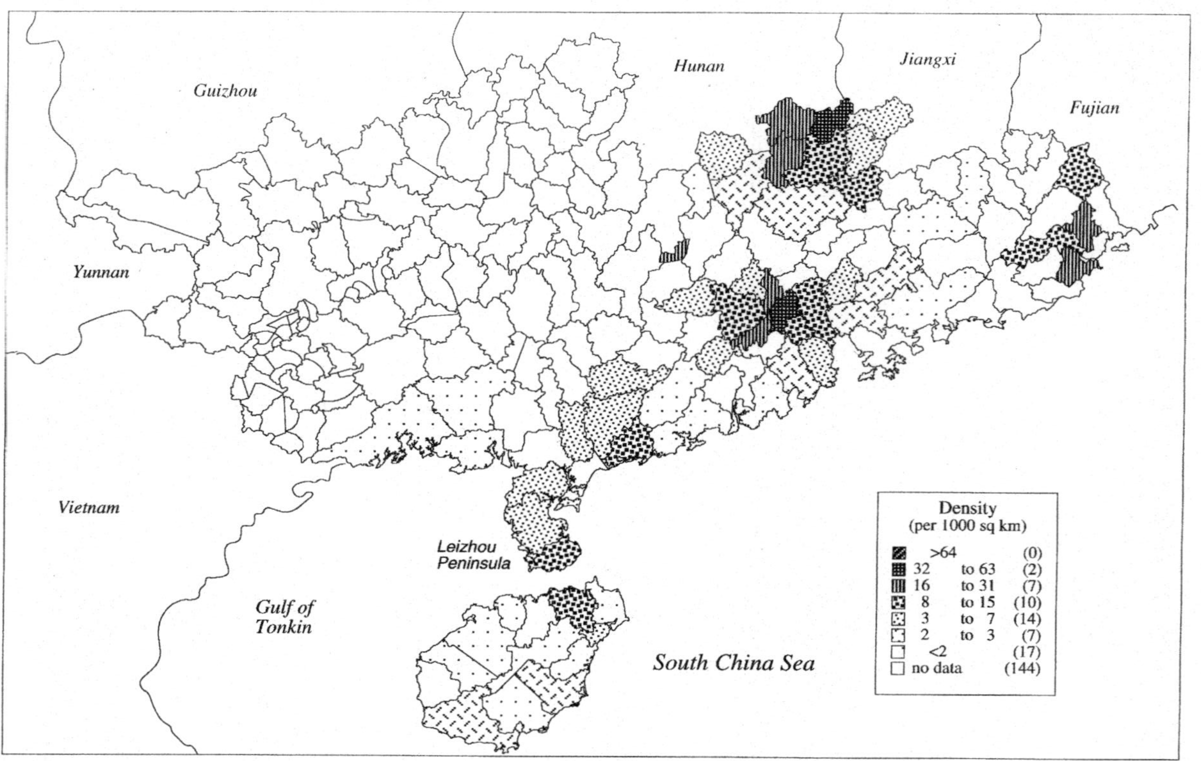

Map. 3.3a. Density of waterworks, ca. 1561

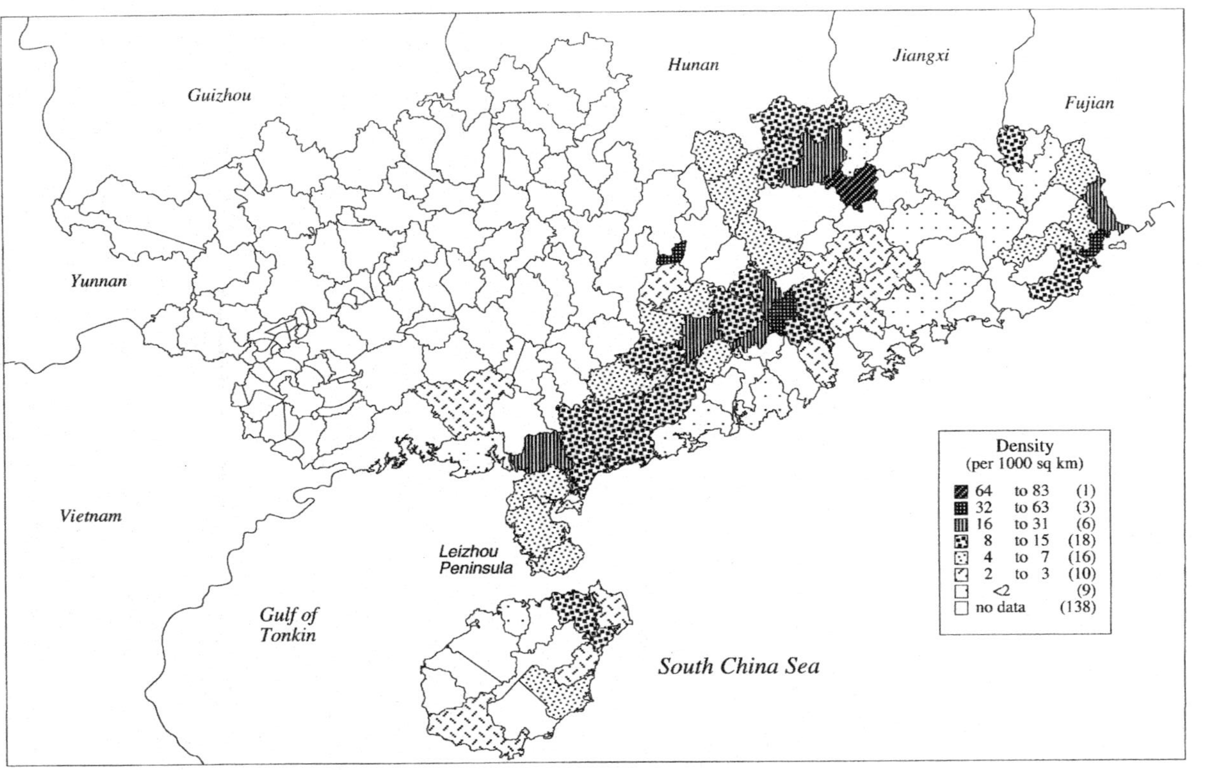

Map 3.3b. Density of waterworks, ca. 1602

wealth would have found it difficult to build the vast water control projects extending for miles along the major rivers, so those had been financed by the state. But the scores of smaller-scale *pi*, *tang*, and *wei tian* were built by families or villages of peasant-farmers hoping to improve the productivity of the fields. So many of these small irrigation projects must have been constructed in the early to middle Ming that they provided a tempting takeover target for unscrupulous local power holders, for in 1441 the Guangdong governor issued a proclamation prohibiting "forcible seizure of small people's [irrigation works] by local power holders (*hao qiang zhanju xiao min*)."[64]

Unfortunately, we cannot get a very clear picture of the Ming (or earlier) water control efforts in Guangxi, for the sources simply do not exist. From the little information to be gleaned from the 1800 edition of the Guangxi provincial gazetteer, just five Song-era waterworks had been constructed, three in the vicinity of Guilin and one each in Pingle and Nanning prefectures.[65] Nearly all of the other water control and irrigation works listed in the 1800 gazetteer are undated and, thus, presumably of a later date. If inferences are worth anything, the 1733 edition of the Guangxi provincial gazetteer did not distinguish water control projects from the general descriptions of the "mountains and the streams" (*shan chuan*), leading one to suspect that whatever water control and irrigation projects there were in Guangxi during the Ming dynasty, they were not many or very noteworthy.[66]

Wet-Rice Cultivation and Double Cropping. The introduction of water control projects from the Song on made wet-rice cultivation possible, and by the fifteenth century considerable tracts of land in Guangdong province had been irrigated. Even on dry-land fields, rice was the major crop, and several more varieties were grown in irrigated paddies. Early- and late-ripening varieties are mentioned in gazetteers printed in the *Yongle dadian* (compiled between 1403 and 1407), raising the question of whether or not double cropping of rice was practiced then.

In Chaozhou prefecture, double cropping of rice was practiced as early as the Song dynasty.[67] In the early Ming, the 1407 *Yongle dadian* records that the

[64] Ibid., 1561 ed., juan 26.

[65] Ibid., 1800 ed., juan 117–20. Not included in this discussion is the famous and ingeniously conceived Ling Qu canal, constructed in the Qin dynasty by Shi Lu, a minister of Qin Shi Huang Di, which was discussed in Chapter 1. Suffice it to say here that the purpose of the Ling Qu canal was transportation, linking the Yangzi River system to Lingnan, not water control or irrigation.

[66] Even the 1985 draft history of Guangxi agriculture, compiled after an exhaustive search of all available local gazetteers, finds little evidence of much irrigation in the Ming and lists only Qing-era (ca. 1800) water control and irrigation works. Mo, *Guangxi nongye jingji shi gao*, 132–33.

[67] "[The people of Chaozhou] boil [sea] water for salt; paddy is harvested twice; and there are five crops of silkworms." *Taiping huan yu ji*, Yue Shi, comp., juan 158: 2b (reprint, Taibei: Wenhai chuban she, 1974).

"paddy can be harvested twice; that which is harvested in the summer in the fifth or sixth month is called 'early rice' (*zao dao*); that which is harvested in the winter in the tenth month is called 'late rice' (*wan dao*)."[68] The wording of the phrase "paddy has been harvested twice" (*gu chang zai shu*) is ambiguous, though: *chang* might mean either "has been," in which case the whole sentence is in the past tense, or "experimented with," in which case double cropping of rice with rice may not have been widespread. Regardless of whether rice was double-cropped with rice or another crop, a surplus was produced enabling exports of "golden city rice" (*jin cheng mi*) to other prefectures, mostly in Fujian.[69]

In Guangzhou prefecture, the *Yongle dadian* lists both early- and late-ripening rice varieties, called locally "one-hundred-day early" and "eighth-month late."[70] But like Chaozhou, it is not clear whether the peasant farmers double-cropped the "one-hundred-day early" variety with rice or with another crop. Whatever the second crop may have been, it was not wheat, which quite explicitly "is not planted."[71] In Wuzhou, another prefecture for which contemporaneous records exist in the *Yongle dadian*, the rice varieties are simply listed; one was presumably the early-ripening Champa rice (the single character *zhan* is listed), along with a few other varieties. Only in Nanning prefecture was the double cropping of rice with rice unambiguously practiced. There, early-ripening rice seeds originating in Champa (*zhancheng mi*) "produce two crops in one year (*yi sui er liang shu*). Much land throughout the province is planted with it (*sheng di duo zhi zhi*)."[72]

If true double cropping of rice was not practiced either at all or only in very few places in Lingnan in the early Ming, by the seventeenth century the evidence of double (and even triple) cropping is incontrovertible. In Cenxi county, south of Wuzhou on a tributary flowing into the West River, the local gazetteer even assigned a specific date to the introduction of double cropping of rice: "Planting an early crop of rice first began during the Tianqi reign (1621–27), [and after that] each year two crops were harvested. The early crop is planted at Jingzhe ["Waking of the Insects," March 5] and harvested in Xiaoshu or Dashu ["Lesser" or "Greater Heat," July 7–23]. The late crop is planted at Mengzhong ["Grain in the Ear," June 6] and harvested in the first month of the winter [mid-November]."[73] In Guangdong, we learn from Qu Dajun, who is so often our reliable observer (albeit from the late seventeenth century), that "it is said that because of the warm climate, three crops [of *gu*, rice] can be harvested annually from the same field in the following rotations:

68 *Chaozhou zhi*, in *Yongle dadian*, vol. 3: 1870.
69 Ibid.
70 *Guangzhou zhi*, in *Yongle dadian*, vol. 3: 1801.
71 Ibid.
72 *Nanning zhi*, in *Yongle dadian*, vol. 4: 2085.
73 *Cenxi xianzhi*, quoted in Mo, *Guangxi nongye jingji shi gao*, 117.

(1) a crop planted in the winter is harvested in the spring; (2) a crop planted in the spring is harvested in the summer; (3) a crop planted in the fall is harvested in the winter."[74] Braudel cites the early-seventeenth-century observations of a Spanish friar: "Father de Las Cortes admired the multiple harvest in the Canton area in 1626. He noted that from the same land, 'they obtain three consecutive harvests in one year, two of rice and one of wheat, with a yield of 40 or 50 to 1, because of the moderate heat, atmospheric conditions and most excellent soil, much better and more fertile than any soil in Spain or Mexico.' "[75] The friar's observations are confirmed by at least one contemporary Chinese source (ca. 1625), who also said that "in Guangdong there are fields which get three harvests; the reason is the warm climate."[76]

Thus, by the seventeenth century, in addition to rice, wheat then was sown. Wheat was to become an important secondary crop in the eighteenth century, but in 1400 it neither was a major crop nor was used for human consumption even where it was grown. In the Yongle-era gazetteers for Nanning and Wuzhou prefectures, wheat is not even mentioned. In Lianzhou department in northern Guangzhou prefecture, "wheat," according to the Yongle-era gazetteer, "is not planted."[77] Only in Chaozhou prefecture was wheat as a crop even mentioned, and then it is glossed with the comment: "Given to other uses. Not eaten."[78] What those "other uses" may have been is not clear, but pig fodder or brewing are possibilities.[79]

By the mid-sixteenth century, wheat may have been grown in northern counties,[80] "but in Guangzhou prefecture," according to the 1561 provincial gazetteer, "it is hot, and if wheat or barley are planted they will not sprout."[81] Seventy years later, though, as seen from Father de Las Cortes's testimony, wheat was being grown in Guangzhou prefecture. By 1700, in much of Guangdong, according to Qu Dajun, the "rice–wheat" rotation was practiced: "There is much wheat and little barley here. After the fall harvest, wheat is planted and in the first month it is harvested."[82] In the early eighteenth century, officials tried in the hill regions to spread the technique of planting wheat after

74 Qu, *Guangdong xin yu*, 371.

75 Braudel, *Civilization and Capitalism, 15th–18th Century*, vol. 1, *The Structures of Everyday Life*, 152.

76 Quoted in Li Hua, "Ming Qing shidai Guangdong nongcun jingji zuowu de fazhan," *Qingshi yanjiu* 3 (1984): 135.

77 *Guangzhou zhi*, in *Yongle dadian*, vol. 3: 1801.

78 *Chaozhou zhi*, in *Yongle dadian*, vol. 3: 1870.

79 In late imperial and modern times, Chinese peasants did not raise crops as animal fodder, especially for pigs or chickens. If peasant farmers in Chaozhou grew wheat as fodder or feed, then they also may have penned the animals to keep them from burning up energy (and hence grain).

80 *Wengyuan xianzhi*, 1557 ed., in *Tian yi ge Ming dai fangzhi xuan kan*, vol. 63.

81 *Guangdong tongzhi*, 1561 ed., juan 22: 1b.

82 Qu, *Guangdong xin yu*, 377–78.

the rice harvest,[83] and by the early nineteenth century Captain Ross saw much wheat in his journey overland from Hainan to Guangzhou in the winter of 1819–20.[84]

Until the middle of the sixteenth century, then, there is little evidence that wheat was grown, and when it was, it was not eaten by humans. But after that, wheat began to assume an increasingly larger role in the crop rotation system of the peasant farmers of Lingnan, being planted in the winter as either a second or a third crop. Along with the spread of double-cropped rice, the inclusion of wheat into the crop rotation thus is a measure of the intensification of agricultural use of land. In the hill regions, one crop of the relatively higher-yielding variety of *geng* rice probably was the rule. Elsewhere, as we have seen, two crops of rice were planted, sometimes in a true rice–rice rotation, or in some areas with the late crop planted in between rows of the early crop.[85] And finally, in the Pearl River and Han River deltas, where irrigation was most developed and population densities highest, peasant-farmers got three crops in the rice–rice–wheat rotation.

During the course of the Ming dynasty, the double cropping of rice with rice thus spread from the few very warm areas such as Nanning, where the climate made the practice relatively easy, to many other parts of Lingnan. Additionally, wheat went from being considered animal fodder to human food and was added to the cropping rotation, either as a second or even third crop following one or two rice harvests. Not only did agricultural production increase, but so too did the productivity of the peasant farming family. The question, of course, is what drove this intensification of agriculture during the Ming.

Three factors are especially noteworthy.[86] In the first place, the size and density of the population increased throughout the Ming. As Boserup argues, increasing population density itself can drive agricultural intensification, and a tripling of the Lingnan population certainly counts as increased population density. There was simply more labor power available to work the land year-round. Second, increased market demand from the middle of the sixteenth century on prompted peasant-farmers to increase output to meet the needs of

[83] According to a Yongzheng-era memorialist: "Last year in the winter [1735] officials in Chaoping county in Pingle prefecture gave out wheat seed and taught the people how to plant it. Now they are reporting a plentiful harvest. Rice-growing villages now have spring wheat to see them through the time between harvests." Memorial dated YZ13.4i.9 in YZCZZ, vol. 24: 507–508.

[84] Ross, "Journal of a Trip Overland from Hainan to Canton in 1819," 25–53.

[85] In Haifeng county, the late-ripening variety thus was called "dweller rice."

[86] A fourth may have been the arrangements for renting land. If landowners collected a fixed rent in kind only on the rice harvests, then tenants had a strong incentive to increase production of rice and to add wheat. Unfortunately, little is known about land tenure relations in the Ming.

the expanding market in and around Guangzhou in the Pearl River delta. I will have more to say about commercialization in the next part of this chapter. And third, the climate also became warmer from about 1550 on, enabling farmers in previously marginal areas to plant a second crop of wheat or rice when previously they would have gotten just one crop of rice; like commercialization, I will examine changing climatic conditions later in this chapter. But the intensification of effort was not the only reason for rising agricultural production; yields also rose.

Harvest Yields. Harvest yields constitute the single best measure of agricultural productivity. When Chinese sources talk about harvest yields, though, they do so not in terms of the seed-to-harvest ratio common to much of early modern Europe, but in terms of the number of *shi* of rice harvest per *mu* of land planted. Estimating per *mu* rice yields is fraught with difficulty and uncertainty the further back in time we look. Indeed, for the early Ming period ca. 1400, there is little evidence of any kind to draw upon. I earlier cited one early Ming source that indicated yields of 1–2 *shi* of unhusked rice on dry-land fields in Qinzhou. In Nanning, the *Guangxi tongzhi* reported that in the fifteenth century the yield from a good harvest was 2 *shi* on the highest quality land.[87] For the sixteenth century, Dwight Perkins gathered rent data from gazetteers that placed yields between 1 and 5 *shi*, with an average of 2.6 *shi* per *mu*.[88] Reviewing the little evidence that there is for the early Ming (ca. 1400), Wang Jianxin concluded that yields for a single crop on dry-land fields probably were just 1 *shi* or so per *mu*, and about 2 *shi* per *mu* for double-cropped fields.[89]

In the late seventeenth century, according to Qu Dajun, rice fields produced 4 *shi* of unhusked rice per *mu* and two crops per year; the yield from the second crop was one-third less than that of the first "because it is a second crop."[90] Evidence from the early eighteenth century confirms Qu's figures: Guangdong province's financial commissioner, Wang Shirui, reported quite unambiguously that the per *mu* yield of the early rice crop was slightly more than 4 *shi*.[91] Further evidence from eighteenth-century rents shows that yields from places scattered throughout Guangdong province averaged about 4 *shi* per *mu*.[92]

The very thin evidence regarding rice yields for the early fifteenth century thus is not inconsistent with the somewhat better data for the late seventeenth

[87] Quoted in Mo, *Guangxi nongye jingji shi gao*, 127.
[88] Perkins, *Agricultural Development in China*, 324.
[89] Wu, "Ming Qing Guangdong liangshi shengchan shuiping shitan," 34.
[90] Qu, *Guandong xin yu*, 374.
[91] Memorial dated YZ7.6.11 in YZHWZZ, vol. 15: 528.
[92] See the table in Chen Chunsheng, *Shichang jizhi yu shehui bianqian – 18 shiji Guangdong mi jia fenxi* (Guangzhou: Zhongshan daxue chuban she, 1992), 25–26.

and eighteenth centuries. Given this data and the intensification of agriculture by the seventeenth century, it is not unreasonable to conclude that around 1400 per harvest (or first-harvest) yields averaged somewhere in the range of 1–2 *shi* per *mu*, increasing to 3–4 *shi* in the seventeenth century.

A few quick calculations show these yield estimates to be plausible, if not probable. If 75 percent of the 1400 acreage was devoted to rice averaging 1 *shi* per *mu*, then in Guangdong (where the data are a bit better), something around 19 million *shi* of rice could have been produced annually. Assuming a per capita consumption of rice around 4 *shi*,[93] then about 4.8 million people could have been sustained by the annual production of rice. Since the population was only about 3 million people, by these calculations Guangdong would have been a rice surplus region. And as we will see later, that indeed was the case.

At the end of the Ming dynasty (around 1640), if one-half of the 30–33 million *mu* under cultivation was devoted to rice and the yields had increased to an average of 2.6 *shi* per *mu*, then about 40 million *shi* of rice was produced. Maintaining the 4 *shi* per capita consumption rate, that would have supported a population of about 10 million. I have estimated that the population was about 9 million in 1640,[94] meaning that almost any decline in yield because of poor harvests would have resulted in grain deficits. The evidence to be examined later supports that conclusion too.

Besides population increases and improvements in yield, the other variable that changed over the 250 years represented in this scenario was the amount of land allotted to rice, decreasing from an estimated 75 to 50 percent of the land under cultivation. With agricultural specialization already evident around 1400 and with substantial commercialization of agriculture occurring after 1550, such a decline in the amount of land devoted to the staple food crop is not unreasonable. To see why, we must turn our attention now to the commercialization of rice.

Commercial Crops, 1400 1550

In 1400, rice was the principal crop in Lingnan, grown on both dry land and in irrigated paddies, yielding one, two, and sometimes three crops annually, depending on local soil, climatic conditions, and water availability. Just as local variations in agricultural conditions affected which type of rice was grown and with what technique, so too did those same variations enable peasant-farmers in different regions to grow crops other than rice. As any casual reader of Chinese gazetteers knows, the section called "local products" (*tu chan* or *wu chan*) listed not just the grains grown locally, but also special agricultural prod-

[93] See the figures in Table 8.1; to obtain the 4 *shi* per capita rate used here, I have combined the rice and sweet potato figures.

[94] See Table 4.1.

ucts, such as sugarcane, tea, mulberry leaves, or fruits, and commodities manufactured locally, such as various kinds of woven fabrics.

Sugarcane. Next to rice, sugarcane was the most important crop grown in many parts of Lingnan. Cane was grown in the Pearl River delta counties, along the southeast coast from Xin'an through the counties in the Han River delta, and nearly everywhere in the southern half of Guangxi along the Xun and Zuo Rivers. In some areas, especially in the deltas and around Nanning, peasant farmers grew so much cane that Qu Dajun noted that "cane fields outnumber rice fields."[95] In Wuzhou prefecture, so much cane was grown along the banks of one West River county that "it looked like a forest."[96] In the late Ming or early Qing, Qu Dajun estimated that 40 percent of the fields in Panyu, Dongguan, and Zengcheng were given over to sugarcane, and 60 percent of the fields in Yangchun. The cane was made into various grades of sugar, sold locally, and exported in substantial quantities. Indeed, all of the sugar in the Chinese empire in Ming times came either from Fujian or Lingnan.[97]

Fruit, Tea, and Indigo. Fruit trees of various kinds were grown throughout Lingnan, but as with sugarcane the areas of most concentrated production tended to be near the larger urban areas. Lingnan had produced fruits for the empire going back at least to Han times; *long-yan,* litchee, oranges, tangerines, and plantains all were grown and either sold fresh locally or dried for export. In Guangdong, the Pearl River delta and the region to the north of Guangzhou grew much fruit. The most famous area was Chen village in Shunde; for 40 *li* around, farmers had planted hundreds of thousands of *long-yan* trees. With so many peasant farmers from Chen village tending the orchards, the village became a major importer of rice in Qing times and the location of a large rice wholesaling operation. A secondary fruit center operated east of Guangzhou around the city of Shilong in Huizhou prefecture.[98]

Other crops grown throughout Lingnan in the early Ming included various fresh vegetables, flowers, and, in hill areas, indigo and tea. Like fruits, tea had

95 Qu Dajun, quoted in Ye and Tan, "Ming Qing Zhu Jiang sanjiaozhou nongye shangyehua yu xushi de fazhan," 16.

96 *Wuzhou zhi,* in *Yongle dadian,* vol. 4: 2203.

97 Sucheta Mazumdar, *A History of the Sugar Industry in China: The Political Economy of a Cash Crop in Guangdong, 1644–1834* (University of California at Los Angeles, Ph.D. dissertation, 1984). Although Mazumdar's thesis focuses upon the Qing period, she provides much useful information both about earlier periods and about commercial crops in general.

98 Ye Xian'en, "Lue lun Zhujiang sanjiaozhou de nongye shangyehua," *Zhongguo shehui jingji shi yanjiu* 2 (1986): 24–25; *Guangxi nongye jingji shi gao* (Nanning: Guangxi minzu chuban she, 1985), 215–16.

a long history in Lingnan, going back to the Han dynasty and was planted in orchards south of Guangzhou or on scattered plots in Zhaoqing, Huizhou, and Chaozhou prefectures. In Guangxi, over 100 varieties of tea were grown in 60 counties, but the most important centers were in Guilin and Wuzhou prefectures, with some in Nanning too.[99] In Guangdong reeds for woven mats were grown in Dongguan and Xin'an, palm fans were grown for similar uses in Xinhui, and fragrant wood incense was manufactured in Dongguan[100] and on much of Hainan Island.

Hemp, Cotton, and Silk. Throughout much of Lingnan, peasant-farmers grew many of the same crops. An interesting and important difference, though, concerns the raw materials for textiles and the different fate of the textile industries in Guangdong and Guangxi, the former based upon cotton and the latter upon hemp.

In Guangxi, peasant-farmers grew three kinds of hemp (*da ma*, *ning ma*, and *ge ma*) from which flaxlike thread was spun and linenlike cloth woven. Both the plants and the technique for making cloth from hemp had been known in Guangxi from very early times, and by the Song Guangxi province ranked third in the empire in production and by the end of the Song ranked second. As the techniques for spinning flax and weaving linen improved and the end product became more refined, demand increased. The tribute quota for silk was commuted to linen, and the cloth was "traded to the four corners [of the empire.]"[101] By the early Ming, peasant-farmers in Guangxi specialized in growing hemp, exchanging it in the market for food. In Zuozhou, peasant-farmers "labor little in [rice] fields, but much at planting hemp." And in Zhongshan county, "workers in the [rice] fields decrease daily, while those planting hemp increase daily. They use the profit to buy food, exchanging much hemp in the market."[102]

Whether the peasant households in Guangxi that grew the hemp also spun and wove is open to question. On the one hand, according to the *Yongle dadian* edition (ca. 1407) of the Nanning gazetteer, "The men farm . . . and the women avail themselves of the market to buy and sell things. The region is not suitable for sericulture, so [the women] only spin hemp and weave it into cloth."[103] On the other hand, two late-sixteenth-century sources[104] imply the existence of specialized weaving households: one mentions that peasant-farmers sold

[99] Ibid., 228. [100] Ibid., 17–18.

[101] Mo, *Guangxi nongye jingji shi gao*, 200–202.

[102] *Guangxi tongzhi*, 1531 ed., quoted in Tan Yanhuan, "Lun Ming Qing shidai Guangxi nongye chanpin de shangpinhua," paper presented at 1987 Shenzhen Conference on Qing Social and Economic History, 2.

[103] *Nanning zhi*, in *Yongle dadian*, vol. 4: 2064–65.

[104] Both quoted in Tan, "Lun Ming Qing shidai Guangxi nongye chanpin de shangpinhua," 2.

their hemp to "dispersed loom households (*sang ji hu*)," and a poem/song captured in the 1587 edition of the *Binzhou zhi* reads:

> Maiden from afar, climb the high loom.
> Spin, whirl, and weave, throw yourself into it;
> Only fear that no hemp grows wild in the hills.
> When the cloth is sold, your money is replenished.[105]

Cotton also was grown, certainly as early as the Tang and Song, but maybe even earlier in the fourth century CE. By the Song, "southerners (*nanfang jen*) comb several score of black seeds from each cotton boll with an iron-toothed roller."[106] The Guangxi evidence examined by Tan Yanhuan suggests rather extensive growing of cotton in Song and Yuan times, as well as spinning and weaving of cotton cloth for export.[107] But if Guangxi weavers exported cotton cloth in the fourteenth century, sometime during the Ming the external demand seems to have dried up. This change probably was related to the growth of the cotton textile industry in Jiangnan, which satisfied the needs of the Chinese empire for cotton cloth. Whatever the cause, by the late Ming few textiles of any kind were exported from Guangxi, being produced for local use only.[108] From then on, opportunities for Guangxi peasant-farmers to export agricultural products would be limited primarily to rice.

Sericulture. In the Pearl River delta, the silk industry developed on a base that had been created first by the "sand flat" fields (*shatan*) and then a particular combination of fish ponds with fruit trees that has struck twentieth-century scientists as exemplifying a form of ecologically sustainable agriculture.[109] From Song times on, fish ponds had been scooped from the swamplands of the upper Pearl River delta.[110] The mud and the muck raked up into embankments above the flood plain protected the ponds from flooding, while the high water table filled the hole with water, and the pond was

[105] Quoted in Tan, "Lun Ming Qing Shidai Guangxi nongye chanpin de shangpinhua." These three tidbits of evidence imply perhaps three kinds of organization of the weaving. The first, from Nanning, implies that the women of the peasant household spun, wove, and marketed the cloth. The second implies specialized weaving households, while the poem could be interpreted to mean that peasant households with spinning wheels and looms hired itinerant female workers on some kind of arrangement, possibly where the weavers purchased the hemp with their own money and then recouped their investment by selling the finished product.

[106] Quoted in Mo, *Guangxi nongye jingji shi gao*, 210.

[107] Tan, "Lun Ming Qing shidai Guangxi nongye chanpin de shangpinhua."

[108] Mo, *Guangxi nongye jingji shi gao*, 211.

[109] "A complete, scientific, man-made ecosystem," in the words of Zhong Gongfu, "Zhujiang sanjiaozhou de 'sang ji yu tang' – yige shui lu xianghu zuoyong de rengong shengtai zitong," *Dili xuebao* 35, no. 3 (Sept. 1980): 200–209.

[110] Ibid., 200–201.

stocked with various kinds of carp fry netted from local waters.[111] On the embankments, peasant-farmers by the early Ming planted mostly fruit trees (*long-yan*, litchee, etc.), giving rise to the "fruit tree and fish pond" (*guo ji yu tang*) combination. The carp fed on organic matter that either dropped or was thrown into the pond, while the muck scooped up from the pond fertilized the fruit trees and the rice fields, and added height to the embankments and more protection for the fish ponds.

The fruit tree and fish pond culture provided a ready-made base for expansion of the silk industry when increased demand warranted. And unlike Guangxi's hemp or cotton textile industries, which had died out, demand for Guangdong silk increased during the last half of the sixteenth century, largely as a result of rising foreign demand. As the demand for silk increased, peasant-farmers replaced the fruit trees with mulberry trees (silk worms feed on mulberry leaves), giving rise to the "mulberry embankment and fish pond" (*cang ji yu tang*) system, and then began digging up even more rice paddies to expand the mulberry embankment and fish pond system. By 1581, according to statistics provided by Ye Xian'en, in the Longshan area of Shunde county, 18 percent of the productive "land" was fish ponds, and when combined with the mulberry trees on the embankments accounted for about 30 percent of the cultivated land area.[112]

The mulberry (or fruit) embankment and fish pond system often is cited as an example of a sustainable, premodern agricultural ecosystem. In any sustainable ecosystem, natural or otherwise, the mineral and energy resources necessary for life are recycled, and the losses from the system are so small that they can be easily replaced (from the sun or by the weathering of rock or the fixation of nitrogen by bacteria). That, in essence, is what the fish pond system accomplished. Silk worm excrement, leaves from the trees, and other organic material were gathered and thrown into the fish pond, providing food for the carp; the fish were harvested annually, with the muck formed from the fish waste and other decomposed organic matter then scooped out and used to fertilize the mulberry trees and rice fields. In the words of a modern ecologist, "There is a closed nutrient recycling loop via decomposition and mineralization in orchards, fields, and ponds. Nutrient export across the system boundaries takes place only with stream runoff, and with sales of plant or animal products."[113]

The ecologists' view of the mulberry and fish pond system is sound up to

[111] In the twentieth century, five kinds of fish were reared in the ponds, all from fry secured from local rivers. See William E. Hoffman, "Preliminary Notes on the Fresh-Water Fish Industry of South China, Especially Kwangtung Province," *Lingnan Science Journal* 8 (Dec. 1929): 167–68.

[112] Ye Xian'en, "Lue lun Zhujiang sanjiaozhou de nongye shangyehua," 22.

[113] Bruenig, *Ecological-Socioeconomic System Analysis and Simulation*, 176.

a point, but it omits from the energy flows a critical part of the ecosystem: human beings and their energy and nutrient needs, much of which were satisfied by food imports. The peasant farmers raising fish and silk worms had to eat, and the food staple was rice. For much of the Ming dynasty, the rice consumed by those in silk-producing areas in the Pearl River delta was available locally or was easily obtained from nearby markets. But by the end of the sixteenth century, the rice was coming from hundreds of miles away. The mulberry and fish pond system thus was not a closed system, but was sustained only by imports of food to sustain the human population of the Pearl River delta.

Certainly, most of the food initially came from nearby sources, perhaps the farmer's own rice paddies that had not been converted into fish ponds. But as time passed and more rice paddies were turned over to sericulture, those farmers had to buy food in markets supplied from ever increasing distances, especially in the Qing dynasty. What was destabilizing about both the local and long-distance trade in food, as we will see in greater detail in later chapters, was the gradual simplification of ecosystems.

Exporting organic material outside the system, then, is a major source of instability in an ecosystem, requiring additional inputs to ensure sustainability. From an economic perspective, this exporting of products from one place to another is the essence of marketing and economic development; in the case of agrarian economies, the products by definition are all organic. Commercial development, then, must be seen as one of the primary forces of ecological change: exports of nutrients "across the system boundary" must be replaced by imports from outside the system, otherwise it is not sustainable. To understand environmental and ecological change in Lingnan, then, a critical question concerns the commercialization of agriculture, in particular of food production.

Commercialization of Agriculture, 1550 1640

Evidence from the first half of the Ming dynasty, roughly the period from 1400 to 1550 that we have been focusing upon until now, paints a picture of an agrarian economy producing a certain amount of commercial crops. It seems unwarranted, though, to conceive of this period as one characterized by the commercialization of agriculture. Indeed, there is little to suggest that the production of commercial crops or marketing activity expanded at a rate greater than the growth of the population. Instead, it seems quite likely that the proportion of the land devoted to commercial crops in 1550 was about what it had been in 1400.

Rice certainly was the dominant crop throughout Lingnan in 1400, but local differences in soil, water, and climate enabled peasant-farmers to specialize in other food and nonfood commodities. And this agricultural specialization sustained local markets to facilitate exchange. Most of the food was produced for use by the peasant family; only in Chaozhou prefecture is there unambiguous evidence that rice had become an exportable commodity. In Guangzhou prefecture, the list of the various kinds of rice, beans, and vegetables that were grown is followed by the following explicit statement: "All of these are for the peasant family's own use; they are not sold to other places."[114] Did this mean that these foodstuffs were not sold in local markets or brought into Guangzhou for sale? Probably not, for markets existed throughout the countryside for the exchange of local goods and for selling exportable commodities like tea, sugar, fruits, and maybe silk and cotton too. What the statement probably meant was that foodstuffs were not exported, but exchanged in periodic markets among local residents. In Guangxi, as noted earlier, peasant-producers exchanged hemp for rice in the local markets.

These exchanges of locally grown food for locally produced cloth were not ecologically unstabilizing, since the energy flows remained within the local system. But when food or cloth was exported beyond the boundaries of an ecosystem, then the system would become increasingly difficult to maintain without additional energy inputs. In a sense, of course, that is what was happening as peasant producers in the Pearl River delta came to rely upon food imports from the West River valley in Guangxi. These food imports did not mean that the Pearl River delta was in ecological trouble, but that without markets to bring food from increasingly distant points of production, a highly specialized mulberry embankment and fish pond system (i.e., one without sources of food for the human population) would not be sustainable.

Periodic Markets and Marketing Systems

Information on early Ming local periodic markets (*xu* or *shi*) is not extensive. The *Yongle dadian* (ca. 1407) lists the number of markets for some counties in Nanning and Guangzhou prefectures. For Qiongzhou prefecture (Hainan Island), a more extensive listing is found in a gazetteer from a later period. Six of the markets in Qiongshan met daily, while the rest of the markets met periodically, probably on a three- or five-day schedule. "In Rong county [Wuzhou prefecture], *shi* are called *xu*, and they meet once in five days."[115] Certainly markets existed throughout Lingnan in 1400, if only in the county city, but records from that period do not exist. The 1561 edition of the *Guangdong tongzhi*, though, lists markets for all counties in the province; regrettably, a similar listing for Guangxi does not exist. Nonetheless, using the 1561 data, a clear sense of market density throughout Guangdong can be conveyed (see Table 3.3 and Maps 3.4a and b).

[114] *Guangzhou zhi*, in *Yongle dadian*, vol. 3: 1802. [115] *Nanning zhi*, in *Yongle dadian*, vol. 4: 2185.

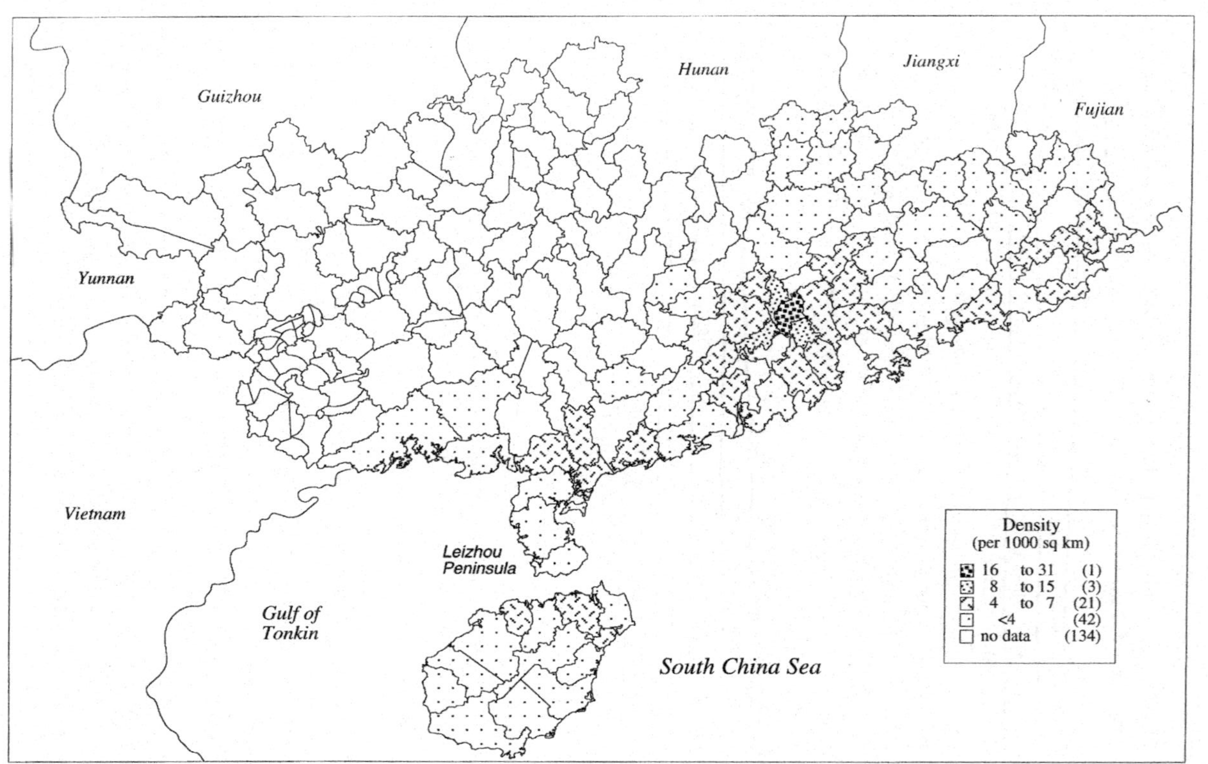

Map. 3.4a. Markets, ca. 1561

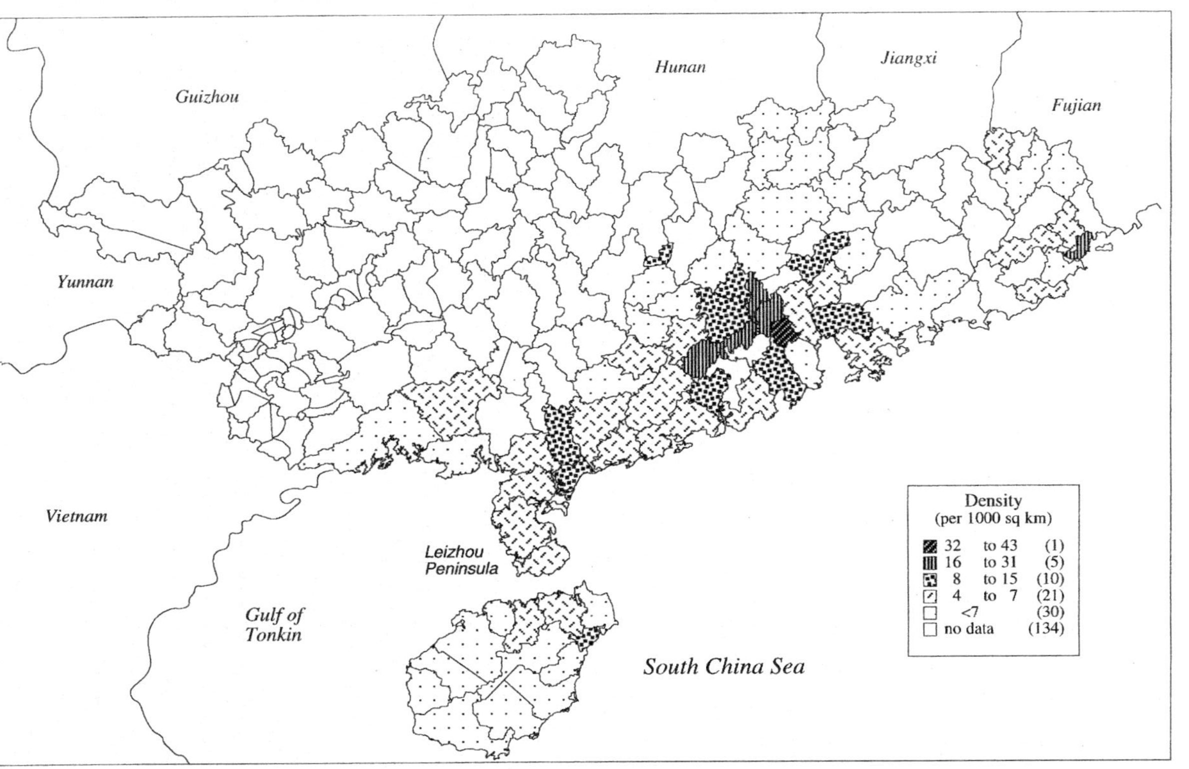

Map. 3.4b. Markets, ca. 1602

Table 3.3. *Markets in Guangdong, 1561 and 1602*

	Number		Per 1,000 sq. km	
Prefecture	1561	1602	1561	1602
Guangzhou	136	234	6.85	11.45
Zhaoqing	69	147	4.34	7.91
Gaozhou	57	79	4.16	5.95
Leizhou	8	41	1.04	4.97
Luoding		30		4.64
Chaozhou	41	56	2.37	4.45
Huizhou	37	18	1.45	3.60
Qiongzhou	66	72	2.56	2.87
Lianzhoufu	19	32	1.17	1.90
Shaozhou	9	18	0.55	0.97
Lianzhou				
Nanxiong				

Table 3.3 lists both the number and density of markets (as measured by the number per 1,000 square kilometers) in the prefectures of Guangdong province in 1561 and 1602. While the number of markets is important, the density is more significant: this measures the number of markets within a 15-kilometer radius, about a three-hour walk from the most distant point. In other words, while in Shaozhou in 1602 there was about one market within walking distance of most peasant farmers, in Gaozhou there were six. Not surprisingly, the area with the greatest density of markets was in the Pearl River delta (in Guangzhou prefecture). Somewhat surprising, though, is the relatively high density of markets in the counties on Hainan Island. Out of 66 counties for which 1561 market data are available, 6 Qiongzhou prefecture counties rank in the top half in terms of market density. Qiongshan county, for instance, ranked 17th just behind Dongguan county in the Pearl River delta. What is even more remarkable is that the number of markets on Hainan in 1561 was a substantial decrease from levels recorded half a century earlier. Thus, even though markets were declining on Hainan Island, reflecting its peripheralization in Lingnan during the Ming dynasty, an "echo" of its former place can be heard in the number of its markets even as late as 1561. But if Hainan Island was declining in the fifteenth and sixteenth centuries, at least as measured by the number of its markets, the Pearl River delta continued to add new markets.

Although data on early Ming markets in Lingnan are scarce, the 1407 *Yongle dadian* edition of the Guangzhou prefecture gazetteer did list the number of markets in four counties (Nanhai, Panyu, Dongguan, and Zengcheng), giving us some hints about the development of markets there from 1400 to the mid-sixteenth century. In these counties, markets increased from 36 in 1407, to 59 in 1561, or an increase of about 60 percent. During the same period, the population may have increased at most by 80 percent. In other words, during the first half of the Ming period, periodic markets in Guangzhou prefecture probably increased at a rate no faster than the population. If the number of periodic markets is an indicator of the pace of economic activity, then while the Lingnan economy did not stagnate during the first half of the Ming dynasty, neither did it grow faster than the population. Indeed, the slow but steady growth in population undoubtedly was the engine for whatever economic growth there was.

From about the middle of the sixteenth century, though, the pace of economic activity accelerated at a rate faster than the growth in population. In the 45-year period from 1561 to 1602, the total number of markets in Guangdong increased from 435 to 762, an increase of 75 percent, a rate far exceeding the population growth for the same period. Furthermore, this rate of increase was more or less evenly spread throughout the province, with a greater rate found in the 4 core counties in the Pearl River delta. Focusing upon the 21 counties comprising the entire Pearl River delta, the number of markets increased from 95 in 1561 to 167 in 1602, an increase of 75 percent.[116] But within the delta, the bulk of the markets were located in just four counties: Shunde, Dongguan, Nanhai, and Xinhui had 75 percent of the total markets. And in those counties, the markets had increased from 59 in 1561 to 115 in 1602, a 95 percent increase. Whether the frequency of their being held also increased is not known, but certainly by the eighteenth century markets in the Pearl River delta and in Chaozhou prefecture had come to meet daily rather than periodically. If any of the markets in the late Ming had come to meet daily, then the intensity of the marketing would have been even greater than the preceding figures suggest.

What happened seems clear enough. In the second half of the sixteenth century, the pace of economic activity accelerated most rapidly in the four Pearl River delta counties making up and surrounding the city of Guangzhou and then spread more generally throughout the entire province. What accounts for this abrupt increase in economic activity? I think two factors were especially important: climatic changes and foreign trade.

Climatic Conditions in Ming Times

In the very broadest terms, Ming China coincided with a global climatic event known as "the Little Ice Age."[117] Defined as the period beginning in the four-

[116] Ye and Tan, "Ming Qing Zhu Jiang sanjiaozhou nongye shangyehua yu xushi de fazhan," 78.
[117] Jean Grove, *The Little Ice Age* (London: Methuen, 1988).

teenth century but "culminating between the mid-sixteenth and the mid-nineteenth century,"[118] the Little Ice Age was characterized by advancing glaciation punctuated by warmer periods lasting several decades, after which colder periods kept the glaciers growing. What caused global temperatures to turn colder during these centuries is a matter of some debate, but climatologists think three "forcing" factors accounted for most of the climatic change. The first was advanced in 1977 by J. A. Eddy, who contended that two periods of almost no sunspot activity – the Sporer Minimum from 1400 to 1510 and the Maunder Minimum from 1645 to 1715 – correspond to, and thus probably caused, the coldest periods of the Little Ice Age. H. H. Lamb's research additionally showed that volcanic activity throws "dust veils" into the atmosphere that significantly cool the earth's surface by blocking radiation from the sun from reaching the earth. More recently, scientists have added the complex and poorly understood interchange of heat between the air and the oceans – summarized as the "El Nino-Southern Oscillation," or ENSO, effect – as another factor.[119] Although not all of the world cooled simultaneously and the period was punctuated by some warmer decades, the concept of the Little Ice Age still conveys the idea of a general global cooling from about 1500 through the middle of the nineteenth century.

The best evidence available indicates that the Little Ice Age affected Ming China. Most of what we know about China's historic temperatures is based upon the pioneering work of Zhu Kezhen, China's noted climatologist. Using records of freezing in the lower Yangzi, snow in the coastal provinces, and Japanese records, Zhu developed a periodization of warmer and colder decades beginning in 1470, when documentary records became more rich.[120] Using a different data set for Guangdong province, the geographer Zheng Sizhong developed a similar periodization[121] (see the "blocks" of cold periods in Figure 6.1). Whatever the temperature trends before 1470 – and they may well have been cold too – what these periodizations show is that at least from 1470 through the middle of the sixteenth century, cooler conditions prevailed in China. From about the mid-sixteenth century through the early seventeenth century, though, temperatures became warmer and more favorable for agriculture.

The relationship of plant growth and agricultural yields to changes in temperature and water supply is very complex and will be discussed in more detail in Chapter 6. Suffice it to say here that it is unlikely that the turn to a slightly

118 Ibid., 1.

119 For a summary of the evidence, see Raymond S. Bradley and Philip D. Jones, eds., *Climate since A.D. 1500* (New York: Routledge, 1992).

120 Zhu, "Zhongguo jin wuqian nian lai qihou bianqian de chubu yanjiu," 486–87.

121 Zheng Sizhong, "1400–1949 nian Guangdong sheng de qihou zhendong ji qi dui liangshi feng kuan de yingxiang," *Dili xuebao* 38, no. 1 (Mar. 1983): 25–32.

warmer climate in the middle of the sixteenth century would have increased the growth rates of any of the important crops such as rice, wheat, or sugarcane. What the warmer conditions meant, though, was that the risk of killing frost early in the growing season or late during the harvest substantially declined. And with less risk, peasant farmers could, with sufficient incentive, add a second or third crop without worrying that either or both would be destroyed by frost. A slightly warmer climate, therefore, made it possible for peasant-farmers to double- or triple-crop. I do not think that warmer conditions alone caused this change in cropping patterns, but when coupled with greater demand for rice, these conditions did not vitiate peasant-farmers' attempts to increase production. But what caused demand to increase?

European Trade and Silver Imports

Although the first Ming emperor had issued a ban on maritime trade shortly after the dynasty was declared, the prohibition never was fully enforced. Some trade did occur – mainly under the guise of normal "tribute" from neighboring countries – but also in the form of "piracy." In the 1520s and 1530s, Japanese pirates raided and traded on the Chinese coast from the mouth of the Yangzi south to Guangdong, joined in the 1540s and 1550s by Chinese trading pirates. Simultaneously, the Portuguese sailed into the South China Sea in the early 1500s looking for and finding trading opportunities, especially after their "discovery" of Japan in 1542–43.[122] With this illegal trade, Japanese and Spanish-American silver bullion began flowing into the Chinese economy as the Portuguese paid for silks, porcelain, and other luxury items with Japanese silver. The flow of silver into the economy was further spurred in the 1570s after the Chinese ban on maritime trade was lifted following the Jiaqing emperor's death in 1567, the nearly simultaneous Spanish colonization of the Philippines and establishment of the Acapulco–Manila silver route, and the Japanese establishment of Nagasaki as their port for the China trade. As Ray Huang concludes, "By 1576 trade between China and the Americas was well established and it continued without interruption into the next century."[123]

Flynn and Giráldez argue that contrary to the conventional wisdom that Europeans had a high demand for Chinese products, the motive force for the trade was the simple fact that "the market value of silver in Ming territory was

[122] Boxer, *South China in the Sixteenth Century*, xxvi.

[123] Ray Huang, "Chia-Ch'ing," in Frederick W. Mote and Denis Twitchett, eds., *The Cambridge History of China*, vol. 7, *The Ming Dynasty, 1368–1644*, part 1 (Cambridge University Press, 1988), 505.

double its value elsewhere," thus ensuring a flow of silver into China.[124] For Lingnan, there were two major trade routes, to Japan and to Manila. Either with their own capital or with silver forwarded by Japanese merchants, Portuguese headed up the Pearl River for biannual fairs in Guangzhou, where they exchanged the silver for the export goods. Those goods, especially the silk and porcelains, then were loaded onto ships bound for Nagasaki. Japanese merchants at Nagasaki bought the Chinese goods with silver, launching another round of trade. Trade through Manila also brought silver into the south China economy. Chinese merchants from Guangdong and Fujian sailed to Manila with their goods, which the Spanish bought with silver from the American mines; from there the silver flowed back to China, and the Chinese commodities found their way to Latin America and Europe.

Von Glahn estimates that each year 50–100 metric tons of Japanese and American silver flowed to China in the period from 1550 to 1645, less in the early years and more in the later year (especially the 1630s).[125] While it is impossible to tell just how much of the total found its way into the Lingnan economy, it is known that in 1636 Portuguese ships transported 75,000 kilograms of Japanese silver to Macao for use at the Guangzhou fairs. My calculations from independent Chinese sources indicate that 75,000–150,000 kilograms is not an unreasonable average annual total. One Chinese source estimated that perhaps 30 percent of the silver imported into Guangdong made its way out in trade north over the Meiling Pass (in return for the porcelains imported from Jingdezhen), which thus amounted to 25,000–50,000 kilograms.[126] The Nanxiong customs house at this pass in 1567 collected 43,000 taels in duty at the rate of 1/30 of the declared value.[127] The value of the goods so taxed thus amounted to 1.3 million taels, or 40,000 kilograms of silver. Even allowing for the fact that this customs figure is for the years before the 1570s expansion of trade, it still makes the 1636 figure plausible.

But how much of an impact did the late Ming influx of silver have on China's economy? There is much debate on the issue. Citing the increase in the money supply and the monetization of the tax system, Atwell has argued that "Japanese and Spanish-American silver played a crucial role in the vig-

[124] Dennis O. Flynn and Arturo Giráldez, "Born with a 'Silver Spoon': The Origin of World Trade in 1571," *Journal of World History*, 6, no. 2 (1995): 206.

[125] Richard von Glahn, "Myth and Reality of China's Seventeenth Century Monetary Crisis," paper presented at the UCLA Center for Chinese Studies seminar, October 1995, 14–15 and Table 5. See also William S. Atwell's articles, "Notes on Silver, Foreign Trade, and the Late Ming Economy," *Ch'ing shih wen-t'i* 3, no. 8 (1977): 1–33; and "International Bullion Flows and the Chinese Economy circa 1530–1650," *Past and Present* 95 (May 1982): 68–90.

[126] Jiang Zulu, "Ming dai Guangzhou de shangye zhongxin diwei yu dongnan yi da bu hui de yincheng," *Zhongguo shehui jingji shi yanjiu*, no. 4 (1990): 25.

[127] *Da Ming huidian*, 1587 ed. (Shanghai: Shang yinshu guan, 1936), juan 35; *Ming shi*, juan 81.

orous economic expansion."[128] Von Glahn, while disagreeing with Atwell on the question of whether or not silver imports declined substantially in the years leading up to the fall of the Ming in 1644, nonetheless agrees that "the impact of silver imports on the late Ming economy, and on the monetary system in particular, was indeed substantial."[129] Goldstone, on the other hand, argues that because the Chinese economy was so large to begin with, "the total volume of European trade was never more than just over 1 percent of China's economy, and it was on average only 0.2–0.3 percent . . . Europe's bullion trade with China was not large enough to be crucial to the workings of the Chinese economy."[130]

Goldstone, it seems to me, overstates his case[131] by measurng the bullion trade against the entire Chinese economy, not by the regions in which it was most important: Jiangnan, the southeast coast, and Lingnan. As noted earlier, perhaps 70 percent of the silver flowing into Guangzhou stayed there. Thus, when seen in terms of China's regional economies, the role of the European trade and of additional supplies of silver in stimulating the economy seems more reasonable. In the second half of the sixteenth century, New World and Japanese silver flowed into Lingnan (and elsewhere) as Europeans and Japanese bought fine Chinese commodities like silk and porcelains. The increased demand for silk – especially great after the Spanish established Manila as their major base of operations in Asia – was met by increased production. As we have already seen, the economy of Lingnan by then was already specialized, with several regions producing various commercial crops. Of particular interest and importance here, though, is the fish pond and fruit tree system that had developed in the Pearl River delta, especially in Shunde, Panyu, and Xiangshan counties. When European demand for silk increased, peasant farmers converted to the mulberry embankment and fish pond system, greatly increasing the supply of mulberry leaves, silkworms, cocoons, and silk. From

[128] William Atwell, "Some Observations of the 'Seventeenth-Century Crisis' in China and Japan," *Journal of Asian Studies* 45, no. 2 (Feb. 1986): 224. For Atwell's more extensive analysis upon which his summary statement is based, see "International Bullion Flows and the Chinese Economy circa 1530–1650," 68–90.

[129] Von Glahn, "Myth and Reality of China's Seventeenth Century Monetary Crisis," 15.

[130] Jack A. Goldstone, *Revolution and Rebellion in the Early Modern World* (Berkeley and Los Angeles: University of California Press, 1991), 372–74. Goldstone continues: "Any claim of a causal link between the decline in the European silver trade and the decline of the Ming dynasty must be viewed as an excess of Eurocentrism, rather than as a historical fact."

[131] In the tradition of Barrington Moore Jr. and Theda Skocpol, Goldstone has a very big thesis about agrarian states and their breakdowns to prove. "I have argued that [the classic state breakdowns of early modern Europe] were not due to the growth of capitalism, or to fortuitous combinations of circumstances. Instead, they were caused by the incapacity of agrarian economies, and of their attendant social and political institutions, to cope with the pressures of sustained population increase. Clearly, if this argument is sound, it should be just as valid for agrarian-bureaucratic states outside Europe." Ibid., 349.

this core region in the Pearl River delta, marketing increased and markets proliferated, spreading throughout all of Lingnan.

Rice-Surplus to Rice-Deficit Region

With the commercialization of the economy, in particular in the Pearl River delta where peasant-farmers gave up growing rice in favor of the silk industry, the declining supply of food from local sources gave rise first to demands that grain exports be halted and then to imports of rice from Guangxi. But this change did not occur until the early 1600s. Prior to that time, Guangdong clearly had been a grain-surplus region. During the Jiaqing period (1522–67), Guangdong had sufficient stocks of grain to supply Guangxi in time of need, and even in the Wanli era (1573–1619), Xie Zhaozhe could still describe Guangdong as a place "with lots of land and cheap rice prices."[132] Contemporaneous documents provide substantial evidence that Guangdong was a grain surplus region and exported grain to other provinces, primarily Fujian. In the coastal regions from the Leizhou Peninsula to Chaozhou, Fujian merchants came in their "white or black ships" to purchase substantial amounts of rice.[133]

But by the middle of the Wanli era (around 1600), protests about rising rice prices prompted Guangdong provincial officials to prohibit Fujian merchants from buying rice in Guangdong. In 1593, 1600, and 1602, officials placed embargoes on the rice trade with Fujian "[to stop] the price increases and the people's outcries," according to one official.[134] The trade nonetheless continued, prompting another official in 1624 once again to ban the trade and to enforce it with executions of those caught running the blockade.[135]

These bureaucratic skirmishes with Fujian rice merchants reflect an important transition in the Lingnan economy, from being a rice surplus, rice-exporting region in the decades (maybe centuries) before 1600, to being a rice-deficit and food-importing region afterwards. Then, turning to Guangxi, merchants from Guangdong journeyed to the rice-producing regions around Gui county in the Xun River valley to procure rice and began establishing warehousing and transshipment facilities in Wuzhou. And this is precisely the time when, as noted earlier in this chapter, peasant farmers in Cenxi county, within easy shipping distance of Wuzhou, began to double-crop rice, most likely exporting their surplus production to the Pearl River delta.[136]

[132] Xie Zhaozhe, *Wu za zu*, quoted in Wu, "Ming Qing Guangdong liangshi shengchan shuiping shitan," 28.

[133] See the numerous gazetteer citations excerpted in ibid., 29.

[134] Regional Inspector (*xun an yu shi*) Wang Youjin in 1593, quoted in ibid., 29.

[135] Regional Inspector Chen Baojin in 1624, quoted in ibid., 29.

[136] See the preceding section entitled "Wet-Rice Cultivation and Double Cropping."

The earliest evidence for the exportation of Guangxi grain comes from the late seventeenth century, but no doubt the grain trade began earlier in the century. According to Qu Dajun, "[Guang]dong has become short of grain, and so depends on [Guang]xi [to supply grain]."[137] From then on, Guangxi became the major source of rice to cover deficits in Guangdong. Where markets in Guangxi had primarily facilitated local exchange, increasingly they linked Guangxi's economy to that of Guangdong. And Guangdong severed its ties to Fujian. This change in trade patterns reflects a deeper change in the agrarian economy as more and more peasant-farmers increased the acreage devoted to nonfood crops by converting paddy to commercial crops, especially in the Pearl River delta with its extensive network of water transportation and rich, alluvial soil.

The development of the silk industry and export trade, the commercialization of the Pearl River delta, the shortage of food grains there, and ultimately the import of rice from the West River valley in Guangxi can be interpreted in ecological terms, and this interpretation points to an important ecological change. In brief, with the increased production and export of silk, the Pearl River delta began losing nutrients across the ecosystem boundary (the silver imported from Japan and America could not be eaten, but it could be used to buy food); to make up for the deficit, food imports were required to maintain the energy of the human population. Since Guangxi was connected to the Pearl River delta via the West River, rice exports from Guangxi flowed into the delta. Where the Pearl River delta and the West River basin in Guangxi previously had been separate ecological systems, they became increasingly linked by commercial forces and market transactions. But does this change mean that these two parts of Lingnan then were in the process of becoming a single ecosystem, with energy and nutrient exchanges ensuring the sustainability of the whole?

There is an ambiguity here. On the one hand, clearly all of Lingnan was becoming knitted together into a common economic unit. On the other hand, the energy flows did tend to be downstream toward the Pearl River delta, where vast quantities of food were consumed and where considerable amounts of silk were exported. The question of whether or not this was an ecologically sustainable agricultural economy turns in part on the extent to which nutrients and energy exported from Guangxi could be replaced. This formulation of course begs the question: How were the energy losses in Guangxi replaced? I do not have a firm answer at this time, but I think that in the long run they probably weren't. Guangxi today is one of the poorest provinces in China, experiencing low (or even declining) per capita agricultural yields: soils have become depleted, hillside erosion is fierce, and modern chemical fertilizers, even if they are widely available, do not add organic material to the soils. The

[137] Qu, *Guangdong xin yu*, 371.

current economic and ecological poverty of Guangxi, I think, is a consequence of the centuries of exports of rice downriver to Guangzhou.

Conclusion

During the centuries spanned by the Ming dynasty (1368–1644), the population and economy of Lingnan recovered and then surpassed the levels reached earlier in Song times. This development was not linear, but underwent a distinct, two-phase process. From 1400 to about 1550, recovery was population driven. But from 1550 on, the process was commercialization driven, with foreign trade stimulating the economy generally and the commercialization of the Pearl River delta in particular. Indeed, over the course of these two-plus centuries, Lingnan began to assume the more familiar core–periphery structure of late imperial times. The concentration of population in the Pearl River delta was a function both of more water control and irrigation projects facilitating more intensive cultivation of the delta, and of the foreign trade centered in the city of Guangzhou. However, other parts of Lingnan underwent processes that might best be called "peripheralization." The clearest case was Hainan Island, which shriveled when its access to foreign trade was severed early in the fifteenth century, but even much of Guangxi province too was peripheralized during the Ming. At one point having a textile export market, Guangxi increasingly developed as a rice monoculture, supplying food downriver to the urban population of Guangzhou and to the commercializing farmers of the Pearl River delta. Commercialization was beginning to link the various regions of Lingnan into a single agroecosystem, with energy losses in the Pearl River delta replaced by rice imports from Guangxi.

If the late Ming population exceeded that attained during the Song, it is not so clear that the amount of land under cultivation – and hence the clearance of forest – surpassed Song levels. Water control and irrigation intensified cultivation of the best lands in the Pearl River delta, and per *mu* yields probably doubled over the two centuries from 1400 to 1600. Furthermore, the greatest increases in the percentage of cultivated land area occurred in those areas that had been devastated by the Mongol invasions – the northern Guangdong prefectures of Shaozhou and Nanxiong, and in the east Huizhou and Chaozhou prefectures – so that the Ming cultivated acreage may well have just reached that of Song times. The relationship of population growth to deforestation in Lingnan thus was complex and not merely a case of a growing population clearing more and more forest to bring the land underneath it under the plow. Instead, the highest population densities were sustained on land in the Pearl River delta not only that had never been forested, but that had been newly created only in the preceding century or so. "Agricultural development without deforestation" might be an apt way to summarize the experience of

Lingnan in the Ming dynasty. What might have happened had this commercialization-driven development continued this way will never be known, for in the middle of the seventeenth century, Lingnan, like the rest of China, was thrown into cataclysm.[138]

[138] The term "cataclysm" comes from the title of Lynn Struve's latest book, *Voices from the Ming–Qing Cataclysm: China in Tigers' Jaws* (New Haven: Yale University Press, 1993).

4

"ALL THE PEOPLE HAVE FLED": WAR AND THE ENVIRONMENT IN THE MID-SEVENTEENTH CENTURY CRISIS, 1644–83

In the eighth month of 1642, residents in a northern ward of the city of Guangzhou were startled by the appearance of a tiger just outside the city wall. Residents of the northern suburbs had not seen a tiger there in decades – maybe a century. Villagers in neighboring Shunde county had reported a tiger attack in 1627,[1] but for the city of Guangzhou itself the last reported tiger attack had been in 1471.

The appearance of this tiger so near the great metropolis thus was unusual. But so too was the way in which the residents handled this unusual tiger. In all of the other recorded incidents of tigers approaching towns or villages in Lingnan, the villagers had the same reaction: to kill the tiger. Now, killing a tiger is no small matter. Certainly, a marksman with a rifle could do it, but seventeenth-century guns weren't called "fowling" pieces or "blunderbusses" for nothing. So too could an archer with poison arrows kill a tiger, but men with that kind of skill and weapons usually were in the army, not at home tilling the vegetable patch. No, the way unarmed villagers approached a tiger was en masse, advancing on the animal behind a thicket of spears and lances until the tiger was cornered and netted. The tiger was then killed, dismembered, and its various body parts sold.

Like most civilized people, seventeenth-century Chinese appropriated nature by making it into commodities. And there was a market demand for nearly all of the tiger's body parts. In Lingnan, tigers were hunted, and not just after an attack on villages. Their pelts were valuable, and other body parts were believed to have regenerative properties.[2] According to an 1839 report in the *China Repository*, "Virtues are ascribed to the ashes of the bones, to the fat, skin, claws, liver, blood, and other parts of the tiger, in many diseases;

[1] *Guangzhou fuzhi*, 1879 ed., juan 79: 10a.

[2] In the twentieth century at least, tiger bones ground into potions or placed in liquor are believed to enhance longevity, while preparations from the penis are believed to increase a man's potency. The trade in tiger and rhino parts is such a current problem that the government of the People's Republic of China has banned trade in tiger parts and rhinoceros horn. See the news report in *The New York Times*, Sunday June 6, 1993, p. 19.

the whiskers are said to be good for toothache."[3] To break a drought, the skull of a tiger sometimes was dragged through a river in order to "arouse the sleeping dragon" and bring rain.[4] All of these beliefs provoked a demand for dead tigers.

So, when the tiger startled the residents of the northern Guangzhou ward, there was reason enough for them to kill the tiger. But that was not what they did. Just one sentence in the Guangzhou gazetteer describes what happened: "The residents captured the tiger, but let it go."[5] After organizing themselves to capture the tiger, a very serious and risky business in itself, they then simply released the tiger! This action is puzzling, wonderful, and quite extraordinary. It is puzzling because we just cannot understand why the residents of that north Guangzhou ward set the tiger free. Today, of course, releasing the tiger is exactly what we wish the residents would have done, and they did. But *why* did they do it? Had a new sensibility about nature and wild things begun to develop among Chinese, or at least urban Chinese in Guangzhou? Had they begun to think differently about their place in the natural world, conceding that some other animals, even if only the magnificent tiger, had a right to live? Or was there a more mundane reason they released the tiger? We just do not know the reason; we just know they let the tiger go. Possibly they experienced the tiger as a portent[6] (as we will see, economically, times had become hard; temperatures had turned colder; rebels in north China were pressing an embattled Ming dynasty to the wall; and epidemics had broken out in the Yangzi River delta) and released it to ward off the dangers that otherwise were sure to be visited upon Lingnan.

Thus, besides being puzzling and wonderful, the release of the tiger in 1642 was quite extraordinary. And to understand how extraordinary, we have to place it into the broader context of what the world was like for Chinese in and around 1642, and that is the main purpose of this chapter. Briefly, the 40-year period beginning in 1644 was one wrought by crisis: civil war, banditry and piracy, peasant uprisings, trade dislocations, and declining harvest yields caused by colder temperatures all combined to make life in those years uncertain at best, unlike any that had preceded or followed. People died from the wars, starvation, and epidemic disease all resulting in a substantial decline in the human population of Lingnan, a decline that was not reversed until the 1680s.

But more than being merely unstable or uncertain, the middle decades of the seventeenth century in Lingnan can be described as a "general crisis." Just as much of the world was caught up in what historians have called "the general

[3] *China Repository* (March 1839), vol. 7: 596–97.

[4] M. W. de Visser, *The Dragon in China and Japan* (Amsterdam: J. Muller, 1913), 119–20.

[5] *Guangzhou fuzhi*, 1879 ed., juan 79: 16a., entry for the eighth month of Chongzheng 14.

[6] I would like to thank Rhoads Murphey for bringing this possibility to my attention.

crisis of the seventeenth century,"[7] so too were the people of Lingnan, at least in the middle decades of that century. So "terribly agonizing" was this period, in the words of one historian, that she called it "the Ming-Qing cataclysm."[8] None of these factors alone "caused" the mid-seventeenth-century crisis in Lingnan, but, when coupled with the political crisis and the resultant warfare, constitute an important historical conjuncture that together constituted the crisis.[9]

In the debate over the underlying causes of the seventeenth-century crisis in China, two opposing positions have been staked out. William Atwell, the

[7] There has been much debate on the extent and causes of the "general crisis." See the essays in Trevor Aston ed., *Crisis in Europe, 1560–1660* (New York: Doubleday, 1967), and in Geoffrey Parker and Leslie M. Smith, eds., *The General Crisis of the Seventeenth Century* (London: Routledge and Kegan Paul, 1978). The extent to which a "general crisis" extended to Asia is taken up in a set of essays in a special issue of *Modern Asian Studies*, 24, no. 4 (1990).

[8] Struve, *Voices from the Ming–Qing Cataclysm.*

[9] As William Atwell has aptly observed, the concept of "general crisis" is somewhat ambiguous as used in the literature on Europe. Let us start with the idea of "crisis." As used initially among European historians looking at the seventeenth century, the term tended toward imprecision, leading to the helpful criticism that "it must be realized that nowadays the crisis is often merely an affirmation of the undisputable fact that something happened in the seventeenth century; the crisis has become a synonym for what historians concerned with other centuries call 'history.'" Building on this critique, Theordore Rabb offered a definition of "crisis" that Atwell subsequently adopted in his analyses of seventeenth-century East Asia: for the term "crisis" to retain any meaning at all, the crisis must be short-lived, maybe in historical perspective as long as two decades, and it must be distinct both from what precedes and from what follows. Atwell then proceeds to argue that the crisis period "falls between the early 1630s and the late 1640s." For south China, the timing of the crisis was a bit later, beginning in the mid-1640s and extending into the late 1650s.

The other part of the concept – "general" – also is laden with ambiguity. It can mean either an event that occurred broadly over a large expanse of territory, such as all of China or East Asia, or a conjuncture of crises affecting a region deeply throughout its society, economy, and polity, to mention just a few of the possible facets of a crisis. In two excellent essays exploring the extent of the general crisis in East Asia, Atwell adopts the former definition stressing the breadth of the crisis across a wide geographic area. As will be used here, though, "general" will signify depth: four and perhaps five different kinds of crises cutting across most aspects of life and livelihood afflicted the people of south China in the middle of the seventeenth century. A demographic crisis, brought about in part by food shortages, epidemic disease, and warfare, resulted in a significant loss of population; an economic crisis was caused in part by declining agricultural production but also by a break in overseas trade and monetary fluctuations, all of which fueled unemployment; banditry and piracy coupled with uprisings of tenants and tenant-serfs ripped the social fabric; and the political crisis of the fall of the Ming and the consolidation of the Qing brought state-sponsored warfare with its attendant death and destruction to south China. An intellectual and cultural crisis could be added to the list, but such an exploration extends beyond the bounds of this study. Our purpose here will be first to describe these crises and then to examine their consequences.

See William S. Atwell, "A Seventeenth-Century 'General Crisis' in East Asia?" *Modern Asian Studies* 24, no. 4 (1990): 664–65; see also his "Some Observations on the 'Seventeenth-Century Crisis' in China and Japan," 223–44.

first to probe the question, has identified a cooler climate, which disrupted harvests and caused grain prices to rise dramatically, exacerbating the ability of peasant families to sustain a living, and the decline in silver imports, disrupting the economy.[10] Richard von Glahn disagrees with Atwell, arguing instead that declines in silver were insufficient to affect the accumulated stock of silver in the Chinese economy adversely, and that, in any event, grain prices increased in the last years of the Ming dynasty, rather than declined as the monetary theory implicit in Atwell's argument would predict.[11] To Jack Goldstone, internal population growth, rather than the external causes cited by Atwell, caused a whole host of problems – from poverty and dislocation of the population to rising prices – that a state whose revenues were based on a land tax collected in depreciating silver was incapable of addressing.[12] To be sure, the rise in population did strain the resources of the Ming empire, and there is evidence of disruptive price increases as well. But I think that for explaining why the crises happened *when* they did, the timing of climatic changes and disruptions in foreign trade strike me as important factors. If a warmer climate and inflows of silver helped us account for the economic expansion that began around 1550, reversals of fortune in both factors contributed to the brewing crisis of the mid-seventeenth century, and that is where I will start trying to explain the circumstances that made the release of the tiger in 1642 so extraordinary.

Climatic Change in the Seventeenth Century

Historians surveying the world in the seventeenth century often have commented on how widespread social and political disorder was – "the times of troubles" in Russia; the English Civil War; peasant uprisings throughout France; and peasant uprisings and the fall of the Ming dynasty in China – and have wondered how coincidental these crises were. In searching for commonalties that might help explain why so much of the world was in disorder, some historians have cited climatic change as a significant factor common to all.[13] Although these seventeenth-century crises also shared other aspects, such as

[10] Ibid., 661–82.

[11] Von Glahn, "Myth and Reality of China's Seventeenth Century Monetary Crisis." This paper is drawn from von Glahn's book, *Fountain of Fortune: Money and Monetary Policy in China, Fourteenth to Seventeenth Century* (Berkeley and Los Angeles: University of California Press, forthcoming).

[12] For a succinct statement of his thesis, see Jack Goldstone, "East and West in the Seventeenth Century: Political Crises in Stuart England, Ottoman Turkey, and Ming China," *Comparative Studies in Society and History* 30, no. 1 (1988): 103–42.

[13] In addition to the sources cited in notes 6, 8, and 10, see also Braudel, *Civilization and Capitalism, 15th–18th Century*, vol. 1, *The Structures of Everyday Life*, 49–51. For at least one part of the world, South Asia, there is little evidence of a general crisis. See John F. Richards, "The Seventeenth-Century Crisis in South Asia," *Modern Asian Studies* 24, no. 4 (1990): 625–38.

all occurring in agrarian regimes incapable of dealing with financial stress (Goldstone's thesis), climatic change was a worldwide phenomenon that did contribute to the general crisis of the seventeenth century.

As I mentioned in the preceding chapter, the Ming dynasty occurred at the onset of the global climatic event known as the "Little Ice Age." Defined as the period from the late-fourteenth to the mid-nineteenth century,[14] the term "Little Ice Age" should not be read to mean uniformly colder temperatures, nor should it be interpreted to mean that each year during this period was colder than those preceding or following. Indeed, even during the Little Ice Age, some years and even decades were rather warm. But on balance, though, global temperatures cooled enough for glaciers to keep growing, rather than receding.

For Lingnan, the characterization of the Little Ice Age as being generally cooler than the preceding period, but with definite warm periods, is confirmed by the documentary evidence. Combing through all of the extant gazetteers for Guangdong province, in 1961 a research team from the Guangdong Provincial Historical Documents Research Group compiled and listed chronologically by kind all citations regarding climatological events, from the fourth to the twentieth century. Quantifying and graphing the citations for cold or freezing weather for the two centuries from the 1490s to the 1680s provides a rough measure of the climatic changes (see Figure 4.1).

Although this chart begins only with the decade of the 1490s, during which time no exceptionally cold spells in Lingnan were recorded, there were in fact only eight citations of cold for the entire fifteenth century (four each in the 1410s and 1480s); the fifteenth century, therefore, was relatively warm. In the sixteenth century, though, the story is quite different. Beginning in 1503, cold spells are first recorded, and then an extreme cold wave covered much of Lingnan in 1510. Following a cold decade in the 1530s, the climate in Lingnan recovered, experiencing just one or two instances of cold per decade until the 1610s. As noted in the preceding chapter, this warmer period coincided with the commercialization of the economy in the second half of the sixteenth century.

But in the seventeenth century, cold waves increased in number, beginning with 10 in the years from 1614 to 1621. In the winter of 1614–15, snow fell not only in the Nanling Mountains to the north of Guangzhou, but as far south as Hengzhou (Nanning) in Guangxi province. Four years later, in the winter of 1618–19, such heavy snow fell in Conghua county just north of Guangzhou that "elders said it had never been like this before";[15] that same winter, snow was reported in the Pearl River delta and as far south as Yangchun county in the southwestern littoral.[16] Cold returned again in 1634, when seven counties reported exceptionally cold conditions, followed 2 years later by another cold

[14] Grove, *The Little Ice Age*, 1.
[15] Ibid., 172. [16] Ibid.

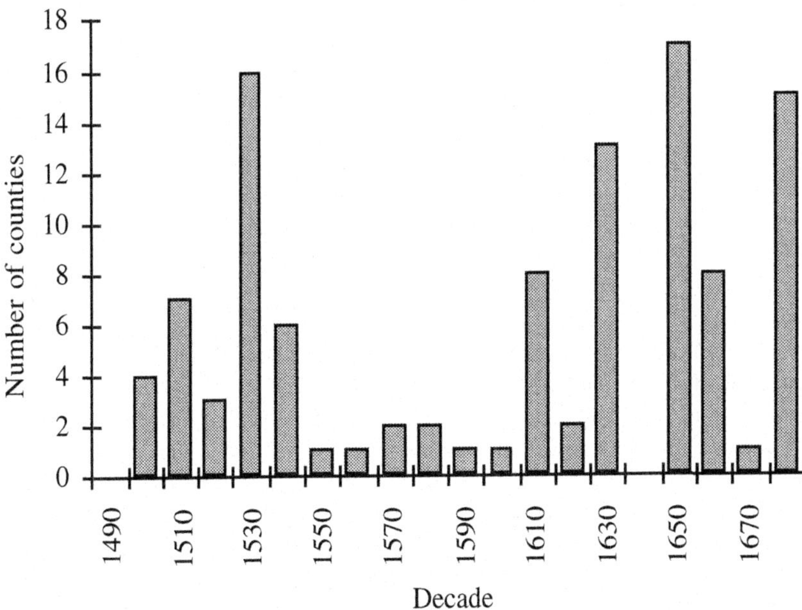

Figure 4.1. Number of counties reporting frost or snow, 1490–1690. Source: Compiled from *Guangdong sheng ziran zaihai shiliao* (Guangzhou: Guangdong sheng wenshi yanjiu guan, 1961).

wave, when residents of coastal Huilai county reported not only snow, frost, and ice four or five inches deep on ponds, but also that they had never experienced anything like it before.[17]

Similarly, the 1650s, 1660s, and 1680s all recorded significant incidences of cold. Only two decades seemed to have escaped the cold: the 1640s and the 1670s. In the latter case, evidence regarding harvest yields that we will examine later in this chapter too suggests that the 1670s were warm. But the 1640s are more problematic, for we cannot be sure why the documentary sources record no cold periods. On the one hand, there may have not been any to record; on the other hand, the massive social and political upheavals of the times may have so overshadowed everything else that colder weather may have escaped notice, or chroniclers simply did not record much that did not seem immediately relevant to the wars between the invading Manchu armies and the Ming loyalists. Overall, though, the documentary record is quite clear that the climatic conditions in Lingnan turned colder in the seventeenth century.

Following the cold snap of 1614, two years of drought began with the late harvest of 1616 and continued until the winter wheat harvest in the spring of

[17] Ibid., 173.

1618. The drought affected the most densely populated parts of Guangzhou and Huizhou prefectures, leading to reports of "dearth" (*ji*), "famine" (*da ji*), and "disturbances" in most of the county cities of eastern Guangdong. Additionally, regular outside supplies of grain to Guishan city (Huizhou) dried up, prompting the prefect to organize a small relief effort.[18]

The significance of the climatic turn toward a colder, drier regime around 1614 lies in the impact these conditions had on agricultural yields.[19] Obviously, droughts, especially those that lasted for more than a single year, so seriously slashed harvest yields that the gazetteers glossed those years as times of hunger (*ji*) or famine (*da ji*), both of which I will refer to as "dearth." But more subtly, lower temperatures and less rain also placed downward pressure on harvest yields. Although good data to demonstrate this phenomenon for the seventeenth century are lacking, we do know from better data in the eighteenth century and from modern studies (which I will examine in more detail in Chapter 6) that cool temperatures lower the grain harvest yields by shortening the growing season: for each day the growing season is shortened, the harvest is skimpier.

In upland areas where peasant-farmers planted just one crop, such as in the northern Guangdong hill region, colder temperatures may have had less of an impact than in the double or triple cropping areas to the south. Even in rich alluvial fields of the Pearl River delta, where farmers could get two or three crops, a shortened growing season could force farmers to choose between harvesting a first crop before it was fully ripe to ensure that the second crop could be planted in time for harvesting, or taking the risk that the second crop would not have sufficient time to ripen, and in the next year lowering the risk of frost damage by planting one less crop altogether. As we saw in the preceding chapter, peasant farmers had responded to the possibilities created by the combination of increased demand for their produce and warmer conditions by adding a second or third crop; the return of colder temperatures would have pushed cropping patterns back to single or double cropping. The incidence of harvest failures, food shortages, and dearth thus increased with the onset of colder temperatures in 1614 (see Figure 4.2), peaking in the middle of the century (I will discuss this period in more detail later in the chapter). But declining harvest yields, food shortages, and an increasing incidence of dearth were not the only problems facing the residents of Lingnan in the second quarter of the seventeenth century.

18 *Huizhou fuzhi*, 1877 ed., juan 17.

19 In discussing the effects of the seventeenth-century crisis on Manchuria, Frederic Wakeman speculates that "the pressure upon the Manchus to find new sources of food must have been increased by the growing cold of the 'little ice age,'" which in turn "may have played no small part in spurring the Manchus to military conquest." *The Great Enterprise* (Berkeley and Los Angeles: University of California Press, 1985), 58, 48.

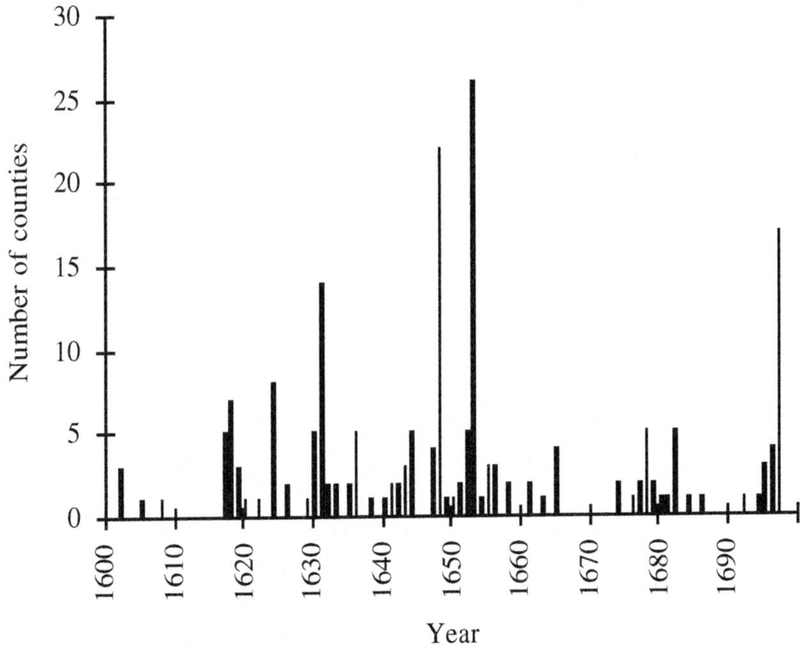

Figure 4.2. Dearth in Guangdong province in the seventeenth century. Source: Compiled from *Guangdong sheng ziran zaihai shiliao* (Guangzhou: Guangdong sheng wenshi yanjiu guan, 1961).

Silver Imports and the Vicissitudes of the International Economy

In the preceding chapter I tied the economic expansion of the mid-sixteenth to mid-seventeenth century to a combination of favorable climatic conditions and foreign demand for Chinese silk and porcelain. If colder temperatures in the early seventeenth century began to constrict agricultural output, so did declining imports of silver hamper the entire economy. That the Lingnan economy had become tied to the silver inflows not just for its expansion and growth but for its very operation can be seen in the aftermath of two disastrous events that severed the trade routes and halted silver imports into Lingnan. In 1639, Japan's Tokugawa Shogunate closed its country and excluded the Portuguese from trading at Nagasaki, thereby destroying the triangular trade route that had enriched Guangdong. And after the Spanish in 1640 massacred 20,000 Chinese in Manila, trade with China through that route dropped off too. These shocks, combined with Chinese hoarding of silver and short-sighted state policies of continuing to collect taxes in silver, substantially reduced the circulation of silver in the Lingnan economy.

Recent work by von Glahn attempts to debunk the thesis that "a sharp fall in silver imports in the 1630s and early 1640s precipitated a monetary crisis that led to the fall of the Ming dynasty in 1644" by arguing (a) that there was not in fact a sharp drop in silver imports, and (b) that the monetary theory (the Fisher equation of exchange) predicting such effects is contradicted by the modern quantity theory of money.[20] Curiously, though, von Glahn's own estimates of silver imports appear to support the case that there was indeed a drop in silver imports: from 572.8 metric tons of silver in the five-year period from 1636 to 1640, to 248.6 metric tons over the years from 1641 to 1645, a drop of over 40 percent.[21] So perhaps the decline in silver imports did affect the economy after all, as Atwell suggests. Certainly, though, this is a very complex issue that cannot be resolved here.

Suffice it to say that, for whatever causes, in Guangdong at least, foreign trade fell sharply, and according to at least one official, money became scarce, as Atwell argues. In a 1647 memorial requesting permission to reestablish the international trade links, the Qing official Tong Yangjia offered his explanation for the economic troubles:

> In the former dynasty [i.e., the Ming] the goods of China and of foreign countries were exchanged and circulated via Guangdong. While the [traders of the] foreign ships and the native merchant princes competed with one another in business, the people were benefited . . . In no year was there a shortage of money.
>
> Later . . . incidents occurred involving the murder of soldiers. Thereupon . . . the Portuguese were no longer allowed in Guangzhou . . . as had been the custom of old. These events occurred in the thirteenth year of Chongzhen (1640) of the former dynasty.
>
> Before long the Chinese merchants were drained of money; goods no longer circulated, the people became impoverished, and the customs duties collected were reduced to little more than 1,000 taels. Thus, it was clearly demonstrated that if the [Portuguese] come to trade, Guangdong profits; but if they do not come, then Guangdong is impoverished.[22]

Although Tong wrongly attributed the decline in commerce solely to the isolation of the Portuguese in Macao, the disruption he noted was unmistakable. With trade severed and silver no longer flowing into Guangdong, not only merchants but others involved in the trade lost their jobs, and unemployed sailors, teamsters, and carters – no longer plying the trade routes up the

20 Von Glahn, "Myth and Reality," 1.

21 Ibid., Table 5. Von Glahn dismisses the impact of this drop by saying that the amount was such a minute amount compared with the accumulated stocks of silver in the Chinese monetary system that it could not have affected price levels.

22 Memorial from Tong Yangjia dated Shunzhi 4.5.3, translated in Fu Lo-shu, *A Documentary Chronicle of Sino-Western Relations (1644–1820)* (Tucson: University of Arizona Press, 1966), vol. 1, 6–7. I have changed Fu's Wade–Giles romanization to pinyin.

North River and through the Meiling Pass – flocked into Guangzhou looking for work, food, or victims. The unemployed also swelled the ranks of bandit gangs, enabling one enterprising leader to pull together a force of 10,000 in 1646.[23]

Banditry and Piracy

Perhaps the economy had begun to slow down as early as the 1620s, for this is the period when local gazetteers begin to make mention of renewed bandit and pirate activities that continued right through the fall of the Ming and for another 20 years into the Qing. The 1620s inaugurated an era of food shortages nearly every 3 or 4 years, accompanied by rising rice prices, reports of famine, and urban disturbances, as well as significant bandit activity. Bandit gangs were most prevalent in several areas of Guangdong province: to the southwest of Guangzhou in Xinhui, Xining, Xiangshan counties; to the north and northeast of Guangzhou in Zengcheng, Conghua, and Longmen counties; in coastal Huizhou prefecture, and in Xin'an county in Guangzhou prefecture to the south of the city of Guangzhou; throughout the hill country along the East River; and in the border region where Guangdong, Fujian, and Jiangxi provinces joined. Bandits may have operated elsewhere as well, but the gazetteers for other areas are not nearly as complete or detailed as those for Guangzhou and Huizhou prefectures.

The size of the bands increased steadily. At first operating in bands reported to be in the hundreds, the ranks of the bandit groups swelled year by year until by the 1630s the bands numbered in the thousands, and groups of 10 or more gangs cooperated to muster tens of thousands of bandits. Targets initially were limited to defenseless villages or market towns,[24] but as the bands grew in size so too did their needs and their targets, until cooperating bands raided or besieged cities in all of the counties just mentioned.[25] Simultaneously, thousands of miners, ironmongers, and charcoal burners in Conghua county began various actions that the authorities variously labeled "uprisings" (*qi*) or "disturbances" (*luan*) beginning with strikes (*ba gong*) in 1623.[26] Complicating matters further, river pirates in the Pearl River estuary and delta, especially in Shunde county, and pirates on the high seas began attacking coastal towns.[27]

By the late 1630s, the bandits, pirates, and miners had marshaled sufficient forces to cooperate on a large scale and, with the collapse of the Ming dynasty in 1644, began besieging county towns such as Xinhui, Xiangshan, Longmen, and Zengcheng, looting county treasuries and chasing away or killing offi-

[23] See the entry for 1646 (Shunzhi 3) in *Xinhui xianzhi*, juan 13.
[24] For example, as in 1628 in Sanshui county. *Guangzhou fuzhi*, 1879 ed., juan 79: 11a.
[25] Ibid., 10a. [26] Ibid., 9a–b. [27] Ibid., 14b.

cials.[28] As the bandits grew in strength and perhaps in ambition too, they attacked military posts.[29] In the countryside, bandit depredations took on the appearance of class warfare as gentry and other wealthy people were marked for abduction or murder.[30]

The authorities and local gentry did what they could to stem the rising tide of bandit activity, and sometimes they were successful, but mostly they were not. Walls had been built around most county and prefectural cities in the mid-1500s, when an earlier high tide of bandit activity prompted defensive measures. By 1640 the abilities of the bandits to besiege cities and overcome their defenses led to a general order (at least in Huizhou prefecture) to reinforce city walls.[31] Beyond these purely defensive measures, the ability of the state to mobilize resources to protect itself against the bandits was limited, especially when compared with state actions in the 1550s. Then, the state mounted aggressive military campaigns involving upwards of 30,000 troops and continuing for nearly a decade to suppress bandits. By the 1630s, the most the state could muster were detachments of a few hundred soldiers to go against the much larger bandit armies. That the military would be ineffective appeared plain to local elites. Where the local gentry had not already been driven away or killed, local leaders formed militia (*tuan lian*) under their command. Some of these gentry-led militia were successful – as in Longmen in 1631[32] or in Xingning in 1651[33] – but by and large, bandits had the upper hand. Indeed, the success of the gentry-led militia in Longmen and Xingning was the exceptional case, just as it was in Tongcheng county in the lower Yangzi at the same time.[34]

The Turning Point in 1644

Declining harvest yields caused by the onset of a cooler climate, the crash of the export-driven economic boom, and the unchecked growth of banditry (which may be seen in part as a consequence of the former two developments), by themselves or perhaps even taken all together, did not constitute the general crisis of the mid-seventeenth century in Lingnan. Indeed, one might imagine such a situation perduring, as perhaps the people living at the time feared. But

[28] Ibid., juan 80: 5a–b. As early as 1630, bandits had beseiged Yong'an, in the upper reaches of the East River. *Huizhou fuzhi*, 1688 ed., juan 5: 10a.

[29] *Huizhou fuzhi*, 1877 ed., juan 17: 49b.

[30] As in 1639 and 1641 in Haifeng county. Ibid., 48b and 49b.

[31] Ibid., 46b.

[32] *Guangzhou fuzhi*, 1879 ed., juan 79: 9b.

[33] *Huizhou fuzhi*, 1877 ed., juan 17: 55b.

[34] Hillary Beattie, "The Alternative to Resistance: The Case of T'ung-ch'eng, Anhwei," in Jonathan D. Spence and John E. Wills Jr., eds., *From Ming to Ch'ing: Conquest, Region, and Continuity in Seventeenth-Century China* (New Haven: Yale University Press, 1979), 239–76.

what happened instead was that the political crisis occasioned by the fall of the Ming and the establishment of the new Qing dynasty in 1644 galvanized these trends into a massive social upheaval and a demographic crisis.

In early 1644, the north China rebel leader Li Zicheng assembled 200,000 of his peasant army for a final campaign against the Ming dynasty and in April entered Beijing, the imperial capital. The last Ming emperor, Chongzhen, hanged himself, and for all practical purposes the Ming dynasty ended with him. But in an amazing twist of fate, when Li Zicheng soon thereafter left Beijing in an attempt to destroy the last Ming army that posed a threat to him, non-Chinese Manchu armies poured south through the Great Wall, occupied Beijing, proclaimed the establishment of a new dynasty, the Qing, and then set about to destroy Li Zicheng's army (which they did within a year) and to chase down the last claimants to the Ming throne (which took another 17 years).

Qing armies did not arrive in Lingnan until late 1646, more than two years after the new dynasty had been proclaimed. Moreover, because of the chaos, the troops had to retake the south once again in 1650. In the meantime, anarchy reigned. Some, perhaps most, of the Ming officials remained in their posts, either declaring for the new dynasty or remaining loyal to the Ming "court" (which had established itself up the West River from Guangzhou in the prefectural town of Zhaoqing), but in any event remaining at their posts; others just walked away. Ming army commanders, who actually commanded few troops, stood their ground trying to decide what to do or made common cause with bandits in ensuring their own survival. Many naval units joined with the pirates they had been charged with controlling. Within any six-month period, many may have taken on any or all of these roles consecutively or simultaneously, so fluid was the situation. Rival camps of Ming claimants engaged in what Struve aptly calls "fratricidal competition,"[35] and to top it all off, the first commander of Qing troops to take Guangdong in 1646, Li Chengdong, "turned" to the Ming in 1648 after being treated shabbily by the Manchus.

If all of this sounds confusing, it was. But it was not the whole of it, either. Political authority was nonexistent, and military might was fragmented. In some areas, local gentry had established self-defense corps to protect themselves and their local areas. But where opposing forces were weak or nonexistent, a new and powerful force began to shake south China: militant peasant uprisings.

The most ferocious and tenacious of these occurred in the Pearl River delta counties, especially in Xinhui, Xinxing, and Xiangshan, but extending west into Gaoyao and north to Qingyuan counties too, where a large number of people who had been held in bondage to their lords and had served them either

[35] Lynn Struve, *The Southern Ming, 1644–1662* (New Haven: Yale University Press, 1984), 101.

in the home or in the fields (as *nu pu* or *dian pu*) rose up in early 1645. The uprisings began in Shunde, but soon spread west to Xinhui and then as far north as Qingyuan. Dubbed the "Associated Bandits" (*she zei*), these former bondservants and servile tenants "killed or chased away their lords and seized the land and houses; the most extreme took [a lord's] wives and children [as prisoners or for their own], and defiled their ancestral graves."[36] According to the Xinhui gazetteer, the Associated Bandits held fast for 20 years, until the early 1660s.[37]

After killing the gentry (the *xiang shen*, *gong sheng*, and *sheng yüan*), the Associated Bandits took towns in Xinhui and Xiangshan counties and probably established some form of political/military structure. Direct evidence for how they were organized is lacking, but the fact that they were called "Associated" and that they then held the regions they had occupied for another decade attests to some organizational ability. And so thorough were they in exterminating their masters and their families that it was not until the 1730s that these counties were resettled and land brought back into production. The bondservants were not the only ones to rise up after the Ming had fallen. In counties all along the eastern coast of Guangdong, peasants (who seem more to fit the classification of tenants) stopped paying rent and taxes and chased away anyone who tried to collect. While not killing their landlords, these acts of defiance too contributed to the social disorder.[38]

In short, in the years immediately following the fall of the Ming dynasty in 1644, a bewildering array of armed groups fighting each other and wanting to extend the area under their control occupied south China: bandits who had grown so numerous as to develop a military-like organization; river pirates and pirates on the high seas; peasant armies organized as the Associated Bandits; former Ming troops who swung between the various Ming contenders, bandits, or the Qing; self-defense corps commanded by gentry-cum-strongmen; Qing armies; turncoat Qing armies; and even, believe it or not, at one point a remnant of Li Zicheng's army.

These armies were not constantly on the move, and fighting among them was episodic. But when armies marched and battles took shape, the results were quite devastating. In Lingnan, the heaviest fighting occurred twice, in 1647 and in 1650, with sporadic "mopping up" campaigns against bandits and Ming loyalists continuing until the mid-1650s. In 1647, the fighting centered in and around the Pearl River delta and involved the Ming loyalists' resistance to Qing rule. The loyalist forces, led by three gentry from the counties around Guangzhou, included some remnant Ming troops but mostly bandits and river

36 Xie Guozhen, *Ming Qing zhi ji dang she yundong* (Taibei: Shangwu yinshu guan, 1967), 277.

37 *Xinhui xianzhi*, 1841 ed., juan 13, entry for 1645 (Shunzhi 2).

38 Fu Yiling, *Ming Qing nongcun shehui jingji* (Xiamen: Shiyong shuju, 1961), 104–45. See also Marks, *Rural Revolution in South China*, ch. 1.

pirates; significantly, the loyalists' troops were not comprised of local self-defense corps. From March through November 1647, the loyalists' armies tried to take county cities all the way from Xin'an in the south to Qingyuan in the north, including an ill-fated siege of Guangzhou itself in August. To counter the loyalists, Qing armies commanded by Li Chengdong marched back and forth throughout the province in the summer "like sweeping leaves in an autumn courtyard."[39] In October and November, the Qing armies isolated the loyalists in Qingyuan and Zengcheng counties and defeated them in major battles; two leaders were captured and executed, while a third committed suicide.

The Demographic Crisis of 1648–53

For the people of Lingnan, 1647 was disastrous. If it is true that an army on the march lives on its stomach, then it is equally true that it forages among the people as it moves. After the depredations of war that engulfed Guangdong during the 1647 growing season, gazetteers record 1648 as a "famine" year, with such reports spread from the easternmost reaches of the province to the westernmost and everywhere in between; few areas were spared. Rice prices rose to 800 wen per *dou*, a price probably 10 times normal and certainly out of reach for any but the wealthiest. In Gaozhou prefecture to the west of Guangzhou, "countless died of starvation."[40] In Xin'an county to the south, "many died of starvation. There was cannibalism; people were sold for food. A major epidemic [hit]; bandits [appeared]. Half the people fled or died. In some villages no one was left."[41]

The epidemic was located primarily to the south and east of Guangzhou, from Huizhou prefecture south to Xin'an; these were areas torn by the fighting between the Ming loyalists and the Qing troops commanded by Li Chengdong. Records from other areas devastated by the Qing troops, especially Qingyuan to the north and Zhaoqing to the west, are at best spotty; those areas too may have had epidemics, but no documents exist to attest either way. What kind of epidemic it was is not at all clear, since the chronicles used the general term "epidemic" (*yi*) to gloss what happened. We can be quite certain that the epidemic was not smallpox. Smallpox was so well known that when it was the cause of the epidemic, it was explicitly labeled *dou yi*. In 1657, for instance, a smallpox outbreak was reported in Jieyang county, along with the variolation techniques for protecting children.[42] Neither did the chroniclers mistake death

[39] Li Chengdong, quoted in Struve, *The Southern Ming*, 124.

[40] Excerpted in *Guangdong sheng ziran zaihai shiliao*, 201.

[41] *Xin'an xianzhi*, 1819 ed., xia juan: 50.

[42] The entry for Shunzhi 14 (1657) includes the following note: "Spring, first month; smallpox. Families engaged doctors to prick the variola and gather scabs. A diluted mixture of the scabs

by starvation for death by epidemic disease, since both kinds of deaths are mentioned separately. And given the coincidence of the epidemic with famine conditions, the epidemic probably was not any of the other contagious diseases so virulent they could spread among an otherwise healthy and well-nourished population. But certainly, simple malnutrition, let alone famine conditions, weakens resistance to any disease.

Whatever the epidemic disease was, it was associated with the Qing troops in one way or another. Prior to 1648, the last mention of an epidemic in the local gazetteers was in 1589–90, when an epidemic killed both animals and people. From then until 1648 when Qing troops pursued Ming loyalists into various parts of Guangdong, no epidemic disease worthy of the name *yi* was mentioned. The Qing troops could have been responsible for the epidemic in two ways, either directly spreading an infection brought from north China or indirectly spreading it by creating conditions conducive to an epidemic.

Qing troops may well have brought an epidemic disease with them as they marched south in 1644–46. The Qing troops were commanded by Li Chengdong, the same general who had suppressed the Jiading loyalists in the Yangzi River delta in 1644–45. As Helen Dunstan has shown, the epidemics that hit that region in 1641 and 1644–44 included dysentery and possibly plague.[43] Given the timing and location of the epidemics in Guangdong, it is possible that the disease – whatever it was – was spread by Qing troops.

Even the death and destruction alone may have created conditions conducive to epidemic disease. According to the Spanish friar Juan de Palafox y Mendoza, who composed a history of the Manchu conquest while in Manila from documents brought to him there:

> [Manchu] outrages could not be committed without frequent Murders and Massacres throughout the whole Countrey; and these were so numerous that the description of the desolation of this Province would require a whole history. The putrid bodies did so infest the Air, that it occasioned a cruel Plague . . . the richest, plentifullest, and most delicious Province in China, lay most dismally ruined . . . and so it remains to this very day (in the 1660s).[44]

Another possibility is that the epidemic was associated with the famine conditions. The famine itself, though, no doubt was caused by the depredations of war, not "natural causes" such as drought or floods. While some counties in Chaozhou prefecture recorded drought conditions and high grain prices,

was stuffed up children's noses to induce [a mild case of smallpox]. After this, none died young." *Chaozhou fuzhi*, 1762 ed., juan 10, 28a.

[43] Helen Dunstan, "The Late Ming Epidemics: A Preliminary Study," *Ch'ing shih wen't'i* 3, no. 3 (Nov. 1975): 1–59.

[44] Juan de Palafox y Mendoza, *The History of the Conquest of China by the Tartars* (London, 1671), 320.

those were not the areas hardest hit by famine and epidemic: the areas visited by troops were. The populations left with little or no food by pilfering troops no doubt turned to unsafe supplies for sustenance, including roots and leaves, carrion, diseased human flesh, and polluted water supplies. These are conditions ripe for dysentery.

That Qing troops formed the link between famine and epidemic disease in 1648 thus seems clear enough. It is also clear that the combination of war, starvation, and disease produced a mortality peak in 1648–49. And it was not yet over, for the tale of woe continued for another five years. The second round was precipitated by the Qing general Li Chengdong. Li had crushed both the Jiangnan and the Guangdong loyalists – bringing for the Manchus the bounty of both of these very rich areas within their grasp – and had expected adequate recognition from the Manchus for doing so. When he felt not properly rewarded for his valuable services, in May 1648 Li declared for the Ming and constrained the civilian governor to go along with him. This act of defiance necessitated a second Qing conquest of south China. The opportunity came a year later when Li was killed trying to extend help to another Ming contingent in Nanchang. In June 1649, Qing troops began moving on Guangdong and Guangxi provinces in two columns from the north. In February 1650 the Ming loyalist court fled up the West River to Wuzhou, while Qing forces moved slowly and deliberately into positions around Guangzhou, which they then besieged for over eight months beginning in March.

When the siege of Guangzhou was broken toward the end of November 1650, Qing troops swept through the city, and for 18 days slaughtered the civilian population. A Jesuit priest described what happened:

> This courage [of the people of Guangzhou in the defense of their city] made the Tartars fall upon a resolution of beating down the walls of the city with their great cannon, which had such an effect that they took it on the 24th of November, 1650 . . . The next day they began to plunder the city; and the sackage continued till the 5th of December, in which they neither spared man, woman, or child; but all whoever came in their way were cruelly put to the sword; nor was there heard any other speech, but kill, – kill these barbarous rebels. Yet they spared some artificers to conserve the necessary arts, as also some strong and lusty men, such as they saw able to carry away the pillage of the city. But finally, December 6th, came out an edict which forbade all further vexation, after they had killed a hundred thousand men, besides those that perished during the siege.[45]

The Dutch estimated that 80,000 died, while Bowra cites unnamed Chinese sources that put the total killed at several hundred thousand.[46] Regardless of

[45] Martin Martini, quoted in E. C. Bowra, "The Manchu Conquest of Canton," *China Review* 1 (1872–73): 91–92.

[46] Ibid., 93.

the actual numbers, it is clear that Guangzhou was devastated and largely depopulated in 1650.

Whatever immediate impact this round of war had on the people of Lingnan is not clear, since the chronicles are silent. But when a typhoon and flood struck Guangdong in 1651 followed by drought in 1652, the weakened and devastated region was plunged into famine once again. This time, though, while reports of famine (*ji* or *da ji)* were as widespread as in the disaster of 1648, the reports of people starving to death and of epidemics came from parts of Guangdong province spared in 1648. In the areas devastated in 1648, most gazetteers reported "only" very high grain prices and people "eating roots and leaves."[47] But on Hainan Island, rice prices reached three taels per *dou*, and there were "too many dead to count. Land is abandoned and few people have returned."[48] In Xiangshan county, "masses died."[49] Epidemics were reported in Gaozhou prefecture[50] and up the West River from Guangzhou in Wuzhou prefecture in Guangxi.[51]

The combined effect of these disasters, of course, was to reduce the size of the human population. I will reconstruct population figures for the whole region a bit later, after I document even more disruption. But for now let me note that the major demographic shock to Lingnan clearly came in the years from 1648 to 1653. During those years, Xin'an county reported, for example, that "half the people fled or died," and Huizhou prefecture reported (in 1652) that in Guishan county (where the prefectural city was situated), "originally the county had 37 *li*. But in successive years of war, famine, and epidemics, many people died, leaving just 24 *li*."[52] Assuming that each *li* contained approximately the same number of families, this represented a 35 percent decline in the population.

While the mortality crisis was caused by the combination of famine and epidemic disease, separating out the causal relationships among famine, disease, and mortality is fraught with difficulty. Contemporary chroniclers seemed to be quite certain in separating out death from starvation and death from epidemic disease: "Many died of starvation," they noted. But modern studies of famine and starvation cast doubt on these certainties.[53] John Post, who has studied these problems extensively in his most recent work on

47 See the entries for 1648 in *Huizhou fuzhi* and *Huilai xianzhi*.

48 Entry for SZ9 (1652), in *Qiongzhou fuzhi*, 1841 ed., juan 42.

49 Entry for SZ9 (1652), in *Xiangshan xianzhi*, 1750 ed., juan 8.

50 Entry for SZ10 (1653), in *Gaozhou fuzhi*, 1827 ed., juan 4.

51 Entry for SZ10 (1653), in *Guangxi tongzhi*, 1733 ed., juan on *ji xiang*.

52 Entry for SZ9 (1652), in *Huizhou fuzhi*, 1877 ed.

53 For a discussion of the "synergies" of the "coincidence" of climatic variability and famine with epidemic disease, see John Walter and Roger Schofield, "Famine, Disease and Crisis Mortality in Early Modern Society," in John Walter and Roger Schofield eds., *Famine, Disease and Crisis Mortality in Early Modern Society* (Cambridge University Press, 1989), esp. 17–21.

eighteenth-century Europe, concludes that "medical opinion today is that starvation is rarely an ascertainable cause of death."[54] Post distinguishes "starvation" from "prolonged undernutrition" and notes that the latter has symptoms in common with dysentery, including bloody diarrhea. Dysentery, furthermore, is spread in times of drought when people drink from muddied or contaminated water sources.[55] Thus, in 1648 and 1652–53 when contemporaries attributed elevated mortality levels to starvation, they may have instead been chronicling dysentery or any of numerous other diseases abetted by malnutrition.

Whatever the ultimate causes of death, Lingnan in 1648 and 1652–53 was in the depths of a mortality crisis attended by, if not caused by, a subsistence crisis. Subsistence crises also reduced fertility until such time as families had more confidence in the future and decided to invest in additional children. Unfortunately, we have no way of even estimating how low fertility dropped during these years of crisis: Did the population even manage a replacement rate, or did fertility fall so low as to precipitate a slow population decline after the crisis years of 1648–53? When reconstructing population figures I will have to make some educated guesses, and because political and economic stability was not reestablished for another 30 years, mine will favor very low fertility rates continuing until 1683.

Relocation of the Coastal Population, 1661–69

The population of south China had little – if any – time to recover from over a decade of war before the Qing embarked upon another stage in its consolidation of power, a stage that, like the first, devastated the people of Lingnan. While the Qing armies had found success on land, control of the high seas and the coastal regions had eluded them. The nominally Ming loyalist Zheng Chenggong (Koxinga) had free run of the southeastern coast and, in fact, even established bases in Fujian province. From there, Zheng ran a massive trading operation, even setting up his own customs houses in the interior of Fujian to regulate trade and collect taxes, besides opposing Qing forces and occasionally battling them. His forces and his presence were not insubstantial threats to Qing power: in 1659 he had mounted an offensive and even threatened to take Nanjing.

In early 1661, as part of a general "get tough" approach to ruling China, the regents for the new Kangxi emperor devised a policy to defeat Zheng Chenggong by severing his ties with the coastal population. To do so, the regents ordered the relocation of the entire coastal population from Zhejiang

[54] John D. Post, *Food Shortage, Climatic Variability, and Epidemic Disease in Preindustrial Europe: The Mortality Peak in the Early 1740s* (Ithaca: Cornell University Press, 1985), 216.

[55] Ibid., 261.

south to the border with Vietnam inland some 50 *li* (about 17 miles), with the intent of creating a swathe of deserted wasteland. And to ensure that the policy was implemented in Guangdong, the regents dispatched two Manchu officials to the province.

Perhaps because of the destructiveness of the implementation of this order from their new Manchu overlords, Chinese sources do not provide much information on what actually happened. Entries in all of the local gazetteers from Chaozhou down to Gaozhou indicate that the order was carried out; in at least two instances (Haifeng county and Gaozhou prefecture) the relocation took place in two stages, first removing the population 30 *li* inland, and then a year or two later the full 50 *li*. At the very least then, the policy was implemented, with the population forcibly relocated inland. Barriers, guard posts, and watchtowers then went up to keep the area devoid of human habitation. A contemporary Spanish source based in the Philippines alleges that the population was not merely relocated, but that the coast was laid waste in "the greatest conflagration and havoc that the world has seen."[56] Another source claims that those who had not relocated by the deadline were "butchered."[57] While it is not known how many in Guangdong lost their lives during the relocation, in Fujian 8,500 were reported to have died.[58]

The barricades remained up and the populace kept away from the coast until 1669, following approval of a memorial from the Guangdong's governor Wang Lairen asking that the policy be rescinded. Governor Wang cited numerous reasons for lifting the ban, including the fact that coastal defenses had been strengthened. In fact, he said, in the two years since he had become governor there had not been a single attack by pirates, but instead people displaced by the relocation order had joined inland bandits, and *they* had become a problem. Indeed, the people of Xinhui county who had been relocated were labeled "the relocated people" and in 1668 were accused of "rebellion."[59] Additionally, the cost of maintaining the barricades was prohibitive, Wang said, amounting to 2.5 million taels annually; the salt gabelle yielded only half that. The cost in materials and labor in constructing and maintaining the watchtowers and barricades was also incalculable. Finally, Wang argued, the forced relocation of hundreds of thousands of people left the land uncultivated so the state lost over 300,000 taels in land taxes.[60]

Coupled with a second edict issued in early 1662 prohibiting all coastal navigation in general and trade with Zheng Chenggong in particular, the reloca-

[56] Diaz, cited in Fu, *A Documentary Chronicle of Sino-Western Relations*, vol. 2: 441, n. 163.

[57] See Bowra, "The Manchu Conquest of Canton," 229.

[58] *Da Qing sheng zu (Kangxi) shi lu.*, cited in Lawrence D. Kessler, *K'ang-shi and the Consolidation of Ch'ing Rule, 1661–1684* (Chicago: University of Chicago Press, 1976), 43.

[59] *Xinhui xianzhi*, 1841 ed., juan 13, 44a.

[60] Wang Lairen's memorial is reprinted in *Guangzhou fuzhi*, 1879 ed., juan 80: 26b–28a.

tion policy had its intended effect of cutting Zheng's supply lines. As an imperial edict put it:

> He has no land on which to produce the wherewithal to maintain human life; the grain, rice, iron, the ship-building timber and other materials are all products from the mainland. . . . In the past . . . merchants and peddlers brought goods of every kind from the interior to the bandits. . . . Since the coastal inhabitants have all moved into the interior, defence [*sic*] and supervision [of the ban on navigation] will be easy. We will no longer allow any one to be as negligent as before.[61]

A measure of the success of the removal of the coastal population and the ban on navigation and coastal trade was Zheng Chenggong's decision in 1661 to abandon the mainland and base his operations on Taiwan, which he then forcibly seized from the Dutch.[62]

The "Shu Huang" of the 1670s

Of course, from the perspective of merchants, traders, and even peasant-producers of grain, the successful isolation of Zheng Chenggong from his mainland sources meant that commerce, and with it the wealth it generated, slumped, a situation that continued until coastal trade was reopened in 1683. As a gazetteer entry for Jieyang county explained: "Peasants [only] till the land and have no other work. Grain was too cheap because bandits and pirates blocked trade."[63] The economic slowdown in the coastal provinces of Guangdong, Fujian, Zhejiang, and even into Jiangxi was so severe that one historian has labeled the period from 1661 to 1683 the "Kangxi depression."[64] In her analysis of the "depression," Kishimoto-Nakayama focuses on the decline in the amount of silver circulating as currency and the depressing effect that had on prices.[65]

The decline in prices during this period was general, affecting not just manufactured goods, wages, rents, and land values, but grain prices as well. The decline in grain prices, though, was caused in part by factors independent of the crash in commerce and the withdrawal of silver from circulation. Where

[61] Imperial edict of SZ18.12.18, translated in Fu, *A Documentary Chronicle*, vol. 1: 28–30.

[62] Zheng Chengdong died shortly afterwards, but his family and his forces remained in control of Taiwan until Qing forces finally conquered them in 1683.

[63] *Chaozhou fuzhi*, 1893 ed., juan 11: 31a.

[64] Mio Kishimoto-Nakayama, "The Kangxi Depression and Early Qing Local Markets," *Late Imperial China*, 10 no. 2 (Apr. 1984): 227–56. See also Atwell, "Some Observations on the 'Seventeenth-Century Crisis' in China and Japan," 234.

[65] Besides the anti-Zheng measures, Kishimoto-Nakayama attributes the withdrawal of silver from circulation to the short-sighted state retrenchment policy of collecting taxes in silver and accumulating treasury reserves rather than placing the taxes back into circulation through state spending.

contemporaries blamed the economic slowdown on the scarcity of silver, the collapse of grain prices was termed a *shu huang*, which might best be translated as "dearth in the midst of plenty."[66]

Before analyzing the *shu huang*, let me begin by describing it. The term was used in the counties of Chaozhou prefecture to describe the oversupply and extremely low price of grain in the 1670s. In Jieyang county, the local gazetteer recorded for 1670: "At this time prices were so low they harmed the peasants, who called it a *shu huang* . . . One tael could purchase 25 *shi* of white rice or 30 *shi* of red rice."[67] In Chaoyang that same year, "there were no boats to conduct trade. One tael could buy 30 *shi* of rice."[68] In nearby Haifeng county, "one *dou* (a tenth of a *shi*) went for three fen (one-hundredth of a tael)."[69] Extremely low prices prevailed throughout Guangdong province. In Huizhou, Guangzhou, Gaozhou, and Zhaoqing prefectures, rice was plentiful and cheap too. In Fujian province, the phenomenon of the extremely low prices lasted until the early 1680s.[70]

To assess just how low these grain prices were, it is helpful to put them into a broader context. First, converting them to the same scale, the reported prices of the *shu huang* were 0.04 to 0.05 tael (liang) per *shi*. Those prices contrast to a price of 0.35–0.40 in 1600,[71] 4.00–5.00 in the crisis year of 1648, and 0.80–0.90 in 1708. The lowest grain prices recorded for the eighteenth century, in 1729, were 0.40–0.60 taels per *shi*. In other words, grain prices during the *shu huang* of the 1670s were one-tenth the lowest price experienced in the eighteenth century, and one-tenth that of 1600.

The causes for the collapse in rice prices are not hard to find, and observers at the time clearly understood at least some of them. First was the severing of trade routes precipitated by Zheng Chenggong's activities and the "relocation of the coastal population." As the Chaoyang gazetteer recorded: "At the time no boats could conduct trade, so rice became too cheap."[72] The Jieyang gazetteer explained it a bit differently: "In Jieyang, [the people] only farmed; there were no other occupations. The reason rice was cheap was that bandits and pirates had closed off the trade routes."[73]

A second reason for the low prices was a succession of very good harvests. As noted at the beginning of this chapter, the seventeenth century was gener-

[66] For an overview, see Chen Zhiping, "Shilun Kangxi chunian dongnan zhu sheng de 'shu huang,' " *Zhongguo shehui jingji shi yanjiu* 2 (1982): 40–46.

[67] *Chaozhou fuzhi*, 1893 ed., juan 11: 31a.

[68] Ibid., 15a.

[69] *Huizhou fuzhi*, 1688 ed., juan 5: 30b.

[70] *Haicheng xianzhi*, juan 18, extracted in Chen Zhiping, " 'Shu huang,' " 40.

[71] See the "memorandum of the detailed selling prices at Canton" in 1600 printed in C. R. Boxer, *The Great Ship from Amacon: Annals of Macao and the Old Japan Trade, 1555–1640* (Lisboa: Centro de Estudos Historicos Ultramarinos, 1963), 184.

[72] *Chaozhou fuzhi*, 1893 ed. [73] Entry for KX10 in ibid.

ally colder than the sixteenth century, with a few exceptions: the decade of the 1670s was one. During the early 1660s, Guangdong experienced drought conditions in one part or another of the province; beginning in 1668, though, the region had seven years of good harvests. The end of the series of droughts certainly improved yields, but the temperature turned warmer too. From 1669 through 1680, there was just one instance of cold (in 1672), and the incidences of drought and flood both decreased. With better climatic conditions, gazetteers throughout much of Guangdong province gloss many of these years as "good years" (*you nian*) or "extremely good years" (*da you nian*). Simply put, in the 1670s climatic conditions were very favorable, resulting in higher yields and bigger harvests than the existing demand could absorb, leading to the *shu huang*.

Understandably, the low grain prices did not benefit the peasant producers. And the state policy of collecting taxes – and of collecting them in silver – only made matters worse. According to the Jieyang gazetteer, "with such low grain prices, peasant-farmers could not pay taxes or support their families, thus much land was abandoned."[74] Even the urban poor suffered in the Kangxi depression. According to Wei Jirui, a secretary of the governor of Zhejiang writing in 1675, when rice prices were high, the rich had money to hire laborers and buy things; but in the 1670s, with grain prices just one-half to one-third of what they had been, the rich had become impoverished, and the poor could not find food.[75] Even with cheap grain prices, "many people [in Jiangxi] died of starvation. Casual laborers and petty peddlers say they like it when grain prices are high because the rich have money, can buy goods and employ laborers. [Only in such circumstances are] the poor able to earn a profitable living."[76] Sayings expressing the mood of the time included the following: "Merchants exchange only bitterness [not goods]" (*shang min jiao ku*) and "The rich become poor; the poor die" (*fuzhe pin; pinzhe si*).[77]

The evidence thus supports the contention that in the 1670s at least, the economy stalled to the point that peasants once again abandoned land rather than pay taxes. Whether depressed conditions continued into the early 1680s, as Kishimoto-Nakayama contends, and whether mortality levels among the urban poor were elevated even with the extremely low grain prices, as the contemporary Wei Jirui alleges, simply are not apparent from available sources.

But like flowers blossoming in the ashes of a wildfire, the *shu huang* of the 1670s foretold the end of the crisis years. Grain was plentiful and prices were low not just because production had resumed, but also because the number of people living in Lingnan had declined (by how much I will attempt to estimate

[74] Quoted in Chen, " 'Shu huang,' " 42. [75] Ibid., 44–45.

[76] Wei Jirui quoted in Kishimoto-Nakayama, "The Kangxi Depression," 231–32.

[77] Chen, " 'Shu huang,' " 45.

in the next section) and because the trade routes that had begun linking the various separate ecosystems of Lingnan into a single larger system had been severed. Grain was not shipped from the West River basin in Guangxi down to the Pearl River delta to farmers who could not sell or export their silk; neither did grain flow from eastern Guangdong to Fujian. But even if local areas had to become more self-sufficient and not rely on food imports, at least the wars, the killing, and the epidemics had stopped. The population may have declined and the land abandoned, but with the *shu huang*, the end of the crisis was in sight – but not yet over.

The End of the Crisis Years

The "revolt of the three feudatories" from 1673–81 inaugurated another period of political and military instability in Lingnan. The story of the revolt has been told elsewhere and will not be repeated here. Suffice it to say that little actual fighting occurred in Lingnan, and even then it was limited to a brief period in 1677–78.[78] Despite the initial threat of the revolt to challenge Qing rule throughout China south of the Yangzi, through a combination of rebel perfidy and uncertainty, unflinching leadership from the Kangxi emperor, and war weariness of the people, the rebels either surrendered or were defeated. By 1681, the feudatories and their privileges, including fiscal, military, and administrative autonomy from the imperial court, had been eliminated, replaced with an administrative structure appointed by the center.

In 1683, the final obstacle to the consolidation of Qing rule was removed when Zheng Chengkong's surviving family and followers surrendered themselves and Taiwan to Qing forces. The disruption to the society and economy of the continued existence of the Zheng family forces on Taiwan came not so much from military depredations, but from the Qing enforcement of the ban on maritime navigation and coastal trade. When in 1678 Zhang Zhixin, then the governor of Guangdong, requested relaxation of the coastal ban "to allow the merchants to construct ships and trade from Guangzhou to Qiongzhou as they please," the Kangxi emperor replied: "Now if We reopen navigation and order merchants to trade freely, We fear that the treacherous people may take this opportunity to communicate with the bandits [the Zheng family] and disturb the people on the seacoasts . . . This prohibition should

[78] When Shang Kexi, the general who had been given virtual possession of Guangdong province and the title Prince Pacifier of the South (*ping nan wang*) for having taken and sacked Guangzhou in 1650, became ill and died in early 1677, his son Zhixin took command and declared his alliance with Wu Sangui. Further fighting occurred when Wu Sangui sent troops into Guangxi and from the north into Guangdong, reaching as far as Shaozhou against his nominal, or former, allies.

not be rescinded too quickly."[79] After Qing forces took Taiwan in late 1683, the ban on coastal navigation and trade was lifted, and four maritime customs posts were established, one of which was in Macao, to reopen trade with Europeans.

Population and Cultivated Land

With the suppression of the three feudatories and the reopening of the coast to normal trade in 1684, a 40-year period of political and military turmoil, of economic dislocation, and of demographic disaster in Lingnan came to an end. The story that has been told in this chapter certainly indicates that those 40 years took a substantial toll, and suggests both that the population declined substantially and that considerable amounts of cultivated land had been abandoned. But the available sources are nearly all subjective accounts, and while some indicated that only "half the population" was left, we do not yet have a quantitative assessment of the impact of those decades of disruption on the size of the population or upon the amount of land under cultivation. The purpose of this section is to attempt to reconstruct those figures.

Population. As discussed in Chapters 2 and 3, the Ming population totals for 1391 are generally considered to be reliable; so too are the Qing population figures for 1776.[80] By moving backward from 1776, and forward from 1391, using various average annual rates of increase of the population for Guangdong and Guangxi provinces and some educated guesses, we can back project population figures for the middle of the seventeenth century.[81]

As I argued in the preceding chapter, during the Ming dynasty the population of Lingnan increased from about 4 million in 1391 to about 12 million in 1640. From that peak, the mid-seventeenth-century crisis reduced the population to less than 10 million by around 1661. If fertility declined below

pop. projection

[79] Memorial dated KX17.9.28, translated in Fu, *A Documentary Chronicle*, vol. 1: 50–51.

[80] On the reliability of these figures, see the classic study by Ho, *Studies on the Population of China.*

[81] For the Qing, the rate of growth in the late eighteenth century can be calculated from generally reliable figures; for Guangdong the rate was 0.757% and for Guangxi 0.515%. These rates of growth can be used for the period beginning in 1685, when peace and stability returned to south China; back projection thus yields 1685 populations of 7.5 million for Guangdong and 3 million for Guangxi. For the 40-year period from 1644 to 1683, I have to make some educated guesses. We know that the population decreased substantially during the demographic crisis of 1648–53 because of elevated mortality levels. We might also assume that fertility dropped off too and probably did not even reach replacement levels; if so, the population would have continued to decline, perhaps reaching a nadir around the time of the relocation of the coastal population in 1661–69. During the 1670s, when grain was so plentiful it was called a *shu huang*, fertility no doubt increased, probably surpassing replacement levels, thereby beginning a period of gradual population increase.

Table 4.1. *Population and land totals, 1391–1685*

	Cultivated land (*mu*)		Population estimates	
Year	Guangdong	Guangxi	Guangdong	Guangxi
1391	23,734,056	10,240,390	3,007,932	1,482,671
1542	25,686,514	9,402,075	*5,500,000*	*2,300,000*
1600	*30,655,400*	*9,853,000*	*7,400,000*	*2,900,000*
1640	*30,655,400*	*9,853,000*	*9,000,000*	*3,400,000*
1650	*19,649,700*	*7,804,800*	*7,500,000*	*3,000,000*
1661	25,083,987	5,393,865	*7,000,000*	*2,800,000*
1685	30,239,255	7,802,451	*7,500,000*	*3,000,000*

Source: Liang Fangzhong, *Zhongguo lidai hukou fiandi fianfa fongji* (Shanghai: Renmin shuban she, 1980) 332–33, 380, 387, 391, 394, 396. Figures in italics are my estimates.

replacement levels, the population would have declined even further. I think the population began to recover slowly during the 1660s and 1670s and then to accelerate substantially after peaceful conditions returned in the 1680s. These population dynamics are summarized in Table 4.1.

Surely, the loss of human life – 2 million people, or about 22 percent – in Lingnan during the crisis years was substantial. But for China overall, Ho estimates that the population probably declined by 33 percent between 1600 and 1650;[82] for Henan and Shandong provinces, Huang lists figures of admittedly "questionable utility" that show a decline of 25 percent for Hebei and 63 percent for Shandong between 1578 and 1685.[83] Perdue does not reconstruct population figures for Hunan, but estimates that the *ding* tax quota declined by 37.5 percent during the same period.[84] If these figures more or less accurately reflect the population decline in various parts of China, then compared with the population loss in other provinces during the Ming–Qing transition, Lingnan suffered less.

Cultivated Land. Data for reconstructing cultivated land figures are a little – but not much – better than for population. During the Ming dynasty, the 1581 survey produced cultivated land figures that are considered reliable.[85] During the Qing, though, no land survey was conducted. The story of why

[82] Ho, *Studies on the Population of China*, 281.

[83] Philip C. C. Huang, *The Peasant Economy and Social Change in North China* (Stanford: Stanford University Press, 1985), 322.

[84] Peter Perdue, *Exhausting the Earth: State and Peasant in Hunan 1500–1850* (Cambridge, MA: Harvard University Press, 1987), 67.

[85] See especially Yeh-chien Wang, *Land Taxation in Imperial China, 1750–1911* (Cambridge, MA: Harvard University Press, 1973), 20–26.

Table 4.2. *Land laid waste, ca. 1650, by prefecture*

	a 1391 Cultivated (million *mu*)	*b* ca. 1600 Yuan-e (million *mu*)	*c* Percent laid waste	*d* ca. 1650 (est.) (million *mu*)
Guangzhou	8.5	9.5		•
Nanxiong	1.0	1.6	*22*	1.2
Shaozhou	1.2	1.7	*22*	1.3
Huizhou	2.8	4.6	*36*	2.9
Chaozhou	2.9	3.1		•
Zhaoqing	3.9	4.4	*42*	2.6
Gaozhou	1.5	1.7		•
Leizhou	1.2	0.5	*22*	0.4
Lianzhoufu	0.7	0.4	*22*	0.3
Qiongzhou	2.0	2.9	*22*	2.3
Total	25.7	30.4		19.8

Sources: Column *a*: *Guangdong tongzhi, 1561 edition*; column *b*: *Guangdong tongzhi, 1731* edition; column *c*: Figs in italics calculated as (1 − *c*) × *b*, bold figures, see text; column *d*: bold figures, see text.

will be told in more detail when I discuss the land reclamation efforts of the Qing state; suffice it to say here that the new Qing state decided during the Kangxi reign (1662–1722) that each locality would adopt the late-sixteenth-century registered land figures as the basis for their tax quotas (the *yuan-e*, or "original tax target"). Officials then reported cultivated land figures by deducting estimates of the amount of land laid waste during the mid–century wars and adding the amount of land reclaimed and reported for tax purposes; that is how the cultivated land figures in Table 4.2 for 1661 and 1685 were derived.

These official estimates provide a first gauge of the amount of destruction during the mid-seventeenth-century crisis. According to the official estimates, by 1661 nearly 25 percent of the land that had been in production in Guangdong by the end of the Ming still was not in production, and nearly half of the land in Guangxi had been abandoned. Since those figures presumably include land that had been brought back into production during the 1650s, the amount of destruction clearly was more than the 1661 figures indicate. Just how much more can be estimated for Guangdong province using county-level figures for three prefectures; unfortunately, similarly disaggregated data are not available for Guangxi.

In Guangzhou, Chaozhou, and Gaozhou prefectures, land reclamation figures for each county are available in prefectural gazetteers (and summarized in Table 4.2). These data show that reclaimed land amounted to 42, 35, and

22 percent of the original tax target (*yuan-e*) in each of those prefectures, respectively, implying that at least that much land had dropped out of production as a result of the mid-seventeenth-century devastation. In order of magnitude, those percentages correspond roughly to the amount of damage those regions suffered as a result of the wars: most in Guangzhou, and least in the more remote Gaozhou prefecture. If those percentages can be used as guides to estimate the amount of land that fell out of production in other prefectures similarly situated, then an estimate for the entire province can be developed. This procedure does not seem unwarranted: land reclamation figures for Haifeng county in Huizhou prefecture amount to 38 percent of the *yuan-e*, close to the 35 percent calculated for neighboring Chaozhou prefecture, and figures for Kaiping county in Zhaoqing prefecture amount to 43 percent of the *yuan-e*, again very close to the 42 percent figure for neighboring Guangzhou prefecture. Using this procedure, I estimate the amount of land in Guangdong remaining in production around 1650 to have declined by about one-third to around 20 million *mu* (see Table. 4.2).

The reconstructed population and cultivated land figures from the late Ming through the early Qing quantify the depth of the mid-seventeenth-century crisis in Lingnan: the population declined by 17–22 percent, while the land in production fell even more precipitously by 35 percent in Guangdong and perhaps by as much as 50 percent in Guangxi. More land was abandoned, then, than can be accounted for by the fall in population. The discrepancy between the two rates of decline can be explained: the land was abandoned not just because people died, but also because they fled from war or taxes and because of the relocation of the coastal population. Many either took to the hills to eke out a living until better times returned or joined up with any of the numerous bandit and pirate gangs operating at the time. This not only accounts for the differential rates of decline, but also explains why land could be reclaimed and brought back into production quickly: additional tillers of the land did not have to be born and raised, but could come back down from the hills to pick up plows.

What condition they found the land in is open to speculation. Had terraces collapsed and the soil eroded? Surely abandoned land had become overgrown with unwanted vegetation, which had to be cleared (probably by burning). What of the irrigation works? Given the amount of time and labor lavished on the maintenance of the various kinds of waterworks, their abandonment for just one year, let alone several, would have been a serious matter. Had embankments fallen apart, sluice gates rotted, irrigation channels clogged with silt from eroded fields? Did swamps reform and anopheles mosquitoes return? Was malaria once more a problem? No doubt these challenges and more confronted farmers as they struggled to bring land back into production.[86]

[86] These questions arise from a reading of McNeill, *The Mountains of the Mediterranean.*

The General Crisis and the Environment

The relationship of the mid-seventeenth-century crisis to the environment of Lingnan was complex. On the one hand, the turn of the climate to a cooler regime played a part in creating the conditions that precipitated the crisis by lowering agricultural yields and making life more precarious for a large number of people. On the other hand, the actions of people both directly and indirectly affected the environment. War and the epidemic disease possibly brought into Lingnan by troops from the north devastated the human population. But then the abandoned farmland had an opportunity to recover its lost fertility, and a forest cover – if only the first stages of a pioneer brush community – could reestablish itself. Certainly the most spectacular regrowth had occurred in the coastal regions from which the human population was removed wholesale. There, barricades and watchtowers kept the people out. And without people, both trees and wildlife returned to the land. In Haifeng county, "because of the relocation of the border, grass and trees have grown in profusion, and tigers have become bold."[87]

With people out of the way, some of the "natural" ecological relationships thus began to reestablish themselves, and to do so quickly. When the mid-seventeenth-century crisis checked the growth of the human population and the commercialization of their economy, it opened the way for other populations and communities, represented by the forests and the tigers, to grow and recover. With only a fixed amount of land to serve as host for human or other populations, the swings in the size and density of the human population affected the size and density of natural populations. And for a moment in the second half of the seventeenth century, wildlife populations in Lingnan grew when the number of people declined.

But does the experience of Lingnan in the mid-seventeenth-century crisis provide a context for understanding why it was that a tiger appeared outside the northern wall of the largest city in south China? On the one hand, the crisis sent the populations of people and tigers into opposite dynamics, with the human population falling while that of tigers increased with the expansion of their habitat. On the other hand, the tiger appeared outside that northern wall in 1642, two years before the fall of the Ming dynasty. Had the threat of bandits forced peasant-farmers to abandon their villages for the safety of the

[87] *Huizhou fuzhi*, 1877 ed., juan 18, entry for KX6. Indeed, tigers became bold not just in Lingnan, but in other parts of China devastated by the wars too. In Hunan province, according to an account written by a young merchant by the name of Wang Hui, conditions there appeared to be very similar to those in Lingnan. Following the soldiers came an epidemic, villages became depopulated, and "with few people on the roads and no signs of life around the houses, tigers and leopards became numerous, and hungry dogs roamed in packs. The massacre having been insufficient to punish people for their sins, the epidemic added more misery." Struve, *Voices from the Ming–Qing Cataclysm*, 159–60.

city, leaving an opening for tigers? Or was the tiger an omen of things to come? In light of what happened afterwards to Guangzhou in particular and Lingnan in general, the residents who let the tiger go may well have been deeply worried about the future.

Conclusion

From the perspective of the people who had survived, the mid-seventeenth-century crisis had been broader, deeper, and longer than a mere economic slowdown or even a deep depression: the population had been decimated by war, famine, and epidemic disease; land was abandoned, agricultural production declined, and grain prices fell; and the coastal closing cut off both foreign and domestic coastal trade and with it the imports of silver and copper that had expanded the money supply and fueled economic growth. Clearly, the 40-year period following the founding of the Qing dynasty was a time few people would have chosen to live through. But, by the turn of the eighteenth century it was clear to contemporaries not only that the dark years had passed, but that there was reason to conclude that economic growth had resumed. What explains the turnaround? If war, disruption of trade (both foreign and domestic), and a colder climate had caused the mid-seventeenth-century crisis, then peace, the resumption of trade (the subject of the next chapter), and warmer temperatures (to be analyzed in Chapter 6) ended it.

5

"RICH HOUSEHOLDS COMPETE TO BUILD SHIPS": OVERSEAS TRADE AND ECONOMIC RECOVERY

The restoration of peaceful conditions in Lingnan provided one condition for the revival of the economy. And while peace itself may have removed obstacles to economic recovery, it did not itself stimulate growth. Yet by the eighteenth century, we know not only that the economy of Lingnan had revived, but that most of China was about to experience one of the best economic climates ever. Moreover, the economic recovery was not gradual, but explosive. What the evidence points to is a sudden, substantial increase in foreign and domestic seaborne trade beginning in 1684 and continuing, albeit with some important changes, right through to the middle of the nineteenth century, driving economic growth and the commercialization of agriculture. In brief, Chinese overseas and foreign trade after 1684 stimulated demand for raw cotton and silk, thereby prompting some peasant-farmers to change their cropping patterns, growing nonfood commercial crops instead of rice, and in turn leading to the further commercialization of rice. By the end of the eighteenth century, the agricultural economy of Lingnan had become thoroughly commercialized, with even peasant-farmers in westernmost Guangxi affected by market demand centered on Guangzhou and the Pearl River delta.

Chinese Overseas Trade

When we think about China's foreign trade in the eighteenth and nineteenth centuries, the image that mostly comes to mind is that of European and American clippers arriving in China's ports and then loading up with tea, silk, sugar, and porcelains bound for their home markets. While it is true that European and American trade became the largest part of China's foreign trade in the second half of the eighteenth century, the largest number of merchants to take to the seas when the Kangxi emperor reopened the coast to trade in 1684–85 were Chinese, plying both the domestic coastal routes and conducting overseas trade with the many states of what the Chinese called the "Nanyang," or the Southern Ocean.[1]

The Nanyang. Chinese merchants and other residents of Lingnan's coastal regions thought of the ocean to the south as being comprised of two parts: the Nan Hai, or South Sea, which was contiguous to the coast and blended with the inland waterways of the Pearl River delta; and the Nanyang, or Southern Ocean, which encompassed both mainland and insular Southeast Asia. The coastline of Guangdong province stretches for some 2,000 miles, and because of the gradual subsidence of the land, it is irregular and dotted with good harbors. Not all of the harbors are deep or sheltered, but there were sufficient places either on the coast or up the coastal rivers for the Kangxi emperor to authorize the establishment of 70 customs houses on the coast of Guangdong when he reopened the coast for trade and shipping.

Many of those customs houses were situated at what the Chinese called "portals onto the sea" (*hai men*), and as Qu Dajun claimed, "The portals onto the Nan Hai are the most numerous [of any in China]." The central and largest portal, the Tiger's Mouth, or Bocca Tigris, as Europeans called it, straddled the Pearl River delta and controlled access to Guangzhou. Qu lists scores of other portals for the "eastern route," that is, up the coast from Xin'an (Hong Kong) to Denghai, and for the "western route," stretching from the Pearl River down the coast, including the Leizhou Peninsula and Lianzhoufu (on the northern shores of the Gulf of Tonkin) (see Map 5.1).[2]

Beyond the coastal waters of the Nan Hai lay the Southern Ocean, or Nanyang. As described by Cushman, the Nanyang "should be conceived of as a circle encompassing the mainland Southeast Asian countries bordering the South China Sea [the Nan Hai] and the Gulf of Siam, i.e., Vietnam, Cambodia and Siam, southern Burma, the Malay Peninsula, Sumatra, western Java, and the north-east coast of Borneo."[3] Stretching from the Tropic of

[1] Jennifer Cushman surely was correct to note that "modern Western scholarship has generally neglected to analyze the role of the overseas junk trade in China's economic development. The primary concern of twentieth-century historians has been with the expansion of Western commercial activities in China, which is legitimate given the greater volume and monetary value of that trade." For her attempt to correct that oversight, see Jennifer Wayne Cushman, *Fields from the Sea: Chinese Junk Trade with Siam during the Late Eighteenth and Early Nineteenth Centuries* (Ithaca: Cornell University Press, 1993), 6. Two other works of note are: Sarasin Viraphol, *Tribute and Profit: Sino-Siamese Trade 1652–1853* (Cambridge, MA: Harvard University Press, 1972), and Ng Chin-keong, *Trade and Society: The Amoy Network on the China Coast, 1683–1735* (Singapore: Singapore University Press, 1983). I have relied heavily on these works for this section.

[2] Qu, *Guangdong xin yu*, 33.

[3] Cushman, *Fields from the Sea*, 4–5. The Philippines, Taiwan, and Japan, although not considered part of the Nanyang, but the "Eastern Ocean" (*dong hai*), also were part of China's junk-trade circuits. Anthony Reid calls attention to "water and forest [as] the dominant elements in the environment of Southeast Asia," with "ubiquitous sealanes," "moderate and predictable"

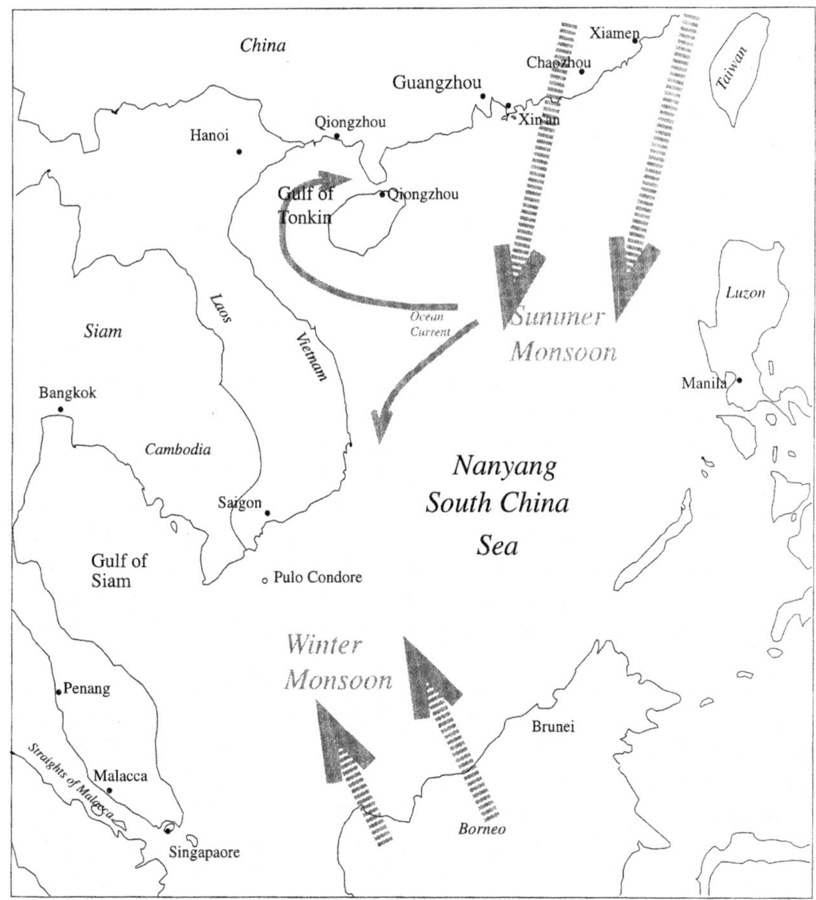

Map 5.1. The Nanyang

Cancer (just north of Guangzhou) to the equator the Nanyang is longer than it is wide, and it lies more or less on a southwest to northeast axis, a shape made to order for the monsoons (see Map 5.1). As soon as the telltale signs of the northeasterly winds of the winter monsoon appeared in December or

winds, and warm water combining to make the Nanyang "more hospitable and inviting a meeting place than that deeper and stormier Mediterranean in the West." A vast supply of wood at the water's edge made the Nanyang "a region uniquely favourable to maritime activity." Anthony Reid, *Southeast Asia in the Age of Commerce, 1450–1680*, vol. 1, *The Lands below the Winds* (New Haven: Yale University Press, 1988), 2. An interesting comparison might be made of the Nanyang with the Mediterranean, but such a comparison is beyond the scope of this book.

January, junks set sail from one of the numerous portals on the sea – the busiest being Guangzhou, Chaozhou, and Haikou (on Hainan Island)[4] – for ports to the south, taking on cargoes in Siam or Malacca and waiting for the winds to change with the summer monsoon. Then in April, gently at first but then with more strength in May, the southerly and southeasterly monsoon winds provided the Chinese junks with the wind power to return home. Ocean currents too facilitated the return voyage, especially for those merchants who plied the Southeast Asian coast up to Tonkin. Easterly currents south of Hainan Island pushed water against the coast of Vietnam, trending then northward into the Gulf of Tonkin before circling westward and through the Hainan Strait separating the island from the Leizhou Peninsula. Chinese junks thus could easily ride the winds and the currents from the Straights of Malacca or the Gulf of Siam right back to ports on Hainan Island, Guangzhou, or Chaozhou.[5]

With both a natural shape and wind and ocean currents conducive to an annual round of trade, Chinese merchants had long maintained trading relations with the countries of the Nanyang, going back at least to Han times,[6] but especially from the eleventh and twelfth centuries, when Chinese traders supplanted Arabs as the primary carriers of goods throughout the Nanyang.[7] But the transition from the Ming to the Qing dynasties, especially the closure of the coast from 1662 through 1683, had severed the trade links between Lingnan and the Nanyang. To be sure, tribute missions from Siam[8] and smuggling kept some goods moving along the old routes,[9] but the legal trade had been virtually extinguished.[10]

Reopening of the Coast for Trade. With the capture of Taiwan in 1683 by Qing forces, though, the last serious challenge to Qing rule was crushed, and

[4] Qu, *Guangdong xin yu*, 33.

[5] Captain William Dampier, perhaps ignorant of the strength of the summer monsoon, found out the hard way how inexorable the winter and summer winds were in determining where one could sail in the South China Sea. Wintering in the Gulf of Siam, Dampier planned on returning to Manila "by the latter End of May [1687], and wait [to pirate] the Acapulco Ship that comes about that time." Setting sail on June 4, Dampier encountered such strong southeasterlies that he was driven, three weeks later and contrary to his plans to raid ships in Manila, to the south China coast near the mouth of the Pearl River estuary. William Dampier, *A New Voyage Round the World* (New York: Dover, 1968), 264ff.

[6] The most comprehensive accounts of this trade can be found in Chen Guanghui, *Zhongguo gudai dui wai maoyi shi* (Guangzhou: Guangdong renmin chuban she, 1985), and Wang Gungwu, *Nanhai maoyi yu Nanyang huaren* (Hong Kong: Zhonghua shuju, 1988).

[7] Cushman, *Fields from the Sea*, 1.

[8] See Viraphol, *Tribute and Profit*, 28.

[9] See Ng, *Trade and Society*, 52–53. See also Viraphol, *Tribute and Profit*, 23–24.

[10] Fan reached this conclusion in *Long Distance Trade and Market Integration in the Ming–Ch'ing Period, 1400–1850*, 239.

the Kangxi emperor then moved quickly to reopen the coast to shipping and foreign trade. And as soon as the emperor did so, Chinese merchants set sail up and down the China coast as well as overseas for ports to the south in the Nanyang and to the north in Japan. The numbers must have been impressive, for the provincial governor Li Shizheng commented that "in any given year, a thousand ships come and go [from Guangdong]."[11] Whether Governor Li had statistics on the numbers of ships passing through the various ports or was just estimating, he does convey the sense of a fairly large fleet of Chinese-owned and -manned junks plying the Nanyang in the years after the coast was opened. Moreover, Governor Li's impression of "a thousand" junks is confirmed by the English Captain Hamilton, who, on a trading mission to Guangzhou in 1703, observed that "there is no Day in the Year but shews 5,000 Sail of Jonks, besides small Boats for other Services, lying before the City."[12]

The number of junks "lying before the City" in 1703 was impressive not merely because of its magnitude, but also because most of that fleet had been built anew only after 1684. By all accounts, the Chinese commercial fleet had been virtually destroyed during the disastrous relocation of the coastal population in 1662. "All oceangoing junks," the order closing the coast had read, "are to be burned; not an inch of wood is allowed to be in the water."[13] Qing troops apparently carried out the order almost to the letter: in Haiyang county "not a junk was left at the docks," and in Xin'an county "not more than one in a hundred junks remained."[14] And yet by 1685, thousands of junks once again sailed the seas. To be sure, not all had been destroyed in the 1660s; some smugglers and pirates had managed to avoid capture, keeping up a small but lucrative trade from new bases in Tonkin or Siam. By and large, though, it seems certain that most of the junks plying the Nanyang had to have been constructed quickly in the years after 1684. "Rich households compete to build ships," one observer wrote at the time.[15] And build they did.

The preferred wood for the structural beams and cross-members of oceangoing junks was cut from the *tie-li*, or "strong-as-iron" tree, that grew in the hill region of western Guangdong province. As the name of the tree implies, the wood had qualities that rendered it very strong relative to its weight and displacement. One such junk with a crew of several hundred men measured 165 feet from stem to stern and 36 feet abreast with a mast 120 feet tall.[16] Indeed, the masts were so impressive that the English privateer Captain

[11] Quoted in Huang Juzhen, "Qingdai qianqi Guangdong de dui wai maoyi," paper presented at the 4th International Conference on Chinese Social and Economic History, 1987, 6.

[12] Hosea Ballou Morse, *The Chronicles of the East India Company Trading to China, 1635–1834* (Taibei: Chengwen Reprint, 1966), vol. 1: 104.

[13] Quoted in Ye, *Guangdong hang yun shi,* 140.

[14] Ibid., 40.

[15] Quoted in Huang, "Qingdai qianqi Guangdong de dui wai maoyi," 6.

[16] Ye, *Guangdong hang yun shi*, 253.

William Dampier had commented on them: "The Main-mast in their biggest Jonks seem to me as big as any Third-Rate Man of Wars Mast in England, and yet not pieced together as ours, but made of one grown Tree; and in all my Travels I never saw any single Tree-masts so big in the body, and yet so well tapered, as I have seen in the Chinese Jonks."[17]

Sometime during the eighteenth century, though, the shipbuilding industry in Guangdong slowed and then came to a virtual halt, for two basic reasons.[18] First, the *tie-li* tree became scarce. I do not know whether the decline in the supply meant that the tree had been eliminated from the forests of Guangdong or that those remaining were so inaccessible as to render continued logging uneconomical. Today, the *tie-li* tree is no longer listed in the botanical studies of Guangdong province, and so I presume it has become extinct. Whether its disappearance coincided with the shipbuilding boom of the late seventeenth and early eighteenth centuries is unknown, but the timing seems reasonable. Hence, as the *tie-li* tree and other wood used to build ships became scarce, the expense increased and it became cheaper to build junks in Siam and Malaya than on the coast of Lingnan. By the 1820s, it cost Chinese merchants 7,400 Spanish silver dollars to build an 8,000-*shi* (476-ton) junk in Siam, 16,000 in Chaozhou prefecture, and 21,000 at Amoy in Fujian. The shipbuilding industry thus shifted from China to Siam and Malaya, where the supplies of wood were plentiful.[19] From 1684 on, then, the trade with the Nanyang stimulated such a burst in the building of ships that the *tie-li* tree vanished from the forests of Lingnan, to be found instead floating in the thousands of junks that plied the coastal and Nanyang trade routes.

Of those thousands, most were smaller one- or two-masted junks plying the coastal trade; the largest, though, with three to five masts, had been built to sail the Nanyang, principally to Siam but also to the Philippines, Malacca, and Batavia. How many oceangoing junks called at ports in Lingnan in any given year is difficult to say, but a variety of sources allow us to get some perspective on the issue. In 1685, the English pirate, adventurer, and author Captain William Dampier arrived in the Philippine Islands intent upon seizing one of the Spanish galleons laden with Mexican silver. At Manila, Dampier observed:

> The Harbour is so large, that some Hundreds of Ships may ride here; and is never without many, both of [the Spaniards'] own and Strangers . . . They do allow the Portuguese to trade here, but the Chinese are the chiefest Mer-

[17] Dampier, *A New Voyage*, 279. Where the wood for the masts came from is not clear; it may have come from the *shui song*, that marvelously straight and exceptionally tall tree that grew in and near the rivers of Lingnan, or from the forests of Siam.

[18] Ye, *Guangdong hang yun shi*, 254.

[19] Viraphol, *Tribute and Profit*, 181. For the same reasons but earlier in the eighteenth century, the English shipbuilding industry expanded from England to the North American colonies.

> chants, and they drive the greatest Trade; for they have commonly twenty, thirty, or forty Jonks in the Harbour at a time, and a great many Merchants constantly residing in the City, besides Shopkeepers and Handy-crafts-men in abundance.[20]

Japanese sources too confirm a large and growing number of Chinese junks at Nagasaki after the China coast was reopened: from 24 junks in 1684 to 73 in 1685, 84 in 1686, 111 in 1687, and 117 in 1688.[21] From 1684 to 1757, a total of 3,017 junks visited Japan; not all of these were from Guangdong, but we can assume that a substantial number were.[22]

But how many were there, and how large and how important to the economy of Lingnan was the trade that was conducted? We can make some estimates by examining data from later periods. Early-nineteenth-century sources put the number of Chinese junks from all ports engaged in the trade with Siam at 150–200,[23] while The *Chinese Repository* estimated in 1833 that

> the whole number of Chinese vessels, annually visiting foreign ports south of Canton, is not probably, less than one hundred; of these one third belong to Canton; six or eight go to Tungking; eighteen or twenty to Cochinchina, Camboja, and Siam; four or five visit the ports of Singapore, Java, Sumatra, and Penang; and as many more find their way to the Celebes, Borneo and the Philippine islands. These vessels never make but one voyage in the year, and always move with the monsoon.[24]

Certainly there were fewer oceangoing junks in 1700 than in 1800; Fan I-chun cites early- to mid-Qianlong-era sources (ca. 1750) stating that up to 40 Guangdong junks had received licenses to trade in the Nanyang.[25] Thus, I think that in the years around 1700, when Fujian-licensed junks (which also stopped in Guangzhou) are added, perhaps 50–100 oceangoing junks traded goods to and from Guangzhou.

At first blush those numbers may not seem like much, but they are – at least when placed into comparative perspective with the size of the European trade (a topic to which I will turn shortly). In the early 1820s, for instance, the amount of goods exported from Siam to China totaled 35,083 tons (with the two-way trade presumably about double that),[26] an amount equivalent to the combined exports from Guangzhou in 1790 carried by British East India Company and American ships.[27] Those comparisons mean that in 1700, Chinese junks were carrying perhaps as much as 20,000 tons of goods back to Lingnan. By com-

20 Dampier, *A New Voyage*, 263. 21 Viraphol, *Tribute and Profit*, 59.

22 Huang, "Qingdai qianqi Guangdong de dui wai maoyi," 7–8.

23 Cushman, *Fields from the Sea*, 86.

24 "Description of the City of Canton," *Chinese Repository* 11, no. 7 (Nov. 1833): 294.

25 Fan, *Long Distance Trade and Market Integration*, 248.

26 Cushman, *Fields from the Sea*, 83. 27 Morse, *Chronicles*, vol. 2, 180.

parison, the volume of European exports from Guangzhou totaled just 500 tons in 1700, 6,071 tons in 1737, and probably did not reach 20,000 tons until the 1770s.[28] In short, Chinese trade with the Nanyang in 1700 was already at a level not reached by the European trade until the 1770s.

To place these trade figures into perspective, some comparisons with Europe might help. According to Jan deVries, for the decade 1731–40, Dutch trade in colonial goods to the Baltic passing through the Danish Sound totaled 16,000 tons, and the maximum yearly tonnage of all European ships trading in Asian waters was about 19,000 tons.[29] And according to Fernand Braudel's estimates, the two-way trade between England and Russia during the eighteenth century (which included considerable quantities of grain) may have amounted to as much as 120,000 tons annually.[30] Thus, the amount of Chinese trade with the Nanyang was about in the middle of the range between Dutch and English trade in Europe.

Chinese customs statistics did not distinguish among the Chinese interport (i.e., domestic) trade, trade throughout the Nanyang, and the European-American trade. Nonetheless, it is possible to gain some perspective on the size of the combined Chinese domestic and Nanyang trade by examining some data from the early eighteenth century. In 1735, the total amount of duty collected by all of China's customs houses totaled 729,000 taels; of that, 37 percent (272,000 taels) was collected in Guangdong alone (see Figure 5.1). The Guangdong total includes customs duty collected from Chinese merchants trading only on the coast, from Chinese merchants trading throughout the Nanyang, and from European ships as well. The latter, however, coming from fewer than 10 ships paying perhaps 3,000 taels each, was as yet relatively a small amount.[31] It therefore seems reasonable to conclude that for Chinese coastal and Nanyang trade, the Guangdong customs house reported duty on the order of 250,000 taels. Assuming that to be a low estimate[32] and that the duty averaged 5 percent ad valorem,[33] then the value of annual Chinese coastal and Nanyang trade approached 5 million taels (about 900 metric tons of silver); that seems

[28] Morse does not provide total European tonnage figures for 1737 to 1790.

[29] Jan deVries, *The Economy of Europe in an Age of Crisis, 1600–1750* (Cambridge University Press, 1976), 120, 131.

[30] Fernand Braudel, *The Wheels of Commerce*, vol. 2 of *Civilization and Capitalism, 15th-18th Century*, Siân Reynolds, trans. (New York: Harper and Row, 1979), 207. Braudel estimated that the trade was conducted on about 400 ships of 300 tons each.

[31] The growth in customs revenue after 1735, but especially around 1777, though, was due mostly to European trade; for a discussion see the section entitled "European Trade."

[32] Smuggling, corruption, and embezzlement lowered the amount of duty reported from that which could have been collected and reported. For a discussion of the nature of the customs statistics, see Fan, *Long Distance Trade and Market Integration*, app. A.

[33] This is a gross estimate only; since duty was levied on each commodity based on volume or weight, not value, reconstructing the ad valorem duty is difficult if not impossible.

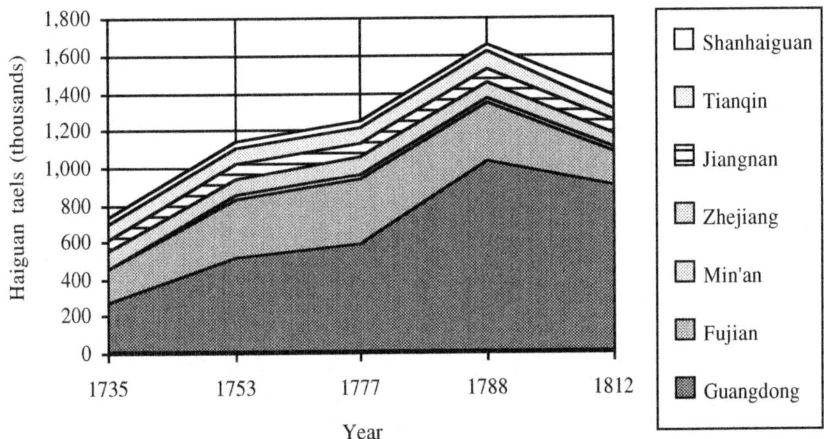

Figure 5.1. Chinese maritime customs revenue, 1735–1812, by province. Source: Adapted from Fan I-chun, *Long Distance Trade and Market Integration in the Ming–Ch'ing Period, 1400–1850*, Stanford University, Ph.D. dissertation, 1992, 241.

to have been a fairly consistent level of trade throughout the eighteenth century.[34] As a portion of all long-distance trade in the Chinese empire at the end of the eighteenth century, that flowing through the customs houses in Guangdong accounted for about a third, as did the Yangzi River and Grand Canal routes.[35] And that was only the licit trade; smuggling added an unknown amount to the total trade.

The trade flows between China and the Nanyang were characterized by Chinese exports of manufactured or processed goods and imports of raw materials and food, in particular rice. According to Cushman, junks from China carried chinaware, earthenware, silk and cotton textiles, brass- and copperware made into utensils or dishes, paper, as well as dried and salted vegetables and fruits and a variety of smaller manufactured items; Viraphol adds ironworks of all kinds – pans, axes, cast iron, metal tubes, and wire – to the list.[36] Imports from Siam included rice, wood for building and for extracting dyes used in the textile industry, raw materials for drugs, hides for farm equipment, various spices, and, importantly, raw cotton.[37]

The Nanyang Trade and Changes in Cropping Patterns. The raw cotton originated in India, was brought to Siam by either Indian, Muslim, or Portuguese

[34] Fan, *Long Distance Trade and Market Integration*, 242–43. [35] Ibid., 129–30.
[36] Viraphol, *Tribute and Profit*, 51. [37] Cushman, *Fields from the Sea*, 82–83, 87.

traders, and was in turn purchased by Chinese merchants. The raw cotton is interesting because it points to aspects of China's coastal trade and to cropping and land use patterns in Lingnan that become increasingly important during the eighteenth and nineteenth centuries. Clearly, the raw cotton was imported in order to be spun and woven into cloth of varying grades, some of which was in turn exported back to Siam as finished goods, but most of which was sold within Lingnan. According to Qu Dajun (writing about 1700), "The cotton cultivated in Guangdong is not sufficient to satisfy the needs of the ten prefectures."[38] The importation of the raw cotton meant that local sources could not satisfy the demand, and so producers looked elsewhere for their supplies. But did this demand then spur the planting of cotton in Lingnan, thereby changing land use patterns? As will be recalled from Chapter 3, the cotton textile industry in Guangxi had dried up sometime during the Ming dynasty, so Qing merchants from Guangzhou could not look there for supplies of raw cotton.

To be sure, some peasant-farmers did plant cotton in and around the Pearl River delta. According to seventeenth-century gazetteers cited by Sucheta Mazumdar (a scholar who has studied extensively the commercialization of agriculture in the Pearl River delta), cotton was planted in rotation with sugarcane in Panyu county. Of all the delta counties, Panyu, it might be recalled, had higher and drier land more suitable to either cotton or sugarcane than lower-lying *shatan* counties like Nanhai. Nonetheless, according to Mazumdar, "Cotton was not grown extensively in the Delta,"[39] and its rotation with sugarcane disappeared sometime in the eighteenth century. It is possible that peasant-farmers had begun to experiment with cotton after coastal trade resumed, responding to the demand of the textile industry in and around the city of Foshan (10 miles west of Guangzhou). But the little evidence that we have indicates that cotton cultivation died out. For whatever reasons – perhaps because of quality, price, or unexpected ecological problems with the cultivation of cotton – the Foshan textile industry turned instead to importing raw cotton not just from India, but also from central and northern China.

Indeed, the importation of raw cotton from the Yangzi River delta constituted one-half of an important coastal trade circuit during the eighteenth century, where merchants brought sugar from Guangdong to the markets of the Yangzi River delta to exchange for raw cotton grown in Jiangsu and Hubei:

> In the Second and Third month, people from Min (Fujian) and Yue (Guangdong) come carrying crystallized sugar (*tanshuang*) to sell. In the autumn they

[38] Qu, *Guangdong xin yu*, 426; also quoted in Mazumdar, *A History of the Sugar Industry in China*, 350, but translated slightly differently.

[39] Mazumdar, *A History of the Sugar Industry*, 292.

> don't buy cloth, but only buy ginned cotton and return. Hundreds and thousands of ships all load up pile upon pile of bags because there [in Guangdong], among themselves, they can spin and weave it.[40]

Mazumdar rightly calls this an "interlinked structure of the sugar–cotton trade" and devotes considerable attention to analyzing how it worked.[41] What is important to note here, though, is that the export trade in cotton textiles woven in Foshan did not stimulate the expansion of cotton cultivation in the Pearl River delta, but instead, because of the trade circuits, of sugarcane. In other words, to obtain raw cotton for the spinners and weavers in Guangdong, merchants established a triangular trade route: sugar produced in Guangdong was sold (or traded) in Jiangnan (in the Yangzi River delta) for raw cotton; the raw cotton then was sold in Guangzhou, the proceeds of which became either profit or capital to finance another round of trade.

The cane was grown in counties on the edge of the Pearl River delta: Panyu, Dongguan, Zengcheng, and Yangchun were the most important. Sugarcane also was grown up the Guangdong coast in Haifeng and Huilai counties, as well as in easternmost counties in Chaozhou prefecture. I suspect that one reason the cane was grown in counties on the fringe of the delta, rather than in the delta itself, was the availability of fuel to boil the cane to refine raw sugar.[42] Because the delta originated as man-made *shatan*, trees for fuel were scarce, but not so in the counties bordering the delta. There, fuel could be obtained from trees growing in nearby hills or even further away, if water transportation were available.

Moreover, to meet the demand for raw cotton, the expansion in the production of sugarcane did not require additional land to be cleared. Rather, what happened is that production was simply switched, on fields already in production, from rice to sugarcane. Doing so required little by way of large capital outlays, which, by contrast, land clearance, swamp drainage, polder construction, or irrigation projects did, thereby putting sugarcane production within the reach of most peasant households. Most of this switching was on land tilled (whether it was owned or rented is a separate question) by peasant-farmers, although Mazumdar does think it possible that merchants or wealthier peasants may have operated large "plantations" with wage labor.[43] Planting sugarcane did have some capital requirements – additional fertilizer and a stake to replace the food that was not being grown – and for peasant-farmers the lack of such capital might have inhibited their willingness to abandon rice for sugarcane.

[40] Quoted in ibid., 350. [41] Ibid., ch. 6.

[42] I would like to thank John McNeill for raising the question of the availability of fuel to refine raw sugar.

[43] Mazumdar, *A History of the Sugar Industry*, 290–91.

To meet this need, sugar merchants advanced small amounts of capital either to peasant-producers, receiving in return a lock on the crop,[44] or to the sugarcane crushers and boilers. As one exquisitely apt description cited by Mazumdar put it:

> Many of the rich merchants in [Chenghai] county buy sugar exactly when it is fully processed . . . Carrying a lot of capital, they go to each district to buy sugar, or else first give (money) on account for the cane crushers and the sheds for boiling sugar, and then get the sugar in this period. There are those who transport the goods themselves, others who stay for the middleman, waiting till the Third or Fourth month for a good Southern wind to rent ocean-going junks and ships. They load on the bags of sugar for sale, going up on the sea route to Suzhou and Tianjin. Then in Autumn when there is the Northeastern wind, they carry back cotton and colored cloths for sale to the county.[45]

In the crop rotation system of many Lingnan peasant-farmers, sugarcane therefore replaced rice, and as the amount of land allotted to sugarcane increased, the amount devoted to rice shrank, more or less on a one-for-one basis. By the middle of the eighteenth century, a substantial portion of the land in several counties had become devoted to sugarcane: "In Panyu, Dongguan, and Zengcheng [counties], 4 out of 10 [peasant-farmers] produce sugar; in Yangchun, 6 out of 10 do. The cane fields almost equal the rice fields."[46] By the nineteenth century, entire villages specialized in only sugarcane.[47] In 1819, for instance, the shipwrecked English Captain J. Ross observed "continued fields of sugar-cane" and "plantations of sugar-cane" on the Leizhou Peninsula and to the north in Gaozhou prefecture.[48]

The process by which peasant-farmers replaced rice fields with sugarcane in order for merchants to purchase raw cotton, of course, is known as the commercialization of agriculture. But what is important to note here about sugarcane is its place in Lingnan's coastal and overseas trade circuits, in particular the linkage with raw cotton. For the demand that spurred the production of sugarcane came not directly for sugar, but for raw cotton that could be spun and woven into thread and cloth that was then sold within Lingnan or exported to the Nanyang. The expansion of trade with the Nanyang following the opening of the coast after 1684 increased demand for cotton cloth and raw cotton. But rather than grow the cotton in Lingnan, it was imported from central and northern China in exchange for locally produced sugar. As demand

[44] Marks, *Rural Revolution in South China*, 99ff.; see also Mazumdar, *A History of the Sugar Industry*, 310.

[45] Mazumdar, *A History of the Sugar Industry*, 351.

[46] Li Diaoyuan, *Yuedong biji* (Shanghai: Huiwentang, 1915), juan 14.

[47] Mazumdar, *A History of the Sugar Industry*, 288.

[48] Ross, "Journey of a Trip Overland from Hainan to Canton in 1819," 237.

increased, the amount of land devoted to rice decreased. An important part of the story of the commercialization of agriculture in the eighteenth and nineteenth centuries therefore has to do with the question of how those peasants who grew sugarcane got their food. This problem of food supply is so important that I will discuss it in much greater detail in subsequent chapters. The point here is that the resumption of Chinese overseas and coastal trade in the late seventeenth and early eighteenth centuries provided the impetus not just to economic expansion following the mid-seventeenth-century crisis, but also to the commercialization and specialization of agriculture in Lingnan.

In other parts of the world, the expansion of sugarcane production had an enormous impact upon the environment, leading to massive and irreversible deforestation and desertification. As Richard Grove has detailed nicely in his recent book, seventeenth- and eighteenth-century European colonial enterprises, especially those organized by the English East India and Dutch East India Companies, opened sugar plantations on tropical islands in the Caribbean and the South Atlantic, leaving islands like Barbados denuded of any forests and others like Mauritius in environmental crisis. In accounting for the differing outcomes on the tropical islands, Grove points to differences between colonizing powers, especially the British and the French, but still it is clear that sugarcane plantations established and run by Europeans to meet the demand for sugar in Europe destroyed many islands' environments.[49]

In Lingnan, the expansion of sugarcane production did not have these disastrous effects. The differences may be obvious, but I think it is important to list them. First, sugarcane in Lingnan replaced rice paddies, not virgin forests. Second, production was organized by the peasant-farming family, not by overseers driving slave labor. And finally, the demand for sugar was mostly domestic, not global. All of these factors contributed to minimizing (at least in comparison with the experience of Barbados) the impact of the expansion of sugarcane production upon the environment of Lingnan, enabling Chinese merchants to create trade circuits that were not premised upon the destruction of forests.

Moreover, the expansion of sugarcane production did not have an "involutionary" impact upon rice culture, unlike the outcome in Indonesia as described by Geertz. Under the "culture system," the Dutch colonists forced Javan peasants to grow sugarcane for export on part of their land while maintaining paddies for rice on the remaining portion. A growing population was sustained by "wet-rice cultivation, with its extraordinary ability to maintain levels of marginal labor productivity by always managing to work one more man in without a serious fall in per-capita income," a process Geertz called

[49] Richard Grove, *Green Imperialism: Colonial Expansion, Tropical Island Edens and the Origins of Environmentalism, 1600–1860* (Cambridge University Press, 1994).

"agricultural involution."[50] Although there is some debate about the extent to which the Javan sugar-producing regions provided for their own subsistence from their rice paddies,[51] the difference with the process in Lingnan is clear: peasant-farmers there substituted sugarcane for rice in response to market stimuli and in turn purchased rice (some or all of which had been imported from Guangxi) in the market.

In summary, several aspects of the Chinese overseas and coastal junk trade are noteworthy. First, by all indications both the volume and the value of the trade, beginning immediately with the lifting of the ban on coastal shipping in 1684–85, were very large, providing the stimulus needed for the economy to begin growing again. Second, the Nanyang demand was mostly for Chinese manufactured goods produced either in or around Guangzhou, or imported to that great emporium from other parts of the empire. The impact of the increased export trade upon Lingnan's agricultural economy was indirect, mediated by the need to import raw cotton: rather than growing cotton, peasant-farmers grew sugarcane, which, after being refined and processed, was exchanged for cotton from central and northern China. After being spun or woven, much of the cotton cloth then was exported to the Nanyang. The increased demand for cotton textiles thus drove the substitution of sugarcane for rice, and although the expansion of cane fields did not result in the clearance of more land to grow sugarcane for sale in the market, it did decrease the amount of rice produced in and around the Pearl River delta and thus increased the market demand for rice.

A similar conversion of rice paddies to a nonfood commodity occurred when the demand for silk increased. And like the demand for cotton textiles that was satisfied by expanding the acreage devoted to sugarcane, the demand for silk had an indirect impact on cropping patterns, increasing the acreage devoted to the fish pond and mulberry tree combination that had first developed in the Ming. The driving force behind the demand for silk, though, was not the coastal or Nanyang trade, but rather the European trade.

European Trade

The story of European and American trade with China – from the reopening of the ports to Europeans in 1685 to the Opium War in 1839–42, the multiport trading system from 1685 to 1760, the rise to dominance of the English, and the use of opium to balance the accounts of the British East India Company – is better known than China's native coastal or Nanyang trade, and

[50] Clifford Geertz, *Agricultural Involution: The Processes of Ecological Change in Indonesia* (Berkeley and Los Angeles: University of California Press, 1963), 80.

[51] See Francesca Bray, *The Rice Economies: Technology and Development in Asian Societies* (Berkeley and Los Angeles: University of California Press, 1994), 117, 178–79.

I will not repeat it here.[52] What I do want to do is to examine those aspects of the trade that are relevant both to understanding the development of the economy of Lingnan in the eighteenth and nineteenth centuries and to changes in cropping patterns.

European trade was layered on top of the base established by the Chinese coastal and Nanyang trade, beginning with just a few ships in the early 1700s, rising only to 20 or so by the middle of the century, and increasing dramatically in the 1780s when the British discovered the Chinese demand for raw cotton. Even the restriction after 1757 of English trade to the single port of Guangzhou did not result in an immediate increase in the amount of trade at Guangzhou. If 250,000 taels of customs revenue represents the amount of Chinese overseas trade, then foreign (i.e., European) trade did not attain that level until the 1770s. By the end of the eighteenth century, though, European trade had eclipsed the Chinese coastal and Nanyang trade, easily reaching four times the Chinese trade. Figure 5.2 shows both the total duty collected by the Guangdong customs houses and the number of European and American ships trading at Guangzhou. Clearly, both the increase in the customs collected and its annual fluctuations are a function of the number of foreign ships arriving in Guangzhou.[53]

The nature of the eighteenth- and nineteenth-century trade between China and Western countries is well known, but a brief summary is warranted. Europeans purchased porcelain, lacquered ware, silk, cotton cloth ("Nankeens"), refined and raw sugar, and, increasingly, tea. Europeans could not trade for these commodities with any of their products or commodities (although they tried) and for the most part paid in silver bullion. As the English demand for tea increased throughout the eighteenth century and the British East India Company (EIC) came to dominate the China trade, the EIC also successfully imported raw cotton from India to pay in part for the tea.

We have already seen the place that the cotton textile industry played in the commercialization of the rural economy through its connection with sugarcane. By all indications, the demand for cotton textiles increased so much during the eighteenth century that increasingly large quantities of raw cotton were imported from India via the EIC. As the EIC's purchases of Chinese products increased, especially to satisfy the growing British thirst for tea, the Company searched for products it could bring in trade and minimize the need to pay in silver. At first it looked like Indian raw cotton would fit the bill.

52 The best and most accessible standard accounts include Frederick Wakeman Jr., *The Fall of Imperial China* (Boston: Free Press, 1975), ch. 7; Jonathan D. Spence, *The Search for Modern China* (New York: Norton, 1990), chs. 6–7; and Immanuel C. Y. Hsü, *The Rise of Modern China*, 3rd edition (New York: Oxford University Press, 1983), chs. 7–8.

53 The correlation coefficient is 0.9, and a linear regression of customs duty on the number of foreign ships has an R^2 value of 0.8.

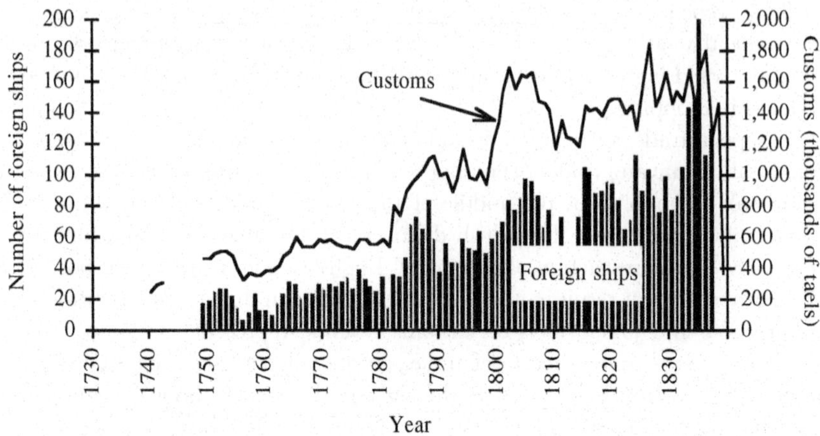

Figure 5.2. Foreign trade at Guangzhou, 1730–1839. Source: Huang Shansheng, "Qing dai Guangdong maoyi ji qi zai Zhougguo jingji shi shang zhi yiyi – yapian zhi yu zhi qian," *Lingnan xuebao* 3 no. 4 (1934): 166–70, 180–84.

Raw cotton imports more than tripled (as measured by value) from 1780 to 1785 and then tripled again from 1795 to 1815 (see Figure 5.3). In terms of weight, the raw cotton imports more than doubled between 1800 and 1830. All or certainly most of this raw cotton then was spun and woven in Foshan, the textile center west of Guangzhou.[54] To be sure, some raw cotton may have been forwarded to the countryside for processing, but it seems more reasonable to assume that the merchants linking the sugarcane–raw cotton trade circuit with north China supplied that market. Thus, I would expect that the Indian raw cotton was processed in Foshan and then sold as finished cloth for the domestic market, with some exported to the Nanyang or to Europe as "Nankeens."

But even with the vast expansion in the import of Indian raw cotton, the balance of trade remained strongly in China's favor (see Figure 5.4). For a while, as John McNeill has recently pointed out, a triangular trade with the Pacific islands helped the Europeans: "European, American, and Australian merchantmen organized the exchange, in which Pacific island products were acquired for Western manufactured goods, then exchanged for Chinese silk and tea."[55] But European demand for, and Chinese exports of, silk and tea

[54] The Foshan cotton textile industry employed "about 50,000 [people]; when there is pressing demand for work the number of laborers is considerably increased; they occupy about 2,500 shops, averaging usually twenty in each shop." *Chinese Repository*, Nov. 1833, 305–306.

[55] John McNeill, "Of Rats and Men: A Synoptic Environmental History of the Island Pacific," *Journal of World History* 5, no. 2 (1994): 319.

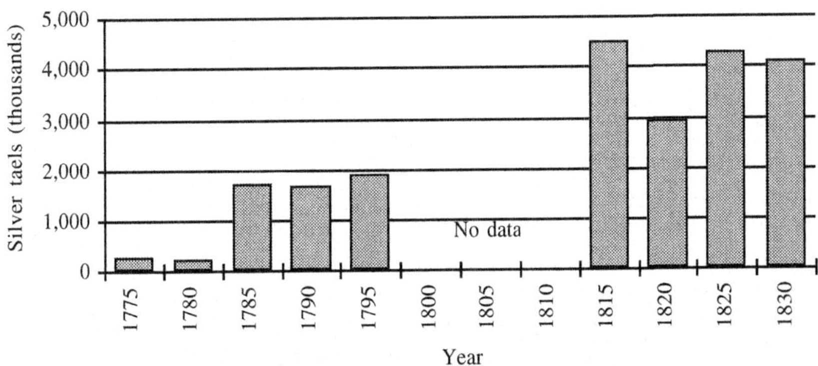

Figure 5.3. Value of Indian raw cotton imports, 1775–1833. Source: Yan Zhongping et al., *Zhonggo jindai jingji tongji ziliao xuanji* (Beijing: Kexue chuban she, 1953), 11.

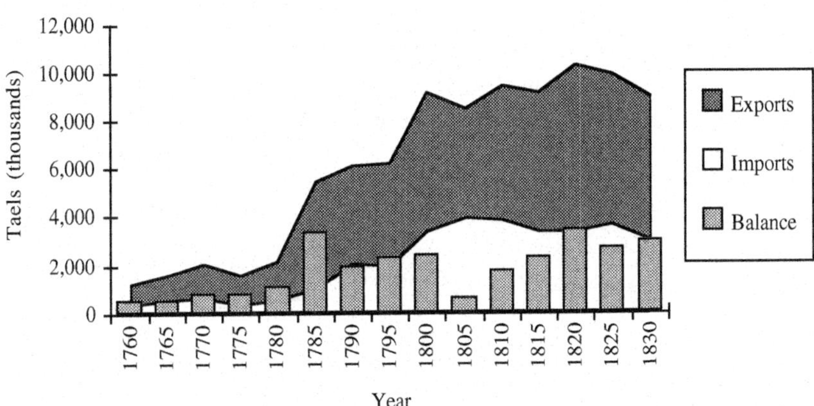

Figure 5.4. China's foreign trade balances, five-year averages, 1760–1833. Source: Adapted from Alvin So, *The South China Silk District: Local Transformation and World-System Theory* (Albany: State University of New York Press, 1986), 57.

increased dramatically in the 1780s, accompanied by a smaller increase in imports – the balance of some 2 million taels annually was in silver bullion imports into Guangzhou, leading to substantial positive balances of trade for China.

If the silver imports lubricated the Lingnan economy, Europeans' reliance on silver bullion to balance their trade deficits was, however, a problem in search of a solution. To stem the flow of silver to China, the EIC had been searching for a commodity that the Chinese would purchase in sufficient quantities to pay for their purchases; raw cotton supplied part of the answer, but it was insufficient, and so silver continued to flow into China. According to data compiled by Yan Zhongping, on-balance millions of taels of silver poured into China in the first decades of the nineteenth century. As is well known, the British increasingly used opium to balance their trade,[56] not merely stemming the flow of silver into China, but reversing it by 1827 (see Figure 5.5).[57]

In effect, China's domestic demand for cotton drove the expanding trade with Europe and North America. Until the early nineteenth century, China probably had the largest industrial capacity of any country in the world – it had the textile manufacturing prowess in centers like Guangzhou and Shanghai – manufacturing raw cotton into finished goods that not only satisfied domestic demand, but provided for the export market too. This provides a new context for understanding the British opium trade. As the story usually gets told, the British EIC turned to opium because Europe's demand for Chinese products, in particular porcelain, tea, and silk, could not be balanced with imports of any other kind. That is only partially true, for there was a large and growing Chinese demand for Indian raw cotton. The Chinese domestic textile market and its circuits of trade, including the sugar–raw cotton exchange linking Guangdong to the lower Yangzi, thus also are important elements in the story. But as it was, the Chinese market for Indian raw cotton did not expand fast enough to sate European appetities for tea and silk, and the EIC did not have the economic power to break the Guangdong textile industry's reliance upon Chinese raw cotton from the Yangzi River delta. With opium pouring into China in the nineteenth century, exports of silk (and tea)[58] increased substantially, pre-

[56] McNeill, "Of Rats and Men," 319. Ironically, the English discovery of opium as the means to balance their trade imbalance with China spelled a reprieve for Pacific island wildlife: "By 1850 Chinese tea could be had without hunting down the last seals or sandalwood. Opium provided the key that unlocked Chinese trade. As the British East India Company converted tracts of Bengal to opium production, China's commercial horizons shifted, and the Pacific trade lapsed into insignificance," 325. For the data, see Yan Zhongping et al., *Zhongguo jindai jingji tongji ziliao xuanji* (Beijing: Kexue Chuban She, 1953), 27–31.

[57] This whole sordid story has been told elsewhere and will not be repeated here. See Hsin-pao Chang, *Commissioner Lin and the Opium War* (New York: Norton, 1970); Peter Ward Fay, *The Opium War, 1840–1842* (Chapel Hill: University of North Carolina Press, 1975); and Arthur Waley, *The Opium War through Chinese Eyes* (Stanford: Stanford University Press, 1958).

[58] Although virtually all tea was exported from the ports of Guangzhou (because of the restrictions on trading), mostly it came from the hills of Fujian and Jiangxi. See Robert Gardella, *Harvesting Mountains: Fujian and the China Tea Trade, 1757–1937* (Berkeley and Los Angeles: University of California Press, 1994). The increased European demand for tea thus had little impact on land use patterns in Guangdong.

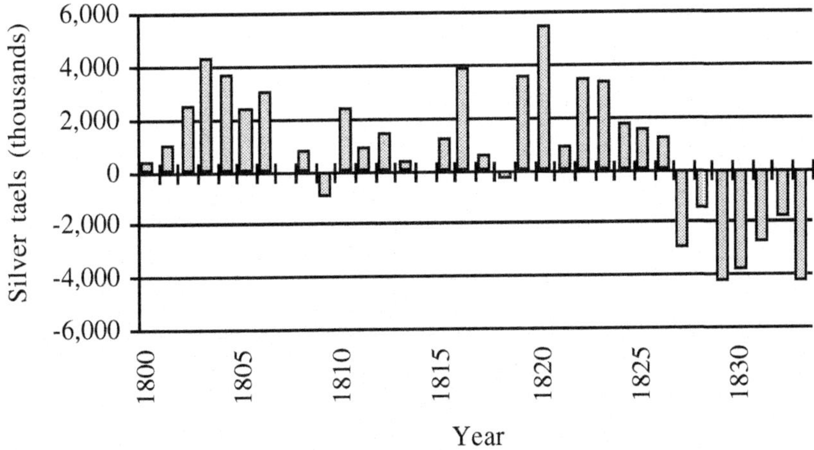

Figure 5.5. Silver flows at Guangzhou, 1800–33. Source: Yan Zhongping et al., *Zhonggo jindai jingji tongji ziliao xuanji* (Beijing: Kexue chuban she, 1953), 31, 32.

cipitating changes in agricultural land use patterns in Guangdong's Pearl River delta.

Silk. Where we can only guess at the amounts of sugar entering the export trade, figures for silk are available[59] and, for the most part, parallel the general pattern for trade between Europe and China. From about 25,000 *piculs* in 1723, exports of Guangdong silk increased steadily for the next century, reaching about 1.1 million *piculs* in 1828 (see Figure 5.6). The trend was virtually linear, with the silk exports increasing by 10,000 *piculs* each year. From 1828 to 1834 the silk exports doubled, largely because the vast increase in the amount of smuggled opium gave the EIC greater resources to buy silk (as well as tea). The Opium War (1839–42) disrupted trade, but afterwards silk exports quickly rebounded to the 1834 level before doubling again from 1850 to 1860. The story of silk exports thus can be characterized by steady if not unspectacular growth during the eighteenth century followed by exponential growth in the 1830s and the 1850s.

To meet this demand, the increased silk production in the eighteenth and nineteenth centuries came not from any technological advances, but from expansion of the tried and true mulberry embankment and fish pond method pioneered centuries earlier (see Chapter 3). According to Alvin So's calcula-

[59] Alvin So, *The South China Silk District: Local Transformation and World-System Theory* (Albany: State University of New York Press, 1986), 80–81.

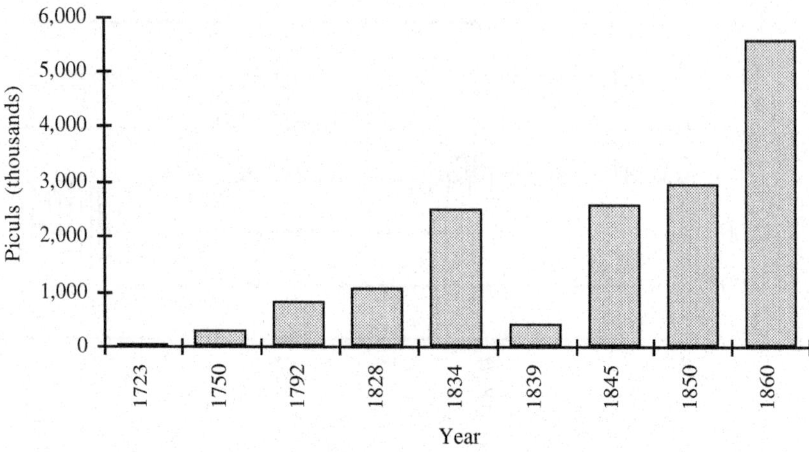

Figure 5.6. Exports of Pearl River delta silk from Guangzhou, 1723–1860. Source: Adapted from Alvin So, *The South China Silk District: Local Transformation and World-System Theory* (Albany: State University of New York Press, 1986), 80–81.

tions, to increase silk exports from 25,000 to 1.1 million *piculs* required expanding the acreage devoted to mulberry trees from 500 to 22,000 *mu*, nearly all of which occurred in the Pearl River delta counties of Nanhai, Shunde, and Xiangshan. However, because of the mulberry tree and fish pond combination, the amount of land converted to the system as a whole was substantially greater. Indeed, So states that the rule of thumb was that "the land in about four-tenths of any given area was dug out and large ponds were formed. The excavated soil was thrown on the other six-tenths of the land, thereby raising the level."[60] Thus, the amount of land converted to the mulberry tree and fish pond combination by 1828 was more than 35,000 *mu* (about 6,000 acres).

Like the expansion of acreage devoted to sugarcane, the increase in the mulberry tree and fish pond system came at the expense of rice paddies. Nanhai and Shunde county gazetteer entries are quite explicit on this point: "Rice fields were turned into mulberry embankments and fish ponds; mulberry bushes were planted on the newly constructed embankments . . . lower part with fishing, upper part with mulberry."[61] By the twentieth century, according to the geographer Trewartha, virtually all the land in Nanhai and Shunde counties had become devoted to sericulture: "From one of the low hills in the delta's specialized mulberry area as far as the eye can reach in any direction,

[60] Ibid., 84–85. [61] Translated and quoted in ibid, 85.

there are closely spaced fields of dark green mulberry shrubs intersected by narrow canals and dotted with ponds of water scattered irregularly between the fields."[62] Demand for silk thus prompted a series of changes in land use patterns in Lingnan, with peasant-farmers in the Pearl River delta converting rice paddies to the mulberry tree and fish pond system.

Unlike the conversion of rice paddy to sugarcane, which peasant farming families could carry out with small advances from sugar merchants, digging the fish ponds and building the embankments and then buying the fish and the mulberry seeds required amounts of capital beyond the reach of peasant-families. Thus, according to both So and Mazumdar, the local gentry elite actively encouraged and funded the conversion of rice paddies to sericulture.[63] However, like sugarcane, peasant farming families, rather than hired laborers or slaves, remained the primary producers of the fish and the mulberry leaves, often with credit advanced by the gentry owners of the land.[64]

Meeting the world demand for silk, then, like sugar, resulted in a particular form of commercialization where land that had been devoted to rice was converted to a crop that was sold on the market, rather than consumed by the peasant family. What this pattern meant was that peasant-producers therefore had to obtain their food not from their farms, but from the market. That this pattern developed is important for our understanding of the relationship between the environment and economy of Lingnan, for one alternative response to the commercial impulse might have been the protection of food-producing land and the creation or clearance of additional land for the new commercial crop.

Other Cash Crops. By the early eighteenth century, peasant-farmers in Guangdong had returned to producing cash, industrial, and commercial crops to such an extent that the province was known as a chronic food-deficit region. During the reign of the Yongzheng emperor (1723–35), officials from both Guangdong and other provinces complained that Guangdong produced just one-half of the rice required to meet the needs of its population because, as one official charged, "coveting profit, [peasant-farmers] have planted much land in *long-yan*, sugarcane, tobacco, and indigo."[65] Peasant-farmers who had turned to commercial crops weren't alone in looking to the market to buy rice; so did a substantial non-farm-working population: "Those who work for wages, who fish, who work in the salt pans and who pick tea outnumber those who work in the fields," one provincial official observed in 1735.[66]

62 Trewartha, quoted in ibid.
63 So, *The South China Silk District*, 86–87; Mazumdar, *A History of the Sugar Industry*, 276.
64 So, *The South China Silk District*, 89–90.
65 Memorial dated Yongzheng 5.4.13, in YZCZZ, vol. 8: 25.
66 Memorial dated YZ 12.9.2, in YZCZZ, vol. 23: 468.

Commercialized agriculture, even in the early decades of the eighteenth century, thus may have claimed half or more of the arable land in Guangdong province. Not only is there little reason to think that that percentage shrank during the eighteenth century, but all the available evidence suggests that peasant-farmers devoted an increasing proportion of their land to commercial and nonfood crops such as sugarcane, mulberry bushes, fruit trees, tobacco, and vegetables, as well as to fish ponds.[67]

Rising prices for silk,[68] and perhaps for other cash commodities and crops as well, provided peasant-farmers with the economic incentive to abandon rice. Calculations by Xu and Wu show that on a five-*mu* farm in the lower Yangzi, farmers could reap five times the income from mulberry leaves as they could from rice.[69] That differential, though, does not mean that peasant-farmers converted all rice paddies into cash crops. In eastern Guangdong, for instance, peasant-farmers were observed strictly dividing their fields between rice and sugar, even though planting sugarcane alone was more "profitable."[70] As James C. Scott reminds us, peasant-farmers often followed the "safety first" principle, where subsistence concerns weighed heavily in their cropping choices.[71] But where peasant-producers could be assured of a regular and cheap market supply of food (this will be taken up in greater detail in Chapter 8), their willingness to devote a larger portion of their land to cash crops increased.

Markets and the Marketing System

As noted in Chapter 3, markets had been an important part of the Lingnan economy from very early times, assuming an important role in the commercialization of the late sixteenth and early seventeenth centuries. The same was to be true in the eighteenth and nineteenth centuries. Markets linked peasant-producers to the export market in Guangzhou and the manufacturing center in Foshan, as well as to the rice market in Wuzhou and Jiangmen. Markets were of various sizes and functions, ranging from small village markets, where peasants exchanged agricultural produce every other day or so, to wholesale warehousing markets, where goods were gathered for shipment to Guangzhou and from there to other parts of China or the world. For commodities for which there was more than a local market, such as raw silk, sugar, or rice,

[67] Ye and Tan, "Lun Zhujiang sanjiaozou de zu tian," ch. 4. See also Mazumdar, *A History of the Sugar Industry*, ch. 5.

[68] Shih Min-hsiung, *The Silk Industry in Ch'ing China*, E-tu Zen Sun, trans. (Ann Arbor: University of Michigan Press, 1976), 46.

[69] Xu and Wu, eds., *Zhongguo zibenzhuyi de mengya*, 207.

[70] Adele Fielde, *A Corner of Cathay* (New York: Macmillan, 1894), 11–12.

[71] James C. Scott, *The Moral Economy of the Peasant: Subsistence and Rebellion in Southeast Asia* (New Haven: Yale University Press, 1976).

Table 5.1. *Market density, ca. 1731*

Markets/1,000 sq. km	Number of counties
0–4	28
4–8	26
8–16	21
16–32	4
32–64	2

merchants sometimes went to the countryside to buy them, or peasant-producers themselves brought the goods to market. However the commodities got there, markets moved agricultural produce or other industrial raw materials from the farm to the city, and manufactured items like cotton cloth back out to the villages.

Market Density. The number of markets in any given area is a rough measure of the level of commercialization of the rural economy. The most complete data available come from the 1731 edition of the Guangdong provincial gazetteer; unfortunately, data from Guangxi province are so scattered as to be virtually useless, so I cannot provide an overall view of Lingnan as a whole. Nonetheless, the data that are available will provide a good picture of Guangdong, and with other nonquantitative data we can begin to imagine how Guangxi fit into the picture too.

Maps 5.2 a and b show the density of markets in Guangdong province. Of the 81 counties for which data are available, the densities range from less than 1 to more than 40 per 1,000 square kilometers. Another way to describe these numbers is that within a radius of 15 kilometers (i.e., about a three-hour walk from the most distant point), there would have been between 1 and 40 markets. Not surprisingly, the Pearl River delta had the densest network of markets; Nanhai and Shunde counties had 44 and 43 markets, respectively, per 1,000 square kilometers. The lowest densities were in Guangning, Ruyuan, and Gan'en counties, each of which had but 1 market in the entire county and was located far from Guangzhou, on the Lingnan periphery. Certainly there was a rough correspondence between density and distance from Guangzhou. But the pattern is not that clean, with pockets of high density in the southwest littoral, on Hainan Island, and to the east and west of Guangzhou. The reason, of course, is that each of these regions had larger markets that served their areas and were linked to the Guangzhou–Foshan urban area (the shape of the distribution of markets in the various regions of Lingnan will be discussed more later). Nonetheless, when classified by density, the counties arrange themselves in a hierarchy with five levels (see Table 5.1; each level represents twice the density of the preceding one).

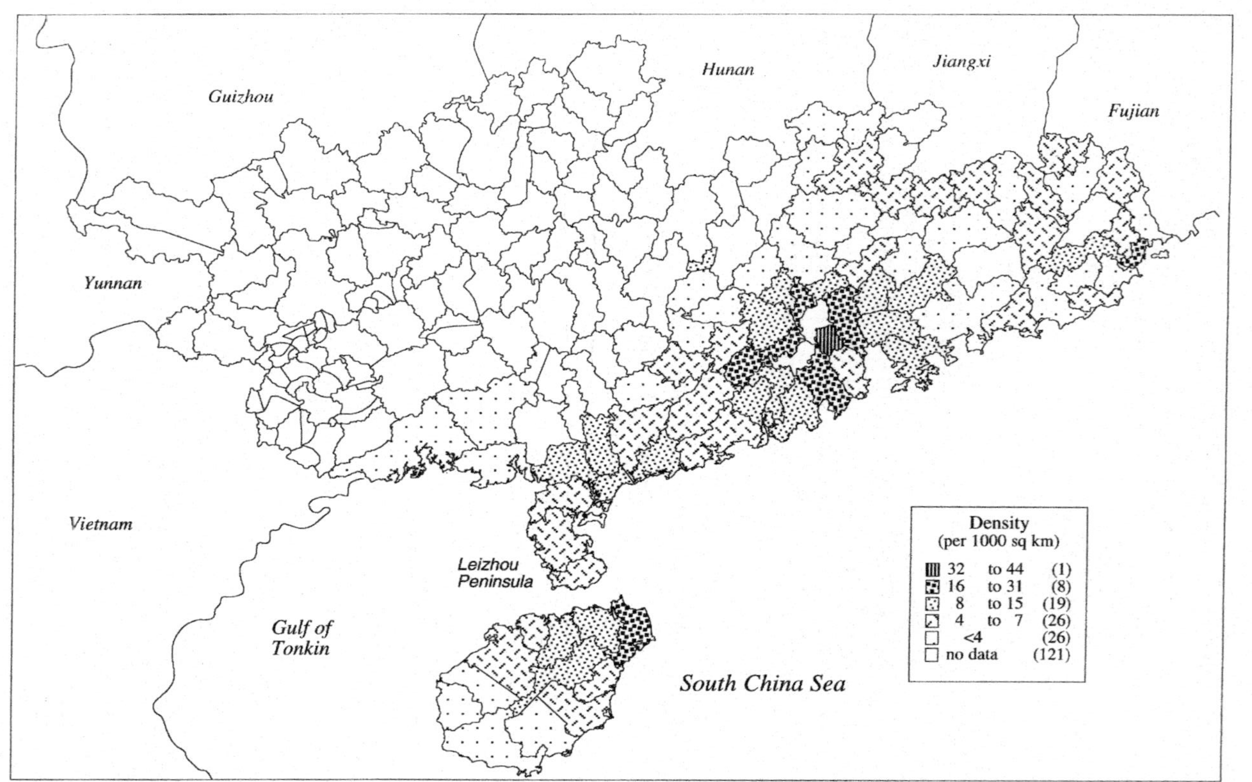

Map 5.2a. Markets, ca. 1731

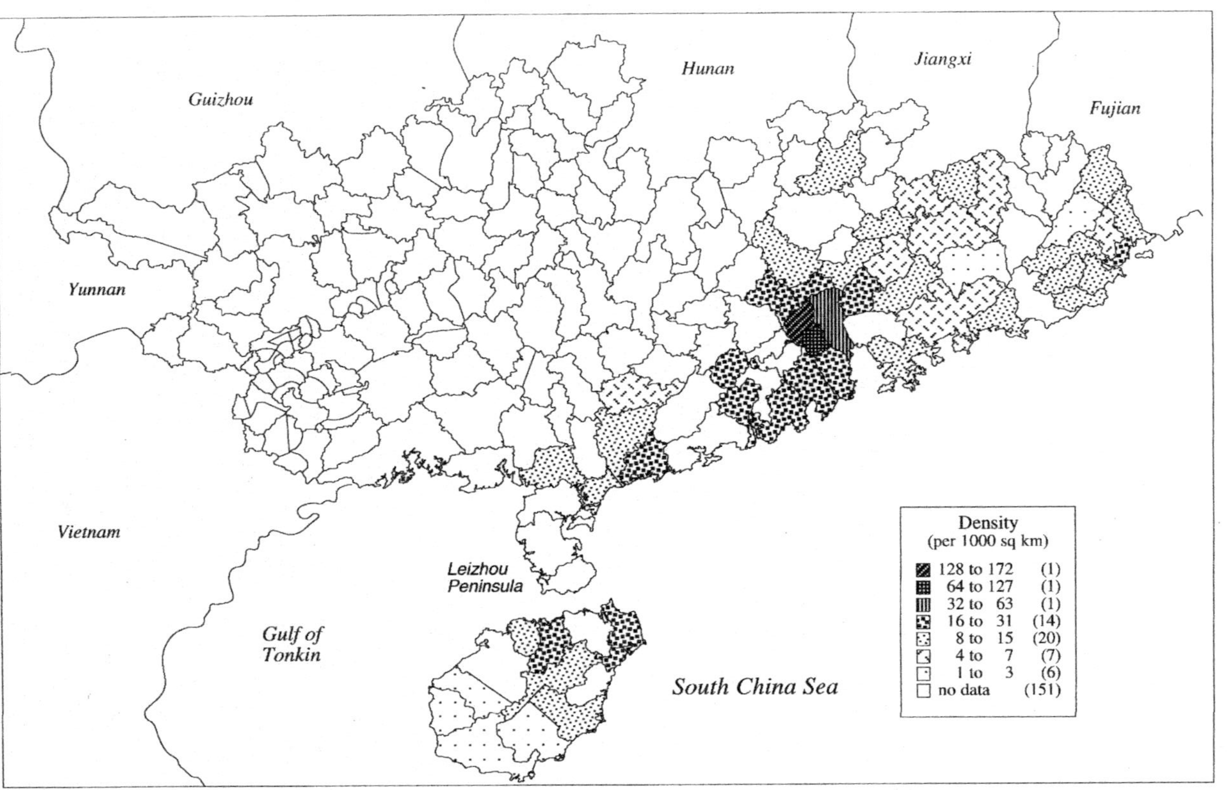

Map 5.2b. Markets, ca. 1890

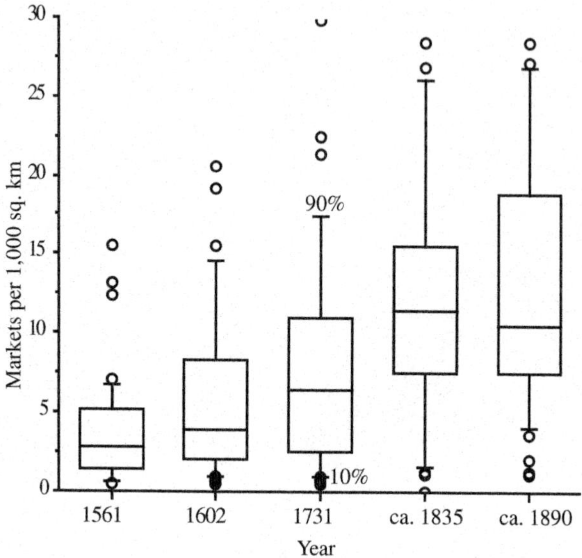

Figure 5.7. Percentile distribution of market density in Lingnan counties, 1561–1890.

Although the data are not as complete for other periods, what are available show that the density of markets increased over time (see Figure 5.7). What the box plots in Figure 5.7 mean is that the middle 50 percent of all counties had between 2 and 7 markets per 1,000 square kilometers in 1731; a century later around 1835, the density of markets for the middle 50 percent had increased to a range between 8 and 15 markets per 1,000 square kilometers. Increasing density, of course, was a function of the increased number of markets. But what Figure 5.7 also shows is that the density of markets increased more or less steadily in all areas of Lingnan, not just in a select few.

That does not mean, of course, that markets in some counties had not increased at a faster pace than in others. Using the classification scheme in Table 5.1 as the basis for selecting representative counties, I have graphed the number of markets in four counties from 1602 to 1890 (see Figure 5.8). What is most notable about Figure 5.8, of course, is the clear way in which Nanhai county broke away from the rest of the pack in the years after 1775. Nanhai, of course, was not simply a county in the Pearl River delta, but was the county most connected with both the silk and the cotton textile industries. Until 1775, the formation of markets in Nanhai did not advance faster than anywhere else in Guangdong, but after the major increase in trade with Europe, the number

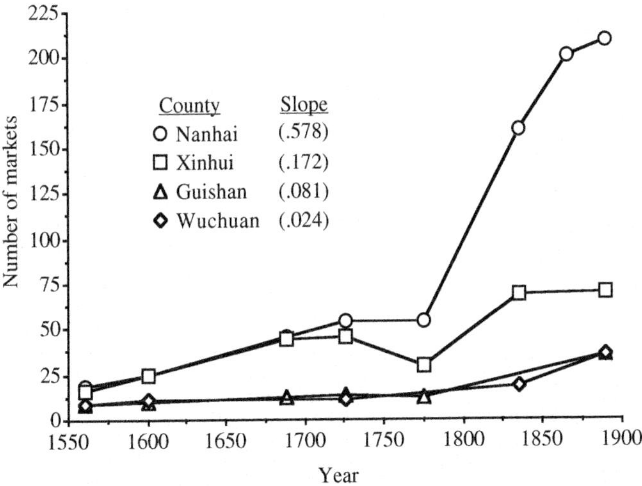

Figure 5.8. Market increase in selected counties, 1561–1890.

of markets there galloped ahead, forming at the rate of about one new market every 2 years, leaving the rest of Guangdong behind, where new markets formed at rates from about one every 40 years (as in Wuchuan) to one every 12 years (as in Guishan).[72]

Patterns of Market Distribution in Lingnan. On a featureless plain, G. William Skinner predicted, markets would tend to arrange themselves hexagonally into nested hierarchies. Lingnan, of course, was not a featureless plain, so market establishment was both constrained and, sometimes, determined by its particular physiography. According to Luo Yixing, a Chinese scholar who has given the matter some thought, Qing-era markets in Lingnan can be classified into three types: (1) more or less evenly distributed (as over the surface of a plate) in the Pearl River delta; (2) a dendritic formation found in the drainage areas of the North, East, and West Rivers and along the coast; and (3) necklaced around Hainan Island (see Figure 5.9).[73]

In all of Lingnan, only the Pearl River delta resembled a featureless plain, and even then that had been built up over the centuries and was crisscrossed with a dense network of irrigation ditches that also served, at high tide, as boat-

[72] These rates are derived from the slope of the trend line for each of those counties (the figures in parentheses in Figure 5.8).

[73] Luo Yixing, "Shi lun Qing dai qian zhong qi Lingnan shichang zhongxin de fenbu tedian," paper presented at the Fourth International Conference on Qing Social and Economic History, Shenzhen, 1987.

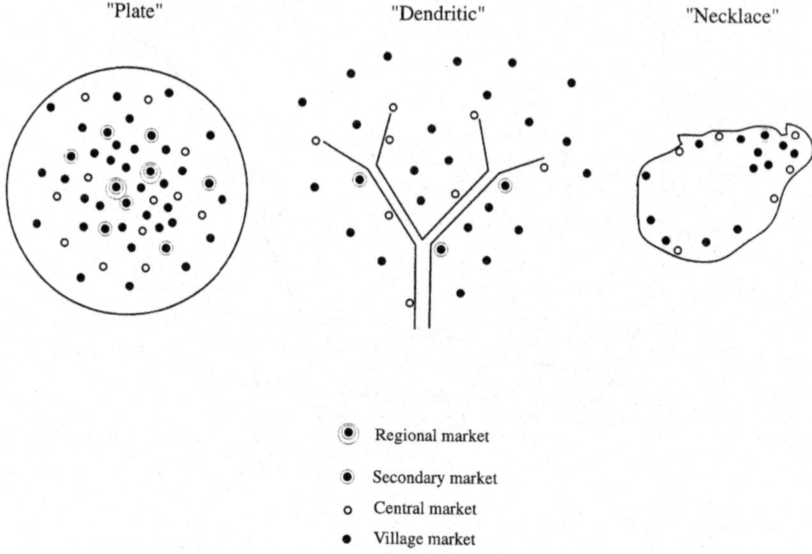

Figure 5.9 Three patterns of market systems in Lingnan (Luo Yixing's model).

carrying waterways. Villages, markets, and towns spread across the delta, like peas on a plate.[74] Elsewhere in Lingnan, the rivers and the coasts gave shape to the pattern of markets. The East, North, and West Rivers all flowed through hill country with little arable land except in the narrow river valleys, while shorter rivers like the Mei or the Jian flowed directly into the ocean. With transportation dependent upon the rivers, markets formed on the rivers, with larger and more important markets such as those in Shaozhou or Sanshui at the confluence of two or more rivers, forming the dendritic pattern. And on Hainan Island, with its mountainous interior, nearly all markets existed on the narrow coastal strip or in the only plain on the northeast corner of the island, rendering the necklace shape.

The Functional Hierarchy of Markets in Lingnan. As the pioneering work of G. William Skinner has demonstrated, markets in late imperial China were not randomly scattered across the countryside, but rather arranged themselves into nested hierarchies that made spatial and functional sense. Skinner classified markets into eight categories, ranging from the lowest level, which he called the "standard marketing system," to the highest, which he termed the

[74] Whether or not these markets could be abstracted into the hexagonal pattern predicted by Skinner is open to further consideration; I will not attempt it here.

"regional metropolis"; in between lay six other kinds of markets, distinguished by their function within the marketing hierarchy.

Like Skinner, Luo Yixing also saw a hierarchy of markets in Lingnan, but instead of eight he classified markets into four categories. In Luo's scheme, the lowest level was the "village market"; next came the "central market," which served 8 to 10 village markets. At the third level were larger secondary markets, which not only served the central markets, but also had direct wholesaling ties to the regional market, which in Lingnan was the Guangzhou–Foshan urban area. Although Luo and Skinner differ on the number of levels in the marketing hierarchy, both do see a hierarchy, and while it is conceivable that their two systems could be reconciled, I prefer to follow Luo's taxonomy for Guangdong. The reason is that Skinner's abstractions presume a featureless plain and nested hierarchies of markets that give peasant-farmers choices about which markets to frequent, whereas Luo's scheme, especially his dendtritic pattern, restricts choices, sometimes to just one market. Monopsony power thus is not likely to emerge in Skinner's scheme, while in Luo's characterization, it is a possible, if not probable, outcome. These differences will matter later in explaining rice price behavior and the structure of the market for rice (see Chapter 8).

In the Pearl River delta, Luo describes all four levels of markets and their interaction. At village markets, which served one or many villages, peasants gathered daily to buy and sell agricultural produce and daily necessities. Mostly without permanent structures or shops, village markets were small-scale affairs, although some in Shunde county specialized in mulberry leaves or rice. At the "central" markets, the next level in Luo's hierarchy, which encompassed 10–20 village markets, peasants could buy farm implements and animals, imported rice, fruit tree stock, fish fry, and silk worm cocoons.

Indeed, what Luo calls the "central" markets played a crucial role in the silk industry, linking peasant-producers of raw silk to the export market in Foshan and Guangzhou. At Dagang market in Shunde, and Chaolian market in Xinhui, merchants from Guangzhou, Foshan, Jiangmen, and Xiangshan purchased raw silk directly from peasant-producers. While some of these markets continued to serve a variety of local needs, a few became specialized in the silk or the fish markets. The market at Jiujiang in Nanhai county dealt only in silk, which then "was shipped to Guangzhou or Foshan for export."[75] And because of the link between silk and fish, Jiujiang was the central market for peasant-families to purchase fish fry, which came from as far away as Qujiang in the north and Chaozhou to the east. Because most of the peasant-farmers in this region had converted to the mulberry embankment and fish pond combination, Jiujiang also became a large market for rice imported from Guangxi. Chen village market in Shunde functioned in much the same way, as did the market in the town of Xinhui.

[75] Luo, "Shi lun Qing dai qian zhong qi Lingnan shichang," 8.

Above the "central" markets in Luo's third level were wholesale markets in larger towns (the secondary markets), where agricultural or forest products were warehoused before being shipped to Guangzhou or Foshan. Jiangmen, which was located at the confluence of the lower reaches of the West and Tan Rivers, was a major port for products arriving from Hainan Island. Other wholesale market centers included Macao, Xi'nan market on the West River in Sanshui, Gaoyao further up the West River in Zhaoqing, and Shilong on the East River in Dongguan.

At the top of the Lingnan marketing hierarchy sat the Guangzhou–Foshan urban area. Foshan housed the cotton and silk textile industries and, in addition, was the location for the final roasting and curing of all the tea that was exported to Europe, as well as a major iron pot manufactory. The urban area was comprised of two cities just a few miles apart – the port of Guangzhou, which served the Nanyang and foreign markets, and Foshan, which captured the products flowing down the West and North Rivers. Of these product flows, the largest and most important was the West River traffic, which linked Foshan directly to the major wholesale rice markets in Wuzhou, Xunzhou, and Guilin.

Where the Pearl River delta contained four levels of markets, in Luo's analysis the dendritic and necklace patterns contained three; of course, if those patterns also are reconceived to include Guangzhou and Foshan, then they too would have four levels. In the dendritic pattern of markets in the East, West, and North River drainage basins, Luo concludes, virtually all of the central and secondary markets in these areas gathered rice from their hinterlands for export downriver to Foshan. A few examples will suffice. As far up the East River as Heyuan, the market exported rice downriver, and even the market in Yong'an, perhaps one of the most remote and least accessible counties in all of Lingnan, exported rice to Heyuan. In Guangxi, two of the three largest rice export markets were on the West River, one in Wuzhou and the other upriver at Xunzhou; a third collected rice from Liuzhou prefecture. Rice merchants from Guangzhou and Foshan established offices (*hui guan*) at all of the third-level markets and were quite active in purchasing rice for the Guangdong market. Indeed, the most important commercial crop throughout the vast Lingnan hinterland drained by these major rivers was rice. So great was market demand for rice by the nineteenth century that peasants in Fengchuan county (up the West River near the border with Guangxi) "ate yams and sweet potatoes in order to sell rice for cash," and in Cangwu and Cenxi counties peasants without immediate access to water transportation carried sacks of rice on their backs to market.[76]

[76] Luo cites more than enough evidence to support his contention that virtually all interior markets connected to Guangzhou by waterways exported rice to the Guangzhou–Foshan–Pearl River delta region. Ibid., 8–15.

In the necklace pattern on Hainan Island, all of the village and central markets fed into the island's largest market at the port of Haikou. Located on the northern tip of the island just opposite the mainland, at the mouth of the largest river on the island, and just a few miles from the prefectural capital of Qiongzhou, Haikou had advantages that other markets on the island did not. Merchant associations from Guangzhou, Foshan, Gaozhou, and Chaozhou all had offices in Haikou, purchasing hardwood, betel nut, coconuts, and incense for export.

By the eighteenth century, then, markets throughout Lingnan linked peasant-farmers specializing in one or another agricultural product not just to other peasant-farmers, but to regional, national, and global markets. In brief, peasant-farmers in the Pearl River delta produced silk for the European market and sugarcane for shipment to markets in central China, and had their food needs met by rice imports from the vast hinterland drained by the East, North, and West Rivers, especially the latter. Rice thus became a commodity just like mulberry leaves, fish, or sugarcane and was no longer grown merely to be consumed on the farm, but sold on the market.

Conclusion

Stimulating and then driving the commercialization of agriculture in Lingnan was the explosive growth of Chinese coastal and foreign trade immediately following the lifting in 1684 of the ban on coastal shipping. Just as demand for cotton cloth stimulated the conversion of rice paddies to sugarcane fields, so did the demand for silk result in the transformation of rice paddies into fish ponds and mulberry tree embankments. When the peasant-farmers in the Pearl River delta turned to these cash crops and commodities, they then looked to the market to supply food. The demand for rice stimulated peasant-farmers along the river systems draining Lingnan to sell their rice downstream, while they substituted New World foods, in particular sweet potatoes, for rice in their diets (more will be said about this in later chapters). The formation of an integrated market for rice is such a large and important topic that it will be the subject of Chapter 8; suffice it to say here that the markets for silk, sugarcane, and cotton turned rice, the basic food staple of most people in Lingnan, into a commodity.

Guangzhou and Foshan comprised the hub of six trade circuits, all interconnected and linked through activities at the center. (1) To get the entire cycle started, merchants contracted with peasant-families growing sugarcane in the counties near Guangzhou (or within easy water access, such as Zengcheng or Yangjiang) for raw sugar, exchanging cotton yarn or cash for the sugar. (2) These merchants then exported raw and refined sugar to Jiangnan, bringing back raw cotton that was spun and woven in Foshan. (3) The cotton cloth and yarn was sold throughout the hinterland to peasant-families, especially in the

West River basin in Guangxi, who in turn sold rice for export to Foshan and Guangzhou. (4) From Foshan, some rice then was sold in markets in the Pearl River delta, where peasants produced raw silk that was shipped to Foshan for finishing there in the silk filatures. (5) From the Nanyang to Foshan and Guangzhou came raw cotton, rice, and dyes, while silk, cotton cloth, and refined sugar, all produced or warehoused in Foshan, were sold to the Nanyang. (6) Europeans purchased silk, cotton goods, and tea in Guangzhou, and brought raw cotton, silver, and opium in return.

The pattern of the commercialization of agriculture in Lingnan thus had several notable features. First, the peasant family farm remained central to the process. While it is true that the landlord-gentry class in the Pearl River delta provided the capital for converting rice paddies to fish ponds and mulberry embankments, neither they nor sugar merchants sought to replace peasant family producers with wage or slave labor.[77] Second, the peasant-farmers who responded to the commercial impulse did so by converting existing rice paddies to sugarcane or sericulture, rather than by clearing or creating new fields upon which to produce the commercial crops and products. Third, the commercialization of agriculture created a dense network of rural markets, where the peasant-producers sold their commercial crops and purchased food. Markets were important not just for the nonfood commercial crops and products, but especially for rice, for peasant-farmers in and around the Pearl River delta would not have responded to the national and world demand for silk and sugar by converting their rice paddies to fish ponds and cane fields without reasonable assurance that they could obtain their food supply from the market. Finally, a highly articulated set of six trade circuits integrated the regional economy of Lingnan and linked it not just with an emerging national market in Jiangnan, but also with the Chinese-dominated overseas trade in the Nanyang and to the growing European world economy.

After coastal trading resumed in 1684, specialization of agricultural production to meet both domestic and foreign demand led to rather far-reaching changes in land use patterns in Lingnan, continuing trends that had first appeared during the late Ming dynasty. A large number of peasant-farmers, now producing ever greater quantities of sugarcane or mulberry leaves for silkworms and less rice, increasingly relied on the market to supply them and their families with food. And market supply of rice depended not just on the skills of peasant-farmers in the river valleys of northern Guangdong or central Guangxi, but on the vagaries of climate too.

[77] Under other social formations, peasant-producers have been compelled to produce nonfood crops as serfs or slaves. But in late imperial China, the economy and the society was based upon a farm managed by peasant-families who made all their own production decisions.

6

"IT NEVER USED TO SNOW": CLIMATIC CHANGE AND AGRICULTURAL PRODUCTIVITY

"The climate has changed," China's Kangxi emperor declared near the end of his 61-year reign in 1717:

> I remember that before 1671, there was already new wheat [from the winter wheat crop] by the 8th day of the fourth month. When I was touring in Jiangnan, by the 18th day of the third month new wheat was available to eat. Now, even by the middle of the fourth month, wheat has not been harvested . . . I have also heard that in Fujian, where it never used to snow, since the beginning of our dynasty, it has.[1]

To the Kangxi emperor, the climate not only seemed to have turned colder during his lifetime, but the cooler climate had noticeably delayed the wheat harvest.[2] Indeed, the colder regime had begun much earlier, as we saw in Chapter 4, with the cold snaps in the early 1610s. Moreover, about the time that the Kangxi emperor commented upon the colder temperatures, the climate was about to change again, this time toward a warmer, wetter regime.

In this chapter I explore the relationship between climatic fluctuation and harvest yields that the Kangxi emperor observed, focusing mostly on the eighteenth century because of the availability of data and sources. In the first part of the chapter, I reconstruct the climate history of Lingnan from 1650 to 1850, examine in a general way the mechanisms by which climatic factors affected agriculture, and chart, using reports from Qing officials, annual fluctuations in harvest yields. Next, after presenting case studies that illustrate the ways in which flooding, cold snaps, and drought affected harvest yields and rice prices,

1 *Da Qing sheng zu (Kangxi) shi lu*, juan 272: 9–10, reprinted in *Qing shi lu Guangxi ziliao ji lu* (Nanning: Guangxi renmin chuban she, 1988), vol. 1: 208.

2 The emperor's observations, moreover, were not merely impressionistic musings. At least since 1693, the Kangxi emperor had been collecting weather reports from Jiangnan; he thus had some knowledge upon which to base his conclusion. And although he was incorrect about it never having snowed in Fujian, he was an astute observer of the connection between changes in the climate and the quality of the harvests. See Xie Tianzuo, "Qihou, shoucheng, liangjia, minqing – du 'Li Xu zouzhe,'" *Zhongguo shehui jingji shi yanjiu*, no. 4 (1984): 17–20.

Decade	Zhu Kezhen	Zheng Sizhong	Marks
1470	cooler	warmer	0
1480	cooler	warmer	2
1490	cooler	warmer	0
1500	cooler	cooler	4
1510	cooler	cooler	1
1520		cooler	1
1530		cooler	4
1540		cooler	4
1550	warmer	cooler	1
1560	warmer	warmer	1
1570	warmer	warmer	2
1580	warmer	warmer	2
1590	warmer	warmer	1
1600	warmer	warmer	1
1610	warmer	warmer	4
1620	cooler	cooler	1
1630	cooler	cooler	3
1640	cooler	cooler	0
1650	cooler	cooler	2
1660	cooler	cooler	3
1670	cooler	cooler	1
1680	cooler	cooler	6
1690	cooler	cooler	3
1700	cooler	cooler	4
1710	cooler	cooler	4
1720	warmer	cooler	3
1730	warmer	cooler	3
1740	warmer	warmer	1
1750	warmer	warmer	4
1760	warmer	warmer	5
1770	warmer	warmer	1
1780	warmer	warmer	5
1790	warmer	warmer	1
1800	warmer	warmer	3
1810	warmer	warmer	3
1820	warmer	warmer	1
1830	cooler	cooler	7
1840	cooler	cooler	3
1850	cooler	cooler	

Figure 6.1. Temperature fluctuations, 1470–1850.

I consider the extent to which pestilence too hurt harvest yields, concluding that climatic variability accounted for all of the significant, regionwide declines in harvests during the eighteenth century and leading to the question of what the people of Lingnan did in response to lessen the riskiness inherent in harvests that varied substantially from one year to the next.

Temperature. Evidence gathered from China's written historical record and recent reconstructions of northern hemisphere temperatures by climatologists enable us to describe climate changes over the two centuries from 1650 to 1850. Figure 6.1 illustrates the findings of three different analyses of the Chinese written record, with the cooler decades placed within boxes for easier identification.

The first column summarizes the findings of the Chinese climatologist Zhu Kezhen. In his classic study of China's historic temperatures, Zhu used phenological evidence and the dates of lakes freezing in the lower Yangzi to estimate the onset of colder temperatures.[3] For our purposes here, what is noteworthy is his identification of the century from the 1620s through the 1710s as cooler, with a warming trend evident from the 1720s on. The second column displays the findings of Zheng Sizhong, a geographer with the Institute of Science in Beijing; Zheng generally agrees with Zhu Kezhen, with the exception that Zheng thinks the colder temperatures extended well into the eighteenth century. To be sure, these categories of "warmer" and "cooler" decades are blunt instruments, being based on the climatologist's assessment of the number of records referring to unusual frosts or freezing, and the periodization too is a rough approximation. But both correspond to what is known about climatic trends reconstructed for other parts of the globe, and thus should be taken seriously as indicators of climatic tendencies in central and south China.

The third column reports my findings gleaned from gazetteer entries noting abnormal cold in Lingnan. What my column reports is simply the number of years in the decade in which one or more counties reported frost, freezing, or snow. If the number of counties reporting cold weather is a rough guide to the severity of the cold and if reports in two or more consecutive years can be taken as indicative of something like a trend, then the coldest periods as recorded in the gazetteers occurred in the 1680s and the 1830s, with shorter cold spells in other decades.[4] Furthermore, volcanic eruptions in the 1680s and 1830s provide reasonable explanations for cooling trends that link the temper-

[3] See especially Zhu, "Zhongguo jin wuqian nian lai qihou bianqian de chubu yanjiu," and Zhang Peiyuan and Gong Gaofa, "Three Cold Episodes in the Climatic History of China," in Ye Duzheng et al., eds., *The Climate of China and Global Climate: Proceedings of the Beijing International Symposium on Climate* (Berlin: Springer, 1987), 38–44.

[4] *Guangdong sheng ziran zaihai shiliao* (Guangzhou: Guangdong sheng wen shi yanjiu guan, 1961), 171–80.

atures in South China to global trends: in 1680 Krakatoa erupted followed by several years of other eruptions, and in 1831 a series of eruptions cooled global temperatures sufficiently to cause massive harvest failures in Japan in 1832 and 1833.[5]

My reconstruction of temperature trends in Lingnan thus generally accords with both Zhu Kezhen and Zheng Sizhong, with the exception that my method identifies the 1760s and the 1780s each as experiencing five years of colder than normal weather. Significantly, these three analyses are confirmed by a recent reconstruction of northern hemisphere temperatures.[6] The Jacoby–D'Arrigo reconstruction (Figure 6.2), based upon their analyses of tree-ring growth in the White Mountains of California, shows annual average temperature departures from the 1951–80 mean.[7] Charting annual temperature fluctuations, the Jacoby–D'Arrigo reconstruction reveals more variability than the decadal summaries of Chinese written materials, but nonetheless tells basically the same story: temperatures increased from a low around 1700 to higher levels for most of the eighteenth century before plunging again after 1807 and bottoming out in the 1830s and 1840s.

In summary, whether literary evidence from China's written sources or tree-ring growth in North America is used, the best available evidence all points to

[5] Lamb, "Volcanic Dust in the Atmosphere," 425–550.

[6] China is unique in the world in having such a long-term historical record from which to extract relevant climatological data; scientists elsewhere have had to develop and calibrate other proxy records from which to reconstruct global temperature trends. Given the length of China's written record and its contribution to reconstructing past climates – as the work by Zhu Kezhen and Zhang De'er has demonstrated – an important question is the extent to which temperature trends are global (or at least hemispheric) rather than merely local. This question is important not merely for those scientists now pondering the connection between climate change and the prospects for global warming, but also for historians (like me) trying to uncover the historic relationships between climate change and food production. Signficantly, recent studies have answered these questions by demonstrating that temperatures in different places in the northern hemisphere are highly correlated: China's temperatures for the period 1880–present show a 0.95 correlation with northern hemisphere temperatures. For a discussion of this issue, see R. S. Bradley et al., "Secular Fluctuations of Temperature over Northern Hemisphere Land Areas and Mainland China since the Mid-19th Century," in Ye et al., *The Climate of China*, 84. Zhang Peiyuan and Gong Gaofa conclude that eighteenth-century European and North American temperature "trends are the same as in China." See Zhang and Gong, "Three Cold Episodes in the Climatic History of China," 43. For graphic depictions of the correlation, see Zhang and Crowley, "Historical Climate Records in China and the Reconstruction of Past Climate," 843. See also Lough et al., "Relationships between the Climates of China and North America," in Ye et al., *The Climate of China*, 89–105.

[7] Jacoby and D'Arrigo, "Reconstructed Northern Hemisphere Annual Temperature since 1671 Based on High-Latitude Tree-Ring Data from North America," 39–59. Their data are used here not just because they are the most reliable reconstruction of northern hemisphere annual temperatures, but also because they most kindly made their database available to me. The chart plots the deviation of temperatures from "present," defined as the mean for 1950–79.

Figure 6.2. Northern hemisphere temperatures, 1671–1972. Source: Gordon C. Jacoby and Rosanne D'Arrigo, "Reconstructed Northern Hemisphere Annual Temperature since 1671 Based on High-Latitude Tree-Ring Data from North America," *Climatic Change* 14 (1989): 39–59.

the same general conclusion about Qing-era temperature trends in Lingnan: after unusually cold temperatures in the 1680s and early 1690s, temperatures warmed in the eighteenth century, plunged in the first half of the nineteenth century with the coldest temperatures being reached in the 1830s, and then warmed again in the second half of the nineteenth century. The Kangxi emperor thus had been right: temperatures during some decades of his reign indeed were colder than "normal." What he could not know, of course, is that coincident with the end of his reign, temperatures had begun to trend upward again.

Rainfall. Thanks to the published results of an important climatological project headed by China's Bureau of Meteorology to quantify and map meteorological data contained in China's written historical records, China's historic rainfall and drought patterns can be analyzed.[8] Since the publication of this work in 1981, researchers have analyzed the data for periodicities and

[8] *Zhongguo jin wubai nian han lao fenbutu ji*, Zhongyang qixiang ju comp. (Beijing: Kexue chuban she, 1981). Both the data and the mapped results from this project must be used carefully. Researchers combed through hundreds of local gazetteers, compiling qualitative comments about the weather, and then quantified those comments on a scale of 1 to 5, with 3 representing "normal" rainfall; reports of extensive drought were quantified as a 5, while reports of extensive flooding were quantified as a 1, with lesser degrees of flood or drought assigned a 2 and a 4, respectively. Certainly, there are limitations inherent in this method, but I can think of no better way of mapping the vast quantity of data culled from the gazetteers and of obtaining a rough sense of changes in rainfall patterns over both time and space.

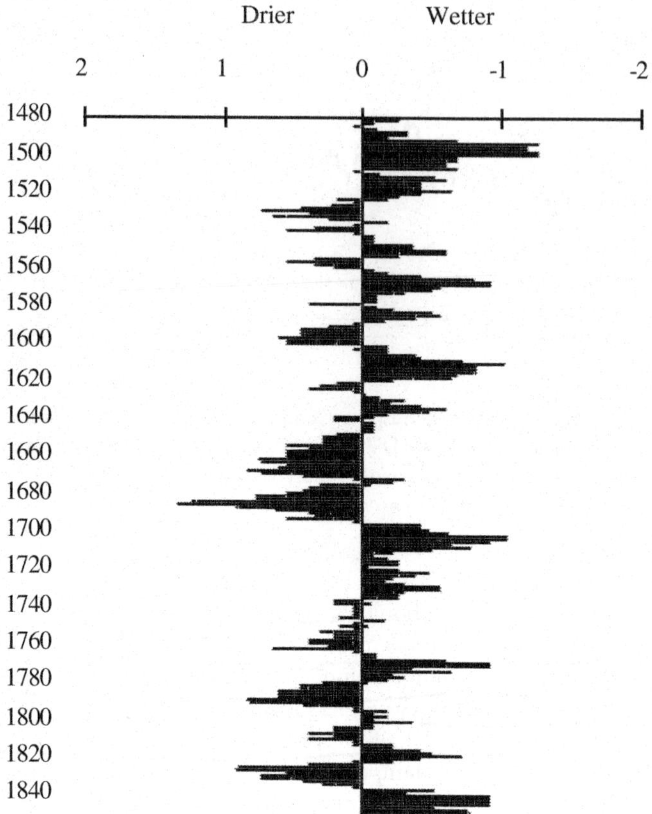

Figure 6.3. Guangzhou wetness index, 1480–1850.

regularities in the patterns of floods and droughts across China[9] and have classified the characteristic patterns into six types.[10]

The historical data compiled by the Bureau of Meteorology cover 10 stations in Lingnan. In the absence of any data recording actual rainfall

[9] See especially Gong Gaofa et al., "Ying yong shiliao feng qian jizai yanjiu Beijing diqu jiang shui liang dui dong xiaomai shoucheng de yingxiang," 444–51; Hameed et al., "An Analysis of Periodicities in the 1470 to 1974 Beijing Precipitation Record," 436–39; and Huang and Wang, "Investigations on Variations of the Subtropical High in the Western Pacific during Historic Times," 427–40.

[10] Wang and Zhao, "Droughts and Floods in China, 1470–1979," in Wigley et al., eds., *Climate and History*, 271–88. The types are: (1a) flood in most of China; (1b) drought in most of China; (2) drought in the Yangzi Valley, flood in other parts; (3) flood in the Yangzi Valley, drought in other parts; (4) flood in south China, drought in north China; and (5) drought in south China, flood in north China.

Table 6.1. *Climatic changes in Lingnan, 1650–1859*

Period	Years wet[a]	Years dry[b]	Climate
1650–64	13	2	Cool and wet
1665–99	11	24	Cool and dry
1700–36	28	9	Warming and wet
1737–88	25	27	Warm and variable
1789–1801	11	2	Warm and wet
1802–38	18	19	Cooling and variable
1839–59	17	5	Cool and wet

[a] Defined as types 1a, 2, or 4; see note 10.
[b] Defined as types 1b, 3, or 5; see note 10.

amounts, the best that the climatologists were able to do is to scour the Chinese written record for reports of floods and droughts, and then to assign, using a scale of 1 to 5 (see note 8), a quantitative value to those qualitative comments. I have used the Bureau's data to construct Figure 6.3, charting what I have called a "wetness index" for the city of Guangzhou from 1480 to 1850. What this chart shows is that the first half of the eighteenth century was wetter than the second half of the seventeenth century, that a drier regime prevailed in the middle of the eighteenth century, and that the latter part of the eighteenth century too was drier. In the nineteenth century, the colder decades from the 1820s through the 1840s were about evenly split between drier and wetter times.

An examination of the frequency of the six flood and drought types for south China for the two centuries beginning in 1650 (chosen to include 50 years on either side of the eighteenth century) shows definable periods marked by general wet or dry conditions, with two variable periods equally divided between types (1737–88 and 1802–38). Combining the temperature trends discussed earlier with both the general classification of flood and drought types and the Guangzhou "wetness index," I have characterized seven distinct climatic regimes in Lingnan from 1650 to 1850 (see Table 6.1).

Compared with the periods before or after, the eighteenth century thus appears generally warmer and wetter. But even within the eighteenth century, three distinct periods can be discerned: 1700–36 was warm and wet, 1737–88 generally was warm with alternating flood and drought periods, and 1789–1801 once again was characterized by a warm and wet climate. Even though I have characterized the eighteenth-century Lingnan climate as generally warm, cold air masses did penetrate the Nanling Mountains and settle over Guangdong; sometimes the cold winter was an isolated occurrence, but at other times the local gazetteers reported consecutive years of cold weather and drought.[11]

Nonetheless, the picture seems clear enough: unusually cold years and decades that had accompanied the mid-seventeenth-century crisis eased by the turn of the eighteenth century, giving way to a more benign and less hostile climate. But so what? What did it matter to the people and peasant-farmers of Lingnan, a region straddling the Tropic of Cancer and experiencing a "subtropical" climate? Was subtropical Lingnan immune from the adverse effects of cold snaps? Or were the climatic fluctuations in southernmost China sufficient to affect harvest yields, just as the Kangxi emperor had claimed happened in the Yangzi River delta? The evidence, I think, shows that even in south China, climatic fluctuations affected harvest yields.

Climate and Agriculture

The ways in which variations in temperature, rainfall, humidity, and solar radiation affect the growth rates and yields of particular food crops, especially cereal grains, are more complex than can be detailed here. Suffice it to say that, like other plants, cereal grains have certain requirements for warmth, moisture, and sunshine during their growing period if they are to mature and be harvested.[12] Too little or too much of any of these factors affects yields, but not necessarily in a linear way.[13] Climatic variability and change thus affect agriculture and harvest yields. Historical studies of the impact of climatic change on European and Japanese agriculture have focused on temperature variations, since cool summers and cold winters in temperate regions have had a greater adverse impact on harvest yields than variations in rainfall.[14] However, in subtropical Lingnan with its dependence on the summer monsoon to bring rainfall, additional attention must be paid to drought and flood.

[11] The relationship between changes in average annual temperatures and precipitation is not uniform and varies considerably around the world. In northern and western Europe, cold summers tended also to be wet; a similar pattern apparently holds for north China too. For central and south China, though, cooler periods have been related to increased frequency of drought. For a discussion, see Zhang and Crowley, "Historical Climate Records," 842–44.

[12] Lamb, *Climate, History and the Modern World*, 282.

[13] Richard W. Katz, "Assessing the Impact of Climatic Change on Food Production," *Climatic Change* 1 (1977): 85–96.

[14] See especially M. L. Parry and T. R. Carter, "The Effect of Climatic Variations on Agricultural Risk," *Climatic Change* 7 (1985): 95–110; and two works by John D. Post, *Food Shortage, Climatic Variability and Epidemic Disease in Preindustrial Europe*, and *The Last Great Subsistence Crisis in the Western World* (Baltimore: Johns Hopkins University Press, 1977). For Japan, see Junsei Kondo, "Volcanic Eruptions, Cool Summers, and Famines in the Northeastern Part of Japan," *Journal of Climate* 1 (Aug. 1988): 775–88.

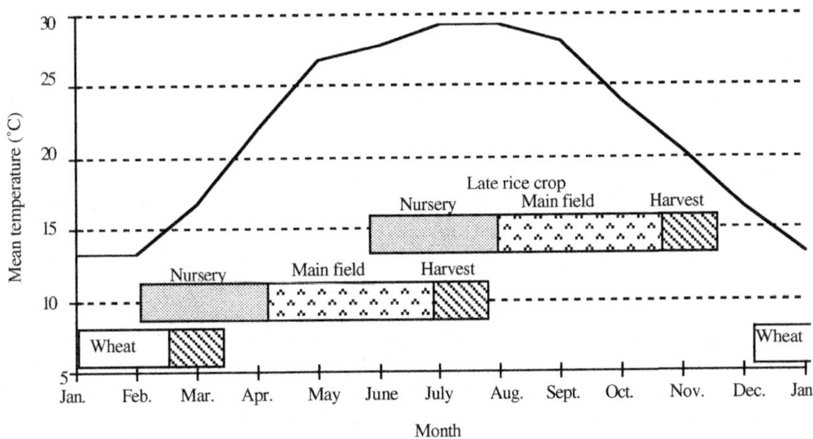

Figure 6.4. Annual cropping cycle.

In eighteenth-century Lingnan, the main crop was rice; wheat, as we saw in Chapter 3, had become a secondary crop. Throughout much of Guangdong province, the annual cropping pattern consisted of two crops of rice followed by wheat or vegetables. In some areas, because either higher elevation or a more northerly location shortened the frost-free growing season to 220–40 days, one crop of rice (rather than two) was followed by wheat or vegetables.

Based upon documentary materials for 1764–65 (two years without any discernible climatic abnormalities such as drought, flood, or extreme cold),[15] I have reconstructed the annual agricultural cycle and charted it underneath a curve of current mean monthly temperatures at Guangzhou (see Figure 6.4).[16] The first, or early, rice crop started around February 1 as seeds germinated and then grew for two months in a nursery before being transplanted to the main field around April 1 (the Qingming festival – held April 4 or 5 – was generally considered to be the time of transplanting); the crop then was harvested in the first two weeks of July. In June, while the first crop was ripening in the field, the second, or late, rice crop started in the nursery beds, being transplanted

[15] See the memorials dated QL29.3.4, in QLCZZ 20: 733; QL29.7.4, in QLCZZ 22: 104; QL29.11.9, in QLCZZ 23: 152; QL30.2i.25, in QLCZZ 24: 247; QL30.7.11, in QLCZZ 25: 476; and QL30.10.24, in QLCZZ 26: 424. An intercalary month is denoted by an "i." For the timing of planting in regions that double-cropped rice, see the memorial dated QL20.6.21, in QLCZZ 11: 801.

[16] The temperature curve in Figure 6.4 is based upon current mean temperatures. The mean annual temperature in 1764–65 may have been about 0.3°C lower than represented in the chart, therefore shifting the curve somewhat lower.

into the field about two weeks after the first crop was harvested. The late rice crop then was harvested from late October to early November; two weeks later the wheat or vegetable crop was planted directly in the field without any prior time sprouting in nursery beds. With just two or three weeks between the harvesting of one crop and the planting of the next, there was hardly an agricultural slack season in the rice–rice–wheat cycle.

Modern researchers have found that the favorable temperature range for the growth of rice is from 15–18°C to 30–33°C and that, within that range, temperatures of 20–22°C generally favor the growth and development of the rice plant; at temperatures below 15°C rice seeds either rot or do not germinate.[17] Under "normal" temperature conditions, then, in January and early February temperatures in Guangdong are below those required for rice; after daily mean temperatures rise to 15°C from middle to late February, seeds could be sprouted in nursery beds. The first crop then was transplanted into the main field just at the optimum temperature – 22°C – and harvested in July at the peak of both temperature and rainfall. For the first rice crop, the critical periods thus were first in the early stage of nursery germination or transplanting when unusual cold could kill the plants, and then while ripening, when a lack of water could desiccate the plants. For the second crop, the danger periods were following transplanting, when drought would pose problems, and in September or October, when unusual cold could kill the ripening crop. The double cropping of rice thus increased the riskiness of crop loss by pushing the sprouting time of the first crop and the ripening of the second crop into times of the year when colder than tolerable temperatures (for rice) were possible.

Cold temperatures affected rice primarily in two ways.[18] First, spring frost could kill the early crop, and fall frost could kill the standing second crop. Both could and did happen. In 1832 in Xingning county in eastern

[17] I. Nishiyama, "Effects of Temperature on the Vegetative Growth of Rice Plants," in International Rice Research Institute, *Proceedings of the Symposium on Climate and Rice* (Los Banos, Philippines: International Rice Research Institute, 1974), 159–85.

[18] S. Yoshida and F. T. Parao, "Climatic Influence on Yield Components of Lowland Rice in the Tropics," in International Rice Research Institute, *Proceedings of the Symposium on Climate and Rice*, 471–94, and K. Munakata, "Effects of Temperature and Light on the Reproductive Growth and Ripening of Rice," in International Rice Research Institute, *Proceedings of the Symposium on Climate and Rice*, 187–210. An additional way in which cold temperatures might have affected harvests was indirectly, by "precipitating" drought. Even if the spring temperatures proved warm enough to germinate seeds, the cold air mass may have disrupted the normal circulation of the North Pacific subtropical high, and with it the arrival of the summer monsoon. The mechanism by which cold temperatures created drought conditions is associated with the annual movement of the North Pacific subtropical high pressure system and the relationship of the movement of this high pressure system to the summer monsoon. For a lucid explanation of this complex phenomenon, see Zhang and Crowley, "Historical Climate Records in China and the Reconstruction of Past Climates," 835.

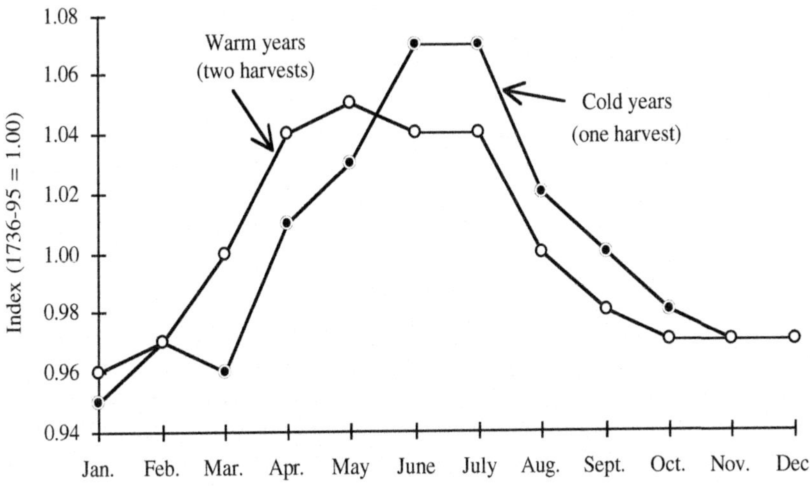

Figure 6.5. Rice prices in cold and warm years at Guilin.

Guangdong, according to the local gazetteer, "spring snow harmed the rice sprouts." And perhaps more commonly than might be expected for a "semi-tropical" climate, frost, and snow in September or October killed the standing crop, as was recorded in 1681 in both Hua and Maoming counties. Both of these examples are from decades already identified as especially cold, but early fall frost killed rice crops in other years as well, as in 1712, 1757, 1763, and 1784.[19]

Second, cold springs with temperatures below 15°C could delay transplanting, forcing peasant-farmers to forgo the spring planting altogether and to follow the single crop of rice with a crop of winter wheat. The strongest evidence for this change in cropping patterns comes from rice prices (see Figure 6.5). During warm years, farmers in Guilin could get two harvests, as evidenced by the behavior of rice prices, peaking twice (in April–May and again in July), after which prices dropped as harvests started coming in. In cold years, though, the peasant-farmers obtained but one harvest, with grain prices peaking once in June–July. Switching from two harvests to one on account of the cold thus reduced the annual yield by 30–40 percent, the amount contributed by double rather than single cropping the land.

Freezing cold and snow in a subtropical region like Lingnan affected more than just the cereal crops. Indeed, comments in the local gazetteers indicate that frost or snow killed trees and grasses, as in 1636, 1690, or 1815. Fruit trees

[19] *Guangdong sheng ziran zaihai shiliao*, 174–77.

and other trees of commercial value all suffered, spreading economic hardship to those who relied upon them for their livelihood. Sometimes farmyard animals – chickens, pigs, and, perhaps, water buffalo – also died, and in a few cases (as in 1532) water froze so deep that fish died. Finally, people froze to death too. The effects of unusual cold in Lingnan thus could be rather widespread, and the broader consequences for the people and the economy should not be overlooked.[20]

Harvest Yields

Anecdotal evidence thus suggests that colder than normal temperatures lowered harvest yields, sometimes dramatically so. But did warmer temperatures improve harvest yields? I have found no anecdotal evidence that suggests an answer either way. But the question of whether climatic changes – either cooling or warming trends – affected harvest yields is very important for understanding the ways in which climatic change affects human societies, especially those like late imperial China that had developed complex economies. For one might imagine cooling temperatures and declining harvest yields to have affected only direct producers who relied solely upon their farms for subsistence, but in economies where food is sold on the market to meet the needs of urban residents or other farmers who produced commercial crops, the effect of variations in harvest yields could have a much broader impact. Under ordinary circumstances,[21] the demand for food from one year to the next was more or less fixed by the size of the population, so variations in supply accounted for almost all of the changes in prices (I will discuss the linkage of harvest yields to rice prices in more detail in Chapter 8). Through the impact on harvest yields, then, climatic changes more broadly influenced the tempo of agrarian economies through the price of food. And in Lingnan, when we speak of food, we mean primarily rice.

Where the Kangxi emperor (1662–1722) had been sufficiently interested in the impact of colder temperatures on harvest yields to comment on it and then to direct his bondservants to collect and report climatological, harvest yield, and grain price data to the throne, he had not systematized his requests for such information or broadened his queries beyond the Yangzi delta. As much as I would like to use evidence from the seventeenth or early eighteenth centuries to demonstrate the ways in which climate change affected harvest yields

[20] Ibid.

[21] One can imagine extraordinary circumstances that would affect the demand for food from one year to the next. Major military campaigns, with the influx of a large number of troops, certainly would affect the demand side of the equation, as happened regularly in Gansu province in the northwest, the staging area for the Qianlong emperor's western military campaigns. For a brief discussion, see Spence, *The Search for Modern China*, 97–99.

in Lingnan, the fact of the matter is that anything more than anecdotal documentation simply does not exist. However, evidence from documents generated during the reigns of the Kangxi emperor's successors does allow us to probe more rigorously the ways in which climatic changes affected harvest yields in Lingnan during the eighteenth century.

Although nothing suggests that either of the Kangxi emperor's two successors, the Yongzheng or Qianlong emperors (reigned 1723–35 and 1736–95, respectively), was aware that the climate during their reigns was warmer than in Kangxi's time or appreciated the fact that conditions had turned more favorable for agriculture, they were nonetheless mindful of the importance of monitoring the food supplies of the empire, and building upon innovations begun during the Kangxi emperor's reign, they developed bureaucratic systems by which local officials routinely reported grain harvest estimates, rainfall amounts, and grain prices to the central government.[22] A vast number of these memorials are extant and available in archives in Beijing and Taibei, making possible a reconstruction of the history of eighteenth-century harvest results.

The memorials reporting harvest yields were of two types: detailed county-level reports for each of the three main harvests (winter wheat, early rice, and late rice), and provincewide harvest figures.[23] The provincial figures probably were averages (how precise is another question) of the county-level estimates, and all were reported in terms of decile blocks (*fen*), which I have chosen to translate as "percent" (e.g., a harvest rated at "8 *fen*" is translated as 80 percent, and one at "over 8 *fen*" as 85 percent). As stipulated in the *Collected Statutes of the Qing Dynasty*, "All estimates of harvest rates are to be memorialized" and rated according to the following definitions:

> Harvest ratings: 80 percent (eight *fen*) and above are plentiful (*feng*); 60 percent (six *fen*) and above are average (*ping*); 50 percent (five *fen*) and below are deficient (*qian*). The reality [of the harvest size] is to be investigated thoroughly and reported. Each year the provincial [authorities] are to estimate the wheat, early rice, and late rice harvests. The governor-general is to memorialize the facts.[24]

22 The grain price reporting system is well known and, thus, will not be discussed here. See Robert B. Marks, "Rice Prices, Food Supply, and Market Structure in Eighteenth-Century South China," *Late Imperial China* 12, no. 2 (Dec. 1991), 64–116; Rawski and Li, eds., *Chinese History in Economic Perspective*, 33–176. For a detailed description see Wang Yeh-chien, "Qing dai de liang jia chenbao zhidu," *Taibei gugong likan* 13, no. 1 (1978): 55–66.

23 The provincial estimates as reported in the routine memorials may have been produced as a result of a bureaucratic struggle over control of information at the beginning of the Qianlong reign, while the county-level estimates became part of the secret palace memorial system. See Beatrice S. Bartlett, *Monarchs and Ministers: The Grand Council in Mid-Ch'ing China, 1723–1820* (Berkeley and Los Angeles: University of California Press, 1991), 164–65.

24 *Da Qing huidian*, juan 21: 17a.

How the harvest estimates were made, or who actually did the estimating, is not at all clear. At the end of the Kangxi reign, the governors of both Guangdong and Guangxi personally investigated harvest yields in areas with possible crop losses.[25] By the early Yongzheng period, the process became routinized through an imperial edict that directed county yamen offices to examine (*yan*) the harvests by asking peasants (*nongmin*).[26] The directive apparently applied to all officials called upon to report on harvests, prices, and the weather: a military commander en route to his new post in Guangxi in 1725 wrote that "according to various villagers," fields near water would harvest 90 percent or so; those in the hills would harvest about 60–70 percent.[27] However the estimates were developed, they clearly were of uneven quality. Even as early as 1729, officials such as Finance Commissioner Wang Shijun commented, "I fear that some [harvest] reports are not factual."[28]

Finally, it should be clear that the reports of harvest ratings based on deciles (*fen*) were blunt, probably impressionistic instruments. An eight- or nine-*fen* harvest tells us nothing about how much grain actually was harvested.[29] Indeed, as population increased, land brought into cultivation, higher levels of productivity achieved, and, hence, larger amounts of grain produced, the harvest ratings remained based on percentages: an eight-*fen* harvest in 1780 certainly was larger than an eight-*fen* harvest in 1736, yet both were glossed as "plentiful" relative to the supply and demand at the time.

Despite the limitations of the harvest rating estimates, Qing officials used them to manage the food supply of the empire and to administer the state granary system.[30] Furthermore, the harvest ratings apparently also became public information, for tenants used the ratings to reduce the amount of rent they were expected to pay landlords.[31] Far from being merely bureaucratic busywork, the Qing officials' harvest rating estimates influenced the way the empire was governed, and even affected private contractual arrangements. Clearly, people at the time put substantial stock in these estimates; what

[25] Memorials dated KX54.4.27, in KXCZZ, doc. no. 1770; and KX55.5.15, in KXCZZ, doc. no. 2103.

[26] Memorial dated YZ2.9.28, in YZCZZ 3: 248.

[27] Memorial dated YZ2.11.7, in YZCZZ 3: 426–27.

[28] Memorial dated YZ7.6.11, in YZCHWZPZZ 15: 528.

[29] During the eighteenth century, yields for the first rice harvest averaged about four *shi* per *mu*. If that yield corresponded to an 85% harvest (i.e., the mode for the series), then the "abundant" (*feng*) or "deficient" (*qian*) harvests yielded somewhat more or less than the four *shi* per *mu*. For a discussion of harvest yields in the lower Yangzi and an attempt to quantify the per *mu* changes over a very long period of time, see Chen Jiaqi, "Ming Qing shiqi qihou bianhua dui tai hu liuyu nongye jingji de yingxiang," *Zhongguo nongshi* 3 (1991): 30–36.

[30] See Pierre-Etienne Will, *Bureaucracy and Famine in Eighteenth-Century China*, Elborg Forster, trans. (Stanford: Stanford University Press, 1990), 110–13.

[31] For the practices in Jiangnan, see Kathryn Bernhardt, *Rents, Taxes, and Peasant Resistance: The Lower Yangzi Region, 1840–1950* (Stanford: Stanford University Press, 1992), 37–39.

might they tell us today about the size and quality of eighteenth-century harvests?

Within the county-level ratings, the range for both the early and late harvest estimates was largely between 70 and 100 percent, implying that officials mostly chose one of four different ratings for the harvest (i.e., 70, 80, 90, or 100 percent). In just 5 cases (out of about 13,000 reports) did officials report countywide harvests at less than 60 percent. The reason for the few cases of countywide ratings below 60 percent may lie with the regulations and procedures for providing relief payments to families stricken by natural disaster and crop loss. According to Pierre-Etienne Will, "No relief payments were to be made when the damage was below or at 50 percent."[32] Natural disasters prompted investigations of villages, with preliminary and final surveys determining the crop loss on a field-by-field and case-by-case basis. Those families that lost more than 50 percent of their crop thus were eligible for monetary relief payments to enable them to purchase food and seed. This being the case, a countywide harvest rating of 50 percent or less would have meant that every farming family in the county would have been eligible for relief, and no county magistrate was about to make that claim. Did the county-level harvest rating estimates of 60–70 percent in 1787 thus mean that in some places the crop loss was 50 percent or more, triggering the relief payments, while harvests of more than 50 percent in other parts of the county "averaged" out to countywide rating estimates of 60–70 percent? Investigations did show some "areas" or "fields" to have less than 50 percent harvests, but not entire counties.[33]

Overall, the early harvest ratings for the eighteenth century averaged 82–83 percent, and the late harvest ratings 84–85 percent, both within the range defined by the *Collected Statutes* as plentiful (*feng*).[34] If officials' harvest rating estimates were a rough guide to harvests, then one could conclude that for most of the Qianlong period (1736–95), Guangdong harvests were good. Given the generally favorable climatic conditions, this conclusion is not unexpected, but it is worth noting that the officials' harvest ratings are consistent with the climatological data.

Although the *Collected Statutes* stipulated that harvest ratings between 60 and 80 percent were average, the historical record in Guangdong indicates that recorded harvests in that range coincided with serious food shortages and conditions described by local officials as "dearth" or "hunger." In 1726, for

[32] Will, *Bureaucreacy and Famine in Eighteenth-Century China*, 113.

[33] Moreover, if the harvest reporting system followed precedents set in the Kangxi era, then harvest estimators distinguished between lowland and upland fields, especially when one or the other had crop losses. See memorials dated KX48.10.2, in KXCZZ, doc. no. 582; KX52.5.27, in KXCZZ, doc. no. 1328; and KX52.7.28, in KXCZZ, doc. no. 1401.

[34] *Da Qing huidian*, juan 21: 17a.

instance, a typhoon hit eastern Guangdong just before the fall harvest, destroying much of the crop. The governor-general reported the fall harvest in Chaozhou and Huizhou prefectures at 60–70 percent[35] but in the winter began substantial relief operations to provide food to the affected areas. Besides purchasing additional grain from Guangxi for reduced price sales (*pingtiao*), officials exhorted merchants to donate money and grain for free distribution to the hungry.[36] Even then, refugees turned up begging in Guangxi.[37] Similarly, in 1786, when a drought prompted Governor-General Sun Shiyi to memorialize that "there is no soil that isn't dry and parched,"[38] the worst harvest reports were in the 60–70 percent range.[39] When the drought continued into 1787 and 18 county gazetteers glossed the year with comments of "drought" (*da han*), "dearth" (*ji*), or "famine" (*da ji*), the provincial authorities rated county harvests no lower than 60 percent.[40]

Certainly, then, climatic variations affected harvest yields. To explore the connections between climate and harvest yields in more detail, I have chosen three case studies with the best available documentation to illustrate the effects of floods (in 1725–27), cold (in 1757–58), and drought (in 1786–87) upon harvest yields.

The 1725–27 Floods and Typhoon. If in Lingnan colder than normal temperatures tended to create atmospheric conditions conducive to drought, then with warming trends the reverse tended to be true as well: warming trends brought more than the usual amount of rains, sometimes causing floods. One instance where this relationship held true and where the documentation exists to chart what happened was over a two-year period from 1725 to 1727.[41]

The crop failures and disaster relief operations in 1725–27 were the result of two separate natural disasters: a West River flood in late 1725, followed a year later by a typhoon in eastern Guangdong, both of which occurred after more than a decade-long warming trend. From 1711 and 1712 lows (when frost in late October killed the standing rice crop in western Guangdong and central

35 Memorial dated YZ4.11.15, in YZCZZ 8: 437.

36 Memorials dated YZ5.3.22, in YZCZZ 9: 309–10; YZ5.3i.25, in YZCZZ 9: 500; and YZ5.3i.25, in YZCZZ 9: 501.

37 Memorial dated YZ5.4.8, in YZCZZ 9: 598–99.

38 Memorial dated QL51.10.18, in QLCZZ 62: 16.

39 Memorials dated QL51.7.4, in QLCZZ 61: 71, and QL51.10.7, in QLCZZ 61: 731–32.

40 Guangdong and Fujian officials' time, energy, and attention in 1787 were taken up with the Lin Shuangwen uprising on Taiwan. See David Alan Ownby, *Communal Violence in Eighteenth Century Southeast China: The Background to the Lin Shuangwen Uprising of 1787* (Cambridge, MA: Harvard University Ph.D. dissertation, 1989).

41 For maps of the extent of the floods, see *Zhongguo jin wubai nian han lao fenbujtu ji*, Zhongyang qixiang ju, comp., 133–34.

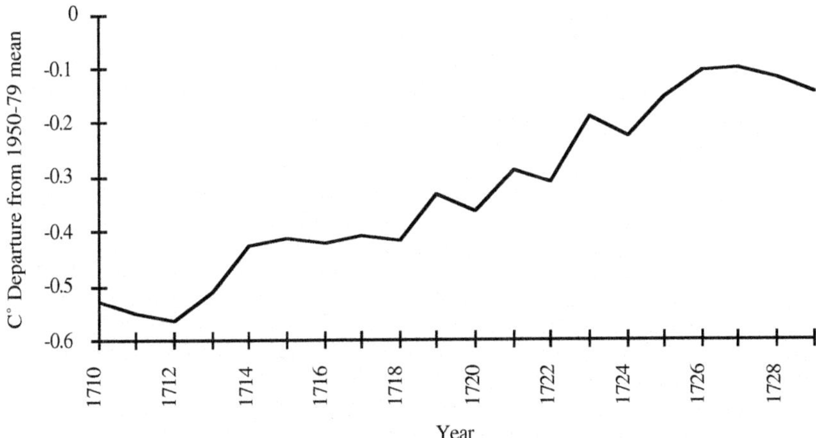

Figure 6.6. Annual temperatures, 1710–29. Source: Same as Figure 6.2.

Guangxi provinces), temperatures rose steadily into the mid-1720s (see Figure 6.6), bringing more moist air masses flowing into south China. Then, in November 1725, flooding along the West River in Guangdong destroyed a significant portion of the standing rice crop in Gaoyao, Sihui, Gaoming, Nanhai, and Sanshui counties. Except for these counties, Governor-General Kong Yuxun reported, the rest of the province would have a plentiful autumn harvest.[42] The counties affected by the flood were classified into two groups: those with fields without a harvest, and those with a loss but "not a disaster (*bu cheng zai*)."[43]

State relief operations spanned the time from the flooding until the spring of 1726. When a good early harvest came in and rice entered the market, provincial officials believed the crisis to have been over. But in September, a typhoon struck eastern Guangdong, destroying the standing rice crop in 11 counties. An investigation determined that 6 counties had a "disaster (*zai*)."[44] Rising to the challenge, provincial officials distributed granary stocks,[45] imported more rice from Guangxi for reduced-price sales, and exhorted the wealthy to contribute money and grain.[46]

42 Memorial dated YZ3.11.15, in YZCZZ 5: 379.

43 Memorial dated YZ4.4.22, in YZCZZ 5: 843.

44 Memorial dated YZ4.9.20, in YZCHWZPZZ, vol. 8: 139–40.

45 Chen Chunsheng, *Shichang jizhi yu shehui bianqian: shiba shiji Guangdong mi jia fenxi* (Xiamen University Ph.D. thesis, 1988), 34.

46 Memorials dated YZ5.3.22, in YZCHWZPZZ 9: 309–10; YZ5.3i.25 in YZCHWZPZZ, vol. 9: 501, and YZ5.4.21, in YZCHWZPZZ 9: 696–97.

Certainly disaster relief operations on this scale reduced the human suffering that otherwise would have come in the wake of the typhoon.[47] Even so, bellelettristic literature described the disaster as a major famine and explicitly mentioned deaths. In Chaozhou the disaster was described as a famine with many deaths. Chenghai county also registered "countless dead," and in Guangzhou there were "people dying one on top of the other along the roads."[48] The governor of Guangxi, Han Liangfu, reported "wandering, hungry people from Guangdong " arriving in Guangxi.[49]

For the state, one consequence of the double disaster was to deplete Guangdong's granary stocks (this topic will be discussed in more detail in the next chapter). By the time the early rice harvest came in and officials could cease relief operations, just 200,000 *shi* remained in the granaries for the entire province. Adding to the officials' woes was the fact that since so much of the grain had to be provided as relief rather than reduced-price sales, there were just 200,000 taels in the provincial treasury to purchase grain to restock the granaries.[50] As late as 1728 the granaries had not yet been restocked, and the governor's orders to local officials to replenish the deficits had not been followed. Fortunately, the 1728 harvests were the best in years, and rice prices fell to their lowest recorded levels. So good were harvests in the next two years as well that in 1729 for the only recorded time in the eighteenth century, Guangdong was self-sufficient in rice supplies.[51]

The 1757–58 Frosts. In searching through the county-level harvest ratings for long periods of consecutive reports, I was fortunate to discover the eight-year period from 1755 to 1762 for which good documentation illustrates the relationships among cold temperatures, drought conditions, harvest ratings, and grain prices. Figure 6.7 relates harvest yield estimates as reported for Shunde county in the Pearl River delta (the bars at the bottom of the chart), with monthly rice prices recorded for Guangzhou prefecture (the line). (The year and month are along the horizontal axis, with "1755.11" meaning, for instance, "November 1755.")

The story begins with the early and late harvests for 1755 rated at 75 and 80 percent, respectively; grain prices then reached a relatively high level of around 2 taels and remained there throughout 1755 and into the first half of 1756. The early harvest in 1756 was excellent (92 percent); rice prices started to fall in June and continued to do so after a good late harvest (85 percent) in

[47] Memorial dated YZ5.5.20, in YZCHWZPZZ 9: 832–33.
[48] Quoted in Chen, thesis, 262–64.
[49] Memorial dated YZ5.4.8, in YZCHWZPZZ 9: 598–99.
[50] Memorial dated YZ5.5.24, in YZCHWZPZZ 9: 845.
[51] Memorial dated YZ7.9.1, in YZCHWZPZZ 16: 580.

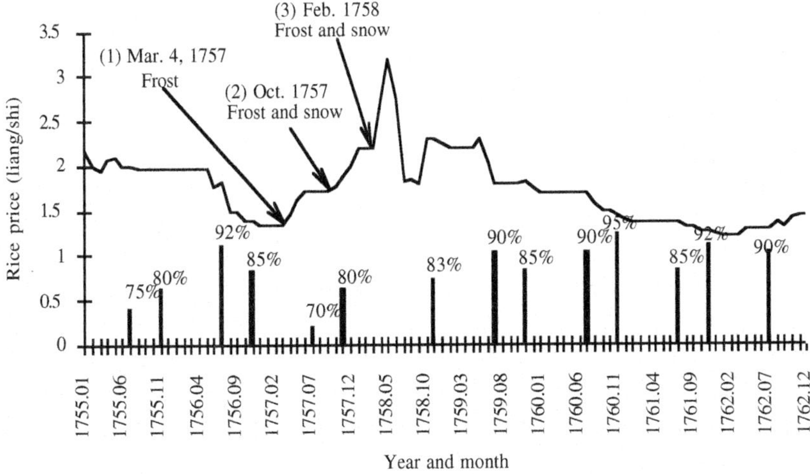

Figure 6.7. Frost, harvest ratings, and monthly rice prices in the Pearl River delta, 1755–62.

November, reaching a low of about 1.5 taels after the late harvest was in. Prices in the spring of 1757 began edging up, as they normally would, until March 3, 1757. Then, on the night of March 4, a cold wave rolled through Lingnan, for killing frost was reported in Xin'an county (the area just north of what is now Hong Kong). As may be recalled from the first part of this chapter, the early rice crop then was growing in nursery beds in preparation for transplanting into the fields, which, under normal circumstances, would have been about one month later.

Immediately after the March 4 frost, grain prices shot up and continued climbing until the early harvest came in. When it did, officials rated it at 70 percent, a "deficient" harvest, which apparently was better than expected, for rice prices leveled off. But then sometime in October – our sources are not specific – frost in Guishan county (75 miles east of Guangzhou) "killed rice plants,"[52] and rice prices in Guangzhou shot up again, leveling off in January 1758 at the peaks reached in 1755–56. And then once again, this time in February 1758, frost and snow were reported in Panyu, Nanhai, Shunde, and Boluo counties in the Pearl River delta,[53] and grain prices skyrocketed to 3.15 taels per *shi*, the highest prices recorded during the eighteenth century. Presumably this frost came too early in February to affect the planting of the early harvest, for grain prices plummeted after the early harvest came in.

[52] Excerpted in *Guangdong sheng ziran zaihai shiliao*, 175.

[53] Excerpted in ibid.

Unfortunately, the officials' early harvest rating estimate for 1758 is missing, but we can imagine it to have been relatively high. The late harvest in 1758 again was good (83 percent), beginning a string of excellent harvests that continued for another four years, resulting in steadily declining grain prices.

The unexpected cold snap in early 1757 affected harvest yields throughout Guangdong province, all the way from the Leizhou Peninsula in the south to Kaijian county in the northwest, where the local gazetteer reported for 1757 that "the early crop was completely lost; the late harvest was deficient."[54] Counties throughout the province reported high grain prices in both 1757 and 1758; some reported "dearth" (*ji*) and some "famine" (*da ji*). And in Gaoyao county, up the West River from Guangzhou, the local gazetteer reported that "on June 2, hungry villagers stole grain from wealthy households."[55]

This brief account of the 1757–58 cold snap reveals much about the relationships among climatic variability, the harvest ratings, and rice prices. First, grain prices shot up immediately after the frosts, considerably in advance of the actual harvests. Rice wholesalers and retailers no doubt played on people's fears that the frost would severely constrict food supplies to push prices up significantly in advance of the harvests. But the behavior of grain prices following each of the three harvests – leveling off or falling – indicates that the harvest was not as deficient as had been feared. The 1757 early harvest rating of 70 percent in Shunde was followed not by increasing prices, but by steadying prices; the same phenomenon can be observed after the 1757 late harvest. Second, when the series of good harvests began in 1758, harvest ratings ranging from 85 to 95 percent were accompanied by generally declining prices, but none that could be directly correlated with the harvest rating. In 1759, for instance, a 90 percent early harvest was followed by a lesser-rated late harvest (85 percent), and yet grain prices continued to decline. While as a general rule it might be expected that better harvests are correlated with declining rice prices, the specifics of the cases (like this one) will make statistical correlations weaker than might be assumed. The explanation (as I will discuss in the next two chapters) is that families, rice wholesalers, and the state all began storing grain, so that runs of good harvests – even if some were slightly smaller than the preceding one – nonetheless added to the stocks of stored grain. Third, the literature on subsistence crises would lead one to suspect that high grain prices are an indictor of elevated mortality. If so, in this instance – when grain prices reached the highest recorded levels in the eighteenth century – the record is silent. The absence of evidence, of course, cannot be construed to mean that mortality did not increase. In other cases the documentary sources do speak to the question; in this case, they do not.

Finally, this case also demonstrates the connection between cold and

[54] Excerpted in ibid., 206. [55] Excerpted in ibid.

drought in Lingnan, for nine counties reported drought conditions in 1758. Apparently, if the cold snap did not kill off the early crop, the ensuing drought decreased the yields. While it is not possible now to sort out which had a greater adverse impact on harvest yields, the combination of cold and drought certainly reduced the harvests in 1757. And that was not the only time such a "one-two" punch hit harvest yields.

The 1786–87 Guangdong Drought and Famine. Beginning with observations of "little rain" just before the 1786 autumn harvest, drought stretched through the end of 1787,[56] probably having been occasioned by significant global cooling of 2–3°C caused by massive volcanic eruptions elsewhere in the northern hemisphere casting a thick veil over the atmosphere and preventing radiation from the sun from reaching the surface of the earth.[57] The cooler temperatures may have blocked the North Pacific subtropical high from its usual path, disrupting the summer monsoon and bringing drought to Lingnan. The areas affected by the drought included the populous, centrally located prefectures in Guangdong most dependent upon imports for their food supplies.

The effect of the drought on food supplies in and around Guangzhou was magnified by two additional factors. After six months of the drought, rivers shriveled so much that the grain boats normally bringing rice into Guangzhou could not navigate the shoals, so market supplies began to dry up.[58] Second, worried provincial officials conducted an audit of granary stocks and discovered, to their alarm, massive deficits.[59] Without granary stocks or imports from Guangxi, by the spring of 1787 the food supply in Guangdong – and especially to Guangzhou – was precarious at best. Officials sent emissaries to the Yangzi Valley to purchase grain and called upon merchants to do the same. The officially purchased grain did not arrive until the fifth month, and then it was distributed not through the ever-normal granaries (to be discussed in the next chapter) but at specially established "depots" (*chang*), and then probably only in Guangzhou.[60] In the meantime, spring rains brought water levels in the West River up so Guangxi grain boats could navigate, and a moderate winter wheat harvest hit the market.[61]

56 For maps, see *Zhongguo jin wubai nian han lao fenbujtu ji*, Zhongyang qixiang ju, comp., 164–65.

57 Major volcanic eruptions in Iceland and then in Japan in 1783 were followed by a series of smaller eruptions in 1785–86, cooling global temperatures for as long as six years afterwards. See Lamb, "Volcanic Dust," 508–509. For a discussion of the impact in Japan, see Kondo, "Volcanic Eruptions, Cool Summers, and Famines in the Northeastern Part of Japan," 775–88.

58 Memorial dated QL52.2.13, in QLCZZ 63: 347.

59 Memorial dated QL51.11.5, in QLCZZ 62: 92–93. Granary deficits will be discussed in greater detail in Chapter 7.

60 Memorial dated QL52.5.27, in QLCZZ 64:524–25.

61 Memorials dated QL52.3.15, in QLCZZ 63: 635–36; and QL52.6.13, in QLCZZ 64: 670.

Moderate rainfall in the spring resulted in a poor early rice harvest, but then little rain fell during the summer of 1787. The provincial authorities appeared unaware that a disaster was building, and only in the ninth month declared a disaster (*zai*). The drought continued through 1787, resulting in the worst late rice harvest in years. Rains came in the spring of 1788, leading to a decent winter wheat harvest and then to "plentiful" early and late rice harvests. The drought was over.

Compared with the energetic response to harvest failure earlier, the response of the state bureaucracy to the 1786–87 drought was anemic. A perusal of the *Qing shi lu* (Veritable records of Qing dynasty) for those years also reveals no attention on the part of the central government, although note is made in the spring of 1788 of a palace memorial from the governor of Guangxi discussing rice prices, granary operations, harvest estimates, and weather reports.[62] The absence of provincial reports to the central government of the drought and the impending disaster and the lack of central government attention to routine matters in Lingnan are partially explained by the fact that the state apparatus was absorbed with the crisis caused by the Lin Shuangwen rebellion on Taiwan, which coincidentally spanned almost exactly the same time frame as the Guangdong drought; Liangguang Governor-General Sun Shiyi was in Taiwan for much of 1787 engaged in military actions, and the *Veritable Records* reflect that concern by including numerous reports about Taiwan. Significantly, the Qianlong emperor did not reprimand Sun for his lack of attention to the Lingnan drought, but instead rewarded him for his role in the suppression of the Lin Shuangwen rebellion.[63] Thus, to the provincial authorities and the central government, the drought, investigations to determine the extent of crop losses, the declaration of a disaster, state relief efforts, the condition of the ever-normal granaries, and the numbers of poor and hungry affected were minor matters not requiring much of their attention. The result was a disaster of historic proportions, the record of which is found not in the palace memorials, but in terse entries in local gazetteers: "famine" (*da ji*), noted several, while others acknowledged that "many died of starvation."[64]

These three case studies all demonstrate the impact adverse climatic conditions could have on harvest yields, even during the generally favorable times of the eighteenth century. The floods in the late 1720s, the cold snap in 1758, and the drought in the late 1780s, though, did not establish general trends that

[62] *Da Qing gao zong (Qianlong) shi lu*, juan 1302: 13b-15a (Taibei: Xinwenfeng chuban gongsi, 1978).

[63] Arthur Hummel, *Eminent Chinese of the Ch'ing period, 1644–1912* (Washington, DC: U.S. Government Printing Office, 1943–44), 680.

[64] For example see *Xin'an xianzhi*, 1819 ed. xia juan: 51; *Guangdong tongzhi*, 1864 ed. juan 81: 7a. All told, I have counted 41 separate references to famine and/or high prices in Guangdong local gazetteers for the 1786–88 drought.

then continued; rather, the eighteenth-century climate in Lingnan simply was quite variable. But not so for the first half of the nineteenth century.

The Cold First Half of the Nineteenth Century. In 1808, the climate turned colder again, with average annual temperatures plummeting nearly 1°C by 1837. European historians have estimated that temperature drops of that magnitude in the sixteenth and seventeenth centuries had the effect of shortening the growing season by about three weeks, the equivalent of raising the elevation by 500 feet.[65] The turn toward a colder climate thus reduced harvest yields and food supplies in Lingnan, and not just for a single year.

In late 1808, gazetteers recorded frost and freezing in counties in the higher elevations, followed in early 1809 by reports of 2–3 inches of snow in counties throughout Guangzhou and Zhaoqing prefectures.[66] Not surprisingly, gazetteers then recorded reports of "dearth" (*ji*) and "famine" (*da ji*) throughout Guangdong province in the spring of 1809.[67] With few rice imports from Guangxi, which by then had become the "rice bowl" for the Pearl River delta and the urban residents of Guangzhou and Foshan (this will be discussed more in Chapter 8), rice prices rose precipitously, and the urban poor demanded relief; ultimately the Foshan charitable granary secured sufficient grain to provide relief to over 50,000 people over a two-week period in early June.[68]

Certainly the temperature drop in 1808 produced a climatic shock to the agricultural ecosystem that the Chinese had created in Lingnan. As temperatures continued to slide downward through the 1810s before leveling out and then recovering somewhat in the 1820s, continuous pressure was placed on the system to provide sufficient food for the populace. How severely that pressure was felt after the 1808 shock is not clear, since the historical record does not speak to widespread harvest failures, rising rice prices, or massive relief efforts again until the 1830s. Perhaps the peasant farmers adjusted to the cooler regime by selecting rice varieties with even shorter maturation periods or by planting a single crop of a higher-yielding variety. However they adjusted, they seem to have successfully weathered such seriously cold temperatures in 1815 that even Hainan Island recorded killing frosts then.

But colder temperatures in the early 1830s once again shocked harvest yields throughout Lingnan. In late 1831, cold was reported from the Pearl River delta to the northern hill region. There, in Xingning county, frost in October

65 See Andrew Appleby, "Epidemics and Famine in the Little Ice Age," *Journal of Interdisciplinary History* 10, no. 4 (Spring 1980): 658; and Parker and Smith, eds., *The General Crisis of the Seventeenth Century*.

66 *Guangdong sheng ziran zaihai shiliao*, 176.

67 Ibid., 209.

68 *Ming Qing Foshan beike wenxian jingji ziliao* (Guangzhou: Guangdong renmin chuban she, 1987), 412.

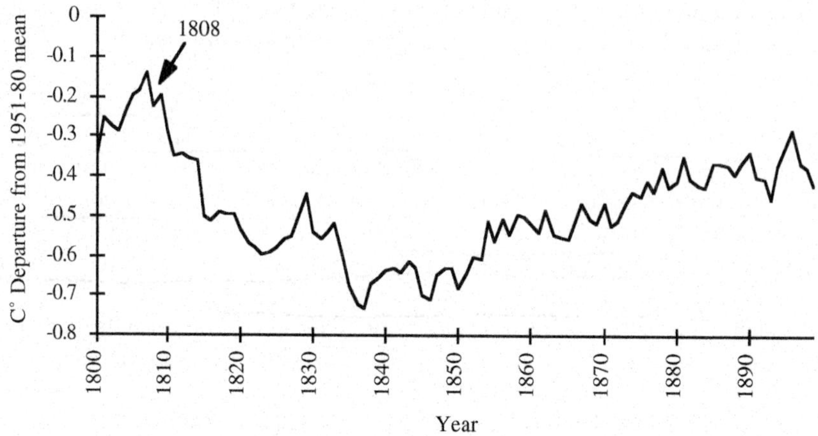

Figure 6.8. Northern hemisphere temperatures, 1800–99. Source: Same as Figure 6.2.

destroyed the late harvest; the same thing happened the next year.[69] Food shortages followed, both in the areas directly affected by the cold and in the Pearl River delta. In Foshan, "very little grain arrived from Guangxi, pushing prices higher," and previously secure supplies from Luoding also dried up. For much of the early 1830s, each spring over 50,000 urban poor received relief food supplies from local granaries. By 1834, the granary managers no longer looked to Guangxi for their supplies, turning instead to Southeast Asian producers, mainly in Siam, for the rice and to European clipper ships to transport the rice to Foshan.[70] As we will see in Chapters 9 and 10, the cold nineteenth century coincided with growing population pressure on the land, exacerbating already pressured food supplies.

In retrospect, we now know that temperatures bottomed out in the 1840s, beginning a warming trend that lasted until the mid-twentieth century. Thus, during the first half or so of the Qing dynasty, temperatures went through a long cycle, from the lows of the middle to late seventeenth century, warming during the eighteenth century, but declining once again in the first half of the nineteenth century. The available documentary evidence suggests that climatic fluctuations did affect harvest yields and food supplies, with colder and drier conditions causing grain shortages and sometimes dearth. While not tied to climatic variations, the size and quality of harvests were influenced by climatic factors, suggesting that conditions were more favorable for farming in the eigh-

[69] *Guangdong sheng ziran zaihai shiliao*, 176.

[70] *Ming Qing Foshan beike wenxian jingji ziliao*, 418–34.

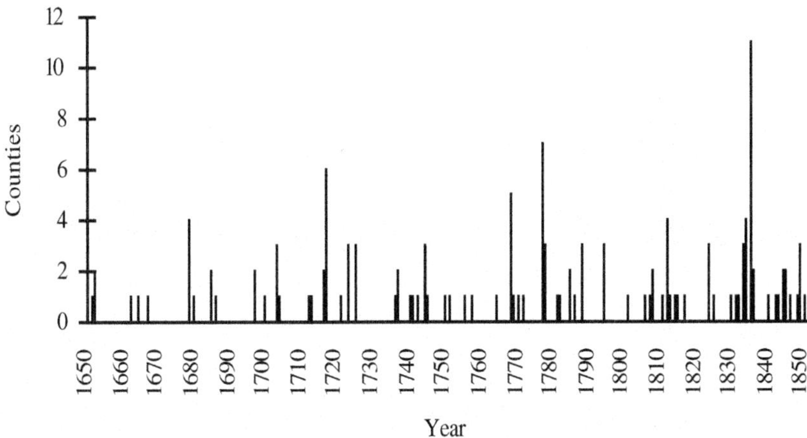

Figure 6.9. Number of counties reporting pestilence, 1650–1850. Source: Compiled from *Guangdong sheng ziran zaihai shiliao*, 157–62.

teenth century than in either the late seventeenth or first half of the nineteenth centuries.

Pestilence

Climatic fluctuations were not the only natural causes of poor harvests, for locusts and other pests too could eat their way through a standing crop. As can be seen in Figure 6.9, pestilence did not strike many counties in any given year, and there were many years free from pests. But four times during those two centuries the number of counties affected totaled five or more. In 1717, the insect damage mostly affected the counties in eastern Guangdong, while in 1768 the affected counties were spread all over the province. In 1777, four of the counties were in Gaozhou prefecture, where locusts damaged enough of the crop that rice prices rose substantially higher than normal. The officials' harvest rating for 1777 fell from what it had been the preceding year (see Figure 6.10), but because 1777 also was a drought year, I do not think that the Gaozhou infestation lowered the harvest yield for the entire province; the drought did that. The most destructive pestilence episode that I have been able to find occurred in 1833–35, when locusts cut a swath through Lingnan starting in the West River valley in Guangxi in 1833, spreading to western Guangdong in 1834, and finally infesting the Pearl River delta in 1835.[71] Unfortunately, neither harvest yield estimates nor reliable price data allow me to probe the extent to which the locusts affected harvest yields, food supplies, and food prices in the mid-1830s.

[71] See the citations for the relevant years in *Guangdong sheng ziran zaihai shiliao*, 157–62.

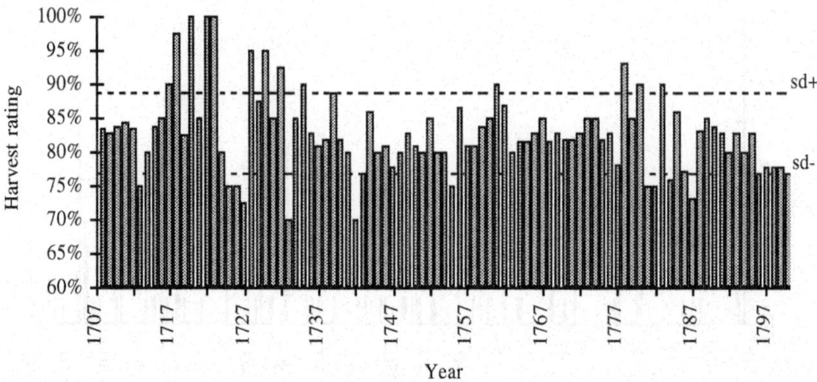

Fig 6.10. Guangdong province harvest ratings, 1707–1800. Source: See note 74.

Thus, although pestilence certainly harmed crops in Lingnan, insect damage tended to be infrequent and limited to a county or two here or there; just three times was the damage concentrated, and only once (in the 1830s) did it affect a broad area. Moreover, none of the eighteenth-century infestations proved big enough to lower the harvest ratings below the range considered normal for the series (see Figure 6.10). In comparison, as I will show later, climatic variability was much more significant in accounting for variation in harvest yields.

The Incidence of Adverse Climatic Conditions

In the case studies examined earlier – freezing cold both in 1757–58 and in the first half of the nineteenth century, drought in 1786–87, and floods in 1725–27 – I documented the linkages among climatic variability, harvest yields, and rice prices.[72] These are not the only instances of climatic factors adversely affecting harvest yields, but they are the ones for which the best documentation exists. Moreover, the officials' harvest rating estimates corresponded to this documentary record, leading to the conclusion not only that the harvest ratings were reasonable estimates of the direction of harvest fluctuations from year to year, but also that climatic changes were the single most important cause of harvest yield fluctuations during the eighteenth century.[73]

[72] For a full explanation offering statistical evidence of these linkages, see Robert B. Marks, "'It Never Used to Snow': Climatic Variability and Harvest Yields in Late Imperial South China, 1650–1850," in Mark Elvin and Liu Ts'ui-jung, eds., *Sediments of Time: Environment and Society in China* (Cambridge University Press, forthcoming).

[73] Asking similar questions about the relationship between climate and harvest yields, the Chinese

These case studies occurred roughly 30 years after each other, but that is not how often farmers could expect poor weather. Farming actually was a very risky business in Lingnan, with the incidence of cold, drought, or flood so high that peasant-farmers could expect to have their harvest reduced with some regularity. How often, though, did harvests decline? Fortunately, we have some evidence to answer this question.

Guangdong Province Harvest Ratings, 1707–1800. Like the county-level harvest ratings, the provincial ratings ranged narrowly between 70 and 100 percent (7 to 10 *fen*), with the mode being in the 80–85 percent range (see Figure 6.10).[74] Even within that range, though, variations are apparent and, I think, meaningful. If a deficient harvest is defined as one that is at least one standard

geographer Zheng Sizhong classified and statistically analyzed over 11,000 citations on climate and harvest from Guangdong gazetteers covering a 500-year period. Zheng's data show: (1) that the incidence of colder than normal temperatures is significantly correlated both with drought and with dearth; (2) that warmer temperatures are significantly correlated with floods; and (3) that typhoons generally are correlated with bumper harvests (by bringing additional rain inland to upland fields). Zheng's conclusions support those reached here. Zheng, "1400–1949 nian Guangdong sheng de qihou zhendong ji qi dui liangshi feng kuan de yingxiang," 25–32. Zheng additionally found (using power spectrum analysis) that droughts tended to exhibit a 30-year recurring cycle.

74 The 94-year time series of Guangdong province harvest ratings charted in Figure 6.10 has been constructed using three sources: (1) the reported provincial figures gleaned from more than a hundred volumes of published palace memorials in KXCZZ, YZCZZ, and QLCZZ provided data for 42 years; (2) for another 32 years, a provincial figure was computed by averaging the county-level estimates; and (3) for 20 years the missing data was reconstructed using a rice price series. This last source requires some explanation.

European economic historians interested in assessing harvest yields, for instance, have not had harvest yield estimates such as those produced by Chinese officials, but have had to rely upon grain price series to deduce harvest qualities. W. G. Hoskins reasoned that annual grain prices substantially above or below what might be considered "normal" reflected unusual harvest conditions. The methodology developed by Hoskins to characterize English harvests based on grain price behavior can be adopted here to augment the gaps in our series of Chinese officials' harvest ratings by determining the departures of mean annual rice prices from "normal" prices, and then estimating what Chinese officials might have reported for those years for which memorials are missing and using these to fill in the gaps in the time series. Hoskins characterized English harvests from 1480 to 1759 as "abundant, good, average, deficient, bad, or dearth" depending on how far annual grain prices deviated from a 31-year moving average. Hoskins used the 31-year moving average on the assumption both that that was the average length of a human generation and that such a long-term average eliminated the effect of monetary changes and population growth from the series. Since Hoskins wrote, a centered 11-year moving average has become the accepted standard for detrending a price series and, thus, is used here. The lacunae in the harvest estimates were calculated from the regression equation of the extant ratings on average annual prices: $y = -0.001x + 0.911$, where y is the harvest rating and x is the price (price is actually the dependent variable, but this equation is the easiest

Table 6.2. *Deficient harvests in Guangdong province*

Year	Cause
1713	Cold
1725–27	Floods, typhoon
1733	Floods
1742–43	Drought
1755	Drought and flood
1781–82	Drought
1784	Cold
1787	Drought

deviation below the mean (i.e., as less than a 77 percent rating, levels that triggered state famine relief activities), then Guangdong experienced deficient harvests in 13 out of the 94 years covered by the time series. Moreover, climatic conditions caused each of those deficient harvests.

Eight times during the eighteenth century, then, (see Table 6.2) the harvest yields sunk far enough for the entire province to have experienced a deficient harvest for one or more consecutive years. The longest interval of reasonably good harvests occurred from 1756 to 1781, while in the first half of the eighteenth century poor harvests happened every decade or so, and in the 1780s alone there were three deficient harvests. These figures, it is important to point out, represent provincewide phenomena: the effects of adverse climatic events were so widespread that most of the province was affected. What these figures do not capture, then, are more localized harvest failures, like those resulting from locusts in 1777 in Gaozhou or the frosts in 1757–58 in the Pearl River delta. To the residents of the Pearl River delta, for instance, the frosts hit quite hard, but the effects were not so widespread as to draw down the harvest yield for the entire province. To gain perspective on how often poor weather affected a particular village's or county's harvest yield, we must add another layer to the provincewide data just presented.

In the absence of county- or provincial-level harvest ratings for the nineteenth century, we need to turn to gazetteer entries. What I have done is simply

form to solve for the harvest rating). Since this regression equation had an R^2 value of 0.102, it is probable that the actual ratings varied from the predicted values.

For a full discussion of this methodology, see W. G. Hoskins's articles, "Harvest Fluctuations and English Economic History, 1480–1619," *Agricultural History Review* 12 (1964): 28–46; and "Harvest Fluctuations and English Economic History, 1620–1759," *Agricultural History Review* 16 (1968): 15–31. Hoskins's work was critiqued by C. J. Harrison, "Grain Price Analysis and Harvest Qualities, 1465–1634," *Agricultural History Review* 19 (1969): 135–55.

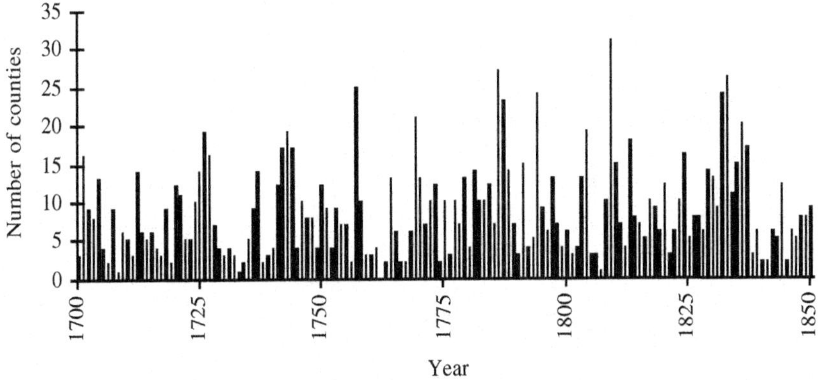

Figure 6.11. Adverse climatic conditions in Guangdong, 1700–1850. Source: Compiled from *Guangdong sheng ziran zaihai shiliao.*

Table 6.3. *Frequency of adverse climatic conditions, 1700–1850 (as measured by the number of counties affected)*

Maximum number of counties affected	Percent of years
0 to 4	29
5 to 9	34
10 to 14	22
15 to 19	9
20 to 25	3
25 to 29	2
30 to 31	1

to aggregate and graph the number of counties in Guangdong province reporting floods, drought, or abnormal cold in any given year (see Figure 6.11). Over the period from 1700 to 1850, an average of 9 counties experienced floods, droughts, or abnormal cold in any given year. In only one year (1762) during that entire period did no county report any adverse weather. In every other year, at least 1 county in Guangdong province had a flood, drought, or cold snap; the worst year was 1809, when 31 counties reported adverse climatic conditions arising from the sharp downward turn in temperatures. The frequency distribution of this data set is listed in Table 6.3. One way of interpreting these data is to say that only about once in seven years (i.e., about 15% of the years), 15 or more counties had adverse weather.

Not all counties got hit with the same regularity; some either were just luckier than others or were more prone to one kind of natural disaster or another. Floods, for instance, visited the Pearl River delta counties nearly every other year, while Longchuan, Xingning, and Wuchuan counties, all in higher elevations, reported a higher incidence of cold. Interestingly, though, so too did Nanhai and Shunde in the Pearl River delta. Drought, on the other hand, appears to have been a bit more randomly scattered throughout Guangdong province.

While patterns of flood and drought were distinctive to Lingnan, I suspect that when Lingnan was exceptionally cold, so too was the rest of China. But in north or even central China, aside from making people uncomfortable, unusual cold probably did not adversely affect agriculture: there were no crops planted in any case. In Lingnan, though, unusual cold in the winter was problematic, precisely because the climate normally allowed peasant-farmers to plant crops all year round. And with the intensification of agriculture that had continued after the recovery from the Ming–Qing transition, more and more peasant-farmers had pushed planting cycles earlier into the spring and harvesting times later into the fall, thereby rendering farming in Lingnan ever more risky.

Conclusion

What the climatological and harvest yield data from Lingnan tell are two slightly different but interesting stories. First, it is clear that climate changed perceptively over the two centuries from 1650 to 1850. From the noticeably colder decades at the end of the seventeenth century, the climate turned warmer during the eighteenth century, before temperatures plunged again in the first half of the nineteenth century. Second, evidence from the eighteenth century demonstrated the ways in which climatic changes affected harvest yields. Generalizing from the eighteenth-century data, it therefore seems reasonable to conclude that the colder climatic regimes in the second half of the seventeenth century and in the first half of the nineteenth century precipitated lower harvest yields during those periods too. But even in the warmer eighteenth century, the climate remained quite variable, sending harvest yields and rice prices up or down virtually every year. To smooth out these ripples, as I will show in the next chapter, both the state and families stored grain from one year to the next, in the process creating institutional responses to the effects of a variable climate upon their supply of food (this will be taken up in greater detail in Chapter 7).

The power of climate to affect harvest yields and the food supply over wide areas of Lingnan thus was very great. Pestilence too reduced harvests, but as we have seen, the losses from locusts or other pests did not send provincial harvest yields significantly below normal; only adverse climatic conditions could do that. Moreover, the likelihood that climatic fluctuations would adversely affect harvest size was quite high. And when the lesser but still real risk of pests destroying crops is added, then the people of Lingnan could be sure of one thing: if they simply stood by and did nothing, the harvest volume (and hence the food supply) from one harvest to the next, and from one year to the next, would be highly variable. So, confronted not with the question of whether climate variability would affect the harvest, but rather with the certainty that it would, the people and the state responded by creating institutions and organizations to lessen the risk that harvest failure would spell disaster.

By the eighteenth century, the people of Lingnan had, over the preceding thousand years, dramatically remade their environment. Farmland had been "built" in an estuary where no land had even existed; the Han Chinese population had grown and expanded into new areas that were cleared for settlement and agriculture, removing the forest cover; irrigation works and wet-rice cultivation improved food supplies and lessened the risk of malaria, thereby increasing the rate of population growth; commercialization spurred the introduction of double and triple cropping; and this highly productive and adaptive agroecological system responded swiftly to the demand for sugarcane and silk, transforming the Pearl River delta into a rice-importing region and the Guangxi Basin into a rice-exporting region. Lingnan no longer was characterized by peasant-farmers growing their own food and selling some crops in the market, but rather by regional specialization.

With food production for the entire population concentrating in fewer and fewer places, and hence with fewer ecosystems sustaining food production, the entire system was becoming more susceptible to shocks brought on by climatically induced disasters. Paradoxically, then, the more the people of Lingnan remade their physical environment in response to commercial and demographic pressures – and thereby seemingly to exert more control over nature – the more impact climatic changes could have on the less diverse agroecosystem. But that was not to be the full story, for social and economic institutions were created that lessened – to the point of severing – the impact of climatic variability upon regional food supplies.

7

"THERE IS ONLY A CERTAIN AMOUNT OF GRAIN PRODUCED":

GRANARIES AND THE ROLE OF THE STATE IN THE FOOD SUPPLY SYSTEM

Peoples and societies nearly everywhere in the world stored grain against the vagaries of weather, markets, invasion, and war, to mention the most obvious causes of food shortages, dearth, famine, and subsistence crises. In China, with its long imperial history, state-managed and state-sponsored granaries supplemented private arrangements by peasant-producers, landowners, and rice shop merchants to store grain from one year to the next. In the Qing dynasty (1644–1911), the success of this combination of state and private efforts, given adequate surpluses from harvests, or at least some bumper years every now and again, meant adequate food supplies even after bad harvests, food prices within ranges tolerable for most or all social classes, and social order, while failure or periodic breakdown of this effort spelled disaster.

State intervention into the management of the food supply system thus was to be one way – albeit an important one – that Chinese society responded to the variation in harvests caused by pestilence or climatic changes. But doing so through the state-managed granary system required such commitment, expertise, and energy on the part of state bureaucrats that they came to look for more efficient ways to ensure the subsistence of the human population of south China by moving rice from grain-surplus to grain-deificit regions via the market rather than by storing it in each and every county. Thus, by the last quarter of the eighteenth century, markets and merchants rather than state granaries and bureaucrats were to be positioned to exert greater influence on land use and cropping patterns in Lingnan. Nonetheless, the state granary system is an important chapter in the story of how the people of south China responded to the challenges their environment placed before them.

The Granary System

State-managed "ever-normal" granaries in China existed from Han times (202 BCE–220 CE), although the idea dates from the Spring and Autumn period (ca. seventh century BCE). In the Northern Song (960–1126), the purpose of the granaries shifted from military provisioning to famine relief, and granaries were established at the county level. When establishing the foundations for their rule over China, the Manchu rulers of the new Qing dynasty thus had a long history of theory and practice to draw upon, although their immediate predecessors, the Ming, had not established an empirewide system of granaries. The Qing, however, starting in the late seventeenth century, did establish a comprehensive empirewide system of granaries, ultimately reaching into each of the 1,300 counties. The outlines of how the Qing granary system was supposed to have worked have been known for some time, and recent scholarly work has presented a comprehensive institutional history of it. Revising earlier assessments of the granary system as little more than plans on paper, the importance of this more recent work has been to demonstrate the extent of granary operations throughout China.[1]

During the eighteenth century, the Qing state established or sponsored three kinds of granaries in Lingnan, as it did elsewhere in the empire. The "ever-normal" granaries (*changping cang*), built in county cities largely in the years after 1690 and managed directly by the county magistrate, had several functions, including famine relief, grain price stabilization, and loans of grain for food and seed in bad years. Community granaries (*she cang*), established in the villages under joint gentry–state control during the 1720s, made loans of grain to peasant-producers but did not sell grain at reduced prices or provide relief. Charity granaries (*yi cang*), established and managed solely by gentry without state intervention at the end of the eighteenth century in a few commercializing areas, provided relief to urban residents. Whereas the ever-normal and community granaries operated throughout Lingnan, before the nineteenth century very few charity granaries existed, and those that did were to be found in large commercial centers, especially in and around the city of Foshan.

Ever-normal Granaries. The theory of the ever-normal granaries was simple enough and was implicit in the name. The granaries would sell grain in the spring when the market price was high and, with the funds accumulated from those sales, purchase grain after the fall harvest when the market price was low, thereby keeping prices moderate for consumers in the spring and supporting prices paid to peasant-producers in the fall. Both grain prices and granary stocks would be "ever normal." Additionally, when the harvest failed or food shortages threatened, the granaries would provide grain for relief operations.

[1] See especially Pierre-Etienne Will and R. Bin Wong, *Nourish the People: The State Civilian Granary System in China, 1650–1850* (Ann Arbor: University of Michigan Press, 1992), ch. 1; and Francesca Bray, *Science and Civilization in China*, vol. 6, part 2, *Agriculture* (Cambridge University Press, 1984), 415–22.

The story of the empirewide accumulation of the granary stocks, which Will and Wong aptly term "grain mobilization by the ever-normal granaries," need not be repeated here.[2] Suffice it to say that the accumulation of stocks in Lingnan broadly fits the pattern and chronology established by them, with stocks of grain accumulated in the first third of the eighteenth century. In Guangdong, nearly all of the granary stocks were accumulated through contributions in exchange for degrees (*juan jian*),[3] while in Guangxi "special levy" (*juan na*) contributions accounted for two-thirds of the granary stocks.[4]

The four to five million *shi* of grain that was stored in the ever-normal granaries in Guangdong and Guangxi provinces was used for two main purposes: price stabilization and famine relief in times of natural disaster.[5] In the preceding chapter, I provided examples of the use of granaries for famine relief.[6] By buying grain in the fall and selling it in the spring, officials intended not only to moderate annual grain price swings, but also to turn over the stock on a two- or three-year cycle to ensure its freshness.[7] Besides these two main functions, the ever-normal granaries supplied grain to other provinces when natural disaster struck, provisioned military garrisons,[8] and loaned grain in time of need.[9]

Community Granaries. Like the ever-normal granaries, the community granaries had precedents predating the Qing dynasty. And like the ever-normal granaries, the establishment of the community granaries happened because

[2] Will and Wong, *Nourish the People*, chs. 2–4.

[3] A provincial financial commisioner's memorial in YZCZZ, vol. 10: 151, claimed that 1,642,000 *shi* of unhusked rice had been contributed. In late imperial China, holding official office was predicated upon holding an imperial degree, which was usually earned through the civil service examination system. As a means of both raising revenue and recognizing other kinds of achievement, the Qing State Sold degrees or awarded them for contributions to worthy causes, as in this case. The degree conferred status, but not the right to hold office.

[4] Memorial dated QL2.7.3, in QLCZZ 2: 838.

[5] Chen, thesis, 299; Will and Wong, *Nourish the People*, 297, 482.

[6] For an additional instance, see the memorials documenting the 1777–78 drought and famine in Guangxi: memorials dated QL42.10.12, in QLCZZ 40: 384–85; QL43.10.19, in QLCZZ 40: 452–53; QL43.2.2, in QLCZZ 42: 8–9; QL43.4.23, in QLCZZ 42: 745; QL43.9.8, in QLCZZ 44: 725; QL43.11.19, in QLCZZ 45: 566–67; QL43.11.16, in QLCZZ 45: 542–43; and QL43.3.15, in QLCZZ 42: 380.

[7] For examples, see the memorials dated YZ1.2.24, in YZCZZ 1: 100–101; KX52.5.27, in KXCZZ 4: 837–41; KX56.5.20, in KXCZZ 7: 914–16; QL17.3.27, in QLCZZ 2: 529; QL33.5.24, in QLCZZ 30: 704; and QL24.3.28, this last one in the Number One Historical Archives in Beijing, Gongzhong zhupi zouzhe; nongye lei; yuxue liangjia; hereafter cited as NYL, QL24.3.28: Box 81.

[8] Chen, thesis, 302–303; for examples, see memorials dated QL 9.2.8, in NYL Box 26, and QL16.4.16, in NYL Box 61.

[9] For examples, see the memorials dated QL33.5.24, in QLCZZ 30: 704; QL28.3.13, in QLCZZ 17: 196; QL33.2.29, in QLCZZ 29: 806; and QL47.5.8, in QLCZZ 51: 647.

the central government encouraged their creation.[10] The community granaries were designed to fill a gap in the operation of the ever-normal granaries. The ever-normal granaries all operated in the county seat, and while some rural residents could trek to town to use them when necessary, most of the rural population could not and did not use the ever-normal granaries. Recognizing this fact, the Kangxi and Yongzheng emperors called for the creation of community granaries in the villages, as well as provided incentives for contributions from both the wealthy and the gentry to stock the granaries.[11] Besides their origin and management, another characteristic distinguishing community granaries in Lingnan from the ever-normal granaries was their limitation of providing only loans, not reduced price sales or famine relief, and only to "those who work the fields."[12] Finally, compared with the ever-normal granaries, the grain stocks managed by the community granaries were small, amounting to just 6 percent of the ever-normal granary stocks in Guangdong.[13]

Granary Deficits. The huge stores of granary stocks put officials, their underlings, granary clerks, rice merchants, store owners and brokers, and military officers into regular contact with rice, money, and each other, providing opportunities for graft, corruption, skimming, and peculation of all kinds imaginable (some quite ingenious).[14] Coupled with the difficulties of restocking the granaries under normal conditions (which I will examine later), managers of granaries in Lingnan came to prefer storing the equivalent of the granary stocks in silver, leading to conditions that higher officials saw as alarming evidence of "deficits," but that local officials saw as a reasonable response to working in a region where private merchants and market forces could much more efficiently manage the storage and movement of grain than they could.

Thus, near the end of his long reign, the Qianlong emperor was receiving so many reports that the granaries had deficits that in 1794 he sarcastically remarked: "The provincial governors report each year that there is no deficit in the granaries. But when suddenly there is a bad year, I am told that is no longer true . . . I know the granaries in each province cannot be full." The reason for the deficits, the emperor came to believe by the end of his reign,

[10] Chen, thesis, 281.

[11] Chen, thesis, 298. See also the memorials dated QL43.6.27, in QLCZZ 43: 563–64, and QL43.6.27, in QLCZZ 43: 563–64.

[12] Chen, thesis, 315.

[13] Memorial dated QL21.1.9, in QLCZZ 16: 42.

[14] For examples, see Chen, thesis, 39–40; memorial dated QL12.2.24, in NYL Box 41; memorial dated QL14.2.10, in the Number One Historical Archives, XKTB dao an, bundle 142; memorial dated QL30.12.9, in QLCZZ 26: 827–36; and Will and Wong, *Nourish the People*, 171ff., 181ff., 225ff.

was that "degenerate officials commonly use their position to remove the grain or even to lend it out at interest."[15]

Confucian precepts deeply ingrained into the minds of state bureaucrats tended to place the blame for any and all shortcomings in administration at the feet of corrupt or degenerate officials; the solution then of course was to select upright officials, and all would be right. To be sure, official corruption and malfeasance probably accounted for some of the granary deficits, but the fact of the matter was, as Will and Wong conclusively demonstrate, that deficits arose simply from the workings of the granaries and because of management and control difficulties. Will argues that the ever-normal granary system had "structural weaknesses" arising from the problems of grain storage and preservation, of selling and restocking efforts, and of collecting loans – in short, because of the very operations the granaries were designed for – that inevitably resulted in shortages and deficits.[16]

Being structural, the problem of deficits emerged with the establishment of the granaries themselves. Thus, it should not be surprising to find evidence of granary deficits early in the eighteenth century. The earliest evidence I have uncovered dates from 1721, when the new governor of Guangxi, Gao Qizhuo, took up his post. As Gao reported to the Kangxi emperor:

> [The matter] of treasury funds and granary stocks is an extremely weighty one, [especially] whether or not there are deficits. Thus, I had to investigate. Investigation shows the provincial treasury with 866,000 taels. I have personally seen [the treasury], and the amount there is not much less [than there should be]. Annual taxes remitted by the counties amount to 326,000 taels, an amount difficult to conceal, and hence there is little shortage. Throughout the province the shortage is only 20,000 taels, and that has an explanation.
>
> I have hastened this year to complete the investigation of granary stocks. The capacity of the ever-normal granaries is 450,000 *shi*. The amount actually in the granaries is 300,000 *shi*. The missing 150,000 shi can be valued at 0.2 taels per *shi* . . . Although the amount of money is small, there is a deficiency, and the difference is not easy to make up.
>
> Since assuming office, I have uncovered the deficits, as follows: Nanning prefect Huang Zhixiao owes 39,000 *shi*; Guilin prefecture associate administrator Li Wo owes 29,000; Guilin prefecture controller general Zhang Honglin owes 13,000; Lingui county magistrate Wang Wenzhen owes 30,000; Hengzhou county magistrate Zhu Tan owes 28,000; Xuanhua county magistrate Zhao Chengzhang owes 16,000; Jiepo county magistrate Ren Tiannan owes 5,000;

15 Excerpted in *Zhongguo lidai shihuo zhi sanbian* (Taibei: Xuehai chuban she, 1972), 2094.
16 Will and Wong, *Nourish the People*, 189ff.

> The rest of the 1,000–2,000 *shi* of deficit is scattered in 17 different places.[17]

This example illustrates an important control measure the Qing state imposed on officials: the "post-transfer audit" (*jiaodai*). Upon taking up a new post, officials were expected to do an audit of the resources for which they were responsible and to make the report of their findings directly to the emperor within a few months of their posting, depending on the size of the administrative unit. Since officials were to remain in one post for no more than three years before being transferred, officials were constantly auditing the accounts of their predecessors. And for good reason: they were personally responsible for any deficits occurring on their watch, and if they were not extremely careful in their audit and missed a deficit, their successor could find it and hold them responsible.[18] In theory, then, grain deficits could have been easily uncovered.

That they weren't attests to the complexities of how the ever-normal granary system really worked, and how it really worked was enough to give any county magistrate nightmares. In the first place, the magistrate had to worry about preserving the grain under his supervision. The problems of grain preservation, large no matter where the magistrate was posted, were accentuated in Lingnan. Because of the warm, moist climate, the general regulations governing the operation of the granaries – selling 30 percent of the stock each year to ensure a complete turnover in three years – simply would not work. As Guangxi Governor Li Fu explained to the Yongzheng emperor upon taking his post: "In three years here the grain is moldy (*mei*); after five years it is rotten (*lan*); and after ten years it has decomposed (*hua*)."[19]

The amount of grain lost to spoilage, then, probably was an important factor in accounting for granary deficits.[20] But of even greater importance were the provisions and prospects for restocking after the fall harvest. Under normal circumstances, restocking would appear to have been routine: grain sold in the spring would be repurchased at lower prices after the fall harvest, resulting in a net gain and extra revenue. After a poor harvest, though, with greater than normal reduced price sales and perhaps some relief efforts, granary managers would have had to purchase even more in the market. If there was a second year of poor harvests, government purchases would push prices higher, and under those market conditions, the receipts from the spring sales would be insufficient to replace the amount sold.

[17] Memorial dated KX60.5.2, in KXCZZ 8: 777–78.

[18] For a description of the procedures, see Will and Wong, *Nourish the People*, 204–18.

[19] Memorial dated YZ2.7.3, in YZCZZ 2: 838.

[20] Will and Wong claim that loss of grain to spoilage or pests was not large; *Nourish the People*, 139–40.

Official Purchases and Restocking Difficulties. Guangdong was a net grain-deficit province, relying on imports (largely from Guangxi) to meet the needs of its population. Officials at the time complained that Guangdong produced only half of the rice it needed, a figure that may or may not have been accurate (see the discussion in Chapter 8 regarding the development of an integrated market for rice). But the point is that officials making decisions about the management of the grain stocks *believed* that Guangdong was a serious grain-deficit region. Under these circumstances, local officials could not easily restock the granaries from local supplies without forcing the prices up too high in the fall, and so had to import grain from other provinces just to stock the ever-normal granaries. The best example of an official caught in this quandary was Guangdong Governor Suchang, who struggled to balance the needs of granary restocking without sucking local markets dry.

When Suchang took up his post in 1751 and checked the inventory of the granary stocks, he discovered deficits amounting to 558,000 *shi* of grain, or about one-sixth of the amount there should have been. Apparently the deficits were not concealed and the result of official corruption, but were logged in granary inventories as "grain not yet repurchased." Concerned that the granaries would not have sufficient grain to sell in the spring, Suchang sent emissaries to Guangxi to purchase grain. For the governor of Guangxi, Dingchang, the appearance of these emissaries was problematic because they triggered price increases in his jurisdiction. In a memorial complaining about these increases, Ding said that local merchants picked up price signals from the weather, harvest results, and merchant activity, but the unexpected appearance of government emissaries from Guangdong was a sure sign of impending price increases. In this instance, the mere appearance of the Guangdong officials had caused rice prices in Guangxi to increase, even after the harvest.[21] So at the Guangxi governor's request, Suchang withdrew the emissaries, saying that "if purchases to replenish Guangdong granaries cause Guangxi rice prices to increase, the purchasing should stop."[22]

The next spring, even with granary stocks low, Suchang ordered reduced price sales and, with success, exhorted the wealthy to sell grain too.[23] That fall, of course, the granary stocks were even lower, and his restocking problem worsened. As he explained to the Qianlong emperor:

> Besides rice, the people [of Guangdong] broadly plant sweet potatoes and secondary grains, which the poor in the mountainous and coastal regions eat. Each year after the harvest rich households store grain; common folk all rely on [granary] reduced price sales to get through the period between harvests. Each year granaries must sell grain, and a lot of grain is sold. This is unlike

[21] Memorial dated QL 16.11.11, in QLCZZ 18: 61–62.
[22] Memorial dated QL16.12.17, in QLCZZ 2: 238.
[23] Memorial dated QL17.3.27, in QLCZZ 2: 529.

other provinces that may not have to sell grain every year . . . [lacunae in original] Each year grain is sold but not replaced.[24]

Taking seriously his responsibility to oversee the proper management of the ever-normal granaries, but with access to Guangxi markets denied, Governor Suchang tried, without success, to restock the granaries from local sources after the 1752 harvest. "Because [locally grown] rice is insufficient to meet consumption needs, grain merchants rely on [imports of] Guangxi rice. Because it rained a lot in the 12th month, little rice has arrived. Thus, rice prices in Guangzhou, Huizhou, and Zhaoqing prefectures have risen. I have ordered a halt to restocking the granaries to ensure local market supplies."[25]

Suchang was now in a bind: How would he ensure food supplies that spring? He decided he wouldn't: "In the time between harvests it is hard for the common people to get their daily food. I have ordered places where prices are rising to sell rice at reduced prices. Those areas that last year sold grain but have not restocked are not ordered to sell grain at reduced prices."[26] The consequences of Suchang's action are not known, but the sources do not record any food supply disasters in the spring of 1753, so Suchang probably was lucky. Following the early rice harvest, Suchang tried once again to restock the granaries but once again had to stop purchases when prices rose. He was in the same bind and saw no solution: "On the one hand I fear [existing] stocks will be insufficient for relief [if needed next spring]; on the other I fear that, after selling, rice granaries will not be able to restock."[27]

As luck would have it, the 1753 autumn harvest was excellent in both Guangdong and Guangxi, just as Suchang left Guangdong to take up another post. His replacement, Henian, walked into a favorable situation and immediately began restocking the ever-normal granaries, first by purchasing 100,000 *shi* from Guangxi in early 1754 and then by continuing restocking efforts in 1755 and 1756. Indeed, the 1756 harvest was so good that the governor-general wrote that "there hasn't been a situation this good for years"[28] and that "granary bins are overflowing and prices are stable."[29]

Suchang was not the only official facing restocking difficulties, and official regulations had acknowledged as early as 1738 that when restocking from purely local sources was not feasible, officials could turn to areas where supplies were adequate and hence prices were stable. The regulations also recognized situations like that confronted by Suchang where purchases from other provinces would be necessary to restock the granaries. But interprovincial pur-

24 Memorial dated QL17.11.8, in QLCZZ 4: 251–53.
25 Memorial dated QL18.1.22, in QLCZZ 4: 713–14.
26 Memorial dated QL18.4.24, in QLCZZ 5: 175–76.
27 Memorial dated QL18.7.16, in QLCZZ 5: 802.
28 Memorial dated QL21.9.17, in QLCZZ 15: 368.
29 Memorial dated QL21.6.17, in QLCZZ 14: 647.

chasing brought its own set of problems, made chronic in Lingnan because Guangdong imported grain to feed the peasant-farmers of the Pearl River delta.

As the Guangxi governor was aware, the appearance of Guangdong emissaries in Guangxi rice markets prompted rice brokers to raise prices. As early as 1737, according to Helen Dunstan, the acting governor of Guangdong "worried that if he notified the Guangxi authorities of Guangdong's intention to make substantial purchases on Guangxi markets, '[the dealers] will get wind of it and raise their prices.'"[30] The solution to this difficulty was finally to stop sending government emissaries to the Guangxi rice market, relying instead upon Foshan rice merchants to carry out the buying (to be discussed more later in this chapter and in Chapter 8).

Managing the routine buying and selling of granary stocks in Guangdong province thus was a major bureaucratic problem for provincial and local officials. A grain-deficit province to begin with, Guangdong could restock its granaries with purchases either from other provinces (a practice occasionally resented and resisted by the governor of Guangxi) or from local Guangdong markets, usually resulting in higher prices that exacerbated rather than relieved food supply problems. Charged on the one hand with maintaining granary stocks, but fearful of increasing prices locally on the other, officials like Suchang found themselves caught on the horns of a bureaucratic dilemma: to restock granary reserves by purchasing from local markets, or not.

Grain Storage "Deficits" and the Increased Use of Silver. Under the best of circumstances, then, the restocking efforts were a major bureaucratic headache, and the best solution was not to hold grain at all, but rather "cash equivalents" in silver taels. Prior to the Kangxi emperor's directive to begin storing up grain, officials had routinely used silver to purchase rice in the market rather than store grain; only during the 50-year period from 1690 through the Yongzheng reign and into the first decade of the Qianlong period did the state place a higher priority on storing grain than using silver. But all along, county magistrates figured that keeping silver in the treasury was better than storing grain, since it did not spoil and was easier to account for. And given the immense and well-stocked rice market in Guangdong, in time of need silver could be easily converted into rice. Keeping the cash equivalent in the treasury instead of the actual grain in local granaries thus was an endemic practice, probably developing along with the granaries themselves.

As early as 1724, Governor Li Fu of Guangxi noted the tendency for granary stocks to be held in silver and salt equivalencies.[31] Rather than over-

30 Helen Dunstan, *An Anthology of Chinese Economic Statecraft, or, The Sprouts of Liberalism* (unpublished manuscript), 1178–79, quoting from *Da Qing gao zong (Qianlong) shi lu*, 53: 20a–b.

31 As an import, salt was in short supply in Guangxi and thus very valuable.

looking the practice, Li energetically pushed for keeping all the stocks as grain. And Li had a project in mind for the revenue generated by regularly selling granary stocks: rebuilding prefectural city walls. When he assumed office, he noted that some 1,600 *zhang* (about 3 miles) of walls around county cities throughout the prefecture, 58 towers, and 3 cannonades needed rebuilding, at an estimated cost of 30,000–40,000 taels. He saw the granary operations as a source of revenue to rebuild city walls, no doubt knowing that such rebuilding got one's name enshrined in county, prefectural, and provincial gazetteers, if not carved on stone steles erected in each city. Governor Li energetically pursued restocking efforts. But the point is that he had a personal agenda.[32] He was the exception that proved the rule: generally, officials preferred to minimize the bureaucratic hazards of storing grain by keeping the ever-normal granary stocks as silver equivalents.

The issue of whether or not to allow officials to stock silver in lieu of grain was debated at the highest levels of the government in the 1740s in the context of addressing the Qianlong emperor's concerns about steady, empirewide increases in grain prices. The Qianlong emperor suspected that the primary cause of the price inflation was his increase in the provincial granary quotas and energetic stocking efforts on the part of provincial officials. Responding to the emperor's 1743 invitation to discuss the causes of the observed price increases, one official argued that all restocking of granaries caused prices to rise, thereby harming the local populace. Accepting the need to find a means of maintaining the state's role in famine and disaster relief, he argued that officials be allowed to keep most of their granary quotas as silver to be distributed directly to the needy:

> Silver is light and insubstantial, easy for the authorities to distribute and easy for the folk to take away. This is its first advantage. Where grain is stored up in the granaries, there is much worry over mildewing and rotting. With silver one avoids this. Should there be embezzlement, it can be brought to light at once. This is the second advantage. The poor get grain to eat, but they must also break up firewood and cook. In that it serves them in their other items of expenditure, the folk set more store by silver. This is the third advantage. The mean folk in their quest for profit have arts of the utmost subtlety. If one affords them some small quantity of silver, they will also be enabled to contrive some hawking trade, and to go after drachms and scruples. Grain in its sluggishness is not as good as silver in its penetration. This is the fourth advantage. Though there may be a famine year, there will of certainty not be exhaustion of all grain supplies. One may have grain and fear the want of silver, but only if one has silver how will one fear the want of grain? This is the fifth advantage.[33]

32 Memorials dated YZ 2.11.26, in YZCZZ 3: 532; and YZ2.12.4, in YZCZZ 3: 565.

33 The translation is from Dunstan, *Anthology*, 1195–96. The original text is from *Huang chao jingshi wen bian*, He Changling, comp., 1827 (reprint, Taibei: Wenhai chuban she, n.d.), 44: 5b–6b.

The Qianlong emperor apparently was not persuaded, and policy remained that of keeping all stocks as grain. The issue arose again in 1748 when the emperor instructed the governors and governors-general to discuss the causes of the continuing rise in grain prices. The emperor received 18 responses, some of which once again proposed eliminating actual grain stocks and using silver instead. After considering the alternatives, the Qianlong emperor chose to reduce each province's target, but not to renounce the policy of keeping stocks in grain.[34] Of relevance here are two points: first, the very fact that the possibility of keeping granary stocks in silver equivalents was discussed at the highest levels of government and was supported by about half of those who responded to the emperor's edict demonstrates that the idea had support and thus was a legitimate practice. The emperor's decree ending the discussion did not explicitly condemn the practice either, thereby keeping the door open to provincial officials for their interpretation. Second, the official making the strongest case not just for the use of silver but for reliance on market forces rather than the state to supply grain in times of crisis was the Liangguang governor-general, Celeng. With Celeng's antipathy toward the practice of stocking grain rather than silver, it should not be surprising that the ever-normal granaries in Guangdong soon abandoned keeping stocks of grain on hand.

Dating the transition in the operation of Guangdong's ever-normal granaries from storing grain to depositing silver in the treasury is approximate, since with the Qianlong emperor's 1749 decision, documents could not openly acknowledge a practice contrary to imperial policy. The only evidence thus is that of actual practice and what can be inferred from the actions and statements of officials trying to manage the granaries. This story dates the abandonment of grain storage by the state to the middle of the Qianlong reign, or somewhere in the 1760s. As we saw earlier, in 1751–53 Governor Suchang struggled mightily with the problems of restocking the granaries. Suchang's restocking efforts – effected in the midst of a court debate on whether or not dependence on the market ought to have been carried further – probably was the last concerted effort in Guangdong to keep grain in granaries; thereafter, silver, merchants, and the market replaced grain, officials, and the state in the management of food supplies in south China, despite the intent of the emperor.

After Suchang's success, references to restocking decline in frequency. In 1755, Guangdong granaries were restocked by imports from Guangxi, and exceptionally good harvests the next year led the governor to report that "granary bins are overflowing and prices are stable."[35] The frost and subsequent price rises in 1757 (discussed in Chapter 6) saw officials opening the

[34] This summary is based upon Dunstan, *Anthology*, 1237–65.

[35] Memorials dated QL20.1.12, in QLCZZ 10: 513; and QL 21.6.17, in QLCZZ 14: 647.

granaries for reduced price sales and noting in 1759 that little grain was sold, even though it was offered for reduced price sales.[36]

Having searched through the extant palace memorials for the Qianlong reign, the last convincing evidence I found that granaries stored actual grain comes from 1764, when a series of palace memorials refer to reduced price sales in the spring totaling 235,200 *shi*, following a halt to repurchasing efforts after the fall harvest because of upward pressure on rice prices. Later reports on granary activities in palace memorials are either formulaic or unconvincing. In 1774, for instance, Governor Debao reported that "in the period between harvests, grain prices get a little high so granaries *should* open and offer reduced price sales."[37] Three years later the governor indicated that he "ordered granary sales *according to regulations*" (emphasis added).[38] More direct evidence dates from 1778, when the Gaozhou prefectural gazetteer records the provincial authorities distributing money, not grain, during the drought and food shortages that year.[39] And in 1783, just five years before the disastrous 1787 drought, Governor Shang'an unconvincingly reported, as if he had just read a description of how he should report, that "those counties which have requested [authorization] to sell grain at reduced prices are ordered to keep 70 percent and sell 30 percent. In expectation of a good harvest, reduce the price by five fen according to regulations. All proceeds must be submitted to the treasury. After the fall harvest those funds will be used to restock the granaries."[40] To be sure, Shang'an may have been led to believe that the ever-normal granaries stored grain, being ignorant of the realities, or at least that some granaries may well have stored grain. But unlike earlier cases of the use of granaries for famine relief, I found no memorials by other officials documenting the amounts of grain distributed.

The available evidence thus points to the mid-1760s as the last time that ever-normal granaries in Guangdong actually held grain as stocks, with the authorities afterwards instead keeping the grain equivalent in silver on hand in the treasury and relying upon merchants and the market to ensure adequate supplies, not just in the time between harvests, but when natural disaster struck as well. The same held true for the community granaries (*she cang*), but because the management of these granaries was delegated to local residents and they were not part of the authorities' official responsibilities, the available sources do not permit as close a dating of the storage of silver in place of grain as with the ever-normal granaries. Nonetheless, the available data on community granary stocks from county gazetteers shows that they too held stocks as the

36 Memorials dated QL21.8.24, in QLCZZ 15: 90; and QL21.9.17, in QLCZZ 15: 368.
37 Memorial dated QL39.4.28, in QLCZZ 35: 443.
38 Memorial dated QL42.5.13, in QLCZZ 38: 605.
39 *Gaozhou fuzhi*, 1890 ed., juan 49: 38a.
40 Memorial dated QL 48.3.21, in QLCZZ 55: 426–27.

silver equivalent of grain.[41] If this evidence is illustrative of what was actually happening with the community granaries, then it appears that the trend toward the replacement of their grain with silver probably began only slightly later than with the ever-normal granaries. And as I will show in more detail in Chapter 8, by the 1760s, officials had come to depend upon the market and private storage rather than state granaries to ensure food supplies.

Charity Granaries. The establishment of charity granaries (*yi cang*) in Guangdong was a direct consequence of the decline toward the end of the eighteenth century in the capabilities of the ever-normal and community granaries to provide relief, especially in urban areas. While some charity granaries had been established in rural counties, the largest and most important charity granary was established in the town of Foshan.[42]

As noted before, Foshan was a commercial and manufacturing town just west of Guangzhou.[43] Favorably situated at the confluence of the West and North Rivers, Foshan was an important trading city with docks, piers, and warehouses servicing various industries, including the rice trade, up and down the rivers. Foshan additionally was known throughout the empire for its high-quality iron cooking pots. The population of Foshan, estimated at perhaps 500,000 by the end of the eighteenth century, was nearly all urban: merchants and their families, cotton textile workers, tea curers, and ironmongers comprised the bulk of the population. An early-nineteenth-century account noted that "there are few farmers and many workers" in Foshan.[44]

The Foshan charity granary was established in 1795 as a direct result of the 1786–87 drought and famine. As we have already seen, by then the ever-normal granaries had no stored grain, and the drought lowered the West River to the point that imports from Guangxi were slow to come. Faced with starving people and babies abandoned along roadsides, the Foshan gentry under the leadership of degree-holder (*juren*) Lao Tong took charge of the emergency.[45] Levying a 5 percent surcharge on the rent of all the shops in Foshan, Lao col-

[41] Chen, *Shichang jizhi yu shehui bianqian* (1992), 241. [42] Chen, thesis, 316–20.

[43] For a recent analysis of Foshan, see David Faure, "What Made Foshan a Town? The Evolution of Rural–Urban Identities in Ming–Qing China," *Late Imperial China* 11, no. 2 (Dec. 1990): 1–31.

[44] *Ming Qing Foshan beike*, 400.

[45] The Foshan charity granary differed from granaries of the same name established in other provinces. Will and Wong have shown that there were two different kinds of granaries established in north and central China with the name "charity granaries." In Zhili province, charity granaries were established around 1750 in rural areas with functions similar to the community granaries in Guangdong, with the exception that the charity granaries could provide famine relief, not just loans. Will and Wong, *Nourish the People*, 69–72. Granaries called *yi cang* also existed in Guangxi and probably were similar in size and function to the rural Zhili charity granaries, but not much is known about them. See memorials dated QL42.11.10, in QLCZZ 40: 736–37; QL43.11.19, in QLCZZ 45: 565; QL46.10.14, in QLCZZ 49: 235; and QL43.11.11, in QLCZZ

lected several thousand taels, purchased rice in Guangxi and arranged for its delivery to the docks in Foshan, then oversaw the establishment and management of the distribution of rice to the hungry.[46]

Lao Tong was so shaken by the 1786–87 disaster that he spent considerable time and energy over the next few years making preparations to ensure that the same never happened again in Foshan.[47] Poring over a vast array of historical documents and publications describing famine relief policies, procedures, and institutions beginning with pre-imperial times, Lao published a compilation in 1794 under the title of *Jiuhuang beilan* (The guide for famine preparedness). The *Guide* included not just historical "how to" descriptions of relief operations, but even recipes for edible plants and grasses.[48] Soliciting contributions from the gentry, Lao succeeded in collecting sufficient funds to build a granary, lay in some initial stocks, and hire two managers. To ensure funds for maintaining granary stocks, Lao gained approval both to levy a toll on ferry crossings to Guangzhou and to collect a fee from each merchant's shop based on the rent paid.[49] In the years after its establishment, the Foshan charity granary increased in size, importance, and centrality to the governance of Foshan, as well as providing for relief in times of harvest failure, food shortages, high prices, and hunger. Professionally managed under gentry trusteeship, the granary developed strong management and control mechanisms that, coupled with secure sources of funding, ensured that it was able to provide urban relief.[50]

Private Storage of Grain

As the state withdrew from direct management of food supplies and relied increasingly on the market, private storage of grain assumed a correspond-

53: 767 for documents listing the size of the charity granary stocks in Guangxi and the amount loaned out. Charity granaries of the rural type found in Guangxi and Zhili thus were unlike the Foshan charity granary. But Will and Wong also describe charity granaries established in Jiangnan, Jiujiang, and Hankou in the 1720s under the leadership of salt merchants (69–70). These urban charity granaries thus appear to be similar to the Foshan granary, but with one important difference: where merchants took the lead in the Yangzi River valley cities, in Foshan gentry controlled the charity granary. The reason for this difference has to do with the very interesting history, told by David Faure, by which the Foshan gentry rose to prominence and maintained their power over and above that of Foshan's substantial merchant class. See David Faure, "What Made Foshan a Town?"

46 *Ming Qing Foshan beike*, 400–401, 411.

47 For a history of the Foshan granary, see Mary Backus Rankin, "Managed by the People: Officials, Gentry, and the Foshan Charitable Granary, 1795–1845," *Late Imperial China* 15, no. 2 (Dec. 1994): 1–52.

48 Lao Tong, *Jiuhuang beilan*, in *Lingnan yishu* 58, *Baibu congshu jicheng* 93 (Taibei: Yiwen chuban she, 1968).

49 *Ming Qing Foshan beike*, 390–91. 50 Ibid., 411–41.

ingly larger role. The amount of grain stored and held over from one harvest to the next by peasant families, landlords and lineages, and rice merchants is difficult to assess and quantify. Unlike the state system, all of these units kept their own accounts and did not report stocks to the state. But in the aggregate the stocks were substantial, as the food supply of 20 million people depended more on them than on the state granaries.

Peasant Storage. That peasant-producers stored grain after the harvest goes without saying. The real questions are: How much? For how long? And did the answers to these questions vary with geography and change with time? Without belaboring the obvious, each peasant family made decisions following the harvest about how much grain to store and how much to sell based on the family's survival strategy and subsistence calculations. Minimally, the peasant family needed to store enough seed to plant the following spring. But beyond that, would it store enough to eat until the next harvest? What if the next harvest were bad? Or would it store more than enough grain? What if the harvest was good? What would it do with the surplus? Answers to all of these questions determined market supplies and grain prices, which in turn affected the peasant family's decision making.

At the most basic level, peasant families prepared to store grain in specially made baskets and, in some places, in granaries as well. Francesca Bray has synthesized the available evidence on peasant storage techniques, demonstrating that peasant families in Guangdong and Guangxi had the facilities to store substantial amounts of grain.[51] Certainly the investment required to buy or make baskets was less than that required to build a granary, and which course was taken depended on the wealth of the family. Since the private granaries were well constructed and rivaled the state granaries, it seems reasonable to assume that, like the state, peasant families with granaries intended to store grain for more than one year; those with just baskets probably stored grain only from one harvest to the next.

Most of the evidence on the patterns of peasant storage comes from officials' memorials on weather and grain prices. With a good fall harvest in 1752, for example, the Guangxi governor reported that "the people are taking the opportunity to stock up."[52] Again in 1777, the governor of Guangxi reported, "Since the abundant early harvest has been sold in the market, very many households now have stored grain."[53] Many other examples could be cited, but the evidence clearly shows peasants storing grain after both early and late rice harvests. I have found no evidence, though, that peasants stored wheat. In fact, because of the difficulties of storing wheat in the humid southern climate and

[51] Bray, *Agriculture*, 381–412. [52] Memorial dated QL17.11.11, in QLCZZ 4: 290.
[53] Memorial dated QL42.7.9, in QLCZZ 39: 320.

the possibility of it molding or even becoming slightly poisonous,[54] most likely wheat was consumed as soon as it was harvested.

Harvests also were the time for peasants to sell grain. Officials reported almost ad nauseam on "new grain" hitting the market as soon as the harvest came in, implying that peasant families sold grain as fast as they could harvest it. But the same sources also indicate that at least some peasant families stored more than enough grain from one harvest to the next and thus had "old grain" to sell when the new harvest came in. In 1753, for example, Guangdong Governor Suchang (who we have already met valiantly trying to restock the ever-normal granaries) expected a good late harvest and so commented, "The grain peasant families have stored will be sold on the market."[55] In Guangxi a year later, following a good early rice harvest, one memorial reported that "families are selling old grain."[56] A decade later, officials reported that with a good late harvest, "peasants will sell the grain they have stored."[57] In fact, in every decade in the eighteenth century, officials commented on peasants selling old grain after a good harvest. One final example from 1782 will suffice: "After the early harvest, peasant families that had stored grain have sold much on the market."[58] Sometimes, peasants gambled and sold grain before the harvest came in, perhaps hoping to realize some larger gains: "When villagers see rain," Liangguang Governor-General Chen Dashou reported in 1751, "they bring rice out of storage to sell, and rice prices do not rise."[59]

The most interesting and specific evidence concerning peasant storage of grain comes from Chen Yuanlong, governor of Guangxi province from 1712 to 1716. Shortly after taking up his post, Chen reported an excellent late rice harvest, at 120 percent of normal and larger than any in recent memory. But while rice prices had initially declined, they then rose 25–50 percent in just one month. Puzzled by the counterintuitive price behavior, Chen reported to the Kangxi emperor:

> In Guangxi, the land is vast and sparsely populated, and there is a surplus of rice. In Guangdong, the population is dense and the land [relatively] scarce; the rice produced there is insufficient to meet demand, so they rely on Guangxi for rice supplies. This year (1712), the price of rice in coastal Guangdong is high, reaching 1.3 or 1.4 taels per *shi*. Thus, merchants gather like clouds in the interior of Guangxi, to the extent that Guangxi rice prices rose 1–2 qian [one-tenth of a tael] in just one month. Local officials are anxious that the poor will be unable to buy rice and have asked that the rice trade be

[54] Bray, *Agriculture*, 471. [55] Memorial dated QL18.10.6, in QLCZZ 6: 361–62.
[56] Memorial dated QL19.6.11, in QLCZZ 8: 751.
[57] Memorial dated QL28.10.8, in QLCZZ 9: 279.
[58] Memorial dated QL47.7.3, in QLCZZ 52: 356.
[59] Memorial dated QL16.1.13, in NYL Box 61.

> suppressed. I presume to think, though, that the people of Guangdong and Guangxi are mutually interdependent.
>
> The imperial court would rather allow some differences between people here and there [i.e., tolerate price differentials] than implement the prohibition on exports. But I fear that the people may be harmed [by unregulated trade]. I only know that the profit to be made from selling rice is not a plan to assure one's future sustenance. [To mediate these conflicting desires, my approach has been] to order local officials to exhort the common people, ordering those who have stored more than eight to nine months of grain to understand this and to sell their surplus to the Guangdong merchants. Grain prices then will level out, and the poor of Guangxi, who know little of storing grain, can be supplied by new grain from the fall harvest.[60]

This text is fraught with ambiguity. What seems certain, though, is that Guangdong merchants were buying rice in Guangxi markets, causing prices to rise. But rather than suppress the trade, which would have lowered prices in Guangxi, Chen allowed it to proceed knowing that the higher prices would tempt peasants to part with their grain, even though "the profit to be made from selling rice is not a plan to assure one's future sustenance." Chen advised finding a balance between sales and storage, suggesting that peasants keep a stock of eight to nine months grain and sell the rest. Doing so would put grain onto the market for both Guangdong merchants and Guangxi poor to buy at moderating prices; everyone would benefit. While it is not clear who "the poor" were in Chen's mind, no doubt they were primarily urban dwellers, since they could buy the new grain hitting the market; peasant-producers would have little need to buy new grain, having just grown it. Thus, if peasant-producers stored eight to nine months' worth of grain, that amount was some three to four months more than needed to see the family from the late rice harvest to either the winter wheat or early rice harvest.

The rhythm to peasant storage of grain thus was tied to the fall harvest. After that harvest, peasant families stored more than enough grain to get them through to the next harvest. If that harvest was good, or even was expected to be good, peasant families sold the "old" grain on the market, expecting to replenish their stores from the new harvest. If the harvest was short, the extra amount stored could see the family through to the next harvest. Under this regime, real subsistence problems could arise only if the entire next harvest was wiped out or there were two consecutive years of poor harvests.

Lineage and Landlord Storage of Grain. If small peasant-producers stored grain on their own account, so too did large lineages and landlords. Indeed,

[60] Memorial dated KX51.11.17, in KXCZZ 4: 538–39.

lineages and landlords had the capital to invest in the substantial private granaries described in considerable detail by Bray,[61] enabling them to store grain for years at a time. Substantial buildings sometimes with more than one "bin" (*jian*) and capable of storing hundreds of *shi* of rice, a landlord's granary was large enough to accommodate several people milling around, as the following summary of a tragicomic accident reveals:

> Liang Shangxi rented land . . . from . . . Chen Wudian and agreed to pay 21 shi in rent. In 1751, Shangxi paid only 5.8 shi and thus was 15.2 shi in arrears. On the 11th day of the ninth month, [Chen] Wudian and his relative Hu Xinlai, together with two carpenters, Li Han'ang and Zeng Yaba, were repairing his granary. Wudian ordered his servant Lin Yuanqing to go with him to Shangxi's house to collect the rent. Shangxi didn't have any money, cursed Wudian for calling on him, and started an argument. Wudian said he would tie up Shangxi's sons Liang Han'ang and Liang Hanhui and file a petition to get the rent. When Shangxi picked up a stick to hit him, Wudian and Yuanqing hurried back to the granary.
>
> A while later, [Shangxi's sons] Han'ang and Hanhui found out what happened and then sought out [Chen] Wudian. [On the way] they passed the door of Woman Zhu [wife of their family's adopted son], and told her about the affair; she too was incensed and went with them to find [Wudian]. [Seeing them come], Wudian became frightened and ran out the back door. At that point, a neighbor, Lai Wenze, invited Woman Zhu in for tea. Hanhui waited at the granary. Han'ang couldn't find Wudian so he too returned to the granary.
>
> At that time, Woman Zhu emerged from Lai's house and heard someone in the granary. Supposing Wudian had returned, she went to have a few words with him. Also hoping to find Wudian, Han'ang rushed in, knocking Lady Zhu over. She hit her head on the corner of a table, whereupon she fell down and hurt her leg. Unable to stand, and with injuries to her head and hand, she was about to die. Han'ang cried for help; Liang Hanhui rushed into the granary and pushed the table onto Lady Zhu, crushing her and breaking both of her legs.[62]

Besides the human drama and tragicomic outcome, this story reveals both that landlords collected rent from tenants and stored it in granaries, and that landlord granaries were so capacious that several people could run around in them. How large were they?[63] A nineteenth-century district magistrate, trying to manage in times of a grain shortage, wrote that "powerful families are permitted to have only a three-year supply of rice. If they have more than that,

[61] Bray, *Agriculture*, 409–12.

[62] *Qing dai dizu boxiao xingtai*, Zhongguo diyi lishi dang'an guan and Zhongguo shehui kexue yuan lishi yanjiu so, comp. (Beijing: Xinhua shudian, 1982), vol. 2: 757–59.

[63] Bray, *Agriculture*, 410.

their rice will be sold at a low price and they will be punished."[64] Three years' worth of stored grain, it seems to me, is a lot of grain, and perhaps most landlord families did not keep that much on hand for their own use. Those who did keep stocks greater than what their family would consume understood how risky farming was in Lingnan (I discussed this in the preceding chapter) and sought to profit from the annual price swings.

The timing of landlord sales of grain thus differed from that of peasant families. Unlike peasants who sold grain immediately after the harvest, whether old or new grain, there is no evidence that landlords sold grain after the harvest. Indeed, with larger and better storage facilities, landlords could afford to wait until prices rose in the spring before selling grain. Faced with the same storage and spoilage problems as the state granaries, landlords too had to sell grain merely to ensure fresh stocks. But they could choose when to sell, and that was when prices were at their highest in the spring.

The amount of grain that families stored on their own account, and hence their chances of survival when a harvest failed, clearly was a function of their wealth and power. In times of harvest failure such as during the droughts, floods, or cold snaps described in Chapter 6, those families with the least amount of stored grain ran out first, while more fortunate peasant families might have been able to hold on until the next harvest – if they didn't have rent to pay. Large landowners with larger stores of grain, though, remained secure and could even profit from the shortages by selling grain at high prices. In times of dearth, the distinction between storing grain and hoarding it blurred, with both officials and those without grain demanding that the wealthy sell their grain.

Rice Brokers, Merchants, and Shops. Just as it proved easier for me to describe than to quantify grain stored by peasant-producers and large landowners, so too is it difficult to gain perspective on the amount of grain stored by rice merchants. But given the extent to which Guangdong and Guangxi provincial officials commented upon the role of rice merchants, especially those from the commercial and industrial city of Foshan, in the interprovincial rice trade, we must assume that the amount of trade was significant. Indeed, the evidence suggests that Foshan was a warehousing center for the rice trade, storing grain imported from Guangxi to supply the needs not just of Foshan, but of Guangzhou as well. With a combined population approaching 1 million in the eighteenth century, Guangzhou and Foshan consumed more than 4 million *shi* of rice each year.[65] An early-nineteenth-century source

[64] Xu Gengqie, *Buziqie zhai man cun* (Taibei: Wenhai chuban she reprint of 1889 text), juan 4: 37a–39b.

[65] Chen, thesis, 96–97.

described the centrality of Foshan grain warehouses: "Grain arriving from all over (*si fang*) is stored at Foshan."[66]

But that is not to say that the Foshan rice merchants had the capacity to store 4 million *shi* at any given time. To be sure, one of the four largest wharves in Foshan was devoted to rice and another to rice bran,[67] but the organization of the collection and distribution channels spread the storage of grain over the year and in different locations. Nonetheless, the general routine was as follows: following the early and late rice harvests, grain was collected from rural Guangxi, loaded onto boats, and shipped to Wuzhou. At Wuzhou the grain was either bagged or loaded in bulk onto boats that carried 100–200 *shi* each. Whatever was not sold downriver was warehoused in Wuzhou.

Upon reaching Foshan, wholesalers (*mi hang* or *liang hang*) unloaded the grain into warehouses at or near the docks, from which they distributed grain to rice shops (*mi bu*) for retail sale. The numbers of wholesalers and retailers is difficult to estimate. Eighteenth-century sources merely mention that there were "several" wholesalers and that one or more rice shops were in every marketplace. In the early twentieth century, Guangzhou alone had 700 retail rice shops.[68] In the eighteenth century, though, there may well have been more. Until 1790, Foshan rice shops were each allowed to stock a maximum of 100 *shi* of grain (a year's supply for five families of five people each); with more than that in storage, rice shop owners were open to charges of hoarding. Following a 1790 petition to the Guangzhou prefect, the authorities allowed the Foshan rice shops to keep up to a maximum of 200 *shi* of rice.[69]

Private storage of rice from harvest to harvest – whether in the baskets of peasant families, in the granaries of landlords, or in the warehouses of rice merchants – therefore was substantial and played an important role in the food supply system. Depending on the size of the harvest and whether or not they had grain left from the previous harvest, peasant-producers sold new or old rice immediately after the harvest, putting downward pressure on prices; landlords collected rice as rent and stored it until prices peaked in the spring before selling it; and rice merchants and brokers warehoused huge amounts in Wuzhou and Foshan. Just how much grain entered the market is a problem I will take up in the next chapter. But with the state too storing grain in the granaries for the first 60 years or so of the eighteenth century, there was considerable demand for stored rice, raising policy questions at the imperial court in Beijing about the best way to manage the food supplies of the Chinese empire.

[66] *Ming Qing Foshan beike*, 344. [67] Ibid., 381–82.

[68] Guangdong yinhang, *Guangzhou mi ye* (Guangzhou: 1936), 86–102.

[69] *Ming Qing Foshan beike*, 343–44; see also David Faure, "What Made Foshan a Town?" 21.

State or Market?

The issue of the appropriate balance between state and private storage of grain was discussed and debated at the imperial court over ten years from 1743 to 1752. As we saw earlier, in both 1743 and 1748, sustained grain price increases alarmed the Qianlong emperor to the point where he issued an edict soliciting comments from officials on the causes of the price increases. According to Helen Dunstan, the Qianlong emperor believed the cause to be the accumulation of granary stocks and hoped the memorialists would write on that topic; the most successful did.[70] In fact, the Qianlong emperor deemed the issue so important that the problem of high grain prices was set as one of the essay topics for the 1748 palace examination. After setting out three possible courses of action – suspending granary purchases, taking stern measures against merchant-hoarders, and forbidding the wealthy to hoard – the emperor discussed only the first:

> There is only a certain amount of grain produced; it stands to reason that if it is accumulated in official hands, there must be shortage for the population. This being so, the harm of its accumulation and the good of its dispersal should be thought upon maturely; yet if one fails to make clear the underlying principle, how shall one cause both sides to benefit?[71]

Of the 18 officials' responses to the emperor's query, most agreed that state intervention in the grain markets caused price increases. Indeed, several officials, in particular Celeng, the governor-general of Guangdong and Guangxi provinces, took, in Dunstan's words, an "anti-interventionist" stance.[72] In fact, Celeng might be seen as a mid-eighteenth-century free trader, extolling the virtues of the market in ensuring adequate food supplies and excoriating the follies of state intervention: "Those things which impede the grain [trade should] all be done away with; . . . official purchasing knowing restraint, commercial transportation may flow free, and . . . grain among the populace becoming day by day more plentiful, a gradual lessening may be looked for in price."[73]

The reasons the governors cited for favoring increased reliance on the market were twofold. The first was an economic consideration: with higher prices, the market itself could be used to ensure that grain would be moved from areas of surplus production and low prices to deficit areas with high

70 Dunstan, *Anthology*, 1237. Intuiting the emperor's desires apparently enhanced an official's career.

71 Edict in *Da Qing gao zong (Qianlong) shi lu*, 313: 33b–34a, translated by Dunstan, in *Anthology*, 1237–38, n. 96.

72 Dunstan, *Anthology*, 1246.

73 Memorial in *Da Qing gao zong (Qianlong) shi lu*, 311: 40a–44b, translated by Dunstan, in *Anthology*, 1248.

prices. The acting governor of Anhui posed an additional reason for abandoning the granaries and relying on the market: "[In Jiangnan], the habituation [of the population] is complete, and no sooner is there flood or drought than they will gaze with outstretched necks. I in my foolishness am of the opinion that the presumptuousness of the population's spirit should be gradually repressed." The most that should be done, according to the governor, was to distribute a little silver and let the poor make their purchases in the market. The market would "discipline the poor" to rely on themselves, not the state, in times of crisis.[74]

The Qianlong emperor ultimately decided in 1749 to reaffirm the place and role of the ever-normal granaries, albeit with smaller "targets" than he had pushed for at the beginning of his reign. With the exception of a brief discussion in 1752, the emperor's 1749 decision effectively ended any further consideration of allowing market forces freer rein. The point to be made here, though, is not that the issue was decided, but that many Qing officials had hoped for a greater role for the market. And although the emperor may have spoken, it was to officials like the Liangguang Governor-General Celeng – who had expressed a decided preference for the market and for the use of silver for relief – that the managers of the ever-normal granaries reported. It should not be too surprising therefore that in Guangdong at least, after the mid-1760s state storage of grain was not the practice but rather the exception, the "storage" of silver was common, and reliance upon the market was usual.

Conclusion

With the Qing state secure and organized by the end of the seventeenth century, state officials began creating granaries to store grain against the vagaries of the weather. Besides providing for famine relief, the state-run ever-normal granaries also were used to stabilize grain prices (buying after the fall harvest and selling before the spring crop was in), to loan grain and seed to peasant-farmers, and to provision the military. Community granaries, established in the countryside, played many of the same roles as the ever-normal granaries, but on a smaller scale.

Although the very operation of the granaries spawned various abuses, for much of the eighteenth century officials in Lingnan effectively mobilized grain for storage, provided relief when needed, and ensured a regular turnover of stocks, both to keep grain fresh and to stabilize grain prices. But by the early years of the Qianlong emperor's reign (1736–95), the abuses in the system, the difficulties of storing the grain in the damp Lingnan climate, and the problems encountered in trying to restock the granaries led many officials in

[74] Memorial in ibid., 311: 28b–29b, translated by Dunstan, in ibid., 1252.

Lingnan to prefer to minimize the bureaucratic hazards of storing grain by keeping silver on hand to buy grain in the market when needed. By the 1760s, the available evidence leads to the conclusion that state officials in Guangdong (and in Guangxi, a decade later) had come to rely on the market to ensure food supplies to urban areas.

Certainly the amount of private storage of grain was substantial. Peasant families stored grain after the harvest, often for more than a year for their own use, sometimes selling surpluses on the market when the incoming harvest looked good. Large lineages and landlords, who collected rent in grain and stored it in their own granaries, sometimes accumulating up to three years' worth of grain at a time, were secure against the worry of food shortages and could profit handsomely by selling grain at higher prices before the harvest came in. Rice brokers, merchants, and rice shops not only had the capacity to buy and warehouse grain, but also had collection and distribution channels that spread the storage of grain throughout the year and in different locations.

When rice prices rose sharply in the 1740s, the Qianlong emperor asked his governors what the proper role of the state in the food supply system of the empire should be. Most governors agreed that state intervention caused prices to rise and therefore favored increased reliance on the market. The emperor decided to reaffirm the place and role of the ever-normal granaries, albeit with smaller targets for stored grain; this decision ended further consideration – at least in the imperial palace – of allowing the market a greater role in the food supply system. But it was local officials who operated the ever-normal granaries, and they preferred storing silver taels with which to buy grain in the market when needed rather than storing it themselves in the granaries. By the 1770s, state storage of grain became unusual, and reliance on the market the normal course of action.

Thus, the storage of grain, whether in state or private hands, was an important response of the people of Lingnan to variations in the size of the harvest (and hence in food supplies, grain prices, and family security) caused by climatic fluctuation and change. But the causal chain linking environmental and economic change did not end there, for the way in which most grain ultimately was stored and moved – in the market – in its turn was to have significant implications for the environment of Lingnan.

8

"TRADE IN RICE IS BRISK": MARKET INTEGRATION AND THE ENVIRONMENT

The state-managed granary system may have been a conscious, institutional response to problems of food supply caused by deficient (or bumper) harvests, but it did not constitute the most important mechanism for moving rice from food-surplus to food-deficit areas. Markets for the sale and purchase of rice dealt with much larger amounts of grain, moved it more frequently and regularly, and did so more efficiently than the granary system. To be sure, handling the food supply of Lingnan was not an either-or case, for as I discussed in the preceding chapter, granaries and markets did function together.

This chapter will examine the markets for, and the prices of, rice. Although this chapter will be more statistical than others in the book, the issues of grain prices and markets are important for understanding both the processes of environmental change in Lingnan and the conditions that sustained significant population growth during the eighteenth century. As an integrated market for rice began to link all regions of Lingnan into a unified market, the West River basin in Guangxi came to specialize in rice for export to Guangzhou and the Pearl River delta, just as peasant-farmers there had begun to specialize in sugar or silk. One consequence of this development was to decrease the number of ecosystems in Lingnan, simplifying the environment and decreasing ecological diversity. Another consequence, though, was to ensure steady supplies of rice at prices that did not increase too rapidly or fluctuate too wildly – despite the adverse effects of climatic shocks – thereby undergirding both further economic expansion and the growth of the population.

Market Integration and Ecological Diversity

As we saw in Chapter 5, to meet market demand for sugar and silk in the eighteenth century, an increasing number of peasant-farmers in and around the Pearl River delta abandoned rice for cash crops, relying on the market rather than their farm to secure their food. Where did the rice come from? How much grain circulated in the market? How dependent were the people of Guangdong – both urban and rural – upon the market to supply their food needs for rice? To analyze the circulation of rice and the development of the market for rice in Lingnan, it is necessary first to estimate the demand for rice in the region and to identify rice-surplus and -deficit areas.

Demand for Food. Assuming a population of about 15 million in 1770[1] and food consumption patterns resembling those documented in the 1940s,[2] we can estimate the amount of food needed to meet the resulting demand (see Table 8.1) and the amount of land required to produce that quantity of food (see Table 8.2). What these calculations show is that, in 1770, about 60 million *shi* of grains of various kinds were required each year to meet the food needs of those 15 million people. Naturally, as the population doubled from about 9 million at the beginning of the eighteenth century to nearly 18 million by 1800, demand for food (and, as we will see in the next chapter, for productive land, too) increased proportionately.

Similar calculations show that those 60 million *shi* of food could have been grown on 16.5 million *mu* of land, assuming the yields listed in Table 8.1. Even if average yields were but half of those estimated, the food needs could have been grown on 33 million *mu* of land. What is significant about these

[1] See Chapter 9 for an explanation of the population estimates.

[2] Measures for grain differed in the Qing and Republican periods. By the 1940s, grain was measured in terms of weight (in *jin*), whereas in the Qing dynasty it was measured in terms of volume (in *shi*). To estimate eighteenth-century food needs, I have converted weights into volume measures. Estimates of annual per capita consumption of rice range from 270 *jin* in the 1930s to 343 *jin* in 1953, or between 1.74 and 2.62 *shi*. The average for the range is 2.17 *shi*, which will be used here on the assumption that the consumption rate in the PRC most likely was higher than during the eighteenth century, while the 1930s rate may well have been lower. The 2.17-*shi* figure also averages differences in wealth and consumption patterns across Guangdong and Guangxi provinces: it may well be, for instance, that Pearl River delta farmers ate more rice than backwoods Guangxi tribesmen. While washing out important regional differences, the average nonetheless allows rough estimates. See Chen Chunsheng, *Qingdai Qianlong nianjian Guangdong de mi jia he mi liang maoyi* (Zhongshan University, M.A. thesis, 1984): 11; Guangdong yinhang, *Guangzhou mi ye*, 2; Wang Yeh-chien, "Food Supply in Eighteenth-Century Fujian," *Late Imperial China* 7, no. 2 (1986): 88, n13. Based upon his analysis of the operation of the ever-normal granaries, Wong estimates that 0.2 *shi* of grain was sufficient to feed a family of four for one week; this equates to an annual per capita consumption of 2.6 *shi* of husked rice; see R. Bin Wong, "State Granaries and Food Supplies in China, 1650–1850: An Assessment," paper presented at 1987 Qing Social and Economic History Conference, Shenzhen. Modern measures of rice consumption are weight measures, while the Qing measure of rice is a volume measure, the "granary *shi*" (*cang shi*). To convert these weight measures to Qing volume measures, the following conversion rates have been used: one Qing granary *shi* = 130 Qing *jin* = 155.168 *jin* (twentieth-century weight) = 77.584 kilograms. Several conversations with Chen Chunsheng helped clear up the confusion regarding the conversion rates. Wang Yeh-chien has used a figure of two *shi* per capita in estimating rice consumption in the Yangzi River delta region in the eighteenth century; see "Food Supply and Grain Prices in the Yangtze Delta in the Eighteenth Century," in *The Second Conference on Modern Chinese Economic History* (Taibei: Academica Sinica Institute of Economics, 1989), 423–59.

Table 8.1. *Food needs for Guangdong province, ca. 1770*

	Per capita consumption of various foods, 1940s (*jin*)		Estimates for eighteenth-century food needs (*shi*)	
Food	Per capita	Percent	Per capita	Total Need
Rice	369.90	83	3.33	49,950,000
Sweet potato	33.15	7	0.30	4,500,000
Yam	3.75	1	0.03	450,000
Beans	9.50	2	0.08	1,200,000
Wheat	5.30	1	0.05	750,000
Other	23.60	5	0.21	3,150,000
Total	445.20	100	4.00	60,000,000

Source: Chen Chunsheng, *Shichang jizhi yu shehui bianqian – 18 shiji Guangdong mi jia fenxi* (Guangzhou: Zhongshan daxue chuban she, 1992), 23.

Table 8.2. *Supply of food in Guangdong province*

	Agricultural yield (*jin/mu*) of various crops, early twentieth century		Estimates for the eighteenth century		
Food	*jin/mu*	As % of rice	Yield *shi/mu*	Food need (*shi*)	Land required (*mu*)
Rice	284.20	100	4.00	49,852,000	12,463,000
Sweet potato	224.00	79	3.15	4,468,000	1,418,413
Yam	130.30	46	1.83	505,000	275,956
Beans	127.20	45	1.79	1,280,000	715,084
Wheat	218.20	77	3.07	714,000	232,573
Other	159.10	56	2.24	3,181,000	1,420,089
Total				60,000,000	16,525,115

Source: Chen Chunsheng, *Shichang jizhi yu shehui bianqian* – 18 *shiji Guangdong mi jia fenxi* (Guangzhou: Zhongshan daxue chuban she, 1992), 26.

calculations, of course, is that total cultivated land area in Guangdong in 1770 amounted to as much as 45 million *mu*,[3] an amount more than sufficient to produce all the food needed by the residents of Guangdong. Indeed, if all of the arable land in Guangdong province had been devoted to food production, the province should have produced a surplus. But not only

[3] See Chapter 9 for a discussion of the estimates of cultivated land.

was Guangdong province not a grain-surplus region; it had become a grain-importing region.

Food Deficit Areas and Grain Circulation. Not all of Guangdong was a grain-deficit area, and as discussed in Chapter 3, the province had not always been a grain importer, developing deficits first in the late sixteenth or early seventeenth century. By the eighteenth century, there were four prefectures in Guangdong with a net food deficit, and probably one deficit prefecture in Guangxi[4]: those were Guangzhou prefecture around Guangzhou and the Pearl River delta, Chaozhou and Jiaying prefectures in easternmost Guangdong, and Hainan Island (Qiongzhou prefecture);[5] in Guangxi, Guilin probably was a net deficit prefecture but only slightly; (see Map 8.1).[6] My best estimate is that Huizhou prefecture was more or less self-sufficient in grain, as were the more remote prefectures in Guangxi (at least in the first half of the eighteenth century). The areas with the greatest exportable grain surplus were along the West River: Zhaoqing prefecture and Luoding in Guangdong, and Wuzhou, Pingle, Xunzhou, and Liuzhou prefectures in Guangxi. The North River prefectures also exported grain to Guangzhou (see Map 8.2). This of course is only a very rough approximation, because within each prefecture no doubt there were counties that constituted grain-surplus and -deficit areas, and the same was true within counties.

Certainly, the largest demand for rice came from the urban area of Guangzhou and Foshan; a combined population of somewhere between 1 and 1.5 million people created a demand for 2.5–3.5 million *shi* of unhusked rice.[7] Perhaps another 250,000–500,000 people lived in and around Chaozhou. Because of the development of sericulture in the Pearl River delta, rice flowed from Foshan to rural markets elsewhere in Guangzhou prefecture, resulting in higher grain prices in rural Shunde than in urban Guangzhou.[8] For Guangdong as a whole, the grain deficit probably fell into a range of 7–13 percent of the total need (or between 3.5 and 7 million *shi* of unhusked rice).[9] Whichever figure is closer to the actual situation in eighteenth-century

4 Chen, *Shichang jizhi*, 1992, 18–29.

5 According to a memorial dated QL18.7.16, in QLCZZ 5: 800–802, Qiongzhou produced only one-half of its food needs; the rest was imported mostly from Gaozhou and Leizhou, with some from overseas.

6 According to a memorial dated QL20.7.9, in QLCZZ 12: 92, "After the repair of the river locks [on the Ling Qu canal] was completed, rice from Chu [i.e., Hunan] arrived [in Guilin] continuously."

7 For a discussion of the population estimates for Guangzhou and Foshan, see Chen, *Shichang jizhi*, 1992, 79–80.

8 See the table in ibid., 82.

9 For the calculations behind this estimate, see Marks, "Rice Prices, Food Supply, and Market Structure in Eighteenth-Century South China," 64–116.

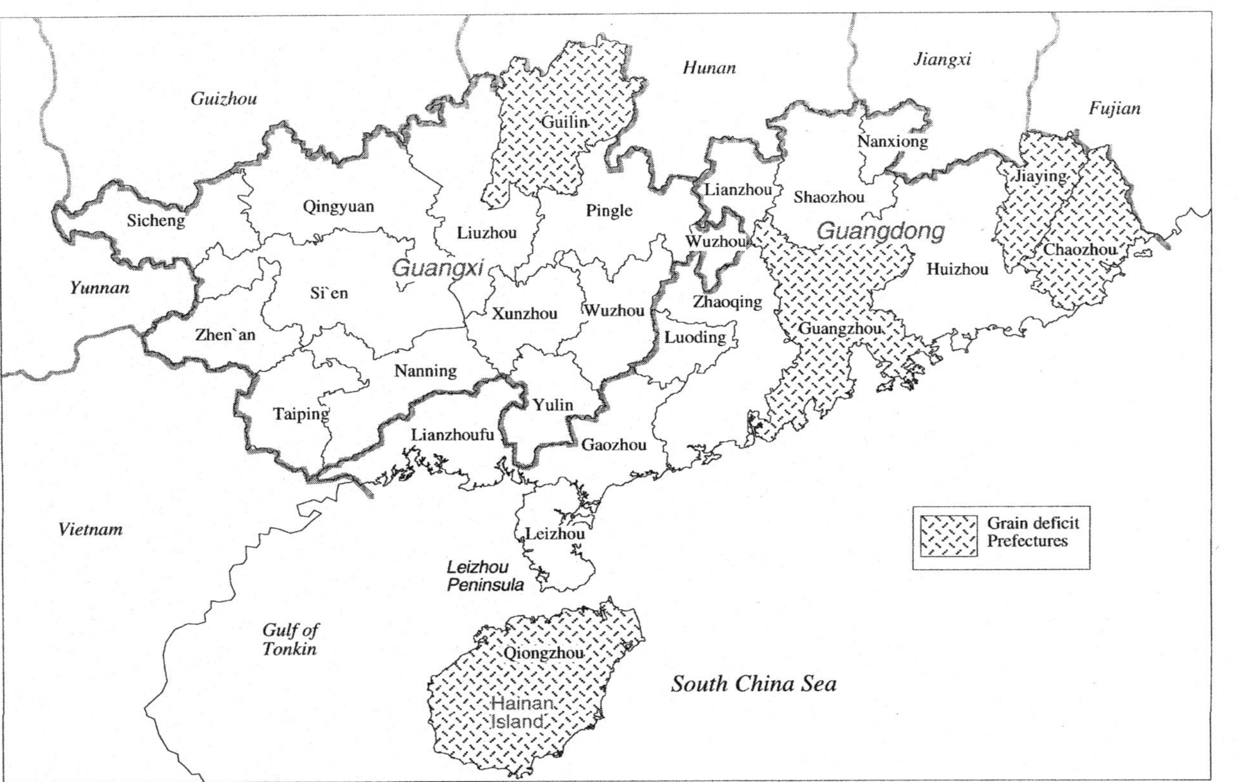

Map 8.1. Grain-deficit prefectures, ca. 1770

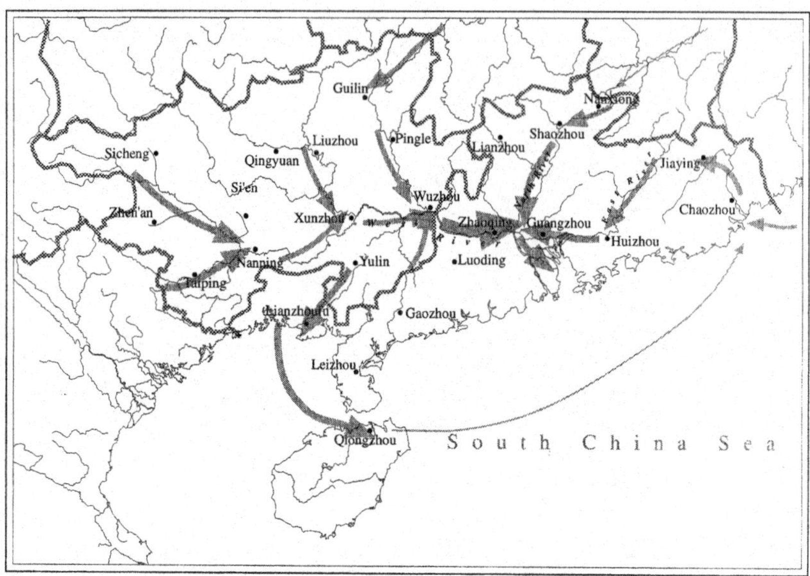

Map 8.2. Grain trade flows, ca. 1770

Guangdong, the grain deficit was considerably less than the 18–19 percent that Wang Yeh-chien has estimated for the Yangzi River delta during the same time period.[10]

Some of Guangzhou's demand for grain was met by other parts of the province. Within Guangdong, rice from Zhaoqing and Luoding moved to Guangzhou down the West River. From the north, Lianzhou exported just a little rice, while Shaozhou prefecture exported considerable quantities to Guangzhou. Some grain came over the Meiling Pass from Jiangxi and some over the Zheling Pass from Hunan, all of which then was gathered at Shaozhou to be shipped down the North River to Guangzhou. Not all grain was then consumed in Guangzhou; some was shipped to Huizhou, and some to the surrounding rural areas where commercial agriculture was most developed. To meet the needs of Chaozhou and Jiaying prefectures, some grain came from coastal Huizhou prefecture, but perhaps the greatest amount came from Taiwan or Siam. Finally, exports from Lianzhou and Gaozhou prefectures met the needs of Hainan Island. Some of this grain then was transshipped to Chaozhou.[11] However much rice flowed from other parts of Guangdong to meet the needs of Guangzhou and Chaozhou, it was insufficient to meet the

[10] Wang, "Food Supply and Grain Prices in the Yangtze Delta in the Eighteenth Century," 429.
[11] Viraphol, *Tribute and Profit*, 82.

needs of those urban areas, for a substantial amount of grain flowed from Guangxi into Guangdong.

From Pingle, Xunzhou, Liuzhou, and Wuzhou prefectures in Guangxi, grain flowed to the city of Wuzhou on the West River, where during the rainy season (April–October) rice was loaded onto boats carrying 5,000–10,000 *shi* of rice for the 10-day trip downstream to Guangzhou. Each day, as much as 200,000–300,000 *jin* (1,500–2,300 *shi*) were handled at one market in Wuzhou.[12] Guilin satisfied its food needs by imports from Hunan, while some of that grain was then transshipped to Wuzhou. How much grain was exported to Guangdong annually? A few scattered references from various officials give us some perspective on the question.[13] In 1715, Guangxi Governor Chen Yuanlong estimated that 618,000 *shi* of husked and unhusked rice were exported between the 6th and 12th months. Fifteen years later, the governor-general of Yunnan, E-er-tai, claimed that "even when the harvest in Guangdong is 'abundant' (*feng*), still 1 to 2 million *shi* are imported from Guangxi." These figures probably are low, for two reasons. First, these amounts were only those upon which officials collected duty; unknown amounts escaped the notice (and taxes) of officials. Second, the officials' estimates lumped husked and unhusked rice together; converting husked to unhusked at the usual rate of 2 to 1 would increase the total too. Taking all of these into consideration, I estimate that something on the order of 3 million *shi* (about 250,000 tons) of unhusked rice were exported annually from Guangxi to Guangdong, enough to have fed 1.5 million people.

As we saw in the preceding chapter, the long-distance movement of grain was organized by both Qing government officials and private merchants, with the role of officials greater in the first half of the Qianlong emperor's reign than in the second half. When prices rose steadily and precipitously in 1741–42 following two years of drought, for example, the market mechanism was inadequate to meet the food needs of Guangzhou, and officials therefore took the initiative. In the summer of 1741, the governor of Guangdong, Wang Anguo, arranged for the importation of 23,000 *shi* of rice from Siam;[14] and in 1742, when even Guangxi suffered shortages because of drought conditions, 40,000 *shi* of tribute grain was diverted from Hubei through Guilin into Guangxi.[15]

To be sure, those were times of crisis. But even in more normal times during the early Qianlong period, official intervention had been deemed necessary to

[12] Guo Songyi, "Qingdai de liangjia maoyi," *Pingjun xuekan*, no. 1 (1985): 298; Ye Xian'en et al., *Guangdong hang yun shi gudai bufen*, 168.

[13] The following quotes are from Chen, *Shichang jizhi*, 45.

[14] Document dated QL7.8.29 printed in *Lishi dang'an* 3 (1985): 1, 7–18. For a discussion of this and other documents regarding the Siam rice trade, see Li Pengnian, "Luelun Qianlong nianjian cong Xianluo yun mi jinkou," *Lishi dang'an* 3 (1985): 83–90.

[15] Memorial dated QL9.2.8, in NYL Box 26.

ensure food supplies to Guangzhou. In the spring of 1747, even after the rains raised the water level in the West River to a point high enough to accommodate the grain boats, Governor-General Celeng reported to the emperor that food prices were rising: "But even after the spring rains, very few merchant grain boats have come. Local periodic markets are having difficulty operating. Now I have sent officials to Wuzhou and Xunzhou to investigate and to urge the grain boats to come and do business."[16] This apparently succeeded, for a month later Celeng memorialized, "Many Guangxi grain boats have arrived and are selling grain everywhere, ensuring a continuous supply."[17]

By "selling grain everywhere," Celeng did not mean that the Guangxi grain boats conducted a lively retail trade from their decks, but rather that they sold their cargoes to one of the several grain brokers (*mi hang*) licensed to serve the Guangzhou metropolitan region. How many of these brokers there were is unknown, but the way the system worked tended to ensure that market forces set prices. As Yang Yingju, a former governor-general, explained: "The merchants were authorized freely to go to the broker of their choice and to deal with him; if the broker in question were even slightly unfair, he would have to fear that the merchant would drop him and go to another one." In the early 1750s, though, the provincial authorities placed the brokers under the control of a "central wharf office" (*zong bu*). After Yang Yingju was appointed acting governor-general in 1754, he found that "the result was that grain prices were soaring" and took action to disband the central wharf office. Governor-General Yang furthermore ordered officials to restock granaries from the market, rather than by requisitioning rice from the Guangxi grain boats.[18] The result of Yang's actions was to lessen official meddling in the grain markets substantially.

Officials thereafter made few references in memorials to their intervention in the market and more to merchants and the market. During the spring of 1759, the governors of both Guangdong and Guangxi commented that "trade in rice is brisk;"[19] the Governor-General of Liangguang also noted that "there are many grain boats coming from Guangxi";[20] another Guangxi official added that "the price of grain is not rising because commoners are selling rice and supplies are plentiful."[21] Even into October as much as 5,000–10,000 *shi* arrived daily from Guangxi.[22] After prices started to rise a bit in November, the gov-

[16] Memorial dated QL12.2.28, in NYL Box 41.

[17] Memorial dated QL12.3.24, in NYL Box 41.

[18] Yang Yingju, memorial dated QL28.6.11, Taibei Palace Museum Gongzhongdang (Palace memorial archives) no. QL 015160. I am grateful to Pierre-Etienne Will for bringing this memorial to my attention and for sharing with me his draft translation.

[19] Memorial dated QL24.3.28, in NYL Box 81.

[20] Ibid.

[21] Ibid.

[22] Memorial dated QL24.9.8, in NYL Box 81.

ernor of Guangdong reported that the Guangxi rice boats returned and remained through December.[23] Even in January, "merchants are conducting business and the market is full of rice."[24] It is clear from these reports that, by the late 1750s, commerce between Guangxi and Guangdong was brisk and that most of the grain movements were organized by merchants.

In reading the memorials of various officials over the 22-year period 1744–65,[25] I got the distinct impression of governors early on struggling with the gargantuan problem of feeding the urban population of Guangzhou, sending officials to Guangxi to find rice supplies, and negotiating (only very occasionally, though) with Siamese merchants, besides managing the state granaries. Twenty years later (by 1765), grain circulation seems much more routine. The picture of a much more efficient market mechanism emerges, with numerous – almost constant – reports of Guangxi grain boats bringing rice to Guangdong and fewer reports about the use of granaries either for relief or to stabilize prices.

One simple measure of the increasing efficiency of the rice market over the course of the eighteenth century is the extent to which monthly rice prices varied. Where markets operated poorly, even moderate fluctuation in harvest yields could send prices up or down; where markets moved rice from areas of surplus to areas of shortages, even when local harvest yields varied wildly because of climatic changes, rice prices overall were more stable. In Table 8.3, we can see that although the price of rice tended to increase throughout the eighteenth century (the column labeled "Mean"), the amount that prices departed from that mean declined steadily (as measured by the standard deviation and the coefficient of variation). Rice prices, in short, became increasingly stable during the eighteenth century.[26] The less volatile rice prices, I think, are attributable to the combination of substantial storage of rice from one year to the next (as discussed in Chapter 7) and the creation of an integrated market for rice, linking virtually all of Lingnan into a single market.

Compared with those for Europe and the United States, these low coefficients of variation for Lingnan imply a fairly integrated market structure with a large amount of storage and intraregional trade. McCloskey and Nash found coefficients of variation ranging from 0.20 to 0.43 in medieval England to 0.26 in Philadelphia (1800–25) and from 0.16 to 0.34 in New York for the period from 1825 to 1914. They conclude that "the typical fall from medieval to modern times, then, was about 0.30 to about 0.24: a variety of climates newly

[23] Memorials dated QL24.10.20, in NYL Box 80; and QL24.11.20, in NYL Box 89.

[24] Memorial dated QL24.12.17, in NYL Box 80.

[25] The memorials published in QLCZZ, which begin only in QL16, have been supplemented by 20 memorials, gleaned from the Number One Historical Archives in Beijing.

[26] I offer a full explanation for rice price behavior in Lingnan in two separate articles: " 'It Never Used To Snow,' " and, with Chen Chunsheng, in "Price Inflation and Its Social, Economic, and Climatic Context in Guangdong, 1707–1800," *T'oung pao* 81, no. 1 (1995): 109–52.

Table 8.3. *Variation of monthly rice prices*

Period	Mean	St. dev	Coef. var
1707–20	0.81	0.23	28.0
1721–40	0.81	0.21	26.0
1741–60	1.42	0.21	14.9
1761–80	1.53	0.16	10.5
1781–1800	1.49	0.11	7.1

Source: Rice price database compiled from memorials (Gongzhong Zhupi zonzhe; nongyelei; liangjia qingdan) in the Number One Historical Archives Beijing; for description, see Marks, "Rice Prices, Food Supply, and Market Structure in Eighteenth-Century South China."

accessible by cheap transport (the Baltic, for example, in the early modern period) was a substitute for a large carryover and had the same effect." By this measure, markets in eighteenth-century Lingnan were more "modern" and efficient than those of Europe and America at a later date.[27]

Market Structure and Integration. The evidence examined thus far – rice price behavior, the import and sale of grain, merchant activity and granary operation, and the actions of merchants and authorities in times of food shortage and scarcity – all indicate both a considerable amount of market activity in Lingnan and the existence of a regional market for grain. In their 1975 analysis of rice prices and markets along the Yangzi River, Ch'uan and Kraus posited four criteria that "should be met if the hypothesis of a large-scale, well-organized trade in grain . . . were true":

1. Prices along a trade route should rise to a peak at the major city;
2. Prices in surplus areas should be lower than those (a) in surrounding higher ground areas and (b) in places further downstream;
3. Prices within short water distance of each other should be virtually identical;
4. Prices should be more stable in producing areas than where grain is in short supply.[28]

Map 8.3 shows the mean price of common rice during the Qianlong period in each of the prefectures. As this map demonstrates, criteria one through three

[27] Donald N. McCloskey and John Nash, "Corn at Interest: The Extent and Cost of Grain Storage in Medieval England," *American Economic Review* 74, no. 1 (Mar. 1984): 177.

[28] Han-shen Ch'uan and Richard A. Kraus, *Mid-Ch'ing Rice Markets and Trade: An Essay in Price History* (Cambridge, MA: Harvard University Press, 1975), 42–43.

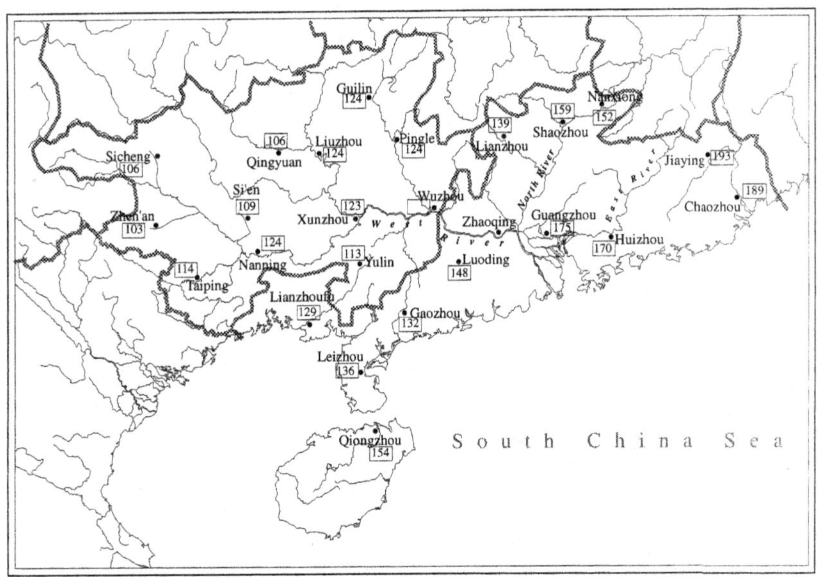

Map 8.3. Mean price of rice, 1736–95

are met for Guangdong and Guangxi provinces, with three exceptions. In eastern Guangdong province, the average price in Jiaying prefecture (193 taels per 100 *shi*) is higher than that downstream in Chaozhou (189). This in fact accords with the documentary evidence which shows that imported grain did in fact flow upstream from Chaozhou to Jiaying. A second case shows Nanning to have a price higher (124) than that downstream at Xunzhou (123). This actually was the case only during the first 20 years of the Qianlong era (1736–55); from 1756 on the price downstream at Xunzhou was higher than that at Nanning. What this does indicate is that Nanning probably was not integrated into the Lingnan market until the mid-1750s. Finally, the map shows the prices at Guilin and Pingle to have been the same (124); this is merely a result of arithmetic rounding, for the price at Guilin was slightly less than that downriver in Pingle.

Correlations of prices and price differences help refine our picture of the Lingnan market.[29] The results are shown in Map 8.4, with each line representing a strong correlation in one of the tests. A "strong correlation" is defined here as being in the highest decile of the correlation coefficients for all pre-

[29] For a full description, analysis, and assessment of the rice price data for Lingnan, see Marks, "Rice Prices, Food Supply, and Market Structure in Eighteenth-Century South China."

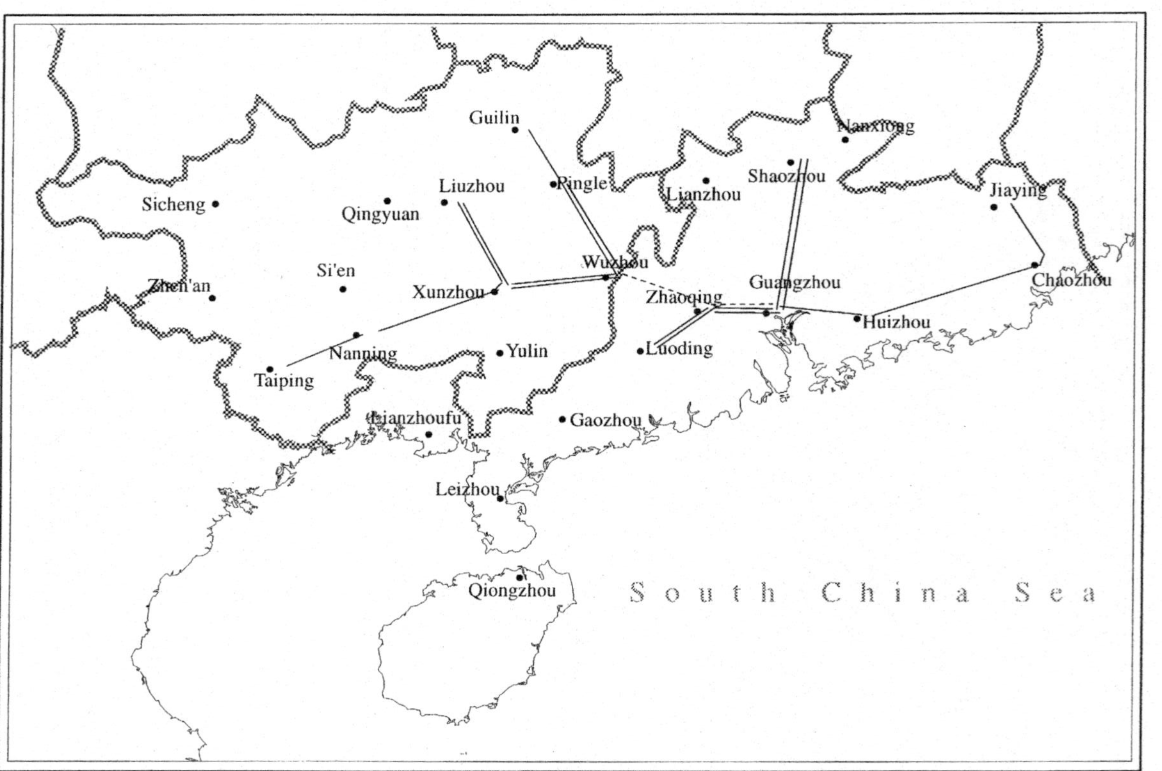

Map 8.4. Structure of the Lingnan rice market

Table 8.4. *Regression of prefectural mean price on Guangzhou mean*

Prefecture	Distance from Guangzhou (km)	Constant	Slope	Std. err.	R^2
Sicheng	1,185	108	−0.013	0.017	−0.001
Qiongzhou	595	94	0.342	0.021	0.319
Qingyuan	540	77	0.167	0.018	0.131
Guilin	510	73	0.285	0.022	0.241
Pingle	405	72	0.300	0.019	0.307
Taiping	720	70	0.254	0.023	0.178
Si'en	720	69	0.227	0.018	0.220
Zhen'an	810	64	0.217	0.022	0.150
Nanning	555	63	0.347	0.024	0.275
Liuzhou	420	62	0.355	0.024	0.293
Leizhou	560	61	0.428	0.019	0.484
Yulin	1,005	56	0.328	0.016	0.426
Jiaying	700	51	0.807	0.027	0.618
Nanxiong	368	50	0.584	0.019	0.613
Xunzhou	420	50	0.420	0.019	0.470
Wuzhou	240	48	0.453	0.020	0.473
Lianzhou	368	46	0.531	0.023	0.485
Chaozhou	560	45	0.821	0.028	0.599
Huizhou	123	40	0.740	0.019	0.738
Lianzhoufu	840	36	0.486	0.020	0.543
Gaozhou	525	28	0.594	0.026	0.484
Shaozhou	280	24	0.773	0.014	0.837
Zhaoqing	88	14	0.897	0.024	0.719
Luoding	210	14	0.761	0.021	0.700

fectures in Guangdong and Guangxi provinces.[30] The dotted line represents a "weak" correlation between Guangzhou and Wuzhou.

The results of a simple regression (Table 8.4) illustrate the extent of market integration: the closer the slope of the regression line approaches 1.0, the stronger the correlation and hence the integration of the market. Loren Brandt has suggested that regressions yield additional data that can be used to analyze the extent of market integration, observing that the intercept of the slope (the "constant" in the table) reflects transaction costs involved in shipping the rice; costs increase with distance, and hence so should the constant in the regression equation.[31] As Table 8.4 shows, the constant does vary with distance from Guangzhou, with three exceptions: Qiongzhou, Yulin, and Leizhou. These are

[30] Rank order (top 10%) rather than absolute value (0.90 or greater) is used as a limiting factor; using 0.90 or greater would include so many places as to make a map quite unintelligible.

[31] For a discussion, see Loren Brandt, *Commercialization and Agricultural Development: Central and Eastern China, 1870–1937* (Cambridge University Press, 1989), ch. 2.

all within close ocean distance from Guangzhou; the higher transaction costs probably are due to increased risk of ocean transport due to weather and pirates.

These statistical analyses confirm the documentary evidence that there was one major rice market in Lingnan centered on Guangzhou, supported by a secondary market feeding into Wuzhou. There are two ambiguities in this formulation worth pondering – the question of the extent to which Chaozhou and Jiaying prefectures in eastern Guangdong and the westernmost prefectures in Guangxi were integrated into this regional market. Let me take the latter case first. In 1738, the governor of Guangxi observed that rice produced in Guilin and other prefectures was exported not just downriver to Guangzhou, but also up the West River into Guizhou province. To relieve the upward pressure on prices in Guilin, the governor proposed splitting the export market, with rice only from western prefectures going to Guizhou, and rice only from the five eastern prefectures exported to Guangzhou.[32] Until the 1760s, when the statistical evidence shows that Nanning was integrated into the Lingnan market (discussed earlier), there is reason to conclude that the exportable rice from western Guangxi thus went not to Guangdong but to Guizhou.

There is also reason to think that easternmost Guangdong was not integrated into the Lingnan market either. As noted earlier, prices in Chaozhou and Jiaying prefectures were higher than those in Guangzhou, the demonstrated center of the Lingnan rice market. Using various statistical methods, I could find no strong correlation between prices in Guangzhou and Chaozhou; strong correlations exist between Huizhou and Jiaying (hence the line on Map 8.4 through Chaozhou connecting Jiaying to Huizhou), but not on through to Guangzhou.

Other documentary evidence also suggests a weak market link between Chaozhou and Guangzhou. In 1748 and 1749, for instance, Guangdong had normal to above normal rainfall, while there was drought in Fujian. Rice prices fell throughout Guangdong, but shot up in Chaozhou. On the other side of the weather coin, when eastern Guangdong, Chaozhou included, experienced dry conditions in 1768 and prices generally rose, they fell in Chaozhou. Other evidence indicates that rice imports into eastern Guangdong came mostly from southern Fujian, Taiwan, and Southeast Asia, although some may have been transshipped from Qiongzhou (Hainan Island).[33] It therefore appears likely that rice price movement in Chaozhou was more closely correlated not with Guangzhou, but with other regions – probably southern Fujian province and Taiwan. Chaozhou and Jiaying prefectures hence were not well integrated into the Liangguang market.

[32] Memorial excerpted in *Da Qing gao zong (Qianlong) shi lu*, juan 83: 43a–b.

[33] Viraphol, *Tribute and Profit*, 82.

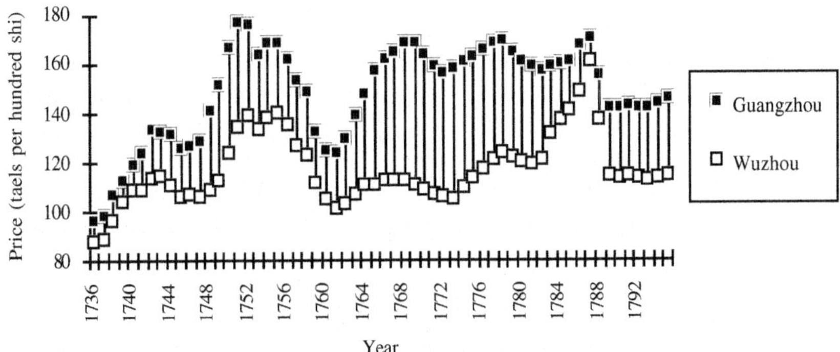

Figure 8.1. Price spread between Guangzhou and Wuzhou, 1736–96. Source: Rice price database compiled from memorials (Gongzhong zhupi zouzhe; nongye lei; liangjia qingdan) in the Number One Historical Archives, Beijing.

In summary, it seems reasonably clear that during the eighteenth century, a well-integrated market for large amounts of common rice had developed in Lingnan, linking peasant-producers in the West River basin of Guangxi to consumers in the Pearl River delta. By the 1760s, even grain prices in westernmost Guangxi jumped to the demand of Guangzhou. A closer look at the relationship between Guangzhou and Wuzhou, though, qualifies that picture somewhat. Despite the documentary evidence of massive grain flows from Wuzhou to Guangzhou, prices between the two cities are not highly correlated. Figure 8.1 compares the mean prices of common rice in the two cities, emphasizing the price differences over the period. As this chart shows, the price spread increased substantially after 1758–62 and stayed that way for another 20 years. Only in the late 1780s with drought and famine conditions did the price gap narrow.

In the absence of any evidence that transaction costs (shipping costs, taxes, tolls, etc.) had increased, a possible explanation of the widening gap is monopsony profits. The West River cuts a pass through a low mountain chain separating the rice-growing districts of Guangxi from Guangdong. Astride the West River and virtually on the Guangxi–Guangdong border, Wuzhou had just one higher level market to which it was oriented: Guangzhou. Once commodities (such as rice) had flowed down the Gui, Xun, and Yu Rivers, which drained Guangxi, to the warehouses at Wuzhou, no alternative to marketing at Guangzhou existed. Geography constrained the choices of sellers in Wuzhou to merchants from Guangzhou and Foshan who had established purchasing offices (*hui guan*) in Wuzhou. Monopsony would explain why rice prices in Wuzhou remained low after 1762, while prices in Guangzhou climbed back up to previous levels, resulting in substantially larger profits for Guangzhou rice merchants and relatively depressed farm prices in Guangxi.

Evidence on riverine transport costs tends to confirm this conclusion. In 1758, the new governor of Guangxi sent a memorial to the palace discussing a request to transfer granary stocks from eastern Guangxi to Yunnan and in it listed transportation costs.[34] Fixed costs included bagging the rice (two bags per *shi* at 0.15 taels per bag) and loading and unloading fees of 0.01 taels per bag at each end. Water transport (going upstream) was 0.03 taels per 100 *li*. The fixed cost of transporting the rice therefore was 0.34 taels per *shi*. Assuming these costs to have been uniform throughout Lingnan, a rough measure of merchant profit can be derived.[35] As Table 8.5 demonstrates, estimated profits at Guangzhou were uniformly higher for Guangxi rice than for rice purchased from within Guangdong.

The Wuzhou–Guangzhou connection therefore appears to be an important exception to a Skinnerian view of the Lingnan macroregion. Because of the dendritic rather than nested hierarchical shape of the marketing system (as discussed in Chapter 5), this is a case where the producers and merchants in a lower-level central place did not have a choice of a higher-level central place in which to market their goods. Instead, geographic and political conditions appear to have made it possible for Foshan or Guangzhou rice merchants to exercise noneconomic power over a lower-level market. Of course, this observation does not contradict Skinner's model, but merely adjusts it to the geographic realities of the Lingnan macroregion. But there can be little doubt that rice flowed from the furthest reaches of Guangxi into markets in Guangdong, linking the cash cropping peasant-farmers of the Pearl River delta with the rice farmers in the West River basin.

Markets and the Environment. That merchants could extract higher profits by locking up the rice trade in Wuzhou than by trading within Guangdong therefore had immense consequences not merely for the economy of Lingnan, but also for land use patterns and the environment. For without the higher profit margins that monopsony virtually guaranteed at Wuzhou, Guangdong merchants may well have sought to meet Guangzhou market demands from other sources. But as it was, those higher profits sent merchants to Wuzhou, stimulating demand for exportable rice throughout the West River basin in Guangxi and precipitating changes in cropping patterns to meet that demand. So just as the Pearl River delta became commercialized in sericul-

[34] Memorial dated QL33.9.16, in QLCZZ 33: 800–801.

[35] Estimated profit = price in Guangzhou − (mean price in place *x* + transportation cost). The transportation costs going downstream to Guangzhou probably were less than these, both because costs transporting rice downstream would be less than those going against the current and because the boats going upstream from Nanning to Yunnan were smaller than those going downstream to Guangzhou.

Table 8.5. *Estimated merchant profits at Guangzhou (per 100 shi of rice)*

Prefecture	Distance from Guangzhou (km)	Mean price	Transport costs	Adjusted price	Estimated profit
Guangzhou		175			
Nanxiong	368	152	11.3	163.3	11.7
Shaozhou	280	159	8.7	167.7	7.3
Huizhou	123	170	4.0	174.0	1.0
Chaozhou	560	189	17.1	206.1	−31.1
Zhaoqing	88	172	2.9	174.9	0.1
Gaozhou	525	132	16.1	148.1	26.9
Leizhou	560	136	17.1	153.1	21.9
Lianzhoufu	840	129	25.5	154.5	20.5
Qiongzhou	595	154	18.2	172.2	2.8
Luoding	210	148	6.6	154.6	20.4
Lianzhou	368	139	11.3	150.3	24.7
Jiaying	700	193	21.3	214.3	−39.3
Guilin	510	124	15.6	139.6	35.4
Pingle	405	124	12.5	136.5	38.5
Wuzhou	240	127	7.5	134.5	40.5
Xunzhou	420	123	12.9	135.9	39.1
Nanning	555	124	17.0	141.0	34.0
Taiping	720	114	21.9	135.9	39.1
Liuzhou	420	124	12.9	136.9	38.1
Qingyuan	540	106	16.5	122.5	52.5
Si'en	720	109	21.9	130.9	44.1
Sicheng	1,185	106	35.9	141.9	33.1
Zhen'an	810	103	24.6	127.6	47.4
Yulin	1,005	113	30.5	143.5	31.5

Source: Same as Figure 8.1.

ture and sugarcane, so too did rice in the West River basin become a commercial crop. The geography of Lingnan thus permitted rice merchants from Guangzhou to dominate the markets in Wuzhou, thereby both stimulating the development of the export rice economy in the West River basin and holding down prices paid to producers.

The development of an integrated market in Lingnan also can be interpreted ecologically. From the estuaries of the Pearl River delta to the wooded hills in the north, communities of organisms were linked in food chains: producers used solar energy to transform inorganic (usually mineral) material from the environment into organic material; consumers fed directly upon the organic material or upon other species; and decomposers like insects, fungi, and bacteria returned the organic material to the inorganic realm, where it was available to be transformed once again into organic material. Energy was transferred from one level to the next, with the producers, consumers, and decomposers forming a single trophic, or food, chain. Most of the energy flows thus occurred within the boundaries of an ecosystem. But energy does flow across ecosystem boundaries, and these cross-system flows constitute a measurement of the stability of an ecosystem: if more energy flows out of a system than into it, the system deteriorates and changes. In a sustainable ecosystem, the energy losses are replaced, for the most part by solar inputs and to a lesser extent by transfers from other systems (e.g., through erosion and siltation).

From this point of view, transfers of food to feed the human population of Lingnan, whether through the market or at the hands of state officials, facilitated energy flows both within and between ecosystems. In fact, where the connections between ecosystems – such as between the river valleys in Guangxi province and the Pearl River delta – may have been negligible in prior times, by the eighteenth century markets began linking those weakly connected ecosystems into a larger, more integrated system. Indeed, where Lingnan earlier may have been a set of nested and interlocked ecosystems, the development of an integrated market for rice may be interpreted as having created a new, larger, but less diverse, ecosystem, breaking down the boundaries between ecosystems. With the Pearl River delta devoted to the mulberry embankment and fish pond combination, many of the counties bordering the delta devoted to sugarcane, and most of the West River basin in Guangxi devoted to rice produced for the export market – each linked through the market into a larger, commercialized whole – the diversity of ecosystems comprising Lingnan declined as a direct result of the creation of an integrated market for food.

Rice Prices, Harvest Yields, and Climate: The Economic and Demographic Implications

Rice flowed from food-surplus regions in Guangxi and elsewhere to the rice-deficit area centered on Guangzhou and the Pearl River delta, not because state officials commandeered grain supplies or even arranged for grain shipments, but because of price signals sent through the market mechanism. Prices in general are a summary statement of a complex set of supply and demand relationships, and rice prices in particular capture and express the relationship between the supply and demand for food at any given moment. Hence, it follows that a long-term price series can provide significant insights into the changing balances between the supply and demand for food,[36] and thus also about the broader ecosystems in which people and their food supply systems were embedded.

[36] Prices also reflect changes in the supply and demand for money, and given China's bimetallic currency system, the exchange ratio of copper cash to the silver tael must be considered. For

Demand for rice was of course conditioned by population size and consumer preferences, and while consumers could switch to sweet potatoes when the price of rice rose too high (and vice versa),[37] in the short run demand for rice was more or less inelastic.[38] With demand constant, variation in supply caused primarily by fluctuation of harvest yields was the primary factor accounting for changes in annual grain prices. When harvests failed and the food supply contracted, grain prices rose; conversely, bumper harvests depressed prices.

The story of the relationship between annual crop yields and rice prices in eighteenth-century Guangdong province is summarized in Figure 8.2.[39] When the officials' harvest ratings are correlated with the price series,[40] the results, as expected, indicate an inverse relationship (see Table 8.6): better

most of the eighteenth century, the exchange rate was more or less stable, deteriorating substantially in the nineteenth century. See Lin Man-houng, *Currency and Society: The Monetary Crisis and Political-Economic Ideology of Early Nineteenth Century China* (Harvard University Ph.D. dissertation, 1989).

37 Following the 1756 harvest, the governor of Guangdong reported: "Throughout the province the price of sweet potatoes and taro is low. For a few coppers (*wen*), the people (*xiao min*) can eat 'til they are full. This hasn't been the case for years." Memorial dated QL 21.8.24 in QLCZZ 15: 237. The reason for the decline in sweet potato prices most likely had less to do with the sweet potato than with rice harvest: as the price of rice came down, those who had been consuming sweet potatoes feasted on rice. Memorial dated QL21.8.24, in QLCZZ 15: 237–38.

38 As Slicher van Bath wrote of grain prices in premodern Europe: "The need for agricultural produce, and especially of bread grain, is practically constant. Since the human stomach has a limited capacity, the consumer does not eat more bread because the price has fallen. The money saved on bread is spent in other ways; the poorer people may spend it on more expensive food . . . or on all sorts of industrial goods . . . When corn [i.e., wheat] is scarce, everyone is afraid of not getting enough; hence the familiar readiness to pay high prices in times of scarcity." B. H. Slicher van Bath, *The Agrarian History of Western Europe, A.D. 500–1800*, Olive Ordish, trans. (London, E. Arnold, 1963): 118–19.

39 The data graphed in Figure 8.2 are averages: the rice price is the average high price of common rice as reported in the 10 prefectures and 3 independent *zhou* that comprise Guangdong province; the harvest rating is the average of the early and late harvest ratings. Since most of the rice in Guangdong was produced by two crops annually, it is prudent to distinguish between the yield of a single harvest and total annual crop yield produced by two harvests. The bars in Figure 8.2 depict the latter. I want to thank Mark Elvin for helping me sharpen this distinction.

40 The correlation of the harvest rating series with the price series presents two methodological problems. First, it is necessary to remove the trend from the price series. Although it might be assumed that the rice price trend in the eighteenth century was to increase more or less in a linear fashion ($y = 1.026x + 76.493$; $R^2 = 0.613$) because of the growing population, the trend actually is best expressed as a wave ($y = 82.571 - 1.116x + 0.079x^2 - 0.001x^3$; $R^2 = 0.775$). (The shape of the wave was determined using standard statistical routines running on the Statview software package.) Several factors account for this shape of the trend line, including population growth, changing monetary exchange rates, and political decisions regarding stocks in the state-managed granary system, but the most important was the development of an integrated

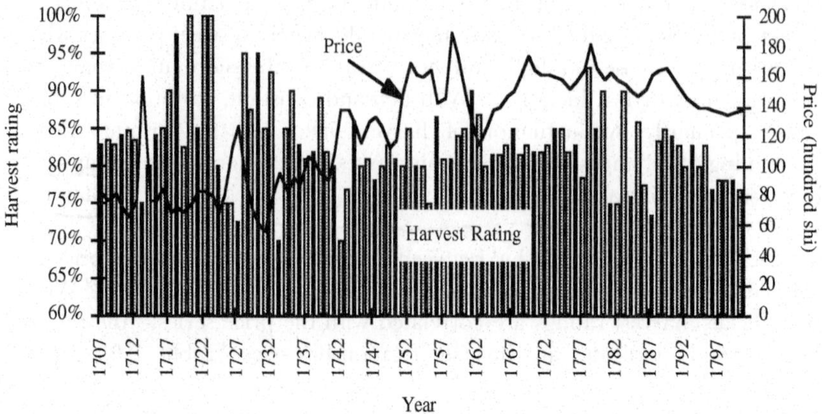

Figure 8.2. Harvest ratings and rice prices, 1707–1800. Sources: Rice price database (see Table 8.3); for the harvest rating, see the sections entitled "Harrest Yields" and "Guangdong Province Harvest Ratings, 1707–1800" in Chapter 6.

harvests tended to depress rice prices, and poorer harvests tended to increase rice prices.

Although this statistical test does demonstrate the expected inverse relationship between harvest yields and rice prices, it also shows that the relationship became weaker during the course of the eighteenth century. This gradual delinking of grain prices from harvest yields is a very important historical development and has to do with the growing power and importance of an integrated market for rice. Until the mid-1750s, officials supervised the grain trade through the regulation of rice brokerage firms (*mi yahang*), creating conditions for profiteering, corruption, and restriction of the rice market; but sometime around 1755, as we saw in the preceding chapter, the governor-general abolished the brokerage system, thereby opening the grain market more widely, lowering prices, and increasing the importation of rice from Guangxi. From that time on, deficient harvests in Guangdong sparked price

market for rice, linking the vast, rice-producing hinterland of Guangxi province to the growing demands of Guangdong province. Detrending the price series eliminates these influences on the movement of prices from one year to the next, making it possible to isolate the impact of annual variation in harvest size upon prices.

Second, if harvest yields influenced rice prices, then harvest yields and rice prices from the same year cannot be used, since the impact of a deficient harvest would be felt in the following year's prices. Thus, to obtain a more accurate reading of the impact of harvest yields on prices, the proper method is to correlate harvest yields with the following year's price. The resulting correlation, then, is between the harvest ratings and the lagged, detrended price series.

Table 8.6. *Correlation of harvest rating with rice price*

Period	*r*
1707–1800	−0.353
1707–1731	−0.413
1731–1758	−0.275
1762–1778	−0.203
1778–1800	−0.157
1762–1800	0.223

Sources: Memorials enclosing rice price and harvest ratings lists in the Number One Historical Archives, Beijing.

increases in Guangxi, with large imports of rice weakening the connection between the harvest ratings and prices in Guangdong. Nonetheless, though weakening, the relationship between harvest size and rice prices remained inverse.

Not surprisingly, this inverse relationship was so obvious that everyone knew it, and officials commented on it nearly continuously in their palace memorials. In 1756, for example, the Liangguang governor-general reported that the early harvest was rated "better than 90 percent." He noted that harvests the two preceding years had been rated much lower, with some counties having harvests rated only 60 percent, and then observed: "This truly is a bountiful year. The granary bins are overflowing, and grain prices moderate daily."[41] The Guangdong governor confirmed: "Throughout the province rice prices are moderating, and there is not a village or a neighborhood with shortages. Truly this is the most abundant harvest year in several."[42]

Given Qing officials' knowledge of how the agrarian economy worked and the fact that officials had their hands on vast mounds of rice price data, harvest ratings estimates, granary stock reports, and even population figures, what is surprising is that no official at the time, at least as far as I am aware, tried to establish a mathematical relationship between the size of the rice harvest and the price of rice.[43] After all, officials were collecting and reporting both harvest

41 Memorial dated QL21.6.17, in QLCZZ 14: 647.

42 Memorial dated QL21.6.17, in QLCZZ 14: 650.

43 The best candidates would have been Li Xu, one of the Kangxi emperor's most trusted officials, and the Kangxi emperor himself. As mentioned earlier, since at least 1693, the emperor had Li Xu report on climate, harvests, and rice prices. Later, in 1715, the emperor appointed Li Xu to oversee an experiment to introduce a second rice crop into the Suzhou area. When Li Xu reported that the results of the second harvest were less than stellar, the emperor reminded him that he had planted both the first and second crops too late. In subsequent years

Table 8.7. *King's law*

	Prices predicted by	
Harvest yield (%)	King	Bouniatian
100	≈1.00	≈1.00
90	1.30	1.28
80	1.80	1.69
70	2.60	2.33
60	3.80	3.43
50	5.50	5.53

ratings and rice prices on a regular basis: Would not some ability to predict price behavior have enhanced their bureaucratic effectiveness?

This question is not an idle one, for Europeans tried to demonstrate not just a relationship between harvest size and grain prices, but also that the relationship could be expressed in mathematical terms. Gregory King (1650–1710), a keen observer of economic activity and population changes in England, sought to establish a regular relationship between an inadequate harvest and cereal prices. "Gregory King's law" posited a geometrical increase in prices for each tenth that the harvest was below normal. Later economists (Jevons and Bouniatian)[44] refined the relationship between harvest yield and grain prices that King had observed, and expressed it mathematically as an equation of the kind $y = a/(x - b)^2$, where y is the index of the price, x is the harvest as a proportion of normal, and a and b are constants.[45]

The results of calculations from these formulas can be seen in Table 8.7. The table shows, for example, that a harvest 90 percent of normal would result in prices about 130 percent of normal, while a harvest just 50 percent of normal would be accompanied by prices nearly five times normal. What these equations model are situations where grain prices changed at rates different

the experiment yielded better results, and Li Xu reported specific harvest yields, both in terms of seed-to-harvest and per *mu* ratios. See Jonathan D. Spence, *Ts'ao Yin and the K'ang-hsi Emperor: Bondservant and Master* (New Haven: Yale University Press, 1966), 278–81.

44 For a discussion of "King's Law," see Slicher van Bath, *The Agrarian History of Western Europe*, 119; Wilhelm Abel, *Agricultural Fluctuations in Europe from the Thirteenth to the Twentieth Centuries* (New York: St. Martin's, 1980), 1–13; and E. A. Wrigley, "Some Reflections on Corn Yields and Prices in Pre-Industrial Economies," in E. A. Wrigley, *People, Cities, and Wealth* (New York: Basil Blackwell, 1987), pp. 92–130.

45 The equations are: Jevons [$y = 0.824/(x - 0.12)^2$]; Bouniatian [$y = 0.757/(x - 0.13)^2$]. Bouniatian's formulation now is taken to be more elegant and will be used in later calculations. For the reasons see Wrigley, "Some Reflections on Corn Yields and Prices in Pre-Industrial Economies," 92–130.

than the changes in harvest size. The reason, according to Slicher van Bath, is that "very slight over-production can make the price drop considerably; the least shortage can drive it up."[46]

King's insight about the mathematical relationship between the size of harvests and changes in grain prices has not only informed classic studies of European agricultural history (such as those by Slicher van Bath and Wilhelm Abel), but has prompted a recent reexamination by E. A. Wrigley of the relationship in Europe between harvest yields and grain prices. In his essay, Wrigley uses King's law to examine numerous issues, including the relationship between consumption and sale of grain, the influence of carryover and storage on prices, the variable impact of rising prices on farmers and consumers, the riskiness of farming strategies, the calculation of harvest yields from price series, and the declining marginal returns to labor.[47] Although Wrigley regarded his essay as "speculative," he did argue that the issue of harvest yields was critically important for understanding the dynamics of European economic history. Clearly, then, modern historians have used King's insights to illuminate aspects of European economic and demographic history. What might King's model tell us about eighteenth-century Lingnan?

Gregory King's Law Applied to China's Harvest Yield Estimates. The fact that Chinese officials did not produce mathematical models of the relationship between harvest size and rice prices does not mean that such models cannot apply to China's agrarian history. The question is: How well do the models suggested by King compare to actual rice price behavior in Guangdong during the eighteenth century? The results for five periods are shown in Table 8.8.

What these data show is that harvest failures in Guangdong province did not cause prices to increase as much as predicted by King's law. In the first two cases, for example, harvest deficiencies of 27 and 21 percent produced price increases of 61 and 45 percent, respectively, not the 80–160 percent increases modeled by King's law. But eighteenth-century Lingnan was not England, after all, and while the general relationship between harvests and prices holds for China, the specific proportions suggested by King's law do not. These data suggest that while eighteenth-century Lingnan rice prices were indeed sensitive to changes in harvest yields, there was less volatility in its price–yield relationship than that in England. Moreover, after 1761, rice prices tended to become even less variable than in the preceding decades, accentuating the difference with the English record. It will also be recalled that just three times in

[46] Slicher van Bath, *The Agrarian History of Western Europe*, 118–19.

[47] Wrigley, "Some Reflections on Corn Yields and Prices in Pre-Industrial Economies," 92–130. Wrigley attributes the articulation of King's law to the economist Davenant, who published works based upon King's unpublished papers.

Table 8.8. *Price changes following abundant or deficient harvests*

Year	Rating (%)	Price
1723	100	79
1726	73	127
Change	−27%	61%
1739	89	95
1742	70	138
Change	−21%	45%
1758	81	189
1761	90	128
Change	11%	−32%
1776	83	156
1777	78	165
Change	−6%	6%
1784	90	151
1787	73	162
Change	−19%	7%

Sources: Same as Table 8.6.

the eighteenth century did Guangdong experience two consecutive years of deficient harvests (see Chapter 7).

Compared with England, this record is rather remarkable. According to W. G. Hoskins's reconstruction of English harvests, during the first 60 years of the eighteenth century (his study ends with 1759), England already had had four periods of 2 or more years of consecutive deficient harvests during which prices increased 25–50 percent over "normal," and he suggests that the remaining 40 years of the century were about the same.[48] In England, in short, there were perhaps six or more times of at least 2 consecutive years of deficient harvests, twice the incidence recorded in Guangdong. The comparison with countries elsewhere in Europe tells much the same story. Across the English Channel, France experienced 16 general famines in the eighteenth century, not to mention numerous local famines; Germany and Italy too had famines more frequently than bumper harvests.[49] In comparative perspective, then, not only

[48] Hoskins, "Harvest Fluctuations and English Economic History," 16. The consecutive years of deficient harvests were 1707–11 (a four-year run), 1727–28, 1739–40, and 1756–57.

[49] Braudel, *The Structures of Everyday Life*, 74.

did Lingnan experience fewer deficient harvests in the eighteenth century than England (and probably the rest of Europe, too), but when the harvest was deficient grain prices in Lingnan tended to increase less than the amount suggested by Gregory King's law.

What accounts for the differences in the harvest record and price histories of Lingnan and England (or continental Europe, too)? Although I have examined the impact of climate on harvest yields, climatic factors are not a likely explanation. As we have already seen, temperature variations are highly correlated around the northern hemisphere, so that both England and China probably experienced similar temperature variations. Explanations thus should look to different institutional arrangements for producing, distributing, and consuming food, including the number of crops harvested annually, the integration and efficiency of markets, and state and private arrangements for storing food.

Perhaps most important, peasant-farmers in much of Lingnan produced two harvests in one year. While it is true that the warmer climate in Lingnan was a necessary condition for double cropping, it was not sufficient: technological improvements coupled with larger labor supplies (a larger, more dense population) pushed the development of double cropping. With the innovation of double cropping, then, over the course of two years Chinese farmers had four harvests, thereby significantly decreasing the risk of losing an entire year's output.

Further reducing the risk of farming in Lingnan, where harvest output was so dependent on rainfall levels and grain price so sensitive to harvest yield, peasant-farmers and state bureaucrats took whatever mitigating measures they could to smooth out the impact of weather on rice production and market supplies. For farmers, managed and manageable irrigation lessened the impact of drier years, which were more usual in the second half of the eighteenth century, while excess rainfall (but not destructive typhoons) had little impact on irrigated fields but certainly improved the yield of dry fields. During the Qianlong period, the state also encouraged and supported water control projects, and evidence (to be presented in the next chapter) suggests that the amount of irrigated land doubled during the course of the eighteenth century.

Grain supplies also improved not only as a function of better control of harvest yields through irrigation, but also because of public and private storage of grain. As we saw in Chapter 7, the Chinese state, primarily through the granary and famine relief system, did what it could to mitigate the harmful effects of food shortages caused by drought or flood, selling granary stocks at discounted prices in the spring before the first harvest came in and providing relief to areas devastated by drought or flood. Clearly, massive state intervention into the grain markets prevented prices from going as high as they otherwise might have in bad times. And over and above better technology and active state intervention into management of the food supply, by the middle of the eighteenth century an integrated market for rice had emerged in Lingnan, linking the economically advanced but chronically food-deficit region in the Pearl River delta to a vast rice-producing hinterland in Guangxi province.[50] All of these factors – improved technology as represented by the extension of irrigation works, the state granary system, and an efficient market mechanism – served to lessen the impact of climatic changes upon harvest yields and rice prices in Lingnan.

By the middle of the eighteenth century, then, an integrated market for rice had formed in Lingnan, becoming increasingly efficient at moving grain from hinterland to city. By then, some 20–28 percent of the rice produced in Guangdong entered the market, and perhaps no more than 40 percent of the cultivated land in Guangdong was devoted to rice production. The grain trade had been jump-started early in the century by state officials seeking to ensure food supplies to Guangzhou, but by the 1760s the rice markets operated with little official intervention: market forces and merchants rather than state politics and bureaucrats efficiently ensured adequate food supplies and hence relatively low and stable rice prices.

This finding has implications for interpretations of China's late imperial economic and demographic history. As Abel summarized the work of Labrousse and Ashton on European economic history, "It culminated in the principle that before the industrial era economic slumps went with high grain prices, economic booms with low prices."[51] Since demand for grain was relatively inelastic and the size of the nonfarm economy relatively small, Labrousse and Ashton reasoned, high grain prices would drain money from the industrial sector, sending it into a slump, and vice versa. Intuitively, this thesis has a compelling logic, and if it is true it means that in Guangdong province at least, the moderate grain prices from the 1760s to the end of the century contributed to the expansion of the nonfarm economy in and around Guangzhou, in particular the textile industry, by ensuring low food prices and hence low wages. Whether or not this relationship held for the whole of China has yet to be determined, but it is an interesting working hypothesis, especially in light of the generally acknowledged economic vitality of the Qianlong era.[52]

Grain prices also are relevant to understanding China's demographic history. Drawing from the insights and conclusions of European historical

[50] See Marks, "Rice Prices, Food Supply, and Market Structure in Eighteenth-Century South China."

[51] Abel, *Agricultural Fluctuations*, 176. Abel was only mildly skeptical of Ashton's formulation: "There is some evidence in favour of this correlation . . . [but] it requires further proof." Andrew Appleby made much the same point in his classic study *Famine in Tudor and Stuart England* (Stanford: Stanford University Press, 1978), 14–15.

[52] See Susan Naquin and Evelyn S. Rawski, *Chinese Society in the Eighteenth Century* (New Haven: Yale University Press, 1987), ch. 4.

demographers, James Lee and others have shown for a particular part of northeastern China, Liaoning, that "virtually all households responded to high prices by reducing fertility and to low prices by increasing fertility." They further suggest that "if all Chinese peasants controlled their fertility in response to economic conditions, then the rise in population during the eighteenth and nineteenth centuries may well have been a direct response to significant advances in economic growth."[53] Like the Labrousse and Ashton thesis, this one too is suggestive of a causal linkage between the low and stable grain prices in Lingnan and the rising population in the second half of the eighteenth century.

Conclusion

The development of an integrated market for rice cut two ways with regard to the environment. On the one hand, by promoting regional agricultural specialization (e.g., the Pearl River delta silk district and the West River rice-exporting district), market forces had simplified the ecosystems of Lingnan. On the other hand, by the second half of the eighteenth century, the large, integrated, and well-stocked market for rice had limited the impact of climatic fluctuations upon grain prices, thereby affecting, as I will discuss later in the Conclusion, population dynamics. Like the state in the first part of the eighteenth century, merchants and the market moved rice from grain-surplus to grain-deficit regions in Lingnan. The market may have done so more efficiently than the state, but it certainly was not the invisible hand that classical economists would like to point to. Rice merchants from Foshan and Guangzhou controlled the Wuzhou market (in part because of the particular geography of that part of Lingnan), not only creating a demand for export rice that peasant-farmers (or landlords) in the West River basin responded to, but also paying prices lower than what they otherwise would have paid. Much of the best farmland in Guangxi thereby became devoted to a single crop – rice – and the peasant-farmers in the Pearl River delta had their food supplies ensured.

Reflecting the increased role of the market, rice prices became increasingly more stable throughout the eighteenth century. Where state intervention earlier in the eighteenth century had sent rice prices wildly gyrating from one year to the next,[54] market forces smoothed out the ripples in price variations

[53] James Lee, Cameron Campbell, and Guofu Tan, "Infanticide and Family Planning in Late Imperial China: The Price and Population History of Rural Liaoning, 1774–1873," in Thomas Rawski and Lillian Li, eds., *Chinese History in Economic Perspective* (Berkeley and Los Angeles: University of California Press, 1992), 167–68, 175.

[54] For the statistical evidence, see Marks and Chen, "Price Inflation and Its Social, Economic, and Climatic Context in Guangdong."

in the latter part of the century, lessening even the power of climatic shocks to send rice prices soaring. While the eighteenth-century agricultural economy certainly was not immune from climatic fluctuations, the state granary system and the market combined to create conditions in which grain prices were more stable and lower than they otherwise might have been. Those conditions would not last into the nineteenth century, but while they did, they proved conducive to the growth of both the economy and the population. And as the population grew during the eighteenth century, pressure upon the land mounted as well.

9

"POPULATION INCREASES DAILY, BUT THE LAND DOES NOT": LAND CLEARANCE IN THE EIGHTEENTH CENTURY

If the commercialization of agriculture was one force driving changes in land use patterns in Lingnan, the other powerful force was population growth. Sometime around 1700 or in the few decades thereafter, Lingnan entered a new era in terms of the number of people living in the region, the amount of land under cultivation, and the relationship between the two. At two previous times – around 1200 during the Southern Song, and around 1600 in the Ming – population and cultivated land areas had reached about the same levels as they did in 1700 (Figure 9.1). But whereas the Song and Ming peaks were followed by substantial population losses and land abandoned because of war, the early-eighteenth-century totals of both population and cultivated land soon were surpassed in the mid-Qing population boom now so familiar to historians.

Because the population and cultivated land areas in the Song and Ming had been about equal to those of 1700, the recovery from the mid-seventeenth-century crisis at first plowed old ground, to pick what seems to be an apt metaphor. Those struggling to bring land back into production in the early Qing chose the best, most easily reclaimable land, and that no doubt in large part was the same land that had caught the eyes of Song and Ming settlers too. To be sure, in Guangxi there was and had been more "virgin" land than in Guangdong, and I will examine some of those differences in this chapter, but by and large those living after 1700, regardless of where in Lingnan they lived, encountered difficulties finding land suitable for cultivation. Settlers pushed into the hills, burning off the forests and damming the rivers, while in the Pearl River delta embankments to create new *shatan* soon obstructed the natural flow of the river. During the course of the eighteenth century, the cumulative efforts of people to plant food in areas previously untouched resulted in another massive remaking of the environment.

The Chinese, of course, called this remaking "land reclamation" (*kaiken*), and to them, it was good. The state supported and encouraged land reclama-

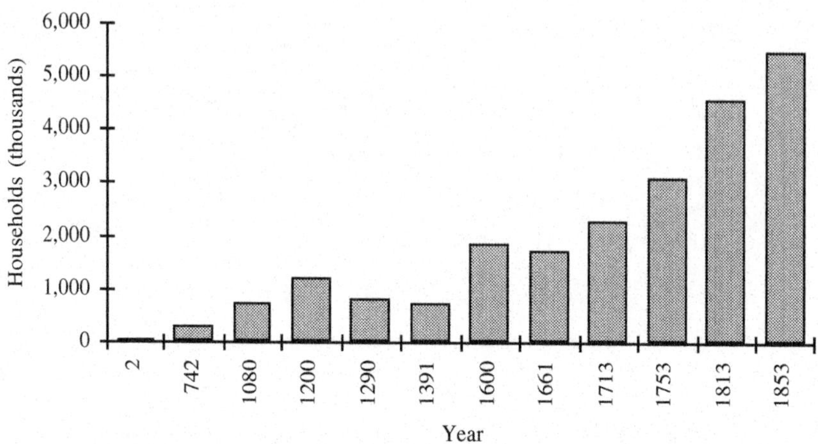

Figure 9.1. Estimated population of Lingnan, 2–1853.

tion with funds, expertise, incentives, and policies designed to accomplish various objectives. In the early years of the dynasty, the new rulers wanted to get land back into production as soon as possible for the strategic reason of providing a tax base for the continued military actions necessary to consolidate Manchu rule over the Chinese empire. The problem then was not understood as too many people on too little land, but precisely the opposite, and early Qing land reclamation policies were geared to getting agricultural production going once again.

But by the end of the Kangxi period (1662–1722), and especially during the Yongzheng emperor's reign (1723–35), officials began to feel the pressure of population upon the resources of the land and became concerned about the food supply of the empire. To the Yongzheng emperor, the problem was that the number of people was outstripping the ability of the cultivated land area to feed them; the solution to him thus was clear – increase the amount of land under the plow. He had, as it were, a "supply side" solution to the problem of food supply. Land reclamation policies then underwent substantial change. Indeed, the story of land reclamation policies in the Yongzheng period is pivotal, and I will examine that episode in some detail. His successor, though, the Qianlong emperor (1736–95), did not think that the problem of food supply was one of a fundamental imbalance between supply and demand, but that the distribution of the existing food supply needed improvement. He thus looked upon grain prices, the role of the state-managed granary system, and grain markets as critical issues in addressing the problem, as we saw in Chapter 8.

Population Growth

With the 1683 capture of Taiwan and the reopening of the coast for shipping and foreign trade, Lingnan (and the rest of China) entered a period of relative peace that reigned for over 150 years. With each day that passed without signs of crisis returning and with increasing confidence in the new-found stability and prosperity, families could form and farm, and the population could recover and grow.

Unlike the Ming, the new Qing state conducted neither a census nor land survey (although a cadastre was contemplated), so very little data exist from which to estimate the size and distribution of the population in the Qing. But using two reasonably reliable later population totals (for the years after 1776 and for 1953), estimates of population increases for the late nineteenth century, and assumptions about annual growth rates consistent with what is known about social and economic conditions, I have estimated the population at 20-year intervals from 1673 to 1953 (see Table 9.1).[1]

[1] The estimates in Table 9.1 were developed starting with the 1953 figures (which come from China's first modern census conducted in that year) and the 1673 figures (which were discussed at the end of Chapter 4), and then estimating a midpoint population figure for 1773 based upon officially reported totals. As Ping-ti Ho pointed out in *Studies on the Population of China, 1368–1953* (47–50), the Qianlong emperor ordered a rigorous recount of the population in 1776 after irregularities in a famine relief effort raised questions about the veracity of the population figures being reported, and the reported figures for both Guangdong and Guangxi show substantial increases for 1776 over previous reports, indicating a substantial upward revision. Whether the 1776 figures for Guangdong and Guangxi represent a recount or just official guesswork is open to question. So I have instead used 1782 figures because the increase from the preceding year was greater than increases for previous or later pairs of years, leading me to suspect that the new governor of Guangdong, Shang'an, had exerted substantial pressure all the way down the bureaucratic ladder for a rigorous count and tallying of the *li-jia* registers. From the 1782 figure, the 1773 estimate was generated by back projection.

From these three data points – 1673, 1773, and 1953 – I estimated "best fit" totals for the other 20-year periods based upon assumptions about the annual rate of growth during those 20-year periods. For Guangdong, the relatively high rates in the decades from 1693 through 1733 correspond with settled conditions and low grain prices, while the lower rate for the 1733–53 period corresponds to a period of increasingly high grain prices. I assume higher rates of population growth from 1753 to 1813, slowing until disturbances of the mid-nineteenth century virtually halted population growth. For 1873, 1893, and 1913, estimates developed in the 1930s by the National Agricultural Experimentation Bureau and the Agricultural Economics Department of Nanjing University have been used. For more on this survey, see Li Wenzhi, ed., *Zhongguo jindai nongye shi ziliao* (Beijing: Sanlian shudian, 1957), vol. 3: 908; and Perkins, *Agricultural Development in China*, 209–10. For Guangxi, the growth rates are consistently lower than for Guangdong until the twentieth century; the rates until 1933 are based on the National Agricultural Experimentation Bureau survey, while I assume a higher 1.4% rate for 1933–53 because of in-migration caused by flight from the Japanese invasion.

Readers may note that my population estimates differ both from the officially reported totals and from the estimates developed by Perkins in *Agricultural Development in China*, 214. The offi-

Table 9.1. *Population and cultivated land estimates, 1673–1953*

	Population (millions)		Cultivated land area (millions of *mu*)		Percent of land area cultivated		Density (per sq. km)		*Mu* (per capita)	
Year	Guangdong	Guangxi	Guangdong	Guangxi	Guangdong	Guangxi	Guangdong	Guangxi	Guangdong	Guangxi
1673	7.0	2.7	30.0	7.5	9	2	31.2	12.2	4.3	2.8
1693	7.9	2.8	33.0	8.9	10	3	35.2	12.6	4.2	3.2
1713	9.6	3.3	37.0	10.3	11	3	42.7	14.9	3.9	3.1
1733	11.7	3.9	40.0	13.3	12	4	52.1	17.6	3.4	3.4
1753	13.2	4.3	43.0	16.3	13	5	58.7	19.4	3.3	3.8
1773	15.2	4.9	45.0	19.3	14	6	67.6	22.1	3.0	3.9
1793	17.1	5.5	47.0	22.3	14	7	76.1	24.8	2.7	4.1
1813	19.3	6.2	49.0	25.3	15	8	85.9	27.9	2.5	4.1
1833	21.3	6.7	51.0	28.3	15	9	94.8	30.2	2.4	4.2
1853	23.5	7.1	53.0	31.2	16	9	104.6	32.0	2.3	4.4
1873	24.5	7.2	53.0	31.2	16	9	109.0	32.4	2.2	4.3
1893	27.1	8.0	53.5	33.8	16	10	120.6	36.0	2.0	4.2
1913	30.0	10.8	53.5	36.5	16	11	133.5	48.6	1.8	3.4
1933	33.8	12.7	54.0	38.4	16	12	150.4	57.2	1.6	3.0
1953	35.9	16.8	54.0	41.8	16	13	159.8	75.7	1.5	2.5

These population estimates show a doubling of Guangdong's population over the century from 1673 to 1773 and a doubling again by 1913. For Guangxi, the rate was slower at first, doubling over a 120-year period from 1673 to 1793, but doubling again from 1793 to 1913 at a rate faster than Guangdong. Given what is known about China's population in general during the Qing and Republican periods, these estimates strike me as reasonable.

Cultivated Land Area

Estimates for cultivated land area have been developed using a procedure similar to that for population, but the level of uncertainty is significantly greater. The reasons for the uncertainty will be discussed in more detail later, but can be briefly summarized here. In the absence of a land survey, the Qing rulers adopted the late-sixteenth-century Ming land and tax survey as their "original targets" (*yuan-e*). For reasons to be discussed later, I think Guangdong can be assumed to have reached those targets in the 1693–1713 period, while Guangxi reached them in 1713–33. Assuming the Ming *yuan-e* to have been reasonably accurate and my assessment of when they were reached not unreasonable, the initial cultivated land figures can be set. A midseries point for the cultivated land area cannot be reconstructed from available data. Unlike the 1776 population figures, none of the later officially reported land figures for the Qing are meaningful; with the Kangxi emperor's 1713 pledge "never to raise taxes" (*yong bu jia fu*), state functionaries had no reason to report any further increases in cultivated land area, and so didn't. For Guangdong and Guangxi, the officially reported Qing cultivated land figures thus never vary much from 33 million and 10 million *mu*, respectively. The methodological problem, of course, is to get from the early Qing figures to the 1953 figures without any midpoint for guidance.

cially reported totals, especially for the nineteenth century, are all much higher than my estimates, probably because the reported figures were simply fabricated rather than annually totalled from the bottom up (see G. William Skinner, "Sichuan's Population in the Nineteenth Century: Lessons from Disaggregated Data," *Late Imperial China* 7 no. 2 (Dec. 1986): 1–79). The differences with Perkins's estimates, though, are only apparent. Perkins too worked backwards from twentieth-century totals and the National Agricultural Experimentation Bureau survey to arrive at an 1851 population figure for Guangdong of 21.7 million, about 2 million less than mine. The reason for the discrepancy, I think, is that Perkins overlooked the administrative changes that removed Lianzhou prefecture (in Republican times called "Qinzhou") and another small area from Guangdong and placed them in Guangxi, representing a population of about 2 million. For a discussion of the Guangxi figures, see Huang Jianlin et al., eds., *Zhongguo Renkou–Guangxi fen ce* (Beijing, Zhongguo caizheng jingji Chuban she 1988), 47, 50. For Perkins's purposes, of course, the national total remained the same, and for my purposes, the total for Guangdong and Guangxi remains the same too.

For Guangdong, I have accepted the Liu–Yeh estimate for 1933,[2] and worked backwards to 1853 using the indexes from the National Agricultural Experimentation Bureau survey.[3] Projecting backwards from there assuming higher annual rates of land reclamation until 1773 than in the 1773–1833 period, I computed the estimates in Table 9.1. I do not think my reconstruction overestimates the amount of land under cultivation, since my estimate of the amount of land added to the total from 1733 to 1793 is about 10 times higher than the reported amounts of land reclaimed. For Guangxi, though, I think the Liu–Yeh estimates for 1933 are too high. I base that conclusion largely on estimates of Guangxi's cultivated land area in the People's Republic to have been about 41.8 million (Qing) *mu*.

Comparing these estimates points to interesting differences between Guangdong and Guangxi, all of which make sense when read in the context of the commercialization of agriculture in Lingnan and consequent changes in land use patterns. Where the amount of cultivated land in Guangdong increased by just 75 percent from 1673 to 1853, in Guangxi it quadrupled over the same period. And while the amount of land (*mu*) per capita fell by about 50 percent in Guangdong from 1673 to 1853, reflecting the greater population density there, in Guangxi the *mu* per capita actually increased, reflecting the increase in the production of rice for the export market. In other words, where agriculture in Guangdong underwent a process of intensification in conjunction with the increased production of cash and nonfood crops, in Guangxi more land was brought into production even as the use of the existing land intensified.

The Intensification of Agriculture

How much agriculture intensified can be judged by surveying changes in cropping patterns that occurred during the eighteenth century. At the beginning of the century, in Guangdong province much of the food-producing crop land in the lower-lying river valleys and in the Pearl River delta was double cropped,[4] either in a rice–rice or a rice–wheat rotation, even in the northern hill region;[5] the eastern Guangdong prefectures of Huizhou and Chaozhou, though, were known as the areas that "plant the most wheat."[6] In Guangxi, by contrast, "there is only one crop of rice. Early crops of wheat or miscellaneous grains

[2] Ta-chung Liu and Kung-chia Yeh, *The Economy of Mainland China: National Income and Economic Development, 1933–1959* (Princeton: Princeton University Press, 1965), Appendix A.

[3] The 1873, 1893, and 1913 index numbers for Guangdong are 101, 101, and 102, respectively; for Guangxi they are 105, 117, and 123. Li Wenzhi, ed., *Zhongguo jindai nongye shi ziliao*, vol. 3: 908.

[4] For cropping patterns in the sixteenth and seventeenth centuries, see Chapter 3.

[5] See memorials dated KX54.4.27, in KXCZZ doc. no. 1770; and YZ6.9.11, in YZCZZ 11: 331–32.

[6] Memorial dated YZ7.3.3, in YZCHWZPZZ 14: 738.

tide the population over between [rice] harvests."[7] But the use of wheat as a second harvest in Guangxi was limited to about 10 percent of the land,[8] and then to rice-exporting areas near Guangdong, such as Wuzhou and Yulin prefectures.[9] In northern Guangxi, though, just one crop of rice was harvested. That pattern began to change, for in 1735 officials reported a program to train peasants how to plant wheat: "Last winter officials in Pingle and Zhaoping counties gave out wheat seed and taught the people how to plant it. Now they are reporting a plentiful harvest. Rice-growing villages now also have spring wheat to see them through the time between [rice] harvests."[10] The picture of the early eighteenth century that emerges thus is one of mostly double cropping in Guangdong and mostly single cropping of rice in Guangxi, with some intensification noted by the 1730s with the introduction of wheat.

By the middle of the eighteenth century, there is clear evidence of further intensification of cropping. In the westernmost Guangxi prefectures of Sicheng, Si'en, and Zhen'an, "the fields in the river valleys have been converted to irrigated rice paddies,"[11] and wheat harvests (as second crops) had expanded to 76 counties.[12] In Guangdong province, officials began paying attention to cropping patterns in an attempt to extend wheat as a second crop into new areas. "Of the different kinds of arable land in Guangdong – higher- or lower-lying land, dry or irrigated – some is suitable for two crops of rice, and some is suitable for a crop of winter wheat and a late rice crop. Peasants differentiate according to the nature of the land and plant accordingly."[13] Apparently it took a while for officials to learn that "not all areas are suited to [wheat]. For example, an experiment in Yong'an yielded a 50 percent harvest (the rest of the province yielded 70 percent)."[14] The failure of this attempt led the governor-general to generalize that "those who plant wheat do so because the winter is relatively warm."[15] Surprisingly, then, there were some places in Guangdong too cold for wheat, and all of these were in counties in the higher elevations (Yong'an, Lechang, Qingyuan, and Kaiping, among others). Additionally, wheat was not planted where the climate was too tropical, as in Qinzhou on the Tonkin Gulf or most of Hainan Island.

By the late eighteenth century, arable land throughout Lingnan was being even more intensively cropped. In Guangdong, "a widespread practice is to

[7] Memorial dated KX60.5.27, in KXCZZ doc. no. 2989.

[8] Memorial dated YZ5.6.24, in YZCHWZPZZ 10: 48–49.

[9] Ibid.

[10] Memorial dated YZ13.4i.9, in YZCZZ 24: 507–508.

[11] Memorial dated QL16.11.3, in QLCZZ 1: 836.

[12] Memorial dated QL17.5.20, in QLCZZ 3: 108. Of those 76, 42 were "Chinese (Han) counties" and 34 "native (*tu*)" counties.

[13] Memorial dated QL18.5.16, in QLCZZ 5: 371.

[14] Memorial dated QL19.4.25, in QLCZZ 8: 106–107.

[15] Memorial dated QL21.4.13, in QLCZZ 14: 178.

plant wheat besides an early and late rice crop."[16] In Guangxi, not only had wheat expanded to 2 more counties (bringing the total to 78),[17] but also double or triple cropping of rice was being practiced even in Guilin. In a mid-1779 memorial, the Guangxi financial commissioner reported that "low-lying fields have much water collected in them, and [the use of] water wheels does not expend human labor . . . *Early* rice is forming grains, and within the month there is likely to be an abundant harvest. The *middle* and *late* rice crops are thick and green."[18] Later that same month, the governor of Guangxi reported upon conditions near Guilin: "seventy to eighty percent of the middle crop already has tassels; 20–30 percent of the late crop has come up luxuriant."[19]

Over the course of the eighteenth century, then, peasant-farmers had intensified their cropping of arable land in Lingnan. By the middle of the century, wheat had spread as a second crop throughout most of Guangxi and Guangdong, and by the end of the century, many areas – even Guilin – in addition to wheat, double cropped rice. The reasons for this intensification of agriculture seem clear enough. First, the population grew and became more dense (in Guangdong, doubling during the eighteenth century from about 40 to 80 people per square kilometer; see Table 9.1), making more labor power available to work the land.[20] Second, commercialization (i.e., the changes in land use patterns to serve the cotton textile and sericulture industries discussed in Chapter 5) prompted peasant-producers throughout the hinterland, but especially in Guangxi, to grow rice for the expanding export market to Guangzhou and the Pearl River delta. Finally, a climate warmer than that in the seventeenth century enabled peasant-farmers to push the edges of the rice-planting envelope earlier in the spring and later in the fall. All of these combined to create a pattern of highly intensive farming of the land in Lingnan by the nineteenth century.

To Europeans, the ability of Chinese farmers to squeeze so much from the land was a source of some amazement, especially when compared with the relatively "backward" techniques found in much of Europe. "By what art can the earth produce subsistence for such numbers?" asked Pierre Poivre, a French agronomist who spent a considerable amount of time investigating agricultural

[16] Memorial dated QL52.3.15, in QLCZZ 63: 635–36.

[17] Memorial dated QL28.4.13, in QLCZZ 17: 443.

[18] Memorial dated QL44.6.9, in QLCZZ 48: 99–100. Emphasis added.

[19] Memorial dated QL44.6.23, in QLCZZ 48: 232–33.

[20] That the intensification of agriculture was driven by increasing population density was first argued by Ester Boserup, *The Conditions of Agricultural Growth: The Economics of Agrarian Change under Population Pressure* (New York: Aldine, 1965). The evidence from Lingnan thus supports Boserup's thesis, but only up to a point, for I think that commercialization also drove intensification, and climate changes made greater intensification possible.

practices throughout Asia in the 1720s, including a stay of several months in Guangzhou:[21]

> Do the Chinese possess any secret arts of multiplying grain and provisions necessary for the nourishment of mankind? To solve my doubts I traversed the fields, I introduced myself among the laborers, who are in general easy, polite, and knowledgeable of the world. I examine, and pursue them through all their operations, and observe that their secret consists simply in manuring the fields judiciously, ploughing them to a considerable depth, sowing them in the proper season, turning to advantage every inch of ground which can produce the most considerable crop, and preferring to every other species of culture that of grain, as by far the most important.[22]

The practice that struck Poivre most was the constant tilling of the land, without allowing for a fallow period: "That which must render this plan of agriculture the more inconceivable to Europeans, is the idea of their never allowing their lands to lie one season fallow . . . [the land thus] yield[s] annually two crops, and in those towards the south often five in two years, without one single season fallow." The reason for the continuous cropping was massive fertilizing: "They are familiar with marl; they employ also common salt, lime, and all sorts of animal dung, but above all that which we throw in our rivers: they make great use of urine, which is carefully stored in every house, and sold to advantage: in a word, everything produced by the earth is re-conveyed to it with the greatest care."[23]

Besides fertilizing and the absence of fallow, Poivre remarked upon the use of every "inch of ground":

> The steepest mountains, even, are rendered accessible . . . At Canton [Guangzhou] . . . you observe mountains cut into terraces . . . Every one of these terraces yields annually a crop of some kind of grain, even rice; and you cannot withhold your admiration, when you behold the water of the river, the canal, or the fountain, which glides by the foot of the mountain, raised from terrace to terrace, even to the summit, by means of a simple mechanism, which two men with ease transport and put in motion.[24]

Certainly the picture that Poivre paints is one of very intensely farmed land, especially around Guangzhou, where peasant-farmers lavished fertilizer, water from irrigation works, and, above all, labor, upon the land in order to obtain two or three crops annually from the same plot.

[21] For more on Pierre Poivre, see Grove, *Green Imperialism*, ch. 5. I thank Professor Grove for drawing my attention to Poivre.

[22] Pierre Poivre, *Travels of a Philosopher, Or, Observations on the Manner and Arts of Various Nations in Africa and Asia*, translated from the French (London, 1769), 146.

[23] Ibid., 153. [24] Ibid., 159.

If the density of population drives the intensification of agriculture, as suggested by Boserup, then variations and changes in population density can be rough guides to when and where agricultural practices intensified in Lingnan. Provincewide estimates are blunt instruments indeed, telling us only in the broadest terms what the population and cultivated land trends were. To be sure, population and land data disaggregated down to the county level would be invaluable, but they simply do not exist. Nonetheless, we can sharpen the provincial picture by comparing changes in population at the prefectural level, using the 1391 population data and 1820 population figures reported in the *Da qing yi tong zhi*. The 1820 data, I think, overstate the size of the population in both Guangdong and Guangxi by about 10 percent; but the relative weights of the populations among the various prefectures probably are reasonable approximations of where the people were and permit a comparison with the 1391 figures (Table 9.2).

The areas that gained relative weight in Guangdong were in the eastern part of the province (Huizhou prefecture) and in the southwestern littoral (Gaozhou); in Guangxi, the greatest gains were to the north and south of the West River (Pingle and Yulin) and in the far west of the province (Nanning, Taiping, Si'en, Sicheng, and Zhen'an prefectures). The biggest percentage losses in Guangdong were the Leizhou Peninsula and Hainan Island, and in Guangxi, Guilin and Wuzhou prefectures. Earlier I discussed the reasons for the relative "underdevelopment" of Leizhou and Hainan Island, but the drop in the relative positions of Guilin and Wuzhou at first glance appears puzzling. The reason for the lesser population growth in those two prefectures, I think, is because they had been settled much earlier than the rest of Guangxi and had mostly filled up during the Ming dynasty, with their populations more than doubling over the 400 years from 1400 to 1800.

Although Guangzhou prefecture declined slightly from 1391 to 1820 in terms of the percentage of the total provincial population, it experienced the largest growth in population and, with about 300 people per square kilometer, was twice as densely populated as Gaozhou, the next most densely populated prefecture (Chaozhou and Jiaying prefectures, which do not belong in the Lingnan macroregion, also had population densities about the same as Gaozhou). The Pearl River delta and the southwest littoral, it may be recalled, had come to specialize in sericulture or sugarcane. In Guangxi, the most densely populated prefectures lay in the south and southeast along the You and West Rivers, from Nanning to Wuzhou. Where Xunzhou, Nanning, and Yulin prefectures were sparsely populated at the beginning of the Ming, by 1820 all had population densities exceeding that of Guilin. In short, the population grew the most dense in those parts of Guangxi exporting rice to Guangzhou. Indeed, all those prefectures that experienced double-digit factor increases in the density of population were the same places where new land was cleared for agriculture.

Table 9.2. *Prefectural population changes, 1391–1820*

	Proportion of the population (%)			Population density (sq. km)		
Prefecture	1391	1820	Change	1391	1820	Factor increase
Guangdong						
Guangzhou	34	29	−5	58	310	5.3
Nanxiong	2	2	−1	21	101	4.9
Shaozhou	3	5	2	7	64	9.8
Huizhou	4	10	6	4	73	17.2
Chaozhou	7	16	9	16	151	9.3
Zhaoqing	15	12	−3	26	135	5.1
Gaozhou	4	11	7	8	150	19.3
Leizhou	16	3	−12	64	84	1.3
Lianzhoufu	2	2	0	5	27	5.9
Qiongzhou	12	6	−5	11	38	3.5
Luoding	1	3	3	3	98	33.7
Lianzhou	n.a.	n.a.	n.a.	n.a.	32	n.a.
Jiaying	n.a.	n.a.	n.a.	n.a.	146	n.a.
Guangxi						
Guilin	27	14	−13	16	43	2.6
Pingle	3	12	9	2	43	22.9
Wuzhou	21	9	−12	25	57	2.3
Xunzhou	6	9	3	7	52	7.4
Nanning	6	11	5	7	63	9.6
Taiping	2	4	2	2	19	8.8
Liuzhou	17	13	−5	15	54	3.7
Qingyuan	8	6	−2	5	19	4.0
Si'en	2	7	5	2	31	17.7
Sicheng	2	4	2	2	19	11.6
Zhen'an	2	4	2	8	80	10.2
Yulin	3	8	4	4	53	12.6

One side of the story told by the population and cultivated land figures from Ming to Qing thus is the intensification of agriculture. And while intensification is an important part of the story, so too were the efforts of peasant-farmers and the state to bring new land into production. One way of thinking about the distinction is that *intensification* led to changes in land *use*, while land *reclamation* led to changes in land *cover*. These were two separate but related processes: changes in the ways in which people used the land, and changes in the land cover itself, in this case from forest to cropland.[25] Where land-use

[25] The distinction between changes in land use and land cover is taken from Meyer and Turner: "The topic of land transformation divides conveniently into two linked components . . . those of land-use and land-cover change. The two terms denote areas of study that have historically

changes had been driven by the process of intensification, land cover changes were shaped by state policy and programs regarding land clearance and reclamation, as well as official responses to the problems raised by the pressure of the human population upon the land.

Early Qing Land Reclamation Policies and Results

Until peaceful conditions returned to Lingnan after 1683, state land reclamation policies had little impact on the amount of land brought back into agricultural production. As noted in Chapter 4, most of the land reclamation work had been carried on by individual families without much regard for state policies. This does not mean that state actions did not affect the pace of land reclamation or that the state did not have land reclamation policies, but only that conditions of war and rebellion rendered them ineffectual. Nonetheless, a summary of land reclamation policies during the Shunzhi (1644–61) and Kangxi reigns (1662–1722) is useful background for understanding the Yongzheng-era (1723–35) and Qianlong-era (1736–95) approaches to land reclamation, the periods when new lands were brought into production and, in some cases, actually created.

Early Qing land reclamation policies during the Shunzhi reign were formulated in the context of the depopulation caused by wars, disease, and famine. We have already seen how devastated Lingnan was in the mid-seventeenth century, but other provinces in north China such as Hebei and Shandong, as well as Sichuan province in west China, had been harder hit, with 50–75 percent of the people gone and equal proportions of land laid waste. Classifying the abandoned land into that "with owners" (*you zhu*) and that "without owners" (*wu zhu*), the state initially tried to settle vagrants on lands with owners. Finding that impossible because settlers wanted to become freeholders rather than tenants, the Shunzhi-era policies soon encouraged peasant-farmers to migrate to those provinces with "ownerless" land where they would be registered as residents rather than as "vagrants" (*liu-min*), given the right to till the land (but not necessarily own it) in perpetuity (*yong jun wei ye*), and extended tax remissions for a varying number of years. To encourage officials to get on top of land reclamation, the state extended incentives to officials to report reclaimed land. Large landowners too were given incentives to bring

been separate . . . Land uses include settlement, cultivation, pasture, rangeland, recreation, and so on. Land-use change at any location may involve either a shift to a different use or an intensification of the existing one . . . Land-cover changes fall into two types, *conversion* and *modification*. The former is a change from one class of land-cover to another: from grassland to cropland, for example. The latter is a change of condition within a land-cover category, such as the thinning of a forest or a change in its composition." William B. Meyer and B. L. Turner II, *Changes in Land Use and Land Cover: A Global Perspective* (New York: Cambridge University Press, 1994), 5.

Table 9.3. *Land reported reclaimed, by province, 1663–69, and by year*

	Amount (100 *mu*)
Province	
Huguang	27,870.07
Henan	26,041.00
Guangdong	10,747.66
Jiangxi	5,670.45
Yunnan	3,659.00
Shandong	3,352.60
Guizhou	695.15
Year	
1663	1,918.89
1664	4,302.50
1665	36,911.66
1666	20,842.12
1667	3,190.50
1668	122.60
1669	10,747.66

Source: Peng Yuxin, *Qing dai tudi kaiken shi* (Beijing: Renmin chuban she, 1965), 46.

land back into production, being extended the offer of a votive tablet commending their public service if they reported 50 *qing* back in production. Despite these incentives, peasant-farmers and landlords skeptical of the intent of the state did their best to hide land from the tax rolls. Peasants feared not just taxes but the more onerous corvée labor obligations, while landlords sought to avoid taxes. Seeking to uncover the hidden land, the state standardized the definition of the unit of land measure (the *mu*) and in 1658 launched land surveys in Shandong and Henan provinces. Besides arousing the resistance of the local elite, the land surveys proved too costly in time and money, and so were abandoned throughout the empire.[26]

Upon the death in 1661 of the Shunzhi emperor and the ascension of the boy-emperor Kangxi, regents for the new emperor adopted a generally "get tough" attitude in reaction to the Shunzhi policies they considered too lax. Knowing that large amounts of land had been hidden from the tax rolls and needing resources to press the military campaign against Zheng

[26] This paragraph is but a brief summary of a more extended treatment provided in Peng, *Qing dai tudi kaiken shi*, 2–34, 36–39. See also Guo Songyi, "Qing chu fengjian guojia ken huang zhengce fenxi," *Qingshi luncong* 2 (1980): 111–38.

Chenggong, the regents mandated that officials ferret out all hidden land and properly report it (i.e., add it to the tax rolls) within four years. The reports of reclaimed land increased, showing a surge in 1665 (see Table 9.3), just prior to the expiration of the deadline. While many of these reported figures represented actual land and the resulting increase in the tax base, many of the reports had been falsified: in those areas, taxes nonetheless increased and fell upon those already on the tax rolls. Rather than pay the increased taxes, many fled. As a result, the state had to back off and, following additional investigations, removed the falsely reported land from the tax rolls.[27]

The relocation of the coastal population in 1662 examined in Chapter 4 was part of the new "get tough" policy. In Guangdong, as we have seen, the policy was relaxed after almost 8 years, while in other areas it was enforced right through to 1683. According to Peng Yuxin, by the time the ban was lifted, nearly 9 million *mu* that had been abandoned in the coastal provinces of Guangdong, Fujian, and Zhejiang during the 22-year ban was reclaimed;[28] in Guangdong province, about 1 million *mu* was brought back into cultivation in 1669 (see the figures in Table 9.3).

During the Kangxi reign as private land reclamation continued apace and in light of the problem of false reporting, the Qing state decided to set the land tax on the basis of the cultivated land figures reported following the 1581 land surveys and reported in registers known as the *Fu yi quan shu* (Books of tax and corvée).[29] Few of these registers survive, but the "original targets" (*yuan-e*), as the late Ming figures came to be known, were recorded in the provincial gazetteers. As reasonably close approximations of the 1581 figures, the Qing *yuan-e* provide us with a sense of the amount and distribution of cultivated land both in the late Ming and in the early eighteenth century.[30] In most of Guangdong, the *yuan-e* targets were reached sometime in the late seventeenth or early eighteenth century, while in Guangxi some prefectures still reported "reclaimable waste" (*huang*) in the 1720s. Presumably most of China had attained the *yuan-e* targets by 1713, for that is when the Kangxi emperor issued his pledge "never to raise taxes."

Population Pressure and Land Reclamation

Concurrent with the *yuan-e* targets being reached and the land tax being fixed, there is evidence that the growing population was beginning to place strains

[27] Peng, *Qing dai tudi kaiken shi*, 45–47, 49–50. [28] Ibid., 61.

[29] See Wang, *Land Taxation in Imperial China*, 21–22; and Peter Perdue, *Exhausting the Earth: State and Peasant in Hunan 1500–1850* (Cambridge: Harvard University Press, 1987): 74–75.

[30] For a description of the methods by which the *yuan–e* were calculated in Hunan province, see Peng, *Qing dai tudi kaiken shi*, 67. See also Perdue, *Exhausting the Earth*, 74–76. As far as I am aware, similarly detailed examples are not available for Guangdong and Guangxi.

upon the supply of easily available land in Lingnan. In the early eighteenth century, people began migrating to other provinces, especially to Sichuan and Guangxi. Following natural disasters or food shortages, people pulled up and headed for Sichuan. As one fellow quoted by a government official explained: "Because of a famine in 1691, my grandfather left for other provinces, ultimately going to Sichuan where there are vast tracts of land. He was fortunate to be able to till the land, and farming became his occupation. After his relatives traveling back and forth [from Guangdong to Sichuan] saw the land in Sichuan, they too migrated. It has been 40 years now since we settled in Sichuan."[31] Similarly, a military officer in the 1720s observed that "several years of natural disasters have caused many people to flee to Sichuan. The reason is that Sichuan has lots of land, while Guangdong is full of people. Food is cheap in Sichuan, so the ignorant masses flock there."[32] Others migrated from Guangdong to Guangxi. Of the 800 members of the Xu lineage in Changle county, for instance, 157 migrated elsewhere during the eighteenth century, 51 of those to Guangxi.[33]

Officials were not unaware of the strain of population on the land. The Guangxi provincial military commander (*ti du*), Han Liangfu, noted that "the population doubled during the Kangxi reign" and that "while the population increases daily, the amount of land under cultivation does not."[34] A few years later, A-ke-dun opined that "throughout the world the population tends to increase; only by bringing land into production can they all be fed."[35] While it is true that these officials were responding to the position taken by the new Yongzheng emperor, according to one Chinese scholar other officials during the Kangxi reign and even the Kangxi emperor himself had commented on the rising population.[36]

What is interesting and significant is that the new Yongzheng emperor connected the rising population with the amount of land under cultivation, and then launched a massive state-supported campaign to bring new land into production. In his edict announcing the land reclamation incentives, the Yongzheng emperor reasoned: "Population has increased of late, so how can [the people] obtain their livelihood? Land reclamation [*kaiken*] is the only solution."[37] For the 13 years of his reign (1723–35), a considerable number of memorials were written on the question of land and land reclamation, leaving

[31] Quoted in Chen, *Shichang jizhi*, 1992, 152.

[32] Quoted in ibid., 153. Given the situation, one wonders how "ignorant" they really were.

[33] Ibid., 155.

[34] Memorial dated YZ2.4i.17, in YZCZZ 2: 582–83.

[35] Memorial dated YZ5.7.1, in YZHWZZ 10: 101–103.

[36] Peng, *Qing dai tudi kaiken shi*, 71.

[37] *Da Qing shi zong (Yongzheng) shi lu* (Taibei: Xinwenfeng chuban gongsi, 1978), edict of YZ1.4, juan 6: 25; see also Song Xixiang, *Zhongguo lidai quan nong kao* (Shanghai: Zhengzhong shuju, 1936), 75.

a written record unique in the Qing dynasty. The Yongzheng land reclamation campaign is significant not because of the actual amount of land that was brought into cultivation, but for what it reveals about the relationship between population and land in Lingnan in the early eighteenth century.

The Yongzheng Emperor and Land Reclamation

Ascending the throne as a mature, 45-year-old adult who had outmaneuvered his sibling rivals (some contemporaries alleged that he usurped it), the Yongzheng emperor had clearly formed ideas about how to rule, many of which represented reactions to what he saw as shortcomings in his father's rulership. Conceiving of himself and his state in more activist terms, and perhaps believing that the Kangxi emperor's relaxed attitudes and practices had led to substantial problems, not the least of which was population growth without commensurate increases in land under cultivation, the Yongzheng emperor signaled his intent to pursue "land reclamation" (*kaiken*) just four months into his reign. To encourage peasant-farmers "to reclaim and report land without interference or obstruction from officials," Yongzheng extended 6-year tax remissions to newly reclaimed paddy land and 10-year remissions to unirrigated land.[38] And in an edict issued eight months later, the Yongzheng emperor placed responsibility on officials "from governors on down" to encourage agriculture (*quan nong*). He ordered that county magistrates annually select one "seasoned farmer" (*lao nong*) who exemplified good farming skills and reward him with an honorary button of the eighth rank.[39]

Guangxi. Among the first officials to respond to the Yongzheng emperor's second edict was the acting governor of Guangxi, Provincial Military Commander (*ti du*) Han Liangfu.[40] In a memorial dated three months after Yongzheng's edict, Han enthusiastically puffed the possibilities for land reclamation in Guangxi province and sketched a plan for bringing the land into production. Guangxi, he said, was sparsely populated with considerable amounts of uncultivated but potentially fertile land.[41]

[38] *Da Qing shi zong (Yongzheng) shi lu*, edict of YZ1.4, juan 6: 25.

[39] "The peasant's lot," the emperor intoned as a preface to selecting one among them to honor, "is hard; his hands and feet are covered with callouses . . . He pays rent and taxes, provides for his parents, and raises his children." Ibid., 25–26.

[40] I have not found a biography of Han, so evidently not much is known about him.

[41] Memorial dated YZ2.4i.17, in YZCZZ 2: 582–83. Han's "proof" that the land was potentially fertile consisted of the observation that dense bamboo stands covered the land. If the old roots could be dug out and the land planted with rice, he reasoned, it would become fertile. Maybe Han never tried to remove bamboo, a nearly impossible task as many a southern California resident can attest.

In Han's estimation, six factors accounted for the land laying unclaimed. First, the virgin lands lay far from existing villages in hills and valleys occupied by Yao and Tong tribesmen, who, it was feared, would steal the ripening grain planted by Han Chinese. Second, the Chinese farming population relied on natural water sources for irrigation and did not know how to drain swamps or build proper weirs (*yan*) or pools (*tang*). Third, the peasants did not know how to plant upland crops (*za liang*). Fourth, they did not know the technique of deep plowing used in other provinces. Fifth, they grew only rice and paid all of their taxes in silver; corvée labor taxes were a function of the amount of land owned, so peasant-farmers feared the long-term consequences of bringing more land into cultivation. And finally, peasants worried that newly cultivated land would be expropriated by local magnates (*hao jin*) just as the crop ripened and that they would be forced to pay them rent.

Han's proposed reclamation plan called for appointing a special official charged with overseeing the reclamation effort, hiring people to teach the necessary farming and water control skills, and protecting the settlers from the aborigines and local power holders. The results, Han promised, would include dense settlement, a decrease in malaria,[42] sufficient food and clothing, and the spread of culture.

In his vermilion rescript on Han's memorial, the Yongzheng emperor commented that "the understanding in this memorial is excellent, (but Han) does not understand the art of planning." He directed Han to work "as one" (*yi de yi xin*) with the newly appointed governor, Li Fu, to manage the effort. For his part, Li Fu had just been appointed governor after a stint in the north and would hold the post for little more than a year.[43] During that time he wrote a memorial pledging that he and Han would work "as one,"[44] and recast Han's analysis and plan into another memorial that was subsequently republished in the collection of statecraft writings on land reclamation.[45]

For his part, Han Liangfu, having been scolded by his sovereign, set about to learn the "art of planning" and reported on his efforts in a 1724 memorial. His reclamation "plan" as presented to the emperor was nothing if not careful

[42] From the time of their military conquest of south China in the mid-seventeenth century, the Manchus had worried about malaria; their troops occupying Guilin in 1650 had been decimated by the disease. The problem continued to be so bad that in 1724 Han Liangfu requested that the usual three-year term of appointment for officials in the malaria-infested regions of Guangxi be shortened to decrease the likelihood that officials would be infected. Memorial dated YZ2.4i.17, in YZCZZ 2: 584.

[43] Hummel, *Emminent Chinese*, 455–57.

[44] Memorial dated YZ2.7.3, in YZCZZ 2: 837.

[45] *Huang chao jingshi wen bian*, juan 34: 34a–36a. Despite embellishments locating the land reclamation efforts in the context of a "doubling" of population during the Kangxi reign, as well as additions of specificity regarding which northern crops would fit conditions in Guangxi, Li Fu's text is lifted whole cloth from Han Liangfu's memorial, leading one to wonder whether this was shameless plagiarism or merely standard bureaucratic practice.

and cautious. Rather than a sweeping, provincewide initiative, Han proposed first doing a survey of a single county that he knew well, uncovering any hitherto unreported reclaimed land and compiling a "reliable" register of all land before developing an approach to reclaiming whatever wasteland might be found. The emperor told him to implement the plan.[46] Had Han achieved any success with his plan, it is not unreasonable to expect that he would have taken credit for it; in the absence of any such documents, though, we have to conclude that the first state-initiated land reclamation effort in Guangxi province was ineffectual.

Having been promoted to the governorship upon Li Fu's departure, Han did not want to be held accountable for his failure to implement the emperor's mandate and so he did the next best thing: he blamed the absence of demonstrable land reclamation in Guangxi upon farming practices in neighboring Guangdong province. Sometime in late 1726 or early 1727, Han complained to the emperor that Guangdong had become so taken with producing commercial crops that only one-half of the province's food needs for rice could be met by local production, the rest being imported from Guangxi.[47] This demand fostered a monoculture in Guangxi agriculture, with the result that no one was willing to open the more marginal lands unsuitable for rice. The Yongzheng emperor apparently agreed with the logic of Han's argument and in early 1727 ordered the governors of Guangdong and Fujian provinces to find a way to convince peasant-farmers in these commercialized areas to convert their fields back to grain production.[48]

The governors of Guangdong and Fujian, Yang Wenqian and Chang Lai, respectively, did not take the challenge lightly but fired off a rejoinder penned by Chang Lai.[49] Chang not only conceded Han's charge that agriculture had become specialized, but defended the specialization as creating greater wealth and called for the emperor to lift restrictions on foreign trade to allow even greater specialization and creation of wealth. The force of Chang's memorial no doubt halted Han's attempt to shift responsibility for his lack of success, for the emperor noted in his rescript on the memorial that he had heard similarly from Yang and the governor-general of Guangdong and Guangxi.

[46] Memorial dated YZ2.9.8, in YZCZZ 3: 155.

[47] I have not found Han's memorial, but from other sources have deduced both its existence and content. See the memorial from Chang Lai dated YZ5.4.13, in YZCZZ 8: 25–26 and the paraphrase of a Yongzheng edict dated YZ5.2, in Song, *Zhongguo lidai quan nong kao*, 76.

[48] Song, *Zhongguo lidai quan nong kao*, 76.

[49] Memorial dated YZ5.4.13, in YZCZZ 8: 25–26. That Chang and Yang had discussed the content of this memorial seems likely both by the extensive references to the situation in Guangdong and the fact that a month earlier they had worked together in a project regarding the maritime customs. See also Yang Wenqian's biography in *Qing shi lie juan* (Taibei: Zhonghua shuju, 1964), juan 13: 43a.

By the middle of his fifth year (1727), the Yongzheng emperor no doubt was becoming as frustrated as Han Liangfu at the inability of officials either to promote land reclamation or to report land that had in fact been brought back into production but not reported to evade taxation. To overcome the latter problem, the Yongzheng emperor ordered provincial officials to ferret out the "hidden land" and, as an incentive to the landholders, forgave all past taxes if they would just register the land.[50]

Guangdong. In the seventh month of 1727, the emperor received yet another memorial from a provincial official – this time from A-ke-dun, an official who held a number of posts in Guangdong and Guangxi from 1726 to 1728 – listing the obstacles in Guangdong to success of officially sponsored land reclamation plans, but with an analysis pointing the way to some accomplishments in Guangdong five years later. A-ke-dun recited the litany of reasons why land was either not being reclaimed or, if land had been reclaimed, it was not being reported and taxed.[51] To address the former, A-ke-dun formulated a six-point plan; to deal with the latter, he dusted off pages from the Shunzhi and Kangxi emperors' policies and proposed incentives to officials for uncovering and reporting land that had not yet been added to the tax rolls.[52] The paltry amount of land reported reclaimed in Guangdong following this memorial indicates both the lack of success that officials there had in coaxing landowners to report land and the lack of the emperor's support for A-ke-dun's proposal.

A-ke-dun's failure was just the latest in the string of unsuccessful attempts at state-sponsored land reclamation efforts in Guangdong. The next abortive attempt came in 1729 and is worth mentioning both for the information conveyed about the situation in Guangdong and as background and contrast for the land reclamation project launched shortly afterwards in Guangxi. In early 1729, the newly appointed financial commissioner for Guangdong province, Wang Shijun, requested permission from the emperor to apply the models of land reclamation pioneered in Zhili and Yunnan provinces to Guangdong. Wang was convinced that considerable reclaimable land remained in Guangdong, and used that argument as the basis for his request to launch a land reclamation project:

> The land area of Guangdong is vast, and the population is densely settled. But those who are engaged in commerce are many, while those who labor in the fields are few, so that the food harvested here is insufficient to meet the

[50] See the the emperor's edict excerpted in *Da Qing huidian shili*, 1875 ed. (Taibei: Wenhai chuban she, 1964), juan 166: 7a.

[51] Memorial dated YZ5.7.1, in YZHWZPZZ 10:101–103.

[52] See Peng, *Qing dai tudi kaiken shi*, 30–31, for the Shunzhi incentives and 43–45 for the Kangxi incentives.

> needs of the populace. Even in a good year rice must be purchased from Guangxi; when there are food shortages, the poor are defenseless.
>
> I have been in Guangdong for four years now, and in each of those years I have traveled [throughout the province] on official business. With my own eyes I have seen reclaimable wasteland in each prefecture; there are none without some, especially Zhaoqing, Gaozhou, Leizhou, and Lianzhoufu prefectures. The reasons given for the unclaimed land [there] include: "It's not on a waterway"; "Small folk don't have the wherewithal to undertake [reclamation]"; or "I once wanted to reclaim land, but I didn't have the right tools." For these reasons reclaimable land in Guangdong goes to waste and the province runs a food deficit.[53]

The Zhili model had been pioneered just a few years earlier and showed signs of success in bringing irrigation and rice production to the north China plain. Under the direction of the Yongzheng emperor's brother, Prince Yinxiang, nearly 600,000 *mu* of land was irrigated and planted in rice. Experienced farmers from the south taught peasants the techniques of planting rice, while rich farmers were enticed to plant rice with promises of low taxes and wealthy persons convicted of crimes could have their sentences commuted if they contributed to the project.[54]

The Yunnan model, developed by another of the emperor's favorites, the governor-general of Yunnan and Guizhou, E-er-tai, was designed to open up the vast frontier for agriculture. In exchange for monetary contributions, degree-holders received grants of land and then recruited tenants to do the actual reclamation.[55] The commonality of both the Zhili and Yunnan models was the enticement of land grants or commuted sentences in exchange for "contributions" (*juan na*) from degree-holders.

Financial Commissioner Wang Shijun was a bit apprehensive about indiscriminately applying the Zhili and Yunnan models to Guangdong, and so proposed instead a one-year trial period. "If rumor of this plan leaked and it did not discriminate by province in extending permission [to participate], all kinds of [Manchu] Bannermen and civilians would come to Guangdong seeking to make contributions."[56] As it was, the emperor did not think that conditions in Guangdong were sufficiently like those in the frontier regions of Yun-Gui or the arid north-China plain to warrant giving his approval, so the plan died.

Wang's memorial, though, did influence the thinking of the Yongzheng emperor about the other aspect of land reclamation that had given him and his officials some difficulty: unreported and untaxed land. To prove his case

[53] Memorial dated YZ7.3.3, in YZCZZ 12: 599.

[54] See Peng, *Qing dai tudi kaiken shi*, 98–99, and Pei Huang, *Autocracy at Work: A Study of the Yongcheng Period, 1723–1735* (Bloomington: Indiana University Press, 1974), 239–40.

[55] *Da Qing huidian shili*, juan 166: 6a–7a.

[56] Memorial dated YZ7.3.3, in YZCZZ 12: 600.

that sufficient reclaimable land existed in Guangdong, Wang had ordered detailed, county-by-county investigations and discovered that only 20–30 percent of the land that had been reclaimed had been reported[57] (as I will discuss later, I think that only 10 percent of reclaimed land was reported). Apparently impressed by Wang's efforts, a month later the emperor ordered all governors to investigate the amount of reclaimable land in their jurisdictions and to come up with plans for lending seed, draught animals, and provisions to settlers (all of which would be repaid within three years).[58] For his part, Wang Shijun proposed using the excess "meltage fees" (a tax surcharge levied to make up for silver lost when melted and recast as ingots) now remaining in the provincial coffer as a source of the loans, and the emperor agreed.[59] In the absence of any further documentation, it is not clear whether this state-promoted approach had any appreciable effect on land reclamation in Guangdong.

The one and only successful state-sponsored land reclamation project in Guangdong was launched in 1732 under the direction of the new governor-general, E-mi-da, but only after a serious false start.[60] E-mi-da's first stab at a project related to land reclamation – a request that the emperor approve a massive water control project costing 400,000 taels – was shot down with a terse "Nonsense!" from the emperor.[61] After this rebuke, E-mi-da turned his attention to the growing bandit problem in Guangdong. One of his first memorials as governor of Guangdong had been on bandits. "The cause [of banditry]," E-mi-da wrote, "can be found in poverty. The number of unemployed here is great." He then went on to suggest that resolution of the bandit problem could be linked to land reclamation in the sparsely populated prefectures of Gaozhou, Leizhou, and Lianzhoufu.[62] Building on this thought, E-mi-da formulated his major policy statement, submitted it to the emperor in mid-1732, and received approval to implement his plan.

There were so many poor, unemployed people in Guangdong, E-mi-da observed, that to find work they had to resort to contraband trade, illegal mining, or banditry, all of which led to disorder. His plan was to resettle the poor – especially those in the "overpopulated" prefectures of Chaozhou and Huizhou – in the sparsely populated regions of western Guangzhou prefecture and in Zhaoqing. His agents for the relocation would be "merchants with

57 Ibid., 599. 58 Edict of YZ7.4, excerpted in Song, *Zhongguo lidai quan nong kao*, 77.

59 Memorial dated YZ7.7.24, in YZCZZ 13: 703.

60 E-mi-da was governor-general of Guangdong, not Guangdong and Guangxi. In early 1730, the Yongzheng emperor had placed Guangxi under E-er-tai, who then became governor-general of Yunnan, Guizhou, and Guangxi. This administrative reallignment was connected with land reclamation plans, as will be noted later.

61 Memorial dated YZ9.7.15, in YZCZZ 18: 560–62.

62 Memorial dated YZ9.2.10, in *Yongzheng zhupi yuzhi*, 1738 ed. reprint (Taibei: Wenhai chuban she, 1965), E-mi-da memorials pt. 1: 19a–20b.

means," who, in return for title to the land would recruit poor families and provide them with shelter, provisions, and capital to get them started. Each merchant would be limited to 100 *mu*, upon which he would settle five tenant families, each with 20 *mu*. In newly created Heshan county alone (one of the areas devastated during the Ming–Qing transition), with its 33,000 *mu* of reclaimable land, E-mi-da figured his plan would result in 6,600 poor families being resettled. In Kaiping and Enping counties, E-mi-da estimated another 10,000–20,000 *mu* was available, with even larger quantities of reclaimable land further south and west in Gaozhou, Lianzhoufu, and Leizhou prefectures. To protect the new tenants from being turned out after laboring to bring the land into production, E-mi-da proposed granting them permanent tenure. In short, this was a win–win–win proposal: the poor would get permanent tenure, merchants would get title to 100 *mu* of land, and the state would transform potential bandit recruits into productive rate payers. The emperor saw it this way too: "For the poor to have such a situation found for them is excellent; make it so."[63]

Over the next two years, E-mi-da implemented his plan and added a few embellishments by expanding the class of people to be resettled to include bandits and the victims of an earlier natural disaster. E-mi-da had linked the bandit problem to the needs for land reclamation early in his tenure in Guangdong, and soon after receiving the emperor's approval for his reclamation plan, he was presented with an opportunity to make the linkage explicit. Bandits on the border between Guangzhou and Zhaoqing prefectures had been holding up merchants and other travelers, disrupting trade and communication along the important West River passage from Guangxi. The offer of rewards soon led to the capture of 55 bandits. Interrogation of the prisoners revealed, though, that 44 of those captured were merely "poor, unemployed people" who had taken to the hills to burn charcoal and that 20 of these were "peasants with farming skills." E-mi-da sought and received the emperor's approval to resettle those 20 in Heshan county. Each tenant was given 20 *mu* of land like the other settlers; but in addition, E-mi-da secured a guarantee from the landowners that the settlers would not return to a life of crime.[64]

Sensing the success he was achieving with his land reclamation plan, in early 1733 E-mi-da proposed resettling refugees from the 1727 and 1732 typhoons in the newly opened territory. The 1727 typhoon had hit eastern Guangdong from Chaozhou on down the coast to the Pearl River estuary just as the fall crop was ripening for harvest (for more detail, see Chapter 6). Homes were blown

[63] Memorial dated YZ10.6.9, in ibid., 56a–58b. Either in calculating or copying, an error was made in reporting the number of poor families that could be settled on the 33,000 *mu*. The printed text gives a figure of 1,600; the correct number should be 6,600.

[64] Memorials dated YZ10.9.19 and YZ10.12.1, in *Yongzheng zhupi yuzhi*, E-mi-da memorials pt. 1: 71a–74b and 83a–85a.

down, dozens were killed, and thousands of homeless, cropless survivors took to the road. According to E-mi-da, many relocated in Guangxi, Sichuan, and Taiwan. Similarly, a 1732 typhoon, while not as devastating, sent "500 a day" into Hunan. Commenting on this situation, E-mi-da proposed sending officials to those areas and recruiting the refugees into the resettlement program. Despite a sweeter land reclamation deal in Sichuan than what they could get in Guangdong (as of 1728, Sichuan officials had been authorized to offer settlers 30 *mu* of irrigated paddy land or 50 *mu* of dry land, and additional increments if they had brothers or sons who had come of age, over 700 families ultimately accepted the offer to return to Guangdong. Nonetheless, the emperor also approved this part of E-mi-da's plan, and hundreds were resettled in Heshan, Enping, and Kaiping counties (all areas afflicted by tenant-serf uprisings in the 1640s–1660s; see Chapter 4).[65]

By early 1735, E-mi-da felt sufficiently confident in the success of his program to report the results to the emperor. In the three targeted counties, over 200,000 *mu* had been resettled by 7,760 tenant farm families; and on the Leizhou Peninsula an additional 63,000 *mu* was being farmed by "more than" 2,500 households.[66] The program was so successful that the Yongzheng emperor helped even further. In a 1734 edict (probably in response to E-mi-da's request) discussed in the *Da Qing huidian shili*, the emperor stated that "the Cantonese only know how to work irrigated land, but not dry land. The land in Gaozhou, Leizhou, Lianzhoufu, and Qiongzhou prefectures is higher and suitable for vegetables and wheat. Settlers [there] are not knowledgeable about dry-land farming and do not have the right tools for the job." The Yongzheng emperor thus "ordered Shandong and Henan provinces to select 20 farmers who excel in dry-land farming and send them to Guangdong to instruct the settlers."[67] Not stopping there, E-mi-da proposed using state funds to develop irrigation works in the newly opened lands, again receiving approval from the emperor.[68]

Simultaneously with informing the emperor of this success story, the provincial governor, Wang Yongbin, sent the emperor another memorial lowering expectations of any further gains in land reclamation in Guangdong. Because of the relative overpopulation of Guangdong and the specialization of the labor force ("Those who work for wages, fish, work in the salt pans, and pick tea outnumber those who work in the fields"), only marginal lands remained. In 1731 provincial officials had stated that over 600,000 *mu* of land was reclaimable, but "in reality the amounts listed are either in the hills or are pebble-sized, so reclamation is difficult." Moreover, the land is "so infertile that

[65] Memorials dated YZ11.3.12, YZ11.5.10, YZ11.10.4, and YZ12.5.4, in ibid. pt. 2: 1a–2b, 3b–6b, 23a–25b, and 50a–51b; *Da Qing huidian shili*, juan 166:7a.

[66] Memorial dated YZ12.5.4, in *Yongzheng zhupi yuzhi*, E-mi-da memorials pt. 2: 50a–51b.

[67] *Da Qing huidian shili*, juan 166: 11a.

[68] Memorial dated YZ13.3.15, in YZCZZ 24: 252–53.

even in a good year the yield would be just one *shi* per *mu*; in a bad year the harvest would be even less and the people, not having enough to eat, would turn to banditry." Governor Wang's solution was to offer lower tax rates on these marginal lands to encourage land reclamation. By this time, though, even the emperor was becoming wary of unrestrained clearing of land in the hills because of the problems of soil erosion. Lands cleared in hilly areas and then planted were soon eroded by the rains, leaving only "stones and bones."[69]

Guangxi Redux. The success of the state-sponsored land reclamation project in Guangdong can be contrasted with a debacle in Guangxi.[70] About the same time that E-mi-da was developing his proposal for a land reclamation project in Guangdong, the governor of Guangxi province, Jin Hong, had been devising a rather different plan. Like Wang Shijun, the Guangdong provincial financial commissioner discussed earlier who had floated a land reclamation plan in 1729, Jin Hong also proposed applying the Yunnan model of land reclamation in his province. Unlike Wang Shijun's proposal, Jin Hong's was approved; and also unlike Wang Shijun himself, Jin Hong was not as cautious about the dangers of carpetbagging. The extension of the Yunnan model of land reclamation to Guangxi happened because the governor-general of Yunnan–Guizhou, E-er-tai, one of the Yongzheng emperor's three favorite officials, wanted it to happen.[71] In early 1730, the emperor placed Guangxi province under E-er-tai's jurisdiction, making him the governor-general of three provinces. Certainly such an administrative move made sense; like Yunnan and Guizhou, Guangxi was a sparsely populated frontier region confronting many of the same issues, including land reclamation and "pacification" of the aboriginal population.

Soon after receiving responsibility for Guangxi, E-er-tai toured the province and reported his observations to the emperor. In addition to assessing the communication and transportation network (no doubt in preparation for military action against aboriginal tribes, should it be necessary), E-er-tai commented on the vast tracts of fertile, uncultivated land that he saw. He reported to the emperor that Jin Hong would be preparing a plan to bring this land into production.[72]

Under the Yunnan model, degree-holders received grants of land in return for contributions (*juan na*), and then recruited tenants to bring the land into production. Additionally, the state would provide start-up funds (loans of 2–3

[69] *Da Qing huidian shili*, juan 166: 10b.

[70] My interpretation of this affair draws heavily upon William T. Rowe, "The State and Land Development in the Mid-Qing: Guangxi Province, 1723–37," unpublished paper presented at the 1992 annual meeting of the American Historical Association. Professor Rowe has kindly consented to my use and citation of his paper.

[71] Ibid., 5–8. [72] Memorial dated YZ13.8.1, in YZCZZ 15: 463–67.

taels for each 10 *mu* cultivated to be repaid over a three-year period).[73] When these incentives yielded less than spectacular results, Jin Hong requested and received in addition the emperor's approval to restore rank to disgraced or demoted officials who assumed responsibility for bringing land into production.[74] No doubt since this provision had already been shown to be an effective tool in the Zhili case, the Yongzheng emperor approved its use in Guangxi.

The results, as Jin Hong reported to the emperor in a series of progress reports, were quite spectacular: by 1735, nearly 500,000 *mu* of land was reported to have been reclaimed, and over 500,000 taels had been contributed.[75] In reality, though, nothing like this happened. Just as Wang Shijun had predicted when he floated his proposal to apply the Yunnan and Zhili models to Guangdong, carpetbagging "bannermen and civilians" from all over had flocked to Guangxi, getting their ranks restored along with title to land in return for contributions. The Guangxi land giveaway, though, did not go unnoticed.

By claiming such huge amounts of newly reclaimed land, Jin Hong also increased the tax liability of the counties within which the land had been reported. Complaints about Jin's management of Guangxi's land reclamation reached the emperor by way of Chen Hongmou, a native of the area around Guilin, then serving as Yunnan's financial commissioner.[76] Chen alleged five faults in Guangxi's land reclamation program that, if true, all pointed to the likely falsification of land reclamation figures.[77] In the imperial rescript on Chen's memorial (apparently not in the Yongzheng emperor's handwriting), the incoming governor-general, Yin-ji-shan, was instructed to investigate and convey his conclusions to the emperor. Yin-ji-shan was either slow or thorough, for his report was not concluded for another two years.[78] In the meantime, Jin Hong reported the ever-increasing amount of land being reclaimed. Even as late as mid-1734, Jin Hong appeared unaware that his management of land reclamation was under investigation and proudly reported an additional 17,000 *mu* reclaimed as a result of nearly 100,000 taels contributed.[79]

Within six months of his 1734 report, though, Jin Hong apparently became aware of the investigation. In his next report submitted in early 1735, Jin recited the history of the Guangxi land reclamation plan and then launched a counterattack against the local gentry. Jin charged that the local gentry, small

[73] *Da Qing huidian shi li*, juan 166: 8b–9a.

[74] Memorials dated YZ10.1.12, in YZCZZ 19: 301–302, and YZ12.12.17, in YZCZZ 23: 894–96.

[75] See Jin Hong's memorials dated YZ10.1.12, in YZCZZ 19: 301–302; YZ11.4.2, in YZCZZ 21: 343; YZ11.11.18, in YZCZZ 22; 351; and YZ12.5.27, in YZCZZ 23: 107.

[76] Without Rowe's account, I would have been unaware of this aspect of the case.

[77] Memorial dated YZ11.3.1, in YZCZZ 21: 194–95.

[78] Memorial dated YZ13.2.4, in YZCZZ 24: 104–108.

[79] Memorial dated YZ12.5.27, in YZCZZ 23: 107.

in number but with a tight grip on local society, had hidden vast amounts of land from taxation, especially in the agriculturally rich prefectures of Guilin, Liuzhou, Xunzhou, and Si'en. Rather than sitting back passively to the challenge that these local gentry posed, Jin asked permission to do a land survey not just to uncover the hidden land, but to address two other issues as well. Noting the absence of "fish-scale" land registers in Guangxi, Jin argued that a cadastral survey could resolve the endless conflict between "gentry and commoners, landlords and tenants" over land rights. Similarly, a land survey would reveal any land that had been reported as reclaimed but not actually in production.[80]

The emperor did not comment on Jin Hong's memorial, and two months later Yin-ji-shan's report was sent to the emperor. Yin-ji-shan summarized Chen Hongmou's charges, and then in detail substantiated each one: the amount of reclaimable land indeed was vastly overstated; Jin Hong and other local officials had "turned falsehoods into truths" in reporting land reclamation figures; restoring cashiered extraprovincial officials' rank in exchange for contributions and title to the land was meaningless (*you ming wu shi*); and a form of "claim jumping" had occurred whereby tillers of hidden land came under the wing of the carpetbaggers.[81] As Yin-ji-shan's report wended its way through the bureaucracy, Jin Hong continued with his land reclamation plan, reporting in May 1735 an additional 20,000 *mu* reclaimed and 100,000 taels received.[82]

What happened after this is not at all clear, for a number of reasons: the Yongzheng emperor died suddenly (in October), throwing the push for land reclamation into question; Jin Hong was called to the capital for an imperial audience with the new Qianlong emperor and then impeached on other charges by the acting governor;[83] and the preservation of officials' memorials from the early Qianlong period is not as complete as for the Yongzheng period. Presumably Yin-ji-shan's report was turned over to E-mi-da sometime in 1735 or 1736, when Guangxi was returned to his jurisdiction as governor-general of Guangdong and Guangxi, for in mid-1737 E-mi-da reported his concerns about the case to the Qianlong emperor.

In brief, E-mi-da did not quite know who to believe or what to do. On the

80 Memorial dated YZ12.12.17, in YZCZZ 23: 894–96.

81 Memorial dated YZ13.2.4, in YZCZZ 24: 104–108.

82 Memorial dated YZ13.4.20, in YZCZZ 24: 414.

83 See the entries in *Da Qing gao zong (Qianlong) shi lu*, juan 18: 14b; juan 24: 2b; juan 39: 24a–b; and juan 40: 25b–26a. Whether or not Jin Hong was summoned to Beijing is unclear. He may have been summoned to explain his inordinate number of memorials on the "Miao problem" in Guangxi, for even after being summoned, Jin continued to report land reclamation figures (see *Da Qing gao zong (Qianlong) shi lu*, juan 32: 7b and 40: 7a). Meanwhile, the acting governor accused Jin of financial misdealings with a state apothecary and shortly afterwards impeached Jin for fiscal mismanagement.

one side stood Chen Hongmou's charges and the existence of untilled land; on the other was the fact that gentry had indeed hidden "not insubstantial amounts of land." Furthermore, E-mi-da had evidence that Chen Hongmou's charges were not completely factual: of the 200,000 *mu* Chen claimed had been falsely reported and of which not a single *mu* actually was tilled, E-mi-da found just 120,000 *mu*. Moreover, E-mi-da found evidence that "substantial amounts of land had in fact been newly reclaimed" and were under the plow. To adjudicate the matter, E-mi-da asked that a senior official be sent to Guangxi. The Qianlong emperor demurred. Since the newly appointed governor of Guangxi, Yang Chaozeng, had not sided with Jin Hong and in fact was partial to Chen Hongmou, he ordered E-mi-da and Yang to prepare a joint memorial on the case.[84]

That memorial was delivered in late 1737. E-mi-da and Yang Chaozeng reported that they had concluded the Guangxi land reclamation investigation – "distinguishing among the land that should be taxed, [the taxes] that should be reduced, and [the taxes] that should be eliminated" – and enclosed a list of the recommended changes. The emperor ordered them to implement their recommendations accordingly.[85]

The list of adjustments to the tax base is not available, so it is not possible to tell just how far taxes were rolled back or how much land was added to the tax rolls either because of the discovery of hidden lands or the confirmation of newly reclaimed land. Whatever the balance may have been, we can be certain that local gentry domination of Guangxi local society, while challenged for a brief moment, had been reaffirmed.[86] Some may have wound up paying slightly higher taxes, but a new, carpetbagging elite had not replaced them.

But the story does not end there. Throughout the empire, provincial officials had acted upon the Yongzheng emperor's decree to bring more land into production and, like Jin Hong, had reported ever-increasing amounts of reclaimed land and thus higher tax quotas. Predictably, this dynamic and the abuses it spawned aroused the opposition of local gentry, like those in Guangxi, whose interests were being challenged,[87] drawing the attention and sympathy

84 *Da Qing gao zong (Qianlong) shi lu*, juan 45: 18b–20b.

85 Ibid., juan 55: 15b–16a.

86 As for Chen Hongmou, he exhibited a display of extremely poor timing, which aroused the emperor's ire. Just after E-mi-da had written to the emperor saying that "Chen Hongmou's memorial was not factual" but before the final, joint memorial from E-mi-da and Yang Chaozeng disposing of the matter, Chen apparently sent another memorial to the throne pushing his case. This time the emperor had had it and sent off a blistering edict to the Grand Council blasting Chen for his impertinence. Ibid., juan 53: 14b–15a.

87 Rowe sees Chen Hongmou as a representative of the local landlord gentry in Guilin and argues that "the Guangxi experience was replicated in much of the empire." Rowe, "The State and Land Development in the mid-Qing," 23.

of higher-level officials, some of whom had the ear of the new emperor. Thus, among the Qianlong emperor's first acts was to change the state land reclamation policy.

The occasion for the policy change was a memorial by Grand Secretary Zhu Shi, sent in the first month of the new emperor's reign. Zhu argued that virtually all productive land had been brought into production and that further, unfettered clearing of marginal land led to erosion and silting of rivers. The newly reclaimed land was so marginally productive that several *mu* had to be combined into one "fiscal *mu*" to yield the tax of one regular *mu*, leading to erroneous suspicions that land had been "hidden." In terms of the state bureaucracy, the rush to report reclaimable land had produced falsified figures, especially in Sichuan, Henan, and (not surprisingly) Guangxi. Finally, Zhu argued, the level of taxation had been set by the Kangxi emperor's promise never to raise taxes, so there was little to be gained by reporting reclaimed land. Zhu Shi concluded by asking that land surveys undertaken in a search for hidden land be called off and that provincial officials audit previously reported figures to uncover and exclude falsifications. The Qianlong emperor replied, "Advice accepted; speedily implement."[88]

Concurrently with the acceptance of Zhu Shi's memorial, the Qianlong emperor issued an edict to all governors and governors-general prohibiting the falsification of land reclamation figures. The emperor pointed out the "especially large" totals for Henan and Fujian provinces, investigation of which showed a large proportion to be without foundation. "In name this is land reclamation, but in reality it is an [unwarranted] increase in taxes."[89]

In the provincial audits conducted over the next few years, a large proportion of the land reportedly reclaimed in the Yongzheng period was struck from the ledgers. In Henan province, for instance, half of the 2 million *mu* reported was found to be unclaimed; and in Hubei, the land reclamation figures were slashed by more than half. Throughout the empire, nearly 4 million *mu* were eliminated from the tax base as having been falsely reported.[90] None of the figures for Guangxi supplied by E-mi-da and Yang Chaozeng to the emperor were reported in the *Qing shi lu*, and that source mentions just 43,530 *mu* excluded from Guangdong province tax rolls (on Hainan Island).[91]

Despite the Qianlong emperor's abandonment of the aggressive state-sponsored land reclamation policy favored by his father, the experience of

[88] Zhu Shi memorial dated YZ13.10.x, summarized in Peng, *Qing dai tudi kaiken shi*, 119–20.

[89] *Da Qing gao zong (Qianlong) shi lu*, juan 4: 37a–38a. Interestingly, the emperor did not mention Guangxi in his list of provincial prevarications, no doubt because the matter was still up in the air. Could Chen Hongmou have missed the significance of this omission from the emperor's list?

[90] Peng, *Qing dai tudi kaiken shi*, 124, gives a total of 3.8 million *mu* compiled from the available written sources. Guangxi is not included in Peng's total.

[91] *Da Qing gao zong (Qianlong) shi lu*, juan 83: 3.

Guangdong and Guangxi provinces as symbolized by the differing plans devised by Jin Hong and E-mi-da left an ambiguous legacy. In Guangxi, the incentives concocted by the provincial officials to lure disgraced officials into large-scale land development schemes proved to be a disaster. In Guangdong on the other hand, E-mi-da's plan successfully resettled unemployed and landless peasants to bring new land into production. Certainly the approaches taken by Jin Hong and E-mi-da partially account for the different outcomes. Where Jin Hong could find takers only with the promise that their rank would be restored, E-mi-da sought out merchants "with means" and limited their land grants to 100 *mu* each. Other than receiving title to the land, the merchants received nothing else in return, and indeed even had to pledge that their settlers would remain law abiding.

Perhaps more important, though, the different outcomes of state-sponsored land reclamation projects in Guangdong and Guangxi provinces point to the ways in which social and economic conditions in the two provinces differed. In Guangdong, population had grown so much and economic specialization had proceeded so far that landlessness, unemployment, and banditry had become serious problems. That the landless and unemployed in Guangdong did not strike out on their own to settle land had to do both with their lack of capital, seed, and provisions and with continuing opportunities for them to scrape together a living on the edges of the urban economy. Economic development also had created a class of wealthy merchants with sufficient capital to invest in land.

In sparsely populated Guangxi, on the other hand, agriculture had become nearly a monoculture producing rice for the Guangdong market. Without population pressure, it is hardly surprising that few ventured on their own to open lands that could not easily produce rice for the expanding Guangdong market. In short, in the early eighteenth century there was apparently insufficient demographic or economic reason to open new lands in Guangxi province. But with population and the demand for rice increasing, settlers in Guangxi too would soon begin opening new land.

Into the Hills and Down to the Valleys

With the ascension of the Qianlong emperor to the throne in late 1735, the Qing state retreated from trying to increase the land under cultivation by giving incentives for large-scale land development projects. Given the policy tone set by Zhu Shi's memorial and the Qianlong emperor's acceptance of the general policy, even modest (and successful) land development projects like E-mi-da's Guangdong plan were too large. Indeed, when the new state policy was articulated in 1740, only the reclamation of "scattered plots" by individual and probably poor peasant families would be encouraged by the state:

> In each province, the population has increased, cultivable land cannot be expanded, and yet the poor have no way to make a living . . . But in mountainous regions with few fields, vacant land on the hill tops is relatively abundant and may be suitable for planting rice or miscellaneous crops . . . Henceforth, all frontier provinces (*bian sheng*) with cultivable scattered plots in the interior are to extend tax exemptions to [Han Chinese] and tribesmen (*yi*) who till these plots.[92]

The interpretation of "frontier provinces" was exceptionally broad, in fact including all provinces with any hilly or mountainous land at all. The scope of "scattered plots" exempted from taxes by statute, though, varied by province. In Guangxi, paddies of 1 *mu* or less and dry land of 3 *mu* or less were tax exempt, while "in those parts of Guangdong, such as hilltops and ridges, where the land slopes, the soil is gravelly and the rain runs off or dissipates, and people are trying to till it, the land is tax exempt."[93] In practice, the tax exemption was extended to the coastal plains of southwest Guangdong province in Gaozhou, Lianzhoufu, and the Leizhou Peninsula, regardless of how much land was tilled.[94]

Under this new policy, a considerable amount of land, most of which was in the hills in the northern and northeastern sections of Guangdong and in the river valleys of western and northern Guangxi, or in the southwestern littoral, was cleared and planted. Officials continued to report the amounts of land cleared, some of which then were listed at various times in the *Qing shi lu*, our only surviving record of the official tally. With missing years and considerable amounts of cleared land left out from the official count, only a fraction of the total has been captured in the official records. For Guangdong, according to figures tabulated from the *Qing shi lu* for the years from 1737 to 1800, about 800,000 *mu* of land was cleared for cultivation, or about 1,500 *mu* per recorded year.[95] In Guangxi the reported amounts were considerably less, just 150,000 *mu*, and most of that was irrigated paddy.

Over the century from 1753 to 1851, official state figures for Lingnan register just a 10 percent increase in the amount of cultivated land, an amount more or less in line with the amount of land reported as reclaimed and added to the tax rolls. These official figures, though, are notoriously inaccurate, not just because the Qing state never conducted a land survey to begin with, but also because of underreporting of new lands brought into cultivation and the conversion of the *mu* from a measure of land area to a measure of tax liabil-

[92] *Da Qing huidian shili*, juan 164; edict quoted in Peng, *Qing dai tudi kaiken shi*, 125.

[93] *Da Qing huidian shili*, juan 164; edict quoted in Peng, *Qing dai tudi kaiken shi*, 127.

[94] Three years earlier, in 1737, the governor of Guangdong had requested and received lower tax rates on "hard to reclaim land" in the southwest littoral. See the brief note discussing Yang Yongbin's memorial in *Da Qing gao zong (Qianlong) shi lu*, juan 37: 2a–b (entries for the second month of QL2).

[95] Chen, *Shichang jizhi*, 1992, 160–62.

ity (two or three *mu* of dry land, for instance, was taxed at the rate of one *mu* of irrigated land and therefore registered as one, not three, *mu*).

However, if the estimates of cultivated land I provided at the beginning of this chapter are more accurate than the Qing figures, then the state added to the official cultivated land figures only about one-tenth of the amount actually reclaimed in the eighteenth and nineteenth centuries. Even if my estimates of cultivated land area are high by 10–20 percent – or even 50 percent, for that matter – the implications are worth mentioning. If the amount of land under cultivation around 1713–33 represented the maximum that had been reached in either the Song or Ming, then all the land that was brought into production after that was being tilled for the first time. And that was not a small amount of land: between 1693 and 1853, an additional 20 million *mu* were brought into production in each Guangdong and Guangxi province, doubling to over 80 million *mu* the cultivated land acreage in Lingnan, most of which was marginal, hilly land. In terms of the percentage of the total Lingnan land area under cultivation, the amount increased from about 7 percent around 1713 to 13 percent in 1853, an increase of some 25,000 square kilometers of land brought under the plow. Importantly, the amount of cultivated land in Guangdong did not increase after 1853, indicating that the limits of cultivable land had been reached by then.[96] Obviously, the vast eighteenth-century land reclamation project had immense implications for the environment of Lingnan, and I will discuss those consequences in the next chapter.

Conclusion

As the population doubled during the eighteenth century, peasant-farmers more intensely farmed land that was already under the plow, and the growing pressure of people on the land prompted the state to promote land reclamation programs. Whether these programs were the large land development schemes of the Yongzheng emperor or the more laissez-faire policies favored by the Qianlong emperor, the land that was brought into cultivation during the eighteenth century was not old, abandoned farmland, but land that had not been farmed before. And because of the way in which land reclamation unfolded during the Qing (with the policies of the Qianlong emperor being the most important), most of the additional 25,000 square kilometers brought under the plow in the eighteenth century were "odd lots" in the hills.

96 In the mid-1980s, there were 48 million *mu* cultivated; see Wu Youwen et al., eds., *Guangdong sheng jingji dili* (Beijing: Xinhua chuban she, 1985), 14–17. One reason for the smaller 1980s total is that with population growth since 1949, towns and cities have expanded over arable land, taking land out of cultivation. See Vaclav Smil, *China's Environmental Crisis: An Inquiry into the Limits of National Development* (Armonk, NY: Sharpe, 1992), 56–57.

Clearly, much land had to have been deforested in the process, as we will see in the next chapter. One can only wonder whether the outcome would have been different had the policies of the Yongzheng emperor been followed instead.

As it was, with the population continuing to grow in the nineteenth century and the limits of cultivable land in Guangdong reached by 1850, a critical point had been reached. How much more intensely could the land be farmed to sustain a growing population? Without modern inputs, in particular of chemical fertilizers and insecticides, how much more could yields be raised? With the technologies then available, how many more people could the land sustain?

To people living on ever-smaller plots of land, though, those were not the questions. For them, with the extent of cultivable land in Guangdong reached by midcentury, with farming techniques as developed as possible, and with yields stagnating, the question became one of obtaining more land at the expense of one's neighbors. Thus, fights between neighbors over land, water, and hills with trees became endemic in Lingnan[97] by the middle of the nineteenth century, contributing to the lineage conflicts and feuds that so distinguished the region,[98] to the conflict between Hakka and Punti (*kejia* and *bendi*, "guests" and "natives"), including the rise of the Taipings in Guangxi province,[99] to the rise of secret societies and sworn brotherhoods,[100] and to the mass uprisings in the 1850s.[101] Given the importance of Lingnan in China's modern (i.e., post–Opium War, ca. 1850) history, I think that the connections between the emerging ecological crisis and the various social movements that originated there are more than coincidental, but making that case is beyond the scope of this book. Suffice it to say here that with population densities in Guangdong increasing from about 60 to 105 persons per square kilometer over the century from 1750 to 1850, many people began developing survival strategies that did not include just farming the land. But the hunger for land affected not merely human relations with other humans. For the clearance of land in the eighteenth and nineteenth centuries precipitated crises for other species as well.

97 For examples in eastern Guangdong, see Marks, *Rural Revolution in South China*, 60–75.

98 See Harry Lamley, "Hsieh-tou: The Pathology of Violence in Southeastern China," *Ch'ing shih wen-t'i* 3 (1977): 1–39.

99 See Jen Yu-wen, *The Taiping Revolutionary Movement* (New Haven: Yale University Press, 1973).

100 See Robert Antony, *Pirates, Bandits, and Brotherhoods: A Study of Crime and Law in Kwangtung Province, 1796–1839* (University of Hawaii, Ph.D. dissertation, 1988).

101 See especially Frederic Wakeman Jr., *Strangers at the Gate: Social Disorder in South China, 1839–1861* (Berkeley and Los Angeles: University of California Press, 1966).

10

"PEOPLE SAID THAT EXTINCTION WAS NOT POSSIBLE":

THE ECOLOGICAL CONSEQUENCES OF LAND CLEARANCE

Opening the hills of Lingnan to cultivation by peasant families was made possible not simply by state policies favoring the development of "scattered plots," but also by New World foods that thrived in dry, hilly land and, where feasible, by irrigation techniques mastered over the centuries. Then, encouraged by the state and armed with new crops and tried-and-true irrigation technologies, settlers headed for the far corners of Lingnan. Peasant-farmers had long tilled the river valleys in northern and northeastern Guangdong, but the record of new dams and reservoirs in the second half of the eighteenth century (to be discussed later) chart additional penetration there,[1] while in Guangxi an official stated in 1751 that in the western highlands under his jurisdiction (Sicheng, Zhen'an and Si'en prefectures along the Zuo River), "all the river valleys have received irrigation and all the hills planted with dry rice."[2] And in 1752, Guangdong Governor Suchang noted that "the poor in the hills of eastern Guangdong all plant sweet potatoes and miscellaneous crops (*za liang*)."[3]

New World Crops

As Governor Suchang makes clear, by the middle of the eighteenth century New World food crops had become an important part of the peasant-farmer's basket of crops. In addition to sweet potatoes, peanuts, maize, and tobacco, all had been brought to China in the sixteenth century by the New World traders who sought silks and porcelains for the European market. And the record is clear that peasant-farmers quickly introduced these new crops into their rotation. In the early sixteenth century, peasant-farmers in the Jiangnan region were planting peanuts, and by the last quarter of that century, peasants

[1] The history of waterworks will be taken up in more detail later in this chapter.
[2] Memorial dated QL16.11.3, in QLCZZ 1: 836.
[3] Memorial dated QL17.11.8, in QLCZZ 4: 251–53.

planted maize in Yunnan and Henan, about the same time that sweet potatoes were being planted in Fujian and Guangdong.[4]

The earliest record of sweet potatoes in Lingnan comes from an entry in the Dongguan county gazetteer in 1580, when one Chen Wen brought back some sweet potatoes from Annam (present-day Vietnam). Another source dates the introduction of sweet potatoes in Chaozhou prefecture to 1584. Whatever the exact date was, it clearly was in the late sixteenth century; within a very short period of time thereafter, sweet potatoes were planted throughout Guangdong province. By the late seventeenth century it was reported, "Sweet potatoes are planted everywhere."[5] In contrast, maize, according to Qu Dajun, "is not eaten much in Lingnan."[6]

Given the importance of the cultivation of maize both to patterns of migration and environmental change in the hills south of the Yangzi River,[7] its absence in Lingnan is curious. Several observers have offered their explanations, mostly extolling the virtues of sweet potatoes. According to Qu Dajun, writing around the turn of the eighteenth century, "The sweet potato has recently been introduced from Luzon. It is very easy to grow, the leaves can be used to fatten pigs, the roots can be fermented into liquor, and they can be dried and stored. In Zidanchengjia (?) where there are many people over 100 years old, they do not eat the five grains but only sweet potatoes."[8] The sweet potato grew rapidly, and in times of harvest failure, according to Xu Guangqi, the author of the late-seventeenth-century *Nong zheng chuan shu*, it "can be used for famine relief."[9] Finally, the sweet potato was a high-yielding crop, producing as much as 10 *shi* per *mu*, a yield exceeding nearly all other crops: "A family with one *mu* can be sustained with one harvest of sweet potatoes."[10] According to Guo Songyi, a modern historian, the reason for the differential acceptance of maize and the sweet potato in Lingnan was threefold: the sweet potato had many uses, it was easy to plant, and it had a high yield.[11] All of these could also be said about maize, so perhaps American corn simply was more unpalatable to the south Chinese than even the sweet potato.

Besides, planting sweet potatoes required "no fertilizer" and "little labor," and they could be planted in hilly, sandy, and dry soil that had little or no other use.[12] In the sugarcane-growing and silk districts, this attribute of the sweet

[4] The classic article on the subject is Ping-ti Ho, "The Introduction of American Food Plants into China," *American Anthropologist* 57 (1955): 191–201.

[5] Sources cited in Chen Shuping, "Yumi he fanshu zai Zhongguo juanfan qingkuang yanjiu," *Zhongguo shehui kexue* 3 (1980): 193–95.

[6] Qu, *Guangdong xin yu*, juan 14.

[7] See Anne Osbourne, "The Local Politics of Land Reclamation in the Lower Yangzi Highlands," *Late Imperial China* 15, no. 1 (June 1994): 1–46.

[8] Quoted in Guo Songyi, "Yumi, fanshu zai Zhongguo juanfan zhong de yi xie wenti," *Qingshi luncong* 7 (1986): 96.

[9] Quoted in ibid., 97.

[10] Quoted in ibid., 102.

[11] Ibid., 96.

[12] Quoted in ibid., 102.

potato was especially noteworthy, for it meant that it did not compete with other crops for land. With increasing demand for sugar, fruits, or silk, peasant-farmers could convert rice paddy to those purposes and simultaneously plant sweet potatoes on previously marginal land, as was the case around the town of Shilong, a fruit and sugar center.[13]

Where sweet potatoes supplemented the diet of the relatively poor, peanuts were a cash crop, sold in the market to pressers for their oils. The peanut shells then were fed to pigs, dumped into fish ponds, or spread as fertilizer on the sugarcane fields. And also unlike sweet potatoes, peanuts actually improved the fertility of marginal soils by fixing nitrogen in the soil.

Tobacco was different from all of the other New World crops. Not only was it a purely commercial crop that could not be eaten; its nutrient demands exhausted the soils. And also unlike sweet potatoes and peanuts, which peasant-farmers in the late sixteenth century clearly had adopted, tobacco was slow to spread in Lingnan, becoming significant only in the eighteenth century. Because of its high market value, tobacco was eminently suited for the scattered plots opened under the Qianlong emperor's land reclamation policy of the 1750s. According to the 1819 edition of the Nanxiong gazetteer, tobacco began to be planted "40 or 50 years ago . . . The profit obtained is much greater than rice. But the tobacco is all planted on the hill tops. As soon as the land is opened, the soil deteriorates and erodes. Any heavy rain silts the rivers and there is fear of imminent flooding. But because of the large profit it is tolerated. The locals [now] are forbidden to open any new land so as to correct the situation."[14]

Ecological Consequences of Land Clearance

The brief entry in the Nanxiong gazetteer highlights two of the most significant ecological impacts of opening hill lands for cultivation: deforestation followed by increased erosion, and siltation of riverbeds. From the northernmost edge of the Lingnan drainage system, silt from newly opened land planted with tobacco or sweet potatoes flowed downstream, past the Sang Yuan Wei levee at the beginning of the Pearl River delta. And just as the Yuan- and Ming-era pioneers in the delta captured the silt to create the *shatan* fields, so too in the eighteenth century did the silt provide the raw material for adding more *shatan* to the delta. This time, though, the new *shatan* did not just extend the cultivated land area, but began to obstruct the flow of water through the delta, increasing the danger of flooding.

Records of serious floods in 1694 and 1743 showed that while *shatan* existed then, they had not impeded the river.[15] But in 1751, when the governor of

[13] Qu Dajun, quoted in Chen, "Yumi he fanshu," 202.

[14] *Nanxiong zhouzhi*, 1819 ed., juan 9: 35a.

[15] Peng, *Qing dai tudi kaiken shi*, 168.

Guangdong province, Suchang, investigated the condition of water flow in the Pearl River delta channels, he concluded that half of the 38 *shatan* dikes in Nanhai, Panyu, and Shunde counties so obstructed the river that he ordered them destroyed. Despite the probable destruction of the offending *shatan*,[16] construction of new ones continued. Finally, in 1765, a year after serious flooding destroyed embankments throughout the delta but especially in Nanhai county, the governor prohibited new construction of *shatan*, prompting greater vigilance of the dikes in the years afterwards. In early 1769, the governor memorialized that "the three prefectures of Guangzhou, Zhaoqing, and Chaozhou all have diked fields (*wei tian*). In the summer and fall, flood waters are held in check by the *wei tian* dikes. During the agricultural slack season, I have ordered district officials to lead owners and tenants in cooperative efforts to strengthen and raise the level of the dikes."[17] Despite concern about flooding, the ban was rescinded three years later on the condition that new *shatan* not obstruct the river,[18] but the condition was not met. By the early nineteenth century, so much *shatan* had been created on both sides of the channel in an area called Wan Ding Sha separating Dongguan from Xiangshan county that gentry leaders from each side fought over which county the *shatan* belonged to, each hoping to secure the rents. Officials split the land between the two counties, awarding 67,000 *mu* to Dongguan.[19]

Water Control and Irrigation

As will be recalled from Chapters 2 and 3, the construction of waterworks in Lingnan had begun in Tang and Song times and continued in the Ming. In the Qing, most of the earlier waterworks were maintained, while the eighteenth-century expansion of population and cultivated land area saw a new building spurt. The construction of the new waterworks did not merely accompany the development of the new land brought into cultivation during the eighteenth century, but in many cases was a condition for transforming land from "waste" into agricultural uses. The Pearl River delta *shatan*, of course, simply would not have existed without embankments; but fields elsewhere in Lingnan too required waterworks either to protect them from flooding or to provide the regular source of water required for wet-rice cultivation. Still other places needed reservoirs to enable peasant-farmers to

[16] Given the wealth and power of the *shatan* owners, Suchang's actions no doubt caused significant turmoil, but because most state memorials from the first 17 years of the Qianlong reign have been lost, the story cannot be told.

[17] Memorial dated QL33.11.14, in QLCZZ 32: 486.

[18] *Nanhai xianzhi*, 1835 ed., juan 16.

[19] Wang, "Qing ji Zhujiang sanjiaozhou de nongtian shuili," 583. The Dongguan gentry had wanted the rents from all the lands to support their academies.

grow more than one crop per year. Water control in Lingnan thus was not of a single type, but of several kinds designed to accomplish different ends.

From the several score of different names given to the waterworks listed in provincial gazetteers, five or six different types can be identified. The first type was designed for flood control and existed mostly to protect urban populations in prefectural or county cities. Called *yu an* or *ti* dikes, these projects were first constructed in Song times and in much of Guangdong had reached their peak numbers by the mid-sixteenth century. Increases in the numbers of *yu an* or *ti* from the Ming through the Qing can be identified only in Panyu county in Guangzhou (no doubt designed to protect the city of Guangzhou), in Chenghai county in Chaozhou prefecture (in the Han River delta where the city of Shantou was developing), and on Hainan Island. In Guangxi, though, several new dikes were constructed in the eighteenth century, especially in Pingle (along the Li River), Wuzhou (along the West River), and Xunzhou (along the Yu and West Rivers).

Related to flood control dikes were the "enclosures" (*ji wei* or *wei tian*) primarily designed to regulate water in *shatan* fields bordering the river channels in the Pearl River delta. The great dikes built at the beginning of the Pearl River delta in the Song – the Sang Yuan Wei, for instance – not only provided flood control, but also made draining the swamps in Sanshui and Nanhai counties possible. Often translated as "polder," the *ji wei* did not keep out tidewaters, but rather freshwater. Where the 1561 edition of the Guangdong provincial gazetteer lists *ji wei* enclosures in Xinhui and Sanshui, the category was dropped in the 1731 edition but returned in the 1822 edition. Between 1561 and 1822, the number of *ji wei* in Xinhui and Sanshui remained constant, but additional ones were built in Nanhai, Shunde, and Xinning counties. Interestingly, in the 1561 gazetteer, *shatan* were distinguished from *ji wei*, but were not listed as a category of waterworks in later editions of the gazetteer.

To make dikes and enclosed fields useful, irrigation structures required openings of various kinds and sophistication, called passages (*guan*), gates (*men*), or sluice gates (*zha*). *Guan* may have been simply depressions in earthen banks that could be filled in with dirt to close off the water flow, while *men* probably were wooden structures that could be lifted to allow water in. The most elaborate were the *zha*, constructed of stone with wooden gates that could be opened and closed depending on the need for water.

A second major category of waterworks included reservoirs called *pi*, *ti*, *tang*, or *keng*. Since each of these had a different name, presumably they were somewhat different. "That which catches overflow waters is called a *tang*," according to a brief definition in the 1731 Guangdong provincial gazetteer, while "that which stores water is called a *keng*."[20] *Pi* and *ti*, on the other hand, were semidamlike structures in streams or rivers designed to back up the water into pools,

[20] *Guangdong tongzhi*, 1731 ed., juan 15.

from which the calmed water could be lifted by hand or waterwheel to the fields. The *pi* dam and *tang* reservoir were the most numerous type of waterworks listed in the provincial gazetteers.

A third type of waterwork consisted of dams (*ba*) and weirs (*yan*). Unlike *pi* or *ti*, which were only partially built into a stream, these structures spanned the watercourse. Dams were designed to block the water more or less completely, while weirs might be seen as low dams over the top of which water continued to flow, while enough backed up behind it to be useful for irrigation purposes. Dams might have been useful directly for irrigation, but it seems that they might have been the anchor of larger, more complex sets of waterworks that included ditches (*gou*), sluices (*han*), or canals (*qu*), all of which comprise a fourth type of waterwork. In Huizhou prefecture, for example, the inhabitants of Changle and Yong'an counties all "relied on canals to direct the water into the fields rather than build *pi* or *tang*."[21]

The fifth type of waterwork consisted of streams, rivers, springs, and wells, all more or less natural phenomena from which water could be lifted, carried, or directed onto fields. In Guixian along the Yu River in Guangxi, for instance, the 1801 edition of the Guangxi provincial gazetteer explicitly noted that "the whole county is along the river so it is easy to irrigate the fields with little else."[22] Also in Shaozhou, Nanning, and Wuzhou prefectures, specific note was made that the inhabitants used waterwheels (*shui che*) to lift the water from the rivers into the fields. Waterwheels moved by human labor, while *niu yun* waterwheels were turned by water buffalo. Where rivers flowed in directions not convenient for farmers, sometimes (or at least once), they were moved. In Hepu county (in the southwestern littoral), where a river flowed in a direction not useful for irrigation, a local official dammed it up and sent it in another direction closer to arable land.[23]

While different kinds of waterworks were fitted to different needs and locations in Lingnan, none represented a new technology. Rather, the story of irrigation and water control in Lingnan mostly is one of the extension of known techniques more broadly throughout the region. In very broad historical terms, the development of water control efforts in Lingnan began in the Song dynasty with flood control in the core regions around the provincial capitals of Guangzhou and Guilin, developed in the Ming into irrigation works in the same areas, and then in the eighteenth century spread into peripheral areas. Using successive generations of provincial gazetteers it is possible to reconstruct a more detailed history of the temporal and spatial development of irrigation works in Lingnan, but the data must be used with care. Like all data in gazetteers, the lists of waterworks may or may not be complete. Second, only a few listings include the length of the structure or amount of land irrigated, so

[21] Ibid. [22] *Guangxi tongzhi*, 1801 ed., juan 24.

[23] Listing for Hepu in the section on Lianzhoufu, *Guangdong tongzhi*, 1864 ed., juan 115–19.

it is not necessarily possible to equate a *pi* dam in Shaozhou with one in Zhaoqing. A third consideration in comparing the lists from successive gazetteers is that it is not clear that the meaning of the terms remained the same from one edition to the next; *shatan* appeared in the 1561 edition, but not later ones, while 63 *ji wei* enclosures appear in the 1822 edition that had not been mentioned in the 1731 edition. Furthermore, over time gaps between nearby *ti* and *wei* might have been connected, reducing the number listed from two to one, when actually there was an increase in the length of the embankment.

These caveats notwithstanding, I think the lists of waterworks in successive provincial gazetteers are both consistent with what else we know about Lingnan and help tell the story. As mentioned earlier, dikes for flood control were mostly all in place by the mid-sixteenth century, with little new construction afterwards. In Guangzhou prefecture, the increases in number of *ti*, *tang*, and *wei* from 1731 to 1822 all occur in those counties where *shatan* emerged: in Nanhai, Shunde, and Sanshui. The greatest increase in the number of reservoirs was in the most peripheral areas. Described in the early eighteenth century as places "where hill land (*shan tian*) constitute the majority of fields,"[24] prefectures such as Nanxiong and Lianzhou in northern Guangdong tripled and doubled the number of irrigation works from 24 in 1733 and to 73 in 1822 and from 36 to 71, respectively. Did this increase mean that irrigated fields came to outnumber dry upland fields by the end of the eighteenth century? Maybe. Smaller but still substantial increases also occurred in Zhaoqing, Gaozhou, Leizhou, and Lianzhoufu prefectures.

In Guangxi in the early eighteenth century there were so few waterworks that the 1733 edition of the provincial gazetteer did not even contain a section on waterworks (*shui li*); what irrigation did exist then was listed in the "mountains and streams" (*shan chuan*) section. Just a few *ti* and *tang* could be identified in 1733: 3 in Lingui, 2 each in Yangchun, Pingle, Xuanhua, Liucheng, and Yishan counties. By 1801, there were 26 in Lingui, 25 in Xuanhua, and 11 in Yishan, not to mention dozens elsewhere. The marvelous Ling Qu canal also had been repaired three times, in 1714, 1731, and 1754.[25]

How much land did these new works irrigate? In the preceding chapter I estimated that in the century from 1753 to 1853 an additional 25,000 square kilometers of land was cleared for agriculture in Lingnan, most of which was in the hill regions where the number of irrigation works likewise increased the most. Unfortunately, we still have little idea of the amount of land irrigated.[26] The best that can be done with the available data, for both the new and older agricultural lands, is to get a rough sense of the density of the

[24] Memorial dated YZ6.9.11, in YZCZZ 11: 331–32.

[25] *Guangxi tongzhi*, 1801 ed., juan 24.

[26] In Nanhai, 6,500 of 12,000 *qing* were irrigated; in Shunde 4,300 of 9,000. See Wang, "Qing jz Zhujiang sanjiaozhou de nongtian shuili," 571, 574.

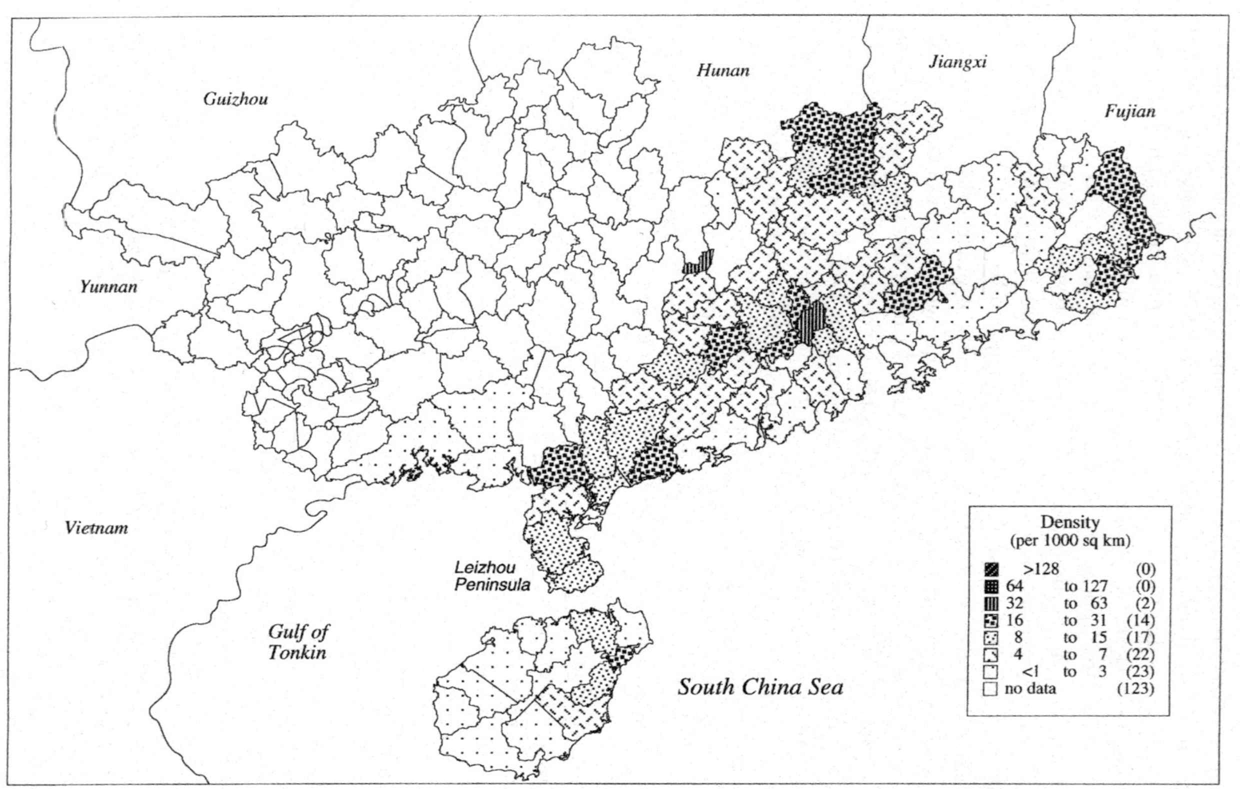

Map 10.1a. Density of waterworks, ca. 1731

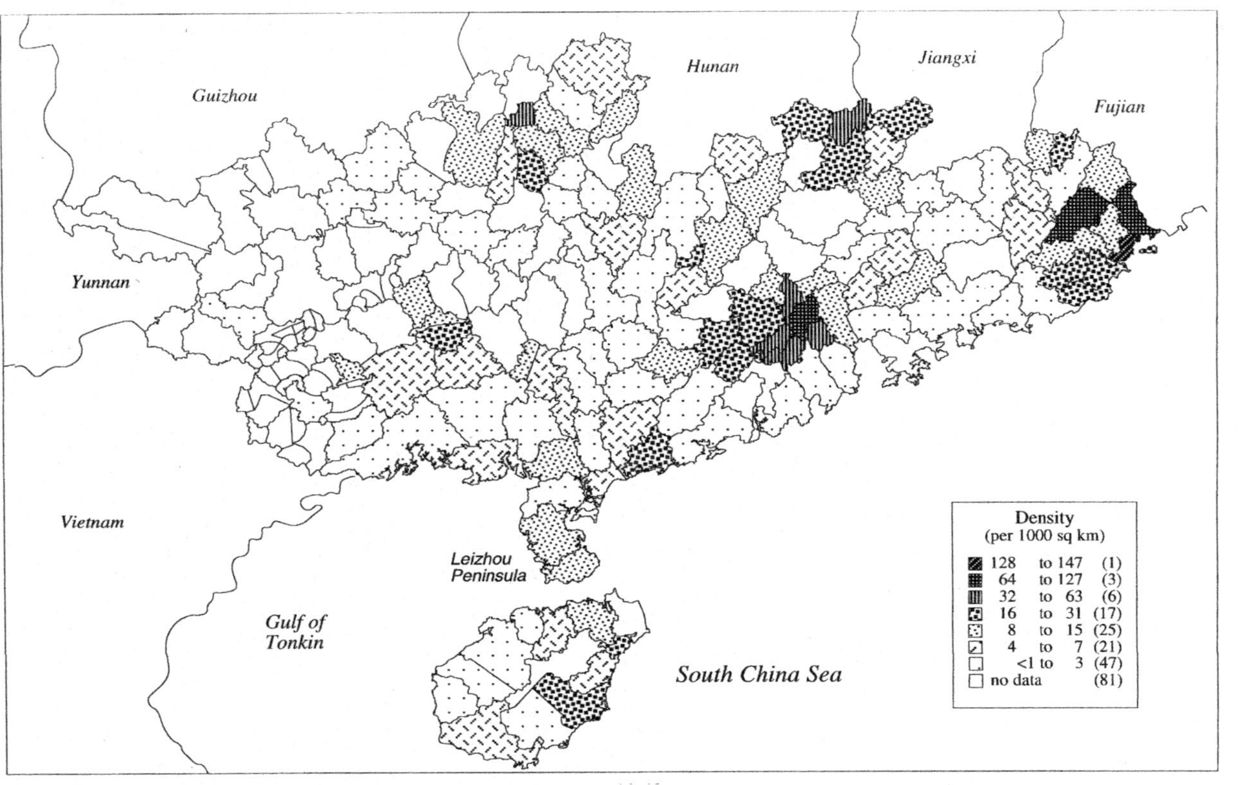

Map 10.1b. Density of waterworks, ca. 1820

waterworks as measured in terms of total area in a county or the amount of cultivated land. These measures are obviously limited – the vast number of projects in Shaozhou prefecture, for instance, no doubt were very small compared with those in Dongguan – but they do provide a rough sense of the proportion of irrigation works to total and cultivated land area (see Maps 10.1a and b).

Around 1820, the counties with the densest network of waterworks (as measured by the number of waterworks per 1,000 square kilometers) were in the Pearl River delta – Nanhai heads the list (at 80 per 100 square kilometers), followed by Sanshui and Shunde (with about 50). But counties to the north – Renhua, Lechang, and Qujiang in Shaozhou prefecture – also appeared high in the rankings (with 30–40 per 1,000 square kilometers). Below that, the rest of the counties in Lingnan each had 10 or fewer recorded waterworks per 1,000 square kilometers in 1820. Part of what this measurement tells is not unexpected – the counties in the Pearl River delta had the highest density of irrigation and water control works, while the river valleys of Guangxi as well as the hill regions of both Guangdong and Guangxi were less densely irrigated.

When the number of waterworks are measured against the amount of cultivated land, a different picture emerges, with peripheral counties in western and northern Guangxi province having the most (more than one per 1,000 *mu*); Nanhai and Shunde counties, by contrast, had less than one waterwork per 10,000 *mu*. But this measurement also shows that not all of the peripheral areas were undeveloped in terms of water control; Taiping prefecture in western Guangxi appears to have been the most advanced of the relatively undeveloped areas of Lingnan. What this measurement also shows, of course, is that peripheral areas had a larger number of smaller irrigation and water control works, and, conversely, that the waterworks in the Pearl River delta were large and complex, serving more than one village.[27]

[27] The investments of labor and capital necesssary to create and then maintain these waterworks were substantial and certainly beyond the reach of individual peasant families. In discussing the *shatan* we have already seen that only the largest and wealthiest of delta lineages had the wherewithal to invest in creating the new lands. Not all of the waterworks were built with private funds; the state invested too. A few of the waterworks listed in the gazetteers were listed as "state-owned" (*guan you*), while the rest presumably were privately owned. Sometimes the state entered into a partnership, as in Qingyuan prefecture when the governor of Guangxi proposed lending 2,400 taels to a local gentry leader to begin construction of a dam, several sluice gates, and seven *ti* for the express purpose of opening new land for cultivation. See the memorial dated QL19.1.11, in QLCZZ 7: 371–72. After being constructed with capital provided by large landowners, tenants were responsible for providing the labor necessary for upkeep. As an example, see memorial dated QL33.11.14, in QLCZZ 32: 486.

Deforestation

The evidence reviewed so far – the growth of the population, the changes in land reclamation policies favoring opening scattered plots in the hills, the spread of New World food crops, and the expansion of water control and irrigation works into previously unirrigated areas – all point to the substantial clearance of land in Lingnan in the eighteenth and nineteenth centuries. The obverse of the story of land clearance is one of deforestation, but since eighteenth- and even nineteenth-century sources do not speak directly to the issue, that story can be pieced together only using later evidence. By the early twentieth century, though, the results were plain to those who began to look. In the hills of northern Guangdong, the forestry expert G. Fenzel observed "vast stretches of flat, barren hills, [with] wild grass growth."[28] Shaw, writing in 1912, found forests in Lingnan only in the upper reaches of the North River in Guangdong and in westernmost Guangxi, on the border with Guizhou province. And in the 1930s, Communists hiding from enemy forces found dense forests on the border with Jiangxi to be virtually impenetrable.[29]

If evidence both from earlier periods and from the twentieth century can be used to illuminate eighteenth-century land clearance practices, fire probably had been used to remove the forest cover and to ready the hillside for planting: "In this process fire is amply used as a pioneer, till, soon, the whole surface of the mountains bordering the valley lies barren from top to bottom."[30] The non-Han Chinese were especially adept at the use of fire:

> The Yao cause tongue-like inlets to be burnt into the forests where he cultivates on the rich soil – still more improved by the ashes – his barley, maize, or sweet potato for two or three years. After this period of crude and transitory cultivation, he . . . moves to another spot for the cultivation of his cereal and potatoes . . . When the soils are clear in this way, a special sort of rice, which grows on the steep slopes without terracing and artificial irrigation, or maize or sweet potatoes are grown.[31]

Land clearance for agriculture was not, of course, the only cause of deforestation. In earlier chapters I have mentioned the logging that was done to provide raw materials for the furniture, building, and shipping industries. And while it is clear that these industries could exhaust the supply of particular kinds of trees (such as the iron wood used in shipbuilding), they did not by themselves clear the land of forest. For that, agriculture clearly played the

28 Fenzel, "On the Natural Conditions Affecting the Introduction of Forestry," 81.

29 Norman Shaw, *China's Forest Trees and Timber Supply* (London: T. Fisher Unwin, 1912), 81–95. Gregor Benton, *Mountain Fires: The Red Army's Three-Year War in South China, 1934–38* (Berkeley and Los Angeles: University of California Press, 1992), 93, 103.

30 Fenzel, "On the Natural Conditions Affecting the Introduction of Forestry," 93.

31 Ibid., 92.

greatest role. But there is more. Wood from forests also had been the major source of fuel for cooking and heating. How much impact this demand for energy contributed to deforestation is not easily estimated, but there is clear evidence from the early nineteenth century that wood was no longer available for use as a fuel, at least in some parts of Lingnan.

According to Captain J. Ross, who traveled overland from Hainan Island to Guangzhou in 1819 following the wreck of his ship, "This part of China is badly supplied with firewood, and the people are obliged to substitute straw, hay, and cow-dung." It was not that there were no trees, but that there were so few: "The country . . . was well cultivated, though hilly, with a few groves of small pines." The reason for the scarcity of forest, of course, is that peasant-farmers had cleared and planted the land, which Ross described as "hilly and poorly cultivated, producing chiefly sweet potatoes, with a sprinkling of other vegetables."[32]

By the early nineteenth century, then, people in Gaozhou prefecture no longer used wood for fuel, but burned straw and dung instead. Certainly this picture has all the earmarks of an energy crisis, with people using for fuel – for cooking, heating, and lighting – the very organic material that had gone into fertilizing the fields.[33] One wonders how widespread this condition was. The population density of Gaozhou in 1820 was 150 people per square kilometer, about the same as Zhaoqing, Chaozhou, and Jiaying and but half of the density of Guangzhou (see Table 9.2). If we assume that areas with about the same population density experienced similar fuel shortages, then the problem was widespread indeed, and it was present as early as 1800.[34]

The vast, treeless grasslands observed in the early twentieth century thus had emerged as a result of a historical process of burning off the forest, planting a crop for 2 or 3 years, and then moving on to another location without replanting trees. By the twentieth century, the Yao tribesmen who Fenzel observed had taken to replanting trees after they moved on; but the Chinese did not do so then and probably had not in earlier times either. After abandoning a cleared hillside, "the land is often invaded so seriously by weeds that

32 Ross, "Journal of a Trip Overland from Hainan to Canton in 1819," 247.

33 For an overview, see Adshead, "An Energy Crisis in Early Modern China," 20–28.

34 Today, of course, the shortage of fuel in the rural areas of China is a critical issue, impinging not just upon economic development, but also on environmental degradation. When I visited the Meiling Pass in early 1994, village women were combing through the hills cutting ferns for cooking the evening meal. By late afternoon, the whole valley was filled with choking smoke from the thousands of stoves. Simply to survive, then, peasant-farmers in this northernmost, mountainous region of Lingnan, which once was heavily forested, remove biomass from the hillsides in order to cook. For conditions in early-twentieth-century Shandong, see Pomeranz, *The Making of a Hinterland*, ch. 3. For contemporary China, see Smil, *China's Environmental Crisis*, 101ff.

further cropping is impossible," according to Robert Pendleton, a botanist who had studied similar processes in the Philippines.[35] After 5 or 10 years, scrub brush might grow and the soil regain some fertility, making it possible to burn it off again. "If, however, the weeds and the brush growing up in the abandoned clearings are removed by annual burning, tree growth has little chance to develop."[36]

And in Lingnan, at least in the twentieth century, peasants habitually burned off the hills every year or two, not only rendering the hills unfit for replanting, but also preventing trees from growing. In Guangxi, Stewart observed that the peasant-farmers "habitually fire most the burnable slopes in the vicinity of the homes during the dry season each year. The continuation of this practice tends to destroy the majority of the species of woody plants and change the aspect of a once richly forested country to that of a hilly or mountainous grassland."[37] In Guangdong too, according to Fenzel, Chinese farmers "annually burn down the grass covering the mountains."[38]

Given the fuel shortage noted earlier, the practice of burning off the hillsides appears somewhat curious, since it would appear to waste a valuable resource. At this point, I do not have any easy answers that would reconcile the two kinds of conflicting evidence. But certainly, those peasant-farmers who burned the grass off the hillsides would have had an alternative fuel source, while those who didn't would have cut the grass from the hills for fuel. Whatever the case may have been, the results were basically the same: removal of forest and the creation of conditions making the regrowth of forest cover unlikely or impossible.

Besides eliminating forests, land clearance by burning, followed by periodic reburning, had an impact on the ability of the watershed to retain rainfall and prevent erosion. On the one hand, the rapid growth of the tough grasses following cultivation retarded soil erosion.[39] Unlike other parts of China where deforestation and shifting cultivation was not followed by the rapid invasion of grasses but by deep soil erosion and the silting of rivers, in Lingnan the grasslands may have prevented extensive soil damage during the summer monsoon. On the other hand, some soil erosion did occur, taking off the thin layer of humus-rich material on the forest floor. When that happened, the ability of the soil to retain water decreased. According to Stewart, the effects upon rivers in Guangxi were clear:

35 Robert Pendleton, "Cogonals and Reforestation with Leucaena Glauca," *Lingnan Science Journal*, 12 no. 3 (Oct. 1933): 555.

36 Ibid., 556.

37 Albert N. Steward, "The Burning of Vegetation on Mountain Land, and Slope Cultivation in Ling Yuin Hsien, Kwangsi Province, China," *Lingnan Science Journal* 13, no. 1 (Jan. 1934): 1.

38 Fenzel, "On the Natural Conditions Affecting the Introduction of Forestry," 42.

39 Pendleton, "Cogonals and Reforestation," 559.

> In Ling Yuin Hsien we found steadily flowing streams in the undisturbed areas of forest at the height of the dry season. At the same time the stream beds in the nearby cultivated and burned-over area were mostly dry. We believe that the preservation or replacement of woody vegetation cover on these slopes would so materially affect the moisture available during the dry season as to be of real economic benefit to the people because it would enable them to grow winter and spring crops, sometimes with the help of irrigation, which it is now impossible to produce on account of the dryness of the soil and the lack of precipitation at that season of the year.[40]

Conversely, of course, with less water retained to seep out and keep the streams flowing in the dry season, more rainfall simply ran off during the summer monsoon, increasing the flow of streams and rivers and, hence, the incidence of flooding.

The immediate question, of course, is whether or not eighteenth-century peasant-farmers too annually burned off the hills after they had cleared them of forest the first time or whether forest might have reestablished itself. Unfortunately, there is little direct evidence, and the little there is, is ambiguous. For instance, when in 1793 Staunton gazed down into Lingnan from the Meiling Pass, he observed "towards the southerly point of the compass . . . a tract of waste and barren ground. The hills scattered over the plain appeared, comparatively to the vast eminence from whence they were viewed, like so many hay-ricks; as is, indeed, the distant appearance of many other Chinese hills."[41] Clearly, Staunton saw at least one scar in the hills, and maybe all of the other hills, having the shape if not the color of "hay-ricks," were covered not with green forest but with grassland.

In the twentieth century, peasant-farmers gave several reasons why they burned off the hills. One was that "after burning off hills the grass ashes wash down the slopes serving as a source of fertilizing material for the lower agricultural land." Pendleton thought this unlikely, since "there are frequently dug contour ditches which carry away the water and eroded material from the hills to prevent flooding of the rice of other low lands."[42] When Fenzel asked "the farmer why he annually burns down the grass covering the mountains . . . [the farmer] stereotypically replies that it is to deprive the robbers, tigers, and snakes of their dens."[43] This answer deserves to be taken seriously and can provide some clues as to when the practice began of annually burning off the hills to prevent the regrowth of forest cover.

Bandits. Banditry certainly was a problem in the eighteenth century and probably had continued unabated for decades. The mid-seventeenth-

40 Steward, "The Burning of Vegetation," 2–3.
41 Staunton, *An Authentic Account*, vol. 2: 213–14.
42 Pendleton, "Cogonals and Reforestation," 557.
43 Fenzel, "On the Natural Conditions Affecting the Introduction of Forestry," 42.

century crisis had spawned a vast number of groups the state had labeled "bandits," and even E-mi-da had justified his land development policies in part to alleviate banditry. But compared with the endemic bandit problem of the 1920s and 1930s, the eighteenth century probably appeared calm. In principle, of course, it is possible to chart the presence of bandits from the numerous entries in the local gazetteers and thereby obtain a rough comparison with the twentieth century. But that exercise might not tell us anything about the peasant-farmer's practice of burning off the hills, since, as adaptable sorts, while they preferred forests, bandits could exist in almost any kind of habitat. But not so tigers. Tigers required a particular habitat – forests – and did not inhabit grasslands.

Tigers. Indeed, along with notations on natural disasters, rebellions, and dragon sightings, the chronicles of local gazetteers are filled with reports of tiger attacks on villages. In 1680, for example, "in Xin'an county, many tigers injured people; [the tigers] were extremely numerous; the attacks stopped by the end of the year."[44] Three years earlier, "hundreds of people" had been injured by tiger attacks in Lianping county.[45] In the southwest littoral, tigers in 1723 attacked so many people and animals in Maoming that 37 people died.[46] In Guangxi province too, tigers entered villages and attacked people and animals, as in Huaiji county in 1752[47] and in Liucheng county in 1696.[48] Villagers thus had reason to fear tigers, and tigers may well have been more threatening to peasant-farmers than bandits.

The relevant and interesting thing about the south China tiger (*P. tigris amoyensis*), though, is its habitat. Unlike lions, which prefer grasslands or savanna, tigers stalk their prey from the cover and the shadows provided by forests.[49] The relationship is pretty simple: no forests, no tigers. The converse also held: where there were tigers, there were forests in Lingnan. And the forest had to have been quite large: recent studies have shown that a single adult tiger requires between 20 and 100 square kilometers of forested habitat to sustain itself, depending on the availability of large game.

44 *Guangzhou fuzhi*, 1879 ed., juan 80–81, *Da shi ji* entry for KX19.

45 *Huizhou fuzhi*, 1877 ed., juan 17–18, *Da shi ji* entry for KX16.

46 *Zhaoqing fuzhi*, 1833 ed., juan 49, *Da shi ji* entry for YZ1.

47 *Wuzhou fuzhi*, 1770 ed., *Da shi ji* entry for QL17.

48 *Liuzhou fuzhi*, 1764 ed., major events entry for KX35.

49 Edward O. Wilson has made the interesting point that while tigers and lions in captivity have been crossbred ("The offspring are called tiglons when the father is a tiger and ligers when the father is a lion"), in the wild, the two species do not "hybridize." Besides radically different behavior (lions are social, while tigers are solitary), "they liked different habitats. Lions stayed mostly in open savanna and grasslands and tigers in forests." Wilson, *The Diversity of Life*, 39. Had lions been anywhere near Lingnan when the burning off of the hills began, lions might have replaced tigers, and the peasant-farmers would have been faced with that old choice: Which do you prefer, the lion or the tiger?

If Chinese peasant-farmers and literate chroniclers paid no attention to forests and failed to comment on the deforestation of the hills, thereby leaving us with no written records from which to reconstruct the story of deforestation, they did note tigers, especially tigers which attacked villages. Since tigers are indicators of forests, reports of tiger attacks in the chronicles of Chinese gazetteers can serve as proxies for forests. Charting the time and place of the tiger attacks thus should produce a picture, however fuzzy, of where the forests were and where they were not. For from the point of view of the Chinese agriculturalists, land reclamation, the clearance of hills, and the annual burning over of the grasslands may have been activities that assured the human population its food supply, but from the point of view of tigers, the same actions constituted the destruction of their habitat. The destruction of tiger habitat by burning off the forest cover reduced the tigers' food supply and contributed both to their willingness to enter villages searching for food and to their willingness to attack and eat people.

The prevalence of "man-eating tigers," according to Charles McDougal (and the appellation, "man-eating," is his), is highest under certain circumstances. Where the incidence of man-eating tigers is low, natural prey (in the case of tigers in Lingnan, primarly deer) is adequate and the encroachment of humans into the environment is gradual. "In some areas tiger habitat has been completely destroyed without man-eating becoming a problem . . . In such cases the tigers were killed off at approximately the same rate that their habitat was removed." But where human encroachment on tiger habitat occurred and where, in addition, there was a reserve of good tiger habitat, tigers "were forced to occupy marginal habitat . . . Tigers forced to occupy areas where their normal food was in short supply supplemented the latter with livestock and also humans."[50] The record of tiger attacks in Lingnan, then, indicated not merely the destruction of tiger habitat, but also the existence of a forest reservoir from which more tigers emerged.

Tiger attacks thus are meaningful indicators simultaneously of forests and of the encroachment of humans into tiger habitat. What does the historical record for Lingnan show? Let us begin by working backwards. Today, just a few tigers survive in the mountains on the border of northern Guangdong and Guangxi, not surprising in light of the extensive deforestation clearly documentable in the twentieth century.[51] In earlier centuries, the distribution of tigers was more general throughout Lingnan. Around 1700, according to Qu Dajun, "There are many tigers in Gaozhou, Leizhou, and Lianzhoufu. Mer-

[50] Charles McDougal, "The Man-Eating Tiger in Geographic and Historical Perspective," in Tilson and Seal, eds., *Tigers of the World*, 445–46.

[51] Lu Huoji, "Habitat Availability and Prospects for Tigers in China," in Tilson and Seal, eds., *Tigers of the World*, 71–74. Lu estimates that 4,000 tigers inhabited the area in 1949, 150–200 in 1981, and 50–80 in the mid-1980s.

chants encounter them." Qu also noted that "in the wilds of Leizhou, there are many deer."[52] For the rest of Lingnan we lack the sweeping generalizations provided by Qu Dajun, but the record of tiger attacks can tell the story. In Guangzhou prefecture, most of the tiger attack records are in the Ming dynasty, with a few in the early Qing. Of interest in the Qing records are those in the first decade of the Kangxi reign when the coastal population was relocated inland. The abandoned fields apparently rapidly reverted to scrub if not actual forest, and with the return of cover came the tigers.[53] Significantly, in Guangzhou prefecture the last tiger attack on record is for 1690. After that, the record of tiger attacks ends, presumably coincident with the destruction of tiger habitat and the elimination of tigers. A similar story can be told about Chaozhou prefecture, where the last recorded tiger attack was in 1708. The last tiger attack in Gaozhou prefecture (which, it may be remembered from the preceding chapter, was second only to Guangzhou in population density in 1820) was recorded in 1723. In Huizhou, though, the records of tiger attacks continue through the eighteenth century, and in Shaozhou prefecture and in Nanxiong (to the north in the Nanling Mountains) the last records are in 1813 and 1815, respectively. Records are more sparse in Guangxi, but in Wuzhou and Xunzhou, the last attacks were scattered from 1752 to 1777.

The records from which to reconstruct tiger attacks in Lingnan no doubt are incomplete – some prefectural gazetteers, such as for Lianzhoufu and Leizhou do not include annual chronicles, and certainly some tiger attacks escaped official notice. Furthermore, tigers lived in areas that did not record any attacks, such as Conghua county, which Qu Dajun said "has many tigers in the hills"[54] and which in the early twentieth century still may have harbored tigers.[55] Nonetheless, I think the story that the record of tiger attacks in Lingnan tells is quite clear. During the mid-seventeenth-century crisis when the human population decreased substantially and forest returned to much of Lingnan, the range of the tigers expanded, even into relatively densely populated areas like Guangzhou prefecture in the Pearl River delta. As population there (and elsewhere) began to recover and forests were cleared for agriculture, tigers and people came into contact. By 1700, tiger habitat probably had been destroyed in and around Guangzhou, while the hills in Guangdong and Guangxi remained forested, as did much of the southwestern littoral. As people moved into the hills and burned off forests, tiger attacks spread outwards, ending in the early nineteenth century in northernmost Guangdong.

[52] Qu, *Guangdong xin yu*, 531, 532.

[53] *Huizhou fuzhi*, 1877 ed., juan 18, *Da shi ji* entry for KX6.

[54] Qu, *Guangdong xin yu*, p. 531.

[55] Shaw writes that tigers could be found 20 miles from Guangzhou in the early twentieth century; if so, the only places that had forest remnants were either surrounding the Buddhist temples at Lofu Mountain east of Guangzhou and at Dinghu Mountain west of Guangzhou, or to the north in Conghua county. Shaw, *China's Forest Trees*, 90.

The record of tiger attacks followed the destruction of their habitat, and the end of tiger attacks in the early nineteenth century dates the nearly complete destruction of tiger habitat in Guangdong by then.

The willingness of Chinese peasant-farmers to destroy tiger habitat may have been due in part to cultural beliefs. In the symbolism of the forces of nature, the tiger and the dragon represented the *yin* and the *yang* of weather: the dragon represented life-giving rain, springtime, and the east, the direction from which the rains came; the tiger symbolized drought, autumn, and the west, the direction from which dry, cold winds came. The rains came, Chinese peasant-farmers believed, when the sleeping dragon arose from the depths of the water and ascended into the heavens, while drought was explained by the unwillingness or inability of the dragon to emerge from the water. In these instances, it was necessary to rouse the dragon, and so a tiger skull was dragged through pools in an attempt to arouse the dragon and bring the rains.[56] It is tempting to think that Chinese peasants, believing that tigers were a baleful influence on the rains, would not have objected to their wholesale destruction. Even if these beliefs did not cause Chinese peasant-farmers to burn off the hills, neither did they provide any restraint.[57] Besides, tigers were dangerous.

The accumulated evidence thus indicates the progressive deforestation of Lingnan in the eighteenth century, coincident with the population and cultivated land areas surpassing previous peaks in the Song and Ming, and with official state policy after 1740 encouraging the clearance of the hill country and the periodic – if not annual – burning of grass off the hills. If, as Ling Daxie has estimated, forests in 1700 had covered about half of the land area of Lingnan, decreasing to 5–10 percent by 1937,[58] then most of that deforestation and loss of habitat occurred during the eighteenth century.

This is not to say that all of Lingnan had been cleared of forest, for that clearly was not the case. Certainly much of the western half of Guangxi remained forested in 1850, and there was sufficient timber in northernmost Guangdong, perhaps as far south as Yingde county (about half-way from

[56] For descriptions of the drought prevention ceremonies, see de Visser, *The Dragon in China and Japan*, 119–20.

[57] The persistence of Chinese attitudes about tigers to the present day can be found, most amazingly, in a 1994 Chinese text: "Large carnivorous animals (including the wolf, tiger, and leopard) and many kinds of poisonous snakes have done great harm to humans and livestock since ancient times. With the gradual clearing of lush forest and swamp vegetation and the rapid increase in population and settlements, harm from carnivorous animals and poisonous snakes has gradually been lessened. Some harmful animals, such as the tiger, have now even become endangered species and have been preserved in natural reserves. Wolves, however, still inflict havoc on human life and livestock in the extensive pastoral areas of China." Zhao, *Geography of China*, 162. Pity the wolf.

[58] Ling, "Wo guo senlin ziyuan de bianqian," 34–35.

Guangzhou to the Nanling Mountains in the north),[59] to sustain a lumber industry into the twentieth century. Traveling north from Guangzhou in 1861, Samuel Bonnery "anchored for the night alongside Timber [*sic*] rafts" in the Pearl River delta, and in Lechang county (in the far north) he noted "groves of dark green firs on the left [bank of the river] – hills in the rear, on both sides, jungly."[60] Traveling south into Guangdong over the Zheling Pass from Hunan province in 1925, Harry Franck commented on the surprise of finding northernmost Guangdong "so mountainous and wooded . . . Evergreen forests gave great quantities of logs, of telegraph-pole size, a hole chopped laboriously in the end of each by which it was dragged down the river and tied into a raft . . . The dull boom of small rafts dropping down the boiling rocky river broke every now and again the stillness, and in the narrow river valley the woodsmen obstructed the public trail . . . with piles of logs." Lest Franck convey the wrong picture of a forested Guangdong, he hastened to add that "even here [i.e., two days' walk from the summit] the old Chinese tendency to destroy forest growths was showing its hand, and great patches of the steep mountain sides had been denuded."[61]

The deforestation of Lingnan thus was not complete by the middle of the nineteenth century, but the process had gone so far as to leave little forest in any areas inhabited by people. Moreover, the forest in the northern Guangdong hills that was left had been cleared in places, rendering an appearance somewhat like swiss cheese, making it possible for some tigers to hang on even into the late twentieth century. But certainly, the rapid growth of the Chinese population from 1700 on and the consequent push to reclaim land for cultivation in the eighteenth and early nineteenth century had seriously altered the environment.

Environmental Change

Besides deforestation, the destruction of habitat, and the extinction of species, land clearance for agriculture in the eighteenth and early nineteenth centuries precipitated other environmental changes as well. Twentieth-century ecologists have shown that the large-scale clearance of tropical and subtropical forests triggers both increased flooding and drought, and they have hypothesized that such deforestation might even affect broader climatic patterns. Without the canopy of the forest to stop the rain, drops hit the uncovered soil with greater force, both eroding the soil and running off rather than slowly percolating in.

59 See the observations of Sir John F. Davis, who wrote an account of the Amherst Mission to Beijing in 1840 and its return to Guangzhou (via the same route as Staunton in 1793), in *Sketches of China* (London: C. Knight, 1841), 155–56.

60 Samuel Bonnery, *Canton to Hankow, Overland* (Canton: Friend of China, 1861), 2, 16.

61 Harry A. Franck, *Roving through South China* (New York: Century, 1925), 642–43.

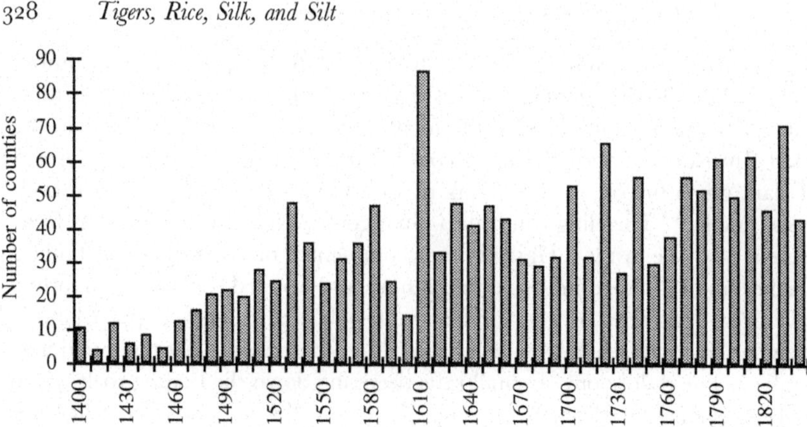

Figure 10.1. Counties afflicted with floods, 1400–1850. Source: Compiled from *Guangdong sheng ziran zaihai shiliao* (Guangzhou: Guangdong sheng wenshi yanjiu guan, 1961), 1–61.

Trees also absorb the sun's energy and release water vapor into the air, so that their removal both increases the temperature on the ground and decreases the amount of water vapor recycled back into the atmosphere.[62]

If the eighteenth- and nineteenth-century land clearance and deforestation in Lingnan had these local effects, they should have been observable in the increased incidence of floods and droughts. Drawing upon the compilation of gazetteer citations of climatic events in Guangdong province, we can chart the number of counties reporting floods and droughts from 1400 to 1850 to see whether or not there are any noticeable changes. Aggregating the data by decade (see Figures 10.1 and 10.2), we can see that the total number of both floods and droughts indeed did tend to increase in this period.[63]

For floods, the increased frequency and scope is more obvious than for droughts and exhibits a pattern that does correlate with what we know about the history of land clearance in Lingnan, increasing by steps from the Ming through the Qing dynasty. From 1460 through 1600, the number of counties reporting drought fluctuated around 20 per decade; after declining during the early Qing, the number increases in the mid-eighteenth century to around 25

[62] Bruenig et al., *Ecological-Socioeconomic System Analysis and Simulation*, 29–30.

[63] Statistical analysis of these data also confirms the upward trend. For floods, the equation for the linear trend has a slope of .106 with an R^2 of .533, and for droughts the slope is .075 with an R^2 of .362. In other words, the incidence of floods and droughts over the entire period tended to impact one additional county each decade.

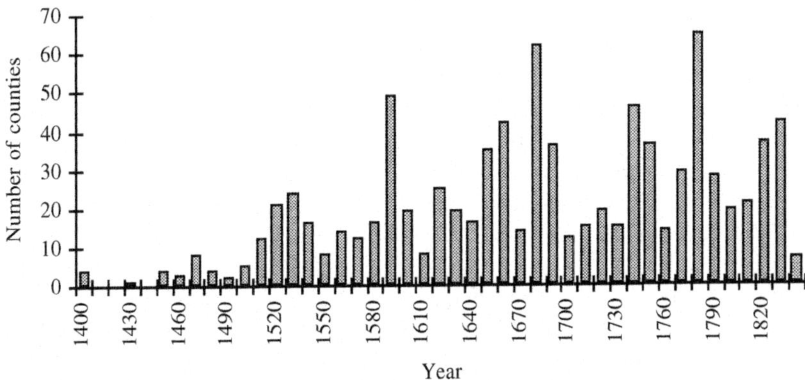

Figure 10.2. Counties afflicted with droughts, 1400–1850. Source: Compiled from *Guangdong sheng ziran zaihai shiliao* (Guangzhou: Guangdong sheng wenshi yanjiu guan, 1961), 62–92.

per decade; and finally, from the 1760s on, the number fluctuates around 40 per decade.

Clearly, the reports of flooding increase in steps that correspond to the history of land clearance. But is there a causal link between the land clearance and increased reports of floods? Certainly that is one possibility, but there are two others as well. In the first instance, it may have been that the incidence of floods did not increase, but merely the reporting of them. It may well be the case that the records for the early fifteenth century are incomplete and that the increase from 1400 to 1480 is a function of more conscientious reporting. By 1500, though, the gazetteer records seem to be quite detailed, so I think that from that time on we can assume that reporting is not a crucial variable in accounting for the number of floods. Second, it may be argued that the increased incidence of flooding may have been associated with climatic changes bringing more rain into Lingnan. But, it may be recalled from Chapter 6, the last decades of the eighteenth century tended to be drier than earlier years; a wetter climate thus cannot account for the increased incidence of flooding. Rather, I think the available evidence points to eighteenth-century deforestation as the primary cause of the increase in flooding.[64]

[64] The amount of rainfall and the extent of land clearance are but two factors that must be taken into account to understand why rain does not get absorbed into the ground but instead runs off into streams and rivers, sometimes overflowing their banks. For an example of the complexity, see Shen Ts'an-hsin, "Non-Hortunian Runoff Generation in the Humid Regions of South China," in Laurence J. C. Ma and Allen G. Noble, eds., *The Environment: Chinese and American Views* (New York: Methuen, 1981), 143–69.

Not only did the incidence of flooding increase, but so too did its severity. The best examples are the 1784 and 1794 floods that breached the Sang Yuan Wei and other levees in the lower reaches of the West and North Rivers. Those levees, it will be recalled, had checked flood waters for centuries. But in 1784, perhaps in part because the river channels had risen with increased silt deposits and perhaps in part because of increased runoff in the upper reaches of the drainage basin, floodwaters overflowed the levees, inundating counties along the West River and in the Pearl River delta. A decade later, floodwaters again breached the levees. In one measure of the extent of the 1794 flooding, relief operations provided for 20,000 families displaced by the floodwaters. As a result of the 1794 floods, local leaders recognized the seriousness of the problem and began to repair and raise the height of the levees.[65]

If the changes in land use increased the incidence of flooding locally in Lingnan, the progressive deforestation may have had a much broader impact on the climate of the rest of China. Ecologists have hypothesized that the elimination of forest in Lingnan likely resulted in lesser humidity reaching north into the interior of China.[66] Until recently, this has remained an interesting hypothesis. But a team of researchers led by Zhang Peiyuan has collected and analyzed an immense amount of historical data on the incidence of drought in China and has concluded that China has indeed become increasingly arid since the thirteenth century.[67]

In Lieu of a Conclusion to This Chapter: Extinction

In terms of the reciprocal relationship between environment and economy in Lingnan, the eighteenth century represented a turning point. Until then, the population and cultivated land area peaks reached twice earlier around 1200 and 1600 had not been surpassed. These earlier maxima probably had left about half of the land area covered with original rain forest. And when populations and cultivated land areas retreated by as much as one-third in the fourteenth and seventeenth centuries, the forest "reclaimed" – if I am allowed to invert the meaning of a key word used in the preceding chapter – land.

By 1800, both the population and the cultivated land area of Lingnan had reached levels twice as high as at any previous time, and by 1853 the limits of cultivable land had been reached in Guangdong. The destruction of forest that accompanied those gains, though, progressed not arithmetically and proportionally, but geometrically. In Guangdong, the 1850 cultivated land area approached the levels reached in the twentieth century when just 10 percent

65 *Sang Yuan Wei zong zhi*, Ming Zhigang, comp. (TZ9 1870), juan 1: 8a–9a.
66 Bruenig et al., *Ecological-Socioeconomic System Analysis and Simulation*, 31.
67 Zhang, "Climate Change and Its Impact on Capital Shift during the Last 2,000 Years in China."

of the land area was left covered with forest. And in Guangxi, while the cultivated land area still had room to expand in the nineteenth and twentieth centuries, there too the forest cover had diminished toward the twentieth-century low of 5 percent. The reason the forest disappeared faster than the population growth was because of the practice of repeatedly burning off the hills. Even on the hills that were cleared and had been planted just once, Chinese peasant-farmers continued the practice of burning the hills to deprive "bandits, tigers, and snakes" of their habitat. This had its effect, at least with respect to tigers, for the final, early-nineteenth-century records of tiger attacks on villagers place tigers only in remote sections of northern Guangdong in the Nanling Mountains, where they have managed to hang on as an endangered species in the remaining pockets of forest cover.

In contrast to the elephant, the other star species that disappeared from Lingnan, the progressive elimination of the tiger population followed a different route. As Edward O. Wilson has recently observed, "For species on the brink, from birds to fungi, the end can come in two ways. Many, like the Morrean tree snails, are taken out by the metaphorical equivalent of a rifle shot – they are erased but the ecosystem from which they are removed is left intact. Others are destroyed by a holocaust, in which the entire ecosystem perishes."[68] As we saw at the beginning of this book, the elephant had been taken out with the "rifle shot," hunted and killed by humans for their tusks and the delicacy of consuming their trunks; otherwise, the environment was left more or less intact. Tigers, on the other hand, were taken out in a "holocaust" with the clearance of forest from Lingnan.

If land clearance destroyed the habitat of the tiger, pushing it to the edge of extinction, the same fate awaited other wildlife too. And while no one seemed concerned about the fate of the tiger, by the early nineteenth century at least one Chinese observer, the compiler of the 1811 edition of the Leizhou gazetteer, Deng Bi'nan, had become conscious of the loss of other species in Lingnan. Whether his consciousness was new and had formed because the rate of the loss of habitat and species had become palpable in his time is not readily apparent. But however his ideas formed, he lamented the passing of various species:

> Because local products come from the land [and because there are changes in the land], the local products too change over time. Of the common ones mentioned in the ancient texts, just 80–90 percent exist today; of the rare ones, just 20–30 percent survive. [Today], there is no land that has not changed, so the times are no longer the same either. Northerners record that Leizhou produced teeth and ivory from black elephants, and noted that in Xuwen there were *bao niu* (a kind of buffalo?). The *Records of Jiaozhou* [probably a fourth-century CE text] say that Xuwen had the giant cen-

[68] Wilson, *The Diversity of Life*, 258.

> tipede . . . The provincial gazetteer records that in the wilds of Leizhou deer were plentiful, and that the "fragrant navel of the civet" could substitute for musk-deer . . . Today these [species] are all extinct. The reason these extinctions were not recorded before is that people then said that extinction was not possible . . . Today it is my task to record for posterity these extinctions in the appendix [to the local products section], [in the hope that my records will be of use] for later research.[69]

Record for posterity only? If so, how lonely is Deng Bi'nan's voice. Was there no one else with whom he could share his sense of loss? Did he feel so alone in his concern that all he could do was record extinctions for posterity? Was he a pioneer who no one else followed? Where did he get his faith that a later researcher – someone like me – would resurrect his lament? And has he recorded those extinctions only for posterity? Or can something yet be done?

[69] *Leizhou fuzhi*, 1811 ed., juan 2: 67a–b.

CONCLUSION

The middle of the nineteenth century has long been seen as a turning point in Chinese history. The Opium War (1839–42) and the Taiping Rebellion (1850–65) are commonly taken to mark the beginning of China's modern history, a history in which the themes of economic development, state formation, and revolution (among others) in the context of a European-dominated capitalist world take center stage in the problematic through which historians interpret Chinese history. But 1850 (or thereabouts) also marks a significant change in terms of the story about Lingnan's environment and economy that I have told here.

By 1850, Lingnan had passed an important divide. As we saw in Chapter 9, the limits of cultivable land were reached by then, and yet the population continued to increase. A colder climate in the first half of the nineteenth century had decreased the already stretched food supplies of the region, and the pressure of people on the land had led to deforestation, the destruction of habitat and ecosystems, and the extinction of an unknown number of species. To be sure, some officials may have become aware of the fate of the wildlife of Lingnan, perhaps presaging an attempt by the state to take corrective action. But China's defeat by Britain in the Opium War began the slow process of switching the presuppositions of the role of the state, from Confucian statecraft concerns for the maintenance of the empire, to "self-strengthening" and competing in the new world of aggressive nation-states,[1] while the Taiping Rebellion focused elites' attention on reconstructing the social bases for their continued dominance of Chinese society. To these social, political, and intellectual crises that wracked China in the second half of the nineteenth century and helped to define what modern China was to become, I think we must now add an environmental crisis. Thus, to understand modern China, we need to understand not just the historical origins of the social and political crises, but also the history of the environment and the making of the environmental crisis.

[1] See Pomeranz, *The Making of a Hinterland.*

As I look back over the long period prior to 1850 covered in this book, five landmarks[2] stand out as particularly significant in the history of the environment and economy in Lingnan. After listing and discussing these five in chronological order, I will then comment on the larger processes that drove environmental change in Lingnan, briefly compare these themes with those in American and European environmental history, discuss environmental change elsewhere in China, and conclude by pondering the question of whose story I have told here.

First among the significant landmarks is the Han Chinese immigrants' acclimatization to malaria during the Song (960–1279) and Yuan (i.e., Mongol, 1279–1368) dynasties.[3] By the dual processes of developing immunity to malaria and of altering the environment through water control projects, Chinese were able to descend from the hill regions of northern Lingnan into the more fertile river valleys, thereby spreading their particular form of settled agriculture and displacing the Tai peoples who had inhabited the lowlands. With more fertile land and close proximity to water supplies, Chinese improved the productivity of the land, enabling a larger and more dense population to be supported. The processes by which Chinese overcame the limitations that malaria had placed upon their ability to settle in the river valleys took not only centuries to unfold, but also perseverance and application of their water control technologies. Even so, malaria continued to be a threat in parts of Guangxi at least into the eighteenth century and possibly later; unlike most of Guangdong, ecological conditions in some areas of Guangxi continued to be ripe for malaria.

The second landmark is the creation of the Pearl River delta. To be sure, natural processes had deposited some alluvium around the islands in the bay, to the south of Guangzhou, but for the most part, people created the delta. Fear of the Mongol invaders sent Chinese refugees in the thirteenth century to those islands in the bay, where they then captured the alluvium and turned it into extremely fertile, well-irrigated agricultural land, ultimately filling in most of the open sea among the islands. Moreover, the amount of alluvium available for capture had increased as a result of human activity: not only did swidden agriculture in the hills increase erosion, but so too may have depopulation and the abandonment of fields and irrigation works after the Mongol conquest; levees in the lower reaches of the West, North, and East Rivers then directed the silt further downstream and into the bay, where it was captured as *shatan*.

The commercialization first of the Pearl River delta and then the rest of

[2] I find somewhat amusing the metaphors we use in discussing environmental history, many of which come from and reflect agricultural values.

[3] No doubt the Han Chinese had faced other deadly tropical diseases too, but a fuller account of the disease gradient than I have been able to provide here will have to await further study.

Lingnan is the third significant development I want to highlight. I see this process as beginning in the mid-sixteenth century and continuing through the eighteenth and nineteenth centuries, albeit interrupted by the mid-seventeenth-century crisis. Markets and the exchange of products obviously had existed for centuries before the sixteenth century, but the creation of new markets was mostly a function of population growth, as in the first 200 years or so of the Ming dynasty. From about 1550 on, peasant-farmers in the Pearl River delta increasingly turned much of their farmland over to producing commodities that were sold in the market, especially silk and sugarcane, and not consumed by the family, although most also kept some farmland in rice or some other food crop. As the farmers in the Pearl River delta changed their land use patterns to producing nonfood crops and commodities, they turned to the market to supplement their food supplies, thereby turning rice into a commercial crop too. By the middle of the eighteenth century, peasant-farmers in the furthest reaches up the East and the West Rivers were selling their rice for export downstream to the Guangzhou–Foshan urban area and the Pearl River delta. To be sure, this process had come to a halt after 1644, but when the emperor reopened the coast for shipping and trade in 1684, the commercialization of the economy surged ahead again.

Then, around 1700, a turning point – the fourth significant development – was reached. Until then, the population had increased and then decreased in two grand cycles, peaking first in the early thirteenth century and then again just before the mid-seventeenth-century crisis. Both of those population peaks had been obliterated by war and foreign conquest, first by the Mongols and then by the Manchus. But after the mid-seventeenth-century crisis, the population of Lingnan reached those two earlier peaks by 1700 and then surpassed them, with the population never declining below the 1700 totals again.

Not surprisingly, the consequences of the population growth forced themselves upon the imperial state as problems that needed to be addressed. To the Yongzheng emperor (1723–35), the problem was one of increasing the food supply, and his favored policy for doing so was to increase the amount of land under cultivation, turning over vast tracts of waste or virgin land to private parties who would develop it. This policy failed when officials falsely reported large amounts of reclaimed land, adding to the tax burden of local landowners. To the Qianlong emperor (1736–95), the problem was that of the most efficient distribution of the existing food supply. He therefore spent much time and energy tracking grain prices, granary supplies, and harvest yields, ultimately allowing merchants and the market rather than officials and the state to manage the food supplies in Lingnan. Significantly, though, neither of these energetic, willful, capable, and intelligent rulers saw population increase itself as a problem: if the Yongzheng emperor was a "productionist," believing that the food supply (and hence the tax revenues too) of the empire could be increased by state-led schemes to bring more land under the plow, the Qianlong emperor was more of a "distributionist," believing that the population growth could be accommodated by allowing market forces to ensure the movement of grain from food-surplus to food-deficit regions.

Finally, I think that the fate of the south China tiger is a significant part of this history. By the early nineteenth century, the tiger had been eliminated from most of Lingnan. To be sure, the tiger had not been driven to extinction, but I think it is clear that so much of the tiger's habitat had been destroyed that it could exist only in those parts of the Nanling Mountains that contained unfragmented blocks of forests. Unfortunately for the tiger, the Qing land policy of allowing peasant families to reclaim odd lots in the hills, the adoption of cash crops like tobacco and indigo by these farmers, and their penchant then for burning off the hills all served to fragment further the forest cover. As a star species, the progressive elimination of the tiger from Lingnan signifies the loss of entire ecosystems, and with them many more species than just the tiger.

These developments are not, of course, explanations for what happened to the environment and economy of Lingnan. But driving those developments, if not explaining them, were three interrelated processes: climate change, population dynamics, and the commercialization of the economy.

The impact of climate on agriculture and food supplies is significant for understanding China's late imperial economy. In his work on China's macroregional cycles of economic development, G. William Skinner speculated that "in an agrarian society where agriculture accounts for the bulk of the national product, it is hardly unreasonable to suppose that a cooling climate could lead to economic distress and depress economic activity" and vice versa.[4] As a variation on the Labrousse thesis regarding eighteenth-century French trade cycles, this connection is broadly true, for the long-term temperature trend during the Qing – rising from the cold 1680s to a peak around 1800 and then dropping to new lows in the 1840s – corresponds to Lingnan's regional economic cycle.

Moreover, the linkage of climatic change to harvest yields and grain prices is relevant to our understanding of the theories of subsistence and demographic crises[5] and their application to China's demographic history. Whether in the classical model (which excludes the effects of epidemic disease) or in the modified form proposed by Dupâquier, both begin with "climatic shocks" to the system and conclude with elevated mortality.[6] Certainly the evidence from

[4] Skinner, "Presidential Address," 285.

[5] For a discussion of the linkages to the economy, see especially Appleby, *Famine in Tudor and Stuart England*, ch. 1.

[6] In the classical model, as summarized by Dupâquier, "demographic crises are caused by poor harvests which are produced by climatic shocks (a rainy spring as in 1693, a 'Siberian' winter as

late imperial Lingnan presented in this book supports these general models of demographic crises: climatic shocks did decrease harvest yields, which in turn elevated grain prices and at times contributed to increased mortality.

But the people of Lingnan did not simply sit back and allow climatic variation to wreak havoc with their harvests and with their lives: they created numerous technological, social, and economic devices and institutions to buffer themselves against the vagaries of the weather. Perhaps most important, peasant-farmers in much of Lingnan produced two harvests in one year. While it is true that the warmer climate in south China was a necessary condition for peasant-farmers to produce two crops, it was not sufficient: technological improvements coupled with a larger, more dense population pushed the development of double cropping, which became a widespread, standard practice during the eighteenth century. With the innovation and spread of double cropping, then, over the course of two years Chinese farmers had four harvests, thereby significantly decreasing the risk of losing an entire year's output. Additionally, the extension of irrigation works into most of Lingnan by the end of the eighteenth century, the establishment of the state granary system in the late seventeenth century, and an efficient market for rice also all served to lessen the impact of climatic changes upon harvest yields and rice prices in Lingnan. This delinking of adverse climate upon the agrarian economy constitutes a significant – and perhaps unique – achievement of a preindustrial civilization.

If the model of demographic crises as suggested by both the classical model and Dupâquier is fundamentally sound – and I think it is – and if the agricultural economy of Lingnan had developed in such a way as to lessen the impact of climatic shocks upon harvest yields and rice prices, then Lingnan most likely experienced fewer and less severe mortality crises than England or France. Since comparable demographic data is virtually nonexistent for China, a full testing of this hypothesis may never be possible. Nonetheless, it does suggest that in Lingnan at least, the linkage between climatic shocks and mortality crises as mediated through the agrarian economy had been substantially weakened, if not altogether severed, earlier than in Europe and without the concurrent creation of an industrial economy. On the one hand, this difference may be seen as a substantial achievement. On the other hand, of course, the population of Lingnan grew steadily from the end of the seventeenth century on, prompting alarm bells within a state administration worried about providing food for a population that nonetheless kept increasing.

in 1709." Critiquing the classical model, Dupâquier includes the role of epidemic disease and fungal plant infections as causal agents in elevating mortality levels. Jacques Dupâquier, "Demographic Crises and Subsistence Crises in France, 1650–1725," in John Walter and Roger Schofield, eds., *Famine, Disease and the Social Order in Early Modern Society* (Cambridge University Press, 1989), 189–99.

The resultant population growth explains, in part, some of the environmental changes in Lingnan, in particular the loss of forest. While climate change alone has been responsible for shifting the lines between forest and grassland in temperate regions, the temperature changes in the past 2,000 years have not been of a magnitude sufficient to account for alterations in the forest cover of Lingnan. Rather, people cleared the land for agriculture, and the more people there were in Lingnan, the more land was cleared. And the more land that was cleared, the less biodiversity there was.

But population and population growth alone cannot explain all of the human-induced environmental change in Lingnan. For the commercialization of the economy too was a powerful force remaking the landscape. Not only did peasant-farmers in the Pearl River delta dig up their rice paddies to make way for fish ponds and mulberry tree embankments, but their consequent need for food transformed much of the agricultural land in the rest of Lingnan into export-oriented rice regions. The particular way in which the economy became commercialized thus can be envisioned in part as a process of displacement: if the peasant-farmers of the Pearl River delta had had to provide all of their own food supplies, either they would have devoted less land to non-food crops and commodities, or they would have brought more land into production. As it was, they could satisfy their food needs through the market stocked with imported rice. But the peasant-farmers up the North or East Rivers or in the West River basin in Guangxi, even though they exported rice downstream, had to obtain their own food supply and so planted New World food crops, in particular the sweet potato, on more marginal land in the hills.

The other way in which commercialization can be envisioned is as a process of specialization. In its simplest formulation for Lingnan, the Pearl River delta was given over mostly to sericulture and sugarcane, while the river valleys specialized in rice for export. One environmental consequence of commercialization thus was the spread of just a few agricultural ecosystems, resulting in a loss of ecosystem diversity. As Donald Worster put it in summarizing similar processes elsewhere, specialization and a market system led to "the radical simplification of the natural ecological order in the number of species found in an area and the intricacy of their interconnections."[7]

Worster attributed this "radical simplification" to "the rise of the capitalistic mode of production," in particular the transition from subsistence-oriented agriculture to a "capitalist agroecosystem." Indeed, the globalization of capitalism and its concomitant – the impact of Europeans upon indigenes elsewhere in the world – combine to form the dominant themes in the environmental history of the Americas, and much of the rest of the world too. As William Cronon concluded in his path-breaking book about colonial America, "Capitalism and environmental degradation went hand in

[7] Worster, *The Wealth of Nature*, 58.

hand."[8] Cronon qualifies this conclusion by rightfully acknowledging that the diseases that Europeans brought and spread to the Indians had nothing to do with capitalism, and Alfred Crosby developed the thesis that "the success of European imperialism has a biological, an ecological, component."[9]

The environmental history of Lingnan shares some similarities to these larger themes. In the first place, what happened to ecosystems in Lingnan and elsewhere – the "radical simplification of the natural ecological order" – appears to have been much the same. But is the story of environmental change in Lingnan to be understood as part of the story of the rise of capitalism? Certainly a case can be made that China was becoming "incorporated" into the emerging capitalist world system from the sixteenth century on,[10] and thus that environmental change in Lingnan, driven by commercialization and the linkage of Lingnan to global markets in silk, sugar, and tea, was part of a worldwide "capitalist transformation of nature."[11] The economy of Lingnan certainly was commercialized, but it also was an integral part of the imperial Chinese state system. The imperial bureaucracy not only produced most of the written documents upon which this history has been based, but also, as I argued in the introduction, distinguishes the Chinese economic system from European capitalism. While markets and commercialization were common to both, in China the imperial state with its "tributary mode of production" (to use Hill Gates's terminology) dominated the market system.

Thus, I think the way that Lingnan fits into Worster's capitalist model is problematic. First, Worster categorizes all agroecosystems as either capitalist or "traditional," the latter characterized by "subsistence strategies."[12] However else one may wish to characterize the Lingnan agroecosystem before the sixteenth century, "subsistence" is not it, if by that is meant something like Worster's example of the Filipino farmers raising up to 40 crops on a single swidden. For even in the early Ming, much of the farming and commodity production in Lingnan had already become specialized, regardless of whether it was rice, barley, sugarcane, or fish ponds, and exchange regularly occurred in the markets spread throughout the countryside. Moreover, by the middle of the eighteenth century, so much of Lingnan's agroecosystem had become commercialized that a larger portion of food entered the market – and markets operated more efficiently – than in England, France, or the United States at the same time.

8 Cronon, *Changes in the Land*, 161.

9 Alfred W. Crosby, *Ecological Imperialism: The Biological Expansion of Europe, 900–1900* (Cambridge University Press, 1986), 135.

10 For the best application of world-systems theory to Chinese history, see Frances V. Moulder, *Japan, China, and the Modern World Economy* (Cambridge University Press, 1977). For a specific case study, see So, *The South China Silk District*.

11 Worster, *The Wealth of Nature*, 57. 12 Ibid., 56.

It makes eminent sense to distinguish market forces and commercialization from capitalism as a driving force of ecological change in China and to conclude that the processes of environmental change in Lingnan, even if they do bear strong resemblance to those elsewhere, cannot be attributed to the "rise of the capitalist mode of production." More important, though, environmental change in Lingnan had more than one cause. To be sure, commercialization was a powerful force. But global climate change and population dynamics in Lingnan too drove economic and environmental change in Lingnan, and those processes had nothing whatsoever to do with the rise and spread of the capitalist mode of production.[13]

The other grand theme in the literature on environmental history (at least of the Americas, Australia, and Oceania) – the encounter of Europeans with indigenes – has its counterpart in Lingnan in the confrontation of Han Chinese with the various non-Han peoples inhabiting Lingnan. In Alfred Crosby's able hands, the puzzle he wants to explain is why the biological exchange between Europeans and the peoples of what he calls the "neo-Europes" – the Americas, Australia, New Zealand – was mostly one way: European diseases, weeds, and animals all overtook the colonies, rather than vice versa.

In Lingnan, though, it was not the indigenous Tai peoples who feared the diseases of the Chinese, but vice versa. Nonetheless, Chinese ultimately did displace the malaria-bearing Tai peoples, but the process took a very long time and involved both Chinese adaptation to the malarial environment and the transformation of that environment through water control projects. Crosby does point out that European attempts to expand elsewhere on the Eurasian and African continents – the Holy Land and the Levant during the Crusades, or the tropics – too were blunted by malaria and other "minute enemies . . . many species of germs, worms, insects, rusts, molds, and what have you attuned to preying on humanity and its servant organisms."[14] The difference between the Chinese and European experience in the tropics is that the Chinese persevered and ultimately settled the previously hostile environments; Europeans had to await the elixir of quinine to conquer the tropics.[15]

[13] Although I think that Worster's problematic might lead to monocausal explanations of environmental change, I think that he is absolutely right in focusing environmental historians' attention upon the problem of detailing how humans secured food from the soil and how that first act is both conditioned by, and then changes, the environment. Whether or not the various ways in which people have accomplished and then institutionalized this process can be called a "mode of production" is a matter of some debate. For a critique of Worster, see William Cronon, "Modes of Prophecy and Production: Placing Nature in History," *Journal of American History* 76, no. 4 (Mar. 1990): 1122–31.

[14] Crosby, *Ecological Imperialism*, 7.

[15] See Daniel R. Headrick, *The Tools of Empire: Technology and European Imperialism in the Nineteenth Century* (New York: Oxford University Press, 1981), 58–95.

Moreover, if Han Chinese did not have their way into Lingnan smoothed by the prior spread of their deadly diseases among the indigenous population, neither does it appear that northern Chinese plants and animals easily spread into Lingnan ecosystems, displacing Lingnan natives. To be sure, wet-rice culture did come to be dominant, but that required that the Chinese actually remake the environment, and while pigs were an important part of the farm economy, they were penned up rather than let loose to root through the forest. The Han Chinese settlement of Lingnan thus was accompanied by very different processes than those Crosby identifies for Europeans spreading into the neo-Europes – and for reasons consistent with Crosby's explanatory framework: Lingnan was not in the same general climatic zone, and being connected with, rather than separated from, the Eurasian continent, its ecosystems hosted a more complex biota than was found in north or central China.[16]

The big themes in the history of environment and economy in Lingnan thus are relevant to those considered important and significant in the broader field of environmental history. But before leaving this topic, I would like to comment upon one of the ways in which China often appears in the environmental history literature and to offer the history of Lingnan as a corrective to what I think is a misunderstanding. When trying to find a foil for the unsustainable, ecologically destructive practices attributed to European or American capitalist farming, historians of those regions sometimes look to Asia or China for examples. Many times they will select the mulberry embankment and fish pond combination practiced in the Pearl River delta, or rice paddy farming in general, as examples of sustainable agriculture. In a very recent example, Alfred Crosby, bemoaning the depletion of soil and water in modern farming, says, "In contrast, we have, for instance, the traditional rice paddy system of southern China, with its sustained and astonishing productivity in rice, vegetables, algae, oysters, carp, pigs, chickens, ducks, and frogs."[17]

However much more diverse the species in the agroecosystems of Lingnan when compared with the wheat, corn, or soy monocultures of North America, it is mistaken to conclude that the Lingnan agroecosystem was any more sustainable. To be sure, the fish pond and mulberry tree combination was a wonderfully ingenious method of minimizing the loss of energy and nutrients beyond the boundaries of that system. And even irrigated rice paddies, relying mostly upon waterborne nutrients to replace those taken up by the rice plants, appear to be ecologically sound. But such perspectives ignore the food and energy needs of the people who farm those agroecosystems.

And as I have shown, the food needs of the people of Lingnan, especially

[16] Crosby, *Ecological Imperialism*, ch. 11.

[17] Alfred W. Crosby, "An Enthusiastic Second," *Journal of American History* 76, no. 4 (Mar. 1990): 1107.

those in the Pearl River delta, transformed the entire Lingnan region – an area about the size of France – into a funnel that concentrated food from that vast region into a densely populated core. Indeed, I have argued that by the middle of the eighteenth century, the market system linked the various parts of Lingnan into a single agroecosystem. That being the case, to look at farming practices in just one part of the system misses the larger picture. And that larger picture is that the system as a whole was not sustainable without greater and greater inputs from outside. Guangxi was literally drained to sustain the Pearl River delta, creating a historical legacy that haunts the people of Guangxi to this day.

The environmental history of Lingnan thus is important for what it can tell us about the questions of global environmental change. But what about China: Was there a broader environmental crisis in China? If so, did it emerge in the nineteenth century, as clearly happened in Lingnan? And how representative is Lingnan's story of environmental change of the rest of China? These are large questions indeed, and perhaps the subjects for other books; here I can only briefly reflect upon them. To be sure, Lingnan was among the last frontiers of Chinese settlement, and thus has a history that developed later than much of the rest of China. On the other hand, it was favorably located and was able to develop quite rapidly from the middle of the sixteenth century on, surpassing many other parts of China in wealth and power by the eighteenth century.

However, little work has been done on late imperial China's environment to enable an extended comparison of Lingnan with other regions. Nonetheless, studies by Peter Perdue on Hunan, Anne Osborne on the lower Yangzi region, and Keith Schoppa on the Xiang Lake region (also in the lower Yangzi region) suggest that those areas too experienced similar problems of land shortage, deforestation, upland erosion, and lowland flooding and that those problems had become critical by the middle of the nineteenth century.[18] If anything, the upland erosion and lowland siltation and flooding were more pronounced along the Yangzi than in Lingnan. Osborne shows how land clearance in the highlands increased the problems of siltation for lowland farmers, causing the state to become involved in trying to solve the problem. Perdue and Schoppa document how Dongting Lake and Xiang Lake both began to be filled with silt, and similar to what happened in Lingnan, peasant-farmers reclaimed land from the new alluvial deposits. Both of those lakes played an important role in absorbing the floodwaters of the Yangzi, just as in Lingnan the flood plains on the lower reaches of the West, North, and East Rivers had – until levees that sent the silt into the Pearl River delta were built. And there,

[18] Perdue, *Exhausting the Earth*; Osborne, "The Local Politics of Land Reclamation in the Lower Yangzi Highlands," 1–46; Keith R. Schoppa, *Xiang Lake – Nine Centuries of Chinese Life* (New Haven: Yale University Press, 1989).

some of the silt was captured as new *shatan*, adding to the extent of the Pearl River delta and obstructing the flow of river water to the sea. This brief comparison thus suggests that the issues and the timing of environmental problems along the Yangzi were similar to those in Lingnan, indicating that broad forces of change were at work, affecting more than just one region of China at a time.

Clearly more research on China's environmental history needs to be undertaken before we can decide whether or not a general environmental crisis had emerged in China by the middle of the nineteenth century. I strongly suspect that one had, and I also suspect that the driving forces of environmental change that I have identified in Lingnan – climate change, population dynamics, and the commercialization of the economy – too are likely to be found in a more comprehensive history of environmental change in late imperial China.

Finally, if history tells a story (and I think it should), the question is whose story have I told here and from what perspective? As I wrote (and rewrote) the book, I was very much aware that my story of the environment of Lingnan could be told, using the sources I had uncovered, from at least three different points of view. Two of those – the Han Chinese and the non-Han indigenes – are fairly obvious, and I have tried to convey something of what the story looked like to them.

To the Han Chinese, the story involved the progressive and successful transformation of an alien landscape into one formed and farmed by settled communities ruled by a distant but benevolent emperor. There was not, of course, a single Chinese story, for peasant-farmers in the Pearl River delta, textile weavers in Foshan, tobacco growers in Nanxiong, or the governor-general in Guangzhou all saw their world somewhat differently. Nonetheless, all these Chinese valued the environmental transformations that created, maintained, or enriched farmland. Or almost all, that is. For at least one person, Deng Bi'nan, the Leizhou prefect in the early nineteenth century, had come to consider the consequences of those environmental changes and to lament the extinction of species that had once inhabited Lingnan.

To the non-Han indigenes, the story line is much different, and regardless of whether they were the Tai lowland tillers of the land or Li inhabitants practicing swidden agriculture, the Han Chinese immigrants precipitated changes in the ways these peoples related to their environment. Indeed, the Han Chinese encounter with the non-Han almost always resulted in their displacement so the Chinese could bring more land under the plow. The process was extremely slow, especially as the Tai had a powerful ally – malaria – that kept the Chinese at bay for centuries. But as Chinese settlers acclimated themselves to Lingnan and controlled the flooding of the lower reaches of the West, North, and East Rivers, malaria receded as a threat. The non-Han resisted the Chinese advance as best they could, but ultimately they had either to accept Chinese overlordship, as most of the Tai agriculturists ultimately did, or to flee to ever more remote fringes of Lingnan – the Li from the coastal plains of the southwest littoral and Hainan Island to the mountains in the center of the island, or the Miao further west in Guangxi – where they continued their mobile, slash-and-burn agriculture. Where the story of the centuries-long remaking of Lingnan to sustain settled, wet-rice agriculture is considered a triumph by Chinese chroniclers, to the Li, Tai, and Miao peoples, it is a story of their displacement from the lands that had supported their ways of life.

To these two basic groups could be added other peoples' perspectives, such as non-Han immigrants like the Yao who confronted both indigenes and Han settlers. But the third perspective I have thought about that informs the story line of this book has been submerged, hidden, lurking in the forest shadows, staying vague in part because of my discomfort in ascribing a "story" or a "perspective" to the nonhuman inhabitants of Lingnan, in particular the tigers. But for a moment I would like to ponder, if the question makes any sense at all, what the environmental and economic transformations that have formed the subject matter of this book might have looked like from the perspective of tigers.

The short answer, I think, is tigricide, if I can extrapolate from the various kinds of mass murder some populations of humans inflict upon others to what humans did to populations of tigers. For just as surely as there is a population history of human inhabitants of Lingnan, so too is there a population history of tigers. Today there are few tigers left in the fragments of forests that still exist in the Nanling Mountains. In 2 CE, when there were perhaps half a million people in Lingnan, there were tens of thousands of tigers. As people captured the energy flows of the Lingnan ecosystems to enable their populations to grow, the habitat for tigers decreased, and thus so too did their food supply, leading to ever smaller tiger populations. To push tigers to the edge of extinction, humans did not need to eliminate all of the forests in Lingnan, but merely to fragment the tigers' preferred habitat into pieces too small – to something on the order of 500 square kilometers – to sustain a viable tiger population.[19]

Both the Han and non-Han Chinese inhabitants of Lingnan contributed to the destruction and fragmentation of tiger habitat. Until about 1700, the human population periodically declined, creating an opportunity for tigers to reclaim some habitat from the humans and, thus, for their numbers to

[19] John Seidensticker attributed the extinction of the Indonesian tiger to the fragmentation of their habitat and the insularity of reserves of less than 500 square kilometers. See Seidensticker, "Large Carnivores and the Consequences of Habitat Insularization." Allan Rabinowitz has used Seidensticker's work and his own field work in "Estimating the Indochinese Tiger *Panthera tigris corbetti* Population in Thailand," *Biological Conservation* 65 (1993): 213–17.

rebound. But around 1700, the human population continued growing, never reverting to a smaller scale that would relieve some pressure on the tiger population. Then, in the middle of the eighteenth century, the Chinese state decided to abandon large-scale land development schemes in favor of individual peasant-farmers bringing odd lots in the hills into production, further fragmenting tiger habitat by spreading Chinese settlers throughout the forests. And when they then began burning off the hills "to deprive the robbers, tigers, and snakes of their dens," what little may have been left of tiger habitat went up in smoke.

Tigers experienced a food shortage, as deer and wild boars disappeared along with the forests. And just as food shortages affect human reproductive strategies and rates, so too can we imagine how the number of tigers declined as fewer cubs were born and survived to adulthood. Did the declining food supply intensify competition among tigers? Did they abandon their territories and poach upon other tigers' turf? We do not know. But tigers certainly competed with the other species at the top of the food chain – humans – for food and for land, leading to their attacks on villages, carrying off pigs or children, depending on what they could get their jaws around.

Although the Han Chinese experienced both tiger attacks and non-Han uprisings as threats to their way of life, I do not mean to impute conscious resistance by tigers to the Han encroachment on their habitat. And while we might imagine what the tigers' perspective on the establishment and expansion of settled agriculture may have been, at this point I have to step back and reaffirm the humanness of the story that I have told. For it is only we humans who can imagine how other species may have experienced us and then tie together many of their generations (and ours) into a single narrative. And by so doing, we connect our history with that of other species and understand that, because extinction is possible (as Deng Bi'nan warned nearly two centuries ago), the elimination of an other species at our hands both diminishes our humanity and impoverishes our history.

BIBLIOGRAPHY

Archival Sources

The archival sources for this book are located primarily in the Number One Historical Archives (Di yi lishi dang'an guan) in Beijing. The rice price data has been transcribed from the price lists catalogued as: Gongzhong zhupi zouzhe; nongye lei; liangjia qingdan (Palace memorials; agriculture section; grain price lists). The harvest yield data and officials' comments about climate come from memorials catalogued as: Gongzhong zhupi zouzhe; nongye lei; yuxue liangjia (Palace memorials; agriculture section; rain, snow, and grain prices; cited as NYL). Other memorials cited in the book are catalogued in the following sections: Gongzhong zhupi zouzhe; nongye lei; tunken (Palace memorials; agriculture section; land reclamation). Gongzhong zhupi zouzhe; nongye lei; tunken gengwu (Palace memorials; agriculture section; land reclamation and land tilling). Gongzhong zhupi zouzhe; xingke tiben; dao an (Palace memorials; board of punishments routine memorials; robberies; cited as XKTB dao an). Neige; xingke tiben; tudi zhaiwu (Grand secretariat; board of punishments routine memorials; land and debt; cited as XKTB). For citations, I have listed the Chinese lunar calendar and reign date, and the box or bundle from the archive.

I have also used the archives of the National Palace Museum (Gugong bowuyuan) in Taibei, Taiwan, in particular the memorials catalogued as Gongzhong dang (Palace memorial archives) or Junji dang (Grand council archives). For citations, I have listed the author of the memorial, the Chinese lunar calendar and reign date, and the catalogue number.

Published Collections of Primary Sources

Da Ming huidian (The Ming code). 1587 ed. Shanghai: Shangwu yinshu guan, 1936.

Da Qing gao zong (Qianlong) shi lu (The veritable records of the Qianlong emperor). Taibei: Xinwenfeng chuban gongsi, 1978.

Da Qing huidian (The Qing code). 1899 ed. Shanghai: Shangwu yinshu guan, 1911.

Da Qing huidian shili (Precedents and regulations supplementing the Qing code). 1875 ed. Taibei: Wenhai chuban she, 1964.

Da Qing sheng zu (Kangxi) shi lu (The veritable records of the Kangxi emperor). Taibei: Xinwenfeng chuban gongsi, 1978.

Da Qing shi chao sheng xun (Imperial edicts from the ten emperors of the Qing dynasty). Taibei: Wenhai chuban she, 1965.

Da Qing shi zong (Yongzheng) shi lu (The veritable records of the Yongzheng emperor). Taibei: Xinwenfeng chuban gongsi, 1978.

Gongzhongdang Kangxi chao zouzhe (Palace memorials from the Kangxi period). Gugong bowuyuan, comp. 9 vols. Taibei: Guoli gugong bowuyuan, 1976–77.

Gongzhongdang Qianlong chao zouzhe (Palace memorials from the Qianlong period). Gugong bowuyuan, comp. 75 vols. Taibei: Guoli gugong bowuyuan, 1982–86.

Gongzhongdang Yongzheng chao zouzhe (Palace memorials from the Yongzheng period). Gugong bowuyuan, comp. 32 vols. Taibei: Guoli gugong bowuyuan, 1977–88.

Guangdong sheng ziran zaihai shiliao (Source materials concerning natural disasters in Guangdong province). Guangzhou: Guangdong sheng wen shi yanjiu guan, 1961.

Huang chao jingshi wen bian (Statecraft writings from our august dynasty). He Changling, comp., 1827. Reprint, Taibei: Wenhai chuban she, n.d.

Huang chao jingshi xubian (Statecraft writings from our august dynasty, continued). Ge Shijun, comp., 1888. Reprint, Taibei: Wenhia chuban she, 1972.

Huang chao jingshi xubian (Statecraft writings from our august dynasty, continued). Sheng Kang, comp., 1897. Reprint, Taibei: Wenhia chuban she, 1972.

KXCZZ. See *Gongzhongdang Kangxi chao zouzhe.*

Liu Xun. *Ling biao lu yi* (Strange records from Lingbiao [Lingnan]). Reprinted in *Qin ding si ku quan shu*, vol. 138. Taibei: Shangwu yinshu guan, 1975.

Ming Qing Foshan beike wenxian jingji ziliao (Economic source materials from Ming- and Qing-era steles in Foshan). Guangzhou: Guangdong renmin chuban she, 1987.

Qing dai dizu boxiao xingtai (Forms of land rent exploitation in the Qing). Zhongguo diyi lishi dang'an guan and Zhongguo shehui kexue yuan lishi yanjiu so, comp. Beijing: Xinhua shudian, 1982.

Qing shi lu Guangxi ziliao ji lu (Source materials on Guangxi from the "veritable records of the Qing"). Nanning: Guangxi renmin chuban she, 1988.

QLCZZ. See *Gongzhongdang Qianlong chao zouzhe.*

Taiping huan yu ji (World almanac of the Taiping era [976–83]). Yue Shi (930–1007), comp. Reprint, Taibei: Wenhai chuban she, 1974.

Wang Anguo, memorial dated QL7.8.29, in *Lishi dang'an* 3 (1985): 17–18.

Yongzheng chao hanwen zhupi zouzhe (Chinese-language palace memorials from the Yongzheng reign). Di yi lishi dang'an guan, comp. 10 vols. Nanjing: Jiangsu guji chuban she, 1989.

Yongzheng zhupi yuzhi (Vermilion rescripts of the Yongzheng emperor). 1738 ed. Reprint, Taibei: Wenhai chuban she, 1965.

Yuanfeng jiu yu zhi (Gazetteer of the nine Yuanfeng-era [1078–85] nations). 1784 ed. Wang Cun (1023–1101), comp. Reprint, Beijing: Zhonghua shuju, 1984.

Yuanhe junxian tuzhi (Yuanhe-era [806–20] gazetteer of prefectures and counties). Li Jifu, comp. Reprint, Beijing: Zhonghua shuju, 1983.

YZCHWZPZZ. See *Yongzheng chao hanwen zhupi zouzhe.*

YZCZZ. See *Gongzhongdang Yongzheng chao zouzhe.*

Zhongguo lidai shihuo zhi sanbian (Three collections from the "economics" sections of China's dynastic histories). Taibei: Xuehai chuban she, 1972.

Zhou Qufei. *Ling wai dai ta* (Explanations of things beyond the passes). 1178 ed. Reprinted in *Qin ding si ku quan shu*, vols. 138–39. Taibei: Shangwu yinshu guan, 1975.

Gazetteers

Note: In the list below, *fuzhi* = "prefecture gazetteer," *tongzhi* = "provincial gazetteer," *xianzhi* = "county gazetteer," *zhouzhi* = "independent department gazetteer," and *zhi* = "gazetteer."

Chaozhou fuzhi. Qing Qianlong 27 (1762).
Chaozhou fuzhi. Qing Guangxu 19 (1893).
Chaozhou zhi. ca. 1407. Reprinted in *Yongle dadian ben difangzhi huikan*, vol. 3. Tokyo: Chubun shupansha, 1980.
Gaozhou fuzhi. Qing Daoguang 7 (1827).
Gaozhou fuzhi. Qing Guangxu 16 (1890).
Guangdong tongzhi. Ming Jiaqing 40 (1561).
Guangdong tongzhi. Ming Wanli 30 (1602).
Guangdong tongzhi. Qing Daoguang 2 (1822).
Guangdong tongzhi. Qing Tongzhi 3 (1864).
Guangdong tongzhi. Qing Yongzheng 9 (1731).
Guangxi tongzhi. Qing Yongzheng 11 (1733).
Guangxi tongzhi. Qing Jiaqing 6 (1801).
Guangzhou fuzhi. Qing Kangxi 12 (1673).
Guangzhou fuzhi. Qing Qianlong 24 (1759).
Guangzhou fuzhi. Qing Guangxu 5 (1879).
Guangzhou zhi. Ca. 1407. Reprinted in *Yongle dadian ben difangzhi huikan*, vol. 3. Tokyo: Chubun shupansha, 1980.
Guilin fuzhi. Qing Guangxu 31 (1905).
Haifeng xianzhi. Qing Qianlong 15 (1750).; revised in Tongzhi 12 (1873). and Minguo 20 (1931)..
Huilai xianzhi. Qing Yongzheng 31; revised as Qing Tongzhi 5 (1866) and Mingguo 19 (1930).
Huizhou fuzhi. Ming Jiaqing 35 (1556).
Huizhou fuzhi. Qing Kangxi 27 (1688).
Huizhou fuzhi. Qing Guangxu 3 (1877).
Jiaying zhouzhi. Qing Xianfeng 3 (1853).
Leizhou fuzhi. Qing Daoguang 16 (1811).
Lianzhou fuzhi. Qing Daoquang 13 (1833).
Lianzhou zhi. Qing Tongzhi 9 (1870).
Liuzhou fuzhi. Qing Qianlong 29 (1764).
Sang Yuan Wei zong zhi. Ming Zhigang, comp. 1870.
Nanhai xianzhi. Qing Daoguang 15 (1835).
Nanhai zhi. Yuan Dade 8 (1304). Reprinted in *Song Yuan fangzhi congkan*, vol. 8. Beijing: Zhonghua shuju, 1990.
Nanning fuzhi. Qing Qianlong 7 (1742).
Nanning zhi. Ca. 1407. Reprinted in *Yongle dadian ben difangzhi huikan*, vol. 4. Tokyo: Chubun shupansha, 1980.
Nanxiong zhouzhi. Qing Jiaqing 24 (1819).
Qingyuan fuzhi. Qing Daoguang 9 (1829).
Qinzhou fuzhi. Qing Daoguang 14 (1834).

Qiongtai zhi. Ming Zhengde 16 (1521). Reprinted in *Tian yi ge Ming dai fangzhi xuan kan,* vols. 60–62. Shanghai: Gu ji shudian, 1982.
Qiongzhou fuzhi. Qing Daoguang 21 (1841).
Shaozhou fuzhi. Qing Tongzhi 13 (1874).
Wengyuan xianzhi. Ming Jiaqing 36 (1557). Reprinted in *Tian yi ge Ming dai fangzhi xuan kan,* vol. 63. Shanghai: Gu ji shudian, 1982.
Wuzhou fuzhi. Qing Qianlong 35 (1770).
Wuzhou zhi. Ca. 1407. Reprinted in *Yongle dadian ben difangzhi huikan,* vol. 4. Tokyo: Chubun shupansha, 1981.
Xiangshan xianzhi. Qing Qianlong 15 (1750).
Xin'an xianzhi. Qing Jiaqing 24 (1819).
Xinhui xiang tuzhi. Hong Kong: Gangzhou xuehui, 1970 reprint of late Qing edition.
Xinhui xianzhi. Qing Daoguang 21 (1841).
Xunzhou fuzhi. Qing Daoguang 6 (1826).
Yangjiang zhi. Mingguo 14 (1925).
Yulin fuzhi. Qing Guangxu 20 (1894).
Zhaoqing fuzhi. Qing Daoguang 13 (1833).
Zhen'an fuzhi. Qing Guangxu 18 (1892).

Dynastic Histories

Han shu. Beijing: Xinhua shuju, 1974.
Ming shi. Beijing: Xinhua shuju, 1974.
Song shi. Beijing: Xinhua shuju, 1974.
Xin Tang shu. Beijing: Xinhua shuju, 1974.
Yuan shi. Beijing: Xinhua shuju, 1974.

Maps

The maps in this book are primarily of two types and are based on different sources. The general maps showing the placement of Lingnan with respect to China, as well as the various maps showing population centers and river systems, I adapted from base maps provided in the World Data Bank by Cartesia software, using the sources listed below.

I produced the maps showing population density or other data, at either the prefectural or county level, using GIS (Geographic Information Systems) software, which is a geographically referenced database with statistical analytic and mapping capability. The initial analysis was conducted using ARC/INFO software, which was then exported to MapInfo, v. 3.0. The base county boundary map, which I adapted to ca. 1820 boundaries using the sources below and then used to construct the prefectural maps, was supplied by CITAS (China in Time and Space). These maps then became the basis for analyzing and mapping the data I had entered into the GIS database.

Guangdong tu (Map of Guangdong). 1866.
Guangxi. Postal Service. 1924.

Guangxi quan sheng di yu tu shuo (Map and explanations of the entire province of Guangxi). 1866.

Guangxi yu di quan tu (Map of Guangxi). 1898.

Huangchao Zhong wai yitong yutu (Imperial maps of China and foreign lands). 1863.

Kuantung [*sic*]. 1898.

Qing dai yi tong ditu (Qing-era maps). Taibei: Guofang yanjiu yuan, 1966 reprint.

Qing Qianlong neifu yutu (Secret imperial palace maps). Beijing: Gugong bowuyuan, 1933 reprint of 1760 map.

Zhongguo jin wubai nian han lao fenbutu ji (Maps of droughts and floods in China for the past 500 years). Zhongyang qixiang ju, comp. Beijing: Kexue chuban she, 1981.

Zhongguo lishi ditu ji (Historical maps of China). Tan Qixiang, editor in chief. 8 vols. Shanghai: Ditu chuban she, 1975–82.

Zhonghua minguo xin chu shi tu (A new atlas of Republican China). 1917.

Zhonghua minguo xin lei fensheng tu (A provincial atlas of Republican China). 1931.

Secondary Sources

Abel, Wilhelm. *Agricultural Fluctuations in Europe from the Thirteenth to the Twentieth Centuries.* New York: St. Martin's, 1980.

Adshead, S. A. M. "An Energy Crisis in Early Modern China." *Ch'ing shih wen-t'i* 3, no. 2 (Dec. 1974): 20–28.

Allaby, Michael. *Dictionary of the Environment.* New York: New York University Press, 1989.

Anderson, E. N. *The Food of China.* New Haven: Yale University Press, 1988.

Antony, Robert. *Pirates, Bandits, and Brotherhoods: A Study of Crime and Law in Kwangtung Province, 1796–1839.* University of Hawaii, Ph.D. dissertation, 1988.

Appleby, Andrew. "Epidemics and Famine in the Little Ice Age." *Journal of Interdisciplinary History* 10, no. 4 (Spring 1980): 643–64.

Famine in Tudor and Stuart England. Stanford: Stanford University Press, 1978.

Archeological Discovery in Eastern Kwangtung: The Major Writings of Fr. Rafael Maglioni (1891–1953). Hong Kong: Hong Kong Archeological Society, 1975.

Aston, Trevor, ed. *Crisis in Europe, 1560–1660.* New York: Doubleday, 1967.

Atwell, William S. "International Bullion Flows and the Chinese Economy circa 1530–1650." *Past and Present* 95 (May 1982): 68–90.

"Notes on Silver, Foreign Trade, and the Late Ming Economy." *Ch'ing shih wen-t'i* 3, no. 8 (1977): 1–33.

"A Seventeenth-Century 'General Crisis' in East Asia?" *Modern Asian Studies* 24, no. 4 (1990): 661–82.

"Some Observations on the 'Seventeenth-Century Crisis' in China and Japan." *Journal of Asian Studies* 45, no. 2 (Feb. 1986): 223–44.

Balazs, Etienne. *Chinese Civilization and Bureaucracy.* New Haven: Yale University Press, 1972.

Banister, Judith. *China's Changing Population.* Stanford: Stanford University Press, 1987.

Bartlett, Beatrice S. *Monarchs and Ministers: The Grand Council in Mid-Ch'ing China, 1723–1820.* Berkeley and Los Angeles: University of California Press, 1991.

Bartlett, H. H. "Fire, Primitive Agriculture, and Grazing in the Tropics." In William L. Thomas, ed. *Man's Role in Changing the Face of the Earth.* Princeton: Princeton University Press, 1955.

Bates, Marston. "Ecology of Anopheline Mosquitoes." In Mark Boyd, ed., *Malariology*. Philadelphia: Saunders 1949.

Beattie, Hillary. "The Alternative to Resistance: The Case of T'ung-ch'eng, Anhwei." In Jonathan D. Spence and John E. Wills Jr., eds., *From Ming to Ch'ing: Conquest, Region, and Continuity in Seventeenth-Century China*. New Haven: Yale University Press, 1979.

Benton, Gregor, *Mountain Fires: The Red Army's Three-Year War in South China, 1934–38*. Berkeley and Los Angeles: University of California Press, 1992.

Bernhardt, Kathryn. *Rents, Taxes, and Peasant Resistance: The Lower Yangzi Region, 1840–1950*. Stanford: Stanford University Press, 1992.

Bonnery, Samuel. *Canton to Hankow, Overland*. Canton: Friend of China, 1861.

Boserup, Ester. *The Conditions of Agricultural Growth: The Economics of Agrarian Change under Population Pressure*. New York: Aldine, 1965.

Economic and Demographic Relationships in Development, T. Paul Schultz, ed. and intro. Baltimore: Johns Hopkins University Press, 1990.

Population and Technological Change: A Study of Long-Term Trends. Chicago: University of Chicago Press, 1981.

Bowra, E. C. "The Manchu Conquest of Canton." *China Review* 1 (July 1872–June 1873): 86–96, 228–37.

Boxer, C. R. *The Great Ship from Amacon: Annals of Macao and the Old Japan Trade, 1555–1640*. Lisboa: Centro de Estudos Historicos Ultramarinos, 1963.

South China in the Sixteenth Century. London: Hakluyt Society, 1953.

Boyd, Mark, ed. *Malariology*. Philadelphia: Saunders 1949.

Bradley, Raymond S., and Philip D. Jones, eds. *Climate since A.D. 1500*. New York: Routledge, 1992.

Bradley, R. S. et al. "Secular Fluctuations of Temperature over Northern Hemisphere Land Areas and Mainland China since the Mid-19th Century." In Ye Duzheng et al., eds., *The Climate of China and Global Climate: Proceedings of the Beijing International Symposium on Climate*. Berlin: Springer, 1987.

Brandt, Loren. *Commercialization and Agricultural Development: Central and Eastern China, 1870–1937*. Cambridge University Press, 1989.

Braudel, Fernand. *Civilization and Capitalism, 15th–18th Century*, vol. 1, *The Structures of Everyday Life*, Siân Reynolds, trans. New York: Harper and Row, 1979.

Civilization and Capitalism, 15th–18th Century, vol. 2, *The Wheels of Commerce*. Sian Reynolds, trans. New York: Harper and Row, 1984.

Civilization and Capitalism, 15th–18th Century, vol. 3, *The Perspective of the World*. Sian Reynolds, trans. New York: Harper and Row, 1984.

The Mediterranean and the Mediterranean World in the Age of Philip II. Siân Reynolds, trans. New York: Harper and Row, 1972.

Bray, Francesca. *Science and Civilization in China*, vol. 6, part 2, *Agriculture*. Cambridge University Press, 1984.

The Rice Economies: Technology and Development in Asian Societies. Berkeley and Los Angeles: University of California Press, 1994.

Brim, John A. "Village Alliance Temples in Hong Kong." In Arthur P. Wolf, ed., *Religion and Ritual in Chinese Society*. Stanford: Stanford University Press, 1974.

Brown, Dee. *Bury My Heart at Wounded Knee*. New York: Holt, Rinehart, & Winston, 1970.

Bruce-Chwatt, L. J. "History of Malaria from Prehistory to Eradication." In Walther H. Wernsdorfer and Sir Ian McGregor, eds., *Malaria: Principles and Practice of Malariology*. Edinburgh: Churchill Livingstone, 1988.

Bruenig, E. F. et al. *Ecological-Socioeconomic System Analysis and Simulation: A Guide for Application of System Analysis to the Conservation, Utilization, and Development of Tropical and Subtropical Land Resources in China.* Bonn: Deutsches Nationalkomitee für das UNESCO Programm Der Mensch und die Biosphäre, 1986.

Chang, Hsin-pao. *Commissioner Lin and the Opium War.* New York: Norton, 1970.

Chang, K. C. *Food in Chinese Culture: Anthropological and Historical Perspectives.* New Haven: Yale University Press, 1977.

Chang, Kwang-chih. *The Archeology of Ancient China*, 4th edition. New Haven: Yale University Press, 1986.

Chao, Kang. *Man and Land in Chinese History: An Economic Analysis.* Stanford: Stanford University Press, 1986.

"Qing zhong qi yi lai liangshi mou chan zhi biandong" (Changes in per mu harvest yields from the mid-Qing on). *Han xue yanjiu* 10, no. 2 (1992): 371–98.

Chaudhuri, K. N. *The Trading World of Asia and the English East India Company 1660–1760.* Cambridge University Press, 1978.

Chen Binyi, editor in chief. *Zhongguo ziran dili* (The natural geography of China), vol. 4, *Dibiao shui* (Surface water). Beijing: Kexue chuban she, 1981.

Zhongguo ziran dili (The natural geography of China), vol. 10, *Lishi ziran dili* (Historical geography). Beijing: Kexue chuban she, 1982.

Chen Chunsheng. "Qingdai Guangdong de yin yuan liutong" (The circulation of silver dollars in Guangdong during the Qing). *Zhongguo qianbi* 1 (1985): 46–53.

"Qingdai Guangdong de zhi qian zhu yu liutong" (The production and circulation of money in Guangdong during the Qing). *Zhongshan daxue yanjiu sheng xue kan* 4 (1984): 81–89.

"Qingdai Guangdong yin qian bi jia" (The copper–silver ratio in Guangdong during the Qing). *Zhongshan daxue xue bao* 1 (1986): 99–104.

Qingdai Qianlong nianjian Guangdong de mi jia he mi liang maoyi. Zhongshan University, M.A. thesis, 1984.

Shichang jizhi yu shehui bianqian: shiba shiji Guangdong mi jia fenxi (Market structure and social change: An analysis of eighteenth-century Guangdong rice prices). Xiamen University, Ph.D. thesis, 1988.

Shichang jizhi yu shehui bianqian – 18 shiji Guangdong mi jia fenxi (Market structure and social change: An analysis of 18th-century Guangdong rice prices). Guangzhou: Zhongshan daxue chuban she, 1992.

Chen Guanghui. *Zhongguo gudai dui wai maoyi shi* (A history of foreign trade in ancient China). Guangzhou: Guangdong renmin chubanshe, 1985.

Chen Jiaqi. "Ming Qing shiqi qihou bianhua dui tai hu liuyu nongye jingji de yingxiang" (The influence of climate change during the Ming and Qing upon the agricultural economy in the Lake Tai region). *Zhongguo nongshi* 3 (1991): 30–36.

Chen Lesu. "Zhujigang shi shi" (A history of Zhujigang). *Xueshu yanjiu* [Guangdong] 6 (1982): 139–51.

Chen Shuping. "Yumi he fanshu zai Zhongguo juanfan qingkuang yanjiu" (A study of the circumstances of the introduction of maize and sweet potatoes into China). *Zhongguo shehui kexue* 3 (1980): 187–204.

Chen Weiming. "Song dai Lingnan zhuliang yu jingji zuowu de shengchan jingying" (The production and management of main crops and industrial crops in Lingnan during the Song). *Zhongguo nongshi* 1 (1990): 20–31.

Chen Yundong. *Kejiaren* (The Hakka). Hong Kong: Lianya chuban she, 1978.

Chen Zhiping. "Shilun Kangxi chunian dongnan zhu sheng de 'shu huang' " (On the crisis of overproduction in the southeast during the early years of the Kangxi reign). *Zhongguo shehui jingji shi yanjiu* 2 (1982): 40–46.

Chou Yuanhe. "Qing dai renkou yanjiu" (Study on population during the Qing). *Zhongguo shehui kexue* 2 (1982): 161–88.

Ch'uan, Han-shen, and Richard A. Kraus. *Mid-Ch'ing Rice Markets and Trade: An Essay in Price History.* Cambridge, MA: Harvard University Press, 1975.

"Course of the Chu Kiang, or Pearl River." *China Repository* 20, no. 2 (Feb. 1851): 105–111, and 20, no. 3 (Mar. 1851): 113–22.

Cressey, George B. *China's Geographic Foundations.* New York: McGraw-Hill, 1934.

Cronon, William. *Changes in the Land: Indians, Colonists, and the Ecology of New England.* New York: Hill & Wang, 1983.

"Modes of Prophecy and Production: Placing Nature in History." *Journal of American History* 76, no. 4 (Mar. 1990): 1122–31.

"A Place for Stories: Nature, History, and Narrative." *Journal of American History* 78, no. 4 (1992): 1347–76.

"The Uses of Environmental History." *Environmental History Review* 17, no. 3 (fall 1993): 1–21.

Crosby, Alfred W. *Ecological Imperialism: The Biological Expansion of Europe, 900–1900.* Cambridge University Press, 1986.

"An Enthusiastic Second." *Journal of American History* 76, no. 4 (Mar. 1990): 1107–10.

Csete, Anne. *A Frontier Minority in the Chinese World: The Li People of Hainan Island from the Han through the High Qing.* State University of New York at Buffalo, Ph.D. dissertation, 1995.

"Qing Management of a Multi-Ethnic Society: The Case of Han–Li Conflict on Hainan in 1767." Paper presented at the Asian Studies annual meeting, Washington, DC, April 7, 1995.

Cushman, Jennifer Wayne. *Fields from the Sea: Chinese Junk Trade with Siam during the Late Eighteenth and Early Nineteenth Centuries.* Ithaca: Cornell University Press, 1993.

Dampier, William. *A New Voyage Round the World.* New York: Dover, 1968.

Daniels, Christian, and Nicholas K. Menzies. In Joseph Needham, ed., *Science and Civilization in China*, vol. 6, part 3, *Agro-industries and Forestry*, Cambridge University Press, 1996.

Davis, John Francis. *Sketches of China; partly during an inland journey of four months, between Peking, Nanking, and Canton; with notices and observations relative to the present war.* London: C. Knight, 1841.

"Description of the City of Canton." *Chinese Repository* 11, no. 4 (Aug. 1833): 145–60; 11, no. 5 (Sept. 1833): 193–211; 11, no. 6 (Oct. 1833): 241–64; 11, no. 7 (Nov. 1833): 289–308.

deVisser, M. W. *The Dragon in China and Japan.* Amsterdam: J. Muller, 1913.

deVries, Jan. *The Economy of Europe in an Age of Crisis, 1600–1750.* Cambridge University Press, 1976.

"Measuring the Impact of Climate on History: The Search for Appropriate Methodologies." In R. I. Rothberg and T. K. Rabb, eds., *Climate and History: Studies in Interdisciplinary History*. Princeton: Princeton University Press, 1981.

Domrös, Manfred, and Peng Gongping. *The Climate of China*. Berlin: Springer, 1988.

du Halde, Jean Baptiste. *The General History of China*. London: J. Watts, 1741.

Dunstan, Helen. *An Anthology of Chinese Economic Statecraft, or, The Sprouts of Liberalism* (unpublished manuscript).

"The Late Ming Epidemics: A Preliminary Study." *Ch'ing shih wen't'i* 3, no. 3 (Nov. 1975): 1–59.

Dupâquier, Jacques. "Demographic Crises and Subsistence Crises in France, 1650–1725." In John Walter and Roger Schofield, eds., *Famine, Disease and the Social Order in Early Modern Society*. Cambridge University Press, 1989.

Eddy, John A. "Climate and the Changing Sun." *Climatic Change* 1 (1977): 173–90.

Edwards, C. A. et al., eds. *Sustainable Agricultural Systems*. Ankeny, Iowa: Soil and Water Conservation Society, 1990.

Ellsaesser, Hugh W. et al. "Global Climatic Trends as Revealed in the Recorded Data." *Reviews of Geophysics* 24, no. 4 (Nov. 1986): 745–92.

Elvin, Mark. *The Pattern of the Chinese Past*. Stanford: Stanford University Press, 1971.

Elvin, Mark, and Liu Ts'ui-jung, eds. *Sediments of Time: Environment and Society in China*. Cambridge University Press, forthcoming.

Fan I-chun. *Long-Distance Trade and Market Integration in the Ming–Ch'ing Period, 1400–1850*. Stanford University, Ph.D. dissertation, 1992.

Faure, David. *The Rural Economy of Pre-Liberation China: Trade Increase and Peasant Livelihood in Jiangsi and Guangdong, 1870 to 1937*. Hong Kong: Oxford University Press East Asian Monographs, 1989.

"What Made Foshan a Town? The Evolution of Rural–Urban Identities in Ming–Qing China." *Late Imperial China* 11, no 2 (Dec. 1990): 1–31.

"The Yao Wars and the Rise of Orthodoxy from the Mid-Ming to the Early Qing." *Association for Asian Studies, Inc. Abstracts of the 1995 Annual Meeting*, 107.

Faust, Ernest Carrol. "An Inquiry into the Prevalence of Malaria in China." *China Medical Journal* 40, no. 10 (Oct. 1926): 938–56.

"Mosquitoes in China and Their Potential Relationship to Human Disease." *Journal of Tropical Medicine and Hygiene* 32, no. 10 (May 1929): 133–37.

Fay, Peter Ward. *The Opium War, 1840–1842*. Chapel Hill: University of North Carolina Press, 1975.

Fenzel, G. "On the Natural Conditions Affecting the Introduction of Forestry as a Branch of Rural Economy in the Province of Kwangtung, Especially in North Kwangtung." *Lingnan Science Journal* 7 (June 1929): 37–97.

"Problems of Reforestation in Kwangtung with Respect to the Climate." *Lingnan Science Journal* 9, nos. 1–2 (June 1930): 97–113.

Fielde, Adele. *A Corner of Cathay*. New York: Macmillan, 1894.

Fiennes, Richard. *Man, Nature and Disease*. London: Weidenfeld and Nicolson, 1964.

Flynn, Dennis O., and Arturo Giráldez. "Born with a 'Silver Spoon': The Origin of World Trade in 1571." *Journal of World History* 6, no. 2 (1995): 201–21.

Fong Kin-lan. "Geological Reconnaissance along the North River of Kwangtung." *Lingnan Science Journal* 8 (Dec. 1929): 701–30.

Franck, Harry A. *Roving through South China*. New York: Century, 1925.

Fu Lo-shu. *A Documentary Chronicle of Sino-Western Relations (1644–1820)*. Tucson: University of Arizona Press, 1966.

Fu Tongxin. "Ming Qing shiqi de Guangdong shatian" (The alluvial fields of Guangdong in the Ming and Qing). In *Ming Qing Guangdong shehui jingji xingtai yanjiu*. Guangzhou: Guangdong renmin chuban she, 1985.

Fu Yiling. *Ming Qing nongcun shehui jingji* (Rural society and economy during the Ming and Qing). Xiamen: Shiyong shuju, 1961.

Fuchs, Walter. *The Mongol Atlas of China*. Beijing: Fu Jen University, 1946.

Fuson, C. G. "The Peoples of Kwangtung: Their Origin, Migrations, and Present Distribution." *Lingnan Science Journal* 7 (June 1929): 5–19.

Galloway, Patrick. "Annual Variations in Deaths by Age, Deaths by Cause, Prices, and Weather in London, 1670–1830." *Population Studies* 39 (1985): 487–505.

"Basic Patterns in Annual Variations in Fertility, Nuptiality, Mortality, and Prices in Pre-industrial Europe." *Population Studies* 42 (1988): 275–303.

"Long-Term Fluctuations in Climate and Population in the Preindustrial Era," *Population and Development Review* 12, no. 1 (Mar. 1986): 1–24.

Gardella, Robert. *Harvesting Mountains: Fujian and the China Tea Trade, 1757–1937*. Berkeley and Los Angeles: University of California Press, 1994.

Gates, Hill. *China's Motor: A Thousand Years of Petty Capitalism*. Ithaca: Cornell University Press, 1996.

Ge Jianxiong. *Zhongguo renkou fazhan* (The development of China's population). Fuzhou: Fujian renmin chuban she, 1991.

Geertz, Clifford. *Agricultural Involution: The Processes of Ecological Change in Indonesia*. Berkeley and Los Angeles: University of California Press, 1963.

Goldstone, Jack A. "East and West in the Seventeenth Century: Political Crises in Stuart England, Ottoman Turkey, and Ming China." *Comparative Studies in Society and History* 30, no. 1 (1988): 103–42.

Revolution and Rebellion in the Early Modern World. Berkeley and Los Angeles: University of California Press, 1991.

Gong Gaofa and Jin Weimin. "Woguo zhiwu wu shiqi de dili fenbu" (On the geographic distribution of phenodate in China). *Dili xuebao* 38, no. 1 (Mar. 1983): 33–40.

Gong Gaofa, Zhang Jinrong, and Zhang Peiyuan. "Ying yong shiliao feng qian jizai yanjiu Beijing diqu jiang shui liang dui dong xiaomai shoucheng de yingxiang" (The use of documentary sources to study the effect of the amount of water on the harvest yields of winter wheat in the Beijing area). *Qixiang xuebao* 41, no. 4 (Nov. 1983): 444–51.

Great Britain Naval Intelligence Division. *China Proper*, vol. 1, *Physical Geography, History, and Peoples*. Geographical Handbook Series. London, 1941.

Grove, Jean. *The Little Ice Age*. London: Methuen, 1988.

Grove, Richard. *Green Imperialism: Colonial Expansion, Tropical Island Edens and the Origins of Environmentalism, 1600–1860*. Cambridge University Press, 1994.

Groveman, Brian S., and Helmut E. Landsberg. "Simulated Northern Hemisphere Temperature Departures." *Geophysical Research Letters* 6, no. 10 (Oct. 1979): 767–69.

Gu Yanwu. *Tianxia junguo li bing shu* (The strategic advantages and disadvantages of all countries in the world), 1879 ed. Shanghai: Shangwu yinshu guan, 1936.

Guangdong lishi xuehui, ed. *Ming Qing Guangdong shehui jingji xingtai yanjiu* (Studies in the social and economic formations of Ming and Qing Guangdong). Guangzhou: Guangdong renmin chuban she, 1985.

Guangdong sheng zhiwu yanjiuso, ed. *Guangdong zhipei* (The botany of Guangdong). Beijing: Kexue chuban she, 1976.

Guangdong yinhang. *Guangzhou mi ye* (The rice industry of Guangzhou). Guangzhou. 1936.

Guangxi nongye jingji shi gao (Draft history of the agricultural economy of Guangxi). Nanning: Guangxi minzu chuban she, 1985.

Guldin, Gregory Eliyu. "Urbanizing the Countryside: Guangzhou, Hong Kong, and the Pearl River Delta." In Gregory Eliyu Guldin, *Urbanizing China*. New York: Greenwood, 1992.

Gumilev, L. N. *Searches for the Imaginary Kingdom of Prester John*, R. E. F. Smith, trans. Cambridge University Press, 1987.

Guo Songyi. "Qing chu fengjian guojia ken huang zhengce fenxi" (An analysis of feudal land reclamation policies at the beginning of the Qing). *Qingshi luncong* 2 (1980): 111–38.

"Qingdai de liangjia maoyi" (Qing rice prices and trade). *Pingjun xuekan*, no. 1 (1985): 289–314.

"Yumi, fanshu zai zhongguo juanfan zhong de yi xie wenti" (A few questions about the introduction of maize and sweet potatoes into China). *Qingshi luncong*, 7 (1986): 80–99.

Hameed, S., et al. "An Analysis of Periodicities in the 1470 to 1974 Beijing Precipitation Record." *Geophysical Research Letters* 10, no. 6 (June 1983): 436–39.

Han Maoli. "Song dai Lingnan diqu nongye dili chutan" (A preliminary investigation of the agricultural geography of Song-era Lingnan). *Lishi dili* 11 (1993): 30–40.

Hansen, James, and Sergei Lebedeff. "Global Surface Air Temperatures: Update through 1987." *Geophysical Research Letter* 15, no. 4 (Apr. 1988): 323–26.

"Global Trends of Measured Surface Air Temperature." *Journal of Geophysical Research* 92, no. D11 (Nov. 20, 1987): 13,345–72.

Harrison, C. J. "Grain Price Analysis and Harvest Qualities, 1465–1634." *Agricultural History Review* 19 (1969): 135–55.

Hartwell, Robert M. "Demographic, Political, and Social Transformations of China, 750–1550." *Harvard Journal of Asiatic Studies* 42, no. 2 (Dec. 1982): 365–442.

"Societal Organization and Demographic Change: Catastrophe, Agrarian Technology, and Interregional Population Trends in Traditional China." Paper presented at the 2ème Congrés international de démographie historique, Paris, June 4–5, 1987.

He Ge'en. "Tang dai Lingnan de xushi" (Tang-era markets in Lingnan). *Shihuo banyuekan* 5, no. 2 (Jan. 1937): 35–37.

Headrick, Daniel R. *The Tools of Empire: Technology and European Imperialism in the Nineteenth Century*. New York: Oxford University Press, 1981.

Hinsch, Bret. "Climatic Change and History in China." *Journal of Asian History* 22 (1988): 131–59.

Ho, Ping-ti. "The Introduction of American Food Plants into China." *American Anthropologist* 57 (1955): 191–201.

Ho Ping-ti (He Bingti). "Nan Song zhi jin tudi shuzi de kaoshi he pingjia" (A critique and assessment of land statistics from the Southern Song to the present). *Zhongguo shehui kexue* 2 (1985): 133–65, and 3 (1985): 125–60.

Studies on the Population of China, 1368–1953. Cambridge, MA: Harvard University Press, 1959.

Hoffman, William E. "Preliminary Notes on the Fresh-Water Fish Industry of South China, Especially Kwangtung Province." *Lingnan Science Journal* 8 (Dec. 1929).

Hoskins, W. G. "Harvest Fluctuations and English Economic History, 1480–1619." *Agricultural History Review* 12 (1964): 28–46.

"Harvest Fluctuations and English Economic History, 1620–1759." *Agricultural History Review* 16 (1968): 15–31.

Hou Wenhui. "The Environmental Crisis in China and the Case for Environmental History Studies." *Environmental History Review* 14, nos. 1–2 (Spring–Summer 1990): 151–58.

Hsü, Immanuel C. Y. *The Rise of Modern China*, 3rd edition. New York: Oxford University Press, 1983.

Hsü, K. J. "Origin of Sedimentary Basins of China." In X. Zhu, ed., *Chinese Sedimentary Basins*. Amsterdam: Elsevier, 1989.

Hu Chunfan et al. "Shilun Qing qianqi de juanmian zhengce" (On the tax remission policy during the Qing). In *Qing shi yanjiu ji*, no. 3. Chongqing: Sichuan renmin chuban she, 1984.

Hua Linfu. "Tangdai shuidao shengchan de dili buqu ji qi bianqian chutan" (A preliminary investigation of the regions of wet rice production in the Tang). *Zhongguo nongshi* 2 (1992): 27–39.

Huang, Pei. *Autocracy at Work: A Study of the Yung-cheng Period, 1723–1735*. Bloomington: Indiana University Press, 1974.

Huang, Philip C. C. *The Peasant Economy and Social Change in North China*. Stanford: Stanford University Press, 1985.

The Peasant Family and Rural Development in the Yangzi Delta, 1350–1988. Stanford: Stanford University Press, 1990.

Huang, Ray. "Chia-Ch'ing." In Frederick W. Mote and Denis Twitchett, eds., *The Cambridge History of China*, vol. 7, *The Ming Dynasty, 1368–1644*, part 1. Cambridge University Press, 1988.

Taxation and Governmental Finance in Sixteenth-Century Ming China. Cambridge University Press, 1974.

Huang Jia-you and Wang Shao-wu. "Investigations on Variations of the Subtropical High in the Western Pacific during Historic Times." *Climatic Change* 7 (1985): 427–40.

Huang Jianlin et al., eds. *Zhongguo renkou – Guangxi fen ce* (China's population – the Guangxi part). Beijing: Zhongguo caizheng jingji chuban she, 1988.

Huang Juzhen. "Qingdai qianqi Guangdong de dui wai maoyi" (Foreign trade of Guangdong in the early Qing). Paper presented in Shenzhen at the 4th International Conference on Chinese Social and Economic History, 1987.

Huang Shansheng. "Qing dai Guangdong maoyi ji qi zai Zhongguo jingji shi shang zhi yiyi – yapian zhi yu zhi qian" (The Qing-era foreign trade of Guangdong prior to the Opium War and its significance in China's economic history). *Lingnan xuebao* 3, no. 4 (1934): 157–96.

Huang Tisong et al. *Guangxi lishi dili* (Historical geography of Guangxi). Guilin: Guangxi minzu chuban she, 1984.

Huda, A. K. Samsul, et al. "Contribution of Climatic Variables in Predicting Rice Yield." *Agricultural Meteorology* 15 (1975): 71–86.

Hughs, J. Donald. "Mencius' Prescriptions for Ancient Chinese Environmental Problems." *Environmental History Review* 13, nos. 3–4 (Fall–Winter 1989): 15–27.

Hummel, Arthur. *Eminent Chinese of the Ch'ing period, 1644–1912.* Washington, DC: U.S. Government Printing Office, 1943–44.

Huntington, Ellsworth. *Climate and Civilization.* New Haven: Yale University Press, 3rd revised edition, 1924.

Hyams, Edward. *Soil and Civilization.* New York: Harper Colophon, 1976.

International Rice Research Institute. *Proceedings of the Symposium on Climate and Rice.* Los Banos, Philippines: IRRI, 1974.

Rice Research and Production in China. Los Banos, Philippines: IRRI, 1979.

Jacoby, Gordon C., and Rosanne D'Arrigo. "Reconstructed Northern Hemisphere Annual Temperature since 1671 Based on High-Latitude Tree-Ring Data from North America." *Climatic Change* 14 (1989): 39–59.

Jen Yu-wen. *The Taiping Revolutionary Movement.* New Haven: Yale University Press, 1973.

Jiang Tao. *Zhongguo jindai renkou shi* (History of China's population in modern times). Yangzhou: Zhejiang renmin chuban she, 1993.

Jiang Yanyu. "Guangxi Han dai nongye kaogu gaishu" (An overview of Han-era agricultural archeology in Guangxi). *Nongye kaogu* 2 (1981): 61–68.

Jiang Zulu. "Ming dai Guangzhou de shangye zhongxin diwei yu dongnan yi da bu hui de xingcheng" (The centrality of the commerce of Guangzhou during the Ming and the formation of the southeast as a single [market]). *Zhongguo shehui jingji shi yanjiu,* no. 4 (1990): 19–29.

Jing Junjian. "Lun Qing dai juanmian zhengce zhong jian zu guiding de bianhua" (On the changes in the rent reduction stipulations in the tax remission policy in the Qing). *Zhongguo jingji shi yanjiu* 1 (1986): 67–80.

"Qing dai mintian zhu dian guanxi zhengce de lishi diwei" (The historical position of the policies regarding the landlord–tenant relationship in the Qing). *Zhongguo jingji shi yanjiu* 2 (1988): 58–71.

Johnson, Graham. "Open for Business, Open to the World: Consequences of Global Incorporation in Guangdong and the Pearl River Delta." In Thomas P. Lyons and Victor Nee, eds., *The Economic Transformation of South China: Reform and Development in the Post-Mao Era.* Ithaca: Cornell University Press, 1994.

Kane, R. P. "Spectral Characteristics of the Series of Annual Rainfall in England and Wales." *Climatic Change* 4 (1988): 77–92.

Kane, Sally, John Reilly and James Tobey. "An Empirical Study of the Economic Effects of Climatic Change on World Agriculture." *Climatic Change* 21 (1992): 17–35.

Kato Shiguru. "Qingdai cunzhen de dingqi shi" (Qing-era village periodic markets), Wang Xingrui, trans. *Shihuo banyuekan* 5, no. 1 (Jan. 1937): 44–65.

Katz, Richard W. "Assessing the Impact of Climatic Change on Food Production." *Climatic Change* 1 (1977): 85–96.

Kessler, Lawrence D. *K'ang-shi and the Consolidation of Ch'ing Rule, 1661–1684.* Chicago: University of Chicago Press, 1976.

King, Frank H. H. *Money and Monetary Policy in China, 1845–1895*. Cambridge: Harvard University Press, 1965.

Kishimoto-Nakayama, Mio. "The Kangxi Depression and Early Qing Local Markets." *Late Imperial China* 10, no. 2 (Apr. 1984): 227–56.

Kondo, Junsei. "Volcanic Eruptions, Cool Summers, and Famines in the Northeastern Part of Japan." *Journal of Climate* 1 (Aug. 1988): 775–88.

"Kwangtung tung-chi, or a General Historical and Statistical Account of the Province of Canton." *China Repository* 12 (June 1843): 309–27.

Ladurie, Emmanuel Le Roy. *Times of Feast, Times of Famine: A History of Climate since the Year 1000*. Barbara Bray, trans. Garden City: Doubleday, 1971.

Latham, A. J. H., and Larry Neal. "The International Market in Rice and Wheat, 1868–1914." *Economic History Review* 36, no. 2 (May 1983): 260–80.

Lamb, H. H. *Climate, History and the Modern World*. London: Methuen, 1982.

"Volcanic Dust in the Atmosphere: With a Chronology and Assessment of Its Meteorological Significance." *Philosophical Transactions of the Royal Society of London*, series A, 266 (July 1970): 425–50.

Lamley, Harry. "Hsieh-tou: The Pathology of Violence in Southeastern China." *Ching shih wen-t'i* 3 (1977): 1–39.

Lao Tong. *Jiuhuang beilan* (A guide to famine preparedness). In *Lingnan yishu*, vol. 58, *Baibu congshu jicheng*, 93. Taibei: Yiwen chuban she, 1968.

Lattimore, Owen. *Studies in Frontier History: Collected Papers 1928–1958*. Paris: Mouton, 1962.

Lee, James, Cameron Campbell, and Guofu Tan. "Infanticide and Family Planning in Late Imperial China: The Price and Population History of Rural Liaoning, 1774–1873." In Thomas Rawski and Lillian Li, eds., *Chinese History in Economic Perspective*. Berkeley and Los Angeles: University of California Press, 1992.

Leemy, Frank. *The Changing Geography of China*. Cambridge: Blackwell, 1993.

Leung, Angela Ki Che. "Organized Medicine in Ming–Qing China: State and Private Medical Institutions in the Lower Yangzi Region." *Late Imperial China* 8, no. 1 (June 1987): 134–65.

Li Diaoyuan. *Yuedong biji* (Sketches of Guangdong). Shanghai: Huiwentang, 1915.

Li Guanchang. "Song dai de Guangxi shehui jingji" (Society and economy in Guangxi during the Song). *Guangxi shifan xueyuan xuebao* 4 (1981): 75–84.

Li Hua. "Ming Qing shidai Guangdong nongcun jingji zuowu de fazhan" (The development of village industrial crops in Guangdong in Ming and Qing times). *Qingshi yanjiu* 3 (1984): 135–49.

"Qing chao qianqi Guangdong de shangye yu shangren" (Guangdong markets and merchants in the early Qing). *Xueshu yanjiu* 2 (1982): 39–44.

Li Pengnian. "Luelun Qianlong nianjian cong Xianluo yun mi jinkou" (On the importation of rice from Siam in the Qianlong period). *Lishi dang'an* 3 (Aug. 1985): 83–90.

Li Wenzhi. *Ming Qing shidai fengjian tudi guanxi de songjie* (The loosening of feudal land relations in the Ming and Qing). Beijing: Zhongguo shehui kexue chuban she, 1993.

Li Wenzhi, ed. *Zhongguo jindai nongye shi ziliao* (Source materials on modern Chinese agriculture), 3 vols. Beijing: Sanlian shudian, 1957.

Li Xiaofang. "Supplement to the Preliminary Standard Classification System for Land

Evaluation in China." In Kenneth Puddle and Wu Chuanjin, eds., *Land Resources of the People's Republic of China.* New York: United Nations University, 1983.

Li Zhuanshi, Li Minghua, and Han Qiangfu, eds. *Lingnan wenhua* (Lingnan culture). Shaoguan: Guangdong renmin chuban she, 1993.

Liang Fang-chung. *The Single-Whip Method of Taxation in China.* Wang Yü-ch'uan, trans. Cambridge: Harvard University Press, 1956.

Liang Fangzhong. *Zhongguo lidai hukou tiandi tianfu tongji* (China's historical population, land, and tax statistics). Shanghai: Renmin chuban she, 1980.

Liang Tingnan. *Yue hai guan zhi* (Guangdong maritime customs gazetteer). In *Jindai Zhongguo shiliao congkan xuji*, vols. 181–84. Taibei: Wenhai chubanshe, 1975.

Liang Xizhe. *Yongzheng di* (The Yongzheng emperor). Changchun: Jilin wenshi chuban she, 1993.

Lin, Man-houng. *Currency and Society: The Monetary Crisis and Political-Economic Ideology of Early Nineteenth Century China.* Harvard University, Ph.D. dissertation, 1989.

Lin Yutang. *The Gay Genius: The Life and Times of Su Tungpo.* New York: John Day, 1947.

Ling Daxie. "Wo guo senlin ziyuan de bianqian" (Changes in the forest cover of China). *Zhongguo nongshi* 2 (1983): 26–36.

Lippit, Victor. *The Economic Development of China.* Armonk, N.Y.: Sharpe, 1987.

Little, Daniel. *Understanding Peasant China: Case Studies in the Philosophy of Social Science.* New Haven: Yale University Press, 1989.

Liu, Ta-chung, and Kung-chia Yeh. *The Economy of Mainland China: National Income and Economic Development, 1933–1959.* Princeton: Princeton University Press, 1965.

Liu Wei. "Qing dai liangjia zouzhe zhidu qianyi" (A simple look at the grain-price memorial system in the Qing). *Qing shi yanjiu tongxun* 3 (1984): 16–19.

Liu Xiwei and Liu Panxiu. "Liu chao shiqi Lingnan diqu de kaifa" (The development of the Lingnan region during the Six Dynasties period). *Zhongguo shi yanjiu* 1 (1991): 3–13.

Liu Zhengdeng. *Zhongguo renkou wenti yanjiu* (Studies on questions of China's population). Beijing: Xinhua shu dian, 1988.

Liu Zhiwei. "Lineages on the Sands: The Case of Shawan." In David Faure and Helen F. Siu, eds., *Down to Earth: The Territorial Bond in South China.* Stanford: Stanford University Press, 1995, pp. 21–43.

"Zongzu yu shatian kaifa – Panyu Shawan He zu de ge'an yanjiu" (Lineages and the beginnings of alluvial fields – a case study of the He lineage of Shawan, Panyu county). *Zhongguo nongshi* 4 (1992): 34–41.

Liverman, Diana. "Forecasting the Impact of Climate on Food Systems: Model Testing and Model Linkage." *Climatic Change* 11 (1987): 267–85.

Lough, J. M., H. C. Fritts, and Wu Xiangding. "Relationships between the Climates of China and North America of the Past Four Centuries: A Comparison of Proxy Records." In Ye Duzheng et al., eds., *The Climate of China and Global Climate: Proceedings of the Beijing International Symposium on Climate.* Berlin: Springer, 1987.

Lu Huoji. "Habitat Availability and Prospects for Tigers in China." In Ronald L. Tilson and Ulysses S. Seal, eds., *Tigers of the World: The Biology, Biopolitics, Management, and Conservation of an Endangered Species.* Park Ridge, N.J.: Noyes, 1987.

Luo Bingdong. "Qing dai qianqi Guangxi nongye jingji de fazhan yu bianhua" (The development and change of the agricultural economy in Guangdong during the early Qing). *Guangxi daxue xuebao* 2 (1980): 65–70.

Luo Hongxing. "Ming zhi Qing qianqi Foshan zhitieye chutan" (A preliminary investigation of steel production in Foshan from the Ming to the early Qing). *Zhongguo shehui jingji shi yanjiu* 4 (1983): 44–54.

Luo Shi ming and Chun ru Han. "Ecological Agriculture in China." In C. A. Edwards et al., eds., *Sustainable Agricultural Systems*. Ankeny, IA: Soil and Water Conservation Society, 1990.

Luo Xianglin. *Kejia yanjiu daolun* (On the study of the Hakka). Beijing: Jiwen shuju, 1933.

Luo Yixing. "Shi lun Qing dai qian zhong qi Lingnan shichang zhongxin de fenbu tedian" (On the differences in marketing systems in Lingnan during the early and middle Qing). Paper presented at the Fourth International Conference on Qing Social and Economic History, Shenzhen, 1987.

Lyons, Thomas P., and Victor Nee, eds. *The Economic Transformation of South China: Reform and Development in the Post-Mao Era*. Ithaca: Cornell University Press, 1994.

Maegraith, Brian. *Adams and Maegraith: Clinical Tropical Diseases*, 9th ed. Oxford: Blackwell Scientific, 1989.

Mao Ze. *Qingdai yapian zhan qian (1644–1840) Guangzhou maoyi yu zhongyang ji difang caizheng de guanxi* (Foreign trade at Guangzhou before the Opium War (1644–1840) and the relationship between central and local governmental finances). Taibei: Donghai University, Ph.D. dissertation, 1979.

Mao Zedong. "The Chinese Revolution and the Chinese Communist Party." In *Selected Works of Mao Tse-tung*. Beijing: Foreign Languages Press, 1967.

Marks, Robert B. " 'It Never Used to Snow': Climatic Variability and Harvest Yields in Late Imperial South China, 1650–1850." In Mark Elvin and Liu Ts'ui-jung, eds., *Sediments of Time: Environment and Society in China*. Cambridge University Press, forthcoming.

"Rice Prices, Food Supply, and Market Structure in Eighteenth-Century South China." *Late Imperial China* 12, no. 2 (Dec. 1991): 64–116.

Rural Revolution in South China: Peasants and the Making of History in Haiteng County, 1570–1930. Madison: University of Wisconsin Press, 1984.

Marks, Robert B., and Chen Chunsheng. "Price Inflation and Its Social, Economic, and Climatic Context in Guangdong, 1707–1800." *T'oung pao* vol. 81, no. 1 (1995): 109–52.

Mazumdar, Sucheta. *A History of the Sugar Industry in China: The Political Economy of a Cash Crop in Guangdong, 1644–1834*. University of California at Los Angeles, Ph.D. dissertation, 1984.

McCloskey, Donald N., and John Nash. "Corn at Interest: The Extent and Cost of Grain Storage in Medieval England." *American Economic Review* 74, no. 1 (Mar. 1984): 174–87.

McDougal, Charles. "The Man-Eating Tiger in Geographic and Historical Perspective." In Ronald L. Tilson and Ulysses S. Seal, eds., *Tigers of the World: The Biology, Biopolitics, Management, and Conservation of an Endangered Species*. Park Ridge, NJ: Noyes, 1987.

McNeill, J. R. *The Mountains of the Mediterranean: An Environmental History*. Cambridge University Press, 1992.

"Of Rats and Men: A Synoptic Environmental History of the Island Pacific." *Journal of World History* 5, no. 2 (1994): 299–349.

McNeill, William H. *Plagues and Peoples*. New York: Doubleday, 1976.

Menzies, Nicholas K. *Forest and Land Management in Imperial China.* New York: St. Martin's, 1994.

"Strategic Space: Exclusion and Inclusion in Wildland Policies in Late Imperial China." *Modern Asian Studies* 26, no. 4 (1992): 719–33.

"A Survey of Customary Law and Control over Trees and Wildlands in China." In Louise Fortman and John W. Bruce, eds., *Whose Trees? Proprietary Dimensions of Forestry.* Boulder, CO: Westview, 1988.

Meyer, William B., and B. L. Turner II. *Changes in Land Use and Land Cover: A Global Perspective.* Cambridge University Press, 1994.

Meyerhoff, Arthur A., et al. *China: Stratigraphy, Paleogeography, and Tectonics.* Boston: Kluwer Academic, 1991.

Ming Qing Guangdong sheng shehui jingji yanjiu hui, ed. *Ming Qing Guangdong shehui jingji yanjiu* (Studies in the society and economy of Guangdong during the Ming and Qing). Guangzhou: Guangdong renmin chuban she, 1987.

Mo Naiqun, ed. *Guangxi nongye jingji shi gao* (Draft history of the agricultural economy of Guangxi). Nanning: Guangxi minzu chuban she, 1985.

Molineaux, L. "The Epidemiology of Human Malaria as an Explanation of Its Distribution, Including Some Implications for Its Control." In Walther H. Wernsdorfer and Sir Ian McGregor, eds., *Malaria: Principles and Practice of Malariology.* Edinburgh: Churchill Livingstone, 1988.

Morita Akira. *Shindai suirishi kenkyu* (Studies on the history of water control in the Qing). Tokyo: Aki shobo, 1974.

Morse, Hosea Ballou. *The Chronicles of the East India Company Trading to China, 1635–1834.* Taibei: Chengwen Reprint, 1966.

Moseley, George. *The Consolidation of the South China Frontier.* Berkeley and Los Angeles: University of California Press, 1973.

Moulder, Frances V. *Japan, China, and the Modern World Economy.* Cambridge University Press, 1977.

Munakata, K. "Effects of Temperature and Light on the Reproductive Growth and Ripening of Rice." In International Rice Research Institute, *Proceedings of the Symposium on Climate and Rice.* Los Banos, Philippines: International Rice Research Institute, 1974.

Murphey, Rhoads. "Deforestation in Modern China." In Richard P. Tucker and J. F. Richards, eds., *Global Deforestation and the Nineteenth-Century World Economy.* Durham: Duke University Press, 1983.

Naquin, Susan, and Evelyn S. Rawski. *Chinese Society in the Eighteenth Century.* New Haven: Yale University Press, 1987.

Needham, Joseph. *Science and Civilization in China,* vol. 4, part 3, *Physics and Physical Technology: Civil Engineering and Nautics.* Cambridge University Press, 1971.

Science in Traditional China. Hong Kong: Chinese University Press, 1981.

Ng Chin-keong. *Trade and Society: The Amoy Network on the China Coast, 1683–1735.* Singapore: Singapore University Press, 1983.

Ng Yen Tak, Chu Kime Yee, and Lai Shing Kou. *Rural Spatial Organization: The Case of Qingyuan.* Hong Kong University Occasional Paper No. 8, 1980.

Nishiyama, I. "Effects of Temperature on the Vegetative Growth of Rice Plants." In International Rice Research Institute, *Proceedings of the Symposium on Climate and Rice.* Los Banos, Philippines: International Rice Research Institute, 1974.

Olivercrona, G. W. "The Flood Problem of Kwangtung." *Lingnan Science Journal* 3, no. 1 (1925).

Oram, P. A. "Sensitivity of Agricultural Production to Climatic Change." *Climatic Change*, 7 (1985): 129–52.

Osborne, Anne. "The Local Politics of Land Reclamation in the Lower Yangzi Highlands." *Late Imperial China* 15, no. 1 (June 1994): 1–46.

Ownby, David Alan. *Communal Violence in Eighteenth Century Southeast China: The Background to the Lin Shuangwen Uprising of 1787*. Harvard University, Ph.D. dissertation, 1989.

Palafox y Mendoza, Juan de. *The History of the Conquest of China by the Tartars*. London, 1671.

Parker, Geoffrey, and L. M. Smith, eds. *The General Crisis of the Seventeenth Century*. London: Routledge and Kegan Paul, 1978.

Parry, M. L., and T. R. Carter. "The Effect of Climatic Variations on Agricultural Risk." *Climatic Change* 7 (1985): 95–110.

Pendleton, Robert. "Cogonals and Reforestation with Leucaena Glauca." *Lingnan Science Journal* 12, no. 4 (Oct. 1933): 555–60.

Peng Shilin and Zhou Shibao. "Guangxi Binyang faxian shiwannian qian de huasheng huashi" (A 100,000-year-old petrified peanut found in Binyang county, Guangxi). *Nongye kaogu* 1 (1981): 17–20.

Peng Xinwei. *Zhongguo huobi shi* (A monetary history of China). Beijing: Renmin chuban she, 1965.

Peng Yuxin. *Qing dai tudi kaiken shi* (A history of land reclamation in the Qing). Beijing: Nongye chuban she, 1990.

Perdue, Peter. *Exhausting the Earth: State and Peasant in Hunan, 1500–1850*. Cambridge, MA: Harvard University Press, 1987.

Perkin, H. J. "Social History." In Fritz Stern, ed., *The Varieties of History: From Voltaire to the Present*. New York: Vintage, 1973.

Perkins, Dwight. *Agricultural Development in China*. Chicago: Aldine, 1968.

Poivre, Pierre. *Travels of a Philosopher; Or, Observations on the Manner and Arts of Various Nations in Africa and Asia*. Translated from the French. London, 1769.

Polanyi, Karl. *The Great Transformation*. Boston: Beacon, 1957.

Pomeranz, Kenneth. *The Making of a Hinterland: State, Society, and Economy in Inland North China, 1853–1937*. Berkeley and Los Angeles: University of California Press, 1993.

Post, John D. *Food Shortage, Climatic Variability, and Epidemic Disease in Preindustrial Europe: The Mortality Peak in the Early 1740s*. Ithaca: Cornell University Press, 1985.

The Last Great Subsistence Crisis in the Western World. Baltimore: Johns Hopkins University Press, 1977.

Priestly, M. B. *Spectral Analysis and Time Series*. London: Academic, 1981.

Qing shi lie juan (Qing biographies). Taibei: Zhonghua shuju, 1964.

Qu Dajun. *Guangdong xin yu* (New sayings about Guangdong). Hong Kong: Zhonghua shuju, 1974 edition of early Qing text.

Quan Hansheng. "Lue lun xin hang lu faxian hou de Zhongguo haiwai maoyi" (On China's foreign trade after the beginning of new shipping routes). In *Zhongguo haiyang fazhan shi lunwen ji*, vol. 5. Taibei: Zhongyang yanjiu yuan zhongshan ren wen shehui kexue yanjiu suo, 1993.

"Meizhou baiyin yu Ming Qing jian Zhongguo haiwai maoyi de guanxi" (The connection between American silver and China's foreign trade in the Ming and Qing). *Xin yazhou bao* 16 (Oct. 15, 1991): 1–22.

"Song dai nanfang de xu shi" (Markets in Song-era south China). In Guoli bianyi guan, ed., *Song shi yanjiu ji*, vol. 6. Taibei: Guoli bianyi guan, 1971–86.

Zhongguo jingji shi luncong (Collected essays on China's economic history). Hong Kong: Xinya yanjiu so, 1972.

Rabinowitz, Allan. "Estimating the Indochinese Tiger *Panthera tigris corbetti* Population in Thailand." *Biological Conservation* 65 (1993): 213–17.

Rankin, Mary Backus. "Managed by the People: Officials, Gentry, and the Foshan Charitable Granary, 1795–1845." *Late Imperial China* 15, no. 2 (Dec. 1994): 1–52.

Rawski, Thomas G., and Lillian M. Li, eds. *Chinese History in Economic Perspective*. Berkeley and Los Angeles: University of California Press, 1992.

Reid, Anthony. *Southeast Asia in the Age of Commerce, 1450–1680*, vol. 1, *The Lands below the Winds*. New Haven: Yale University Press, 1988.

Ren Jishun et al. *Geotectonic Evolution of China*. Beijing: Science Press, 1987.

Richards, John F. "The Seventeenth-Century Crisis in South Asia." *Modern Asian Studies* 24, no. 4 (1990): 625–38.

Richardson, S. D. *Forests and Forestry in China*. Washington, DC: Island Press, 1990.

Ross, J. "Journal of a Trip Overland from Hainan to Canton in 1819." *Chinese Repository* 18, no. 5 (May 1849): 225–53.

Rowe, William T. "The State and Land Development in the Mid-Qing: Guangxi Province, 1723–37." Paper presented at the 1992 annual meeting of the American Historical Association.

Sakamoto, C. et al. "Climate and Global Grain Yield Variability." *Climate Change* 2 (1980): 349–61.

Sands, Barbara, and Ramon H. Myers. "The Spatial Approach to Chinese History: A Test." *Journal of Asian Studies* 45, 4 (Aug. 1986): 721–43.

Schafer, Edward H. *Shore of Pearls*. Berkeley and Los Angeles: University of California Press, 1970.

The Vermilion Bird: T'ang Images of the South. Berkeley and Los Angeles: University of California Press, 1967.

Schoppa. Keith R. *Xiang Lake – Nine Centuries of Chinese Life*. New Haven: Yale University Press, 1989.

Scott, H. Harold. *A History of Tropical Medicine*. Baltimore: Williams and Wilkins, 1939.

Scott, James C. *The Moral Economy of the Peasant: Subsistence and Rebellion in Southeast Asia*. New Haven: Yale University Press, 1976.

Seidensticker, John. "Large Carnivores and the Consequences of Habitat Insularization: Ecology and Conservation of Tigers in Indonesia and Bangladesh." In S. D. Miller and D. D. Everett, eds., *Cats of the World: Biology, Conservation, and Management*. Washington, DC: National Wildlife Federation, 1986.

Shaw, Norman. *China's Forest Trees and Timber Supply*. London: T. Fisher Unwin, 1912.

Shen Ts'an-hsin. "Non-Hortunian Runoff Generation in the Humid Regions of South China." In Laurence J. C. Ma and Allen G. Noble, eds., *The Environment: Chinese and American Views*. New York: Methuen, 1981.

Shepherd, John Robert. *Statecraft and Political Economy on the Taiwan Frontier, 1600–1800*. Stanford: Stanford University Press, 1993.

Shiba, Yoshinobu. *Commerce and Society in Sung China*. Mark Elvin, trans. Ann Arbor: University of Michigan Press, 1970.

Shih Min-hsiung. *The Silk Industry in Ch'ing China*. E-tu Zen Sun, trans. Ann Arbor: University of Michigan Press, 1976.

Siu, Helen. *Agents and Victims in South China: Accomplices in Rural Revolution*. New Haven: Yale University Press, 1989.

Skinner, G. William. "Cities and the Hierarchy of Local Systems." In G. William Skinner, ed., *The City in Late Imperial China*. Stanford: Stanford University Press, 1977.

The City in Late Imperial China. Stanford: Stanford University Press, 1977.

"Differential Development in Lingnan." In Thomas P. Lyons and Victor Nee, eds., *The Economic Transformation of South China: Reform and Development in the Post-Mao Era*. Ithaca: Cornell University Press, 1994.

"Presidential Address: The Structure of Chinese History." *Journal of Asian Studies* 45, no. 2 (Feb. 1985): 271–92.

"Regional Urbanization in Nineteenth-Century China." In G. William Skinner, ed., *The City in Late Imperial China*. Stanford: Stanford University Press, 1977.

"Sichuan's Population in the Nineteenth Century: Lessons from Disaggregated Data. *Late Imperial China* 7, no. 2 (Dec. 1986):1–79.

Slicher van Bath, B. H. *The Agrarian History of Western Europe, 500–1800*. Olive Ordish, trans. London: E. Arndd, 1963.

Smil, Vaclav. *China's Environmental Crisis: An Inquiry into the Limits of National Development*. Armonk, NY: Sharpe, 1992.

So, Alvin. *The South China Silk District: Local Transformation and World-System Theory*. Albany: State University of New York Press, 1986.

Song Xixiang. *Zhongguo lidai quan nong kao* (A study of exhorting agriculture in Chinese history). Shanghai: Zhengzhong shuju, 1936.

Song Yingxing. *Tiangong kaiwu*. Ttrans. by E-tu Zen Sun and Shiou-Chuan Sun as *T'ien-kung k'ai-wu: Chinese Technology in the Seventeenth Century*. University Park: Pennsylvania State University Press, 1966.

Spence, Jonathan D. *The Search for Modern China*. New York: Norton, 1990.

Ts'ao Yin and the K'ang-hsi Emperor: Bondservant and Master. New Haven: Yale University Press, 1966.

Staunton, Sir George L. *An Authentic Account of an Embassy from the King of Great Britain to the Emperor of China*. Philadelphia, 1799.

Steward, Albert N. "The Burning of Vegetation on Mountain Land, and Slope Cultivation in Ling Yuin Hsien, Kwangsi Province, China." *Lingnan Science Journal*, 13, no. 1 (Jan. 1934): 1–7.

Struve, Lynn. *The Southern Ming, 1644–1662*. New Haven: Yale University Press, 1984.

Voices from the Ming–Qing Cataclysm: China in Tigers' Jaws. New Haven: Yale University Press, 1993.

Su Guangchang. "Song dai de Guangxi shehui jingji" (The society and economy of Guangxi during the Song). *Guangxi shifan xueyuan xuebao* 4 (1981): 75–84.

Sun Wenliang, Zhang Jie, and Zheng Quanshui. *Qianlong di* (The Qianlong emperor). Changchun: Jilin wenshi chuban she, 1993.

Tan Bangjie. "Status and Problems of Captive Tigers in China." In Ronald L. Tilson and Ulysses S. Seal, eds., *Tigers of the World: The Biology, Biopolitics, Management, and Conservation of an Endangered Species*. Park Ridge, NJ: Noyes, 1987.

Tan Yanhuan. "Lun Ming Qing shidai Guangxi nongye chanpin de shangpinhua" (On the commercialization of agricultural produce in Guangxi during the Ming and Qing). Paper presented at 1987 Shenzhen Conference on Qing Social and Economic History.

Thomas, William L., ed. *Man's Role in Changing the Face of the Earth.* Chicago: University of Chicago Press, 1956.

Tilly, Charles. *Coercion, Capital and European States, AD 990–1990.* Cambridge, MA: Basil Blackwell, 1990.

Tilson, Ronald L., and Ulysses S. Seal, eds. *Tigers of the World: The Biology, Biopolitics, Management, and Conservation of an Endangered Species.* Park Ridge, NJ: Noyes, 1987.

Todhunter, P. E. et al. "Effects of Monsoonal Fluctuations on Grains in China, part 1, Climatic Conditions for 1961–1975." *Journal of Climate* 2 (Jan. 1989): 5–37.

"Topography of Kwangtung." *The China Repository* 12 (Feb. 1843): 88–93.

Tregar, Thomas. R. *A Geography of China.* London: University of London Press, 1966.

Tsang Wah-moon. *The Centricity of Development of Lingnan in T'ang Dynasty.* Hong Kong: Chinese University of Hong Kong Press, 1973.

Tuan, Yi-fu. *China.* London: Longman Group, 1970.

"Discrepancies between Environmental Attitude and Behavior: Examples from Europe and China." *The Canadian Geographer* 12, no. 3 (1968): 176–91.

Tucker, Mary Evelyn. "The Relevance of Chinese Neo-Confucianism for the Reverence of Nature." *Environmental History Review* 15, no. 2 (Summer 1991): 55–69.

Tucker, Richard P., and J. F. Richards, eds. *Global Deforestation and the Nineteenth-Century World Economy.* Durham: Duke University Press, 1983.

Turner, B. L. et al., eds. *The Earth as Transformed by Human Action: Global and Regional Changes in the Biosphere of the Past 300 Years.* Cambridge University Press, 1990.

van der Sprenkel, Otto. "Population Statistics of Ming China." *Bulletin of the School of Oriental and African Studies* 15, no. 2 (1953): 289–326.

Van Slyke, Lyman P. *Yangtze: Nature, History, and the River.* Reading, MA: Addison-Wesley, 1988.

Viraphol, Sarasin. *Tribute and Profit: Sino-Siamese Trade, 1652–1853.* Cambridge, MA: Harvard University Press, 1972.

von Glahn, Richard. "Myth and Reality of China's Seventeenth Century Monetary Crisis." Paper presented at the UCLA Center for Chinese Studies seminar, October 1995.

Wakeman, Frederic, Jr. *The Fall of Imperial China.* Boston: Free Press, 1975.

The Great Enterprise. Berkeley and Los Angeles: University of California Press, 1985.

Strangers at the Gate: Social Disorder in South China, 1839–1861. Berkeley and Los Angeles: University of California Press, 1966.

Waley, Arthur. *The Opium War through Chinese Eyes.* Stanford: Stanford University Press, 1958.

Wallerstein, Immanuel. *The Modern World System*, vol. 1, *Capitalist Agriculture and the Origins of the European World-Economy in the Sixteenth Century.* New York: Academic, 1977.

Walter, John, and Roger Schofield. "Famine, Disease and Crisis Mortality in Early Modern Society." In John Walter and Roger Schofield, eds., *Famine, Disease and Crisis Mortality in Early Modern Society.* Cambridge University Press, 1989.

Wang Chi-wu. *The Forests of China.* Cambridge, MA: Harvard University Press, 1961.

Wang Daorui. "Qing dai liangjia zoubao zhidu de queli ji qi zuoyong" (The verification and function of the Qing grain-price reporting system). *Lishi dang'an* 4 (1987): 80–86.

Wang, Yeh-chien. "Food Supply and Grain Prices in the Yangtze Delta in the Eighteenth Century." In *The Second Conference on Modern Chinese Economic History*. Taibei: Academica Sinica Institute of Economics, 1989, pp. 423–59.

"Food Supply in Eighteenth-Century Fujian." *Late Imperial China* 7, no. 2 (1986): 80–117.

Land Taxation in Imperial China, 1750–1911. Cambridge, MA: Harvard University Press, 1973.

"Qing dai de liang jia chenbao zhidu" (The grain-price reporting system in the Qing). *Taibei gugong likan* 13, no. 1 (1978): 53–66.

Wang Gungwu. *Nan Hai maoyi yu Nanyang huaren* (Commerce in the Nan Hai and overseas Chinese in the Nanyang). Hong Kong: Zhonghua shuju, 1988.

Wang Hongyue and Liu Ruchong. "Guangdong Foshan zibenzhuyi mengya de jidian tanlun" (A few points for discussion about the sprouts of capitalism in Foshan, Guangdong). *Zhongguo lishi bowuguan guankan* 2 (1980): 58–79.

Wang Lunghua and Liu Shengli, comps. *Zhongguo nongxue shi (chu gao)* (A draft history of Chinese agronomy). Beijing: Xinhua shudian, 1984.

Wang Pao-kuan. "On the Relationship between Winter Thunder and the Climatic Change in China jn the Past 2,200 Years." *Climatic Change* 3 (1980): 37–46.

Wang Ping. "Qing ji Zhujiang sanjiaozhou de nongtian shuili" (Agricultural irrigation in the Pearl River delta during the Qing). In *Jindai Zhongguo quyu shi yanjiu taolunhui wenji*. Taibei: Academica Sinica Institute of Modern History, 1986.

Wang Qiang, editor in chief. *Zhongguo daozuo xue* (Chinese rice culture). Beijing: Xinhua shudian, 1986.

Wang Shao-wu, Zhao Zong-ci, and Chen Zhen-hua. "Reconstruction of the Summer Rainfall Regime for the Last 500 Years in China." *GeoJournal* 5, no. 2 (1981): 117–22.

Wang Shao-wu and Zhao Zong-ci. "Droughts and Floods in China, 1470–1979." In T. M. L. Wigley et al., eds., *Climate and History: Studies in Past Climates and Their Impact on Man*. Cambridge University Press, 1981.

Wang Yumin. "'Ming chu quan guo renkou kao zhi yi" (A study on the population of China at the beginning of the Ming). *Lishi yanjiu* 3 (1990): 55–64.

Watson, James Lee. *A Chinese Emigrant Community: The Man Lineage in Hong Kong and London*. University of California at Berkeley, Ph.D. dissertation, 1972.

Wernsdorfer, Walther H., and Sir Ian McGregor. *Malaria: Principles and Practice of Malariology*. Edinburgh: Churchill Livingstone, 1988.

Wiens, Harold J. *Han Chinese Expansion in South China*. Hamden, Conn.: Shoe String Press, 1967.

Wigley, T. M. L., et al., eds. *Climate and History: Studies in Past Climates and Their Impact on Man*. Cambridge University Press, 1981

Wilkinson, Endymion. *Studies in Chinese Price History*. Princeton University, Ph.D. dissertation, 1970.

Will, Pierre-Etienne. *Bureaucracy and Famine in Eighteenth-Century China*. Elborg Forster trans. Stanford: Stanford University Press, 1990.

"State Intervention in the Administration of a Hydraulic Infrastructure: The

Example of Hubei Province in Late Imperial Times." In Stuart Schram, ed., *The Scope of State Power in China.* New York: St. Martin's, 1985.

Will, Pierre-Etienne, and R. Bin Wong. *Nourish the People: The State Civilian Granary System in China, 1650–1850.* Ann Arbor: University of Michigan Press, 1992.

Wills, John E., Jr. "Maritime Asia, 1500–1800: The Interactive Emergence of European Domination." *American Historical Review* 98, no. 1 (Feb. 1993): 83–105.

Wilson, Edward O. *The Diversity of Life.* Cambridge, MA: Harvard University Press, 1992.

Wong, K. Chimin, and Wu Lien-teh. *History of Chinese Medicine, Being a Chronicle of Medical Happenings in China from Ancient Times to the Present Period.* Tientsin (Tianjin): Tientsin Press, 1932.

Wong, R. Bin. "State Granaries and Food Supplies in China, 1650–1850: An Assessment." Paper presented at the 1987 Qing Social and Economic History Conference, Shenzhen.

Worster, Donald. *Dust Bowl: The Southern Plains in the 1930s.* New York: Oxford University Press, 1979.

"Transformations of the Earth: Toward an Agroecological Perspective in History." *Journal of American History* 76, no. 4 (Mar. 1990): 1087–106.

The Wealth of Nature: Environmental History and the Ecological Imagination. New York: Oxford University Press, 1993.

Wrigley, E. A. "Some Reflections on Corn Yields and Prices in Pre-industrial Economies." In E. A. Wrigley, *People, Cities, and Wealth.* New York: Basil Blackwell, 1987.

Wu Jianxin. "Ming Qing Guangdong liangshi shengchan shuiping shitan" (A preliminary investigation of harvest yields in Guangdong during the Ming and Qing). *Zhongguo nongshi* 4 (1990): 28–37.

"Qingdai Guangdong liangshi zhengce shulue" (An overview of food policies in Guangdong during the Qing period). *Zhongguo nongshi* 3 (1990): 59–67.

Wu Youwen et al., eds. *Guangdong sheng jingji dili* (An economic geography of Guangdong province). Beijing: Xinhua chuban she, 1985.

Xiang Peilon, Tan Bangjie, and Jia Xianggang. "South China Tiger Recovery Program." In Ronald T. Tilson and Ulysses S. Seal, eds., *Tigers of the World: The Biology, Biopolitics, Management, and Conservation of an Endangered Species.* Park Ridge, NJ: Noyes, 1987.

Xiao Yishan. *Qing dai tong shi* (A general history of the Qing). Beijing: Xinhua shudian, 1986.

Xie Guozhen. *Ming Qing zhi ji dang she yundong* (The party movement in the late Ming and early Qing). Taibei: Shangwu yinshu guan, 1967.

Xie Tianzuo. "Qihou, shoucheng, liangjia, minqing – du 'Li Xu zouzhe' " (Climate, harvests, grain prices, and the people's morale – reading 'The palace memorials of Li Xu'). *Zhongguo shehui jingji shi yanjiu,* no. 4 (1984): 17–20.

Xu Dixin and Wu Chengming, eds. *Zhongguo zibenzhuyi de mengya* (The sprouts of capitalism in China). Beijing: Renmin chuban she, 1985.

Xu Gengqie. *Buziqie zhai man cun* (Desultory musings from a studio of discontent). Taibei: Wenhai chuban she reprint of 1889 text.

Xu Hengbin. "Han dai Guangdong nongye shengchan chutan" (A preliminary investigation of agricultural production in Guangdong during the Han). *Nongye kaogu* 2 (1981): 56–60.

Xu Junming. *Lingnan lishi dili lun ji* (Essays on the historical geography of Lingnan). Guangzhou: Zhongshan daxue xuebao bianji, 1990.

Yan Zhongping et al. *Zhongguo jindai jingji tongji ziliao xuanji* (Selected economic statistical materials for modern China). Beijing: Kexue chuban she, 1953.

Yang, C. K. *Chinese Communist Society: The Family and the Village (A Chinese Village in Early Communist Transition)*. Cambridge, MA: MIT Press, 1959.

Yang Guozhen. *Ming Qing tudi qinyue wenshu yanjiu* (Studies of land contracts from the Ming and Qing). Beijing: Renmin chuban she, 1988.

Yang Qiqiao. *Yongzheng di ji qi mi zou zhidu yanjiu* (A study of the Yongzheng emperor and his secret palace memorial system). Hong Kong: Sanlian shu dian, 1985.

Ye Duzheng et al., eds. *The Climate of China and Global Climate: Proceedings of the Beijing International Symposium on Climate*. Berlin: Springer, 1987.

Ye Xian'en. "Lue lun Zhujiang sanjiaozhou de nongye shangyehua" (An overview of the commercialization of the Pearl River delta). *Zhongguo shehui jingji shi yanjiu*, no. 2 (1986): 16–29.

Ye Xian'en, ed. *Qing dai chuyu shehui jingji yanjiu* (Studies in the regional social and economic history of the Qing period). Beijing: Zhonghua shu ju, 1992.

Ye Xian'en and Tan Dihua. "Lun Zhujiang sanjiaozou de zu tian" (On lineage lands in the Pearl River delta). In *Ming Qing Guangdong shehui jingji xingtai yanjiu*. Guangzhou: Guangdong renmin chuban she, 1985.

"Ming Qing Zhu Jiang sanjiaozhou nongye shangyehua yu xushi de fazhan" (The commercialization of agriculture in the Pearl River delta during the Ming and the Qing and market development). *Guangdong shehui kexue* 2 (1984): 73–90.

Ye Xian'en, Tan Dihua, and Luo Yixing. *Guangdong hang yun shi gudai bufen* (The history of shipping in Guangdong in ancient times). Beijing: Renmin jiaotong chuban she, 1989.

Ye Yineng, ed. *Zhongguo lidai panshi nong zheng shi* (A general history of China's agricultural policies). Nanjing: Dongnan daxue chuban she, 1991.

Yoshida, S., and F. T. Parao. "Climatic Influence on Yield Components of Lowland Rice in the Tropics." In International Rice Research Institute, *Proceedings of the Symposium on Climate and Rice*. Los Banos, Philippines: International Rice Research Institute, 1974.

Yoshino, Masatoshi M., ed. *Climate and Agricultural Land Use in Monsoon China*. Tokyo: University of Tokyo Press, 1984.

Zeng Huaman (Tsang Wah-moon). *Tangdai lingnan fazhan de gaixinxing* (The centricity of development of Lingnan in T'ang dynasty). Hong Kong: Hong Kong University Press, 1973.

Zeng Zhaoxian. "Cong lishi dimaoxue kan Guangzhou cheng fazhan wenti" (Looking at the question of the development of Guangzhou city from the perspective of historical physiography). *Lishi dili* 4 (1986): 28–41.

Zhang De'er. "Zhongguo nanbu jin 500 nian dongji wendu bianhua de rogan tezheng" (A few points about the temperature change over the past 500 years in the southern part of China). *Kexue tongbao* 6 (1980): 270–72.

Zhang Jiacheng and Thomas B. Crowley. "Historical Climate Records in China and the Reconstruction of Past Climate." *Journal of Climate* 2 (Aug. 1989): 833–49.

Zhang Jiacheng and Lin Zhiguang. *Climate of China*. Ding Tan, trans. New York: Wiley, 1992.

Zhang Peiyuan and Gong Gaofa. "Three Cold Episodes in the Climatic History of China." In Ye Duzheng et al., eds., *The Climate of China and Global Climate: Proceedings of the Beijing International Symposium on Climate.* Berlin: Springer, 1987.

Zhang Peiyuan, et. al. "Climate Change and Its Impact on Capital Shift during the Last 2,000 Years in China." Paper presented at the Conference on the History of the Environment in China, Hong Kong, December 13–18, 1993.

Zhang Yongda, et al. *Leizhou bandao de zhipei* (The flora of the Leizhou peninsula). Shanghai: Xinhua shu ju, 1957.

Zhao Songqiao. *Geography of China: Environment, Resources, Population, and Development.* New York: Wiley, 1994.

Zheng Sizhong. "1400–1949 nian Guangdong sheng de qihou zhendong ji qi dui liangshi feng kuan de yingxiang" (Climatic fluctuation and its effect on food production during the period 1400–1949 in Guangdong province). *Dili xuebao* 38, no.1 (Mar. 1983): 25–32.

Zhong Gongfu. "Zhujiang sanjiaozhou de 'sang ji yu tang' – yige shui lu xianghu zuoyong de rengong shengtai zitong" (The 'mulberry embankment fish pond' in the Pearl River delta – a useful man-made land and water ecological system). *Dili xuebao* 35, no. 3 (Sept. 1980): 200–209.

Zhou Kangxie. *Guangzhou shi yange shilue* (An outline history of the administrative changes of Guangzhou). Hong Kong: Zongwen shudian, 1972.

Zhou Yuanhe. "Zhujiang sanjiaozhou de chenglu guocheng" (The process by which the Pearl River delta became land). *Lishi dili* 5 (1987): 58–69.

Zhou Yuanlian. *Shunzhi di* (The Shunzhi emperor). Changchun: Jilin wenshi chuban she, 1993.

Zhu, X., ed. *Chinese Sedimentary Basins.* New York: Elsevier, 1989.

Zhu Kezhen. "Zhongguo jin wuqian nian lai qihou bianqian de chubu yanjiu" (A preliminary study of climatic change in China over the past 5,000 years). *Kaogu xuebao,* no. 1 (1972). Reprinted in Zhu Kezhen, *Zhu Kezhen wen ji.* Beijing: Kexue chuban she, 1979.

Zhu Kezhen and Zhang Baogun. *Zhongguo zhi yuliang* (The rainfall of China). Beijing: Ziyuan weiyuan hui, 1936.

Zhu Yuncheng, comp. *Zhongguo renkou – Guangdong fence* (China's population – the Guangdong part) Beijing: Xinhua shudian, 1988.

Zhuang Jifa. *Gugong dang'an shu yao* (An introduction to the palace archives). Taibei: Gugong congkan, 1983.

INDEX

CPSIA information can be obtained
at www.ICGtesting.com
Printed in the USA
LVOW13s1933150118
562985LV00012B/750/P